Professional Visual Basic 6 XML

James Britt
Teun Duynstee

Wrox Press Ltd. ®

Professional Visual Basic 6 XML

Published by Wrox Press Ltd
Arden House, 1102 Warwick Road, Acock's Green, Birmingham B27 6BH, UK
Printed in USA
ISBN 1-861003-32-3

Trademark Acknowledgements

Credits

Authors
James Britt
Teun Duynstee

Additional Material
Kevin Williams

Technical Editors
Dianne Parker
Adrian Young

Managing Editor
Dominic Lowe

Development Editor
Peter Morgan

Project Manager
Tony Berry

Index
Michael Brinkman

Technical Reviewers
Rich Bonneau
Matt Bortniker
Joe Bustos
Michael Corning
Robert Chang
Steve Danielson
Robin Dewson
Mike Erickson
Tony Greening
Sumit Pal
Richard Ward
Helmut Watson

Design / Layout
Tom Bartlett
Mark Burdett
William Fallon
Jonathan Jones
Laurent Lafon

Cover Design
Shelley Frazier
Chris Morris

About the Authors

James Britt

James Britt wears many hats at Logic Milestone, a company providing Web site hosting and design, software development, and e-commerce solutions. James lives in the United States, and, when not designing or coding Internet applications, composes noisy music and experiments with graphic design. He occasionally goes outside and hikes in the desert, but not too often. He can be contacted at JBritt@logicmilestone.com

Acknowledgements

Along the way in both my private life and professional career, I've been lucky to make the acquaintance of several smart, talented people with the patience and heart to really teach me how to improve my craft. In particular, I'd like to thank Michael Guidone and Shad Gates, who often swelled my brain with their remarkable insight and experience.

I'd especially like to thank Rose, for her enduring love and tolerance of an (occasionally) over-caffeinated geek.

Teun Duynstee

Teun Duynstee is lead developer at Macaw, a Dutch cutting edge Web-building and consulting firm, specializing in building complex enterprise Web-applications on the Windows DNA platform. What he likes to do most are enthusing others with the great new possibilities of Web technology and sleeping late. You can reach him at teun.duynstee@macaw.nl or duynstee@email.com

Acknowledgements

It seems customary to think up an incredibly long list of people here that made extremely important contributions to this book. I will try not to. Sure, there are some that must be mentioned. All the people at Wrox working on my late-in texts, giving kind comments for example. Everyone that read my chapters when they were not yet nicely edited. And of course everyone who encouraged me to do this. Two thank-yous however go before all others: Roel and Maarten from Macaw, for making it possible for me to work on a book and still sleep sometimes, and finally there is Marjolein; it was her time too that I used to make this the best book I could.

Thanks to all of you and all others!

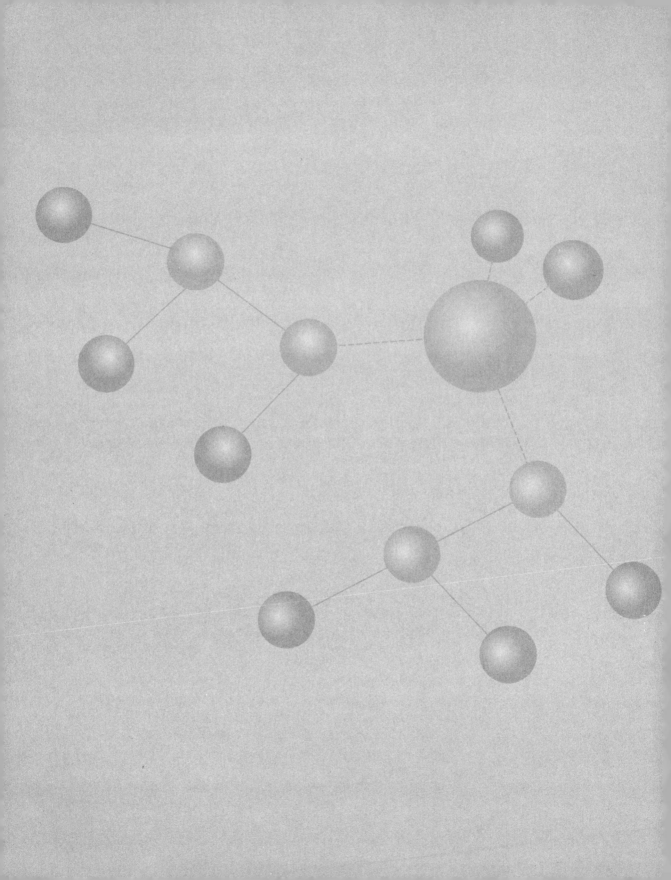

Table of Contents

Introduction   **1**

Chapter 1: Introduction to XML   **7**

Markup Languages   8
    HTML   8
    SGML   9
What Is XML?   11
    XML as a Data Format   12
    XML for Web Pages   12
    Object Method Parameter Encoding and RPC Protocol 12
    XML and Open Exchange   13
    The Flexibility of XML   13
    XML is Easy to Read   14
    XML is Platform Independent   14
Why XML and VB?   15
    When to Use XML   15
    When Not to Use XML   17
XML Basics   17
    Digging Into the Syntax   18
        XML Anatomy   19
        Elements   19
        Attributes   21
        Text   24
        Entities   25
        Character References   26
        CDATA   27
        Encodings   28
        Comments   29
        Processing Instructions   29

Well-formed versus Valid   30
XML Namespaces   30
The World of Parsers   33
Microsoft Internet Explorer Parser   33
James Clark's Expat   34
Vivid Creations ActiveDOM   34
DataChannel XJ Parser   34
IBM xml4j   34
Apache Xerces   34

Chapter 2: XML Validation   **37**

Why Validation is Necessary   37
Validation is Optional   39
Validation Using DTDs   41
Syntax Elements in a DTD   43
Testing Validity with a DTD   51
Limitations of DTDs   57
Validation Using XML Schemas   58
The Concept of a Schema   58
Datatypes   60
The Available Elements   64
Example of an MS Schema   70
Comparing the MS Schema and XML Schema   74
Choosing Whether to Use a DTD or a Schema   75

Chapter 3: Programming the Document Object Model   **79**

Introduction   80
A Little History   80
The Idea Behind the DOM   81
DOM Requirements   82
Language and Platform Independent   82
Core DOM for Both HTML and XML   82

Independent of the User Interface 83

Accessable Elements of the Document 84

Some Limitations of the DOM 84

Objects in the DOM 84

The Fundamental DOM Interfaces 85

The Microsoft parseError Object 98

Platform Neutrality of XML and the DOM 99

Generic Node Methods 102

Wrapper Functions for Manipulating the DOM 103

Specific Node Interfaces 116

Extended Interfaces 125

Microsoft Specific Extensions 130

Putting It All Together 130

Using the DOM in Visual Basic Applications 138

A Test Program to Manipulate the DOM 138

Displaying the Nodes in a Tree Control 150

SAX 154

Where to Find SAX 155

When to Use SAX 155

Chapter 4: Using XML Queries and Transformations 161

XPath Query Syntax 162

Different Axes 162

Different Node Tests 164

Building a Path 165

Selecting Subsets 166

Built-in Functions 169

IE5 Conformance 172

XSLT 173

How Transformation Works 174

Some Good XSLT Processors 175

XSLT Elements – Composing the XSLT Stylesheet   176
    Pre-defined Templates   182
    Elements that Generate Output Elements   184
    Commands   194
    What if Several Templates Match?   196
    Control of Flow   199
    Variables and Parameters   201
    Top Level Settings   203
    Built-in Functions   210
Simplified Syntax   214
XSLT Language Extensions   214
The IE5 Implementation   215
    Tricks for using MSXML 2.0   217
XSLT Examples   218
Giving Style to XML   222
Using CSS in HTML   223
Using CSS in XML   224
Using XSLT for Adding Style   226
Client Side XSLT Styling   231

Chapter 5: Linking with XPointer and XLink   **235**

Restrictions of Linking in HTML   236
The Link: Concept and Representation   237
What Should an XML Browser Do?   237
XPointer   238
Standard XPointer Syntax   238
    Shorthand Notations   238
Examples of Using XPath in XPointer   239
Extensions to XPath   240
XPointer Functions   243
Empty Result Sets   245

XLink   245
   Recognizing an Element as a Link   246
   Simple Link   247
   Extended Link   251
   Out-of-Line Links   257
Elements Overview   259

Chapter 6: Maximizing Performance of XML Applications   263

Loading Tree Views on Demand   264
Asynchronous Loading of Large Documents   268
Using SAX with Large XML Documents   270
Accessing Nodes by ID   273
   Making a Custom Index   275
Performance Tester Application   276
   Constructing a Simple Document from Scratch   277
   Parsing With and Without Validation   281
   Using an Inline or an External DTD   281
   Parsing Using DOM or SAX   282
   Apartment-Threaded Versus Free-Threaded Access 283
   General and Specific XPath Queries   284
   Transformation by XSLT Versus the DOM   284
Summary of Performance Issues   286

Chapter 7: Introducing the Sample Application   289

Building a Distributed Application   290
Why XML Files?   291
Communication and Distributed Applications   292
   XML over the Wire   293
     XML-RPC   293
     SOAP   297
     Making Requests   299
     Getting a Response   301

Returning Error Information   301
Writing SOAP Client/Server Code   304
The SOAP Client/Server Application   329

Current Efforts to Standardize Web Transactions   351
BizTalk   352
OASIS   354
What to Use – Schema, DTD, or Neither?   355

Chapter 8: Developing an XML Editor   365

Data Entry and Parsing   365
Building an ActiveX XML Text Box   366
Dynamic Resource Files   370
The Product Information Editor Application   375
Creating the Tab Control   375
Setting Up frmMain   380
Coding the Data Entry Fields   380
Coding the Menu   384
The Editing Options Menu   392

Chapter 9: Storing and Retrieving XML Data   397

Building Web Objects in VB   398
What about WebClasses?   398
Building for MTS   399
Designing the Request Handlers   400
Data Services   402
Converting an ADO Recordset to XML   404
Executing SQL   405
The XML File Server   407
Writing Files to Disk   409
Writing the XML File   410
Changes to the SoapUtils Class   412

SOAP Transactions   416
    The Web Transaction Utilities Class   416
    The Back-End Application Class   431
    The SOAP Wrappers Class   434
Additions to the Product File Editor   437

Chapter 10: Using a VB Component to Implement Linking   455

Chosen Approach   457
  Simple Links   458
  Extended Links   459
  Component Functionality   460
  Component Output   461
The XLink Component   463
  Object Model Overview   463
  The Implementation   468
  The User Interface   484
    The HTML Page   484
    The Stylesheet   486
    The ASP Page   487

Chapter 11: Distributed Objects   491

The Application Architecture   491
Posting Purchase Requests to a Remote Application   493
Moving Information in a Distributed Application   495
  Purchase Order Posting Classes   497
The Wrox Store Web Site   503
  Designing the Web Site   513
    Configuring global.asa   515
    The Default Page   516
    The Search Page   517
    The Search Results Page   518
    Resolving XLinks   519
    Purchasing Items   521
The SOAP Server   526

Chapter 12: Transforming and Transmitting the Data   537

Outline of the Solution   538
The Basic Application   539
   Reading the Message   540
      Checking Stock   542
      Changing Inventory Level   542
      Checking Reorder Requirements   543
   Transforming the Reorder Information   543
      Creating a Default Reorder Document   543
      Transforming to Another Schema   545
      Transforming to CSV   546
      Transforming to Human Readable Format   547
   Transferring Information   548
      The Dummy Transfer   549
      Transfer Using HTTP   549
      Transfer Using e-mail   550

Chapter 13: Converting Word To XML   553

Introduction   553
   Scripting Word   554
Word-XML Conversion Application   555
   The WordXml DLL   555
   The Word Template   566
   Test Document   567

Appendix A: XML Document Object Model   571

The Base DOM Objects   571
   NamedNodeMap Object   572
   Node Object   573
   NodeList Object   575

The High-Level DOM Objects   575
    Attribute or Attr Object   576
    CDATASection Object   579
    CharacterData Object   582
    Comment Object   585
    Document Object   588
    DocumentFragment Object   592
    DocumentType Object   595
    Element Object   597
    Entity Object   600
    EntityReference Object   603
    Implementation Object   605
    Notation Object   605
    ProcessingInstruction Object   608
    Text Object   610
IE5-Specific XML Parser Objects   613
    HttpRequest Object   614
    ParseError Object   615
    Runtime Object   616
The DOM NodeTypes   621
    IDOMNodeType Enumeration   621

Appendix B: SAX 1.0: The Simple API for XML   625

Class Hierarchy   626
    AttributeList Class   626
    DocumentHandler Class   628
    DTDHandler Class   632
    EntityResolver Class   633
    ErrorHandler Class   635
    HandlerBase Class   636
    InputSource Class   638
    Locator Class   641
    Parser Class   642

SAXException Class   645

SAXParseException Class   646

Appendix C: XPath Reference   651

General Introduction   651

Axes   652

Node Tests   654

Functions   655

A Few Examples of XPath Expressions   661

Appendix D: XSLT Reference   663

Elements   663

Functions   677

Inherited XPath Functions   679

XSLT Types   679

Appendix E: XLink/XPointer Reference   683

XLink   683

Namespace   683

Simple Links   683

Extended Links   684

XPointer   687

Syntax   687

XPointer Extensions to XPath   687

Appendix F: Support and Errata   691

Introduction

XML, the Extensible Markup Language, is a platform-independent language for describing data. The XML and related specifications, as well as the Document Object Model, have all been developed with language independence in mind. This was done to allow *any* programmer to use these powerful protocols and object models in their own language of choice, thus providing a huge development potential for the XML community.

As the programming language with the largest developer-base, VB has a surprisingly low amount of publications on XML development to choose from. In this book we will show the VB community how to take advantage of the latest XML technology. Possible applications are innumerable – think of 'passing complex data from one application to another' (importing data from other systems is a very common enterprise scenario), 'passing data from the client to the server in a multi-tier environment', 'storing your user settings or user documents in your own XML format' and many more.

What Does this Book Cover?

We will cover the standards and ready-to-use components of XML in a step-by-step way, assuming no prior XML knowledge. As we get to know more and more features of XML and related technologies, we will expand the sample application with the newly learned items.

The book will cover the XML 1.0 recommendation, the XML Namespaces 1.0 recommendation, the DOM 1.0 recommendation, the SAX 1.0 standard, the XPath recommendation as implemented in Internet Explorer 5, the XSLT recommendation and the current implementation in IE5, and Microsoft's extensions to the DOM as implemented in IE5. In all subjects, we will stress which functionality is based on an open standard and which constitutes vendor-specific (mainly Microsoft) extensions.

We will focus on using VB6, but most features that weren't present in version 5 will not be used.

Who Is this Book For?

This book is for intermediate to advanced VB programmers who have little or no knowledge of XML. It will be helpful if you are familiar with several Internet techniques (on the Microsoft platform), such as (D)HTML, Active Server Pages, client-side scripting with JScript and/or VBScript. You should have at least a *basic* understanding of three-tier architectures like Microsoft DNA.

If you have read or heard a bit about XML and wonder how to use it best, building on your existing programming skills, then this book is for you!

How is this Book Structured?

The book is divided into two parts. The first part (Chapters 1 to 6) explains the background theory, using small code samples to illustrate how to use XML. The second part (Chapters 7 to 13) demonstrates putting that theory into practice, by presenting and describing a comprehensive case study. Further discussions are presented on some of the more advanced concepts introduced in the earlier chapters.

Chapter 1 – Introduction to XML

This introductory chapter covers the fundamentals of XML, including why it was developed, where it can be useful, how XML and VB can work together, and basic concepts such as the anatomy of XML documents and the terminology used. Also included is a discussion of the currently available XML parsers.

Chapter 2 – XML Validation

This chapter discusses validating XML documents using Document Type Definitions and Schemas. Both the W3C and Microsoft implementations of schemas are considered, and comparisons are made between the validation methods.

Chapter 3 – Programming the Document Object Model

The DOM (Document Object Model) is described and we learn how to program using its objects, methods and properties. The SAX (Simple API for XML) model is also discussed.

Chapter 4 – Using XML Queries and Transformations

In this chapter we look at how to query XML using XPath, and how to transform it using XSLT. This includes adding style to XML documents using CSS and XSL stylesheets.

Chapter 5 – Linking with XPointer and XLink

Chapter 5 shows how to incorporate simple and complex linking to external resources into XML documents using the XPointer and XLink languages.

Chapter 6 – Maximizing Performance of XML Applications

Having covered all the XML essentials, we now look at some tips to get better performance from our XML documents, and how to handle large documents.

Chapter 7 – Introducing the Sample Application

At this point we introduce the sample application – an online store, incorporating XML data files and XML stored in a SQL Server 7 database, VB components and a web-based front end. The use of SOAP as a transport protocol for our XML files is discussed and we develop a VB component to handle many of the SOAP transactions. This chapter takes an in depth look at the benefits of validating, and discusses the BizTalk and OASIS initiatives to provide a repository of standard schema.

Chapter 8 – Developing an XML Editor

In this chapter a VB application is developed – an editor for creating and editing product information documents in XML. The editor utilizes the DOM and XML-to-HTML transformations.

Chapter 9 – Storing and Retrieving XML Data

This chapter shows how to use a VB component for storing and retrieving XML data in a SQL Server 7 database and text files.

Chapter 10 – Using a VB Component to Implement Linking

Chapter 10 covers the creation of a VB component to implement linking when XML is transformed into HTML. This allows us to display HTML incorporating data from our SQL Server database, with links to our XML files that reside on a separate server.

Chapter 11 – Distributed Objects

In this chapter we create a simple web-based user interface (using ASP techniques) to allow a user to search for, select and purchase items in our database of products. We also program an MTS object to handle all requests, moving information around in our distributed application. This involves using a SOAP server to enable communication across platforms.

Chapter 12 – Transforming and Transmitting the Data

The sample application is completed by looking at a system for reordering products from our suppliers, which involves *transforming* XML data into other formats (different XML, HTML, and plain text) and then *transmitting* the transformed data to other platforms.

Chapter 13 – Converting Word to XML

In this mini case-study an application is developed to convert Word documents into XML, using a VB DLL called from a Word macro.

There are also 6 reference Appendices:

Appendix A – DOM Reference

Appendix B – SAX Reference

Appendix C – XPath Reference

Appendix D – XSLT Reference

Appendix E – XLink/XPointer Reference

Appendix F – Support and Errata

What You Need to Use this Book

As well as intermediate to advanced knowledge of VB, basic familiarity with web programming techniques is assumed (for example HTML, ASP) and the ability to use simple databases is required.

To develop and run all of the examples and the entire case study you'll need to have the following software:

- ❑ Visual Basic 6
- ❑ Visual Studio Service Pack 3
- ❑ Microsoft XML parser 2.0 (supplied with IE5)
- ❑ IIS 4.0
- ❑ ADO 2.1
- ❑ SQL Server 7
- ❑ Microsoft Transaction Server 2.0
- ❑ CDO for NTS 1.2 (supplied with NT Option Pack)
- ❑ Microsoft XML parser 2.6 "web release" preview (for XLinking in Chapters 5 and 10)
- ❑ Vivid Creations ActiveSAX library (for performance testing in Chapter 6)
- ❑ Microsoft Message Queue (for the last part of the main sample application)
- ❑ Microsoft Word 97 or 2000 (for building a macro in Chapter 13)

The complete source code for the case study is available for download from:
http://www.wrox.com

Conventions

To help you get the most from the text and keep track of what's happening, we've used a number of conventions throughout the book.

For instance:

> **These boxes hold important, not-to-be forgotten information that is directly relevant to the surrounding text.**

While the background style is used for asides to the current discussion.

As for styles in the text:

❑   When we introduce them, we **highlight** important words

❑   We show keyboard strokes like this: *Ctrl-A*

❑   We show filenames and code within the text like so. doGet ()

❑   Text on user interfaces (and URLs) is shown as: Menu

We present code in two different ways:

```
In our code examples, the code foreground style shows new, important,
    pertinent code
while code background shows code that's less important in the present context,
    or which has been seen before.
```

Tell Us What You Think

We've worked hard to make this book as useful to you as possible, so we'd like to know what you think. We're always keen to know what it is you want and need to know.

We appreciate feedback on our efforts and take both criticism and praise on board in our future editorial efforts. If you've anything to say, let us know via e-mail:

feedback@wrox.com

or via the feedback links on our web site:

http://www.wrox.com

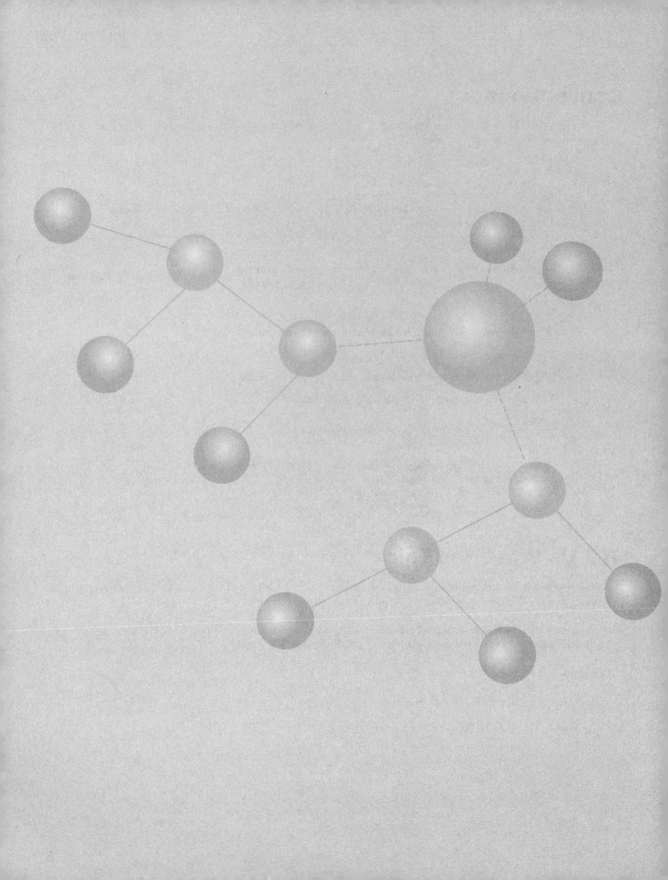

Introduction to XML

The goal of this first chapter is to provide a fundamental understanding of XML, the Extensible Markup Language. XML is in many ways similar to HTML, so you may already have a grasp of the basic ideas behind markup languages. XML also has some important differences from HTML, primarily the concept of *extensibility*, so this chapter inevitably contains some amount of technical detail.

In this chapter we'll cover all of the essential parts of XML. There may be cases where brief references are made to terms and syntax that may be unfamiliar. Where an understanding of some detail is essential for understanding an example, a brief explanation is given alongside the example, with more detail given further on in the chapter.

We begin with a very simple definition of XML as a markup language, and explain what a markup language is. We continue with a comparison to two other markup languages, SGML and HTML, and point out some problems those languages have.

We take a look at when to use XML, and the circumstances when its use is not appropriate, and show how XML compares to other text and data processing technologies, such as ADO and conventional word processors. We also look at the different areas where XML can be used, and why it can be valuable to a Visual Basic developer.

We then give some basic examples of XML, and work through the details of the many aspects of the XML specification. This part can be a bit technical, but it serves to provide a firm foundation for further work.

Finally, we give an overview of available XML processing tools.

Markup Languages

XML stands for **Extensible Markup Language**. If you've ever written a web page, then you have some experience with a markup language. It's a way to describe the characteristics (such as formatting or logical structure) of textual information, using specially formatted text. Typically, this involves using **tags** (enclosed by "<" and ">" characters) to delineated pieces of text, with the **contents** of the tags providing information about the textual information between the tags. This is essentially how XML works.

To understand why XML was invented, it's helpful to look at two other markup languages. We have **HTML** (**Hyper Text Markup Language**) for the web, and if you want a more feature-rich markup language for, say, complex printed documents, there's **SGML** (**Standard Generalized Markup Language**), the markup language specification from which HTML was derived. So why invent a new one? Well, there were problems. To put it simply, HTML is too inflexible, and SGML too complex for the needs of most users; the former offers only a relatively small set of markup facilities intended for browser rendering and, while the latter provides almost endless options, the development of a document requires a fairly steep learning curve.

HTML

HTML is easy to learn, and does a fairly good job of defining basic web page layout and hypertext linking, but it tells you nothing about *what* it is that you're presenting. For example, suppose you wanted to create a web page providing information about famous writers. You might include the author's name, a list of some books, perhaps the author's date of birth. It might look something like this:

```
<HTML>
 <HEAD>
 <TITLE>Famous Writers</TITLE>
 </HEAD>
 <BODY>
 <H1>Mark Twain</H1>
 <B>Born:</B> <FONT color="blue">1835</FONT><BR>
 <B>Nationality:</B> <FONT color="blue">American</FONT><BR>
 <P>Mark Twain, whose real name was Samuel Langhorne
    Clemens, is the author of the classic American novel
    <I> The Adventures of Tom Sawyer</I>, and short stories
    such as <I> The Celebrated Jumping Frog of Calaveras
    County</I>.
 </P>
 </BODY>
</HTML>
```

While this might look nice in a web browser, the HTML only describes the *presentation* of data, but says nothing about its real *structure* or *meaning*. Any perceived structure is purely visual and incidental. There's no <NAME> element, no <DATE> element, and the <TITLE> element may only refer to the title of the web page, not the title of any books. HTML markup does not provide any *semantic* information, such as why certain text is presented in a given way, or what role it plays in the document. For example, rendering a date in a different color might make it visually distinct, but <FONT color="blue"> does nothing to suggest the nature of the data being displayed. If you wanted to programmatically parse this page to extract particular types of information, it would be difficult to determine what the markup was intended to convey.

Let's say you wanted to extract a summary of a web page. There are various ways to do this, but they largely rely on certain assumptions about natural languages and how people tend to order information in paragraphs. Generally speaking, the important ideas are found at the beginning of a paragraph. A summarization tool could go through our sample web page and locate the HTML elements. The tool should correctly figure out that this page is about famous authors (since that's exactly what the TITLE element says), and would likely include "Mark Twain" in the summary, since his name is marked with <H1> tags. But how would it fare in picking out the titles of Twain's works? Italicized text serves to tell a human reader that it is meant to be thought of differently from normal text, but a proper understanding requires knowledge of the context in which it is used. The <I> tag alone does not give enough information for a text parser to know what the author meant.

This is true not only of HTML, but most word processing software as well. While many people extol the value of WYSIWYG (What You See Is What You Get) tools, critics of such an approach have coined a variant on this acronym: HTML is a case of WYSIAYG, or What You See Is All You Get.

SGML

In 1974, Charles Goldfarb, Ed Mosher and Ray Lorie invented SGML, the Standard Generalized Markup Language. SGML allows you painstaking control over every piece of text, detailing what types of element are used, and where they are allowed to go. If you were to create your famous writers document using SGML, you could define your own <NAME> and <DATE> elements. Furthermore, you could assign attributes to the elements to give them more meaning, for example <DATE type="birth">. However, the power of SGML comes with a cost; it can be difficult to learn, and it is hard to write software to handle SGML properly. All SGML documents must have a **Document Type Definition** (**DTD**) file that defines what elements and attributes are allowed, and how they may be used. DTDs (as you'll see later) have their own special syntax and, as they grow in complexity, become more difficult to write.

XML also uses DTDs, and while the rules have been somewhat simplified, they can be still be difficult to develop. We'll take a look at DTDs and the related topic of Schemas in Chapter 2.

The SGML editor must be able to parse the DTD, restrict the user's text entry to just the defined elements, and make sure that the elements are only used in the prescribed way. SGML does, however, allow the use of abbreviated end tags, and even the omission of end tags, as long as the document structure can be unambiguously determined from the DTD.

If we were to create our famous writers page in SGML, it might look like this:

```
<!DOCTYPE authors system "authors.dtd">
<Authors>
 <PageTitle>Famous Writers
 <MainBody>
 <Name type="author">Mark Twain</>
 <bold>Born:</> <date type="birth">1835</>
 <bold>Nationality</> <Nationality>American</>
 <para> Mark Twain, whose real name was Samuel Langhorne
    Clemens, is the author of the classic American novel
    <title type="novel">Tom Sawyer</>, and short stories such
```

```
      as <title type="shortstory">The Celebrated Jumping Frog of
      Calaveras County</>.
  </>
</Authors>
```

This is better, at least from the perspective of improved use of semantic information. However, it requires that a DTD be created (in this case "authors.dtd") that properly defines how elements must be used. In this example, the DTD must have defined that the Authors element may only contain a single MainBody element; therefore the end tag for the Authors element implies the end of the MainBody element. Likewise, the PageTitle element must not be allowed to contain any other elements; the opening MainBody tag indicates the end of the PageTitle element content. Any software written to parse this document must be able to handle the DTD and use that information to correctly resolve the abbreviated or missing end tags. While these shortcuts may make it easier to create the document markup, it adds significant complexity to the development of parsing programs.

The amount of work required to prepare SGML documents, and the cost of SGML tools, kept many developers from adopting it. What was needed was some kind of middle ground, a markup language that was easier to learn and use, and easier to write software for, yet powerful enough to express sophisticated content.

So, the members of the **World Wide Web Consortium** (**W3C**), an international organization created to promote the development of common protocols for the World Wide Web, put their collective heads together, and on February 10 1998 they issued their recommendation for XML version 1.0. According to the recommendation, which can be seen in full at http://www.w3.org/TR/1998/REC-xml-19980210, the design goals for XML were:

❑   XML shall be straightforwardly usable over the Internet

❑   XML shall support a wide variety of applications

❑   XML shall be compatible with SGML

❑   It shall be easy to write programs that process XML documents

❑   The number of optional features in XML is to be kept to the absolute minimum, ideally zero

❑   XML documents should be legible to humans and be reasonably clear

❑   The XML design should be prepared quickly

❑   The design of XML shall be formal and concise

❑   XML documents shall be easy to create

❑   Terseness in XML markup is of minimal importance

By the way, Tim Bray, one of the authors of the recommendation, has created an annotated version of the recommendation, which you can find at http://www.xml.com/axml/testaxml.htm. It does a very good job of clarifying the occasionally arcane definitions or ambiguous statements in the recommendation. For example, in explaining the goal that the design should be prepared quickly, he states, "This goal was motivated largely by fear. We perceived that many of the Net's powers-that-be did not share our desire for widespread use of open, non-proprietary, textual data formats. We believed that if we didn't toss XML's hat into the ring soon, the web's obvious need for extensibility would be met by some combination of binary gibberish and proprietary kludges." Explaining the role of "terseness" he writes, "The historical reason for this goal is that the complexity and difficulty of SGML was greatly increased by its use of minimization, i.e. the omission of pieces of markup, in the interest of terseness. In the case of XML, whenever there was a conflict between conciseness and clarity, clarity won."

The result is a markup language with remarkably few requirements, but with enough range to essentially achieve what both HTML and SGML do, but with greater flexibility than HTML, and with a lower cost (both in time and money) than SGML.

But What *is* XML?

The simplest definition is that XML is "text that follows certain rules". The rules are very similar to those for creating HTML, but stricter, and with some enhancements. For example, in XML, all elements must have a closing tag. In HTML, forms often use INPUT elements. You typically see something like this:

```
<INPUT type='text' name='user' size='4'>
```

This may be acceptable to web browsers, but XML requires that you "close" the element, either by providing a closing tag, or by using a specific notation (a forward slash immediately before the closing "greater than" character) to indicate that the element is "empty" (i.e. it does not hold any text data):

```
<INPUT type='text' name='user' size='4'></INPUT>
```

or:

```
<INPUT type='text' name='user' size='4'/>
```

Extensibility

Because it follows these rules, applications can know what to expect and decide how to handle it. Using our INPUT example, an XML parser, upon encountering "/>", would know that the element has been closed. If it encounters just the ">" character, it will expect that the following text belongs to the INPUT element. However, unlike HTML, the rules are concerned with the markup syntax, not the qualities of a specific set of elements. This allows XML to be a simple, standard data format, without coercing you to use a fixed set of elements. In fact, while the XML recommendation goes to great lengths in describing how to develop your markup, it does not require the use of any specific elements. This is what makes the language *extensible*. So long as an XML document adheres to the rules of XML syntax, the creator of the document is free to employ any set of markup tags that seems appropriate. For example, in HTML, if you want to indicate that some text is part of a hierarchy, you can use header tags (H1, H2, etc.). But you may feel that these are too broad to express a more complex document structure. In XML, you may freely design your own set of tags that are more descriptive, such as <ABSTRACT> or <PROLOG>.

XML as a Data Format

XML can be a "smart" data format: XML documents describe themselves by combining descriptive markup with text. Think about CSV (comma-separated variable) data. It too is a textual data format, consisting simply of blocks of text delimited by commas, but much of the information about the data (what's frequently called the **metadata**), such as data types, often lives outside the actual data file. Furthermore, CSV is one-dimensional; you can't express complex data hierarchies. Also, if a user decides to change the number of fields in the file, the programs designed to read the file (which expect to find a fixed number of fields) will break. XML, being a markup language, allows you to mix content and metadata together. This is what happens in HTML files, where markup tags (the metadata) are used to organize the content. Unlike HTML, XML allows you to invent your own elements to define the data as you see fit. You can use nested elements to describe sophisticated data structures.

Because you can freely define the data, you can use it in any number of places. For example, many Visual Basic programs rely on INI files or the registry for configuration information. XML files could be used instead, allowing for a much richer set of possibilities when defining program information. INI files do not define hierarchical data, and there are circumstances where registry entries cannot be written. For example, if there are a large number of applications installed, HKEY_CLASSES_ROOT may become very large and, according to Microsoft, if one of the structures in the System.dat file takes up too much space in conventional memory, the registry cannot be accessed. It is also easier (and safer) for a user to read a disk file to inspect application settings than it is to run regedit.

XML for Web Pages

XML was devised with the Internet in mind. By combining XML with **CSS** (**Cascading Style Sheets**) or **XSL** (the **Extensible Stylesheet Language**), which are both discussed later, XML pages can be transformed into HTML for display in web browsers. Most browsers in use today cannot perform the XML+XSL or XML+CSS rendering – the transformation to HTML must be done before the page is sent to the browser. But at least one browser, Internet Explorer 5, and its update IE 5.5, can perform native XML, XSL and CSS processing because of a built-in XML parser. (XSL and CSS are covered later in this book, in Chapter 4, and this is the same parser we'll be using in our sample application.) However, relying on the client to perform the XML/XSL transformation limits your users to IE5.

Object Method Parameter Encoding and RPC Protocol

Besides being a possible alternative to web page markup, XML can be used to describe object method parameters. For example, when writing a Visual Basic COM object, you can have your method accept a single parameter of type String. That string would be an XML document describing the parameter/value pairs for the method. Should you need to alter your method to accept additional parameters, you can safely do so without breaking your interface.

Because the parameter list is simple text, it can be sent over any number of protocols. Combined with HTTP, XML offers a way to perform platform-independent **remote procedure calls** (**RPC**s). One problem with using DCOM or CORBA is that they use network ports that may be blocked by firewalls. However, HTTP port 80 is generally open. Encoding your method invocation in XML, and sending it via HTTP to port 80, allows you to get past this block.

> *In DCOM, when the client wishes to contact the server, the respective Service Control Managers communicate over port 135. When a remote object is then bound to a client, another port is dynamically allocated for the connection. The range of ports from which this might come is fairly wide, from 1024 to 65535. Leaving all of these open can present a severe security risk. It is possible, however, to configure DCOM to work with firewalls; see "Using Distributed COM with Firewalls" on the MSDN web site, at http://msdn.microsoft.com/library/backgrnd/html/msdn_dcomfirewall.htm. However, it requires that the client know the actual IP address of the server, which may constrain the development and deployment of your application.*

Imagine this scenario: you have a web site running on IIS, and an XML string is posted to an Active Server Page. The page looks at the XML and decides which object to load to handle the request. The request is processed, the object returns an answer, and an XML string containing the results is sent back to the caller. Your web site acts as a middle-tier request handler available to any application on any platform that can speak HTTP. Furthermore, this same logic could be implemented on a UNIX box running Apache, with the request dispatcher written in Perl. From the point of view of the object making the initial request, it is irrelevant how the HTTP POST is handled, and remote objects can be placed on whatever platform is most appropriate. If you write your Visual Basic objects to use XML over HTTP, they can speak to remote objects on any platform. If your remote objects know how to handle this invocation method, they are available to clients on any platform. Thus, XML can be used to pass information to and from an intermediate web server.

Microsoft has been involved in the development of a specification called **SOAP**, or **Simple Object Access Protocol**. SOAP defines a standard syntax for communicating with remote objects, and for describing various data types and data structures. SOAP is discussed in more detail later in this book, in Chapter 7.

So, we've seen that while it is convenient to think of XML as a data format, or as a document description language, the notions of "data" and "document" need to be expanded in order to appreciate the full value of XML.

XML and Open Exchange

Since XML is text, it is easy to exchange. Using text means you don't have to bother with decoding complex, proprietary data formats. Think of the overhead that would be incurred in trying to convert a binary Microsoft Office document into another format. Working with text makes it easy to transform one XML structure to another. In fact, since this was seen to be such a common task, another member of the XML family, **XSLT** (the **Extensible Stylesheet Language** for **Transformations**), has been developed to handle transformations. XSLT is discussed in depth in Chapter 4. Briefly, it is a language that uses XML syntax to define how XML documents can be transformed into other XML documents.

The Flexibility of XML

XML is flexible. Because you define the elements you need, and the relationship between these elements, XML allows you to express extremely complex data structures. However, since all the data structures employ common XML syntax, a single XML parsing tool can be used on every XML document.

Writing data from inside a running application to a file, or sending it to another system, has always been a tough task. Apart from the work involved in planning the format, parsers had to be written to process and check the validity of the data. The XML standard gives developers the tools to create document formats much faster, allows reuse of the parser code (or rather, the use of code written by other users) and provides a formal means to specify document types with other developers.

XML is Easy to Read

XML is both human and machine-readable. One of the lessons the W3C learned from HTML and SGML is that the more comprehensible the standard, the more successful it will become. One factor leading to the wide adoption of HTML was that, when you first came across it you probably thought, "Hey, I can do that too". (You may have said the same thing about SGML as well, but I'll bet it took you longer to do it.) The easier it is to write standards-compliant software, the cheaper and more plentiful the tools will be.

An important aspect of XML, which applies to both human and machine readers, is that XML is quite strict when it comes to the use of closing tags. An early draft of XML allowed the use of generic closing tags (</>) on the belief that the correct matching start tag could be deduced from the structure of the document. However, it was decided that allowing this would make it harder to write processing software, and harder for the human eye to pick out the structure, so it was dropped. A major reason for this is that a closing tag may be left out by mistake. The absence of any element name in a closing tag makes it harder for a reader to pick this out, and a program that is parsing a document with a missing closing tag might not know that something was wrong until the very end of the document was reached. It is much easier to detect this when each closing tag tells you to which element it belongs.

XML is Platform Independent

There is nothing in the XML specification that favors one platform over another. XML is pure text, which makes it a platform-neutral data format. Just to be clear on this, the specification states that allowable characters are tab, carriage return, line feed, and the legal graphic characters of Unicode and ISO/IEC 10646 (see http://www.unicode.org/unicode/techwork.html for more details). This simplicity is essential when trying to exchange data between any two arbitrary systems. It has tremendous value even when all of your applications are on the same platform. For example, you may use Internet Explorer as your main web browser, and have a large number of bookmarks. It would be nice if these were available to you when you use, say, Netscape Navigator. It would be handy if they shared a common format. In fact, a language exists called **XBEL**, the **Extensible Bookmark Exchange Language**, which is a browser-neutral way to define web site bookmarks. Bookmarks created using XBEL can be imported (using the proper tools) into most browsers.

The use of XML as a common exchange format will become of greater practical value as more vendors support XML as a native format in word processing software. Office 2000 currently has some limited XML features, and Corel's WordPerfect 9 has XML support. Currently, when converting a document from one binary format to another, some amount of formatting is lost or corrupted. Exporting a document using an industry standard DTD would mean the ability to edit your work in a variety of tools without distortion.

So Why XML and VB?

There is nothing in the XML specification that would require or imply the use of any particular programming language. In fact, any language that can handle text can handle XML. Thus, the choice of which programming language to use becomes a matter of personal preference and experience. So, perhaps the best reason to use Visual Basic (and a reason why you bought this book) is because you already know it!

If you are *not* familiar with VB, then this book will demonstrate how XML can be used to enhance the features of Visual Basic by exploiting its value as a rapid development tool. Because there is an XML standard, numerous component developers are producing ready-to-use XML parsing tools that can be easily manipulated with Visual Basic. One of the great things about Visual Basic is that it lets you use third-party components within the context of a robust development environment. Even though XML is language independent, some languages can have a larger developer community and more supporting tools available.

On the Windows platform, the easiest available free tool for parsing and manipulating XML is the MSXML COM object from Microsoft. If you have Internet Explorer 5 installed, then you already have it. (If you have IE 4, Microsoft provides an updated parser that can be downloaded from their web site. We'll explain how to get this in Chapter 3.) With the task of parsing the XML handled by a COM object, you are free to use your knowledge of VB to handle the application logic.

Microsoft has shown a strong commitment to the development of the XML standard, and the momentum of Microsoft alone would probably be enough to make things happen in this area. As a tools vendor, Microsoft has invested much time and effort to provide resources for the VB developer community, and has suggested that in future releases of VB, XML-specific features will be included. Though XML programming is essentially platform and language independent, the availability of such pre-built objects may be a strong factor in deciding which language to use.

Overall there is no real advantage of using VB when compared to other languages. Other languages that have significant XML developer communities and available tools are Java, C, C++, Perl, and Python.

When to Use XML

While much has been made of XML as an Internet technology, it is not limited to the web. It is useful in any circumstance where data is passed between applications or objects. Whenever you are dealing with information that is more complex than a simple string or integer value, you may consider using XML to store or exchange it with other systems. If you expect others to use your files, or you want to use files from someone else, you should consider using an XML-based data format.

Examples

To demonstrate how XML adds value, let's look at a couple of examples.

Scenario No. 1

First, imagine a software development company. Before a single line of code is written, a fair amount of technical documentation needs to be created. Suppose that, as often happens, these documents are written using a common word processing program, such as Microsoft Word. So, the company acquires scores of documents describing each piece of software: what it does, how it works, what business requirements it handles, and so on. The authors use PCs running Windows, but the network servers are UNIX boxes, and the documents are stored there. So, one day the company decides to see how many of their products are web-enabled. Well, how should they do this? They could run an indexing program against all of their documents, but it would have to know how to parse the Word binary format. And then, what should it look for? Would the mere presence of the words "Internet" or "web" really tell them enough about what products, or what parts of products, had Internet capability? If you've ever used an Internet search engine, then you have some idea of how hard it can be to locate a document containing a somewhat abstract idea.

Now suppose that they had decided to store their documents as XML. Since they had relatively complete freedom in choosing how to mark up the content, they could have selected elements that describe what each part of a document is for. At the very least, they could have used tags such as or <requirements>, so that they could restrict text searches to those areas of the document likely to contain fundamental information. If they were more diligent, then they would have used additional elements to provide a more fine-grained description of the content, such as using tags to indicate the names of related products. They could then avail themselves of any number of free tools to locate and query the XML. In addition to providing a more robust searching capability, having documents in XML would give them far greater publishing options. If they wanted to make their documents available through a web browser, they could use XSLT to transform the data to HTML. If they needed to print the documents, they could transform them to PDF, RTF, or Postscript.

Compound documents could be created by selecting tagged sections from individual documents and combining them in order to produce output. Because the XML documents would be plain text, other applications could easily extract the data. For example, by parsing the text, building INSERT statements, and populating a table, they could create a product database. The separation of content from presentation means that the data is available to any number of applications, each of which might need to use the data in a unique way.

Scenario No. 2

Here's another example. This same software company has grown quite large, and has produced different applications, in various languages, that run on different platforms. They have a large Oracle database application that runs on Solaris, and they have some Java applications that provide various functions for talking to the database. There are some C programs floating around and, of course, some VB applications. As they continue development, they begin to see that some desired features already exist in some form or another in an existing program. To fully make use of their investment, they decide to make the existing functionality openly available by exposing XML interfaces (meaning that the public methods take XML strings as parameters, and return XML strings as the response). Rather than redo the same set of functions in a new application, they modify the older applications to allow transaction requests via socket requests. An application could listen on a given port, waiting for a connection, and when one comes, XML could be passed in, the request handled, and XML sent back out. New applications could now request services from any of the existing applications, regardless of platform. The Java application that creates nice summarized financial reports can offer them to the VB application that populates a database with monthly sales figures. That same service can be called from a Word document using Visual Basic for Applications (VBA). A VBA macro can make a network call, pull back XML, use the Microsoft XML parser to hold the results, and output text based on the content. It's hard to emphasize enough the value of using a robust, standard, text-based data format.

When Not to Use XML

Well, you should not use it just because it's so hot and all the hip magazines (or books) write about it. XML comes with a cost. The verbose use of tags and attributes adds considerable bulk to data, particularly when compared to binary formats. Transforming XML into another format (such as HTML) takes time and resources. You can create your own file-based database using XML, but remember that a database might require a good deal of disk I/O and lookup activity, tasks for which most database applications have been optimized. As the number of files grows, you would need to pay close attention to how your files and directories are organized to reduce the path to the data you want and the number of file reads to extract it. For example, if you were looking for a set of files whose data pertain to certain dates, it would be helpful to set up subdirectories based on date ranges and store your files by date groups, making it easier to pinpoint a specific directory with fewer files to examine.

If you're managing a great number of extremely large documents you may find that you really do need the full power of SGML. Despite their similarities, XML and SGML are not functionally equivalent, and sometimes XML just won't do everything you need.

XML will not replace HTML. Since XML does not intrinsically contain any presentation information, XML documents will need to be transformed into some rendering format. While much of this can happen dynamically before being viewed by a user, the overhead for doing this might make it more practical to directly create some documents in HTML.

XML will not replace ADO (ActiveX Data Objects). There is some overlap: XML and disconnected recordsets can both be used to pass fairly complex data around. However, XML lacks most of the functionality ADO has in connected scenarios for retrieving, modifying and displaying data from databases. In a disconnected scenario, XML is much more flexible than a recordset could ever be, implementing links and complex hierarchies, being able to move data structures from a Windows machine to a UNIX box or a mainframe. But, since XML is strictly text, it does not by itself provide any built-in methods for manipulation. XML will most likely be used in *conjunction* with ADO to take advantage of what each has to offer.

This is not intended to scare you off using XML in any way you choose. As you go through this book, you'll see a variety of ways to use XML in place of more traditional methods. You'll also learn how to avoid or minimize the potential problems you may find with XML. What's important, as with any technology, is to understand just what it can do, and learn enough to make informed decisions.

XML Basics

Let's start taking a look at some XML. Here is a sample XML document:

```
<tag/>
```

Here's another one:

```
<?xml version="1.0" encoding="utf-8"?>
<example number="1">
 <sample>
  This is some sample content
 </sample>
```

```
<!-- This is a comment -->
<sample type="next">
 Sometimes we want to include <![CDATA[odds & ends]]>in our document.
</sample>
<moretext>
 <p>
  Content &amp; markup are different things
 </p>
</moretext>
</example>
```

Digging Into the Syntax

Hmm. What does this tell us? Well, XML documents can range from the extremely simple to the highly complex. It looks very much like HTML, but there can be some peculiar markup characters. Let's take a look at some of the guts of XML to see just how it works. We'll look at some comparisons to HTML and SGML, and get a sense of what makes XML unique. Then we'll dive into the fundamental syntax of XML.

It's Just Like HTML and SGML, but ...

Like both HTML and SGML, XML uses the familiar `<TAG>` format to indicate markup elements. Unlike HTML (but like SGML), XML allows you to make up your own tags and attributes. However, like HTML, but unlike SGML, you don't need a DTD (though you may use one if you like). Unlike SGML and HTML, XML elements must have a complete closing tag. For example, you must use `<TAG>Some text</TAG>`. (The exception is an *empty* element, which is written as `<TAG/>`.)

Here's a table to help make the comparison:

XML	HTML/SGML
Opening and closing tags must have identical names: `<Tag>Some text</Tag>`	This is the same in SGML; in HTML, there is no distinction for case: `<Tag>Some text<TAG>` is acceptable in HTML
The creator of an XML document may invent element and attribute names	This is the same in SGML; in HTML, the elements and attributes are restricted to a predefined set. (Beginning with Microsoft's IE 4, document authors could invent attributes and refer to them in script; they are referred to as "expando" properties. With IE5, HTML documents could also have custom elements. This is not available in other browsers, and not standard HTML)

XML	HTML/SGML
All closing tags must have the name of the element (with the exception of empty elements, which are dicussed later in this chapter). You may not abbreviate closing tags: OK: `<Tag>Some text</Tag>` Not OK: `<Tag>Some text</>` Not OK: `<Tag>Some text`	In SGML, all elements must have a closing tag (except for empty elements), but the closing tag may be abbreviated: `<Tag>Some text</>` In HTML, some elements may be used without a closing tag: ` `, or `<input type="text" name="test">`
XML documents are not required to use a DTD or schema	In SGML, a document must have a DTD; SGML does not use schemas In HTML, reference to a DTD is optional; HTML does not use schemas

XML is case-sensitive. `<TAG>Some text</tag>` is not proper XML because `TAG` and `tag` are not the same.

XML Anatomy

XML has only one data type: `String`. More specifically, XML is composed of characters as defined by ISO/IEC 10646; the legal graphic characters of Unicode and ISO/IEC 10646: tab, carriage return, and line feed are allowed. While everything in an XML document is a character, a distinction is made between **text** and **markup**. Text (or more specifically, **character data**) is what you would normally think of as the actual content of a document, the part that contains the information you're generally really interested in. The markup is all of the other stuff that gives structure and meaning to the text, as well as providing additional information to the XML parser. By reserving certain characters and character combinations, XML parsers can recognize when they are looking at content and when they are looking at markup.

Elements

These are the familiar `<TAG>` things. An XML document must have a single **root element**, also known as the **document element**, optionally containing text and markup. If there are other elements besides the root element, then they must be contained within the root element. The root element is not required to have any **content**, though practical uses of such a document may be limited. Nonetheless, it doesn't take much to create a minimal XML document.

Elements may optionally contain content:

```
<p>Here's my content!</p>
```

Any element with content must have complete start and end tags. If an element does not have any content then it may be written as a single tag:

```
<p/>
```

> Note that `<p></p>` and `<p/>` are considered equivalent.

A word about nomenclature: the words "tag" and "element" are often used interchangeably. This is not correct. A tag gives a name to an element; it describes an element type. Tags contain an element type name, and may also contain attribute names. Elements (except for empty ones) have two tags: a start tag and an end tag. According to Charles Goldfarb (The XML Handbook, 1998, ISBN 0-13-081152-1, pp60) there is no such thing as a "tag name". Having helped invent SGML, he should know. But this can get confusing. The W3C specification document for DOM Level 1 makes frequent reference to "tag names" when discussing element nodes, such as in the description of the `getElementsByTagName` *method:*

"Returns a NodeList of all the Elements with a given tag name in the order in which they would be encountered in a preorder traversal of the Document tree."

(A preorder traversal is the order you would encounter the elements if you viewed the XML as a single string.)

We will cover `getElementsByTagName` in Chapter 3, but we can take a quick look at it here to help clarify the terminology. The method is used to retrieve a list of elements from an XML document. So, if your document has some number of Item elements, then we could call `getElementsByTagName("Item")`. The definition is referring to the name of the desired elements as the "tag name". Don't be too concerned about the reference to nodes and trees; they are not essential for this chapter, and will be discussed in depth in Chapter 3.

Elements may contain other elements. The elements must be properly nested; that is, the elements may not overlap. For example the following would not be correct:

```
<b><i>This is wrong</b></i>
```

The correct syntax would be:

```
<b><i>This is right</i></b>
```

Elements may also contain any other type of markup, as well as plain text. Exceptions to this would depend on whether or not the document is using a DTD, and how that element is defined in the DTD. It is possible to define elements so that they may only contain other elements, but not character data, or to define elements that may not have any content whatsoever.

Element names may be anything you like, with a few restrictions. Names must begin with either a letter or an underscore (_). The remaining characters may be any letter, digit, underscore, period, or hyphen (but not spaces). Names may not begin with 'xml', 'XML', or any upper/lower case combination; these have been reserved for future use.

Note that element names are fully international; you are free to use international characters in names, as in:

```
<Gästebuch>Deutsche</Gästebuch>
```

You may have seen XML elements that look like this:

```
<xsl:value-of select="Item" />
```

The use of the colon (:) indicates that a *namespace* is being used to distinguish the element name. In this case, the xsl namespace is being used with the value-of element. We discuss namespaces later in this chapter.

Attributes

Elements may have **attributes**. An attribute is a name/value pair assigned to an element. For example:

```
<TAG id="123"> This has an id attribute</TAG>
```

Attribute values must be enclosed in either single or double quotes. The attribute value may contain quote marks, so long as they are not the same type of quotes used to enclose the value. For example:

```
<TAG quote="There's an apostrophe in here!" />
<TAG quote='Define "apostrophe"' />
```

You may be required to use **entity references** inside of attribute values if you want to have both types of quote marks in your data. Use " for the double quote character, and ' for the single quote character:

```
<TAG quote="There&apos;s the word &quot;apostrophe&quot; again " />
```

Keep in mind that XML documents are often created programmatically, and you may not always know exactly which quote character is acceptable. It is a good practice to use the quote character entities for all character data to avoid possible confusion. Entities are discussed in more detail later in this section.

Attribute names may not be repeated inside of a tag, for example:

```
<X id="1" id="2">This is not correct</X>
```

Each attribute name in an element must be unique. However, attribute names are case-sensitive, so the following is perfectly legal, but may lead to confusion:

```
<X name="John" NAME="Doe">Not a good idea</X>
```

If you are using a DTD with your document then there may be additional constraints on certain attribute types. DTDs and the mechanics of declaring attributes are discussed in the next chapter, so we won't go into all of the details here. But it is useful to understand the concepts behind ID and IDREF attributes because they give your document additional power.

If you use an attribute, which in your DTD you declare to be of type ID, then its value must be unique throughout the document for all other ID-type attribute values. Further, attributes of type IDREF must have a value that matches that of a corresponding ID attribute. Many IDREFs may refer to the same ID.

Typically you would want to name these types of attributes 'ID', or 'IDREF', but it's the DTD declaration, not the actual name, that determines their role. So you can pick whatever name suits your purposes. Once you have these types of attributes, you can use them to behave as element cross-references, in much the same way as, with a database, you would use a foreign key to index a table on a primary key.

Let's see how this works. Suppose we have the following document. Up top is the DTD declaration.

```
<?xml version="1.0"?>
<!-- Note that we need to have -->
<!-- DTD information for this! -->
<!DOCTYPE doc [
 <!ELEMENT doc (product|part)>
 <!ELEMENT part (#PCDATA)>
 <!ATTLIST part idref IDREFS #IMPLIED >
 <!ELEMENT product (#PCDATA)>
 <!ATTLIST product id ID #IMPLIED prodnum CDATA #IMPLIED >
]>
```

Don't worry about the syntax in the above code, as it will be explained in Chapter 2. What I want you to look at is the XML content below:

```
<doc>
 <product my-id="123">foo</product>
 <product my-id="456">bar</product>
 <part my-idref="123">spring</part>
 <part my-idref="123">lever</part>
 <part my-idref="456">sprocket</part>
 <part my-idref="456">little plastic piece</part>
</doc>
```

You'll notice that the relationship between products and parts is not inherent in the structure of the document. However, because we are using ID and IDREF attributes, we can programmatically extract this information. For example, if we wanted to render this document, we could use XSL to find the related pieces of data, and display them in a more visually connected manner:

```
<xsl:template match="product">
  <xsl:variable name="ref" select="@id" />
  <b>
    <h2>Product: </h2><h3><xsl:value-of select="."/></h3>
    <h2>Parts</h2>
    <xsl:for-each select="//*[@idref=$ref]">
    <xsl:value-of select="."/><br/>
    </xsl:for-each>
  </b>
</xsl:template>
```

Again, don't worry about the syntax in the above code; it is purely illustrative.

Manipulating XML is explained in Chapter 3, 'Programming the Document Object Model', and Chapter 4, 'Using XML Queries and Transformations'. DTD declarations may also be used to restrict attributes to a specific set of values, to assign default attribute values, and to assign entity data to attribute values, as explained in Chapter 2, 'XML Validation'.

Element or Attribute?

As you start to design XML documents, you will run into the "element or attribute" question. That is, when should something be an element, and when should it be an attribute? There is nothing in the XML specification that dictates how to design documents, so you need to look at the type of data you are trying to represent, how that data will be accessed, and how the different pieces of data relate to each other.

For example, suppose we wanted to describe a product from a catalog. One option is to use elements only:

```
<product>
  <name>Wonder Widget</name>
  <prodid>123</prodid>
  <cost>100.00</cost>
  <currency>USD</currency>
  <weight>10</weight>
  <weightunit>kilograms</weightunit>
  <description>Expensive little item</description>
</product>
```

While this is perfectly fine XML, it makes no distinction between data meant for display, and data meant to clarify other data. Let's try it using only attributes:

```
<product prodid="123" name="Wonder Widget"
cost="100.000" currency="USD" weight="10"
weightunit ="kilograms"
description="Expensive little item"/>
```

Well, that works too, but it can be a little hard to read and pick out the salient data. Let's try it one more time, combining elements and attributes:

```
<product prodid="123">
  <name>Wonder Widget</name>
  <cost currency="USD">100.00</cost>
  <weight weightunit ="kilograms">10</weight>
  <description>Expensive little item</description>
</product>
```

The use of attributes here does two things. First, it better couples primary data (what it is, what it costs, how much it weighs) with clarification data (the product ID, the currency type, and the unit of weight measurement). Second, it helps reduce the overall size of your file without sacrificing readability.

Another way of looking at this is to use elements for data that is primarily intended for display, and attributes for data that provides instructions on how the data should be rendered. (There is nothing to stop you from doing this the other way around, should you care to make things more difficult for yourself!) Or, for the literarily inclined, elements are like nouns and verbs, and attributes are like adjectives and adverbs.

Here are some basic comparisons between elements and attributes:

Quality	Elements	Attributes
May have default values	No	Yes
May be referenced by index	Yes	No (except through the `NamedNodeMap` interface, which, as we'll see in Chapter 3, can provide a list of attributes)
May have child elements	Yes	No
May be repeated	Yes	No
May contain unparsed entities	Yes	No
May have a data type	No	Yes
Whitespace can be ignored	Yes	No
Have an intrinsic order	Yes	No

Finally, your choices may depend on your code. Some parsers are better at retrieving attributes than elements. If you are looking to use recursion to travel though the content of an XML document then it may be better to use elements only.

An interesting discussion of this question may be found on the OASIS website, at http://www.oasis-open.org/cover/elementsAndAttrs.html

Text

Text is all the information surrounded by markup. As we mentioned earlier, more technically, this type of text is referred to as character data. Text may be any XML-allowed character (tab, carriage return, line feed, and the legal graphic characters of Unicode and ISO/IEC 10646) with a few exceptions. You may not use the ampersand character (&) or the left angle bracket or "less than" symbol (<) because they have special meanings. The left angle bracket indicates the beginning of an element tag whereas the ampersand indicates the use of an entity. If you want to use these characters then you need to use their entity references, much like in HTML. These are explained in the following section.

Entities

Entities are a way of substituting text. They are similar to the #include directive found in some programming languages. For example, you may want to include the same copyright information in numerous documents. You can use an entity to define a piece of text that will be replaced by the contents of your copyright data. Later on in your document, you use the entity reference where you would like this data to appear.

Entity references begin with the ampersand character and end with a semicolon. Examples of entity references would be   (non-breaking space) or > ("greater than" symbol >) which are often used in HTML documents. Entities must be declared before being referenced, though XML gives you some for free: & (the ampersand &), < (the left angle bracket <), " (the double quote ") and ' (the apostrophe '). These are called *pre-declared* or *predefined* entities. They are the only entities that you may use without a declaration (One common problem XML newcomers encounter is trying to use the   entity reference, which is very common in HTML. This must be declared in XML before it is used, though you may also use , which is a different kind of reference that we'll cover in just a moment.)

Entities must be declared inside a DTD. DTDs are often referenced as external documents, but they may also be defined directly inside the XML document. For those documents that do not require a DTD, but do need to use entities, the internal DTD notation can be used to declare the entities. DTDs are discussed in depth in Chapter 2, but for now I will use the internal declaration notation.

How an entity is declared (in other words, the specific notation syntax) depends on what type of entity you want it to be. There are several types of entities: *internal* and *external*, *parsed* and *unparsed*, and *general* or *parameter*. All entities are some combination of these types, though not all combinations make sense. Here are some examples:

```
<!DOCTYPE EXAMPLE [
<!ENTITY internalparsed
"Greetings from the internal parsed entity!" >
] >
<EXAMPLE>
   <TEXT>&internalparsed;</TEXT>
</EXAMPLE>
```

```
<!DOCTYPE EXAMPLE [
<!ENTITY externalparsed
SYSTEM "http://www.somehost.com/extparsed.ent" >
] >
<EXAMPLE>
   <TEXT>&externalparsed;</TEXT>
</EXAMPLE>
```

Both of these are examples of general parsed entities; parameter entities are for use only inside the DTD. The notation is basically the same, except a percent sign (%) is added between the ENTITY keyword and the entity name. The percent sign serves to tell the parser it is looking at a parameter entity.

Unparsed entities are used to refer to a resource that might not be text, or, if it is text, might not be valid XML. Because of this, an unparsed entity is always external. Unparsed entities are a way to include all those things that don't fit neatly into the world of text, such as image or sound files, without the XML parser complaining about character sequences it cannot understand.

The declaration for an unparsed entity is similar to that of a general parsed entity, except that it must have an associated **notation**, which identifies the format of the unparsed entity. Since we eventually want some application to handle the unparsed entity, the notation provides the information on how to process it. XML does not specify what name you can give the notation – you can name it whatever you like. In general, the notation would refer to a file type that the parsing application would know how to recognize and handle. An example would be the inclusion of a graphic file; the DTD would contain this entity declaration:

```
<!ENTITY AuthorGIF
    "http://www.wrox.com/images/author.gif"
NDATA gif>
```

Then, in your XML document, you could have:

```
<IMG src="AuthorGIF"/>
```

Note: if you are using a DTD, then this only works if the attribute being assigned an entity value has been declared as type ENTITY. Also be aware that unparsed entities do not use the leading "&" and trailing ";". Instead, they are directly referenced using the entity name.

One final note: every XML document itself is also an entity, called the **document entity**. It is the root of the entity tree and the starting point for XML processors.

Character References

Character references are similar to entities in that they allow you to use a symbolic reference in place of other text. Character references are always replacements for single characters, and begin with '&#'. Like entities, they end with a semicolon. In between these delimiters is a decimal representation of the character's location in the ISO/IEC 10646 character set. For example, the familiar   (non-breaking space) could also be encoded as . This is a handy notation to know if you are writing XML, which you intend to be rendered as HTML. The non-breaking space is often useful for controlling, for example, how empty <TD> elements appear. But it is not one of the pre-declared entities, and if you want to use it you need to explicitly define it in a DTD (either internally or externally). Unless you have other reasons for needing a DTD, it can be easier to just use the character reference. Alternatively, a character reference may begin with '&#x' to indicate a hexadecimal representation. So, you can also represent the non-breaking space as .

You can think of a character set as an array. You index into the array with some number, and get back some particular character. For example, suppose we had an array called ascii, and it held all of the ASCII characters. So, ascii[65] would give you the letter "A". (In fact, this is what happens in Visual Basic when you write Chr$(65).)

There are, however, many different "arrays" for various collections of characters. These different collections were devised because people write in different languages that use their own unique characters. ISO/IEC 10646 is a character set created to provide a greater, international, range of characters than ASCII. We'll take a closer look at character sets when we discuss character encoding and Unicode later on.

CDATA

Sometimes you want your document's content to contain characters or character sequences that are not allowed by the XML syntax. For example, the left-angle bracket (<) is a reserved XML character, so you can't just write this:

```
<bad> 2 < 4</bad>
```

Of course, you can use the entity reference for this:

```
<good> 2 &lt; 4</good>
```

However, if your intended document content becomes a bit more involved, the use of entity references diminishes readability. If you are trying to display sample HTML code, then this is what the use of entity references would give you:

```
<sample> Sample table:
&lt;table border="0">
 &lt;tr>
  &lt;td>Data goes here&lt;/td>
 &lt;/tr>
&lt;/table>
</sample>
```

Instead, you can mark your text as CDATA. CDATA stands for "character data", and the CDATA markup tells the XML processor to stop parsing the text as XML. It allows the marked text to pass through. Using the CDATA element we can rewrite our example like this:

```
<sample>
Sample table:
<![CDATA[
<table border="0">
 <tr>
  <td>Data goes here</td>
 </tr>
</table>
]]>
</sample>
```

The syntax for CDATA is:

```
<![CDATA[ your text here ]]>
```

At the risk of stating the obvious, be aware that one thing you can't put inside of a CDATA section is, of course, the end-of-CDATA string: ']]>'. This is an unlikely, but certainly feasible, text string that you might actually enter by mistake. So, if the parser starts throwing out inexplicable error messages, this is something to take a look at.

Encodings

For a computer to display text it needs to take some binary data and render it according to some defined translating format. What may not be so obvious is exactly what that rendering format is. You may use a variety of text editors, which appear to represent your text equally well, but the binary representation may be different. The text may be stored as ASCII, which uses single bytes to represent characters (and really only uses seven of the eight bits available), or ISO 8859-1, (also known as Latin 1), which uses eights bits to define the characters in most European languages. Or it may be using a **code page**. A code page defines a standard set of characters, and different code pages exist for different locales. Code pages can be referred to by a specific number; for example, the Windows code page for English is 1252. Most code pages use standard ASCII characters for the first 128 characters, but beyond that the character sets diverge.

Generally, you don't need to think about these things. If you edit some text in Notepad, save it out to disk, and then load it into Word, everything works fine. However, if you're using characters outside of the ASCII range, you might see some problems as you move the text to other editors. If the editor does not know what character set is intended, or is only able to render a single, incompatible character set, then you run the risk of having your text appear mangled.

For example, Microsoft Word allows you to insert special characters into a document. So, we may decide to write something like this:

```
1 • 2
```

(We've used a symbol from the "Mathematical Operators" set.)

Now we decide to save our file as text, so that we may work on it in another editor, and decide to use UTF-8 as the encoding. However, when we view the file in Notepad, we see something like this:

```
1â% 2
```

The particular set of bits Word used to save our file as text do not quite match up with those used by Notepad when reading a file, because Notepad does not understand UTF-8.

Unicode

Such problems are brought about because eight bits does not provide enough room to uniquely define all of the written characters in use around the world. To get around this limitation, **Unicode** was devised. According to "*The Unicode Standard, Version 3.0*', available at http://www.unicode.org/index.html, the design goals of the Unicode Standard were:

❑ **Universal:** The repertoire must be large enough to encompass all characters that are likely to be used in general text interchange, including those in major international, national, and industry character sets.

❑ **Efficient:** Plain text, composed of a sequence of fixed-width characters, provides an extremely useful model because it is simple to parse. Software does not have to maintain state, look for special escape sequences, or search forward or backward through text to identify characters.

❑ **Uniform:** A fixed character code allows efficient sorting, searching, displaying, and editing of text.

❑ **Unambiguous:** Any given 16-bit value always represents the same character.

To allow XML to be international, the W3C decided that XML processors must handle Unicode characters. In the absence of any explicit encoding declaration the default encoding is UTF-8, meaning each character is represented by one or more bytes. An alternative encoding may be declared in the XML prolog, the processing instruction found at the start of many XML documents:

```
<?xml version="1.0" encoding="iso-8859-1"?>
```

If you are writing your XML in an ASCII editor then your file can use the default encoding, but be sure that it is true ASCII, and not the Windows code page. Some text editors, such as the version of Notepad that ships with Windows 2000, allow you to explicitly set the encoding type. If you are not sure what encoding is being used, check the documentation for your editor.

Comments

XML comments use the familiar HTML comment notation. For example:

```
<!--comments look like this. -->
```

Comments may appear anywhere you like, outside of other markup text, but you may not nest comments:

```
<!--Comments like
<!-- these -->
will get you in trouble -->
```

Note that the XML specification states that XML processors are not required to retrieve the comment text, and comments are not considered to be part of the document's character data. Typically, XML parsers will provide access to comment text, but they are really intended only for human readers of XML documents. Do not use comments with the expectation that they will be retrievable by the XML parser, because there is no guarantee of that happening. Finally, a double-hyphen (--) may not be used inside a comment, so as to maintain compatibility with SGML.

Processing Instructions

Processing instructions, often referred to as **PIs**, are a way to provide instructions for the application processing the XML. Processing instructions use a special tag syntax, consisting of the standard "<" and ">" tag characters, plus corresponding "?" characters, as in this example:

```
<?SomePI Some data goes here ?>
```

The most notable PI is the one often found at the very top of many XML documents:

```
<?xml version="1.0"?>
```

What you might think of as the PI name (SomePI, in our example) is referred to as the **target**, and specifies the application for which the instruction is intended. The 'xml' target (and 'XML', 'Xml' etc.) is reserved. The text following the target, and separated by a whitespace character, is the PI **data**. An interesting feature of processing instructions is that they may contain characters that would be illegal elsewhere in the XML text. One possible use for PIs is to notate your XML document for parsing by a non-XML parser.

If you were to create your own processing instruction, it would look something like this:

```
<?MyApp BEGIN-EXTRACT ?>
```

In this example, the application `MyApp` would be able to determine what to do when it saw the `BEGIN-EXTRACT` string, perhaps using it to copy a section of the document.

Like comments, processing instructions are not considered part of the document's character data, but they are available to the XML parser.

Well-formed versus Valid

Documents that adhere to the XML syntax specification are referred to as **well-formed**. According to the XML specification, XML parsers are required to indicate an error if they encounter a document that is not well-formed, for example if it does not have correctly formatted closing tags. This is in contrast to most web browsers, which accept and render (albeit with much variety) poorly constructed HTML – there are many HTML editing tools that create HTML code that may or may not be properly displayed by the browser. Such inconsistency is not acceptable in XML.

The structure of an XML document may optionally be defined by a DTD. A document that follows the rules of its DTD is considered **valid**. Note that, if a document does not have a DTD, it is not considered *invalid* – without a DTD the concept of validation doesn't apply. Validation can only occur when there is a DTD. Likewise, only the presence of a DTD can tell you if a document is invalid.

If a document is found to be valid, then it must also be well-formed. A parser cannot get to the point of checking the validity of the document if it didn't make it past the well-formed check. However, a document can be well-formed without being valid.

Whether or not a document needs a DTD depends on your particular circumstances. For example, DTDs can define default values for attributes, enabling you to construct documents without having to explicitly repeat this attribute, unless the value is different from the default. On the other hand, XML documents are often created and used entirely by software, and each part of the process may not always know what elements are to be expected at every step along the way. By avoiding validation, you allow your program to embrace the philosophy of "Ignore what you don't understand". XML documents can be built up by aggregating other XML documents, and the program need only look for and process the parts it is coded for, disregarding elements intended for other processes. Validation is covered in detail in Chapter 2.

XML Namespaces

XML allows you to make up your own element names, which is a good thing. This gives you the flexibility to name your elements in a way that has meaning for you or the intended recipient without having to conform to a predefined set of elements that may only loosely (or worse, incorrectly) describe your data. Of course, if *you* can do this, then so can anybody else. However, this can lead to problems when users start exchanging documents. Suppose, for example, that I send you a document containing `<date>` elements. You receive something like this:

```
<invoice>
 <date>19990301</date>
 <!-- other elements ... -->
</invoice>
```

Well, what does that date mean? Depending on your part of the world, that string of digits could refer to March 1 1999, January 3 1999, or perhaps something else altogether. The problem is compounded if you are constructing an XML document by pulling together fragments from multiple sources (for example, using a linking mechanism such as XLink, which we discuss in Chapter 5). However, if you knew something about the source of that element, and if you could uniquely identify it, then you can determine how to handle it. **Namespaces** were devised to do just that. When you declare a namespace, and use that namespace with your elements, you indicate how the elements are defined.

Namespaces allow overlapping use of the same tags (for elements and attributes) within a given set of documents without fear of clashes. This is very similar to scoping of variable names within typical programming languages. They become particularly useful when a set of elements is made available to a wide group of people. Application software needs to be sure that the use of a particular element is meant to refer to a member of that special set, and that the element was not used because someone just made it up. For example, in Chapter 4 we discuss XSLT, which transforms XML so that its data can be viewed in an HTML browser. However, XSLT is itself XML, and the markup defining XSLT has special meaning. Anyone can use a tag called `apply-template`, but when used with the `xsl` namespace we know that it refers to a specific definition of that element. In this case, the use of the `xsl` prefix on an element fully qualifies it as belonging to the XSL namespace.

A Detailed Example

Suppose we ran a news service, and wanted to send a news article to the printer, which, being a modern "with-it" printer, has printing applications that understand XML. We want to specify some special printing instructions, but we also want to make sure that the layout markup doesn't get confused with the news article markup. Luckily, for us, the "Society of With-it Printers" has recognized this, and has created a set of elements to be used for printing instructions. And, as their name would suggest, they've even implemented a namespace for it. So, we send this document:

```
<?xml version="1.0"?>
<swp:article xmlns:swp='http://www.swp.org/xml/swp1.0'>
  <swp:header>
    <swp:date>20000103</swp:date>
    <swp:author>Sam Clemens</swp:author>
    <swp:title>Author's notes discovered</swp:title>
  </swp:header>
  <swp:body>
    <para>
    Yesterday, <date format="ISO8601">2000-02-16</date>,
    a rare manuscript of <title>A Connecticut Yankee in King
    Arthur's Court</title>, by the American author
    <author>Mark Twain</author>, was discovered at a
    garage sale in New England
    </para>
  </swp:body>
</swp:article>
```

Now, you'll notice that some of the elements have a peculiar syntax. The use of the colon in the element name indicates that a namespace is being used. The swp prefix allows the parser to distinguish between the date element in the header and the date element in the actual article. When the printer application processes this document, it will know that the name of the author of the article should be treated differently from the name of the author mentioned in the article, that is to say "Sam Clemens" and "Mark Twain" will be treated differently.

A namespace can be declared in two ways. It can be defined in the root element of the document, or it can be defined on any specific element. For example, suppose we needed to use some additional markup, defined by a different namespace. Imagine that a namespace was defined for ISO date formats. Then, we could use:

```
<iso:date xmlns:iso="http://www.w3.org/TR/NOTE-datetime">
2000-02-16
</iso:date>
```

This is a little more unwieldy, but allows us to mix up the use of numerous namespaces in a single document.

How do Namespace Declarations Work?

You'll notice that we declared the iso namespace using the xmlns:iso attribute and assigning what looks like a web site address. So, you may wonder, where did that address come from? You might also wonder if the XML parser actually goes out and fetches something from that address. Well, the answer to the second question is no. The reason for this has to do with what the "web address" is intended to mean.

A namespace is distinguished by referring to a **URI**, or **Uniform Resource Identifier**; a URL (Uniform Resource Locator), such as a web address, is a special type of URI. However, URIs can point to other resources besides web pages, such as FTP sites (ftp://ftp.wrox.com), e-mail addresses (mailto:biff@someplace.com), or local files (file:///c:/MyDoc.txt). The general format is to specify a protocol, followed by the characters "://", and followed by whatever text would comprise a valid path or address for the resource.

According to RFC 2396, "A Uniform Resource Identifier (URI) is a compact string of characters used for identifying an abstract or physical resource."

Regarding URLs, it states: "A URI can be further classified as a locator, a name, or both. The term 'Uniform Resource Locator' (URL) refers to the subset of URIs that identify resources via a representation of their primary access mechanism (e.g., their network 'location'), rather than identifying the resource by name or by some other attribute(s) of that resource".

Another term, Uniform Resource Name (URN) refers to the subset of URIs that are required to remain globally unique and persistent even when the resource ceases to exist or becomes unavailable.

The URI specification is intended to provide a general syntax for all locatable resources, encompassing the existing Internet addressing schemes as well as allowing for the definition of new ones. Perhaps most interesting is this definition from the RFC of a resource:

"A resource can be anything that has identity. Familiar examples include an electronic document, an image, a service (e.g., 'today's weather report for Los Angeles'), and a collection of other resources. Not all resources are network 'retrievable'; e.g., human beings, corporations, and bound books in a library can also be considered resources."

This can present a problem to an XML processing application, which, though possibly having the ability to retrieve Internet documents, is unlikely to know how to resolve all possible URIs. And what this means for namespaces is that there is no requirement that an XML parser be able to do this. However, there is some value in specifying a retrievable file, so that any *user* who is interested in knowing just what the namespace is intended for can obtain a readable document.

> The upshot of this is that the URI specifying the identifier for the namespace does not have to be a retrievable resource or even an existing one. All it has to be is globally unique.

The World of Parsers

So, we have a format for representing data. Now we want to use it. That's where the XML processor, or **parser**, comes in. A parser is a program that is able to read in an XML document, determine if it is well-formed, and possibly check that it is valid. Parsers typically expose some interface into the document to allow you to retrieve or manipulate the contents, and we'll look at this in Chapter 3, when we discuss the Document Object Model. A blessing of open standards is that any vendor is free to go ahead and implement software to do this processing, and a number of companies (and individuals) have done so. Let's take a look at some of the parsers available.

Microsoft Internet Explorer Parser

Microsoft was quick out of the gate with an XML parser, shipped with Internet Explorer 4. It implemented an early draft of the XML specification, as well as an early version of XSL. Developers could access the XML features by setting a reference to the MSXML DLL. With the release of IE 5, the XML implementation was upgraded to reflect the XML version 1 specification. The XSL specification was still a draft, though Microsoft upgraded its code to reflect the changes since IE 4; XSL written for that first version will no longer work. When XSLT became a recommendation in December of 1999, Microsoft moved once again to upgrade the parser, though at the time this book was going to press it had not yet implemented the full XSLT recommendation.

The IE5 parser is the one we will use to describe the programming of the DOM (Chapter 3) and to implement the main application described in the book. We'll discuss the implications of using alternative parsers in Chapter 3.

James Clark's Expat

Expat is an XML 1.0 parser toolkit written in C. It has found its way into a number of open source projects, including Mozilla and the Perl XML modules. It is not a validating XML processor (it will check that a document is well-formed, but does not validate against a DTD), but it is extremely quick. Expat can be downloaded from ftp://ftp.jclark.com/pub/xml/expat.zip. It includes Win32 executables and Win32 import libraries. It is free for both private and commercial use.

Vivid Creations ActiveDOM

When a large, influential software company includes a robust XML parser as a reusable COM object in the world's most popular web browser, there would seem to be little incentive for other companies to build the same thing. However, Vivid Creations (http://www.vivid-creations.com) has done just that, and more. The company offers several XML tools, including ActiveDOM and ActiveSAX. ActiveDOM is a re-distributable COM object implementing the W3C Level 1 DOM specification. It is very much like the Microsoft parser; in fact, it implements most of the extended interfaces that Microsoft included in MSXML.DLL. However, unlike the Microsoft object, it does not do any XSL transformations, but it does not require the installation of Internet Explorer in order to run, a requirement that may cause some concerns with potential recipients of your application if they go with MSXML.

ActiveSAX implements the SAX (Simple API for XML) interface, a specification designed by the XML community at large. We'll take a look at ActiveSAX when we discuss the SAX interface in Chapter 3.

Both ActiveDOM and ActiveSAX are commercial products, but a demonstration version of these tools may be downloaded from the Vivid Creations web site.

DataChannel XJ Parser

DataChannel, a business solutions software company, worked with Microsoft to produce an early XML parser written in Java. Their website (http://xdev.datachannel.com/directory/xml_parser.html) provides a link to get their most recent version. However, they state that since XML parsers have now become easily and freely available, they are no longer doing parser development. They have opted instead to use the xml4j parser from IBM.

IBM xml4j

IBM has made a strong commitment to XML. Their AlphaWorks site (http://www.alphaworks.ibm.com) offers a number of XML tools and applications, including the xml4j parser. This is another parser written in Java, and it includes limited support for the 9/24/1999 XML Schema Working Draft, and limited support for DOM Level 2, and support for SAX 2. The parser is free, though there are some licensing restrictions regarding its use.

Apache Xerces

With the increasing use of XML by web servers to deliver content, the Apache Software Foundation moved to include native XML support in the Apache web server. The Xerces sub-project of the Apache XML Project (http://xml.apache.org/) has resulted in XML parsers in Java and C++, plus a Perl wrapper for the C++ parser. These tools are in beta, but aim to support DOM Level 1 and Level 2, as well as the SAX 2 interface. They are free and the distribution of the code is controlled by the GNU Public License.

Summary

This chapter introduced markup languages, and highlighted some aspects of two older markup languages, HTML and SGML. We have seen that XML is another markup language, and was created to help solve some problems that existed with both HTML and SGML – by reducing the complexity of SGML, and increasing the flexibility of HTML through the use of extensibility.

We took a look at the main features of XML, the roles XML can play, and how a Visual Basic programmer can use XML. Later in the chapter, we looked at the details of XML, explaining the fundamental syntax of the language, and discussed the subject of XML namespaces.

Finally, some of the XML parsers available for developers were reviewed, a list that is bound to rise as more and more software companies develop XML products. However, for this book we shall be concentrating on the Microsoft parser.

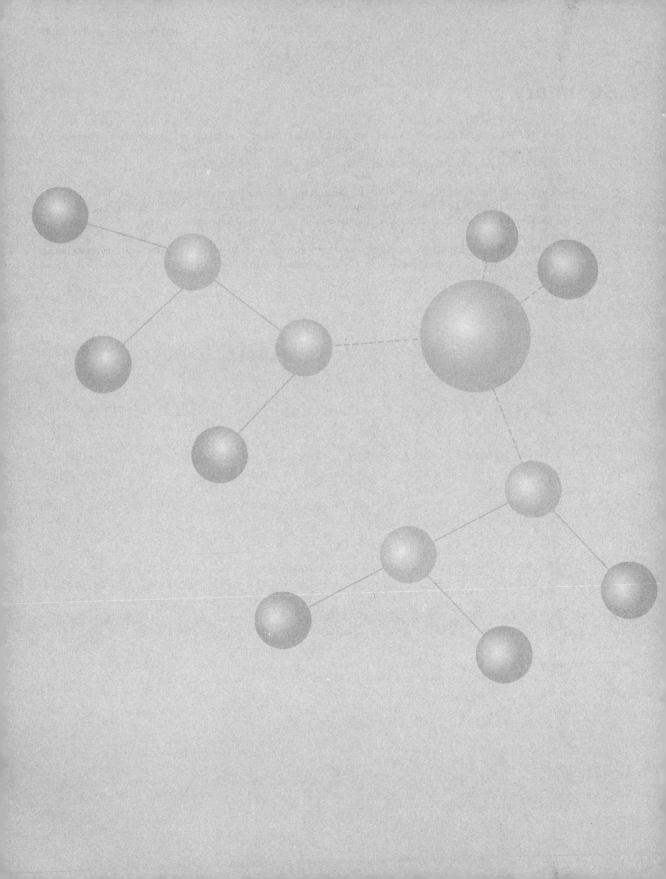

XML Validation

We saw in Chapter 1 that XML gives us the tools to describe our data in a very flexible way. We can choose our tag names freely. We can choose a hierarchical data structure or a plain table of fields, just as we see fit. However, the freedom to express our data in whatever format we choose does bring with it a new problem: it can become unclear what a certain piece of markup actually means; we as individuals are free to design such markup however we desire. If we want to share information with others, we need a way to specify how the documents should be structured and to describe rules for using our custom-built tags. We can then check the validity of the XML documents, in other words whether they conform to our rules.

In this chapter we will have a look at:

- ❏ How you can specify validation rules for a document type, using both standard DTD (Document Type Definition) syntax and the emerging standard, XML Schema

- ❏ How to declare an XML document as conforming to a certain document type

- ❏ How to use validation rules for creating relations between several parts of the data inside your document (creating a kind of referential integrity as found in relational databases)

Why Validation is Necessary

Let's look at an example: suppose user A wants to store information about the members of his or her family. An application could be created consisting of a simple user interface into which data is entered. XML could be used to mark up the stored data, which would consist of the name of each family member, and the name and type of any household pets. The XML file created might look like this:

```
<?xml version="1.0"?>
<FAMILY>
  <PERSON name="Freddy"/>
  <PERSON name="Margie"/>
  <PERSON name="Gerald"/>
  <PERSON name="Petra"/>
  <PET name="Bonzo" type="dog"/>
  <PET name="Arnie" type="cat"/>
</FAMILY>
```

However, a different user, B, creates a similar application to store exactly the same information, but in a very different format, as follows:

```
<?xml version="1.0"?>
<FAMILY>
  <PERSONS>
    <PERSON>Freddy</PERSON>
    <PERSON>Margie</PERSON>
    <PERSON>Gerald</PERSON>
    <PERSON>Petra </PERSON>
  </PERSONS>
  <PETS>
    <PET species="dog">Bonzo</PET>
    <PET species="cat">Arnie</PET>
  </PETS>
</FAMILY>
```

Both are well-formed XML documents. For a human reader, it is more or less obvious that both files contain the same information. Both users will be able to create an application that stores and retrieves this information.

However, problems arise as soon as a user wants to share his information with others. Each of the applications can read and write only one format. What we would like to do is create a *common* format and update our applications to support this. Any of the applications should be able to:

❑   Write its information to a file in the specified format

❑   Read its information from a file in the specified format

❑   Check if an arbitrary file conforms to the specified format

We will also need a formal way to describe the shared format, so we can have a fixed document that everyone agrees on. This document would hold a set of rules that every file in the common format should follow.

The XML specification includes a way to do just that: a formal way to describe a format, called the **validation** rules. Inside the XML document, we can specify what kind of document it is by referring to a set of rules. These rules are generally described in a separate document, although they can also be contained within the XML document itself. If the document follows the rules, it is considered 'valid'. Examples of the rules you can impose on a document are:

❑   A FAMILY element can hold only PERSON elements and PET elements

❑   The species attribute on the PET element can only have the values 'cat' and 'dog'

The XML recommendation specifies a standardized way of specifying validation rules for a document. This syntax is called **Document Type Definition** (**DTD**) and was inherited from the SGML world. The good thing about DTDs is that they are an official recommendation (by the W3C), and every validating parser must be able to use them.

XML parsers come in two kinds: validating and non-validating. A validating parser will not only parse the XML, checking it is well-formed, but will also check if the document conforms to any specified document type. If you want to be sure that the document you receive conforms to the specification, before processing the content, a validating parser will save you a ton of work. If the document isn't valid, the parser will raise an error.

DTDs have some limitations as well, especially in terms of flexibility. Some vendors, among them Microsoft, are in the process of developing a new way for specifying validation rules, called the XML **Schema**. However, all vendors support DTD validation.

Both methods will be covered here. Often, you will prefer to use DTDs, because you want to be sure that every parser supports your document type. Sometimes, however, you will need the extended functionality of XML Schema. This will probably become more and more common when the XML Schema finally becomes a standard.

Validation is Optional

Although validation is one of the key features of the XML specification, you don't have to use validation if you don't want to. When the XML specification was originally drawn up, it was a simplification of SGML. SGML documents must *always* specify validation rules. To make it simpler to use, XML documents do not need validation rules. This means that if no document type is specified, any well-formed document is valid. So, you can leave out the specification of rules and bypass the validation process altogether, but why would anyone choose to do this? There are several reasons, but the most important are performance and extensibility.

First, validation affects *performance*; it takes processor time to check the validity of a document every time you parse it. You may have a system that allows for importing and displaying certain data in XML format. When you import data and want to be sure that it conforms to the document specification, you will want to apply validation rules. However, when the information is imported, accepted and stored in the system, you will undoubtedly want to retrieve and display the data again and again. You already know that the document is valid, because if it were not, it would have been rejected when it was imported. So validating the document every time you want to read it is a waste of time. In this case, you would use a non-validating parser, or remove the declaration of the document type from the document (something we'll discuss later on).

The second important argument for not validating your documents is *extensibility*, the ability to extend your document format without confusing applications that know only the unextended format. Let's consider the case of the XML documents describing family members that we discussed earlier. Let's suppose that we choose the first syntax (that of user A) as the industry standard for describing families. User A might decide to extend the application to include the age of each family member as an additional age attribute on the PERSON element:

```
<?xml version="1.0"?>
<FAMILY>
  <PERSON name="Freddy" age="48"/>
  <PERSON name="Margie" age="32"/>
  <PERSON name="Gerald" age="8"/>
  <PERSON name="Petra" age="5"/>
  <PET name="Bonzo" type="dog"/>
  <PET name="Arnie" type="cat"/>
</FAMILY>
```

However, if we do this and keep referring to the same rule set, the validating parser would raise an error, even if we use a separate namespace for our `age` attribute. If we refer to a new rule set, older applications will no longer recognize our document to be of the common format. With the validation syntax of the XML recommendation, it is not possible to declare that an element can have *any* attribute, you must be very specific. (By not using validation rules, the old application wouldn't mind an extra attribute – it would just ignore it.)

Choosing Whether or Not to Validate

When you are programming software in Visual Basic and you want to output strings to the Immediate window, you might write the following code:

```
Sub DebugOutput(outputString as String)
  Debug.Print outputString
End Sub
```

If you pass the `Sub` a string, it will print it in the Immediate window. However, if you pass it a `DateTime` value, it will automatically convert this to a `String` and output it. This behavior (making the best of a type mismatch) is called 'weak typing' or 'loose typing'. A programming language like C or Java would never let you get away with passing a date into a function that accepts only strings – the compiler would raise an error. Such behavior is called 'strong typing'.

The question of whether you should use validation in your project is more or less analogous to choosing whether to use a strongly typed or a weakly typed programming language. It is a trade-off between flexibility and robustness. A validated document contains the exact structure of data that your application expects to find. If anything is different, your application will not be able to process it. For some applications that is a *desired* behavior, for others it is not.

Suppose you have an application that processes bank transactions. A request in XML comes in, and you make the changes and return a message of confirmation, also in XML. If a request comes in that is a bit strange but which does not cause any runtime errors in your application, the results could be disastrous. If the format expected was:

```
<transaction to_account="123456789" amount="10000" currency="ITL"/>
```

and the format received is:

```
<transaction to_account="123456789" amount="10000" currenc="ITL"/>
```

the banking application might decide to transfer $10,000 (dollars being the default currency) instead of 10,000 Italian lira.

If, on the other hand, your application receives articles written by several authors and you want to process them and place them on your web site, the situation is very different. You may not care very much if the content authors deliver is sometimes badly formed XML, as long as it can be processed and the result displayed correctly. If one of the authors forgets to enter the keywords attribute, the article can still be displayed for the visitors of the web site. In a content serving business, it is a serious problem to have your customers waiting for the validation of their article.

In the end, it depends upon the business case you are working on. If flexibility and speed are important, you should not be validating all of your documents. If robustness and reliability are key values, validation should be performed.

An interesting way to use validation rules is the following: in the process of specifying a common syntax, a formal set of validation rules is used. All implementers of the standard have to be able to process any document that is valid according to the set of rules agreed upon. During development of the system, the validation rules are used to check if the output files are valid and well formed. However, as soon as all development and testing is done, we know that the system(s) has been proven to produce valid documents and is able to process any valid document in a predictable way. Then we can remove validation for performance reasons. The formal description of the document type remains available for new vendors who want to use the common document type. In case of any problem (for example if system A cannot import the file produced by system B), the validation rules can be used by a referee to resolve which party should change its code.

Validation Using DTDs

Often the best way to get to know a new technology is to dive straight into it. Although the syntax of DTDs is not as intuitive to web developers as that of XML itself, it should be possible to make some sense of it. So here is a DTD describing the family member application example we saw earlier (along with the original XML file):

```
<?xml version="1.0"?>
<!DOCTYPE FAMILY [
  <!-- DTD for family -->
  <!ELEMENT FAMILY (PERSON+, PET*)>
  <!ELEMENT PERSON EMPTY>
  <!ATTLIST PERSON
        name CDATA #REQUIRED
  >
  <!ELEMENT PET EMPTY>
  <!ATTLIST PET
        name CDATA #REQUIRED
        type (dog|cat) #REQUIRED
  >
]>
<FAMILY>
  <PERSON name="Freddy"/>
  <PERSON name="Margie"/>
  <PERSON name="Gerald"/>
  <PERSON name="Petra"/>
```

```
      <PET name="Bonzo" type="dog"/>
      <PET name="Arnie" type="cat"/>
</FAMILY>
```

This is a validated version of user A's code sample from earlier in this chapter. Only the first part of the document has changed. It now includes a DOCTYPE declaration. If you take your time, you would probably be able to figure it out yourself, but to speed thing up a bit, we will step through it together. The first line of the XML document remains unchanged.

```
<?xml version="1.0"?>
```

The second line begins the declaration of the document type and contains only the name of the document element (FAMILY):

```
<!DOCTYPE FAMILY [
```

The definition continues in the lines that follow. The full content of the DTD is embraced by square brackets ([]), and the actual XML data follows on afterwards. In this way you include the full DTD in the XML document, which is probably the simplest way to specify the DTD. There are other ways, such as referencing a URL, which we'll come back to later.

This next line is a comment, just as in an XML file. The <!-- and --> delimit the comment text:

```
<!-- DTD for family -->
```

This line specifies a rule for any FAMILY element in the XML document:

```
<!ELEMENT FAMILY (PERSON+, PET*)>
```

It states that any FAMILY element in a valid document should contain:

- ❑ First, one or more PERSON elements.
- ❑ Then, zero or more PET elements. The order of the elements is determined by the above sequence, so the PET elements must come after the PERSON elements.

PERSON and PET should both be specified in the DTD.

The number of occurrences is specified by appending a symbol to the element name (called a **multiplier**). In this case, one or more PERSON elements must be present and zero or more PET elements.

Multiplier	Meaning
*	'any number', 'zero or more'
+	'one or more'
?	'zero or one'
	'exactly one'

For example, the following line would allow for one PERSON element and a maximum of one PET element:

```
<!ELEMENT FAMILY (PERSON, PET?)>
```

Take a look at these lines in the DTD:

```
<!ELEMENT PERSON EMPTY>
<!ATTLIST PERSON
    name CDATA #REQUIRED
>
```

They describe the rules for any of the PERSON elements in the document. What it means is this: PERSON elements do not have child elements, that is elements within elements, which is why the word EMPTY is used. They contain a single, mandatory (#REQUIRED) attribute called name. The ATTLIST declaration can hold many attributes for a single element type. The CDATA keyword specifies possible values for the attribute, which in this case are character strings.

The PET element is slightly different, as you can see:

```
<!ELEMENT PET EMPTY>
<!ATTLIST PET
    name CDATA #REQUIRED
    type (dog|cat) #REQUIRED
>
```

It looks very much like the PERSON element, except for the additional attribute: type. Like name, type is a required attribute, but its values are restricted to the literals dog or cat. It is not so hard to imagine cases where this document type would need to be extended.

Thus the DTD defines the elements that the data must contain and in what quantities, and the number and values of any attributes within the elements. Now that we have seen a simple example, we'll get into the full DTD syntax.

Syntax Elements in a DTD

DOCTYPE

DOCTYPE is the root element for any DTD. It is also one of the simplest to understand. The DOCTYPE declaration declares what kind of document this is.

```
<!DOCTYPE NAME CONTENT>
```

There are two parts to the declaration. The **name** should be the same as the root element of the described XML document. In our example, the root element of the document is FAMILY, so the DOCTYPE must be declared with the name FAMILY.

Then the **content** is inserted before the closing angle bracket. There are two ways to define the allowable content for a document type. The first is **inline**, as shown in the sample in the previous section:

```
<!DOCTYPE NAME [
...DTD content here
]>
```

The second method of specifying content uses an **external reference**, which can be a separate file referred to through a URL. The external reference uses the keywords SYSTEM and PUBLIC:

```
<!DOCTYPE FAMILY SYSTEM "http://www.ourcomp.com/dtd/family.dtd">
<!DOCTYPE FAMILY PUBLIC "-//OurComp//Family DTD//EN"
"http://www.ourcomp.com/dtd/family.dtd">
```

If the SYSTEM keyword is used, we are telling the XML parser to look for content in the URL directly after the keyword.

The PUBLIC keyword is more complex. It is a bit like SYSTEM, but is followed by two parameters, first a **public identifier** (a unique name) and then a URL. The XML parser will first check if it knows the public identifier. If so, it can go on to request the content, which will often be stored locally. However, if the parser doesn't know the identifier, it will use the URL, just like the SYSTEM keyword. This declaration will often be used for content that belongs to published XML-based standards. An example of such a standard is XHTML. XHTML is a reformulation of HTML in XML. Future HTML browsers will certainly have the DTDs for XHTML 1.0 pre-installed. The parser will not have to fetch it from a URL every time to check the validity of an XHTML document. XHTML 1.0 is referred to with this document type declaration:

```
<!DOCTYPE
html PUBLIC "-//W3C//DTD XHTML 1.0 Strict//EN"
"http://www.w3.org/TR/xhtml1/DTD/xhtml1-strict.dtd">
```

The syntax for a PUBLIC identifier is a **Formal Public Identifier** (ISO 9070). This is an international standard to refer to electronic documents. It is not as cryptic as it looks; it consists of four parts that are divided by double slashes. The first part indicates that the DTD referred to is a standard indicator, it can be 'ISO' for ISO standards, '+' for standards from registered standards bodies, and '-' for non-registered standards. W3C is not a registered standards body in the sense of ISO 9070, so normally you will see the '-' used. The second part identifies the owner of the DTD, W3C in this case, the third part names the described document. The fourth and last part is a language code (using ISO 639) to indicate the language of the DTD. The code for English is 'EN'. Other codings can be found at http://www.oasis-open.org/cover/iso639a.html.

Unlike SGML, XML requires you to enter a URL after the public identifier, because you cannot be sure that the parser will be able to find it. The DOCTYPE declarations that many HTML editors generate in their documents often don't carry a URL and are, strictly speaking, not well-formed XML.

What are URIs, URLs, URNs?

You are probably familiar with what a URL is, but what are those other terms that are used more and more often?

URL	Uniform Resource Locator. A URL is a unique way to identify a specific resource on the Internet. It specifies a protocol (http, ftp), a server location (www.wrox.com) and a path (/famschem.xml).
URN	Uniform Resource Name. A location-independent way to refer to an online resource. They start with the reserved dummy protocol urn:. The exact form of the URN means nothing about the place where one could find the document it refers to. The application must recognise the URN and know where to find the resource (or know where to ask). The nice thing about URNs is that they are not bound to a specific server machine and can be moved transparently. An example: urn:schemas-microsoft-com:datatypes This is the URN that IE5 uses as a namespace URI for datatypes.
URI	Uniform Resource Identifier. This is a superset of all URLs and all URNs. When we talk about XML, the term URI is often used for URL. URI is just the more generic term. It is expected that more URNs will be used in the future.

ELEMENT

The most common DTD element is the ELEMENT declaration. Its use is to declare that elements of the specified name can occur in this document type. As we have seen already, it also contains information about the element's content. The generic syntax for an element declaration is like this:

```
<!ELEMENT NAME CONTENT >
```

Here NAME represents, of course, the name of the declared element. The name must be a valid XML name, so it cannot contain whitespace and must start with a letter or underscore. Also, by definition, no name should start with the letters 'XML'. Names starting with 'XML' are reserved for future extensions to the XML standard. The same name cannot be declared twice in a DTD.

The CONTENT part is more complex. It specifies what can be contained between the start tag and closing tag of the declared element. This does not include any attribute that the element may carry – the attributes are declared separately.

EMPTY

The simplest value for CONTENT is EMPTY. An element that is declared as EMPTY can't contain any sub-elements or text. So if we declare an element as:

```
<!ELEMENT MY_ELEMENT EMPTY>
```

The following lines would be valid uses of the MY_ELEMENT element:

```
<MY_ELEMENT/>
```

or:

```
<MY_ELEMENT></MY_ELEMENT>
```

These lines, however, would be illegal:

```
<MY_ELEMENT>Some content</MY_ELEMENT>
```

or:

```
<MY_ELEMENT>
</MY_ELEMENT>
```

Note that whitespace is also considered to be content and parsers should not allow empty elements to contain spaces, tabs or new lines.

ANY

If the content for an element is declared as being ANY, it can contain any element content that is itself valid.

```
<!ELEMENT MY_ELEMENT ANY>
```

This does not mean that it can contain just anything; for instance, it cannot contain character data. It can only contain *elements* that are declared elsewhere in the DTD. So this line would be OK:

```
<MY_ELEMENT><SOME_OTHER_DECLARED_ELEMENT/></MY_ELEMENT>
```

while this would be illegal:

```
<MY_ELEMENT>My content</MY_ELEMENT>
```

#PCDATA

If the content of an element is declared as #PCDATA, it can only contain parsed character data (which is what PCDATA stands for). Character data can be any textual content that does not contain child elements. The text can contain CDATA sections, for data that will not be parsed. Therefore, if we declare:

```
<!ELEMENT MY_ELEMENT #PCDATA>
```

then the following would be valid uses of the MY_ELEMENT element:

```
<MY_ELEMENT>Just some text about whatever we feel like.</MY_ELEMENT>
<MY_ELEMENT />
<MY_ELEMENT>Some text with an <![CDATA[ unparsed section ]]> in it.</MY_ELEMENT>
```

However, this line would be illegal:

```
<MY_ELEMENT>Some <B>bold</B> content </MY_ELEMENT>
```

It is illegal because the MY_ELEMENT element contains another element (the B element), while it has been declared as containing only character data.

Element Content

The most common case for an element is to contain several elements of other types. For these elements the element declaration specifies exactly which elements are allowed to appear as child elements. In the example for the simple DTD we declared above, the FAMILY element contains both PERSON elements and PET elements. There we saw the use of the comma to append several element types in a set order and the use of multipliers to indicate the quantity. So the following definition:

```
<!ELEMENT MY_ELEMENT (EL1, EL2+, EL3?, EL4*)>
```

allows for any combination of child elements where the first is of type EL1, followed by one or more elements of the type EL2, possibly followed by one element of type EL3 (the ? means 'zero or one'), and then finally some (zero or more) elements of type EL4. Elements must always occur in that exact order. Note that parentheses enclose the element content declaration.

By placing the pipe symbol (|) inside the content declaration, we can indicate that one of several options must be chosen. So the following line:

```
<!ELEMENT MY_ELEMENT (EL1|EL2+)>
```

means that the element content of a MY_ELEMENT element must consist of either one single EL1 element, or one or more EL2 elements.

These combinations can be very complex and have an arbitrary number of parenthesis levels indicating processing order (inner parentheses first). By carefully combining commas, pipes and parentheses, you can describe quite complex rules for the content. However, what this method cannot describe is character data intermixed with element content. Character data combined with element content, such as the kind of document that is common in HTML, is only possible in a special case of content declaration called 'mixed'.

An element type with a mixed content model has a declaration which takes the following form:

```
<!ELEMENT MY_ELEMENT (#PCDATA|EL1|EL2|EL3|EL4)*>
```

In the mixed content model, you cannot specify more complex rules than these and it is not possible to use the ANY keyword. This is a limitation of the DTD language. You must specify all possible elements that may occur within the declared element. In document types like HTML 3.2, where almost all elements can occur within almost all other elements, the DTD can grow to gigantic proportions (although other features in the DTD syntax help to lessen the burden).

ATTLIST

What the ELEMENT declaration does for the enclosed content of a declared element, the ATTLIST declaration does for the attributes that can be used on a declared element. There can be only one ATTLIST declaration for each element type. The syntax looks like this:

```
<!ATTLIST NAME
     ATT_NAME TYPE DEFAULT
     ...
 >
```

NAME refers to the name of the element type the attribute list belongs to. The second line can occur one or more times, each occurrence defining another attribute. For readability the different attribute definitions are normally separated by line feeds, but any whitespace will do. ATT_NAME is the name of the attribute. The TYPE part defines what the content of the attribute can be, the DEFAULT part refers to default values of the attribute.

Attribute Types

CDATA

The most common type for an attribute is CDATA, which can hold any piece of character data.

Enumeration

The enumerated type is the one we used before for the type attribute of the PET element. We specified that it could only contain the values cat or dog by declaring the attribute as:

```
<!ATTLIST PET
     type (cat|dog) #REQUIRED
 >
```

The enumeration of the literal values cat and dog can be as long as you like. So if we want to change the DTD to accept additional types, we could replace (cat|dog) with (cat|dog|parrot|seal|squirrel).

ID

Attributes of type ID are declared to uniquely identify the element that holds them. Therefore an ID attribute can only hold a value that does not occur in any other ID type attribute in the whole document. Also, the value of an ID type attribute must conform to the same rules as the names of elements and attributes; it must start with either a letter or an underscore. If you try to parse a document that has two elements with ID attributes with identical values, the parser will raise an error.

IDREF/IDREFS

IDREF attributes are what make ID attributes useful and interesting. An attribute with type IDREF can hold any value, as long as there is another element in the document that has an ID attribute with exactly that value. IDREFS is more or less the same thing, but can hold more than one reference, separated by whitespace. This allows for very interesting constructs that are like relational integrity in relational databases.

In our example XML format describing families, it would be useful to describe relationships between the various members of the family. An important relation between family members is the parent-child relation. To store this relationship in our XML format, we can create a `prsid` attribute of type `ID` for each person and a `parent-of` attribute of type `IDREFS`. The `parent-of` attribute can only hold values that occur in the same document as an `ID` attribute value. So if a person has a `parent-of` attribute containing an ID value that is not available in the document, the document is not valid.

An example of a DTD describing this situation is shown:

```
<!-- DTD for family -->
<!ELEMENT FAMILY (PERSON+)>
<!ELEMENT PERSON EMPTY>
<!ATTLIST PERSON
     prsid ID #REQUIRED
     parent-of IDREFS #IMPLIED
     name CDATA #REQUIRED
>
```

(See later for the explanation of the #REQUIRED and #IMPLIED labels.)

The above definition would make this XML fragment valid:

```
<FAMILY>
  <PERSON prsid="p_1" parent-of="p_3 p_4" name="Freddy"/>
  <PERSON prsid ="p_2" name="Margie"/>
  <PERSON prsid ="p_3" name="Gerald"/>
  <PERSON prsid ="p_4" name="Petra"/>
</FAMILY>
```

Here the `parent-of` attribute of the PERSON element with name Freddy has references to two other PERSON elements. If a reference is made to a person whose details are not available in this document, an error occurs. So, this is not valid, because there is no element with an ID of value p_5:

```
<PERSON prsid="p_1" parent-of="p_3 p_4 p_5" name="Freddy"/>
```

NMTOKEN/NMTOKENS

Attributes of type NMTOKEN can contain any value that conforms to the same rules as element names do. NMTOKENS can hold several of these values, separated by whitespace. The use of NMTOKEN attributes is fairly limited. An example of using NMTOKENS attributes could be in an automated process that receives a daily document containing changes in the logon information of the network. We can use a DTD like this:

```
<!ELEMENT ACCOUNT_CHANGES (ADDED, REMOVED)>
<!ELEMENT ADDED EMPTY>
<!ELEMENT REMOVED EMPTY>
<!ATTLIST ADDED
     userids NMTOKENS #REQUIRED
>
<!ATTLIST REMOVED
     userids NMTOKENS #REQUIRED
>
```

This would create an XML document like this:

```
<ACCOUNT_CHANGES>
    <ADDED userids="JohnB PatrickD ArthurC"/>
        <REMOVED userids="RoelB MaartenS"/>
</ACCOUNT_CHANGES>
```

Using an attribute of type NMTOKENS, we can have the XML parser check that a name does not contain any strange characters. Using the ID/IDREF method here would force us to include a full list of all usernames available in the system.

Some examples of information that has the form of an NMTOKEN are: class names, security identifiers, server names and property names.

ENTITY and NOTATION

These are special attributes which we will explain more fully later on. They can be used to make attributes refer to resources that are not part of the document.

Different Default Values

The third part of the declaration of an attribute specifies its default value. There are three basic options. The first is to supply a literal string value where, for example, one of an enumerated type is declared as the default. In our example DTD, this would be written as follows:

```
<!ATTLIST PET
        type (cat|dog) "cat"
>
```

If this DTD is used and no type attribute is specified, applications using this data file will assume that the value is cat. There is no difference between an attribute explicitly set to cat and an omitted attribute defaulting to cat.

Sometimes, however, the default value is also the only possible value. In these cases, the #FIXED keyword must be used before the literal value. An example would look like this:

```
<!ATTLIST PET
        type CDATA #FIXED "cat"
>
```

A fixed attribute can be left out and it will default to the fixed value, but if you specify a value, it must be the one and only valid value. Often, these fixed attributes are used to maintain backward compatibility with previous versions of a data format.

#REQUIRED

The default value #REQUIRED means that the attribute must always be explicitly declared. If this is the case, a default value has no meaning. Validating parsers will raise an error if they encounter an element that lacks an attribute declared as #REQUIRED.

#IMPLIED

If the #IMPLIED value is used, this means that there is no default value at all for the attribute. If the attribute is declared as #IMPLIED and the author does not specify the value of the attribute, then the attribute does not exist and the parser will not inform its client application of any attribute.

Testing Validity with a DTD

Now that we have come this far through the theory, we deserve to have some fun. Let's try it out. In the XML sources directory of the code download, you'll find a file called `validated_family.xml`. It contains a description of a family with a document type declaration included:

```
<?xml version="1.0"?>
<!DOCTYPE FAMILY [
    <!ELEMENT FAMILY (PERSON+, PET*)>
    <!ELEMENT PERSON EMPTY>
    <!ATTLIST PERSON
        name CDATA #REQUIRED
>
    <!ELEMENT PET EMPTY>
    <!ATTLIST PET
        name CDATA #REQUIRED
        type (cat|dog) #REQUIRED
    >
]>
<FAMILY>
  <PERSON name="Freddy" />
  <PERSON name="Maartje" />
  <PERSON name="Gerard"/>
  <PERSON name="Peter"/>
  <PET name="Bonzo" type="dog"/>
  <PET name="Arnie" type="cat"/>
</FAMILY>
```

It can be very interesting and instructive to change the code for either the XML source or the DTD and run it through a validating parser. The parser in IE5 is a good validating parser, but when you just load an XML document into IE5, it will not validate. The MSXML parser can have validation turned off. When IE5 loads a document, it turns validation in the parser off. So, to test validity, we must use the parser object from our own code and have validation turned on. In the code download you'll find a VB project called `TreeView.vbp` that does just that.

The user interface of this application looks like this:

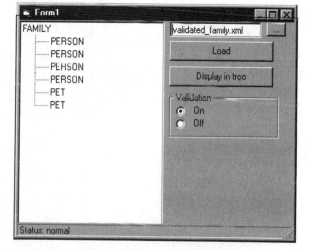

Now we will make changes to either the XML content or the DTD and watch the error messages from the parser.

1. Add an undeclared attribute to an element:

```
<PERSON name="Freddy" age="20"/>
```

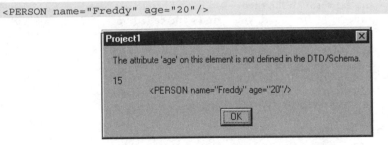

2. Add a child element to an element declared as EMPTY:

```
<PERSON name="Freddy"><CHILD/></PERSON>
```

> **Project1**
>
> Element content is invalid according to the DTD/Schema.
>
> 15
>
>   <PERSON name="Freddy"><CHILD/></PERSON>
>
> OK

3. Change the order of elements in a way that is not allowed by the declaration:

```
<FAMILY>
  <PET name="Bonzo" type="dog"/>
  <PERSON name="Freddy"/>
```

> **Project1**
>
> Element content is invalid according to the DTD/Schema.
> Expecting: PERSON.
>
> 15
>
>   <PET name="Bonzo" type="dog"/>
>
> OK

4. Make the name attribute type ID and give two elements identical name attributes:

```
<?xml version="1.0"?>
<!DOCTYPE FAMILY [
    <!ELEMENT FAMILY (PERSON+, PET*)>
    <!ELEMENT PERSON EMPTY>
    <!ATTLIST PERSON
        name ID #REQUIRED
>
    <!ELEMENT PET EMPTY>
    <!ATTLIST PET
        name ID #REQUIRED
        type (cat|dog) #REQUIRED
    >
]>
<FAMILY>
  <PERSON name="Freddy"/>
  <PERSON name="Maartje" />
  <PERSON name="Gerard"/>
  <PERSON name="Peter"/>
        <PET name="Peter" type="dog"/>
  <PET name="Arnie" type="cat"/>
</FAMILY>
```

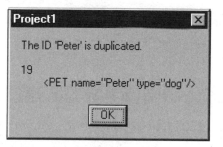

5. Use a wrong value for the type attribute on PET:

```
        <PET name="Bonzo" type="parrot"/>
```

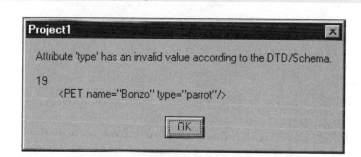

Look at the error messages the sample application shows you. These error messages can be very instructive.

ENTITY

The next element in the DTD syntax which we'll look at is the ENTITY element. Entities are references to other content. This other content can be a piece of text, but can also be a very large external file. The most well known entities are the standard entities, such as <, which represents the 'less than' symbol (<). Declaring your own custom entities can be useful to make management of the content easier (text that is used very often can be declared once and the entity can be used in many places).

Entities always have two parts, the **declaration** and the **reference**. Declaring an entity is done inside the DTD. Here we declare the entity &currency; to represent $ (the entity declaration):

```
<!DOCTYPE MYDOC
<!ENTITY currency "$" >
>
```

And here we refer to it in the XML content (the entity reference):

```
<MYDOC>
   Cost: &currency; 1500.00
</MYDOC>
```

The XML parser will convert the code &currency; to $ automatically.

There are two distinct kinds of entities, called 'general entities' and 'parameter entities'. We will have a look at both.

General Entities

General entities are the ones we saw in the previous example. & is a typical example of a reference to a general entity. Some entities can be used without declaring them first. They are defined in the XML specification. These are:

Entity	Replacement Text
&amp;	&
&lt;	<
&gt;	>
&quot;	"
&apos;	'
覫 (any hex value)	The Unicode character indicated by the hex value
Ӓ (any decimal value)	The Unicode character indicated by the decimal value

Declaring General Entities

When you declare custom entities, you will probably use them to define some fragments of standard text that you want to appear in several places in your applications, but that you want to define in a central place. Think of defining &comp_name_adrr; as holding your company's name and address. In any XML document you want this text to appear, you just include the entity reference &comp_name_adrr;.

The declaration of a custom entity looks like this:

```
<!ENTITY comp_name_addr "Our company &#x0D; 1, Our road &#x0D; Somewheresbury, UK
&#x0D;" >
```

So we have two parts, the *name* and the *replacement text*. Note that the replacement text itself is supposed to be a well-formed XML fragment and may therefore not include characters like & or <. In this sample we included some newline characters with the reference .

External Entities

Sometimes the replacement text of an entity can be very long, or sometimes we don't want to include the text in the DTD itself for manageability or security reasons. In such cases, it is possible to refer to an external file that holds the replacement text. This can be done with the keywords SYSTEM and PUBLIC, just like referring to an external DTD from the XML document:

```
<!ENTITY comp_name_addr SYSTEM "http://www.ourcomp.com/snippets/comp_addr.xml">
<!ENTITY comp_name_addr PUBLIC "-//OurCompany//DTD snippet Company name and
address//EN" "http://www.ourcomp.com/snippets/comp_addr.xml">
```

Note that, just as with literal values, the content of the document referred to must be well-formed XML.

Parameter Entities

There are special kinds of entities that will only be encountered in more complex DTDs. They are called **parameter entities** and are actually only used within the DTD itself. They are meant to keep DTD files smaller and more structured. The declaration of a parameter entity looks like this:

```
<!ENTITY % addr_details "street, city, country">
```

With this line of code, we assign the literal value between the quotes to the entity addr_details. It can be referenced from within the DTD using %addr_details;, as follows:

```
<!ELEMENT CONTACT (firstname, lastname, %addr_details;, phone)>
```

This is especially useful when the combination of child elements occurs in many places in the DTD. Most official DTDs, such as the one for XHTML, are full of parameter entities, which keeps them more or less readable and manageable.

Parameter entities must always be declared before they are used. The content of a parameter entity should always be properly nested itself. This means that if a parenthesis is used in an entity, its matching parenthesis should be present in the same entity declaration. The same rule forbids entities to have a value that ends or starts with a connector symbol, such as a comma or pipe. These declarations are all illegal:

```
<!ENTITY % addr_details "street, city,">
<!ENTITY % addr_start "(street, city,">
<!ENTITY % addr_end "country)">
```

And these are correct:

```
<!ENTITY % addr_details "street, city">
<!ENTITY % addr_details "(street, city)">
```

External Parameter Entities

If you declare an external entity and then reference it, you can include external files into your DTD. Doing so will create a DTD from reusable fragments. A very common reusable fragment is the entity declaration for HTML. Normally, you cannot use entities other than the five standard entities (&<>"') in an XML file. Even very common HTML entities such as   and © must be declared in the DTD in order to be valid (or even well-formed) XML. You can include all these HTML entities for the ISO Latin 1 character set (HTML is not Unicode, so the codes depend on the character set) in one PUBLIC external entity declaration:

```
<!ENTITY % HTMLlat1 PUBLIC
   "-//W3C//ENTITIES Latin 1 for XHTML//EN"
   "http://www.w3.org/TR/xhtml1/DTD/xhtml-lat1.ent">
%HTMLlat1;
```

If you would like to include symbols, such as Greek characters, in your document, the following entity declaration will allow you to use α and the others:

```
<!ENTITY % HTMLsymbol PUBLIC
   "-//W3C//ENTITIES Symbols for XHTML//EN"
   "http://www.w3.org/TR/xhtml1/DTD/xhtml-symbol.ent">
%HTMLsymbol;
```

NOTATION

Notations are strange beasts. You will not encounter them often, but it's good to know that they are around and can be used. Their purpose is to be able to use non-XML content in XML. Think of binary content like GIF images or non-valid text content. This content should never be parsed by the XML parser, but we can provide an external application to the XML parser that knows how to handle this non-XML content. As an example, we will use a GIF image as unparsed external content.

```
<!NOTATION gif SYSTEM "iexplore.exe">
<!ENTITY logo SYSTEM "http://www.ourcomp.com/Images/btssmall.gif" NDATA gif>
<!ELEMENT PIC EMPTY>
<!ATTLIST PIC
   loc ENTITY #REQUIRED
 >
```

There is a lot to see in this little sample. First the NOTATION declaration. It has a name (gif) and a PUBLIC or SYSTEM reference to a processing application. In this case we use iexplore.exe as the reference. An application could get this string from the XML parser and use Internet Explorer to show the binary content to a user.

Then follows an ENTITY declaration, which first refers to a SYSTEM external content file, but it has appended the keyword NDATA (non-parsed data) and a reference to a declared notation (gif). Then, we see an element declaration with an attribute declared as type ENTITY. In the document we could now use:

```
<PIC loc="&logo;"/>
```

The value of the loc attribute is an unparsed entity. Because this entity is known to be non-XML, it is not parsed by the XML parser and will not be included in the XML document as a parsed entity would. The loc attribute is effectively pointing to some GIF file and the XML parser will notify iexplore.exe of the existence of such a reference.

Attributes of type ENTITY can only refer to unparsed entities.

Of course, you could just have an attribute of type CDATA and include the URL of the GIF file there. The application would know what to do with GIFs, and in the majority of cases that's just what you would do. Still, this technique gives you the opportunity to reference other files from an XML document using XML itself.

Limitations of DTDs

The DTD syntax for validating documents is derived from the DTD syntax used in SGML. There are definitely some limitations to DTDs as a validation syntax. Some are related to the validation functionality and flexibility itself:

- ❑ You cannot specify elements to appear in an undefined order. You have two choices: ordered child elements or the mixed content model, which allows you no influence on the permitted number of child elements.

- ❑ There is no way to specify the type of any text content. The type specification possible on attributes is useful, but does not include such simple types as integers or dates.

- ❑ There is no 'free content model'. The content model of a DTD is closed. This means that every element you use must be declared. An open content model would specify that any element is allowable, unless specified otherwise. The closed content model of DTDs seriously hinders evolving standards. We want a free content model, where the developer of the validation rules can choose a closed or an open model.

Other reasons for thinking up another validation syntax are more esthetic in nature – for example, why is the syntax for validation different from XML itself? After all, XML is supposed to be able to handle any kind of data, so this should include validation rules. An additional benefit to using some XML-based validation syntax is that tools and APIs for modifying XML content could also be used to edit the validation rules. We'll investigate these tools in later chapters.

Validation Using XML Schemas

To overcome the limitations of DTDs, several proposals for better methods have been proposed. Among these are:

- ❑ XML Schema, a W3C project

- ❑ Document Content Description (DCD), an initiative by IBM and Microsoft, building on top of the W3C Resource Description Framework (RDF) project

- ❑ Schema for OO XML (SOX)

- ❑ XML-Data/XML Schema from Microsoft (which is a subset of DCD)

For the future, the XML Schema project from the W3C is the most probable standard to emerge. However, this standard is still in the stage of 'Working Draft' and the editors have announced that the current release (December 17, 1999) will still suffer significant revisions and changes. This already makes it difficult to work with their current specification.

The MSXML COM objects carry an implementation of what Microsoft calls XML Schema. This is not the same thing as the W3C project, although both syntaxes look pretty much alike. In this chapter we will call the IE5 implementation of XML Schema the 'MS Schema'. Wherever we use the term 'XML Schema', we refer to the current W3C project's Working Draft.

MS Schema was built using syntax from two other initiatives. First, the XML-Data proposal that Microsoft made to the W3C specifies several new data types that were not available in DTD-validated XML. Second, the DCD syntax Microsoft was working on with IBM was the model for the structural syntax. We will cover the current Microsoft implementation here and after that indicate what the differences are between it and the Working Draft of the W3C. It is important to be aware of the fact that XML Schema is not yet a standard and the MS Schema will probably never be a standard. On the other hand, Microsoft is using its current Schema implementation in so many of its new technologies that it will probably invest in backward compatibility of its own objects.

The Concept of a Schema

The concept of the MS Schema is very much like DTDs. The key differences are:

- ❑ The schemas are formulated in XML. This means that you don't have to learn a new syntax, and that all the tools, libraries, etc., for the creation and manipulation of XML can also be used for schemas.

- ❑ The content model of an XML Schema can be either 'open' or 'closed'. This means that it is possible to include unspecified elements. This allows for future extensions to be added, whilst keeping the documents valid against the old rules.

The MS Schema specification consists of two separate parts, the Datatype specification and the Structure specification. The **Datatype** specification deals with specifying datatypes that extend further than the attribute types in DTDs and #PCDATA content for elements. The **Structure** specification deals with which elements can appear in which context and what values (datatypes) they can hold.

The MS Schema syntax uses XML namespaces to let the parser know which elements are content and which are part of the schema. The nodes that are part of the structural specification use the namespace 'urn:schemas-microsoft-com:xml-data', while nodes that are part of the datatype specification use the namespace 'urn:schemas-microsoft-com:datatypes'. In the examples in this chapter, we will often leave the namespace declaration out, to improve readability. The prefix s: is used for the xml-data namespace and the prefix dt: is used for the datatype namespace.

To give you an idea of what it looks like, we will first have a short look at some sample code before we dive into theory again.

```
<s:Schema  xmlns:s='urn:schemas-microsoft-com:xml-data'
  xmlns:dt='urn:schemas-microsoft-com:datatypes'>

  <s:ElementType name="PERSON" >
    <s:AttributeType name="name" />
    <s:attribute type="name" />
  </s:ElementType>

  <s:ElementType name="PET" >
    <s:AttributeType name="name" />
    <s:attribute type="name" />
  </s:ElementType>

  <s:ElementType name="FAMILY" order="seq" content="eltOnly">
    <s:element type="PERSON" minOccurs="1"/>
    <s:element type="PET" minOccurs="0"/>
  </s:ElementType>
</s:Schema>
```

This is an MS Schema specifying a format identical to the one specified by the DTD at the start of the chapter. It uses two namespaces, one for elements that define the *structure* of the document and one for elements and attributes that define a *datatype*. In this example only structural relations are defined, so the second namespace is not used. We can see that three different element types are defined using the element s:ElementType. For example the definition of PERSON:

```
<s:ElementType name="PERSON" >
  <s:AttributeType name="name" />
  <s:attribute type="name" />
</s:ElementType>
```

It defines the name of the element in the name attribute and holds two children. One, the s:AttributeType, defines a certain kind of attribute (with name name). The other one, s:attribute, specifies that this type of attribute can occur in this very place (as part of the PERSON element). The type attribute of s:attribute refers to the name attribute of s:AttributeType.

The MS Schema syntax uses separate elements to define the existence of a type of element and to indicate the place in the document where it may appear.

Further down we see the definition of the FAMILY element:

```
<s:ElementType name="FAMILY" order="seq" content="eltOnly">
  <s:element type="PERSON" minOccurs="1"/>
  <s:element type="PET" minOccurs="0"/>
</s:ElementType>
```

Here again we see how s:element is used to indicate the presence of an element type that has been declared in another place (using s:ElementType). This is analogous to the s:attribute/s:AttributeType combination.

The schema can be referenced from an XML file like this:

```
<?xml version="1.0"?>
<FAMILY  xmlns="x-schema:famschem.xml">
  <PERSON name="Freddy" />
  <PERSON name="Maartje" />
  <PERSON name="Gerard"/>
  <PERSON name="Peter"/>
  <PET name="Bonzo"/>
</FAMILY>
```

The schema that defines the rules for the content is declared by a namespace declaration of a special kind. The protocol of such a namespace is x-schema, and it refers to an external URI. The URI here is a relative one (famschem.xml), but is can also refer to another server:

```
<FAMILY  xmlns="x-schema:http://www.wrox.com/famschem.xml">
```

It is not yet possible to create inline schemas in IE5.

Datatypes

The most obvious advantage of using the MS Schema compared to using DTDs is the extended support for datatypes. In standard XML with a DTD, every value, be it a text node or an attribute value, is a *string* value. If you code the following:

```
<PERSON age="28"/>
```

the age attribute of the PERSON element has the string value "28", not the numeric value 28. All the type declarations possible in a DTD are subdivisions of the string type: enumerated types, ID, IDREF. From the perspective of the XML parser, every value is a string value.

In the XML-Data specification, that has changed. It was drawn up to facilitate the use of XML for transferring database content. To do that, you need some support for all the different datatypes available in the several database management systems. A simple example of a datatype is the integer, coded as int. There are several ways to specify a datatype for an element's content. If the content of a certain element must be of a specified type, you can add a dt attribute in the datatypes namespace to the element. This would look like this:

```
<shoes xmlns:dt="urn:schemas-microsoft-com:datatypes" />
 <sizes id="mens">
  <size dt:dt="int">8</size>
  <size dt:dt="int">10</size>
  <size dt:dt="int">12</size>
 </sizes>
</shoes>
```

If you use an XML parser that knows this syntax, it will recognize the namespace and check if the elements have the correct content. IE5 will raise an error when it encounters this:

```
<size dt:dt="int">a10</size>
```

The specification for XML-Data specifies a new group of datatypes as an extension to the existing DTD types, which it calls 'primitive types'. The primitive types map exactly to the types in DTDs to guarantee that DTD functionality is a subset of Schema functionality. The second set implements datatypes as they are used in most programming languages and databases: integer, boolean, uri, etc.

Primitive Types		
Name	**Description**	**Remarks**
entity	Represents the XML ENTITY type	
entities	Represents the XML ENTITIES type	
enumeration	Represents an enumerated type (supported on attributes only)	Defining several possible values: (cat|dog)
id	Represents the XML ID type	
idref	Represents the XML IDREF type	
idrefs	Represents the XML IDREFS type	
nmtoken	Represents the XML NMTOKEN type	
nmtokens	Represents the XML NMTOKENS type	
notation	Represents a NOTATION type	
string	Represents a string type	This is the default type in DTD syntax. For elements: #PCDATA, for attributes: CDATA

Extension Types		
Name	**Description**	**Compares to VB Type**
`bin.base64`	MIME-style Base64 encoded binary BLOB.	
`bin.hex`	Hexadecimal digits representing octets.	
`boolean`	0 or 1, where 0 is equivalent to `false` and 1 is equivalent to `true`.	`Boolean`
`char`	String, one character long.	`Byte`
`date`	Date in a subset of ISO 8601 format, without the time data. For example: "1994-11-05".	`Date`
`dateTime`	Date in a subset of ISO 8601 format, with optional time and no optional zone. Fractional seconds can be as precise as nanoseconds. For example, "1988-04-07T18:39:09".	`Date`
`dateTime.tz`	Date in a subset of ISO 8601 format, with optional time and optional zone. Fractional seconds can be as precise as nanoseconds. For example: "1988-04-07T18:39:09-08:00".	`Date`
`fixed.14.4`	Same as "number" but no more than 14 digits to the left of the decimal point, and no more than 4 to the right.	`Decimal`
`float`	Real number, with no limit on digits; can potentially have a leading sign, fractional digits, and optionally an exponent. Punctuation as in U.S. English. Values range from 1.7976931348623157E+308 to 2.2250738585072014E-308.	`Double`
`int`	Number, with optional sign, no fractions, and no exponent. Uses four bytes, identical to `i4`.	`Long`

Name	Description	Compares to VB Type
number	Number, with no limit on digits; can potentially have a leading sign, fractional digits, and optionally an exponent. Punctuation as in U.S. English. (Values have same range as most significant number, R8, 1.7976931348623157E+308 to 2.2250738585072014E-308.)	Double
time	Time in a subset of ISO 8601 format, with no date and no time zone. For example: "08:15:27".	Date
time.tz	Time in a subset of ISO 8601 format, with no date but optional time zone. For example: "08:1527-05:00".	Date
i1	Integer represented in one byte. A number, with optional sign, no fractions, no exponent. For example: 1, 127, -128.	Byte
i2	Integer represented in two bytes. A number, with optional sign, no fractions, no exponent. For example: 1, 703, -32768.	Integer
i4	Integer represented in four bytes. A number, with optional sign, no fractions, no exponent. For example: 1, 703, -32768, 148343, 1000000000.	Long
r4	Real number, with seven digit precision; can potentially have a leading sign, fractional digits, and optionally an exponent. Punctuation as in U.S. English. Values range from 3.40282347E+38F to 1.17549435E-38F.	Single
r8	Real number, with 15 digit precision; can potentially have a leading sign, fractional digits, and optionally an exponent. Punctuation as in U.S. English. Values range from 1.7976931348623157E+308 to 2.2250738585072014E-308.	Double
ui1	Unsigned integer. A number, unsigned, no fractions, no exponent. For example: 1, 255.	Byte

Name	Description	Compares to VB Type
ui2	Unsigned integer, two bytes. A number, unsigned, no fractions, no exponent. For example: 1, 255, 65535.	Integer
ui4	Unsigned integer, four bytes. A number, unsigned, no fractions, no exponent. For example: 1, 703, 3000000000.	Long
uri	Universal Resource Identifier (URI). For example, urn:schemas-microsoft-com:Office9.	N/A
uuid	Hexadecimal digits representing octets, optional embedded hyphens that are ignored. For example: 333C7BC4-460F-11D0-BC04-0080C7055A83.	String

These types all refer to the MS Schema. The specification process for the XML Schema has in the mean time reshuffled all of the datatypes and made up new names. The full XML Schema (once specified and implemented) will probably support all of these types and a mechanism to define your own types.

Where to Use Extension Types and Primitive Types

The specification for XML-Data intended the extended datatypes to be used both on element content and attribute values. However, this is not the case in the IE 5.0 implementation. The primitive types can currently only be used on attribute values, just like when you use a DTD. The extension values can only be used on element content. So you cannot create an element embracing an NMTOKEN value, but you also cannot specify an attribute as being an int. This really weakens the concept of XML-Data. After all, it is most often the information in attribute values that needs to be typed in.

In release 5.01 of IE, support has been implemented for extension types in attributes. Microsoft has promised that primitive types will be supported in element content later.

The Available Elements

The second part of the MS Schema consists of the structural rules for elements and their position relative to each other. Its function is more or less identical to the ELEMENT and ATTRLIST declarations from the DTD syntax.

Schema

The root element of every MS Schema is a Schema element. It holds the namespace declaration for the MS Schema elements and can have a name attribute.

```
<Schema name="any name"
    xmlns="urn:schemas-microsoft-com:xml-data"
    xmlns:dt="urn:schemas-microsoft-com:datatypes">
```

Note that in this case we chose to declare that the default namespace (the namespace to be used when no prefix is placed before a name) is 'urn:schemas-microsoft-com:xml-data'. This is why we can just use Schema elements instead of s:Schema elements as we did in the previous example.

The namespaces can have any prefix. In this case we chose to use the default namespace for the Schema elements and the dt prefix for the datatype references. The name attribute has no purpose other than being an identifier for referring to this particular schema. No functionality uses the name attribute at the moment.

Possible child elements for the Schema element are:

❑   ElementType

❑   AttributeType

❑   description

The last of these is used to store a descriptive text string. The first two are discussed fully below.

ElementType

ElementType allows us to specify a certain kind of element. It is very much like the <!ELEMENT> declaration from the DTD. The content description for the element appears as child elements of the ElementType element. It can have several attributes: content, model, order and name.

content

The content attribute can have one of the following values:

Value	Meaning
mixed	The element can contain both text and child elements. This is the default value.
eltOnly	The element can hold child elements, but not text content.
textOnly	The element can hold only text, not child elements. Note that if the content model is set to open, the element can hold child elements, but only undeclared elements.
empty	Equivalent to the EMPTY keyword from the DTD syntax. If content is set to empty, no content is allowed (no elements, no text, no whitespace even).

model

The `model` attribute provides a new feature not found with DTD syntax, and illustrates the advantage of Schemas over DTDs. The DTD specifies exactly which child elements can appear inside an element. If another element type is created later, inserting it always violates the DTD rules. This is a pity, because it more or less prevents us from thinking up new elements once we use the DTD, and we can not easily change the specification. This behavior is called a 'closed content model'. A DTD always has a closed content model. MS Schema will allow us to choose an alternative 'open content model' – which is the default. This means that *any* child element, even if it has not been previously mentioned, can legally be used. If the unexpected child element is in the same namespace as its parent, it must be declared in the schema in order to be legal, but it does not have to be declared as a possible child element. If the unexpected element is in another namespace, everything is legal, providing that it is legal in its own namespace. The `model` attribute's value can either be `open` or `closed`.

An interesting situation is when the model is open, but the element `content` attribute is `textOnly`. Child elements can be inserted, so long as they are *unknown* to the schema.

order

The `order` attribute specifies the allowable order of the elements describing the content. Three values are available:

Value	Meaning
one	Only one of the list of child elements can appear. This child element can be a group holding several others.
seq	Child elements must appear in exactly the same order as they appear in the schema.
many	Child elements can appear in any order. If the content type is `mixed`, the order must be `many`. This is the default value.

If the `order` attribute of an `ElementType` is set to `one` or `seq`, the `content` attribute must be set to `eltOnly`.

name

The `name` attribute specifies exactly that – the name of the element type. Thus the two samples of code below are identical:

```
<Schema xmlns="urn:schemas-microsoft-com:xml-data">
  <ElementType name="PERSON" content="empty"/>
</Schema>
```

```
<!DOCTYPE [
  <!ELEMENT PERSON EMPTY>
]>
```

Examples illustrating the use of these attributes will be given in due course.

Child Elements of ElementType

The `ElementType` element can hold these child elements:

- ❑   element
- ❑   AttributeType
- ❑   attribute
- ❑   group
- ❑   description
- ❑   datatype

element

The `element` element is a reference to an existing `ElementType` in the schema. It specifies the possible appearance of an instance of the element type in a certain location. The possible attributes are:

Name	Meaning
type	References the name attribute of a declared element type.
minOccurs	Specifies the minimum number of occurrences of the elements in this context. Has values of 0 or 1.
maxOccurs	Specifies the maximum number of occurrences of the elements in this context. Has values of 1 or * (* means unlimited).

The attributes `minOccurs` and `maxOccurs` can only be used when the `content` attribute of the parent element is set to `eltOnly`. If it is set to `mixed` (which is the default), the number of child elements cannot be restricted.

The `element` element cannot have child elements itself.

```
<ElementType name="class" order="many">
  <element type="teacher" minOccurs="1"/>
  <element type="student"/>
</ElementType>
<ElementType name="teacher" content="empty">
<ElementType name="student" content="empty">
```

This example describes three different element types for a document. The `class` element can hold both `teacher` elements and `student` elements. There should be at least one `teacher` and an arbitrary number of `students`. The `student` and `teacher` elements can be in any order, but they cannot hold any content.

AttributeType

`AttributeType` allows us to declare a certain kind of attribute. This can be done within the `ElementType` element, or outside, thus allowing us to use the same definition for an attribute in several `ElementTypes`. The possible attributes for an `AttributeType` element are:

- ❑ default
- ❑ name
- ❑ required

The function of the name attribute is identical to that of the name in `ElementType`. It is a name to be referred to from the `attribute` element which is an instance of the attribute type defined by this element. The `default` attribute holds the default value for this attribute. It must be a valid value for the type defined by the `dt:type` attribute.

The `required` attribute can only have the values yes and no. It has no default value. If the `AttributeType` has no value, the behavior is specified by the `attribute` element that refers to this `AttributeType`.

When an attribute has a `default` value defined and the `required` attribute is set to yes, then the defined attribute must always have the default value (identical to using the #FIXED keyword in DTDs).

The `AttributeType` element can hold these child elements, which don't really need explaining:

- ❑ datatype
- ❑ description

attribute

The `attribute` element specifies an instance of an `AttributeType` declared in the same document. This is analogous to the `ElementType/element` pair. An `attribute` element can only appear within an `ElementType` element. On this element we can find these attributes:

- ❑ default – specifies the default value for this attribute. It can overrule any default specified by the referred `AttributeType` element.
- ❑ type – holds the name of an `AttributeType` element in the schema.
- ❑ required – can overrule the setting on the `AttributeType`.

The `attribute` element cannot hold any child elements. After all, attributes in the XML document that is being described cannot have children. Look at how we used `s:attribute` and `s:AttributeType` in the example schema to define the name attribute on the PET element:

```
<s:ElementType name="PET" >
  <s:AttributeType name="name" />
  <s:attribute type="name" />
</s:ElementType>
```

group

The group element can be used to group elements together. This can be used to create more complex content models. The group element can have the attributes:

Name	Meaning
order	Specifies the allowable order and number of the elements within the group.
minOccurs	Specifies the minimum number of times the group must appear. Has values of 0 or 1.
maxOccurs	Specifies the maximum number of times the group can appear. Has values of 1 or *. (The * means 'unlimited'.)

So this schema fragment:

```
<ElementType name="x" order="one">
  <group order="seq">
    <element type="x1"/>
    <element type="y1"/>
  </group>
  <group order="many">
    <element type="x2"/>
    <element type="y2"/>
  </group>
</ElementType>
```

would make this a valid XML fragment:

```
<x>
  <x1/><y1/>
</x>
<x>
  <x2/><y2/><x2/>
</x>
```

The group element can hold these child elements, which are self-explanatory:

❑   description

❑   element

description

The description element can be used as a child to almost all other schema elements to add documentation about the schema, implementation details and rationale behind a certain content model. It cannot have any child elements. For example:

```
<s:ElementType name="FAMILY" order="seq" content="eltOnly">
  <s:element type="PERSON" minOccurs="1"/>
  <s:element type="PET" minOccurs="0"/>
  <s:description>The FAMILY element can only be valid if it holds at least one
  PERSON element.</s:description>
</s:ElementType>
```

datatype

To add data type information to the schema, we include the `datatype` element within an `ElementType` or `AttributeType` element. The `datatype` element holds a `type` attribute from the XML-Data namespace. So if the content of a certain element should be a valid URI, we would define:

```
<ElementType name="x">
  <datatype dt:type="uri"/>
</ElementType>
```

It is also possible to add a `dt:type` attribute directly to the `ElementType` or `AttributeType` element. So the type declaration shown below is exactly the same as that shown above:

```
<ElementType name="x" dt:type="uri"/>
```

If you declare an attribute with type `enumeration`, you have to add an additional `dt:values` attribute holding a list of whitespace-separated values:

```
<AttributeType name="species" dt:type="enumeration" dt:values="cat dog"/>
```

Note that the current implementation will not allow the type `enumeration` for elements, only attributes.

The `datatype` element cannot hold any child elements.

Example of an MS Schema

Let's have a look at a schema that declares a few element and attribute types and the relations between them. Try to figure it out from the code first. After that we'll explain each part separately.

```
<s:Schema xmlns:s="urn:schemas-microsoft-com:xml-data" xmlns:dt="urn:schemas-
microsoft-com:datatypes">
    <s:ElementType name="school" order="many" content="eltOnly" model="closed">
        <s:element type="class"/>
        <s:element type="course"/>
    </s:ElementType>

    <s:ElementType name="fullname" content="textOnly"/>
    <s:ElementType name="lastname"/>
    <s:ElementType name="firstname"/>

    <s:ElementType name="student" content="eltOnly" order="seq">
        <s:element type="firstname"/>
        <s:element type="lastname"/>
    </s:ElementType>

    <s:ElementType name="teacher" content="eltOnly" order="one">
        <s:element type="fullname" maxOccurs="1"/>
        <s:group order="seq">
          <s:element type="firstname"/>
          <s:element type="lastname"/>
        </s:group>
```

```
     </s:ElementType>

     <s:ElementType name="course" content="eltOnly">
        <s:AttributeType name="courseID" dt:type="id"/>
        <s:attribute type="courseID"/>
        <s:element type="teacher" maxOccurs="1"/>
     </s:ElementType>

     <s:ElementType name="class" content="eltOnly" model="closed" order="many">
        <s:AttributeType name="name" dt:type="string"/>
        <s:attribute type="name"/>
        <s:AttributeType name="courses" dt:type="idrefs" required="yes"/>
        <s:attribute type="courses" />
        <s:element type="student"/>
     </s:ElementType>

  </s:Schema>
```

This is quite a lot of code, but it is not as complicated as it looks. We will just start at the beginning and work our way down. The first line of the schema document is used for the Schema element and namespace declarations. This tells the parser that all elements in the s namespace must be interpreted as belonging to an MS Schema declaration and all nodes prefixed with dt: get their meaning from the XML-Data specification:

```
  <s:Schema xmlns:s="urn:schemas-microsoft-com:xml-data" xmlns:dt="urn:schemas-
  microsoft-com:datatypes">
```

Here is our first element declaration:

```
     <s:ElementType name="school" order="many" content="eltOnly" model="closed">
        <s:element type="class"/>
        <s:element type="course"/>
     </s:ElementType>
```

A school element is defined which can hold any number of classes and courses in any order (i.e. order="many"), but nothing else – no additional elements or text are allowed (model="closed"). The referred element types class and course will apparently be defined later on. There follows three very simple declarations:

```
     <s:ElementType name="fullname" content="textOnly"/>
     <s:ElementType name="lastname"/>
     <s:ElementType name="firstname"/>
```

The fullname element can hold only text. The content and model of the lastname and firstname elements are not defined. The default values model="open" and content="mixed" therefore apply.

In this section, the element types `student` and `teacher` are defined:

```
<s:ElementType name="student" content="eltOnly" order="seq">
   <s:element type="firstname"/>
   <s:element type="lastname"/>
</s:ElementType>

<s:ElementType name="teacher" content="eltOnly" order="one">
   <s:element type="fullname" maxOccurs="1"/>
   <s:group order="seq">
     <s:element type="firstname"/>
     <s:element type="lastname"/>
   </s:group>
</s:ElementType>
```

The `student` element is fairly simple. Its content `model` is open, to allow for later additions. The order of the content elements is set to sequential (`seq`) and therefore the `content` is `eltOnly` (`order` `seq` or `one` can only be used with `content="eltOnly"`). The `student` element can hold `firstname` elements and `lastname` elements.

The `teacher` element can be used in two ways. It can behave just like a `student` element, holding `firstname` and `lastname` elements. But it can also hold a `fullname` element. Only one `fullname` element is allowed.

Now we come to defining the `course` element:

```
<s:ElementType name="course" content="eltOnly">
   <s:AttributeType name="courseID" dt:type="id"/>
   <s:attribute type="courseID"/>
   <s:element type="teacher" maxOccurs="1"/>
</s:ElementType>
```

The `course` element has one attribute, called `courseID`. The `courseID` attribute is of type ID, so only one course with the same name may exist in a document. This also places some restrictions on the valid `courseID` values (no whitespace, must start with a letter or underscore). This `courseID` will be used in the `class` element to indicate which courses are given to a class.

The `course` element can hold only elements as content (`eltOnly`). This setting is chosen to constrain the number of `teacher` elements to a maximum of 1 (`maxOccurs` can only be used when `content="eltOnly"`). The content `model` is not specified and defaults to open, which means that elements other than `teacher` can be added freely.

Finally we come to the `class` element:

```
<s:ElementType name="class" content="eltOnly" model="closed" order="many">
   <s:AttributeType name="name" dt:type="string"/>
   <s:attribute type="name"/>
   <s:AttributeType name="courses" dt:type="idrefs" required="yes"/>
   <s:attribute type="courses" />
   <s:element type="student"/>
</s:ElementType>
```

This is the most interesting thing in our schema. It has a `closed` content `model` and can therefore not hold anything other than the specified `student` elements. The `class` element carries two attributes: a name attribute that is just a string and a `courses` attribute. This `courses` attribute holds all `courseID`s for the courses that this class receives. The `courseID`s must be separated by whitespace.

A document conforming to this schema might contain the following fragment:

```
<class name="VWO1a" courses="English Math1">
  <student>
    <firstname>Frankie</firstname>
    <lastname>McCourt</lastname>
  </student>
  … more students …
</class>
<course  courseID="Math1">
  <teacher>
    <firstname>Theo</firstname>
    <lastname>Jones</lastname>
  </teacher>
</course>
<course  courseID="French">
  <teacher><fullname>Prof. Bob</fullname>
  </teacher>
</course>
<course  courseID="English">
  <teacher>
    <firstname>Brian</firstname>
    <lastname>Donaldson</lastname>
  </teacher>
</course>
```

Note how the `courseID`s are referenced from the `class` element.

It is very interesting to load this document into a validating parser and see if it works, and even more interesting is to see what the error messages look like when you change the content to an invalid format. You can use the `TreeDOM.exe` application from the source code download to try this. A document conforming to this schema is in the download, called `Schema_class.xml`.

Here are some interesting invalidity messages. If you try to reference a non-existing `courseID`, you will get this:

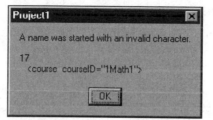

If you place the `lastname` and `firstname` elements in the wrong order, you will get this:

```
Project1                                    [X]

Element content is invalid according to the DTD/Schema.
Expecting: firstname.

5
           <lastname>McCourt</lastname>

                  [ OK ]
```

Comparing the MS Schema and XML Schema

The MS Schema implementation will probably be replaced by the XML Schema specification from the W3C. However, the current status of the specification is that of Working Draft, and the editors have warned that significant changes are still to be made. Many of the paragraphs in the specification are still not agreed on by all participating parties. For now, it is not very useful to learn the syntax of the XML Schema, because the standard is still changing too fast. This very situation, along with the resulting absence of implementations, is the main reason for the delay in the process of specifying XML Schema. Instead of covering the XML Schema in its current form, we will touch on some topics where the XML Schema will probably be extended or changed compared to the MS Schema implementation.

Merging of element and ElementType, attribute and AttributeType

In the MS Schema, the `ElementType` element defines an element *type*, and an `element` element refers to an *instance* of that type. In the XML Schema, both will be done with one element: `element`. It will be used for both *defining* an element type and *referring* to an instance of that type. Defining an element type will be done like this:

```
<s:element name="PERSON">
   <!-- content definition goes here -->
</s:element>
```

and referring to an instance of that type will be done like this:

```
<s:element ref="PERSON"/>
```

The same goes for `AttributeType` and `attribute`. They will both be replaced by `attribute`.

Complex Type Declarations

In the XML Schema it will be possible to define a complex type, which has a template that can be used for defining other elements. So, for example, the following code:

```
<complexType name='Address'>
   <element name='street' type='string'/>
   <element name='city' type='string'/>
   <element name='state' type='string'/>
</ complexType >
```

would create a fixed set of elements that form an Address. This can be used when declaring new element types that contain all these sub-elements:

```
<element name='PurchaseOrder'>
 <element name='shipTo' type='Address'/>
 <element name='shipFrom' type='Address'/>
 <!- other content -->
</element>
```

Creating New Datatypes

Apart from the quite complete list of built-in datatypes, XML Schemas will support the creation of user-defined types. This will allow the grouping of existing types, but also the modifying of existing types by defining legal values. This can be the setting of maximum and minimum values, but also formatting rules for string values. The following code defines two attributes, attr1 and attr2. Both can only hold integer values, but the value of attr1 must be a positive integer less than twenty – the intUnderTwenty type was created with this specification:

```
<simpleType name='intUnderTwenty' base='int'>
 <maxExclusive>20</maxExclusive>
</datatype>

<attribute name='attr1' type='intUnderTwenty' />

<attribute name='attr2' type='int'/>
```

Choosing Whether to Use a DTD or a Schema

Once the XML Schema specification has become a recommendation and is widely implemented by parser vendors, it will probably be the best choice for defining the content of a document type. But what should we choose for the time being? The XML Schema is not yet implemented outside demonstration software; the MS Schema works, but will eventually be superseded by the XML Schema; and DTDs seem a bit old-fashioned and lack some functionality that you need for making documents extensible and for working with namespaces. There are a few strategies that make sense:

❑   Don't use validation at all. This saves you a lot of trouble, and if your application doesn't really need all this checking of content, it's a perfectly respectable strategy.

❑   Use DTDs. They have been proven to work, and all validating XML must support DTDs. So they are the safest bet, for now, and are platform independent (an advantage over the MS Schema), which will help when porting code. They are currently available and will continue to be. However, some features, such as data type support, will have to be left out, due to the inflexibility of the DTD model. Also, validating documents with several namespaces is very hard to achieve, if not impossible.

❑ Use the MS Schema now, and convert to the XML Schema later. The MS Schema works, and offers the most important advantages that the XML Schema will. It can be used now, provided that you restrict yourself to using the MSXML library. There is no platform independence on offer here. For you, as a VB developer, being tied to the Windows platform will not be an issue and using the MS Schema is a feasible option. However, you will encounter problems when you want to send your documents to partners who use other platforms and vendors. Converting to the standardized XML Schema when it arrives will probably be an easy task, because its functionality will be a superset of the functionality of MS Schema – it will probably be achieved using an XSLT stylesheet.

Summary

This chapter has shown you why validation is such an important part of working with XML. The shared schema definition actually gives meaning to your data. Still, in many cases you will not bother with validation and will use your data unvalidated. That's fine too. XML was intended to be used pragmatically and if you don't need validation, leave it out. Make sure though that you understand what it is all about.

To summarize, in this chapter we saw:

❑ That the same data can be described in different formats in XML

❑ That we can use validation rules to specify the format we expect

❑ That we can let a validating parser check if an XML document indeed conforms to this specification

❑ How to describe validation rules using DTDs

❑ How to describe validation rules using the MS Schema

❑ A few of the features that the XML Schema will deliver once it is fully specified and implemented

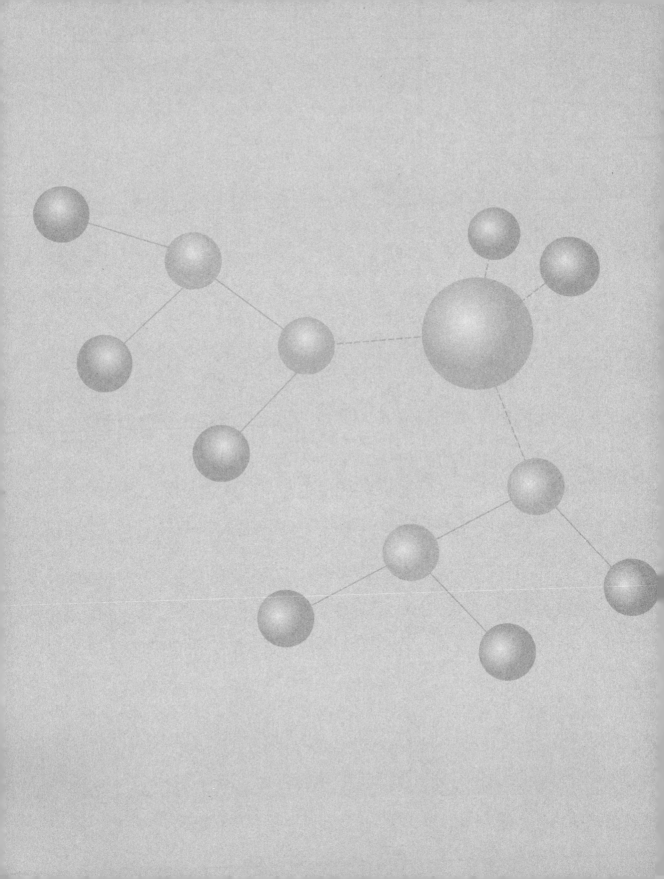

Programming the Document Object Model

Having looked at the basics of XML, and the two methods of validating XML code (the DTD and the Schema), this chapter introduces the **DOM**, or **Document Object Model**, which is the standard way of representing XML data for programmatic purposes. It describes the W3C DOM Level 1 recommendation, and explains how this is implemented in Microsoft's XML parser. As the chapter progresses, we shall see where the MS implementation adds to the basic DOM specification, and the features that are not supported by Level 1 of the DOM standard, but which should be included in the DOM Level 2 implementation.

Throughout the chapter we will present some example code showing how different objects and methods are used. As we will see, the DOM is based on the concept of an abstract **node interface**, which defines a general set of methods and properties for DOM objects. The abstract node interface is used to derive an assortment of specific node types, such as element nodes and attribute nodes. However, the pervasive use of a single interface for a variety of node types can lead to some potentially confusing situations. This is because not every specific node type implements the abstract node interface in exactly the same way. Furthermore, Microsoft's implementation of the DOM has its own quirks, and code that appears to conform to how the DOM *should* behave may not always work as expected. As a result of this, many common DOM tasks require a number of preparatory steps (such as the creation of intermediate objects, and testing for potentially illegal parameter values) before you can actually perform the desired action. To make using the DOM easier, we will develop a class project that provides wrapper functions for performing many DOM tasks, in order to hide the complexity and to offer better error handling.

The code samples fall into two categories: small bits of sample code intended to demonstrate syntax, and specific functions intended for our class project. The syntax samples can generally be run by creating a Visual Basic application project with a single form, and entering the code into the `Form_Load` subroutine. Any code that defines a *specific* function or subroutine is intended for our class project. The class project will result in an ActiveX DLL that should make DOM life a little easier in other programs.

We will also present some small but complete programs for manipulating the DOM.

At the end of the chapter we will take a look at another way of handling XML: **SAX** (the Simple API for XML), and give a sample program demonstrating how it works.

Introduction

XML gives us a standard way to describe and encode complex, structured data, and a way to validate it. We can now start building applications that use and modify data encoded according to this standard. Many of the tasks these applications will have to perform are more or less standard. From the perspective of code reuse, parsing, manipulating and querying XML data from a stream should be done with a set of generic XML editing objects. To prevent the creation of several competing object models, as had happened for HTML (where Netscape and Microsoft implemented similar, but not-quite-the-same, scripting models for their browsers), the W3C included the manipulation of XML documents into the specification process for the HTML Document Object Model. This provided one core object model, with extensions provided for HTML-specific options.

This standardized object model allows developers who have worked on an XML application, on one specific platform or in one specific programming language, to make use of their experience in any other platform or language, as long as a standard DOM implementation is available.

A Little History

When Netscape Communications released version 2.0 of its Navigator web browser, it added a remarkable feature – a scripting language that could, among other things, *interact* with the contents of the browser. This language was called JavaScript (due to some misplaced association with the Java programming language). Microsoft, not to be outdone, implemented its own version of JavaScript, called JScript, with the release of Internet Explorer 3.0. However, because there was no agreement on exactly what parts of the HTML document should be controlled, or how, the scripting languages differed. It was (and still is) difficult to write client-side script to run correctly on multiple browsers. To alleviate these problems, the W3C set about creating a standard to define the DOM, or Document Object Model, building on the experiences of both Netscape and Microsoft.

On October 1 1998, the W3C released its recommendation. According to the introduction, which can be viewed at http://www.w3.org/TR/1998/REC-DOM-Level-1-19981001/introduction.html, "*[t]he Document Object Model (DOM) is an application programming interface (API) for HTML and XML documents. It defines the logical structure of documents and the way a document is accessed and manipulated.*"

Ideally, this would provide a well-defined specification that would be implemented in all future browsers, allowing client-side script to behave identically in products from every vendor.

The Idea Behind the DOM

The DOM is basically a structured view of an XML document. While, strictly speaking, an XML document is a linear sequence of characters, it can be more useful to look at it in other ways. You can think of it as a conventional document with embedded layout codes, or as a series of elements with starting and ending tags raising events (the SAX view, which we'll discuss a little later), or as a "tree" with each element being a branch or a leaf. The DOM views an XML document as a tree of nodes, a node being an object with which it can interact. In this model, each element is a node, and each node may contain its own sub-tree of nodes. At the very top of each document is a root node.

Let's take a look at an XML document, and see just how it maps out against the DOM. Here's a simple XML document that could be used to describe e-mail:

```
<?xml version="1.0"?>
<email>
 <header>
  <to>Mary Shelley</to>
  <from>Lord Byron</from>
  <cc></cc>
  <subject>Your new book</subject>
 </header>
 <body>
  How were the reviews?
 </body>
</email>
```

If we were to represent this as a set of nodes, it would look like this:

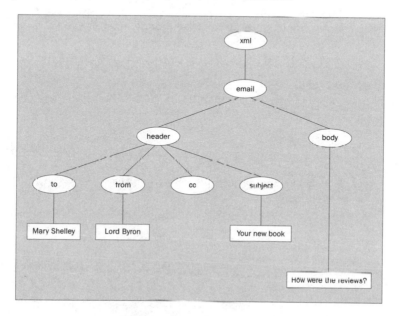

One of the useful things about this node diagram is that it exposes certain structural aspects that might not be so obvious from simply viewing the document text. For one thing, we can see that our root element (email) has two immediate child nodes, header and body. As far as the DOM is concerned, these two nodes are *siblings* – they're at the same level in the hierarchy. The DOM allows us to easily find such relationships in a document. The diagram also includes the text we would expect to appear in a rendered version of this document; in the DOM, such character data is also represented as nodes.

If this were a Visual Basic object, we might want to be able to manipulate these nodes, and perhaps inspect or change their values. The object might be called the DocumentObject, with a collection of Node types. So we would have something like DocumentObject.Node(index).value, which would allow us to inspect a particular node. This is basically what the XML DOM does. It provides an API into an XML or HTML document as if it were a structured, addressable object.

DOM Requirements

When working to define the DOM, the W3C set some requirements for the final product, four of which are described here.

Language and Platform Independent

The specification needed to be designed without favoring any particular platform or language. The API defines a set of methods and properties, but does not dictate how they are to be implemented. DOMs have been written for most major operating systems, in such languages as Python, Perl, Java, and C++.

Core DOM for Both HTML and XML

The same object model is applicable to both HTML and XML documents, and as a result Cascading Style Sheets (CSS) work the same way for both types of documents. If you have Internet Explorer 5 you can see this for yourself. For example, open up a text editor and enter this code:

```
<?xml version="1.0"?>
<?xml-stylesheet type="text/css" href="xmlcss.css" ?>
<sample>
  <foo>This looks different ...
  </foo>
  <bar> ... from this.
  </bar>
</sample>
```

Save it as xmlcss.xml. Now create another text file, and enter this:

```
foo {
display:block;
color:red;
}
bar {
  display:block;
  color:blue;
}
```

Save this file as `xmlcss.css`, in the same directory as `xmlcss.xml`. Load `xmlcss.xml` into IE5. See what happens if you edit `xmlcss.xml` and remove the second line, which instructs the XML parser to load and process the CSS file.

The results should look like this before the line was removed (left) and afterwards (right):

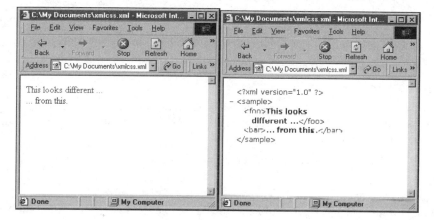

The DOM specification is divided into two parts: the **core DOM**, and the **HTML DOM**. The core DOM is required for XML functionality, and is the foundation for the HTML DOM. The core DOM specification defines a set of fundamental interfaces, which must be implemented by any compliant DOM object.

Extensions for HTML

HTML documents differ from XML documents in a number of significant ways. For example, since HTML documents are typically viewed in a browser window, the `window` object is a parent of the `document` object. Also, HTML documents, being primarily presentation objects, have features that are not found in XML documents, such as forms and images. (You might think that XML documents can have these too, but technically they can only have elements *named* IMG or FORM. Elements with these names do not have any intrinsic meaning, without some external program predisposed to interpret them.)

HTML documents are also a specific type of SGML document with a defined DTD. If we know that a document is HTML, then we know that it has (or should have) certain elements and attributes. For example, an HTML document has HEAD and BODY elements. The BODY element has certain attributes, such as `bgcolor` and `text`. Owing to this, the HTML DOM provides specific interfaces to certain aspects of an HTML document, and builds on the scripting model devised by Microsoft and Netscape. It is the basis for DHTML (Dynamic HTML), whereby you can use client-side script (typically JavaScript or VBScript) to directly access and manipulate the HTML elements in your document.

Independent of the User Interface

There is nothing in the specification that says how an XML document is to be rendered, or even if it is to be rendered at all. Presentation is completely divorced from content. This is an extremely important concept. When you bind your data to a presentation method, you bind it to a presentation program. This limits what applications can use the data, and introduces extraneous information. An example of this would be preparing a document in RTF (Rich Text Format). The use of the document requires that an application know how to interpret RTF, and the copious amounts of formatting text used by RTF is not the data you are primarily interested in.

Accessable Elements of the Document

The DOM has to allow full access to elements, and provide the ability to add and remove elements.

Some Limitations of the DOM

❑ The DOM specification does not provide any means for validation against a schema.

❑ There is no interface definition for rendering the DOM contents with XSL.

❑ There are no methods to control access to the DOM.

❑ The DOM does not raise any events.

❑ The DOM specification does not cover thread safety. There are no requirements governing how the DOM is implemented, and so there are no guarantees about what kind of threading model will be used by any vendor.

❑ There is no structural model for the internal subset and the external subset of an XML document.

Although the DOM bears a passing resemblance to DHTML, it does not define all of the functionality typically found in DHTML, particularly event handling.

Objects in the DOM

In this section we'll get down to the nitty-gritty, by examining the fundamental methods and attributes of the DOM, learning about nodes, and developing some code to help us manipulate our XML. We'll use the XML parser provided by Microsoft in Internet Explorer 5.

> *We're using the Microsoft XML parser because it's readily available, and free. The parser implements the W3C DOM, but also provides additional methods and properties that are not part of the recommendation. Because we are interested in using the DOM as defined in the recommendation, and to avoid dependencies on any one implementation, we will mainly use those features that are covered by the recommendation, though we will point out some vendor-specific features too.*

To develop in Visual Basic using the Microsoft XML parser you need to either have Internet Explorer 5 installed, or Internet Explorer 4 and the Microsoft redistributable parser.

When you open up the Visual Basic IDE and create a new standard EXE project, go to Project | References, and set a reference to the Microsoft XML object. If you are using the redistributable COM object and have IE 4 installed, then you may see two references to Microsoft XML. Make sure you select version 2.

We'll be developing a class to implement some DOM wrapper methods that will make it easier to perform some fundamental DOM operations and to provide more robust error handling. The ultimate goal is to have a set of methods that hide some of the complexity of manipulating the DOM. We'll also provide some code snippets to demonstrate how some methods may be called.

The Fundamental DOM Interfaces

These are essential parts of the DOM specification. We'll begin our exploration by examining some basic (though perhaps less interesting) features of the DOM, then move on to discussing the Node interface. Finally we'll look at the NodeList and the NamedNodeMap objects.

Type: DOMString

Because the DOM is intended to be implementation-independent, the specification defines the data type DOMString as a sequence of 16-bit quantities. DOMString values must be encoded using UTF-16, a text-encoding method that uses two bytes to represent a character. For our purpose, using Visual Basic, a DOMString is simply a Unicode String type.

Exception: DOMException

DOM operations that cannot be performed, perhaps because there is no valid object to work with, or because the particular node type does not allow the operation, are required to raise a DOM exception. Curiously, the Microsoft implementation does not provide for this. If you attempt to manipulate a node in an improper way, then you'll receive a COM error, but the error does not give you any DOM-specific error information. We'll get back to this little detail in a moment when we cover just what a node is supposed to do. First we'll cover the exceptions as defined in the specification.

The DOM recommendation defines the following exception code constants:

Exception Code	When Raised	Integer Value
INDEX_SIZE_ERR	If the index or size is negative, or greater than the allowed value	1
DOMSTRING_SIZE_ERR	If the specified range of text does not fit into a DOMString	2
HIERARCHY_REQUEST_ERR	If any node is inserted where it doesn't belong	3
WRONG_DOCUMENT_ERR	If a node occurs in a different document from the one that created it	4
INVALID_CHARACTER_ERR	If an invalid character is specified, such as in a name	5
NO_DATA_ALLOWED_ERR	If data is specified for a node which does not support data	6
NO_MODIFICATION_ALLOWED_ERR	If an attempt is made to modify an object where modifications are not allowed	7

Table continued on following page

Exception Code	When Raised	Integer Value
NOT_FOUND_ERR	If an attempt is made to reference a node in a context where it does not exist	8
NOT_SUPPORTED_ERR	If the implementation does not support the type of object requested	9
INUSE_ATTRIBUTE_ERR	If an attempt is made to add an attribute that is already in use elsewhere	10

We'll see just when these exceptions are raised by specific operations as we move through the DOM interface definitions.

For our DOM wrapper class, let's begin by opening a new Visual Basic standard ActiveX project. We've called the project WroxXml, but of course you're free to pick any name you like. (Later on we'll build a standard application to try out our class.) Add a class and call it CDomFunctions. Now let's define our DOMException enumerated type:

```
Public Enum DOMException
    NO_ERROR = 0
    INDEX_SIZE_ERR = 1
    DOMSTRING_SIZE_ERR = 2
    HIERARCHY_REQUEST_ERR = 3
    WRONG_DOCUMENT_ERR = 4
    INVALID_CHARACTER_ERR = 5
    NO_DATA_ALLOWED_ERR = 6
    NO_MODIFICATION_ALLOWED_ERR = 7
    NOT_FOUND_ERR = 8
    NOT_SUPPORTED_ERR = 9
    INUSE_ATTRIBUTE_ERR = 10
    UNKNOWN = 99
End Enum
```

We've added two additional values, NO_ERROR and UNKNOWN, for those cases where we need to return a value of type DOMException, even though none has occurred, and for when our code encounters an error that does not fit neatly into the defined DOMException categories.

We'll also define a set of general purpose error information properties to make error handling a little cleaner. First we'll declare some private variables to hold the information:

```
Private m_strErrorDescription As String
Private m_lngErrorNumber As Long
Private m_strErrorSource As String
Private m_DomError As DOMException
```

And then add some public property methods to allow read-only access to the outside world:

```
Public Property Get ErrorDescription() As String
    ErrorDescription = m_strErrorDescription
End Property

Public Property Get domError() As DOMException
    domError = m_DomError
End Property

Public Property Get ErrorNumber() As Long
    ErrorNumber = m_lngErrorNumber
End Property

Public Property Get ErrorSource() As String
    ErrorSource = m_strErrorSource
End Property
```

Now we'll add some private methods to set and clear these values:

```
Private Sub ClearErrorInfo()
    m_strErrorDescription = ""
    m_lngErrorNumber = 0
    m_strErrorSource = ""
    m_DomError = NO_ERROR
End Sub

Private Sub SetErrorInfo(lngErrNum As Long, strErrDesc As String, _
                  strErrSource As String, DomErr As DOMException)
    m_strErrorDescription = strErrDesc
    m_lngErrorNumber = lngErrNum
    m_strErrorSource = strErrSource
    m_DomError = DomErr
End Sub
```

When we start writing the DOM wrapper functions we'll use these to provide error information in an easy-to-access format.

Interface: DOMImplementation

As we said earlier, the DOM specification consists of two sections: the core XML part, and the HTML part. Some DOM implementations might offer both parts, or they may only provide the core interface (as is the case with the Microsoft parser). The DOMImplementation interface provides a single method, hasFeature, to query the object to see what it offers. This method has two parameters: feature and version, both of type DomString.

> *An interface is a specification for what a set of methods is expected to look like. It defines method signatures; what each method is called, the data types for the arguments (if any), and the data type for the return value (if any). An interface is used to provide a template, which must then be implemented by a specific class. We'll take a closer look at interfaces in Chapter 8, 'Developing an XML Editor'.*

Right now, the only useful values for `feature` are "XML" or "HTML"; case does not matter. The `version` parameter refers to the version of the DOM. In DOM Level 1 this value is "1.0".

This method returns a Boolean value. The specification states that if the version is not specified, then support for any version of the feature should return a value of `True`. In practice, though, the Microsoft parser implementation requires *both* parameters, and using an empty string will produce a value of `False`, which would incorrectly suggest that *no* version is supported.

Here's an example of calling this method. (Microsoft has chosen to expose the `IXMLDOMImplementation` object with the name `implementation`, which provides the `hasFeature` method.) Create a new project, and add a reference to the Microsoft XML object. (This is not part of our class project, but simply a sample of how to call this method.) Add this code to the `Form_Load` subroutine:

```
Private Sub Form_Load()
    Dim objDOM As MSXML.DOMDocument
    Set objDOM = New MSXML.DOMDocument

    Debug.Print objDOM.implementation.hasFeature("XML", "1.0")
    ' Returns True
    Debug.Print objDOM.implementation.hasFeature("HTML", "1.0")
    ' Returns False
    Debug.Print objDOM.implementation.hasFeature("XML", "")
    ' Returns False
End Sub
```

We should note here that we've declared `objDOM` as an `MSXML.DOMDocument` object. This is the object we use to manage the DOM; the `DOMDocument` object implements the `Document` interface, which provides all of our required methods and objects. It includes methods and properties to obtain or create all of the other XML DOM interfaces. We'll be digging into the `Document` interface in a moment.

Interface: DocumentFragment

The specification describes the `DocumentFragment` as a 'lightweight' or 'minimal' `Document` object. What this means is that a `DocumentFragment` object is much like an XML `Document` object but without the complete object model features or overhead. It is useful for managing chunks of your XML document without having to instantiate a whole new DOM object. The `DocumentFragment` is a node; it may have zero or more child nodes, which could be the top (root) nodes of any sub-trees. `DocumentFragments` do not have to be well-formed XML documents – such documents must have a single root node, and a `DocumentFragment` may have multiple child (and therefore root) nodes. Alternatively, the fragment may contain just a single text node, i.e. a piece of raw data, which by itself cannot be well-formed XML.

Bear in mind that a fragment is not necessarily a complete XML document; it is a temporary collection of node objects. It will not have a reference to a DTD, so there is no way of determining if a fragment is valid. If the fragment is not at least a minimal XML document (e.g., it has a single root element) then it cannot be considered well-formed. This can be compared with extracting a sub-string from a paragraph; the sub-string may itself be a complete, valid sentence, but it is also quite possible that it is just a collection of words, or even just a set of letters, which would not be a valid sentence.

The DocumentFragment acts as a temporary parent node. When a DocumentFragment is inserted as a child node of any other node, it is the fragment's child nodes which are inserted, and not the DocumentFragment node itself. Thus, the document fragment acts as a temporary container for the child nodes. So, for example, you could use the DocumentFragment to construct a series of nodes that are intended to exist as sibling nodes under some other node.

Here's a graphical example of the process of creating new nodes under a document fragment and inserting those nodes into a document. We begin with a document tree:

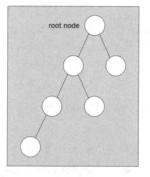

And then we create new nodes under a document fragment:

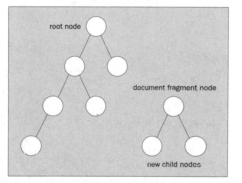

We then insert the new nodes into our document:

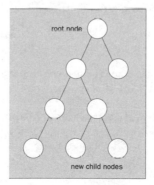

Interface: Document

The Document interface is our main gateway to the entire XML or HTML document. It represents the root of the document node tree. The Document is itself a node, but because no other nodes can exist outside a Document object, it provides additional methods for creating other nodes.

The Document object has three attributes:

doctype

This is the Document Type Declaration (DTD) associated with the document. If the XML document does not have a document type, then this value is null. Otherwise, the attribute points to a doctype node (discussed later in this chapter). The DOM Level 1 specification does not provide any means for editing a DTD, so this is a read-only attribute.

implementation

This is a reference to a DOMImplementation object that implements the hasFeature method described earlier.

documentElement

This attribute returns a reference to the root node of the document. We'll examine this object in more detail later on.

Here's an example of using these attributes – you can insert this code into the same Form_Load example given previously:

```
If Not objDOM.doctype Is Nothing Then
    MsgBox objDOM.doctype.Name, vbInformation
End If

If Not objDOM.documentElement Is Nothing Then
    MsgBox objDOM.documentElement.nodeName, vbInformation
End If

If Not objDOM.implementation Is Nothing Then
    MsgBox objDOM.implementation.hasFeature("XML", "1.0"), vbInformation
End If
```

The Document object also provides a number of object factory methods, used to create instances of various types of nodes:

createElement (String tagName)

This method creates a new Element object and returns a reference to it. The element type (its "tag name") is set by the parameter tagName and is case-sensitive.

For HTML, though, the case of the tag name is irrelevant; the specification for the HTML DOM states that HTML tag names are to be mapped to the uppercase version of the element type. You can use lowercase (or mixed case), and the DOM will consider it the equivalent of the all-uppercase version.

This method will raise an INVALID_CHARACTER_ERR DOMException if the tag name contains any invalid characters.

Let's take a look at how we would use this in Visual Basic with the Microsoft parser. (By the way, this is not part of our DOM wrapper class; this is just some "here's how you do it" example code. We will later build upon what's shown here to create a more robust method for managing the creation of Element nodes.)

```
' First we declare our objects and a string variable:

Dim objDOM As MSXML.DOMDocument
Dim elNode As MSXML.IXMLDOMElement
Dim strTagName As String

' We'll give our string variable a value
strTagName = "Test"

' Now get a new DOMDocument:
Set objDOM = New DOMDocument
```

Note that we have declared elNode using a reference to an interface class; this specifies the methods it is expected to implement. We need to use the DOMDocument to create a specific instance of this object, using the createElement method:

```
' Now call createElement to get a new Element object
Set elNode = objDOM.createElement(strTagName)
MsgBox elNode.baseName
```

There are a few things that need further explanation. First, we've created a new element, but it doesn't yet belong to the DOMDocument. That will be easy enough to fix once we get to the appendChild method later on. However, there is another subtler problem. If you tried this code for yourself (for example, by adding a form to our project and entering the code in the form onLoad event) then set the value of strTagName to '1Test' and run it. You should get run-time error number 5, "Invalid procedure call or argument". This is because we tried to create an Element object with an invalid tag name. As you may recall from Chapter 1, tag names may not begin with a digit. However, according to the DOM specification, this will raise the INVALID_CHARACTER_ERR DOMException, but it doesn't. This is something you'll need to keep in mind when using the Microsoft parser – you may experience COM exceptions due to specific violations of the DOM specification, and you'll need a way to handle them gracefully.

createDocumentFragment()

This method creates an instance of an empty DocumentFragment object. There are no parameters, and it does not raise any exceptions. This method has the following syntax:

```
Dim objDOM as MSXML.DOMDocument
Set objDOM = New DOMDocument
Dim docFragNode As IXMLDOMDocumentFragment
Set docFragNode = objDOM.createDocumentFragment()
```

Once you have a reference to a DocumentFragment you can begin adding child nodes to it, as we'll see later on.

createTextNode (String sNodeData)

This creates a new Text node, with the value of parameter sNodeData, which is used to set the node's data. Again, it does not raise any exceptions. The syntax is as follows:

```
Dim objDOM as MSXML.DOMDocument
Set objDOM = New DOMDocument
Dim textNode As IXMLDOMText
Set textNode = objDOM.createTextNode("Hello!")
```

Text nodes are always leaf nodes, that is to say they may not have child nodes.

createComment (String sNodeData)

This is used to create a new Comment node object, with the sNodeData parameter containing the value of the node. It does not raise any exceptions, and uses the following syntax:

```
Dim objDOM as MSXML.DOMDocument
Set objDOM = New DOMDocument
Dim commentNode As IXMLDOMComment
Set commentNode = objDOM.createComment("This is a comment!")
```

createCDATASection (String sNodeData)

This is used to create a new CDATASection node; the value is set to the parameter sNodeData. If you try to call this on an HTML DOM object, this method will raise the NOT_SUPPORTED_ERR exception. It has the following syntax:

```
Dim objDOM as MSXML.DOMDocument
Set objDOM = New DOMDocument
Dim cdataNode As IXMLDOMCDATASection
Set cdataNode = objDOM.createCDATASection("1 < 2")
```

If you recall the restrictions on what text a CDATA section may contain, then you may wonder what would happen if we were to try this:

```
Set cdataNode = objDOM.createCDATASection("<![CDATA[!]]>")
```

If you thought "Run-time error 5", you'd be right. If you haven't already guessed, none of the node creation methods of the MSXML object raise DOMException errors. If we try to insert invalid text into a CDATA section, the DOM specification doesn't tell us what exception to raise. It is the Microsoft parser that will complain. When calling createCDATASection, it is advisable to trap any possible errors in circumstances when the CDATA text is invalid:

```
Dim objDOM as MSXML.DOMDocument
Set objDOM = New DOMDocument
Dim cdataNode As IXMLDOMCDATASection
On Error Resume Next
Set cdataNode = objDOM.createCDATASection("1 < 2")
```

```
If Err.Number <> 0 Then
    ' Some error handling code
End If
```

AddCDATA Utility Function

Rather than doing this each time a CDATA section is added, the following function can be used in a class project to handle any possible errors. The code starts like this:

```
Public Function AddCDATA(oDOM As DOMDocument, _
                 oPNode As IXMLDOMNode, _
                 sCDATAContent As String _
                 ) As Boolean
    On Error GoTo ErrHand

    Dim oNode As MSXML.IXMLDOMNode
    Dim elNode As MSXML.IXMLDOMCDATASection
    Dim bResults As Boolean

    Call ClearErrorInfo
```

The function requires the particular DOMDocument we are using (since we need it to call the createCDATASection method), the parent node on which the CDATA section is added, followed by the CDATA content itself. First, a test is carried out to make sure that the CDATA content doesn't include the forbidden "]]>" string:

```
If (InStr(sCDATAContent, "]]>")) Then
    bResults = False
    Call SetErrorInfo(-1, "Invalid character string: ']]>' ", _
        "CDomFunctions.AddCDATA", INVALID_CHARACTER_ERR)
```

If this string is absent, a second check verifies that the intended parent node type allows CDATA sections. Only document fragments, entity references, and elements may include CDATA:

```
Else
    Select Case oPNode.NodeType
        Case NODE_DOCUMENT_FRAGMENT, NODE_ENTITY_REFERENCE, NODE_ELEMENT:
```

If the parent node is acceptable, createCDATASection is called to create a new CDATA node:

```
            Set elNode = oDOM.createCDATASection(sCDATAContent)
```

The new node is appended to the parent node, and the bResults parameter is set to True:

```
            Set oNode = oPNode.appendChild(elNode)
            bResults = True
```

Note that this code jumps ahead of us a bit because it involves the use of the appendChild DOM method. The real value in creating a new node is that you may add it to an existing document object. The AddCDATA function we are presenting here should give the general idea of how this is done. We'll examine the appendChild method further on and build other class methods for handling the addition of various nodes.

If the parent node is the wrong type, bResults is set to False and error information is recorded:

```
          Case Else
                bResults = False
                Call SetErrorInfo(-1, "Invalid parent node type.", _
                    "CDomFunctions.AddCDATA", HIERARCHY_REQUEST_ERR)
          End Select
    End If
```

Finally, code is included to handle unexpected errors:

```
ErrHand:
    If Err.Number <> 0 Then
        Call SetErrorInfo(Err.Number, Err.Description, "CDomFunctions." & _
            Err.Source, UNKNOWN)
        bResults = False
    End If
    AddCDATA = bResults
End Function
```

createProcessingInstruction (String sTarget, String sInstruction)

This creates a new XML ProcessingInstruction node, with the target specified by the sTarget parameter and the instructions given by the sInstruction parameter. This method has the syntax shown:

```
Dim objDOM as MSXML.DOMDocument
Set objDOM = New DOMDocument
Dim piNode As MSXML.IXMLDOMProcessingInstruction
Set piNode = objDOM.createProcessingInstruction("MyApp", _
             "Some instruction for MyApp")
```

An INVALID_CHARACTER_ERR exception will be raised if you try to use any invalid characters; a NOT_SUPPORTED_ERR exception will be raised if you try to call this method on an HTML DOM object.

createAttribute (String sAttrName)

This method is used to create a new Attribute object with the name given by the sAttrName parameter. As we'll see when we examine the different node types, once we have our attribute node we can then add it to an Element, and set the value using the Element node's setAttribute method. The syntax for this method is as follows:

```
Dim attrNode As IXMLDOMAttribute
Set attrNode = objDOM.createAttribute(sAttrName)
```

An INVALID_CHARACTER_ERR exception will be raised if the specified name contains an invalid character.

createEntityReference (String sEntityRefName)

This creates a new EntityReference node object, with the name of the entity specified by the sEntityRefName parameter, for example:

```
Dim entrefNode As MSXML.IXMLDOMEntityReference
Set entrefNode = objDOM.CreateEntityReference("gt")
```

Here we are creating an entity reference for the greater-than symbol, which in the textual XML document would appear as >.

An INVALID_CHARACTER_ERR exception will be raised if the specified name contains an invalid character; a NOT_SUPPORTED_ERR exception will be raised if this method is called on an HTML DOM object.

getElementsByTagName (String sTagName)

This is a different sort of DOMDocument method. Given a tag name, the method will search through the entire DOM collection of elements and return a NodeList object containing all element nodes with the given tag name. The element nodes are ordered just as they would appear in the source document if you walked the tree using a preorder traversal (i.e., the same order the elements would occur if the document was viewed as a single string). An example of the syntax is:

```
MsgBox objDOM.getElementsByTagName("SomeElement").length
```

If you use the special '*' tag name value then *all* of the element nodes are returned in the NodeList.

> *The Microsoft implementation of this has an interesting feature: if you specify an empty string for the tag name, the method returns a node list containing every node (including attributes, processing instructions, and so on) in the document, not just the element nodes.*

Something's Missing

We've just looked at the DOMDocument object, which will let us manipulate our XML, but how do we get our document into the DOM in the first place? Well, we could build the document from scratch, using various DOM methods, but this would be a tedious way of achieving this. And there are certain things we couldn't even do, because some properties of the DOM (such as the doctype attribute) are read-only. The DOM Level 1 specification does not provide any means to simply load XML text into the DOM (this is intended to be addressed in the DOM Level 2 recommendation). It presumes that the document is there, and then describes how to work with it.

The Microsoft parser provides two extensions for getting XML into the DOM, load and loadXML. Both methods take a single string parameter; the load method expects a URI to a document, and the loadXML method takes a literal XML string. Both methods return a Boolean value to indicate if the XML was loaded correctly.

> *Note that these methods are not part of the W3C recommendation, and that other DOM implementations provide different methods for loading text into a DOM. Until the DOM Level 2 standard is official, and each vendor implements a compliant DOM object; the specifics will vary from one implementation to another.*

Loading a document is not the only feature not yet included in the DOM specification. Once you have a document in the DOM, and have taken great trouble to tweak it, you will probably want to save it back to disk. Once again, the DOM specification says nothing about this procedure. However, Microsoft has thoughtfully included a method called `save`, which takes a destination file name as a parameter. For example, here's a small sample for loading and saving an XML document (in this case, a collection of quotations):

```
Dim objDom As MSXML.DOMDocument
Set objDom = New MSXML.DOMDocument
objDom.async = False
objDom.load "http://starship.python.net/crew/amk/quotations/quotations.xml"
objDom.save "c:/quotations.xml"
```

The `load` method takes a URL to an XML document, and goes and retrieves it, parsing it into the DOM. Note that we used another Microsoft-specific property, `async`; when loading from an XML source, you have the option of doing so either synchronously or asynchronously. If you set `async` to `True`, the document will load in the background while code execution continues. Since we do not want to save the document until it has been completely loaded in to the DOM, we set `async` to `False`.

The Microsoft parser also provides some events to notify you of changes in the state of the DOM. If you decide to do an asynchronous document retrieval, you would need to catch the following two events:

ondataavailable

This event fires each time a new chunk of data has arrived. You may check the status of the download state by inspecting the `readyState` property.

The `readyState` property may have one of these `Long` values:

Value	Meaning
1 (LOADING)	The load is in progress, reading persisted properties. It has not yet started parsing data.
2 (LOADED)	Completed reading the persisted properties, reading and parsing data. However, the object model is not yet available.
3 (INTERACTIVE)	Some data has been read and parsed, and the object model is now available on the partially retrieved data set. Although the object model is available during this state, it is read-only.
4 (COMPLETED)	All done!

onreadystatechange

This event fires whenever the `readyState` property has changed. Here's a small example of loading and saving asynchronously:

Start a new project, with a reference to the Microsoft XML object. Declare the object using the `WithEvents` keyword so that we can catch the events:

```
Option Explicit
Dim WithEvents objDom As DOMDocument
Dim g_sFilename As String
```

We also use a global variable that holds the name for the local file.

Create a subroutine to start the async download:

```
Sub FetchAndSaveAsync(sURL As String, sFile As String)
    g_ sFilename = sFile
    objDom.async = True
    objDom.Load sURL
End Sub
```

Create another subroutine, which we'll call from the objDom_onreadystatechange event:

```
Sub SaveOnReady()
    objDom.save sFilename
    sFilename = ""
End Sub
```

Now add some code to objDom_onreadystatechange to call SaveOnReady when all of the data is available:

```
Private Sub objDom_onreadystatechange()
    Debug.Print "readyState = " & objDom.readyState & ": " & Now
    If (Len(sFilename) > 0) And (objDom.readyState = 4) Then
        SaveOnReady
        Debug.Print "Called SaveOnReady"
    End If
End Sub
```

The Debug.Print statement lets us watch the progress of the download state.

In the Form_Load subroutine, add these lines:

```
Private Sub Form_Load()
    Set objDom = New DOMDocument
    FetchAndSaveAsync
"http://starship.python.net/crew/amk/quotations/quotations.xml", "C:/MyFile.xml"
End Sub
```

When the form loads, it calls FetchAndSave, which initializes the XML URL and the file name variable. The DOMDocument begins downloading; each time the readyState property changes, it fires the onreadystatechange event. When the ready state tells us that the document has finished loading (and we have a name for the local file), the code calls SaveOnReady, which writes the XML to disk and clears the file name variable.

The Microsoft parseError Object

Microsoft has implemented an additional object to track parsing errors, the parseError object. This is not part of the W3C DOM specification, but is extremely useful in figuring out why a document hasn't correctly loaded into the DOM object. ParseError provides these properties:

Property	Description
errorCode	The error code
Filepos	The absolute file position in the XML document containing the error
Line	The line number in the XML document where the error occurred
Linepos	The character position in the line containing the error
Reason	The cause of the error
SrcText	The data where the error occurred
url	The URL of the XML document containing the error

Let's take a look at loading some bad XML, and see what these errors tell us. You can try this code by creating a new project and putting this code into the Form_Load subroutine:

```
Dim oDOM as MSXML.DOMDocument
Set oDOM = New MSXML.DOMDocument

oDOM.loadXML ("<s>X</f>")
With oDOM.parseError
    Debug.Print.errorCode    ' -1072896659
    Debug.Print.filepos      ' 6
    Debug.Print.Line         ' 1
    Debug.Print.linepos      ' 7
    Debug.Print.reason       ' End tag 'f' does not match the start tag 's'.
    Debug.Print.srcText      ' <s>X</f>
    Debug.Print.url          ' Does not print anything
End With
```

You should see the following output in the Immediate window of the IDE:

```
-1072896659
 6
 1
 7
End tag 'f' does not match the start tag 's'.

<s>X</f>
```

You'll notice that the errorCode value is cryptic. Luckily, the srcText value provides a much better explanation of the problem. The url value is empty when loading literal XML.

Platform Neutrality of XML and the DOM

The XML and DOM specifications were intended to be platform neutral. There is a tremendous advantage to coding to a standard, as opposed to investing in vendor specific interfaces. By sticking to a public specification, you keep yourself open to a choice of XML parsers and DOM implementations. If you find a new one that runs faster or is more faithful to the specification, then you can swap components. However, much can be said for an implementation that provides additional methods that ease your coding. This may not be such a problem with the Microsoft parser. For example, Vivid Creations offers ActiveDOM, an XML parser COM object that implements most of the same interfaces as the Microsoft parser, but does not include any XSL transformation methods. However, it does include the parseError object. Unlike the Microsoft parser, it's not free, but it also doesn't require that Internet Explorer be installed in order to run, which is something to consider when planning to distribute your application.

If you want to be extra safe, you could wrap all calls to load and loadXML in another function, and call that function to load your XML. If you change DOM implementations, and the new object has a different method for loading XML, you just need to change your code in one place.

The DOM specification does not provide a method for retrieving the XML from a DOM. There are methods for obtaining the values of individual nodes, but to get the full contents of the DOM you would have to recursively walk through the object and construct a string representation. Both the Microsoft and Vivid Creations parsers provide a Node method called simply xml. It returns a string containing all of the XML contained in that node tree. You can call this method on a node to retrieve the node's XML. Again, because this is not part of the DOM specification, you may want to wrap this call in another function to avoid filling your code with references to a non-specification method.

> **Some of the sample code in this chapter will make straight calls to the load, loadXML, and xml methods for the sake of simplicity, but your production code should have another layer of abstraction to isolate them.**

Interface: Node

Finally, we come to the center of the DOM – the node itself. Having described some ancillary objects, and various methods for *creating* nodes, we can get to the actual details of the real workhorse of the DOM. The node is the fundamental unit of the DOM. There are several types of node objects; some may have child nodes, while others (called **leaf nodes**) are end points. The node interface defines a set of generic methods and attributes, but not every one of these is applicable to every node type. For example, there is a childNodes attribute that returns a NodeList containing the children of a given node. However, the Text node does not have any child nodes, so the childNodes attribute does not apply. The following table lists the different node types:

Node Types

Node Type	Allowed Child Nodes	Constant Name	Constant Value
Element	Element, Text, Comment, ProcessingInstruction, CDATASection, EntityReference	ELEMENT_NODE	1
Attr	Text, EntityReference	ATTRIBUTE_NODE	2
Text	No children	TEXT_NODE	3
CDATASection	No children	CDATA_SECTION_NODE	4
Entity Reference	Element, ProcessingInstruction, Comment, Text, CDATASection, EntityReference	ENTITY_REFERENCE_NODE	5
Entity	Element, ProcessingInstruction, Comment, Text, CDATASection, EntityReference	ENTITY_NODE	6
Processing Instruction	No children	PROCESSING_INSTRUCTION_NODE	7
Comment	No children	COMMENT_NODE	8
Document	Element (maximum of one), ProcessingInstruction, Comment, DocumentType	DOCUMENT_NODE	9
DocumentType	No children	DOCUMENT_TYPE_NODE	10
Document Fragment	Element, ProcessingInstruction, Comment, Text, CDATASection, EntityReference	DOCUMENT_FRAGMENT_NODE	11
Notation	No children	NOTATION_NODE	12

The Microsoft parser provides constant definitions for these, so we do not need to duplicate that in our DOM wrapper class. We just use the constants provided by the Microsoft parser.

Now let's look at the generic node attributes. As you'll note from the third column of the following table, some of these are read-only. Furthermore, the values of nodeName and nodeValue depend on what type of node you are referring to. For example, the node value for an Element node is always null, while the node value of an Attr node is its string content.

> *A frequent source of confusion is trying to get at the text children of an element by referring to the element's nodeValue property. Elements do not have a value. However, they may contain child nodes, such as Text or EntityReference nodes, and it is the value of these nodes that you must retrieve.*

Node Attributes

Attribute Name	Details	Exceptions on Setting	Exceptions on Retrieving
nodeName	The name of this node, depending on its type.	None	None
nodeValue	The value of this node, depending on its type.	DOMException NO_ MODIFICATION _ALLOWED_ ERR: Raised when the node is read-only.	DOMException DOMSTRING_ SIZE_ERR: Raised when it would return more characters than fit in a DOMString variable on the implementation platform.
nodeType	A code representing the type of the underlying object.	None	None
parentNode	The parent of the node. All nodes except Document, DocumentFragment, and Attr may have a parent. However, if a node has just been created and not yet added to the tree, or if it has been removed from the tree, this value is null.	None	None
childNodes	A NodeList that contains all children of this node. If there are no children, this is a NodeList containing no nodes. The content of the returned NodeList is "live" in the sense that, changes to the children of the node object that it was created from are immediately reflected in the nodes returned by the NodeList accessors; it is not a static snapshot of the content of the node. This is true for every NodeList, including the ones returned by the getElementsByTagName method.	None	None

Table continued on following page

Attribute Name	Details	Exceptions on Setting	Exceptions on Retrieving
firstChild	The first child of this node. If there is no such node, this returns null.	Not Applicable	Not Applicable
lastChild	The last child of this node. If there is no such node, this returns null.	Not Applicable	Not Applicable
previous Sibling	The node immediately preceding this node. If there is no such node, this returns null.	Not Applicable	Not Applicable
nextSibling	The node immediately following this node. If there is no such node, this returns null.	Not Applicable	Not Applicable
attributes	A NamedNodeMap containing the attributes of this node (if it is an Element) or null otherwise.	Not Applicable	Not Applicable
owner Document	The Document object associated with this node. This is also the Document object used to create new nodes. When this node is a Document, this is null.	Not Applicable	Not Applicable

Generic Node Methods

Finally, here are the generic node methods. We'll spend a bit more time with these to see exactly how they are used.

appendChild (Node newChild)

This method will add the node newChild to the end of the list of children of this node. If an attempt is made to add a node that already exists in the tree, it will first be removed, along with any child nodes it may contain, and the corresponding data. If the new child is a DocumentFragment node, then the entire contents of the document fragment are moved into the child list of this node you are manipulating. The method returns a reference to the node just added.

A HIERARCHY_REQUEST_ERR exception will be raised if an attempt is made to add a node where no child nodes are allowed, or if the node we are trying to append is one of the node's ancestors. A WRONG_DOCUMENT_ERR exception will be raised if the new child node that is being appended was created in a different document from that of the parent node. A NO_MODIFICATION_ALLOWED_ERR exception will be raised if the node is read-only.

Let's see how this works with adding a new `Element` node:

```
Dim objDOM As MSXML.DOMDocument
Dim pNode as MSXML.IXMLDOMNode
Dim oNode As MSXML.IXMLDOMNode
Dim elNode As MSXML.IXMLDOMElement

Set objDOM = New MSXML.DOMDocument
objDOM.load sSomeXmlUrl

' Let's grab a reference to the root node
Set pNode = objDOM.documentElement
' Use the DOMDocument object factory method to create a new
' element node
Set elNode = objDOM.createElement("Test")
' Now append the node
Set oNode = pNode.appendChild(elNode)
```

As we noted before, certain operations will raise a `DOMException` error under certain circumstances. We also saw that different node types only allow certain types of child nodes, or perhaps no children at all. Creating new nodes and appending them to existing nodes is a common operation in many XML DOM applications. Every time you want to append a node, you would have to check to make sure that:

- ❏ The node accepted the child node
- ❏ The new node was properly named
- ❏ The parent node allowed modifications

Wrapper Functions for Manipulating the DOM

Rather than spreading duplicate code around, let's create a wrapper method in our class project for adding `Element` nodes, that handles this for us. The function `AddElement` will take the following arguments:

- ❏ `oDOM`, a reference to our `DOMDocument` object
- ❏ `oPNode`, the parent node to receive the new child
- ❏ `sElementName`, the tag name we wish to give our new element
- ❏ `sElementContent`, any text content we wish to have for our new element

AddElement

```
Public Function AddElement(oDOM As DOMDocument, _
                oPNode As IXMLDOMNode, _
                sElementName As String, _
                sElementContent As String _
                ) As Boolean
    On Error GoTo ErrHand
    Dim oNode As MSXML.IXMLDOMNode
    Dim elNode As MSXML.IXMLDOMElement
    Dim bResults As Boolean
```

```
        Call ClearErrorInfo
        ' Need to check that the element name is valid
        If Not ValidateElementType(sElementName) Then
            AddElement = False
            Call SetErrorInfo(-1, "Invalid element type", _
                "CDomFunctions.AddElement", INVALID_CHARACTER_ERR)
            bResults = False
        Else
            Select Case oPNode.NodeType
                Case NODE_DOCUMENT, NODE_DOCUMENT_FRAGMENT, _
                    NODE_ENTITY_REFERENCE, NODE_ELEMENT:
                    Set elNode = oDOM.createElement(sElementName)
                    Set oNode = oPNode.appendChild(elNode)
                    If (Len(sElementContent)) Then
                        oNode.Text = sElementContent
                    End If
                    bResults = True
                Case Else
                    bResults = False
                    Call SetErrorInfo(-1, "Invalid parent node type.", _
                        "CDomFunctions.AddElement", HIERARCHY_REQUEST_ERR)
            End Select
        End If
        Exit Function

Errhand:
    If Err.Number <> 0 Then
        bResults = False
        Call SetErrorInfo(Err.Number, Err.Description, _
            "CDomFunctions." & Err.Source, UNKNOWN)
    End If
    AddElement = bResults
End Function
```

ValidateElementType

Here's the code for validating the Element tag name:

```
Public Function ValidateElementType(strTagName As String) As Boolean
    ' An element tag name may begin with only certain characters.
    ' Rather than test for all of them, let's get the parser to do it ...
    Dim oDOM As DOMDocument
    Dim sXML As String

    Set oDOM = New DOMDocument

    sXML = "<" & strTagName & "/>"
    If Not oDOM.loadXML(sXML) Then
        ValidateElementType = False
    Exit Function
    End If
    ValidateElementType = True
End Function
```

AddElementXML

Another approach to adding an element node is to create a string version of the Element first. We can take advantage of the fact that a single element can serve as a stand-alone XML document to verify that it is well-formed and to parse its contents.

```
Public Function AddElementXML(oDOM As DOMDocument, _
        oPNode As IXMLDOMNode, _
        sElementXML As String _
        ) As Boolean
    On Error GoTo ErrHand
    Dim oNode As MSXML.IXMLDOMNode
    Dim elNode As MSXML.IXMLDOMElement
    Dim oTempDOM As DOMDocument
    Dim nIdx As Integer
    Dim strParserErr As String
    Dim domErr As DOMException

    Call ClearErrorInfo

    Set oTempDOM = New DOMDocument
    If Not (oTempDOM.loadXML(sElementXML)) Then
        AddElementXML = False
        strParserErr = oTempDOM.parseError.reason
        If InStr(strParserErr, "name was started with an invalid character") Then
            domErr = INVALID_CHARACTER_ERR
        Else
            domErr = UNKNOWN
        End If
        Call SetErrorInfo(-1, "Invalid element XML: " & strParserErr, _
                                "CDomFunctions.AddElementXML", domErr)
        AddElementXML = False
        Exit Function
    End If

    Select Case oPNode.nodeType
        Case NODE_DOCUMENT, NODE_DOCUMENT_FRAGMENT, NODE_ENTITY_REFERENCE, _
                NODE_ELEMENT:
            Set elNode = oDOM.createElement(oTempDOM.documentElement.nodeName)
            Set oNode = oPNode.appendChild(elNode)
            If (Len(oTempDOM.documentElement.Text)) Then
                oNode.Text = oTempDOM.documentElement.Text
            End If
            If (oTempDOM.documentElement.Attributes.length > 0) Then
                With oTempDOM.documentElement.Attributes
                    For nIdx = 0 To oTempDOM.documentElement.Attributes.length - 1
                        If Not (AddAttribute(oDOM, oNode, .Item(nIdx).nodeName, _
                            .Item(nIdx).nodeValue)) Then
                            AddElementXML = False
                            Call SetErrorInfo(-1, "Error adding attribute.", _
                                "CDomFunctions.AddElementXML", UNKNOWN)
                            Exit Function
                        End If
                    Next
```

```
                        End With
                End If
                AddElementXML = True
            Case Else
                AddElementXML = False
                Call SetErrorInfo(-1, "Invalid parent node type.", _
                        "CDomFunctions.AddElementXML", HIERARCHY_REQUEST_ERR)
        End Select
        Exit Function

ErrHand:
    If Err.Number <> 0 Then
        AddElementXML = False
        Call SetErrorInfo(Err.Number, Err.Description, "CDomFunctions." & _
                    Err.Source, UNKNOWN)
    End If
End Function
```

AddAttribute

In the following code, we have jumped ahead of ourselves a little, by having it handle not only the creation and addition of an element but also the addition of attributes and element content. So, here's the code for AddAttribute:

```
Public Function AddAttribute(oDOM As DOMDocument, _
            oElement As IXMLDOMElement, _
            sName As String, _
            sValue As String, _
            Optional bReplace As Boolean = False _
            ) As Boolean
    On Error GoTo ErrHand
    Dim oAttr As IXMLDOMAttribute
    Call ClearErrorInfo

    ' First see if the attribute already exists ...
    If (Not oElement.Attributes.getNamedItem(sName) Is Nothing) Then
        If bReplace = False Then
            AddAttribute = False
            Exit Function
        End If
    End If
    Set oAttr = oDOM.createAttribute(sName)

    oElement.setAttribute sName, sValue
    AddAttribute = True
    Exit Function

ErrHand:
    If Err.Number <> 0 Then
        Call SetErrorInfo(Err.Number, Err.Description, "CDomFunctions." &_
                    Err.Source, UNKNOWN)
        AddAttribute = False
    End If
End Function
```

Adding a Processing Instruction

Similar functions can be created for managing the addition of the other node types. We'll take a look now at one for adding a processing instruction (PI). Only certain nodes may contain processing instructions. To add a PI, we need to check the node type of the intended parent. We'll add a function to our class project to handle this for us. The method takes four parameters: the DOM document we are using, the intended parent node for the PI, a string for the name of the PI target, and a string for the PI's instructions:

```
Public Function AddPI(oDOM As DOMDocument, _
                      oPNode As IXMLDOMNode, _
                      sTarget As String, _
                      sValue As String _
                      ) As Boolean
    On Error GoTo ErrHand
```

We declare a PI node for our process, and a Boolean to hold the function response:

```
    Dim piNode As MSXML.IXMLDOMProcessingInstruction
    Dim bResults As Boolean
```

We'll clear any error information, and then check the node type of the intended parent node. If the parent node is one of the allowed types, we call `createProcessingInstruction`, passing it the target name and the instruction text:

```
    Call ClearErrorInfo

    Select Case oPNode.NodeType
        Case NODE_DOCUMENT, NODE_DOCUMENT_FRAGMENT, _
            NODE_ENTITY_REFERENCE, NODE_ELEMENT:
            Set piNode = oDOM.createProcessingInstruction(sTarget, sValue)
```

We then append the new PI node to the parent node, and set our return value:

```
            oPNode.appendChild piNode
            bResults = True
```

If the parent node is the wrong type, we set the error information and return value:

```
        Case Else
            bResults = False
            Call SetErrorInfo(-1, "Invalid parent node type.", _
                "CDomFunctions.AddPI", HIERARCHY_REQUEST_ERR)
    End Select
```

We have some basic error trapping, and return our response:

```
ErrHand:
    If Err.Number <> 0 Then
        bResults = False
```

```
            Call SetErrorInfo(Err.Number, Err.Description, "CDomFunctions." _
                & Err.Source, UNKNOWN)
        End If
        AddPI = bResults
    End Function
```

Adding a Comment

Adding a Comment node is very similar. The function takes the following parameters:

- ❑ oDOM, a reference to our DOMDocument object

- ❑ oPNode, the parent node to receive the new child

- ❑ sContent, the text that goes inside of the comment

```
    Public Function AddComment(oDOM As DOMDocument, _
                    oPNode As IXMLDOMNode, _
                    sContent As String _
                    ) As Boolean
        On Error GoTo ErrHand

        Dim elNode As MSXML.IXMLDOMComment
        Dim bResults As Boolean

        Call ClearErrorInfo
```

After setting up the function variables and clearing any error data, we check that the parent node can accept a Comment node. If the parent node is of a correct type, then createComment is called to get a new Comment node, the node is appended to the parent node, and the return value is set to True:

```
        Select Case oPNode.NodeType
            Case NODE_DOCUMENT_FRAGMENT, NODE_DOCUMENT, NODE_ENTITY_REFERENCE, _
                NODE_ELEMENT:
                Set elNode = oDOM.createComment(sContent)
                oPNode.appendChild elNode
                bResults = True
```

If the parent node is the wrong type to accept a Comment node, we'll register the error data and set the return type to False:

```
            Case Else
                bResults = False
                Call SetErrorInfo(-1, "Invalid parent node type.", _
                    "CDomFunctions.AddComment", HIERARCHY_REQUEST_ERR)
        End Select
        Exit Function

    ErrHand:
        If Err.Number <> 0 Then
            Call SetErrorInfo(Err.Number, Err.Description, "CDomFunctions." & _
                Err.Source, UNKNOWN)
            bResults = False
```

```
        End If
        AddComment = bResults
    End Function
```

insertBefore (node newChild, node refNode)

The insertBefore method is similar to appendChild, except that the referring node (refNode) is treated as a sibling rather than a parent. The parent node is the one the method is called from. As the name suggests, the new node is inserted before the referring node; the result being that both nodes share the same parent. The specification states that if the referring node is null, then the new node is inserted at the end of the list of children of the calling node. If the new node already exists as a child, then it is first removed. The method returns a reference to the newly inserted node.

This method will raise a HIERARCHY_REQUEST_ERR exception if the parent node cannot accept a child node of the type of the new node, or if the new node is an ancestor of the calling node. A WRONG_DOCUMENT_ERR exception will be raised if an attempt is made to insert a node from another DOM object. If the calling node is read-only, then a NO_MODIFICATION_ALLOWED_ERR exception will be raised. Finally, if the referring node is not actually a child of the calling node then a NOT_FOUND_ERR exception will be raised.

The InsertElementBefore Function

Let's see how this works in practice. We'll write a function to handle the insertion of a new Element, much like the AddElement function above.

```
Public Function InsertElementBefore(oDOM As DOMDocument, _
                 oRefNode As IXMLDOMNode, _
                 sElementName As String, _
                 sElementContent As String _
                 ) As Boolean
    On Error GoTo Errhand
    Dim oNode As MSXML.IXMLDOMNode
    Dim elNode As MSXML.IXMLDOMElement
    Dim oPNode As IXMLDOMNode
    Call ClearErrorInfo

    ' Check that the element name is valid
    If Not ValidateElementType(sElementName) Then
        InsertElementBefore = False
        Call SetErrorInfo( 1, "Invalid element type", _
            "CDomFunctions.InsertElementBefore", INVALID_CHARACTER_ERR)
        Exit Function
    End If

    Set oPNode = oRefNode.parentNode
    ' Check that the parent of the referring node will accept an Element node
    Select Case oPNode.NodeType
        Case NODE_DOCUMENT, NODE_DOCUMENT_FRAGMENT, NODE_ENTITY_REFERENCE, _
            NODE_ELEMENT:
            Set elNode = oDOM.createElement(sElementName)
            Set oNode = oPNode.insertBefore(elNode, oRefNode)
            If (Len(sElementContent)) Then
                oNode.Text = sElementContent
            End If
```

```
                        InsertElementBefore = True
            Case Else
                InsertElementBefore = False
                Call SetErrorInfo(-1, "Invalid parent node type.", _
                    "CDomFunctions.InsertElementBefore", HIERARCHY_REQUEST_ERR)
        End Select
        Exit Function

    Errhand:
        If Err.Number <> 0 Then
            InsertElementBefore = False
            Call SetErrorInfo(Err.Number, Err.Description, _
                "CDomFunctions.InsertElementBefore " & Err.Source, UNKNOWN)
        End If
    End Function
```

The Microsoft parser will indeed catch certain anomalies, such as trying to pass a referring node that's really a sibling of the calling node. However, it throws a COM exception that doesn't explain the error in terms of the DOM. The above function gets the correct parent node for the insertBefore *method. However, the parser does not care whether the new* Element *node was created from another DOM object – the function creates the new element from scratch, using a single* DOMDocument *object. However, a wrapper function that takes an instance of a node as a parameter would need to check that the new node is from the same document as the calling node. Otherwise, if you were to use a node from another DOM, it would be inserted without any complaints from the parser.*

replaceChild (node newChild, node oldChild)

If, instead of adding a node, we wanted to replace a node, then this is the method that would be used. This method replaces the oldChild with newChild, and returns a reference to the old node. A HIERARCHY_REQUEST_ERR exception will be raised if an attempt is made to replace a node with a new node whose type is not accepted by the parent node, or if an attempt is made to replace an ancestor node. A WRONG_DOCUMENT_ERR exception will be raised if the replacement node came from a different DOM object. A NO_MODIFICATION_ALLOWED_ERR exception will be raised if this node is read-only. Finally, a NOT_FOUND_ERR exception should be raised if the node we're trying to replace isn't really a child node.

removeChild (node oldChild)

As the name suggests, this method is used to remove the node passed as the parameter. It returns a reference to the removed node. If the parent node is read-only, a NO_MODIFICATION_ALLOWED_ERR exception will be raised. If the node that is to be removed is not a child of the calling node, a NOT_FOUND_ERR exception will be raised.

hasChildNodes

The W3C threw this in as a "convenience method"; it checks if the node has any children; it returns either 'true' (if it has) or 'false' (if it hasn't).

cloneNode (Boolean deep)

If there's a particular node you want to copy from one place in the DOM to another, then you can clone it. The `cloneNode` method returns a reference to a new, duplicate node. The `deep` parameter can be either `'true'` or `'false'`; if `true`, the method will return a duplicate node, along with copies of all of the node's child nodes. This is particularly useful when cloning `Element` nodes. The text contained in an element is a separate node (or possibly a set of nodes). If you want to clone the whole element, text and all, then you need to set `deep` to `true`. However, element attributes are included in the clone regardless of the value of `deep`. You should also be aware that the returned node, like any other newly instanced node, does not have a parent node.

Interface: NodeList

Now we'll look at another object, one that lets us work with groups of nodes. A `NodeList` is an ordered collection of nodes. It is the object returned by all methods and properties that can return more than one node, such as `getElementsByName`. The nodes in a `NodeList` do not necessarily have any sibling or parent-child relationships, but they must be part of the same document.

The `NodeList` has a single attribute, `length`, which is the number of nodes in the list. There is also one method: `item`, which takes an `Integer` as its parameter, `index`. The `item` method returns a reference to the node specified by `index`. Indexing is zero-based; if the index is greater than or equal to the number of nodes in the list, the method returns null.

> When using this method with the Microsoft parser, you need to check for `Is Nothing` rather than `IsNull` because of the way Microsoft has chosen to implement it.

An example of the syntax is as follows:

```
Dim oNodeList As IXMLDOMNodeList
' Look for elements that don't exist …
Set oNodeList = objDOM. GetElementsByTagName("SomeNonexistentTag")

MsgBox IsNull (oNodeList (0) )        ' Displays "false"
MsgBox (oNodeList (0) Is Nothing)     ' Displays "true"
```

Interface: NamedNodeMap

The `NamedNodeMap` is similar to the `NodeList` except that it allows you to reference items by name or by an index number. It is like a hash array or a collection. Note that, while an index number may reference the items in a `NamedNodeMap`, there is no implied order to the nodes. If you want to add a new node, there is no guarantee that the previously existing nodes could still be indexed as before. Thus, an integer index is useful for iterating through the members, but cannot be relied on to always point to the same specific entry once the list has been modified. The `NamedNodeMap` is a "live" object, meaning that if you alter any of the items in the list, the changes are propagated back to the source node.

The `NamedNodeMap` interface is provided by `DOMDocument.notations`, `DOMDocument.entities`, and all the nodes that implement the `Attributes` attribute. Consequently, a `NamedNodeMap` will only contain nodes of type `Notation`, `Entity`, or `Attr`, depending on the object you are using.

The NamedNodeMap has these methods:

getNamedItem (String sName)

getNamedItem returns a reference to the node with name sName. It returns null if no matching node was found, for example:

```
' Assuming objDOM holds "<doc a='1' b='2'>test</doc>"
Dim oMap As IXMLDOMNamedNodeMap
Set oMap = objDOM.childNodes(0).Attributes
MsgBox oMap.getNamedItem("a").nodeValue
```

setNamedItem (node nodeArg)

This method allows you to add a new node to the NamedNodeMap. If a node with the same name is present, then that node will be replaced. setNamedItem returns null if you are adding a node; if a node is replaced, a reference to that node is returned.

A WRONG_DOCUMENT_ERR DOMException will be raised if the node argument comes from a different DOM object than the DOM that created the NamedNodeMap. If the NamedNodeMap is read-only, a NO_MODIFICATION_ALLOWED_ERR exception will be raised. If the node argument is an Attr node that is an attribute of another Element node, then an INUSE_ATTRIBUTE_ERR exception will be raised. If you want to reuse an Attr node then you must first clone the Attr node.

Notations and entities are read-only; trying to add or replace either of these will raise an error.

> *The Microsoft parser shows some interesting behavior here. Adding a new Attr node returns a reference to that new node, rather than returning null. Furthermore, if a node is replaced, the method returns a reference to the new node, rather than to the replaced node.*

An Example of Creating and Using a NamedNodeMap

First we define our variables:

```
Dim oDOM As DOMDocument
Dim oMap As IXMLDOMNamedNodeMap
Dim oAttr As IXMLDOMAttribute
Dim oNode As IXMLDOMNode
```

Then set the DOM object:

```
Set oDOM = New DOMDocument
```

And load some text:

```
oDOM.loadXML "<doc a='1' b='2'>test</doc>"
```

First we'll see how many items are in NamedNodeMap for the root element's attributes:

```
Set oMap = oDOM.childNodes(0).Attributes
Debug.Print "Map length = " & oMap.length
```

This should print "Map length = 2"

Now we want to add a new attribute. We create a new attribute node, give it a value, and use setNamedItem to add it to the namedNodeMap:

```
Set oAttr = oDOM.createAttribute("new")
oAttr.nodeValue = "Hello"
Set oNode = oMap.setNamedItem(oAttr)
```

We've set oNode to the return value. Now we want to see how the length of the map has changed, and what the method call returned:

```
Debug.Print oNode.baseName & " = " & oNode.nodeValue & _
                    "; map length = " & oMap.length
```

Now we get the output: "new = Hello; map length = 3"

Well, we've added the node, but rather than being null (as the recommendation dictates), oNode has been given a reference to the newly added node.

Now we'll try adding another node, but this time it will have the same name as an existing node:

```
Set oAttr = oDOM.createAttribute("new")
oAttr.nodeValue = "new value"
Set oNode = oMap.setNamedItem(oAttr)
```

Now we check our new values:

```
Debug.Print oNode.baseName & " = " & oNode.nodeValue & _
                    "; map length = " & oMap.length
```

And we get this output: "new = new value; map length = 3"

The map has not gained a new node; we've replaced the new attribute with another value. But rather than giving us a reference to the old node (where the nodeValue would be "Hello"), we've been given a reference to the node we just added.

The return value is the same regardless of whether we are adding or replacing a node. Suppose we wanted to add new attributes to an element, but only if the attribute does not already exist. According to the W3C specification, replacing a node should give a reference to the old node; if the return value for setNamedItem is not null, we could repeat the replace operation, using the old node, to restore the original value. The Microsoft version does not give us this information, so we need to do a little extra work.

Wrapper Functions for NamedNodeMap Methods

Let's write a wrapper function for this. We'll pass in the node we want to set, and the `NamedNodeMap` we're using:

```
Public Function SetNamedItem(oNode As IXMLDOMNode, _
        oMap As IXMLDOMNamedNodeMap) As IXMLDOMNode
    Dim sName As String
    Dim oNodeTemp As IXMLDOMNode
    sName = oNode.baseName

    If oMap.getNamedItem(sName) Is Nothing Then
        ' This is a new node. Return a Nothing node object
        Set SetNamedItem = oNodeTemp
        oMap.setNamedItem oNode
    Else ' We're replacing. Return the replaced node
        Set SetNamedItem = oMap.getNamedItem(sName)
        oMap.setNamedItem oNode
    End If
End Function
```

Redoing our first example, you can call the function like this. This part is the same:

```
Dim oDOM As DOMDocument
Dim oMap As IXMLDOMNamedNodeMap
Dim oAttr As IXMLDOMAttribute
Dim oNode As IXMLDOMNode

Set oDOM = New DOMDocument

oDOM.loadXML "<doc a='1' b='2'>test</doc>"

Set oMap = oDOM.childNodes(0).Attributes
Debug.Print "Map length = " & oMap.length

Set oAttr = oDOM.createAttribute("new")
oAttr.nodeValue = "Hello"
```

We use the wrapper function to perform the node addition. It should return a value of `Nothing`, since we've added a new attribute. The `If` check will only run if something very unpredictable happens:

```
Set oNode = SetNamedItem(oAttr, oMap)
' This should never be run
If Not oNode Is Nothing Then
    Debug.Print oNode.baseName & " = " & oNode.nodeValue & _
                "; map length = " & oMap.length
End If
```

We then add a node with the same name, which should replace the previously added node:

```
Set oAttr = oDOM.createAttribute("new")
oAttr.nodeValue = "new value"
Set oNode = SetNamedItem(oAttr, oMap)
```

Now we should get a reference to the replaced node:

```
Debug.Print oNode.baseName & " = " & oNode.nodeValue & _
                "; map length = " & oMap.length
```

This will print the revised output: "new = Hello; map length = 3"

removeNamedItem (String sNodeName)

This method removes the node specified by sNodeName. However, if you try to remove an Attr node, and that node has a default value (which would need to have been defined in a DTD), that node will be automatically replaced. This method should return the node being removed or, if no such node exists, return null and raise a NOT_FOUND_ERR exception.

The Microsoft parser will raise a run-time error if we try to remove a non-existent node, so we'll write another wrapper function to trap this:

```
Public Function RemoveNamedItem(oNode As IXMLDOMNode, _
                                oMap As IXMLDOMNamedNodeMap) As IXMLDOMNode
    Dim sName As String    ,
    Dim oNodeTemp As IXMLDOMNode
    sName = oNode.baseName
    If oMap.getNamedItem(sName) Is Nothing Then
        ' This node doesn't exist, so we can't remove it.
        ' Return a Nothing node object
        Set RemoveNamedItem = oNodeTemp
    Else ' Remove the node and return a reference to the old node
        Set RemoveNamedItem = oMap.getNamedItem(sName)
        oMap.removeNamedItem oNode
    End If
End Function
```

item (Integer nIndex)

The item method returns the node indexed by the nIndex parameter. If the index is out-of-bounds for the NamedNodeMap, it returns null. Indexing begins at zero. The specification states that this method raises no exceptions, but you should really test the index before trying to retrieve a node. First, let's take a look at the single NamedNodeMap attribute: length.

length

This returns the number of nodes in the NamedNodeMap. So, for example, to safely retrieve a node by index, we can do this as follows:

```
Dim nIndex as Integer

...

If (nIndex < oMap.length) And (nIndex > -1) then
    Set oNode = oMap.item(nIndex)
End if
```

Specific Node Interfaces

In addition to the generic node interface, the DOM provides a set of node-type specific interfaces that inherit from the base node object. Because of this, you'll notice that the IntelliSense feature in the Visual Basic IDE will display all of the methods and properties for any of the specific node types (such as IXMLDOMAttribute), but not all of these methods and properties will work with all node types. If you try and use any of these "phantom" methods or properties a run-time error will result.

Interface: Attr

The Attr node provides an interface to the attributes of an Element. The DOM specification states that attributes are not considered to be child nodes of an Element, and so are not viewed as part of the document tree. As a result, the base node attributes parentNode, previousSibling, and nextSibling should have null values when applied to attributes. But, if attributes are not part of the tree, then what are they? Well, they are properties, which describe the element and are thus bound to the given element. When the DOM specification was drawn up, this approach was taken to make it easier for DOM implementations to give default attributes to elements when defined in a DTD. If an attribute is defined in a DTD, then that definition will restrict the allowable values the Attr node may have. Attributes that have been declared with a default value automatically exist for the element types that they have been defined for. If a declared attribute has not been explicitly set to a particular value, then the attribute takes the default value that has been specified. If there is no default value, then the attribute does not exist on any element until deliberately added.

Attr nodes may not be the immediate children of a DocumentFragment, though they can be part of an Element that resides in a DocumentFragment.

In XML, where the value of an attribute can contain entity references, the child nodes of the Attr node provide a representation in which entity references are not expanded; these child nodes may be either Text or EntityReference nodes. Because the attribute type may be unknown, there are no tokenized attribute values. The W3C specification grants some flexibility on how a parser resolves entity references. It may choose to replace the reference with the corresponding text when the document is first parsed into the DOM, or may wait until the entity is accessed through one of the DOM's methods, such as the childNodes method on the EntityReference node. The Attr node itself has several attributes.

String name

As you might expect, this returns the attribute's name and is read-only. To change the name of an attribute you must first delete it, then add a new attribute with the new name, and assign it a value.

Boolean specified

The specified attribute returns true if the attribute was assigned a value in either the original document or through a DOM interface. If the attribute obtained its value from the default value defined in a DTD, then it returns false. However, if an attribute with a default value has had its value explicitly assigned (even if its value was the same as the default value) then specified would return true. Finally, if the attribute was removed, but it has been defined in a DTD with a default value, it will automatically be replaced, and set to the default value, and specified will be set to false. This attribute is read-only.

String value

This returns the value of the attribute as a string. Character and general entity references are replaced with their corresponding values. When an attribute's value is set, the DOM creates a Text node with the unparsed contents of the string.

Interface: Element

This is the node type you'll probably be spending most of your time with. Aside from holding the character data for your DOM, Elements may also have Attr nodes, which represent the attributes of the element. Element nodes have one attribute:

String tagName

This is a read-only attribute that provides the tag name, or type, of the Element.

Element Node Methods

getAttribute(String sAttrName)

getAttribute takes the name of an attribute, and returns that attribute's value as a string. If the attribute has not been given a value (and has no default value), then an empty string is returned. The specification says that this method does not raise any exceptions; with the Microsoft parser, if you call this method with the name of a non-existent attribute, it returns Null. However, trying to retrieve an attribute value using an illegal attribute name (e.g., names beginning with a digit or backslash) or an empty string will cause a run-time error.

setAttribute (String sAttrName, String sAttrValue)

This method sets the value, given by sAttrValue, of an attribute specified by sAttrName. The attribute value is not parsed when set. For example, if the value contains an entity reference, the ampersand character (and the remaining entity reference string) would be stored as exactly that. Care must be taken when retrieving this value, as it will be seen as containing a special character, and not the parsed value of the entity. A better way to assign an entity reference to an attribute is to construct the attribute using an Attr node with an EntityReference node, and then use the setAttributeNode method (described soon) to assign it. This method will raise an INVALID_CHARACTER_ERR DOMException if the specified attribute name contains an invalid character, and a NO_MODIFICATION_ALLOWED_ERR exception if the Element is read-only.

removeAttribute (String sAttrName)

This will remove the attribute specified by sAttrName; if the attribute has been defined in a DTD with a default value then it will automatically be replaced. Unlike the removeNamedItem method of the NamedNodeMap, this method does not return anything. A NO_MODIFICATION_ALLOWED_ERR DOMException will be raised if the Element is read-only.

getAttributeNode (String sAttrName)

The getAttributeNode method returns a reference to the node named by sAttrName. The specification says that this method should return null if the named attribute doesn't exist; the Microsoft parser will throw a run-time error. To avoid this, we can write a simple wrapper function for this, similar to the RemoveNamedItem function we saw earlier:

```
Public Function GetAttributeNode (oEL As IXMLDOMElement, sAttrname As String) _
         As IXMLDOMAttribute
    Dim oAttrTemp As IXMLDOMAttribute

    If Not IsNull(oEL.getAttribute(sAttrname)) Then
        Set GetAttributeNode = oEL.getAttributeNode(sAttrname)
    Else
        Set GetAttributeNode = oAttrTemp
    End If
End Function
```

setAttributeNode (attr newAttr)

This method will add an `Attr` node to the current `Element`. If an attribute already exists with the same name as the one being added, it will be replaced. `SetAttributeNode` will return a reference to the replaced node, or will return `Null` if a new node is added.

A `WRONG_DOCUMENT_ERR` `DOMException` will be raised if the new `Attr` node comes from a DOM object other than the `Element` node. If the element is read-only, a `NO_MODIFICATION_ALLOWED_ERR` exception will be raised. If the new `Attr` node is an attribute of another `Element` then an `INUSE_ATTRIBUTE_ERR` exception will be raised. To reuse an `Attr` node you must first clone it.

> *The Microsoft parser implementation will return `Nothing`, rather than `Null`, if a new node is added.*

removeAttributeNode (attr oldAttr)

This will remove the `Attr` node specified by `oldAttr`. If you remove an attribute defined with a default value it will be automatically replaced. The method returns the node that was removed. If the `Attr` node does not exist in the `Element`, a `NOT_FOUND_ERR` `DOMException` will be raised. If the `Element` is read-only, a `NO_MODIFICATION_ALLOWED_ERR` exception will be raised.

The Microsoft parser will raise a run-time error if you try to remove a non-existent node. To prevent this, we need to test that the node exists before attempting to remove it:

```
Public Function RemoveAttributeNode (_
         oEl As IXMLDOMElement, oAttr As IXMLDOMAttribute) As IXMLDOMAttribute
    Dim oAttrTemp As IXMLDOMAttribute
    Dim sAttrName As String
    sAttrName = oAttr.Name

    If Not IsNull(oEl.getAttribute(sAttrName)) Then
        ' The attribute exists, so we can remove it and return the removed node
        Set RemoveAttributeNode = oEl.removeAttributeNode(oAttr)
    Else
        ' Return a Nothing node
        Set RemoveAttributeNode = oAttrTemp
    End If
End Function
```

You can use this function to remove an `Attr` node; to test if a node was actually removed, call the function as follows:

First declare the variables, initialize the DOM and give it some XML (as we have done before):

```
Dim oDOM As DOMDocument
Dim oAttr As IXMLDOMAttribute
Dim oElement As IXMLDOMElement
Dim oAttrToRemove As IXMLDOMAttribute
Set oDOM = New DOMDocument
oDOM.loadXML "<doc a='1' b='2'>test</doc>"
```

Set `oElement` to the first document element, and `oAttrToRemove` to the element's first attribute:

```
Set oElement = oDOM.childNodes(0)
Set oAttrToRemove = oElement.Attributes.Item(0)
```

Now remove the attribute, and test the return value:

```
Set oAttr = RemoveAttributeNode(oElement, oAttrToRemove)
If (oAttr Is Nothing) Then
    Debug.Print "Attribute not found."
Else
    Debug.Print "Attribute " & oAttr.baseName & " removed."
End If
```

getElementsByTagName (String sTagName)

This method performs a search on all of the child elements of the `Element` node and returns a `NodeList` containing all of the `Elements` whose type match the parameter `sTagName`. The nodes are returned in the same order as you would encounter them when viewing the document as a string. So, for example, if we have this XML:

```
<doc>
  <Item>These</Item>
  <Object>
    <Item>are</Item>
    <Tag>
      <Item>the</Item>
    </Tag>
  </Object>
  <Item>items</Item>
</doc>
```

The elements in the node list would be in this order:

```
<Item>These</Item>
<Item>are</Item>
<Item>the</Item>
<Item>items</Item>
```

Setting sTagName to '*' will return all child Elements.

> *The specification states that this method raises no exceptions but, as described earlier in the 'Interface:Node' section, trying to locate elements using an invalid tag name will cause the Microsoft parser to raise a run-time error.*

normalize ()

Using the addChild method of the Node object, you can add Text nodes to Element nodes. If you add multiple Text nodes to an Element, you end up with what appears to be a single string that is actually spread out over multiple nodes. You may prefer, however, to have the complete text contained in one Text node. The normalize method alters all of the Text nodes in the Element's subtree so that all adjacent Text nodes (i.e. Text nodes of the same Element) are merged into one.

Here's a diagram to illustrate this: we start with an element that contains a single child text node:

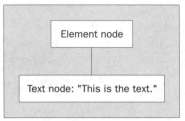

When we add new text, the element will contain two text nodes:

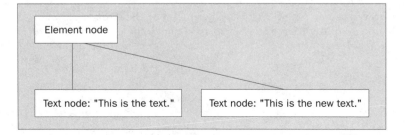

Calling normalize combines the text nodes into one:

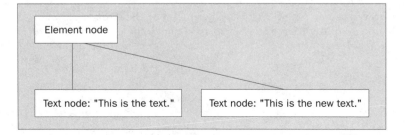

To see how this works, let's build a wrapper function so that we can safely add Text nodes. Not all nodes will accept Text child nodes, and the Microsoft parser will complain if we're not careful:

```
Public Function AddTextNode(oDOM As DOMDocument, _
            oPNode As IXMLDOMNode, _
            sValue As String _
            ) As Boolean
    On Error GoTo ErrHand
    Dim oNode As MSXML.IXMLDOMNode
    Dim elNode As MSXML.IXMLDOMText

    Call ClearErrorInfo

    Select Case oPNode.nodeType
        Case NODE_ATTRIBUTE, NODE_DOCUMENT_FRAGMENT, NODE_ENTITY_REFERENCE, _
                NODE_ELEMENT:
            Set elNode = oDOM.createTextNode(sValue)
            Set oNode = oPNode.appendChild(elNode)
            AddTextNode = True
        Case Else
            AddTextNode = False
            Call SetErrorInfo(-1, "Invalid parent node type.", _
                "CDomFunctions.AddTextNode", HIERARCHY_REQUEST_ERR)
    End Select
    Exit Function

ErrHand:
    If Err.Number <> 0 Then
        AddTextNode = False
        Call SetErrorInfo(Err.Number, Err.Description, _
                    "CDomFunctions." & Err.Source, UNKNOWN)
    End If
End Function
```

Now let's look at an example to see how adding text changes the total number of an Element's child nodes:

```
    Dim oElNode As IXMLDOMElement
    Set oDOM = New DOMDocument
    oDOM.loadXML ("<TEST>Hello!</TEST>")

    Set oElNode = oDOM.childNodes(0)
    ' Prints 1
    Debug.Print "Element TEST has " & oElNode.childNodes.length & _
                    " children"
    Call dw.AddTextNode(oDOM, oElNode, "one")
    ' Prints 2
    Debug.Print "Element TEST has " & oElNode.childNodes.length & _
                    " children"
    Call dw.AddTextNode(objDOM, oElNode, "two")
    ' Prints 3
    Debug.Print "Element TEST has " & oElNode.childNodes.length & _
                    " children"
```

```
oElNode.normalize
' Prints 1
Debug.Print "Element TEST has " & oElNode.childNodes.length & _
               " children"
```

Interface: Text

The Text node is the object that holds the character data of your document. When a document is first loaded, the character data for an Element is placed into a single Text node. Adding more character data will create additional Text nodes, which can be combined using the normalize method. This is handy for reformatting your DOM structure for certain XPointer functions, which may not be able to handle multiple Text nodes. XPointer is discussed in Chapter 5, 'Linking with XPointer and XLink'.

The Text node has a single method:

splitText (Integer nOffset)

This method allows you to split a Text node into two adjacent Text nodes. The breakpoint is specified by the nOffset parameter, an integer index into the Text node value starting at zero. The original Text node retains all of the character data up to but not including the offset demarcation; a new Text node is created adjacent to the original node, containing the remaining text. A reference to the new Text node is returned.

This method will raise an INDEX_SIZE_ERR DOMException if the offset is negative or greater than the length of the Text node value. If the node is read-only, a NO_MODIFICATION_ALLOWED_ERR exception will be raised.

The Microsoft parser will raise a run-time error if the offset is negative or larger than the length of the node value. To safely split a Text node, we can use this wrapper function to check the length of the node:

```
Public Function SplitTextNode(oTextNode As IXMLDOMText, _
              nOffset As Integer) As IXMLDOMText
   Dim oTempTextNode As IXMLDOMText
   If (nOffset < 0) Or (nOffset > Len(oTextNode.nodeValue)) Then
       Set SplitTextNode = oTempTextNode
       Call SetErrorInfo(-1, "Offset out-of-bounds", _
              "CDomFunctions.SplitTextNode", INDEX_SIZE_ERR)
   Else
       Set SplitTextNode = oTextNode.splitText(nOffset)
   End If
End Function
```

We can call this function and test the results, like this:

```
Dim oDOM As DOMDocument
Dim oElement As IXMLDOMElement
Dim oNewTextNode As IXMLDOMText
Dim oTextNode As IXMLDOMText

Set oDOM = New DOMDocument
oDOM.loadXML "<doc a='1' b='2'>test</doc>"
```

```
      Set oElement = oDOM.childNodes(0)
      Set oTextNode = oElement.childNodes(0)
      Set oNewTextNode = SplitTextNode(oTextNode, 2)

      If (oNewTextNode Is Nothing) Then
          Debug.Print "Index out of bounds!"
      Else
          Debug.Print "New text node contains " & oNewTextNode.nodeValue
      End If
```

Interface: Comment

The Comment node represents comments inside your DOM document. There are no methods or properties; the Comment is defined simply as type CharacterData.

Interface: CharacterData

Along with Elements, character data is important in XML DOM programming. The DOM specification extends the Node object with the CharacterData interface for managing the document text. There is no actual CharacterData object, but some other objects (such as the Text node) do inherit from the CharacterData interface, making it a virtual class.

CharacterData has these attributes:

data

The data attribute represents the character data of the node, and is used to either retrieve or set the character data of the node. A NO_MODIFICATION_ALLOWED_ERR DOMException will be raised if the node is read-only. If the text returned is too large to fit into a String variable (however, given that a String can hold up to 2 billion characters, this is highly unlikely) then a DOMSTRING_SIZE_ERR exception will be raised.

length

Like the Visual Basic Len() function, this returns the number of characters in the node's data. Since CharacterData nodes may be empty, this may return zero.

CharacterData Interface Methods

substringData (Integer nOffset, Integer nCount)

This retrieves a substring from the data contents. The substring begins at the character at location nOffset, and contains the following characters up to nCount-1, using zero-based indexing, which means that if an offset of zero is specified, and a count of four, then characters zero through three will be returned.

If nCount points past the end of the data, then all the character data from nOffset are returned. If nOffset is less than zero or greater than the length of the data then an INDEX_SIZE_ERR DOMException will be raised. If the text returned is too large to fit into a String variable then a DOMSTRING_SIZE_ERR exception will be raised.

As with the data attribute, the Microsoft parser will raise a run-time error if the offset is negative or larger than the length of the data string.

appendData (String sNewData)

The appendData method adds new data to the end of the node's existing character data. A NO_MODIFICATION_ALLOWED_ERR DOMException will be raised if the node is read-only.

insertData(Integer nOffset, String sData)

This will insert the sData string into the node's existing data at the location specified by nOffset. If nOffset is negative or greater than the length of the node's data minus 1, an INDEX_SIZE_ERR DOMException will be raised. If the node is read-only, a NO_MODIFICATION_ALLOWED_ERR exception will be raised.

To prevent a run-time error from the Microsoft parser, if nOffset is out of bounds, we can use this wrapper function:

```
Public Function TextInsertData(oTextNode As IXMLDOMText, _
                     nOffset As Integer, sData As String) As Boolean
    If (nOffset < 0) Or (nOffset > Len(oTextNode.Data) - 1) Then
        TextInsertData = False
        Call SetErrorInfo(-1, "Offset out-of-bounds", _
                   "CDomFunctions.TextInsertData", INDEX_SIZE_ERR)
    Else
        Call oTextNode.insertData(nOffset, sData)
        TextInsertData = True
    End If
End Function
```

deleteData (Integer nOffset, Integer nCount)

Structurally similar to substringData, deleteData will remove a substring from the node's data string, beginning at the character designated by nOffset, for the total number of characters specified by nCount. If nOffset is negative or greater than one less than the length of the node's data, an INDEX_SIZE_ERR DOMException will be raised. If the node is read-only, a NO_MODIFICATION_ALLOWED_ERR exception will be raised.

Again, we need to look for possible errors, so the following function can be used:

```
Public Function TextDeleteData(oTextNode As IXMLDOMText, _
                     nOffset As Integer, nCount As Integer) As Boolean
    If (nOffset < 0) Or (nOffset > Len(oTextNode.Data) - 1) Then
        TextDeleteData = False
        Call SetErrorInfo(-1, "Offset out-of-bounds", _
                   "CDomFunctions.TextDeleteData", INDEX_SIZE_ERR)
    Else
        Call oTextNode.deleteData(nOffset, nCount)
        TextDeleteData = True
    End If
End Function
```

replaceData (Integer nOffset, Integer nCount, String sData)

Another way to add to character data is to replace some or all of the text with a different string. replaceData finds a substring starting at nOffset, for length nCount, and replaces it with sData. If the nCount defines a string that extends past the length of the character data, then the extra length is ignored and all of the text from nOffset to the end of the character data is replaced. If nOffset is negative or greater than one less than the length of the node's data, an INDEX_SIZE_ERR DOMexception will be raised. If the node is read only, a NO_MODIFICATION_ALLOWED_ERR exception will be raised.

Our wrapper function is as follows:

```
Public Function TextReplaceData(oTextNode As IXMLDOMText, _
                 nOffset As Integer, nCount As Integer, sData As String) _
                 As Boolean
    If (nOffset < 0) Or (nOffset > Len(oTextNode.Data) - 1) Then
        TextReplaceData = False
        Call SetErrorInfo(-1, "Offset out-of-bounds", _
                     "CDomFunctions.TextReplaceData", INDEX_SIZE_ERR)
    Else
        Call oTextNode.replaceData(nOffset, nCount, sData)
        TextReplaceData = True
    End If
End Function
```

Extended Interfaces

Because of the differences between XML and HTML documents, there are certain objects that apply only to the XML DOM, referred to in the specification as "extended interfaces." These are only required to be implemented in the XML DOM.

Interface: CDATASection

You may recall from Chapter 1 that CDATA sections allow us to mark sections of character data so that the parser does not try to interpret them as markup text. For example, if this were in your document, the parser would complain about the "less than" symbol, <, thinking it was the beginning of a start tag:

```
<lessthan> 4 < 5 </lessthan>
```

By wrapping this in CDATA notation, we can prevent this:

```
<lessthan> <![CDATA[ 4 < 5 ]]> </lessthan>
```

(Refer to Chapter 1 for further details on CDATA notation.)

The CDATASection interface is derived from CharacterData via the Text object. Although the normalize method will combine adjacent Text nodes, it does not do the same for adjacent CDATASection nodes.

The CDATASection object does not have its own methods or attributes. We can use the createCDATASection method from the Document object to add CDATA nodes. Because only certain nodes are allowed to have CDATA children, we'll implement a function to check the insertion, which will also check that the intended content of the CDATA section doesn't contain illegal markup:

```
Public Function AddCDATA(oDOM As DOMDocument, _
          oPNode As IXMLDOMNode, _
          sElementContent As String _
          ) As Boolean
    On Error GoTo ErrHand
    Dim oNode As MSXML.IXMLDOMNode
    Dim elNode As MSXML.IXMLDOMCDATASection

    Call ClearErrorInfo
    ' <![CDATA[<greeting>Hello, world!</greeting>]]>
    ' We need to check that the string we're assigning to the CDATA section
    ' doesn't contain the "end of CDATA section" character combination: ]]>
    If (InStr(sElementContent, "]]>")) Then
        AddCDATA = False
        Call SetErrorInfo(-1, "Invalid character string: ']]>' ", _
                "CDomFunctions.AddCDATA", _
                INVALID_CHARACTER_ERR)
        Exit Function
    End If

    Select Case oPNode.nodeType
    ' DocumentFragment, EntityReference, and Element nodes.
        Case NODE_DOCUMENT_FRAGMENT, NODE_ENTITY_REFERENCE, NODE_ELEMENT:
            Set elNode = oDOM.createCDATASection(sElementContent)
            Set oNode = oPNode.appendChild(elNode)
            AddCDATA = True
        Case Else
            AddCDATA = False
            Call SetErrorInfo(-1, "Invalid parent node type.", _
                    "CDomFunctions.AddCDATA", HIERARCHY_REQUEST_ERR)
    End Select
    Exit Function

ErrHand:
    If Err.Number <> 0 Then
        Call SetErrorInfo(Err.Number, Err.Description, _
                    "CDomFunctions." & Err.Source, UNKNOWN)
        AddCDATA = False
    End If
End Function
```

Interface: DocumentType

Your XML document may contain an explicit reference to a doctype, either through a reference to an external DTD, or through the inclusion of the DTD content. Every document has a doctype, and the absence of an explicit declaration sets the doctype value to null. Although the doctype may contain structural definitions for elements and attributes, as well as entities and notions, the DOM only provides methods for getting at those last two. Furthermore, the DocumentType node is read-only; the W3C was unsure of how the possible use of namespaces and XML Schemas would affect this.

The DocumentType has these attributes:

name

This is the name of your DTD (and therefore the element type of your root element).

entities

The entities attribute provides a NamedNodeMap interface into the entity definitions, both internal and external, given in the doctype. Duplicate entity declarations are ignored. Parameter entities (for example, <!ENTITY % wrox "Wrox"> are not accessible because they are only used by the DTD.

Entities may not be edited.

notations

The notations attribute is a NamedNodeMap interface into the notations declared in the DTD. You may not edit notations. Each notation attribute also implements the Notation interface, described next.

Interface: Notation

Notations are used to define the format of an unparsed entity (such as when you wish to have an entity reference a JPEG image file and need to define just what that file format is) or to declare the target of a processing instruction (PI).

The name of the Notation is obtained by using the nodeName attribute, which is inherited from the Node interface. Notations also have these additional attributes:

publicId

This is the public identifier of the notation. If the public identifier was not specified, this is null.

systemId

This is the system identifier of this notation. If the system identifier was not specified, this is null.

Interface: Entity

This interface provides the means for referencing entities (both parsed and unparsed) contained in the DTD. The name of the entity is obtained through the use of the nodeName attribute, inherited from the Node object.

Parsed Entity nodes may have child nodes, but only if the parser expands the entity. However, this is not required of non-validating XML processors. If the Entity is expanded, its child list will contain the text and entities that constitute the parsed Entity. Otherwise, the child list is empty.

An Entity node cannot be edited. However, it can be cloned, and each of the document's EntityReference nodes can be replaced with the contents of the Entity clone. The clone's contents can then be edited. All the descendants of an Entity node are read-only; an Entity node does not have any parent node.

Entity nodes have these attributes:

publicId

This is the public identifier associated with the Entity, if specified. If the public identifier was not specified, this is null.

systemId

This is the URI where the contents of the Entity may be found. If no systemId was given then this is null.

notationName

This provides the name of the notation for the Entity. Parsed entities, which do not use notations, return null.

Interface: EntityReference

Once an Entity has been declared, it may be used in the document text. The EntityReference node represents the interface to these references. Note that the DOM specification states that XML processors have the option of completely expanding entities before the DOM tree is constructed, so it is possible that the DOM will not contain any EntityReference nodes even though the source document contains them. This is what the Microsoft parser does. The pre-declared entities (such as for the "<" character <), and character references, are also automatically expanded when the document is first parsed, so the DOM will present these with their Unicode equivalent value, not an entity reference.

If you add an EntityReference node that corresponds to a defined Entity, then the EntityReference node will have the same child nodes as the Entity declaration. It is possible to add EntityReference nodes that do not have an Entity declaration, in which case the child node list will be empty. Of course, if you do not remedy this, and you attempt to re-parse your document, it will be invalid because you have an undeclared Entity floating around.

For example, suppose we start with this XML document:

```
<doc>
    <item>Here is some text</item>
</doc>
```

Using the DOM, we might add a new element containing an entity reference, giving this document:

```
<doc>
    <item>Here is some text</item>
    <copyright>&copy; 2000</ copyright >
</doc>
```

We save the DOM contents, and then later try to reload it. But now the document has an undeclared entity reference (in this case, the copyright symbol often used in HTML), so we receive an error.

The EntityReference node inherits from the Node object; the EntityReference name can be obtained from nodeName; childNodes may be used to get to any of the sub-nodes of the reference to inspect their values.

Note that, with the Microsoft parser, if you add an EntityReference node corresponding to a pre-declared entity, and later try to take a look at its child nodes, you won't find any.

Here's a wrapper function for adding EntityReference nodes that checks that the node is being inserted under a legal parent node:

```
Public Function AddEntityReference(oDOM As DOMDocument, _
            oPNode As IXMLDOMNode, _
            sEntity As String _
            ) As Boolean
    On Error GoTo ErrHand
    Dim oNode As MSXML.IXMLDOMNode
    Dim entrefNode As MSXML.IXMLDOMEntityReference

    Call ClearErrorInfo

    Select Case oPNode.nodeType
        Case NODE_ATTRIBUTE, NODE_DOCUMENT_FRAGMENT, NODE_ENTITY_REFERENCE, _
                NODE_ELEMENT:
            Set entrefNode = oDOM.createEntityReference(sEntity)
            Set oNode = oPNode.appendChild(entrefNode)
            AddEntityReference = True
        Case Else
            AddEntityReference = False
            Call SetErrorInfo(-1, "Invalid parent node type.", _
                "CDomFunctions.AddEntityReference", HIERARCHY_REQUEST_ERR)
    End Select
    Exit Function

ErrHand:
    If Err.Number <> 0 Then
        AddEntityReference = False
        Call SetErrorInfo(Err.Number, Err.Description, "CDomFunctions." & _
                    Err.Source, UNKNOWN)
    End If
End Function
```

Here's an example of how we can call the function:

```
Dim oNode As IXMLDOMNode
Dim dw As WroxXML.CDomFunctions
Set oNode = objDOM.selectNodes("//").Item(1)
If Not dw.AddEntity(objDOM, oNode, "lt") Then
    Debug.print = "Add entity reference failed." & vbCrLf & dw.GetErrorInfoXML()
Else
    Debug.print = "Entity reference added."
End If
```

Interface: *ProcessingInstruction*

This is the `ProcessingInstruction` (PI) object. PIs are used to hold information for various applications that might process your document, and occur within `<?` and `?>` delimiters at the top of your XML documents. The `ProcessingInstruction` node has these attributes:

target

The text immediately following the "`<?`" is the target of the PI; it allows applications to recognize the instruction.

data

This is the processing data for the processor to act on, and includes all of the text, that is not whitespace, from the first character after the target until the end of the PI markup.

Trying to set a read-only PI node will raise a `NO_MODIFICATION_ALLOWED_ERR DOMException`.

Microsoft Specific Extensions

Microsoft has fully implemented the DOM core for XML, but also added some extra functionality. Always bear in mind that these are not standardized. Some of these extensions can prove very handy though, so you may want to use them, but it will tie you to the Microsoft parser. We will only cover a select few in this book – we have already used the `load`, `parseError` and `save` functions. Wherever we come across others in the remainder of this book, they will be explained. The full set is covered in Alex Homer's *"IE5 XML Programmer's Reference"* (ISBN 1-861001-57-6) from Wrox Press.

Putting It All Together

To give an example of manipulating the DOM, let's look at a few programs. First, since we've been building up a collection of DOM manipulation functions, we'll take our class project and use it in an application. We just need to add a few more functions to allow for some generalized behavior. The first will give us a more general means for adding nodes.

This function allows you to pass some general parameters to create a specified node. It takes these arguments:

- ❑ oDOM, the DOMDocument we're working with
- ❑ nIndex, an Integer that specifies what node we want to add to
- ❑ nNodeType, a DOMNodeType that tells what sort of node we want to add
- ❑ sNodeName, a String holding the name of the node
- ❑ sNodeContent, a String holding the node's content

The AddNode Function

```
Public Function AddNode(oDOM As DOMDocument, nIndex As Integer, _
                    nNodeType As DOMNodeType, _
                    sNodeName As String, _
                    sNodeContent As String _
                    ) As Boolean

    Dim oNode As IXMLDOMNode
    Dim bResults as Boolean
    bResults = True
```

After declaring a generic Node object to serve as the parent node for the new node, and a variable to hold our function response, which we optimistically set to True – which will be changed if our attempt at adding the node fails, we check to see if the node index is within bounds, using IsNodeIndexOK, described just after this function. If it is, then we use selectNodes to get a NodeList holding all of our nodes, and use the node index to get a reference to the desired node:

```
    If (IsNodeIndexOK(oDOM, nIndex)) Then
        Set oNode = oDOM.selectNodes("//").Item(nIndex)
```

We then take a look at the type of node we want to insert, and try to insert it, using the corresponding wrapper function in our class. We check the results of the wrapper function to see if we have to change our minds about what to return:

```
    Select Case nNodeType
        Case NODE_ELEMENT
            If Not AddElement(oDOM, oNode, sNodeName, sNodeContent) Then
                bResults = False
            End If
        Case NODE_ATTRIBUTE
            If Not AddAttribute(oDOM, oNode, sNodeName, sNodeContent) Then
                bResults = False
            End If
        Case NODE_TEXT
            If Not AddTextNode(oDOM, oNode, sNodeContent) Then
                bResults = False
            End If
        Case NODE_CDATA_SECTION
            If Not AddCDATA(oDOM, oNode, sNodeContent) Then
                bResults = False
            End If
        Case NODE_ENTITY_REFERENCE
            If Not AddEntityReference(oDOM, oNode, sNodeName) Then
                bResults = False
            End If
        Case NODE_PROCESSING_INSTRUCTION
            If Not AddPI(oDOM, oNode, sNodeName, sNodeContent) Then
                bResults = False
            End If
        Case NODE_COMMENT
            If Not AddComment(oDOM, oNode, sNodeContent) Then
                bResults = False
```

```
                    End If
          Case NODE_ENTITY, NODE_DOCUMENT, NODE_DOCUMENT_TYPE, _
                NODE_DOCUMENT_FRAGMENT, NODE_NOTATION
              bResults = False
              Call SetErrorInfo(-1, "Not implemented", _
                  "CDomFunctions.AddNode", NOT_SUPPORTED_ERR)
          Case Else
              bResults = False
              Call SetErrorInfo(-1, "Unknown parent node type", _
                  "CDomFunctions.AddNode", NOT_SUPPORTED_ERR)
      End Select
```

For those cases where we don't have a wrapper function, we set the error information to indicate that the request isn't supported. If the node index we passed was out of bounds, we set our return value to False and register an INDEX_SIZE_ERR error. Finally, we return our results:

```
    Else
        bResults = False
        Call SetErrorInfo(-1, "Parent node index out-of-bounds.", _
            "CDomFunctions.AddNode", INDEX_SIZE_ERR)
    End If

    AddNode = bResults
End Function
```

Checking that the node index is within range is a matter of getting a list of all the nodes and checking the length of the list:

The IsNodeIndexOK Function

```
Public Function IsNodeIndexOK(oDOM As DOMDocument, nIndex As Integer) As Boolean
    If nIndex < 0 Then
        IsNodeIndexOK = False
    ElseIf nIndex > (oDOM.selectNodes("//").length - 1) Then
        IsNodeIndexOK = False
    Else
        IsNodeIndexOK = True
    End If
End Function
```

The SearchAndReplace Function

Now let's write a function to do something handy, such as search and replace. We'll try to make it as generic as possible; our function will accept a starting node, an element type, the value to search for, and the new value to replace it with.

```
Public Function SearchAndReplace(oPNode As IXMLDOMNode, _
                                 DomNodeTargetNodeType As DOMNodeType, _
                                 sOldText As String, _
                                 sNewText As String, _
                                 Optional bLastFoundValue As Variant _
                                 ) As Boolean
    On Error GoTo ErrHand
```

```
        Dim strTemp As String
        Dim nIdx As Integer
        Dim bFoundIt As Boolean
```

This is a recursive function; it will call itself as it walks through the DOM looking for text it can replace. We need to pass along the `Boolean` value `bLastFoundValue` to keep track of whether we have found and replaced anything along the way. This is an optional value that we do not pass when we first call this function. We use the `IsMissing` method to see if this has been explicitly passed in, or if it was omitted. Visual Basic has an "interesting" quirk: if you use an optional parameter that is not one of the intrinsic VB data types (such as `String`, `Integer`, `Boolean`, etc.) then the `IsMissing` function will always return `False`. So, even though we will be using it as a `Boolean`, we declare it as a `Variant`:

```
        If (Not bLastFoundValue) And (Not IsMissing(bLastFoundValue)) Then
        SearchAndReplace = False
        Call SetErrorInfo(-1, "Text not found", _
            "CDomFunctions.SearchAndReplace", NOT_FOUND_ERR)
    End If

    'Default to False; we'll change this value if we actually replace anything
    If (IsMissing(bLastFoundValue)) Then
        bLastFoundValue = False
    End If

    bFoundIt = CBool(bLastFoundValue)
```

We want to walk through the `oPNode` tree of nodes, looking for nodes of `DomNodeTargetNodeType`. If we find any, we want to see if it contains text we can search for and replace. First, we need to see if the target node type can actually have any text. If not, then we return `False` and set the error information:

```
    Select Case DomNodeTargetNodeType
        Case NODE_ENTITY, NODE_DOCUMENT_TYPE, NODE_NOTATION, NODE_ENTITY_REFERENCE
            SearchAndReplace = False
            Call SetErrorInfo(-1, "Node and children are read-only", _
                "CDomFunctions.SearchAndReplace", NO_MODIFICATION_ALLOWED_ERR)
            Exit Function
        Case Else
```

Now, we see if `oPNode` is the type we're looking for:

```
        If DomNodeTargetNodeType = oPNode.NodeType Then
```

Let's determine what we can replace. If the target type is `Element` or `Attr`, we'll interpret this to mean search and replace on the child nodes. We examine the node type, and if it can contain text, we place the node value into a temporary string, perform the replace on that string, and then set the node value to the altered text:

```
            Select Case oPNode.NodeType
                Case NODE_TEXT, NODE_CDATA_SECTION, NODE_COMMENT, _
                    NODE_PROCESSING_INSTRUCTION
                    strTemp = oPNode.nodeValue
```

```
                    If InStr(strTemp, sOldText) Then
                        strTemp = Replace(strTemp, sOldText, sNewText)
                        oPNode.nodeValue = strTemp
                        SearchAndReplace = True
                        bFoundIt = True
                        Call ClearErrorInfo
                    End If
```

If we are looking at a document fragment or element node, then we want to replace the text in any child text nodes:

```
                Case NODE_DOCUMENT_FRAGMENT, NODE_ELEMENT
                    For nIdx = 0 To oPNode.childNodes.length - 1
                        If (oPNode.childNodes(nIdx).NodeType = NODE_TEXT) Then
                            strTemp = oPNode.childNodes(nIdx).nodeValue
                            If InStr(strTemp, sOldText) Then
                                strTemp = Replace(strTemp, sOldText, sNewText)
                                oPNode.childNodes(nIdx).nodeValue = strTemp
                                SearchAndReplace = True
                                Call ClearErrorInfo
                                bFoundIt = True
                            End If
```

If we find any non-text nodes, we call `SearchAndReplace`, passing in the current node:

```
                        ElseIf (oPNode.childNodes(nIdx).NodeType = _
                            NODE_ELEMENT) Then
                            bFoundIt = bFoundIt Or _
                                SearchAndReplace(oPNode.childNodes(nIdx), _
                                DomNodeTargetNodeType, sOldText, _
                                sNewText, bFoundIt)
                        End If
                    Next
```

And if we run across any node types we can not handle, we set our error data and quit:

```
                Case Else
                    ' Error
                    SearchAndReplace = False
                    Call SetErrorInfo(-1, "Unexpected node type", _
                        "CDomFunctions.SearchAndReplace", UNKNOWN)
                    Exit Function
            End Select
```

Now, it may be the case we are trying to replace text in attributes; in that case, we need to see if the parent node is an element, iterate through the `NamedNodeMap` of the attributes, and do the replace on each of those:

```
            Else
                If (DomNodeTargetNodeType = NODE_ATTRIBUTE) Then
                    If oPNode.NodeType = NODE_ELEMENT Then
```

```
                    For nIdx = 0 To oPNode.Attributes.length - 1
                        strTemp = oPNode.Attributes(0).nodeValue
                        If InStr(strTemp, sOldText) Then
                            strTemp = Replace(strTemp, sOldText, sNewText)
                            oPNode.Attributes(0).nodeValue = strTemp
                            SearchAndReplace = True
                            bFoundIt = True
                            Call ClearErrorInfo
                        End If
                    Next
                End If
            End If
```

We also want to look at the parent node's children to continue walking the DOM tree, in case the parent node itself does not have any text or attributes:

```
            ' Look at the parent node's children
            If oPNode.childNodes.length > 0 Then
                For nIdx = 0 To oPNode.childNodes.length - 1
                    bFoundIt = bFoundIt Or _
                        SearchAndReplace(oPNode.childNodes(nIdx), _
                        DomNodeTargetNodeType, sOldText, sNewText, bFoundIt)
                Next
            Else
```

If we've got this far, and the parent node has no children, then we're finished, and we exit:

```
                SearchAndReplace = bFoundIt
            End If
        End If
    End Select
    Exit Function
```

We have a bit of error handling code at the end in case something unexpected happens:

```
ErrHand:
    If Err.Number <> 0 Then
        SearchAndReplace = False
        Call SetErrorInfo(Err.Number, Err.Description, _
            "CDomFunctions.SearchAndReplace " & Err.Source, UNKNOWN)
    End If
End Function
```

This function makes some assumptions about desired behavior. For example, if you want to do a search and replace on Elements, the code looks at the Text child nodes of the element, since the nodeValue of an Element is always null. Likewise, this code will change the data value of a PI, but not the target. Finally, you might want to call normalize on the parent node before passing it in, or perhaps modify the function to take an optional parameter to normalize the text nodes in the function.

The SearchAndReplaceElementType Function

Let's try our hand at a variation on this. Suppose we wanted to search and replace Element types. For example, say your document has a number of elements like this:

```
<SIZE unit="meters">12</SIZE>
```

But, in fact, they all refer to the width of something, and we would rather it look like this:

```
<WIDTH unit="meters">12</WIDTH>
```

It would be handy to have a method to go and change the appropriate Element types. However, the Element type is read-only. You could, of course, do this with XSLT, but that's not part of the DOM. Instead, we'll take a starting node, and walk the tree looking for Elements matching a given type. Each time we find a match we'll create a new node, giving it the new tag name, and copy over any attributes and child nodes. Then we'll delete the old node.

```
Public Function SearchAndReplaceElementType( _
                        oDOM As DOMDocument, _
                        oNode As IXMLDOMNode, _
                        sOldType As String, _
                        sNewType As String, _
                        Optional bFoundIt As Variant _
                            ) As Boolean


    On Error GoTo ErrHand

    Dim oTempEl As IXMLDOMElement
    Dim oAttr As IXMLDOMAttribute
    Dim oPNode As IXMLDOMNode
    Dim nIdx As Integer
    Dim oFrag As IXMLDOMDocumentFragment
    Dim nChildCount As Integer
    Dim bReplacedIt As Boolean
```

We begin by declaring a few local node types we'll use as temporary objects, and check the value of the bFoundIt parameter. This is also a recursive function, and works much like the previous one:

```
    If (Not CBool(bFoundIt)) And (Not IsMissing(bFoundIt)) Then
        SearchAndReplaceElementType = False
        Call SetErrorInfo(-1, "Type not found", _
            "CDomFunctions.SearchAndReplaceElementType", NOT_FOUND_ERR)
    End If
    'Default to False; we'll change this value if we actually replace anything
    If IsMissing(bFoundIt) Then
        bFoundIt = False
    End If

    bReplacedIt = CBool(bFoundIt)
```

We then look at the node type of the parent node passed in. If it's an Element, then we want to create a new element (using the sNewType value), and add to it all of the child nodes of the element we intend to replace:

```
Select Case oNode.NodeType
Case NODE_ELEMENT
    If oNode.baseName = sOldType Then
        Set oTempEl = oDOM.createElement(sNewType)
        For nIdx = 0 To oNode.childNodes.length - 1
            Call oTempEl.appendChild(oNode.childNodes(nIdx).cloneNode(True))
        Next
        For nIdx = 0 To oNode.Attributes.length - 1
            Call AddAttribute(oDOM, oTempEl, oNode.Attributes(nIdx).nodeName, _
                oNode.Attributes(nIdx).nodeValue)
        Next
```

We then get a reference to the original element's parent node, and call the replaceChild DOM method:

```
        Set oPNode = oNode.parentNode
        Call oPNode.replaceChild(oTempEl, oNode)
        SearchAndReplaceElementType = True
        bReplacedIt = True
        Call ClearErrorInfo
    End If
```

Now we want to walk the DOM tree below the element, and call SearchAndReplaceElementType for each child node:

```
    For nIdx = 0 To oNode.childNodes.length - 1
        bReplacedIt = bReplacedIt Or _
            SearchAndReplaceElementType(oDOM, oNode.childNodes(nIdx), _
                                sOldType, sNewType, bReplacedIt)
    Next
```

In case we are looking at the Document node or a document fragment, we will just call SearchAndReplaceElementType for each child element:

```
Case NODE_DOCUMENT, NODE_DOCUMENT_FRAGMENT
    For nIdx = 0 To oNode.childNodes.length - 1
        bReplacedIt = bReplacedIt Or SearchAndReplaceElementType(oDOM, _
            oNode.childNodes(nIdx), sOldType, sNewType, bReplacedIt)
    Next
```

Finally, if the node we're looking at cannot have any child elements, we just set a return value and exit:

```
Case Else
    SearchAndReplaceElementType = bReplacedIt
    Exit Function
End Select
```

```
        Exit Function

    ErrHand:
        If Err.Number <> 0 Then
            SearchAndReplaceElementType = False
            Call SetErrorInfo(Err.Number, Err.Description, _
                "CDomFunctions.SearchAndReplaceElementType" & Err.Source, UNKNOWN)
        End If
    End Function
```

Now we have covered all the functions in the CDomFunctions class, we can package them up in an ActiveX component.

Using the DOM in Visual Basic Applications

A Test Program to Manipulate the DOM

The test application will use the functions wrapped in the WroxXML DLL to demonstrate loading an XML file, inspecting DOM properties, and modifying the DOM. It consists of a Module file and two forms, and uses a reference to the MSXML DLL as well as a reference to the Wrox XML DLL. The project can be downloaded from the Wrox web site; it is called DOMTest and, like all the samples in this chapter, is in the Chapter 3 folder.

First, we use the module to declare a global DOMDocument variable so that it is available to both forms:

```
' mod1.bas
Option Explicit
Global objDOM As MSXML.DOMDocument        ' Our DOM object
```

Defining the Main Form

The primary form, frmMain, looks like this:

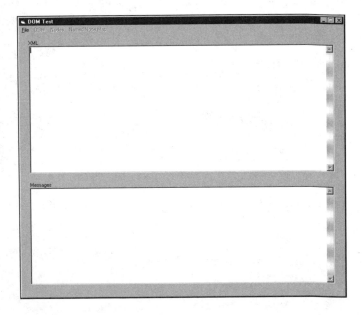

It has two textboxes, `txtXML` for displaying a loaded XML file, and `txtMessages` for displaying any messages from the code.

We declare a variable, `dw`, for our DOM wrapper functions object, a `String` for the name of the file, and a variable of our user-defined type, `DOMException`:

```
'************************************************************
' Simple application to load and manipulate the XML DOM
' frmMain
'************************************************************
Option Explicit
Dim dw As WroxXml.CDomFunctions
Dim strFilename As String
Dim domErr As WroxXml.DOMException
```

Loading the Form

We use the `Form_Load` subroutine to initialize our objects:

```
Private Sub Form_Load()
    Set objDOM = New DOMDocument
    Set dw = New CDomFunctions
End Sub
```

Implementing the File Menu

Our form also has a set of menu items. The first menu heading is called File. It has a submenu item for Open. This routine displays a FileOpen dialog box, and calls `LoadDocument` to load the file into the DOM – this function is described shortly. If the load is successful, the other menu items are enabled, otherwise an error message is displayed:

```
Private Sub mnuOpen_Click()
    On Error GoTo ErrHand
    Dim strFilefilter As String
    strFilefilter = "XML Files (*.xml)|*.xml|All Files (*.*)|*.*"
    strFilename = ""

    With dlgOpen
        .FileName = ""
        .CancelError = True
        .Filter = strFilefilter
        .ShowOpen
    End With

    strFilename = dlgOpen.FileName

    If (Len(strFilename) > 0) Then
        If Not LoadDocument(strFilename) Then
            MsgBox "Error loading XML document", vbExclamation, "XML load error"
            strFilename = ""
        Else
            mnuSave.Enabled = True
            mnuDOM.Enabled = True
```

```
                    mnuNodes.Enabled = True
                    mnuNamedNodeMap.Enabled = True
                End If
        End If
        Exit Function

    ErrHand:
        If (Err.Number <> 0) And (Err.Number <> cdlCancel) Then
            Call ShowError(Err)
        End If
    End Sub
```

The `LoadDocument` function does the actual loading of the file into the DOM:

```
Function LoadDocument(strFilename As String) As Boolean
    On Error GoTo ErrHand

    objDOM.async = False
```

We've set the `async` property to `False` so that we wait until the file has finished loading. If the load works, we display the contents of the DOM in `txtXML`:

```
    If (objDOM.Load(strFilename)) Then
        txtXML = objDOM.xml
        LoadDocument = True
        txtMessages = "Document " & strFilename & " loaded successfully."
        lblXml = "Contents of " & strFilename
```

If there's an error parsing the file, we display the parsing error information:

```
    Else
        txtMessages = objDOM.parseError.reason
        lblXml = "XML"
        LoadDocument = False
    End If
    Exit Function

ErrHand:
        Call ShowError(Err)
        LoadDocument = False
End Function
```

To save the contents of the DOM, we have a submenu item called <u>S</u>ave:

```
Private Sub mnuSave_Click()
    If Len(strFilename) Then
        objDOM.save (strFilename)
    End If
End Sub
```

There's also a submenu item for Exit:

```
Private Sub mnuExit_Click()
    End
End Sub
```

Implementing the DOM Menu

We have a second menu called DOM, which holds some submenu items for doing DOM inspections. The first one is called Root, and simply displays information about the root element of the document:

```
Private Sub mnuRoot_Click()
    Call ShowRootElement(objDOM)
End Sub
```

ShowRootElement starts like this:

```
Sub ShowRootElement(oDOM As DOMDocument)
    On Error GoTo ErrHand
    Dim sDocumentElement As String
    sDocumentElement = ""
```

First we check that we have something loaded in the DOM. It gives an example of using the Microsoft-specific DOM method xml, which returns the contents of the DOM as a string:

```
    If (Len(objDOM.xml)) Then
```

If we have something in the DOM, we get the nodeName property of the documentElement object of the DOM:

```
        sDocumentElement = objDOM.documentElement.nodeName
        txtMessages = "The root element is " & sDocumentElement
```

Otherwise, we display an error message:

```
    Else
        MsgBox "There is no root element", vbExclamation, "Show Root Element"
    End If
    Exit Function

ErrHand:
    If Err.Number <> 0 Then
        Call ShowError(Err)
    End If
End Sub
```

Next we have a submenu item, Count nodes, that calls CountNodes:

```
Private Sub mnuCountNodes_Click()
    Call CountNodes(objDOM)
End Sub
```

And here is `CountNodes`:

```
Sub CountNodes(objDOM As DOMDocument)
    On Error GoTo ErrHand
    Dim nNodeCount As Integer

    nNodeCount = objDOM.selectNodes("//").length
    If (nNodeCount) Then
        txtMessages = "The document has " & CStr(nNodeCount) & " nodes."
    Else
        MsgBox "There are no nodes.", vbInformation, "Node count"
    End If
    Exit Function

ErrHand:
    If Err.Number <> 0 Then
        Call ShowError(Err)
    End If
End Sub
```

The function simply gets the length of a `NodeList` (which is what `selectNodes` exposes) where we select all of the nodes. Next is a submenu item, **Count elements,** to count the number of elements in the DOM:

```
Private Sub mnuCountElements_Click()
    Call CountElements(objDOM)
End Sub
```

`CountElements` starts like this:

```
Sub CountElements(objDOM As DOMDocument)
    On Error GoTo ErrHand
    Dim nNodeCount As Integer
    Dim nIdx As Integer
```

We call `getElementsByTagName` using the special "get all elements" parameter (the "*"), and take the length of the list:

```
    nNodeCount = objDOM.getElementsByTagName("*").length
```

If the length is non-zero the count is displayed, otherwise an error message is displayed:

```
    If (nNodeCount) Then
        txtMessages = "The document has " & CStr(nNodeCount) & " elements."
    Else
        MsgBox "There are no elements.", vbInformation, "Element count"
    End If
    Exit Function

ErrHand:
    If Err.Number <> 0 Then
```

```
            Call ShowError(Err)
        End If
    End Sub
```

There's also a submenu item for listing all of the elements, **List Elements**:

```
    Private Sub mnuListElements_Click()
        Call ListElements(objDOM)
    End Sub
```

`ListElements` also uses `getElementsByTagName("*")`, but then goes on to retrieve some element information:

```
    Sub ListElements(oDOM As DOMDocument)
        On Error GoTo ErrHand
        Dim sNodeList As String
        Dim nNodeCount As Integer
        Dim oEl As IXMLDOMElement

        sNodeList = ""
        nElCount = 0
```

We iterate through all of the elements in the document:

```
        For nNodeCount = 0 To oDOM.getElementsByTagName("*").length - 1
```

And set our `oEl` object to the current element in the list:

```
            Set oEl = oDOM.getElementsByTagName("*").Item(nNodeCount)
```

We then call `nodeName` to get the element type, and use our wrapper function `GetElementText` to get the text content of the element:

```
            sNodeList = sNodeList & CStr(nElCount) & ": Element name: " & _
                oEl.nodeName & vbTab & "Element text: " & _
                dw.GetElementText(oEl) & vbCrLf
        Next
```

If there were any elements, we display the results; otherwise we display an error message:

```
        If (Len(sNodeList)) Then
            txtMessages = sNodeList
        Else
            MsgBox "There are no elements.", vbInformation, "Element list"
        End If
        Exit Function

    ErrHand:
        If Err.Number <> 0 Then
```

```
            Call ShowError(Err)
        End If
    End Sub
```

We also have a submenu item called **List nodes**. It displays information about all of the nodes in the document:

```
Private Sub mnuListNodes_Click()
    txtMessages = ListNodes(objDOM.documentElement, 1)
End Sub
```

`ListNodes` takes a reference to a node, and an integer to specify the indentation of the display:

```
Function ListNodes(oNode As IXMLDOMNode, nLevel As Integer) As String
    On Error GoTo ErrHand
    Dim nIdx As Integer
    Dim sTemp As String
```

We first display some basic information about the node we are given:

```
    sTemp = String(nLevel, vbTab) & "Name: " & vbTab & oNode.nodeName & vbCrLf
    sTemp = sTemp & String(nLevel, vbTab) & "Value: " & vbTab & _
        oNode.nodeValue & vbCrLf
    sTemp = sTemp & String(nLevel, vbTab) & "Type: " & vbTab & _
        oNode.nodeTypeString & vbCrLf
```

We also look to see if the node has attributes, and if it does, we display information about them as well:

```
    If Not oNode.Attributes Is Nothing Then
        If (oNode.Attributes.length > 0) Then
            sTemp = sTemp & String(nLevel, vbTab) & "Attributes" & vbCrLf
            For nIdx = 0 To oNode.Attributes.length - 1
                sTemp = sTemp & String(nLevel + 1, vbTab) & "Name: " & _
                    vbTab & oNode.Attributes(nIdx).nodeName & vbTab & "Value: " & _
                    vbTab & oNode.Attributes(nIdx).nodeValue & vbCrLf
            Next
        End If
    End If
```

We also want to see if the node has any children, and if there are any, then we call `ListNodes` on those:

```
    If (oNode.childNodes.length > 0) Then
        For nIdx = 0 To oNode.childNodes.length - 1
            sTemp = sTemp & ListNodes(oNode.childNodes(nIdx), nLevel + 1)
        Next
    End If
    ListNodes= sTemp
    Exit Function
```

```
ErrHand:
    If Err.Number <> 0 Then
        Call ShowError(Err)
    End If
End Function
```

Finally, the DOM menu has two other items, Implementation and Doctype, for displaying some implementation information and the document's doctype:

```
Private Sub mnuImplementation_Click()
    If Not objDOM.implementation Is Nothing Then
        MsgBox objDOM.implementation.hasFeature("XML", "1.0"), vbInformation
    Else
        MsgBox "The IDOMImplementation object is null."
    End If
End Sub
```

```
Private Sub mnuDoctype_Click()
    Dim sDoctype As String
    If Not objDOM.doctype Is Nothing Then
        sDoctype = objDOM.doctype.Name
        MsgBox sDoctype, vbInformation
    Else
        MsgBox "No doctype!", vbExclamation
    End If
End Sub
```

Implementing the Nodes Menu

Our next menu, Nodes, is for node manipulation. It has three submenu items: Inspect node, Add node, and Search and replace. To inspect a node, we display an InputBox to prompt the user for a node number:

```
Private Sub mnuInspectNode_Click()
    Dim nNodeIndex As Integer
    Dim nNodeCount As Integer
    nNodeCount = objDOM.selectNodes("//").length - 1
    nNodeIndex = InputBox("Enter a node index value, 0 to " _
        & CStr(nNodeCount), "Inspect node", 0)
```

We then call InspectNode, passing the node index:

```
    Call InspectNode(nNodeIndex)
End Sub
```

InspectNode will take the node index, locate the node, and display some information about it:

```
Sub InspectNode(nNodeIndex As Integer)
    On Error GoTo ErrHand
    Dim oNode As MSXML.IXMLDOMNode
```

```
        Dim strNodeInfo As String
        Dim nIdx As Integer
        strNodeInfo = ""
```

We first check that the index is not out of bounds:

```
        If Not dw.IsNodeIndexOK(objDOM, nNodeIndex) Then
            MsgBox "Node index out-of-bounds", vbExclamation, "Inspect Node Error"
            Exit Sub
```

If it's OK, we select the node, and begin building up a string of node information:

```
        Else
            Set oNode = objDOM.selectNodes("//").Item(nNodeIndex)
            strNodeInfo = "Node index: " & vbTab & CStr(nNodeIndex) & vbCrLf

            With oNode
                strNodeInfo = strNodeInfo & "Node name: " & vbTab & _
                    .nodeName & vbCrLf
                strNodeInfo = strNodeInfo & "Node type: " & vbTab & _
                    .nodeTypeString & vbCrLf
```

If we've selected an `Element` node, then we'll pull out the details about its attributes as well:

```
                If (.NodeType = NODE_ELEMENT) Then
                    strNodeInfo = strNodeInfo & "Attributes:" & vbCrLf
                    If (.Attributes.length > 0) Then
                        For nIdx = 0 To .Attributes.length - 1
                            strNodeInfo = strNodeInfo & vbTab & vbTab & "Name =  '" & _
                            .Attributes(nIdx).baseName & "' " & vbTab & "Value = '" & _
                            .Attributes(nIdx).Text & "'" & vbCrLf
                        Next
                    Else
                        strNodeInfo = strNodeInfo & vbTab & vbTab & "None." & vbCrLf
                    End If
                End If
```

We check the assorted node properties to construct the string:

```
                strNodeInfo = strNodeInfo & "Number of child nodes: " & vbTab & _
                    .childNodes.length & vbCrLf
                strNodeInfo = strNodeInfo & "Data type:" & vbTab & .dataType & vbCrLf
                If Not (.definition Is Nothing) Then
                    strNodeInfo = strNodeInfo & "Definition: " & vbTab & _
                        .definition & vbCrLf
                End If
                strNodeInfo = strNodeInfo & "Namespace URI:" & vbTab & _
                    .namespaceURI & vbCrLf

                If Not (.nextSibling Is Nothing) Then
                    strNodeInfo = strNodeInfo & "nextSibling:" & vbTab & _
                        .nextSibling.baseName & vbCrLf
```

```
            End If
            strNodeInfo = strNodeInfo & "Node typed value : " & vbTab & _
                 .nodeTypedValue & vbCrLf
            strNodeInfo = strNodeInfo & "Node type : " & vbTab & _
                 .NodeType & vbCrLf
            strNodeInfo = strNodeInfo & "Node value: " & vbTab & _
                 .nodeValue & vbCrLf
            strNodeInfo = strNodeInfo & "Node owner document element name: " _
                 & vbTab & .ownerDocument.documentElement.tagName & vbCrLf
            strNodeInfo = strNodeInfo & "Node XML: " & vbTab & .xml & vbCrLf
        End With
    End If
```

Finally we display the data:

```
        txtMessages = strNodeInfo
        Exit Function

    ErrHand:
        If Err.Number <> 0 Then
            Call ShowError(Err)
        End If
    End Sub
```

The Add node menu item uses our second form, frmAddNode, which looks like this:

The code for the form is fairly simple. We want to prompt the user for some information about a new node to add to the DOM. The form has a text box for the node name (txtNodeName), a list box for the node type (lstNodeType), a text box for the parent node index number (txtPNodeIdx), a text box for specifying the node's content (txtNodeContent), and two buttons, OKButton and CancelButton.

We declare an object for our `CDomFunctions` class, and when the form loads it populates the list box with the available node types:

```
'*********************************************************
' Application to load and manipulate the XML DOM - frmAddNode
'*********************************************************
Option Explicit
Dim df As CDomFunctions

Private Sub Form_Load()
                                                        'Literal value
    lstNodeType.AddItem ("NODE_INVALID")                '0
    lstNodeType.AddItem ("NODE_ELEMENT")                '1
    lstNodeType.AddItem ("NODE_ATTRIBUTE")              '2
    lstNodeType.AddItem ("NODE_TEXT")                   '3
    lstNodeType.AddItem ("NODE_CDATA_SECTION")          '4
    lstNodeType.AddItem ("NODE_ENTITY_REFERENCE")       '5
    lstNodeType.AddItem ("NODE_ENTITY")                 '6
    lstNodeType.AddItem ("NODE_PROCESSING_INSTRUCTION") '7
    lstNodeType.AddItem ("NODE_COMMENT")                '8
    lstNodeType.AddItem ("NODE_DOCUMENT")               '9
    lstNodeType.AddItem ("NODE_DOCUMENT_TYPE")          '10
    lstNodeType.AddItem ("NODE_DOCUMENT_FRAGMENT")      '11
    lstNodeType.AddItem ("NODE_NOTATION")               '12

    Set df = New CDomFunctions
End Sub
```

After the user has entered some options, the **OK** button takes the data and passes it to the `AddNode` method of the `CDomFunctions` class. If all goes well, we update the text in the `frmMain_txtXML` text box and go away:

```
Private Sub OKButton_Click()
    Dim oDOM As DOMDocument
    If (df.AddNode(objDOM, txtPNodeIdx, lstNodeType.ListIndex, _
        txtNodeName, txtNodeContent)) Then
        frmMain.txtMessages = "Node added OK!"
        frmMain.txtXML = objDOM.xml
        Unload Me
```

If there's a problem, we display an error message:

```
    Else
        MsgBox df.ErrorDescription & vbCrLf & df.ErrorSource, vbExclamation, _
            "Error " & CStr(df.ErrorNumber)
    End If
End Sub
```

The Cancel button simply unloads the form:

```
Private Sub CancelButton_Click()
    Unload Me
End Sub
```

Search and Replace

Meanwhile, back at frmMain, the last submenu item for <u>N</u>odes is Search and Replace. This prompts the user with two input boxes: one to get an element type to find, and the other to get the new element type:

```
Private Sub mnuSearchAndReplace_Click()
    Dim sOldElementType As String
    Dim sNewElementType As String
    sOldElementType = InputBox("Element type to find", "Search & Replace")
    sNewElementType = InputBox("New Element type", "Search & Replace")
    Call ReplaceElementType(sOldElementType, sNewElementType)
End Sub
```

The strings are then passed on to ReplaceElementType. We want to start at the top, so we get a reference to the document root node, and call SearchAndReplaceElementType from our DOM function wrapper class:

```
Sub ReplaceElementType(sOldElType As String, sNewElType As String)
    Dim oNode As IXMLDOMNode

    Set oNode = objDOM.documentElement
    If dw.SearchAndReplaceElementType(objDOM, oNode, sOldElType, sNewElType) Then
        txtXML = objDOM.xml
        txtMessages = "Replace complete."
    Else
        txtXML = objDOM.xml
        txtMessages = "Error!" & vbCrLf & dw.GetErrorInfoXML()
    End If
End Sub
```

If we manage to replace any nodes, the updated XML is displayed in txtXML. Otherwise, we display an error message.

We also have a little routine for displaying any error information:

```
Sub ShowError(e As ErrObject)
    If e.Number <> 0 Then
        MsgBox e.Description, vbExclamation, "Error " & CStr(e.Number) & _
            " " & e.Source
    End If
End Sub
```

Implementing the Named Node Map Menu

The final menu, Named Node <u>M</u>ap, has just one item: <u>D</u>isplay map nodes, which iterates through the node list and displays the attributes:

```
Function DisplayMapNodes(oDOM As DOMDocument, strSelect As String) As Boolean
    Dim oNodeList As IXMLDOMNodeList
    Dim nAttIdx As Integer
    Dim nIdx As Integer
    Set oNodeList = oDOM.selectNodes("//*[@*]")
```

```
    If Not oNodeList Is Nothing Then
        txtMessages = ""
        For nIdx = 0 To oNodeList.length - 1
            txtMessages = txtMessages & "Name: " & _
                          oNodeList.Item(nIdx).nodeName & vbTab & _
                          "Value: " & oNodeList(nIdx).nodeValue & vbCrLf
            For nAttIdx = 0 To oNodeList(nIdx).Attributes.length - 1
                txtMessages = txtMessages & vbTab & "Att name: " & _
                    oNodeList(nIdx).Attributes(nAttIdx).nodeName & vbTab & _
                    "Value: " & oNodeList(nIdx).Attributes(nAttIdx).nodeValue & _
                    vbCrLf
            Next
        Next nIdx
    Else
        txtMessages = "Node map is null"
    End If
End Function
```

This is an example of the kind of activity that you can do with this application; the screenshot opposite shows a list of elements in the **Messages** box:

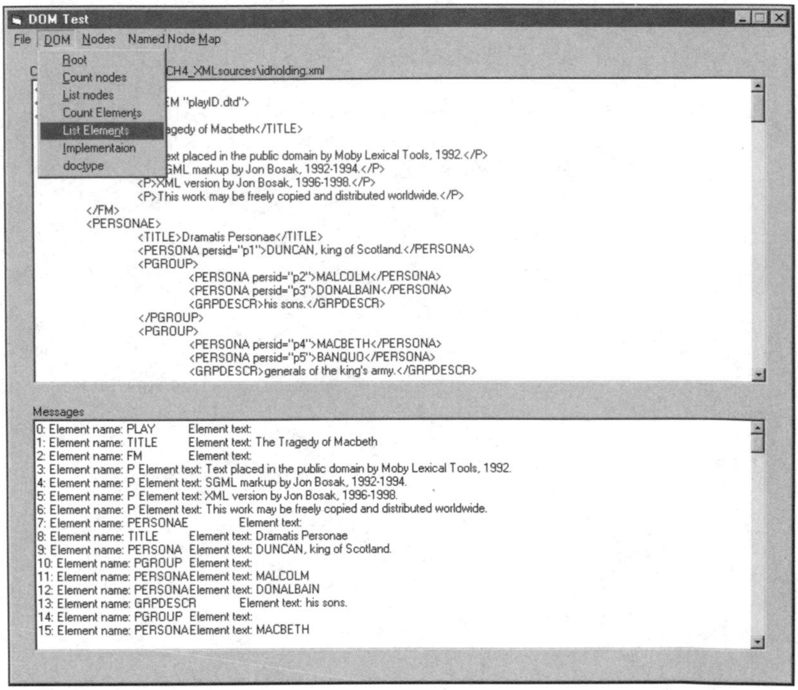

Displaying the Nodes in a Tree Control

In the next application, we'll build a simple program that reads in an XML file and populates a tree view control. The project requires a form, a status bar, a text box to contain the name of a local file to load, three command buttons (Load, Display and a button linked to the File Chooser common control), and the tree view control itself. In addition two radio buttons are included to switch validation on or off (off being the default). The project is called TreeView, and can be downloaded from the Wrox web site.

Note that, to make the project a little more interesting, you will be able to rearrange the nodes in the display window by using drag and drop.

Here is the complete code for the form:

```
Option Explicit
Dim oDoc As MSXML.DOMDocument
Dim bLoaded As Boolean
Dim indrag As Boolean
Dim bValidate As Boolean

Private Sub optValidOn_Click(Index As Integer)
    bValidate = True
    MsgBox "Validation on"
End Sub

Private Sub optValidOff_Click()
    bValidate = False
End Sub

Private Sub btnLoad_Click()
    Set oDoc = New DOMDocument
    oDoc.async = False
    If bValidate = False Then
        oDoc.validateOnParse = False
    Else
        oDoc.validateOnParse = True
    End If
    oDoc.Load "file:///" & txtFile.Text
    If oDoc.parseError.errorCode = 0 Then
        MsgBox "Succeeded"
        bLoaded = True
    Else
        MsgBox oDoc.parseError.reason & vbCrLf & oDoc.parseError.Line & vbCrLf & _
            oDoc.parseError.srcText
    End If
End Sub

Private Sub btnDisplay_Click()
    tvwNodeTree.Nodes.Clear
    AddNode oDoc.documentElement
End Sub

Private Sub btnFileChoose_Click()
    dlgFileChoose.FileName = txtFile.Text
    dlgFileChoose.ShowOpen
    txtFile.Text = dlgFileChoose.FileName
End Sub

Private Sub AddNode(ByRef oElem As IXMLDOMNode, Optional ByRef oTreeNode As Node)
    Dim oNewNode As Node
    Dim oNodeList As IXMLDOMNodeList
    Dim i As Long
```

```
        If oTreeNode Is Nothing Then
            Set oNewNode = tvwNodeTree.Nodes.Add
            oNewNode.Expanded = True
        Else
            Set oNewNode = tvwNodeTree.Nodes.Add(oTreeNode, tvwChild)
            oNewNode.Expanded = False
        End If

        oNewNode.Text = oElem.nodeName
        Set oNewNode.Tag = oElem
        Set oNodeList = oElem.childNodes
        For i = 0 To oNodeList.length - 1
            AddNode oNodeList.Item(i), oNewNode
        Next
End Sub

Private Sub tvwNodeTree_DragDrop(Source As Control, x As Single, y As Single)
    Dim oTargetElement As IXMLDOMNode
    Dim oDraggedNode As IXMLDOMNode

    If tvwNodeTree.DropHighlight Is Nothing Then
        Set tvwNodeTree.DropHighlight = Nothing
        indrag = False
        Exit Sub
    Else
        If tvwNodeTree.SelectedItem.Index = tvwNodeTree.DropHighlight.Index Then _
                Exit Sub
        Debug.Print tvwNodeTree.SelectedItem.Text & " dropped on " & _
            tvwNodeTree.DropHighlight.Text
        Set oDraggedNode = tvwNodeTree.SelectedItem.Tag
        Set oTargetElement = tvwNodeTree.DropHighlight.Tag
        If oTargetElement.nodeType = NODE_ELEMENT Then
            oTargetElement.insertBefore oDraggedNode, oTargetElement.firstChild
            Set tvwNodeTree.SelectedItem.Parent = tvwNodeTree.DropHighlight
        End If
        Set tvwNodeTree.DropHighlight = Nothing
        indrag = False
    End If
End Sub

Private Sub tvwNodeTree_DragOver(Source As Control, x As Single, _
        y As Single, State As Integer)
    If indrag = True Then
        ' Set DropHighlight to the mouse's coordinates.
        Set tvwNodeTree.DropHighlight = tvwNodeTree.HitTest(x, y)
    End If
End Sub

Private Sub tvwNodeTree_MouseDown(Button As Integer, Shift As Integer, _
        x As Single, y As Single)
    stbStatus.SimpleText = "MouseDown"
    tvwNodeTree.SelectedItem = tvwNodeTree.HitTest(x, y)
End Sub
```

```
Private Sub tvwNodeTree_MouseMove(Button As Integer, Shift As Integer, _
        x As Single, y As Single)

    If Button = vbLeftButton Then        ' Signal a Drag operation.
        indrag = True ' Set the flag to true.
        ' Set the drag icon with the CreateDragImage method.
        If Not tvwNodeTree.SelectedItem Is Nothing Then
            tvwNodeTree.DragIcon = tvwNodeTree.SelectedItem.CreateDragImage
        End If
        tvwNodeTree.Drag vbBeginDrag       ' Drag operation.
    End If
End Sub
```

This is how the project works. When you run the project, you get an empty dialog such as that shown in the left hand diagram below. Press the ... button at the top right of the box and choose an XML file from the list. Press Load and then Display in tree and the parsed file will appear in the left hand window as shown in the right hand diagram below:

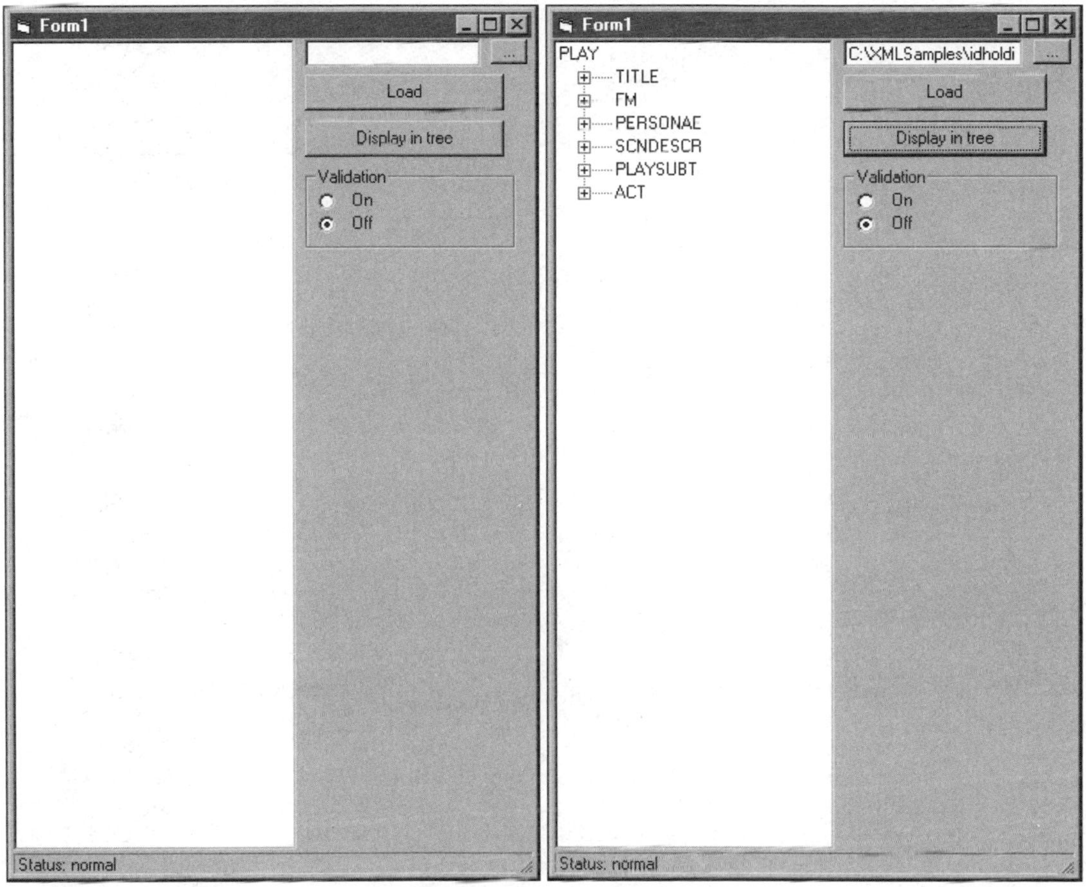

Now you can play with the tree as much as you wish, including moving nodes about. The figure opposite shows a drag-and drop in progress with the chosen PERSONA node being moved under the TITLE node:

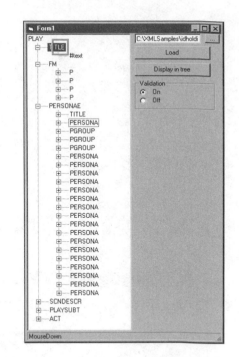

SAX

Before the DOM was heralded as the standard interface for accessing XML data, another object model for handling XML data was designed. Unlike the DOM, it was created independently by the XML community. According to David Megginson:

> "John Tigue, of DataChannel, was the first to attempt to develop an XML API collaboratively on the XML-DEV mailing list with his earlier XAPI-J.
>
> The process of developing SAX itself started on Saturday 13 December 1997, mainly as a result [of] the persistence of Peter Murray-Rust. Peter is the author of the free Java-based XML browser JUMBO, and after going through the headaches of supporting three different XML parsers with their own proprietary APIs, he insisted that parser writers should all support a common Java event-based API, which he code-named YAXPAPI (for Yet Another XML Parser API)."

David Megginson maintains a web site at http://www.megginson.com/SAX/ for SAX news and downloads.

Murray-Rust began a conversation with Megginson and Tim Bray (one of the editors of the XML recommendation) to devise a single, standard event-based API for XML parsers. The discussion was held on the xml-dev mailing list, and there were contributions from many list subscribers. SAX 1.0 was released on Monday 11 May 1998.

SAX, or **Simple API for XML**, is far less feature-rich than the DOM because it was designed just to provide a standard parser interface optimized for handling large documents.

SAX is an event-based model. When using it, the application registers with the parser for receiving parsing events. So, for example, when the parser runs, it calls an event handler every time the start or end of an element is encountered. It's up to the application programmer to build an internal representation of the document. A common use of SAX is to build temporary document fragments and act on each of them as they are built. The parser can only give information about the content at the very moment of parsing it. This makes its use somewhat limited, but SAX parsers can be very fast.

Interestingly, SAX does not "see" the XML data as a tree of nodes, but merely as a stream of events. A result of this is that a SAX parser cannot tell if a document is well-formed or not. If the closing tag of the root element is missing, it will not be caught until the end of the document is reached. Nonetheless, SAX is invaluable for processing documents whose size would overwhelm the memory-intensive DOM.

> *Note that SAX is not a W3C recommendation; it's a "standard" by virtue of the XML community's collective consent. It is not a competitor to the DOM, but an alternative, whose use depends on the particular XML processing needs. Microsoft does not currently provide a SAX parser, but there is sufficient support for the SAX interface in the general XML community that it will survive without any help from Redmond.*

Where to Find SAX

The Microsoft object model does not support the SAX interfaces. However, Vivid Creations (http://www.vivid-creations.com) offers **ActiveSAX**, a SAX parser ActiveX control you can use with Visual Basic.

When to Use SAX

If You Have a Need for Speed

Before you can do anything with the DOM, the application must first read and parse the entire document. It must identify each node type to construct and then build an internal representation. So, if you wanted to check the document root element type, you'd have to wait until the closing root tag was read in before you could call any DOM methods A SAX parser, on the other hand, simply reads through the file and fires events whenever it recognizes the parts of the document tree. When the event handler for the first element is raised, you can retrieve whatever information you are looking for, such as the element type, then stop reading any more of the document file.

If You Don't Need to Make Alterations to the Document

SAX will just tell you what's there; if you need to change anything, you would need to catch every event, grab the data, make your changes, and build a new document from the results. However, many applications only need to locate certain pieces of information. For example, you can store complex configuration data in an XML file, and use a SAX parser to quickly read through it and set your application.

If You're Interested in a Very Small Part of the Contained Data

Using a SAX parser, you can pick and choose what to do with each event that is raised, ignoring those which don't interest you. You don't have that option with the DOM, where there is overhead for the entire document regardless of its value to your application.

Here's a simple program, called SAXTest, which uses the ActiveSAX object. It reads a file and displays the content information. It uses a form with a single, multi-line text box:

```
Option Explicit
Dim nIndent As Integer
Dim WithEvents oSax As SAXLib.SAXParser

Private Sub Form_Load()
    Set oSax = New SAXParser
    nIndent = 0
    oSax.parseFile ("c:\SomeFile.xml")
End Sub

Private Sub oSax_characters(ByVal sCharacter As String, ByVal iLength As Long)
    txtMessages = txtMessages & String(nIndent, vbTab) & _
            "Text content is " & sCharacter & "; _
            length = " & iLength & vbCrLf
End Sub

Private Sub oSax_comment(ByVal sComment As String)
    txtMessages = txtMessages & String(nIndent, vbTab) & _
            "<!-- " & sComment & " -->" & vbCrLf
End Sub

Private Sub oSax_endDocument()
    txtMessages = txtMessages & String(nIndent, vbTab) & _
            "End of Document" & vbCrLf
    nIndent = nIndent - 1
End Sub

Private Sub oSax_endElement(ByVal sName As String)
    txtMessages = txtMessages & String(nIndent, vbTab) & _
            "End of element " & sName & vbCrLf
    nIndent = nIndent - 1
End Sub

Private Sub oSax_processingInstruction(ByVal sTarget As String, _
                            ByVal sData As String)
    txtMessages = txtMessages & String(nIndent, vbTab) & _
            "PI: target = " & sTarget & "; data = " & sData & vbCrLf
End Sub

Private Sub oSax_startDocument()
    nIndent = nIndent + 1
    txtMessages = txtMessages & String(nIndent, vbTab) & _
            "Start of document" & vbCrLf
End Sub
```

```
Private Sub oSax_startElement(ByVal sName As String, _
                        ByVal pAttributeList As SAXLib.ISAXAttributeList)
    Dim oSaxAttr As SAXAttributeList
    Dim nIdx As Integer
    nIndent = nIndent + 1
    txtMessages = txtMessages & String(nIndent, vbTab) & _
            "Start of Element: Name = " & sName & vbCrLf
    Set oSaxAttr = pAttributeList
    txtMessages = txtMessages & String(nIndent, vbTab) & _
            "There are " & oSaxAttr.getLength & " attributes." & vbCrLf
    For nIdx = 0 To oSaxAttr.getLength - 1
        txtMessages = txtMessages & String(nIndent + 2, vbTab) & _
            "Name = " & oSaxAttr.getName(nIdx) & _
            "; Value = " & oSaxAttr.getValue(nIdx) & vbCrLf
    Next
End Sub
```

The result is a dialog very similar to that of the TreeView example, only it has just one button, **Display in tree**. Note that the XML document is not loaded – it is parsed directly from the file. Note also that the text nodes are not designated "#text" as in TreeView but have their correct values:

We will show a performance-testing program that also tests DOM – SAX when we look at performance in Chapter 6.

Summary

In this chapter we took a look at where the DOM came from, and why it was important to develop a standard model. We saw that the DOM represents XML text as a collection of nodes, which are objects that expose methods and properties for manipulating the data. We then took a detailed walk though the different DOM methods and properties, and the various types of nodes the DOM provides.

We built a class of wrapper functions to help mask the various steps required to perform common basic DOM functions, like adding nodes. We also developed a few additional functions to help perform some more sophisticated tasks, such as doing a search and replace on text data, or a search and replace on element types. We built a sample application to try out these methods and to see how the DOM functions work in practice.

We also built a small application to allow us to view and manipulate a DOM through a tree-view control.

We also examined the SAX interface, and saw that it offers a different approach to XML processing, by treating an XML string as a series of events. Finally, we demonstrated SAX using the freely available `ActiveSAX` object from Vivid Creations.

Appendix A provides a reference to the Document Object Model; Appendix B covers the SAX model.

In the next chapter we'll take a look at how we can query and transform XML.

Using XML Queries and Transformations

Now we have an easy and platform-independent method of describing XML data, validating its type as we wish and modifying and reading it programmatically. So we basically have a transportable miniature database. No surprise then that when you start to work with it, you'll feel the need for a query mechanism. Using the DOM, you can get to each and every node in your document, but it can get tiresome, maneuvering through the hierarchies of children to find that single node you are interested in.

What we would like to have is an XML version of SQL. We would like to say "Get me all nodes of type X that have descendants of type Y". Many initiatives in this direction have been started up. There were some working groups specifying only a query language, but query mechanisms were also part of the drafts under development for transformation (XSLT) and linking technologies (XPointer). Then the W3C joined efforts with some of the working groups to specify **XPath**. XPath is a simple syntax to select a subset of the nodes in a document. It now has recommendation status and is used in both the XSLT and XPointer standards (as we'll see later in this chapter and in the next chapter).

Later in this chapter you will understand the importance of XPath in the context of *transforming* one document type to another, but first we will look at using XPath as a pure *querying* tool. In the initial release of IE5, a basic version of XPath implementation was included (then called **XQL**). Once XPath and XSLT gained recommendation status, Microsoft promised to deliver a fully compliant implementation of XPath and XSLT soon, and in January 2000 Microsoft shipped a developers preview of the MSXML library. In the appendices for XPath and XSLT (Appendix C and D respectively), you can find exactly which features are supported in which releases.

We will work with the full version of XPath in this chapter. If you want to program for the MSXML library that came with IE5 originally (if you cannot update to the newer version on all installed versions), you are restricted to a subset of XPath. We will indicate what can be used in the earlier IE5 versions in a separate section.

Be aware of the fact that several (more powerful) XML query languages are still under development. These include a syntax called XQL, that has firm support from IBM, and an initiative from the W3C, called XML Query, which is still in the first stages of specification. At the moment, XPath is the only way that has reached recommendation status and it looks like it will be a long time before anything else will.

This chapter will cover:

- ❏ XPath for querying a document
- ❏ XSLT for transforming a document
- ❏ Styling a document with Cascading Style Sheets
- ❏ Styling a document by using transformations (XSLT)

XPath Query Syntax

Before we get into the syntax of an XPath query, we have to discuss the concept of a **context node**. In XPath, a query is not automatically done over the whole of the content, but always has a starting point or context node. This can be any node in the node tree that constitutes the document. From this "fixed point" you can issue queries like "*give me all your children*". This kind of query only makes sense if there is a starting point defined. This starting point may be the root node, of course, which would query the entire document.

> **This may seem a bit abstract now, but just remember: an XPath query is done from a certain starting point in the document.**

Different Axes

Have a look at the following XPath query:

```
descendant::TABLE
```

This query would translate to plain English as: "Get the TABLE elements from all descendants (children, children's children, etc) of the context node". The first part of this query, descendant, is called the **axis** of the query. The second part, TABLE, is called the **node test**. The axis is the searching direction; if a node along the specified axis conforms to the node test, it is included in the result set. These patterns can be very complex and can have subqueries in them. We will look at that later. First, we will list all available axes that can be used in a query:

Axis	Description
child	All direct children of the context node. Excludes attributes.
descendant	All children and children's children etc... Excludes attributes.
parent	The direct parent (and only the direct parent) of the context node (if any).
ancestor	All ancestors of the context node. Always includes the root node (unless the root node is the context node).
following-sibling	All siblings to the context node that appear later in the document.
preceding-sibling	All siblings to the context node that appear earlier in the document.
following	All nodes in the document that come after it (in document order).
preceding	All nodes in the document that come before it (in document order).
attribute	Contains the attributes of the context node.
namespace	Contains the namespace nodes of the context node. This includes an entry for the default namespace and the implicitly declared XML namespace.
self	Only the context node itself.
descendant-or-self	All descendants and the context node itself.
ancestor-or-self	All ancestors and the context node itself.

The ancestor, descendant, following, preceding and self axes partition the document. This means that these five axes together contain all nodes of the tree (except attributes and namespaces), but do not overlap. This means that an ancestor is not on the preceding axis and that a descendant is not on the following axis, as illustrated in the following diagram:

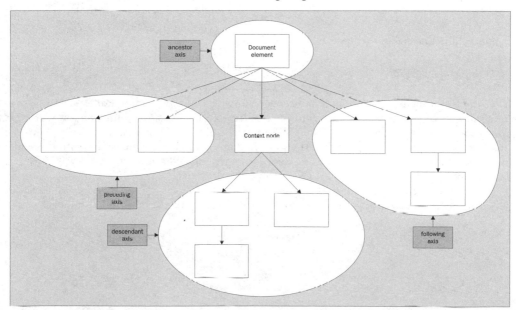

Different Node Tests

The sample we showed before used a literal name (TABLE) as a node test. This is only one of the ways to specify what a selected node should look like. Other valid values are:

- ❑   text() – which is true for all text nodes.

- ❑   * – which is true for any node of the principal type and every axis has its own principal node type. For most axes the principal node type is 'element', but for the attribute axis it is 'attribute' and for the namespace axis, the principal type is 'namespace'.

- ❑   comment() – which is true for all comment nodes.

- ❑   processing-instruction() – which is true for all processing instruction nodes.

- ❑   node() – which is true for all nodes

These node type tests take no arguments. Only the processing-instruction can be passed a literal; if an argument is passed, the node test is only true for a processing instruction that has a name equal to the argument.

The following are examples of XPath queries using different axes and node tests. This selects all descendant elements from the context node:

```
descendant::*
```

This selects the name attribute from the context node:

```
attribute::name
```

This selects the parent node of the context node:

```
parent::*
```

This selects all namespaces that are valid in the context node:

```
namespace::*
```

This means that it includes the default namespace, the xml namespace, any namespaces that are declared in the context node, and any namespaces declared in ancestors of the context node that have not been overruled by declarations in their children. The overruling of a namespace happens when one element declares a prefix to a certain URI and a child node declares a namespace with the same prefix, but with another URI. In this case, the first declaration is removed and becomes invisible from nodes that are descendants of the element with the second declaration.

Finally, this query selects all comment nodes that are a direct child of the context node:

```
child::comment()
```

Building a Path

Several of the XPath expressions we have seen up until now can be appended to each other to form a longer expression. This is done in a way similar to building a full directory path from several directory names: by separating them with forward slashes. The first expression in the path is evaluated in the original context; the result set from this expression forms the context for the next. Each of the nodes in the result set is used as context for the expression that follows, and all the results of each query are combined to one result set at the end. This would work as follows: this command selects the `parent` element of all `name` elements along the `descendant` axis of our context node:

```
descendant::name/parent::*
```

This selects all `text` nodes from `paragraph` elements that are children of `chapter` elements that are children of `book` elements that are children of our context node:

```
child::book/child::chapter/child::paragraph/child::text()
```

Absolute vs. Relative Paths

Just as with directory paths, we can make the XPath expression *absolute* by prefixing a slash. This sets the expression context to the document root. This is not the root element (compare with the `documentElement` attribute of the `DOMDocument` object in the DOM), but the parent of the root element (compare with the `DOMDocument` object itself). This example would select all attributes on the root element:

```
/child::*/attribute::*
```

However, the next example would select nothing, because the document root cannot carry attributes:

```
/attribute::*
```

An XPath that consists of only a slash (/) always refers to the document root.

Abbreviated Form / IE5 Compatible Form

The abbreviated notation of XPath is intended to keep the queries shorter. But the most important reason to learn the shorthand notation is that it used to be the full notation (according to the working draft) at the moment that the first release of IE5 hit the shops. In fact, it wasn't even called XPath back then, but was part of the XSL specification, which was later split up in three parts. (More on that later in this chapter.) That's why in IE5, only the shorthand syntax of XPath is implemented (in January 2000; Microsoft released a preview of the newer version of the library, which will support the full XPath specification). The main rules for the abbreviated syntax are:

Shorthand Rule	Example
The `child` axis is the default axis	`TABLE` equals `child::TABLE`
The `attribute` axis can be abbreviated to the prefix @	`@name` equals `attribute::name`

Table Continued on Following Page

Shorthand Rule	Example
The `self` axis can be abbreviated to `.`	`.` equals `self::*`
The `parent` axis can be abbreviated to `..`	`..` equals `parent::*`
The `descendant` axis can be abbreviated to `//`	`//*` equals `/descendant::*`
	`.//*` equals `descendant::*`

So these XPath expressions are valid in the IE5 implementation. The first command returns all ID attributes from TABLE elements in the whole document:

```
//TABLE/@ID
```

While this returns all text nodes that are children of PARAGRAPH elements that are children of CHAPTER elements that are children of the context element:

```
CHAPTER/PARAGRAPH/text()
```

Selecting Subsets

Now we have seen most of the basic elements of building XPaths. There is only one more to discuss: **predicates**. Predicates are a way to select a subset from a result set in an XPath (or part of an XPath). An XPath with a predicate looks like this:

```
<axis>:<node-test>[<predicate expression>]
```

We have already seen the axis and node test. Now the predicate expression gets appended in square brackets. Basically, what the predicate does is place a filter on the result set. For each node in the set, the XPath processor will test the predicate expression.

The Expression is True/False

If the expression evaluates to true, the node remains in the result set; if it evaluates to false, the node is removed. The predicate can contain special XPath functions (we will see those later, although we already met with text(), comment() etc.), numeric values and XPath expressions. This XPath expression would return the second child element named chapter from the context node.

```
child::chapter[position() < 2]
```

The position() function returns the position of the context node in its set. The set is the result of the node test child::chapter. For the first node in the set, position() will return 1, for the second 2, etc. The expression position() < 2 evaluates to true only for the first and second chapter elements found.

The Expression Returns a Number

If the expression evaluates to a numerical value *n*, it is only true for the *n*th node. If the value is 2, only the second node in the set will remain in the set, the rest will be deleted. The next example will return only the first `chapter` element found among the children of the context node.

```
child::chapter[1]
```

The number can also be the result of a calculation. The `last()` function returns the number of nodes in the result set of the current context node. Using this numeric value we can select the last `chapter`:

```
child::chapter[last()]
```

The Expression Returns a Node Set

If the result of the expression is a node set, the context node is included if there are nodes in the node set. The context node is deleted if the returned node set is empty. The expression can itself be an XPath expression (with axes, node tests and predicates). The inner XPath is evaluated with the outer XPath result as its context. This is a powerful concept; it allows us to make sub-querying constructions. The next example selects only those `chapter` elements that have `para` elements among their children:

```
child::chapter[child::para]
```

The outer XPath expression selects all `chapter` elements from the children of the context node. Then, taking each of these `chapter` elements as context, it tries to select `para` elements from their children. The chapters that have an empty set of results are removed from the result set of the outer XPath expression.

This query selects all messages that are a `descendant` of the context query and have an `ID` attribute. Note that the results of this query are the `message` elements, not the `ID` attributes:

```
descendant::message[attribute::ID]
```

Here a node, the attribute `confidentiality`, is compared with a literal string value:

```
descendant::message[attribute::confidentiality='secret']
```

In these cases, XPath compares the string value of the node with the literal string value. If they are identical, the expression is true. If the literal is numerical, the string value of the node is converted to a numerical value and then compared. If a node set is compared with a literal value, the expression is true if one of the elements in the set is identical to the literal value. If two node sets are compared, the result is true if any one node from the first can be matched with any one node from the second.

So in the example above, the predicate is true, if the context node has a `confidentiality` attribute with value `'secret'`. Only if this is the case will the `message` will be selected.

Note that with this form of comparing, these two expressions are *not* identical:

```
descendant::*[attribute::*='Teun']
descendant::*[not(attribute::*!='Teun')]
```

The first query selects all descendants that have an attribute with value 'Teun'. The second one selects only descendants with *all* attributes set to 'Teun' (!= means 'not equal to'). If you don't immediately understand this, try to figure out when this query evaluates to true:

```
descendant::*[attribute::*!='Teun']
```

It selects all descendants that have an attribute that does **not** have the value 'Teun'. The reverse of this is selecting all descendants that have **no** attribute that does **not** have the value 'Teun', which is identical to selecting only descendants that have all attributes set to the value 'Teun'. In expressions like these, you can use the following operators:

=	Equal to.
!=	Not equal to.
<, <=, >, >=	Less than, less than or equal to, greater than, greater than or equal to.
and, or	Logical and, or.
+, -, *	Addition, subtraction, multiplication. Because – can be part of a valid name and * can be used to indicate an arbitrary name, you have to make sure they cannot be interpreted wrongly by leaving whitespace before the operator.
div	Division (floating point).
mod	Integer remainder of a division.
|	Union of two node sets (creates a new node set holding all elements in the two node sets).

The filtered result set returned by an XPath expression with a predicate expression can be further filtered by appending another predicate to it. This example selects the fifth `employee` that has a `function` child element with the value 'manager'. We first select all `employee` nodes along the `descendant` axis, and then filter them with the `[function='manager']` predicate. From this filtered result set, we again filter only the fifth element with the predicate `[5]`:

```
descendant::employee[function='manager'][5]
```

The following example looks very much the same, but selects the fifth `employee` element, but only if it has a `child` element of type `function` with the value 'manager'. Otherwise it will return an empty node set:

```
descendant::employee[5][function='manager']
```

Built-in Functions

As we have already seen, in the writing of predicates, functions that perform complex operations are very handy, if not absolutely necessary. Some of them we have already seen in some of the samples presented. We will show some important functions here, but all other built-in functions specified by the XPath recommendation are listed in Appendix C.

Node Set Functions

last()

The last() function returns the index number of the last node in the context. For example, this command selects the chapter elements (along the child axis, which is the default axis in the shorthand notation) that have exactly 5 paragraph children:

```
chapter[paragraph[last() = 5]]
```

position()

The position() function returns the position of the current context node in the current result set. For example, this command selects the chapter children that have a fifth paragraph:

```
chapter[paragraph[position() = 5]]
```

Note that here we create a predicate to filter the results of the outer expression, and this predicate uses an XPath expression that also has a predicate. This recursive use of XPath expressions in predicates is a powerful way to create sub-queries.

count(node set)

The count() function returns the number of nodes in the node set passed to it. This seems identical to the last() function, but it isn't; the context it works on is different. It can be used to do more or less equal things, but the syntax would be different. This example selects the chapters with exactly five paragraph children (identical to the example for the last() function):

```
chapter[count(paragraph) = 5]
```

Whereas this selects the chapters with five or more paragraph children (identical to the example for the position() function):

```
chapter[count(paragraph) >= 5]
```

id(object)

The id() function returns nodes that have the specified ID attribute. If the object passed to the function is a node set, each of the elements is converted to its string value. The function then returns all elements in the document that have one of the ID values in the set.

If the passed object is anything else, the query parser tries to convert it to a string and returns the element from the document that has this string for an ID. This can, by definition, be only one element, for example:

```
id(//book[@publisher = 'WROX']/@authors)
```

This query returns all nodes that have an ID that matches the content of the `authors` attributes on books that have their publisher attribute set to `'WROX'`. This kind of query can be extremely powerful. However, they demand that the document is validated against a schema or DTD, because without validation, the processor cannot know which attributes are IDs. For doing things like this with invalidated documents, see the section on using keys.

namespace-uri(node-set)

If your application has to act only on information in a specific namespace (this is in fact very probable as soon as you are building real applications), you will love the `namespace-uri()` function. It returns a string containing the URI of the namespace of the passed node set. Normally, the node set you pass will only contain one node. In fact, if you pass a node set containing multiple nodes, the function will use the first node in the set. So, if the node you pass is an element of type `mydata:chapter`, the function will look for the declaration of the `mydata` namespace and will return the value of the URI used there.

This next query will return all elements in the specified namespace:

```
//*[namespace-uri() = 'http://www.w3.org/1999/XSL/Transform']
```

String Functions

For the handling of strings, several functions are included. We will not get into these in very much depth. Most are what you would expect from string handling functions. They cover concatenation, comparing and manipulating strings, and selecting a substring from a string. We will show just a few functions here; refer to Appendix C for the complete list.

string(object)

This function converts the passed object to a string. This may be a Boolean value that is converted to `'true'`, or a number value converted to its string value (i.e. the number 3 would be converted to the string "3"). If a node set is passed, the first node in the set is used.

starts-with(string, string)

This is for checking if the first string starts with the second string. The function returns true if so, otherwise false. For example, this query returns all `employee` elements that have a `last-name` attribute that starts with an `'A'`:

```
descendant::employee[starts-with(@last-name, "A")]
```

Note the use of the shorthand notation `@last-name` for `attribute::last-name`.

translate(string, string, string)

The `translate` function takes a string and, character-by-character, translates characters which match the second string into the corresponding characters in the third string. This is the only way to convert from lower to upper case in XPath. That would look like this (with extra whitespace added for readability). This code would translate the employee last names to upper case and then select those employees whose last names begin with A:

```
descendant::employee[
  starts-with(
    translate(@last-name,
              "abcdefghijklmnopqrstuvwxyz",
              "ABCDEFGHIJKLMNOPQRSTUVWXYZ"),
    "A"
  )
]
```

If the second string has more characters than the third string, these extra characters will be removed from the first string. If the third string has more characters than the second string, the extra characters are ignored.

Number Functions

As for strings, a set of functions is available for number handling, but we will not list them all here. They are available in Appendix C. We will show a few of the most important and instructive examples.

number(object)

The number() function converts any passed value to a number. Its behaviour depends on the type of the passed parameter. Some possible situations:

- ❑ If a string is passed, the value of the string is converted to the mathematical value that it displays (following the IEE 754 standard).
- ❑ If a Boolean value is passed, true is converted to 1, false to 0.
- ❑ If a node set is passed, it is first converted to a string (as if using the string() function). Then the string is converted to a number.

The number function has no support for language-specific formats. The string value passed in should be of a language neutral format.

sum(node set)

The sum() function returns the sum of the numerical values of all passed nodes. The numerical value is the result of the conversion of their string values. For example, this query selects the industry elements that have customer elements as children, whose totalturnover attributes sum to an amount larger than 1 million:

```
//industry[sum(customer/@totalturnover) > 1000000]
```

round(number)

The round() function is a typical number function. It rounds a floating point value to the nearest integer value. Other ways of making an integer from a floating point value are floor() and ceiling().

Boolean Functions

The functions that handle Boolean values are not very special. The only really useful one is the not() function, which converts a Boolean value to its opposite. Other than that, there are the true() and false() functions that always return true and false respectively, and the lang() function that can be used to check the language of the content (if this is indicated with the xml:lang attribute).

IE5 Conformance

IE5 implements a subset of XPath. If you are developing for the MSXML objects in the initial IE5 release, you have to know what features are implemented in XPath and which are not. Microsoft has committed to implementing the full standard in all later versions. It is unclear what backward compatibility will exist with syntax elements that are not part of the W3C recommendation. Here we will show the differences between the IE5 implementation and the W3C recommendation 1.0.

Axes

IE5 knows only the abbreviated syntax for axis and node test. You cannot use the syntax with a double colon. This limits the number of axes, because not all XPath axes have an abbreviated form (for example namespace, ancestor, following, preceding).

Functions

Not all of the built-in functions of XPath are supported in IE5. The most notable difference is the last() function which is called end() in IE5. Also, many functions are not supported at all. Here is a full list of the supported functions in IE5:

- ❑ attribute() returns all attribute nodes of the context node.
- ❑ cdata() returns all CDATA nodes that are children of the context node.
- ❑ comment() returns all comment nodes that are children of the context node.
- ❑ date() casts a value to date format.
- ❑ element() returns all elements that are children of the context node.
- ❑ end() is synonymous to last() in the XPath recommendation.
- ❑ index() returns the index number of the node within its parent.
- ❑ node() returns all nodes (except attributes and the root node) that are children of the context node.
- ❑ nodeName() returns the tag name (includes namespace prefix).
- ❑ nodeType() returns a number indicating the node type.
- ❑ number() casts values to number format.
- ❑ pi() returns all processing instruction nodes that are children of the context node.
- ❑ text() returns all nodes that represent a text value, that are children of the context node. This includes both text nodes and CDATA nodes.
- ❑ textnode() returns all text nodes that are children of the context node.
- ❑ value() returns the value of an element or attribute.

Examples

In the source code download, you will find a small Visual Basic application, called `XPathTester.vbp`, which allows you to both practice the writing of XPath queries and test their performance. If you start the application, you will see this form:

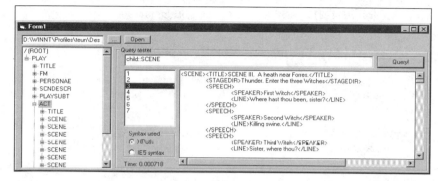

The **Query tester** frame can be used once an XML document is loaded. After loading such a document (take a big one like `Macbeth.xml`), you can see the structure of the document in the tree view control to the left. If you select a node and type an XPath expression in the **Query** text box, you can execute this query, using the selected node as your context node. All matching nodes are listed in the list box. If you click a list item, the underlying XML source is shown in the text box on the right. Note that the number of seconds needed for performing the query is shown directly under the list box. Use this application to practice writing queries. Notice how more specific queries have a better performance than very general ones. Also, queries that specify the structural relations of elements are much faster than queries specifying the text content of elements and attributes.

XSLT

In Chapter 2 we saw how we can specify the XML format that our application can work with using validation rules. When we want to exchange information with other applications, it would be nice if everyone would use the same document types (that is use the same validation rules). However, it is inevitable that, for comparable types of data, several document types will emerge. Some repositories will emerge, where schemas and DTDs can be stored and shared. Often these are industry-wide initiatives. However, several schemas for the same data will exist.

Therefore, it would be very handy to have a tool or tools to convert a document from one schema to another. These would consist of a set of rules that describe exactly how and where a piece of content in document type A should appear in document type B. These rules might as well be described in XML themselves. This is exactly what XSLT is – a language to specify how to transform an XML document of one type to another document type.

To be completely honest with you, when the XSLT initiative was started, this was not the goal. Back then it was called XSL (eXtensible Stylesheet Language) and its target was to convert an XML document to HTML. The specification was divided into two parts: the **transformation** part (which became **XSLT**) and the **formatting objects** part (**XSL-FO**). This decision was made because the development of the two parts of the XSL specification happened at different rates. Indeed, XSLT has recently become recommended, though XSL-FO is still in the early stages of development. In addition, the XSL query language, included in the earlier XSL specification, was removed and combined with the path syntax in XPointer to form XPath.

So we have two recommendations: XPath and XSLT, and some specifications that will still undergo serious changes. As XSL-FO is still so premature, it will not be covered in this book.

When the work was in progress, the editors started to understand that the fields of application of their work were much broader than just creating HTML. This is still one of the purposes of XSLT, but only one of many. In the remainder of this chapter we will focus on the broader possibilities of XSLT, and will show how to use it for HTML generation at the end of the chapter.

How Transformation Works

Transforming an XML document from one format into another always involves three documents: the **source** document, the **destination** document and the document holding the **transformation rules**, the XSLT stylesheet:

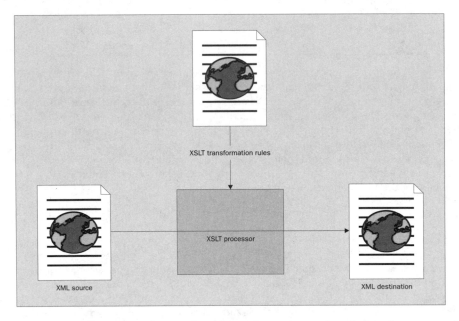

Each stylesheet in XSLT consists of a number of templates. A **template** defines how a certain kind of content in the source document appears in the destination document. A template always has an XPath expression that describes what nodes in the source the template applies to.

Most programming languages start their execution at a specific place in the program code (in Visual Basic, this is Sub Main()). XSLT is different. It starts with the data and searches for the right code to execute with that data. When a document is transformed with an XSLT stylesheet, the start node is the document root. Now the following steps will be taken:

1. The processor searches for the most suitable template in the stylesheet for transforming this node. (We'll talk about what makes a template suitable later).

2. This template defines certain output nodes, which are added to the result document.

3. The template can also specify which nodes should be processed next. For all of these nodes, go to step 1.

The process ends when no more nodes are specified to process next. The most common form is that every template tells the processor to continue by processing the children of the current node. This makes sure that all nodes will get processed and that no infinite loops can occur.

Programming stylesheets is an art of its own and the very recursive nature of the task will sometimes puzzle the average VB programmer. It can help to think of a template as an event handler. At the start of the transformation, the event for processing the root is raised. The processor selects the best handler and executes this. This event handler produces nodes in the output document, but can also raise events itself. For all of these raised events, the XSLT processor will again search in the stylesheet for handlers, etc...

Before we look at writing stylesheets, let's take a look at the other requirement for transformations – XSLT processors.

Some Good XSLT Processors

At the time of writing, the XSLT specification was still very fresh, so implementations of the full specification were still scarce. The best one at the time was **SAXON** (at least the best implementation that I could find). SAXON is implemented in Java, with source code available, but also a Win32 binary can be downloaded (http://users.iclway.co.uk/mhkay/saxon/). This can be called as follows:

```
saxon -o destination.xml source.xml stylesheet.xsl
```

Another well-known implementation is **XT** by James Clark. Clark was one of the main contributors to the XSLT specification and has always tried to keep his implementation following the specification as close as possible. At the time of writing there were still a few features unimplemented in XT, but a full version will undoubtedly be released (download from www.jclark.com/xml/xt.html). Like SAXON, XT is distributed as Java classes and code, but can also be downloaded in binary form, allowing use like this:

```
xt source.xml stylesheet.xsl destination.xml
```

The third implementation that should be mentioned in a book for VB programmers is the Microsoft MSXML library. The version available at the time of writing was dated March 1999, and is therefore rather out-of-date. Microsoft has promised that the full specification will be included in a next release. The fact that these libraries can be used as COM objects from VB code or scripting gives them a huge advantage over the command-line based competition. The performance of the MSXML library is much better than that of the Java-based implementations at the moment, but of course, implementations with different functionality are hard to compare.

To give developers a head start when the newer library is released, Microsoft has published a 'developers preview' in January 2000 (this is the same preview that was mentioned when we discussed XPath). This preview can be used side by side with the older library and partially implements the final specification of XSLT. (Check Appendix D to see exactly which parts are implemented). With the MSXML library, you could do something like:

```
Dim oDoc as new DOMDocument
Dim oXSLT as new DOMDocument
```

```
oDoc.async = false
oXSLT.async = false

oDoc.load "http://www.comp.com/sourceDocument.xml"
oXSLT.load "http://www.comp.com/stylesheet.xsl"

sResult = oDoc.transformNode(oXSLT)
```

The `transformNode` method returns a string holding the full transformed document. The current version of MSXML can be downloaded from http://msdn.microsoft.com/downloads/tools/xmlparser/xmlredist.exe, and the developers preview from http://msdn.microsoft.com/downloads/webtechnology/xml/msxml.asp.

XSLT Elements – Composing the XSLT Stylesheet

An XSLT document defines rules for transforming a specific kind of XML document into another kind of document. These rules are themselves defined in an XML-based document syntax. Most of this chapter will be used to describe all of the available elements in an XSLT document.

To differentiate the XSLT-specific elements in a stylesheet from other XML content, XSLT uses namespaces. The official XSLT namespace is `http://www.w3.org/1999/XSL/Transform`. Remember that this URI does not necessarily point to any resource. It only specifies to the XSLT processor that these elements are part of an XSLT stylesheet. In this chapter we will always use the `xsl` namespace prefix for XSLT elements. This assumes that all our stylesheets contain this namespace declaration:

```
xmlns:xsl="http://www.w3.org/1999/XSL/Transform"
```

For example, if we talk about the `template` element in the XSLT namespace, we will display it as `xsl:template`. Remember that this URL is not pointing to anything special. It is only used as a unique identifier to make these elements unique from all other kinds of elements (that are not specifying an XSLT stylesheet).

stylesheet

The root element of any XSLT stylesheet document is normally the `stylesheet` element (exceptions are the `transform` element and the simplified syntax; both will be explained later). It holds a number of templates and can hold some more elements that specify settings. Elements that can appear in the `stylesheet` element (and only there) are called top level elements. An example of a `stylesheet` element is shown:

```
<xsl:stylesheet
  id = id
  extension-element-prefixes = tokens
  exclude-result-prefixes = tokens
  version = number>
</xsl:stylesheet>
```

The version attribute of the `stylesheet` element is necessary to ensure that later additions to the XSLT specification can be implemented without changing the old stylesheets. The current version is 1.0. When newer versions of the recommendation are specified, the version number can be increased (but the namespace for XSLT will remain stable, including the '1999'). If the version is set to anything higher than 1.0, this will also affect the way a 1.0 processor works. The processor will switch on forward compatibility mode. In this mode, the processor ignores any unknown elements or elements in unexpected places. You will rarely use the other attributes of the `stylesheet` element, but we'll discuss them here briefly anyway.

With the `extension-element-prefixes` attribute, it is possible to assign a number of namespace prefixes, other than the defined XSLT prefix, as XSLT extension prefixes. This tells the XSLT processors that support any extensions to watch out for these namespace extensions. They might be extensions that it knows. The prefixes must be defined namespaces.

If the source document contains namespace declarations, these will normally automatically appear in the result document as well. The only exception is the XSLT declaration itself. If there are any other namespaces in the source document that you do not want to show up in the output, these can be excluded with the `exclude-result-prefixes` attribute.

Just to give you the idea, we'll have a look at an extremely simple stylesheet here. We'll use some elements that we have not described yet, but we'll describe what happens afterwards.

```
<?xml version="1.0"?>
<xsl:stylesheet xmlns:xsl=" http://www.w3.org/1999/XSL/Transform" version="1.0">
  <xsl:template match="/">
    <root_node/>
  </xsl:template>
</xsl:stylesheet>
```

You will recognize the `stylesheet` element carrying the namespace declaration to indicate that this is an XSLT stylesheet. Inside the stylesheet is one `xsl:template` element. This element has a `match` attribute set to "/" and a child element `root_node`. This template matches ('is a suitable template for') the document root (indicated by '/'). The only content of the template is the `root_node` element. This is not an XSLT element, but a literal element that is added to the output when this template is executed. When this stylesheet is used to transform an arbitrary XML document, the processor will start processing the document root of the source document. It will find a suitable template in the stylesheet (the only template we have) and use it to process the document root. The only thing the template does is create a `root_node` element in the output document. This stylesheet will transform an arbitrary XML source document to:

```
<root_node/>
```

transform

The `transform` element is synonymous to the `stylesheet` element. It is included because the uses for XSLT have grown much wider than just giving style to XML content, but the stylesheet is still the most common way to define a transformation. Functionally, there is no difference.

import

To construct a stylesheet from several reusable fragments, the XSLT specification supports the importing of external stylesheet document fragments. This is done with either the `import` or `include` elements, for example:

```
<xsl:import href=uri-reference/>
```

The document retrieved from the URI should be a stylesheet document itself and the children of the `stylesheet` element are imported directly into the main stylesheet. The `import` element can only be used as a top-level element and must appear before any of the `template` elements in the document. If the XSLT processor is trying to match a node in the source document to a template in the stylesheet, it will first try to use one of the templates in the importing document before trying to use one of the imported templates. This allows for creating rules that are used in many stylesheets. Rules can be overridden by defining one of the rules again locally.

Both the `import` and the `include` elements may never reference themselves (not even indirectly).

include

The `include` element is the simpler brother of the `import` element:

```
<xsl:include href=uri-reference/>
```

It just *inserts* the rules from the referenced URI. These are parsed as if they were in the original document.

Like the `import` element, `include` can only appear at the top-level. There is no restriction on the location of this element in the document (unlike `import`).

template

The `template` element is one of the main building blocks of an XSLT stylesheet. It consists of two parts, the **matching pattern** and the **implementation**. Roughly, you can say that the pattern defines which nodes will be acceptable as input for the template. The implementation defines what the output will look like. We will cover the implementation later, when we discuss the elements that generate output.

```
<xsl:template
  match = pattern
  name = qname
  priority = number
  mode = qname>
  <!-- Content: implementation-->
</xsl:template>
```

The attributes `name`, `priority` and `mode` are used to differentiate between several templates that match on the same node. In these cases several rules exist for preference of templates over each other. In the section titled "*What if Several Templates Match?*" we will show the use of these attributes.

The `match` attribute holds the matching pattern for the template. The matching pattern defines for which nodes in the source document this template is the appropriate processing rule. The syntax used is a subset of XPath. It contains only the `child` and `attribute` axes (but it is also legal to use "`//`" from the abbreviated syntax, so the `descendant` axis is also available). A template matches a node, if the node is part of the result set of the pattern from any available context, which basically says that a node should be "selectable" with the pattern. We'll take a look at a few examples to clear this up.

Imagine that we are processing a document with chapters and paragraphs. The paragraphs are marked up with the element `para`, the chapters with `chapter`. We will look at possible values for the match attribute of the `xsl:template` element. This matches any `para` element that has a `chapter` element as a parent:

```
<xsl:template match="child::chapter/child::para">
</xsl:template>
```

Note that this will only work when the `chapter` element has a parent node. This parent node is the context we need to select the `para` element from with this pattern. Fortunately, all elements have a parent (the root element has the document root for a parent), so this pattern matches all `para` elements that have a `chapter` as a parent. This example will match with all `para` elements:

```
<xsl:template match="para">
</xsl:template>
```

This matches any `para` element as well as any `chapter` element:

```
<xsl:template match="(chapter|para)">
</xsl:template>
```

This matches any `para` element that has a `chapter` element as an ancestor:

```
<xsl:template match="chapter//para">
</xsl:template>
```

This matches the root node:

```
<xsl:template match="/">
</xsl:template>
```

This matches all nodes but not attributes and the root:

```
<xsl:template match="node()">
</xsl:template>
```

This matches any `para` element, which is the first `para` child of its parent:

```
<xsl:template match="para[position() = 1]">
</xsl:template>
```

This matches any `title` attribute (not an element that has a `title` attribute):

```
<xsl:template match="@title">
</xsl:template>
```

This matches only the odd-numbered `para` elements within its parent:

```
<xsl:template match="para[position() mod 2 = 1]">
</xsl:template>
```

Two interesting extra functions that you can use in the pattern are `id()` and `key()`. `id('someLiteral')` evaluates to the node that has `'someLiteral'` as its ID value. This pattern matches all `para` elements that are children of the element with its ID attribute set to `'Table1'`:

```
<xsl:template match="id('Table1')/para">
</xsl:template>
```

Note that the ID attribute is not necessarily called `ID` – it can be any attribute that is declared as having type ID in the DTD or Schema. The `key()` method does something similar, but refers to defined keys instead of elements by ID. Refer to the section covering the `xsl:key` element to learn more about the `key()` method.

apply-templates

In the simple and rather non-functional example we looked at in the paragraph about the `stylesheet` element, we had only one template. This template matched on the document root. When the XSLT processor starts transforming a document with that stylesheet, it will first search for a template to match the document root. Our only template does this, so it is executed. It generates an output element and processing is stopped. All content held by nodes other than the document root is not processed. We need a way to tell the processor to carry on processing another node.

```
<xsl:apply-templates
    select = node set-expression
    mode = qname>
</xsl:apply-templates>
```

This is done using the `xsl:apply-templates` element. It selects the nodes that should be processed next using an XPath expression. The nodes in the node set that is selected by this XPath expression will become the new context nodes. For these new context nodes, the processor will search a new matching template. The transformed output of these nodes will appear within the output generated by the current template.

You may compare the use of the `apply-templates` element with calling a subroutine in a procedural programming language. There are only two possible attributes for the `apply-templates` element: `select` and `mode`.

The `select` attribute is the more important one. It specifies which nodes should be transformed now and have their transformed output shown. It holds an XPath expression. The expression is evaluated with the current context node. For each node in the result set, the processor will search for the appropriate template and transform it.

The default value for the `select` attribute is `'child::node()'`. This matches all child nodes, but not attributes.

Let's make a few changes to our example and use `xsl:apply-templates`:

```
<?xml version="1.0"?>
<xsl:stylesheet xmlns:xsl=" http://www.w3.org/1999/XSL/Transform" version="1.0">
  <xsl:template match="/">
    <root_node>
      <xsl:apply-templates/>
    </root_node>
  </xsl:template>

  <xsl:template match="*">
    <result_node>
      <xsl:apply-templates/>
    </result_node>
  </xsl:template>
</xsl:stylesheet>
```

Now we'll use the following source document to test the transformation:

```
<?xml version="1.0" ?>
<FAMILY>
  <PERSON name="Freddy" />
  <PERSON name="Maartje" />
  <PERSON name="Gerard"/>
  <PERSON name="Peter"/>
  <PET name="Bonzo" type="dog"/>
  <PET name="Arnie" type="cat"/>
</FAMILY>
```

Let's first have a look at the changes in the stylesheet. Something was added to the original template: the root_node element now has a child element: `xsl:apply-templates`. This means that when the template is executed, the root_node element will still output a root_node element in the output document, but between outputting the start tag and the end tag, it will try to process all nodes that are selected by the `xsl:apply-templates` element. This element has no `select` attribute, so that defaults to `child::node()`, which selects all child nodes of the current context (excluding attributes).

Another change is that we added a new template, matching on "*". All it does is generate a result_node element in the output document (which does not mean anything, it is just test output). This node too has an `xsl:apply-templates` child element.

We saved the sample XML source as `family.xml` and the stylesheet as `test.xsl`. Then we called the SAXON processor like this:

```
saxon -o destination.xml family.xml test.xsl
```

We'll follow the XSLT processor step-by-step as it creates an output document from the sample source document and our test stylesheet:

1. Try to match the root to one of the templates: the first template matches.

2. Process the implementation of the first template, using the root as the context node.

3. The implementation causes the output of a `root_node` element to the destination document and tells us to process all the child nodes of the root. These are only the XML declaration (`<?xml version="1.0"?>`) and the `FAMILY` element.

4. The XML declaration has no matching template, and will not be processed. The `FAMILY` element matches the second template.

5. The implementation causes the output of a `result_node` element to the destination document (as a child of the `root_node` element) and tells us to process all the child nodes of the `FAMILY`. These are all `PERSON` and `PET` elements.

6. The processor tries to match the `PERSON` element to one of the templates: the second template matches.

7. The second template generates a `result_node` element in the output and tells the processor to process the children of the element. It finds no children.

8. Steps 6 and 7 are repeated for all `PERSON` and `PET` elements.

The result of all this processing looks like this:

```
<root_node>
  <result_node>
    <result_node/>
    <result_node/>
    <result_node/>
    <result_node/>
    <result_node/>
    <result_node/>
  </result_node>
</root_node>
```

The outer element (`root_node`) is the transformed result of the document root; the element within the `root_node` is the transformed result of the `FAMILY` element in the source. All of the `PERSON` and `PET` elements are transformed to the six empty `result_node` elements.

So, what about the `mode` attribute? We will discuss that in the section "*What if Several Templates Match?*"

Pre-defined Templates

Apart from the templates that *you* will define and implement, two default templates are provided for free. These templates can be overruled by creating a template that matches the same nodes. We haven't covered the implementation of templates yet, but still it can be instructive to see what real implemented templates look like:

```
<xsl:template match="*|/">
  <xsl:apply-templates/>
</xsl:template>

<xsl:template match="text()|@*">
  <xsl:value-of select="."/>
</xsl:template>
```

What do we see? There are two templates defined. One matches all elements and the root (`* | /`). The other one matches both text nodes and all attributes. The implementation of the templates is fairly simple. The first one has only an `xsl:apply-templates` element. The implementation of the second template uses another element: `xsl:value-of`. This element generates text output containing the string value of the context node.

Now suppose that we try to transform the sample source document (`family.xml`) using only the built-in templates. What would happen? The document root would be matched by the first built-in template, matching on "`* | /`", i.e. any node including the root. The only thing this template does is call `xsl:apply-templates` with no `select` attribute. This will cause the processor to process all child nodes (but not attributes).

The result of our sample source, transformed by only built-in templates, would be an empty document. If it contained any text nodes, these would appear in the output. But although no output appears in the result, all nodes in the document have been processed. This is an important fact. The default templates will process all nodes in the document.

If you implement your own template, you will specify specific output for the element you are matching. But if you ever want the children of this element to become the context node, you must also make sure that you pass the context to them. One of the most common mistakes is using a stylesheet like this:

```
<?xml version="1.0"?>
<xsl:stylesheet xmlns:xsl="http://www.w3.org/1999/XSL/Transform">
<xsl:template match="/">
    <HTML><BODY>
    </BODY></HTML>
</xsl:template>

<xsl:template match="*">
    <!--some content here -->
</xsl:template>
</xsl:stylesheet>
```

Note that the first template contains no `xsl:apply-templates` element. This means that after processing the document root and outputting a document like this:

```
<HTML>
  <BODY/>
</HTML>
```

the processor will stop. The context is not passed to any other node, so the XSLT processor assumes that the job is done. We must change that template to:

```
<xsl:template match="/">
   <HTML><BODY>
      <xsl:apply-templates/>
   </BODY></HTML>
</xsl:template>
```

> **Forgetting to pass the context from a node to its children is one of the most common mistakes when developing XSLT documents.**

Of course, you may have good reasons to do it on purpose. Often, you don't want all nodes to appear in the destination document and you may decide not to pass focus to them at all. That's fine, as long as it is a *deliberate* decision to leave out `apply-templates`.

Elements that Generate Output Elements

The most easily understandable elements in an XSLT document are the literals. They must be any fragment of valid XML and should not be in the XSLT namespace, that is any XML content within the `xsl:template` element that is not prefixed `xsl:` is passed on to the result document. The output to the destination document is identical to the literal value in the XSLT document. This can be a piece of text, but also a tree of XML nodes.

This template will output a LITERALS element for each PERSON element it is used on (we have actually seen this already in the example for the `xsl:template` element). If the PERSON element has any child elements or attributes, these will not be included in the destination document:

```
<xsl:template match="PERSON">
   <LITERALS/>
</xsl:template>
```

Literal values can include both text and XML elements. Other nodes, like comments and processing instructions, cannot be output as literal values. A literal value must always be a well-formed piece of XML. So we cannot generate only an opening tag. This would prevent the XSLT document from being well-formed.

value-of

The `value-of` element generates the string value of the specified node in the destination document.

The `select` attribute indicates which node's value should be output. It contains an XPath expression that is evaluated in the template's context. For example, this code would generate the text string in the destination document with the value of the `name` attribute of the matched PERSON element:

```
<xsl:template match="PERSON">
   <xsl:value-of select="@name"/>
</xsl:template>
```

copy

The `copy` element creates a node in the destination document with the same node name and node type as the context node. The `copy` element will not copy any children or attributes of an element. An example of using this element would be:

```
<xsl:template match="PERSON|PET">
  <xsl:copy/>
</xsl:template>
```

This template will output a PERSON element for each matched PERSON element in the source document and a PET element for each matched PET element in the source document. Any attributes of the copied elements will not show up in the destination document.

copy-of

The copy-of element is used to copy a set of nodes to the destination document. The select attribute can be used to indicate which nodes are to be copied. Unlike the copy element, copy-of will copy all children and all attributes of an element.

The copy-of element is very much like the value-of element, except that copy-of does not convert the selected node to a string value and that copy-of will copy all selected nodes, not only the first, for example:

```
<xsl:template match="PERSON">
  <xsl:copy>
    <xsl:copy-of select="@name"/>
  </xsl:copy>
</xsl:template>
```

This template creates a PERSON element for each matched PERSON element in the source document and copies any existing name attribute into it. Note how the copying of the attribute is placed within the copying of the element.

```
<xsl:template match="PERSON">
  <xsl:copy-of select="."/>
</xsl:template>
```

This template will copy a PERSON element with all its attributes and children (and further descendants) to the destination document for each matched PERSON element in the source.

element

The element element (how meta can you get?) allows us to create elements in the destination document. You must use the name attribute to specify the element name. The namespace of the created element can be set using the optional namespace attribute. If you include a namespace attribute, the XSLT engine may decide to change the prefix you specified in the name attribute. The local name (everything after the colon) will remain intact.

```
<xsl:template match="PERSON">
  <xsl:element name="PERSONAL_DATA"/>
</xsl:template>
```

This template will produce exactly the same output as the example for literals. You may wonder why you would ever use the element element if you can use literals. The extra value is in the fact that the name and namespace attributes are not normal attributes, but 'attribute value templates'. We will explain about those later.

attribute

The `attribute` element generates attributes in the destination document. It works in the same way as the `element` element, but inserting attributes is bound to some limitations:

❑   You may not insert an attribute in an element after child elements have been added to that element.

❑   You can only use this in the context of an element. Adding an attribute to a `comment` node is not allowed.

❑   Within the `attribute` element, no nodes may be generated other than text nodes. Attribute nodes can not have child nodes.

This template will create a `species` attribute for each matched `type` attribute, inserting the value of the `type` attribute in the `species` attribute:

```
<xsl:template match="@type">
  <xsl:attribute name="species">
    <xsl:value-of/>
  </xsl:attribute>
</xsl:template>
```

Attribute Value Templates

The `attribute` element is often used to create attributes in the output that have a calculated name. Because their value is not fixed, they cannot be specified in a literal element, or can they? XSLT specifies a special kind of attribute, called **attribute value templates**. All literal attributes in XSLT are value templates, but many attributes on predefined XSLT elements are as well. An attribute value template can contain an expression part that is evaluated before execution of the element the attribute is in. The expression must be placed in curly braces, so this code:

```
<LITERAL some="blah{4+5}"/>
```

would create this node in the output:

```
<LITERAL some="blah9"/>
```

The expression can also be an XPath expression. Using attribute value templates, the following transformation can be made much more readable than it is with `attribute` elements, so this code:

```
<photograph>
  <url>img/pic.jpg</url>
  <size width="40"/>
</photograph>

<xsl:template match="photograph">
<img src="{url}" width="{size/@width}"/>
</xsl:template>
```

would create:

```
<img src="img/pic.jpg" width="40"/>
```

You cannot use nested braces. If you need to specify a {, use a double brace: {{. Check Appendix D to find out which attributes can be used as value templates.

A Stylesheet Example

Before we go on with any theory, we will now have a look at a sample. Remember the two XML documents specifying information about a family? It was the first code sample of Chapter 2.

We will create a transformation document to convert documents of type A into documents of type B. To work along and try the result of several elements, you may want to use a tool that allows you to see source, rules and destination documents side by side. Some good commercial tools exist, but we suggest using the free open source tool under development by some members of the VBXML mailing list. It is called **XSLTester** and can be downloaded from www.vbxml.com. The sample XSL files can be downloaded from the Wrox web site.

First we define a template that matches the root of the document and outputs all standard elements:

```
<xsl:template match="/">
  <FAMILY>
    <PERSONS>
    <xsl:apply-templates select="FAMILY/PERSON"/>
    </PERSONS>
    <PETS>
    <xsl:apply-templates select="FAMILY/PET"/>
    </PETS>
  </FAMILY>
</xsl:template>
```

The template generates a framework for the document and specifies the places where other content should appear. In this case, it specifies the PERSON and PET elements to appear in two different places. Note how two XPath expressions are used to invoke new transformations to occur.

For each of the PERSON elements, we want to do a simple transformation: instead of having the name in a name attribute, it should be the content of the element:

```
<xsl:template match="PERSON">
  <PERSON>
    <xsl:value-of select="@name"/>
  </PERSON>
</xsl:template>
```

The PET element needs a more complex transformation. Like the PERSON element, it has its name attribute transformed into the element content. But the PET element in the source document also has a type attribute. In the destination syntax, this attribute is called species. We achieve this transformation with this template:

```
<xsl:template match="PET">
  <PET>
    <xsl:attribute name="species">
      <xsl:value-of select="@type"/>
    </xsl:attribute>
    <xsl:value-of select="@name"/>
```

```
     </PET>
   </xsl:template>
```

There it is – our first complete and functional XSLT document. Using MSXML, we could program a VB application that does this transformation containing code like this:

```
Dim oDocFormatA as new DOMDocument 'Object to hold the format we cannot handle
Dim oDocFormatB as new DOMDocument 'Object that holds the format we know
Dim oXSLT as new DOMDocument         'Object that holds the XSLT stylesheet

oDocFormatA.async = false
oXSLT.async = false

oDocFormatA.load "D:\sourceDocument.xml"
oXSLT.load "D:\stylesheet.xsl"

oDocFormatB.loadXML( oDocFormatA.transformNode(oXSLT))
' Now save this string or process it further
```

text

The text element creates a text node in the destination document, holding the content of the original text element. This can also be achieved using literal text, but the text attribute will also be included if it contains only whitespace. Including whitespace is the main reason for using the text element. See the sections on strip-space and preserve-space for more information on whitespace stripping. So these two templates are functionally identical:

```
<xsl:template match="PERSON">
  <xsl:text>A person element found</xsl:text>
</xsl:template>
```

```
<xsl:template match="PERSON">
  A person element found
</xsl:template>
```

processing-instruction

The processing-instruction element generates a processing instruction in the destination document. The syntax for creating a processing instruction is different from that for elements. So this code:

```
<xsl:processing-instruction name="xml-stylesheet">
  href="style.xsl" type="text/xsl"
</xsl:processing-instruction>
```

would generate in the destination document:

```
<?xml-stylesheet href="style.xsl" type="text/xsl"?>
```

This would be typical for an XSLT document that is used for pre-processing – specifying the transformation rules for the next step. Look at the very end of this chapter to see what the effect of this processing instruction is.

> **The attributes of the processing instruction (`href` and `type`) must be created as a text node instead of attributes. This is because the content of the processing instruction does not necessarily use an XML-based syntax.**

The `name` attribute must contain a valid name for a processing instruction. This means that it cannot be 'xml' and therefore cannot be used to generate the XML declaration itself. To learn about how to create XML declarations, see the section on the `xsl:output` element.

It is not allowed to create any node other than a text node within the processing instruction element. It is also forbidden to create textual content holding the string '?>' – it will be interpreted as the end of the processing instruction.

comment

The `comment` element is the only way to create comments in the destination document – a comment in the source document would be ignored, because it will not be parsed anyway. So this code:

```
<xsl:comment>This file was generated using XSLT</xsl:comment>
```

would generate this line in the destination document:

```
<!-- This file was generated using XSLT-->
```

It can, of course, not have any other content than text nodes.

number

The `number` element is a special one. It is more or less a numerical conversion tool. It creates a numeric value in the output and has a ton of attributes for specifying which number and format should be output:

```
<xsl:number
   value = number-expression
   level = "single" | "multiple" | "any"
   count = pattern
   from = pattern
   format = { string }
   grouping-separator = { char }
   grouping-size = { number }
/>
```

The simplest way to use the `number` element is by specifying the numeric value that should be output using the `value` attribute. The `value` attribute is evaluated and converted to a number (as if using the `number` function). This number is rounded to an integer value and converted back to a string value. So this code would output the index number of the context node (relative to its parent) followed by a dot and a space:

```
<xsl:number value="position()" format="1. "/>
```

The attributes of the number element can be separated into two groups: those necessary to *calculate* the numeric value and those necessary to *format* the numerical value into a string.

Number Calculation Example

As we saw earlier, the simplest way to calculate the number that will be output to the destination document is using the value attribute. Any expression that can be converted to a number can be used here. A more complex, but in some cases very powerful, way to calculate the number is using the level, count and from attributes. It is used whenever the value property is not used.

We will explain the workings of the number element by example. Imagine an XML document containing the full text of a book. The book is divided into chapters (CH elements), sections (SEC elements) and paragraphs (P elements). Within a paragraph, we want to create a paragraph title, including the chapter number, section number, paragraph number, etc. These numbers are not really content; they follow from the structure of the content. We would really like Chapter 1 to be called 'Introduction', not '1. Introduction'. Still, in the final hardcopy (or web page or Acrobat document etc.) we want the number to show up. So we will let the XSLT processor do the counting and insert the numbering on the fly. This is exactly what the number element is good at. Let's have a look at our book document:

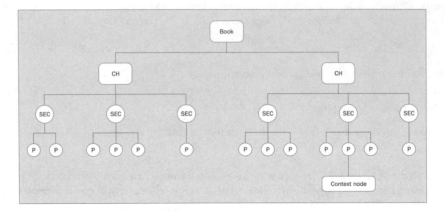

level attribute

We are transforming the context node at the bottom of the diagram. There are three modes for counting nodes, 'single', 'multiple' and 'any'. The counting mode is set using the level attribute. The default mode is 'single'.

```
level='single'
```

The count attribute specifies which kind of nodes you want to count. If the level attribute is set to 'single', the processor will search along the ancestor axis for a node that matches the count attribute. If the count attribute is empty, it uses the context node itself. Once the processor has found a matching ancestor, it counts the number of preceding siblings that also match the count attribute and adds one. It's quite complex, right? Look at the diagram above. Suppose we want to display the paragraph number of the paragraph our context node is part of. That would be 2 – i.e. it is the second paragraph in the section. To display this the following code would be used:

```
<xsl:number level='single' count='P'/>
```

The processor goes up from the context node until it finds a node that matched 'P'. Then it looks at this node's preceding siblings and counts the number of them that match the count attribute (1). It adds one to that, returning 2. The chapter number would similarly be returned by:

```
<xsl:number level='single' count='CH'/>
```

The from attribute allows us to look only at a part of the ancestor axis. If the from attribute is specified, the processor will first search for an ancestor that matches the from attribute. After that, it will search for the node that will be counted using the count attribute, but it will not look past the node that was matched by the from attribute. This allows you to narrow down the counting to a subtree of the document.

Using the 'multiple' mode is very much like the 'single' mode, but it can return more values at once:

```
level='multiple'
```

This is useful for creating paragraph numbers like §2.2.2. The processor will search along the ancestor axis for all nodes matching the count attribute. Each matching node will be used to calculate a number (just like in single mode, counting preceding siblings). A list of numbers is returned, in document order. Therefore this line will return a list with the current chapter number, section number and paragraph number, in that order:

```
<xsl:number level='multiple' count='CH|SEC|P'/>
```

It is up to the number-to-string formatting attributes to output this list as an understandable format.

Note that you may run into trouble if your document structure is not as clean as in this sample. If chapters are not siblings of each other, the numbering will go wrong. Also, try to think about what happens if P elements are not only part of SEC elements, but can also appear directly in a CH element. The P elements would become siblings to the SEC elements and be included in the section numbering.

If the level attribute is set to 'any', the processor counts all nodes matching the pattern in the count attribute that occur in the document before the context node (including the context node itself and its ancestors):

```
level='any'
```

This can be used for counting the number of a certain kind of node throughout the document (typically 'notes' and 'diagrams'). If the from attribute is specified, the processor searches backward from the context node for the first node matching that specified by the from attribute. Then it counts all nodes matching the count attribute between the 'from node' and the context node.

Let's look at a few examples using the document structure from the diagram:

XSLT Element	Number Value
`<xsl:number level='single' count='CH|SEC' />`	2
`<xsl:number level='multiple' count='CH|SEC' />`	2, 2
`<xsl:number level='any' count='CH|SEC' />`	7
`<xsl:number level='any' count='P' />`	11
`<xsl:number level='any' count='P' from='CH'/>`	5

To output numeric values as a string, the `number` element specifies a set of attributes. We will not cover all details of formatting numeric values here. Numbering is a lot more complicated than you probably think. Ways of numbering include the obvious ones such as Arabic numbers (1, 2, 3, ...), letters (a, b, c, ...) and Roman numbers (I, II, III, ...). But there are many more. Think of all languages using other character sets. Even many languages that use normal Latin characters use other letter orders when counting. Some languages (Hebrew, Greek) have a special non-alphabetic order of letters especially for numbering. While the specification more or less tries to address these issues, in this book we will assume that you want to use one of the numbering types mentioned above, and will refrain from using traditional Georgian numbering! If you need to use more exotic numbering types, check if the XSLT implementation supports them. Most implementations will not.

format attribute

The most important attribute for formatting numbers is the `format` attribute. The `format` attribute specifies the formatting for a list of numeric values. The format string consists of alphanumeric parts, separated by non-alphanumeric parts. When a list of numbers is formatted, the nth alphanumeric part of the format is used for the nth number. If there are more numbers than formats, the last format is used for the remaining numbers. The default format (to be used if nothing is specified or if the specified format is not supported by the XSLT implementation) is '1'. These are the most common formats:

Format String	Name	Example
"1"	Arabic	1, 2, 3, 4, ...
"I"	Roman capitals	I, II, III, IV, ...
"i"	Roman lower	i, ii, iii, iv, ...
"a"	Alphabetic lower	a, b, c, d, ..., z, aa, ab, ...
"A"	Alphabetic capitals	A, B, C, D, ...
"01"	Arabic with trailing zero	01, 02, 03, ..., 10, 11, 12, ...

The non-alphanumeric characters that are used to separate the formats appear in the output separating the formatted numbers. The default separator is the period.

Here are some examples (again referring to the previous diagram):

XSLT Element	Output
`<xsl:number level='single' count='CH|SEC' format="A"/>`	B
`<xsl:number level='multiple' count='CH|SEC' format="A i"/>`	B ii
`<xsl:number level='any' count='CH|SEC' format="I" />`	VII
`<xsl:number level='any' count='P' format="a"/>`	k
`<xsl:number level='any' count='P' from='CH' format="§1"/>`	§5

Apart from the `format` attribute, the `number` element can carry the `grouping-separator` and `grouping-size` attributes. Their use is very simple and we will only show a few examples:

XSLT Element	Output
`<xsl:number value='1000000' grouping-size='3' grouping-separator='.'/>`	1.000.000
`<xsl:number value='1000000' grouping-size='2' grouping-separator=','/>`	1,00,00,00
`<xsl:number value='999' grouping-size='1' grouping-separator=':' format='i'/>`	c:m:x:c:i:x

Think about that last one! Of course you would never use this format in real life. If only one of these attributes is specified, then no grouping happens at all.

eval and script

First of all a warning: be careful – the `eval` and `script` elements are not specified in the XSLT recommendation. They are Microsoft extensions, available only in their MSXML implementation. So, if you want to be able to switch XSLT implementations later on, do not use these features.

Still, the elements are so convenient that we will cover them here. After all, most Visual Basic programmers will be using the MSXML library anyway. It is the most widely available implementation on the Windows platform. Microsoft has stated that they will continue support for the `eval` and `script` elements in later versions, so if you plan to stick with Microsoft, there is no reason for not using `eval`.

So what is it then? The `eval` element allows you to generate a text node in the destination document using script. If you have created Active Server Pages or Windows Scripting Host scripts before, you will be familiar with the ActiveX Scripting Engine. This is a generic scripting platform that several languages can be plugged into. Standard available scripting languages are VBScript and JScript.

The `script` node can hold a piece of script that can hold function definitions. These can be called from the `eval` element.

This way you can do something like this:

```
<xsl:template match="TEMP[@scale='F']">
  <xsl:eval language="VBScript">
      Celsius(this.getAttribute('value'))
  </xsl:eval>
</xsl:template>

<xsl:script language="VBScript"><![CDATA[
  Function Celsius(fDegrees)
    Celsius = (fDegrees - 32) * 5 / 9
  End Function
  ]]>
</xsl:script>
```

If this template is used on an XML element like this:

```
<TEMP scale="F" value="80"/>
```

it would generate this in the output document:

```
26.66666667
```

Using this extension, more complex calculations can be placed inside the script block. As scripting languages will sometimes contain characters that are not allowable in XML, it is good practice to place the script blocks in CDATA nodes.

The eval element contains a function call to the Celsius function in the script element. The return value of the function is outputted by the eval element to the destination document. Note the use of this to refer to the context node.

Functions defined inside a script element can be called from an eval element, but also from attributes that are evaluated as an expression (see for example the if element in the section "*Control of Flow*").

Commands

apply-templates

The xsl:apply-templates element is the most typical example of a command element (an element that starts the processing of a node). Because it is so important, we have already covered it before. However, there are more ways to invoke another template.

apply-imports

When we described the import element, we saw that sometimes the main XSLT document contains templates that match the same XPath expression as one of the templates in the imported document. In these cases, the template in the main document overrides the imported template. Using this feature, XSLT authors can create new transformations based on existing ones, extending them with new templates or changing existing templates. If you are familiar with object-oriented design, you will like this idea.

194

If you are overruling a template in your document, you will often want to invoke the original template from your newer implementation. Let's look at an example.

The source document contains data about books and the data about a book's author is always coded in an AUTHOR tag. A typical AUTHOR tag looks like this:

```
<AUTHOR firstname="Teun" lastname="Duynstee" initials="L.W.A." nobelprize="no"/>
```

Several different XSLT transformations exist in our organization, all dealing with book information. Some repeating transformations were put together in a stylesheet that is frequently imported into other XSLT documents. It looks like this:

```
<?xml version="1.0"?>
<xsl:stylesheet xmlns:xsl="http://www.w3.org/1999/XSL/Transform">
<!-- many other templates -->

<xsl:template match="AUTHOR">
   <xsl:value-of match="@firstname"/>
   <xsl:text> </xsl:text>
   <xsl:value-of match="@lastname"/>
</xsl:template>

</xsl:stylesheet>
```

The template transforms any matched AUTHOR attribute to a text node consisting of the firstname attribute joined to the lastname attribute by a single space. In our sample source, the output would be something like:

```
Teun Duynstee
```

Now we want to write an XSLT document that will transform XML data about a book into an HTML document. In the HTML document, the author's full name should appear, formatted in italics. We already have a transformation rule that creates the full name of the author, but it does no formatting. We can now import the standard author transformation and modify it slightly in our overriding template:

```
<?xml version="1.0"?>
<xsl:stylesheet xmlns:xsl="http://www.w3.org/1999/XSL/Transform">
<xsl:import href="booklib.xsl"/>

<xsl:template match="AUTHOR">
   <I><xsl:apply-import/></I>
</xsl:template>

</xsl:stylesheet>
```

The new template just specifies the literal element I that will cause italic fonts in HTML, and inside the I element, it calls the template which it overrules from the import. The result would be this:

```
<I>Teun Duynstee</I>
```

call-template

The `call-template` element is another element that can be used to organize the templates in your document. For calling a template with `call-template`, the template must have a name attribute. It works like `apply-templates`, but there is no change of context node. In fact `call-template` is very much like calling a function in a procedural programming language. Here's an example:

```
<xsl:template name="fullname output">
  <xsl:value-of match="@firstname"/>
  <xsl:text> </xsl:text>
  <xsl:value-of match="@lastname"/>
</xsl:template>

<xsl:template match="AUTHOR[@nobelprize='no']">
  <xsl:call-template name="fullname output"/>
</xsl:template>

<xsl:template match="AUTHOR[@nobelprize='yes']">
  <B>
  <xsl:call-template name="fullname output"/>
  </B>
</xsl:template>
```

The two templates for AUTHOR elements (for Nobel prize winners and others) both call the same template for formatting the attributes into a full name string.

If a template is called by name the `match` attribute is ignored and vice versa.

What if Several Templates Match?

If the XSLT processor is searching for a template to use for transforming a certain node, it's possible that it will find several templates that match (and are of the same mode – check the following section on *Modes*). The XSLT specification defines a set of rules to determine which template is the most appropriate. These rules are quite complex, but the general idea is not so hard to understand. In order of increasing importance:

❑ An imported template is less important than one associated with the document (i.e. not imported).

❑ The template imported later is more important than one imported earlier.

❑ A high priority template is more important than a low priority template.

❑ A more specific `match` attribute is more important than a more general matching expression.

When the processor starts searching for an appropriate template, it first creates a set of all available templates. From this set, it removes all templates that don't match. After that it removes templates that have a lower import precedence than others. When several documents are imported, and especially when imports are nested, things can get rather complicated. What the processor does is to build a tree of imported documents. Suppose Document A imports B and C (in that order), B imports D and C imports E, the tree would look like this:

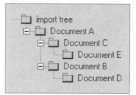

Note how Document B is lower in the tree than Document C. This is because imports that occur later in the document prevail over imports done before. The higher in the tree a document is (in an absolute sense, not in a hierarchical sense), the higher the import precedence. The built-in templates are treated as if they are imported at the very beginning of the main document and therefore have the lowest priority of all.

If several templates remain (i.e. there is more than one matching template in the same document), the template with the highest priority is chosen. The priority of a template can be set using the `priority` attribute on the `template` element. This attribute can have any numeric value, both positive and negative. If the `priority` attribute is not set, a default priority is calculated for the template. This default priority depends on the `match` attribute. It is always a value between –0.5 and 0.5. Priority values are assigned as follows:

Kind of Pattern	Examples	Priority

Specified name along the `child` or `attribute` axis	`child::PARA`
	`TITLE`
	`@fullname`
		0

Unspecified name along the `child` or `attribute` axis	`*` `attribute::*`	-0.25

Only a node test	`node()`
	`text()`
	`processing-instruction()`
		-0.5

All other cases	`PARA/LINE`
	`preceding::*`
	`*[@*='yes']`
		0.5

If several templates exist in the same document with the same priority it causes an error, but most XSLT processors will not stall but will instead pick the one nearest to the bottom of the document. This happens quite often. In many cases, developers use no `priority` attributes. Because many matching patterns cause a priority of 0.5, templates with the same priority will no doubt occur.

Modes

If you need to have some templates used in some special cases, but not always, you can try using different modes. The mode attribute is an optional attribute on both the `template` and `apply-templates` elements. By calling `apply-templates` with the mode attribute set, you instruct the processor to use only templates that have the same mode attribute. This way, you can create several sets of templates that don't interfere with each other. Each mode also has its own built-in templates.

Looking at the code sample below, we have two templates now that both match on AUTHOR, but one is in the default mode and the other one in the formal mode:

```
<xsl:template match="AUTHOR">
  <xsl:value-of match="@firstname"/>
  <xsl:text> </xsl:text>
  <xsl:value-of match="@lastname"/>
</xsl:template>

<xsl:template match="AUTHOR" mode="formal">
  <xsl:value-of match="@initials"/>
  <xsl:text> </xsl:text>
  <xsl:value-of match="@lastname"/>
</xsl:template>

<xsl:template match="BOOK[@target-audience='management']">
  Authors:
  <xsl:apply-templates select="AUTHOR" mode="formal"/>
</xsl:template>
```

In formal mode, the name of the author is generated in a more formal format (using initials instead of first name). The template that processes the content of BOOK elements that have their target-audience attribute set to 'management' decides to display the authors' names in a formal way using the 'formal' mode. Presumably, other templates invoke the default templates for AUTHOR. Removing all templates with another mode attribute from the set happens before anything else.

The IE5 Case

When IE5 was released, the XSLT specification was far from ready, so the implementation shipped in IE5 does not conform to the recommendation, more on that in the section "*The IE5 Implementation*". One word of caution though should be mentioned here. The MSXML library in IE5 *does not implement any of the rules* for assessing priorities between templates. The strategy followed by the IE5 XSLT engine is shockingly simple – it tries to find a matching template in the document from the bottom upwards. As soon as it finds one, it stops. This means that templates placed lower in the document automatically have a higher priority. For example, if you had this code:

```
<xsl:template match="AUTHOR">
  <I><xsl:value-of select="@name"/></I>
</xsl:template>

<xsl:template match="*">
  <xsl:apply-templates/>
</xsl:template>
```

IE5 will never use the first template, because it will always find and use the lower one, which matches AUTHOR elements just as well as the first template. Be aware of this behavior when developing for IE5.

message

A very special and not very commonly used element is the message element. It is designed to give stylesheet authors the opportunity to issue warnings and error messages at certain times. Only one attribute can be specified: terminate. If terminate is set to yes, the processor stops after issuing the message, if it is set to no, the processor will attempt to continue.

The specification does not specify what a processor should do when such a message is issued. Possibilities could include raising errors, displaying message boxes, or writing to a log file. The command line based processors mentioned before (SAXON and XT) will generate a message on the console, while the developers preview of MSXML does not yet implement xsl:message.

The content of the message element will be the content of the issued message. This example will display a warning whenever the stylesheet is used on a PET element:

```
<xsl:template match="PET">
  <xsl:message>
    Warning: Displaying information on pets is not yet implemented
  </xsl:message>
</xsl:template>
```

Control of Flow

Like most programming languages, XSLT includes a few keywords to let you control the flow of the processing. These include the if/then construct, while loops and some extras. Like anything in XSLT, these features are implemented as XML elements.

if

The if element does one of the most common things in programming – checking a condition and executing an action if the condition is met. A simple example is:

```
<xsl:template match="AUTHOR">
  <xsl:if test="@name">
    <I><xsl:value-of select="@name"/></I>
  </xsl:if>
</xsl:template>
```

The if element has a test attribute. If the XPath expression in it returns false (an empty node list), the content of the element is not executed. In the example, the XPath query @name returns true if an attribute with name name exists. The if element cannot be combined with an else element (as is common in many languages). If you need an else, you have to use the choose/when/otherwise construct. Several if elements can be used nested.

choose/when/otherwise

For more complex choices the choose, when and otherwise elements can be used. The elements when and otherwise can only be used within a choose element. The processor will check every when element from the top down. A when element works exactly like an if element. The first time the test attribute returns true, the content of that when element is executed. After this, the processor jumps past the choose element without further checking. If none of the when elements can be executed, the otherwise element will be executed (if there is one).

```
<xsl:template match="AUTHOR">
  <xsl:choose>
    <xsl:when test="@name = 'Duynstee'">
      <B><xsl:value-of select="@name"/></B>
    </xsl:when>
    <xsl:when test="@name">
```

```
      <I><xsl:value-of select="@name"/></I>
   </xsl:when>
   <xsl:otherwise>
     No name available
   </xsl:otherwise>
  <xsl:choose>
 </xsl:template>
```

In this example, the name attribute of the AUTHOR element we are processing is first checked for being 'Duynstee'. If it is, the value of the attribute is generated in the output as content of a B element and the processor jumps past the xsl:choose element in the stylesheet. If it is not, the next check is performed. If this is the case, the value of the name attribute is generated as content of an I element. If the second check fails too, then (and only then) will the processor execute the content of the xsl:otherwise element, which means generating the string 'No name available'.

for-each

For looping through a set of nodes, XSLT specifies the for-each element. The for-each element has a select attribute holding an XPath expression. The content of the for-each element is executed for each result from this query. Inside the loop, the context is moved to the current result set element.

```
<xsl:template match="PUBLISHER">
<xsl:for-each select="child::BOOK">
  <xsl:value-of select="attribute::title"/>
  <xsl:for-each select="child::AUTHOR">
     <xsl:value-of select="attribute::name"/>
  </ xsl:for-each>
  <xsl:text>&#13;</xsl:text><!--Insert a new line after each book -->
</ xsl:for-each>

</xsl:template>
```

In this example, for-each elements are nested. Because the context moves with the for-each loop, the select attribute of the inner loop is evaluated in the context of the results of the outer loop. This is of course what you would expect.

Note that there is not much difference between an apply-templates element with an appropriate template and a for-each loop. Basically, a for-each loop is an in-line template. However, a for-each loop is generally more easy to read, but separating the content over several templates makes reuse of the inner template easier.

sort

Whenever XSLT iterates along a set of nodes, it can be useful to set the order of iteration. By default this is always document order, but the destination format may expect another order (or you are transforming data to HTML and you need to display it in a set order).

Sorting can be used on the elements apply-templates and for-each. The sort element is inserted as a child element of the apply-templates or for-each element. Consider this example:

```
<xsl:template match="FAMILY">
  <xsl:apply-templates select="PERSON">
    <xsl:sort select="@lastname"/>
    <xsl:sort select="@firstname"/>
```

```
    </xsl:apply-templates>
  </xsl:template>
```

The `select` attribute holds an XPath expression. This expression is evaluated for each of the nodes in the set. The result of this expression determines the position in the sorted set.

By inserting multiple `sort` elements, the result set can be sorted primarily on the first criterion, and secondarily on the second one. In this case, the `apply-templates` element selects a set of all PERSON elements. These are sorted first on their `lastname` attribute, then on their `firstname` attribute. Only after the sorting does the XSLT processor start searching for the appropriate matching templates.

A number of extra optional attributes can be used with the `sort` element. The most important ones are:

❑ `order`, for specifying 'ascending' or 'descending' sort order.

❑ `data-type`, for sorting numerically or alphabetically. The default is alphabetically, causing 10 to be smaller than 9. Available values for `data-type` are 'text' and 'number'. Other values can also be used, but the meaning is not specified by the XSLT specification.

❑ `case-order`, for specifying lower first or upper-first. When case-order is lower-first, A sorts after a. There is no functionality for case insensitivity.

Variables and Parameters

Once you have read this section, you will have found out that its title is a bit deceptive. You, as a programmer, have certain expectations about a new programming language when you start learning it. One of them is that you expect it to be possible to store values in variables, change them and retrieve them later. Although XSLT has an element called `variable`, you actually cannot do much with it. This may sound unbelievable, but it is a result of the way XSLT works that you cannot have variables. This is a thing that beginner XSLT programmers have many difficulties grasping.

variable

A variable in XSLT is really not what we would call a variable in VB, but more like a constant. The syntax for declaring a variable is like this:

```
<xsl:variable name="x" select="2"/>
```

Or you can declare it like this:

```
<xsl:variable name="x">2</xsl:variable>
```

These syntaxes are equivalent, but note that the first example uses an XPath expression and the second one uses an included fragment of XML. This causes the first variable to hold the numeric value 2 and the second one the string value '2'.

The value of a `variable` can be used in expressions and attribute value templates. The reference to a variable's value is done with `$variablename`, for example:

```
<xsl:variable name="x" value="2"/>
...
<xsl:value-of select="item[$x]"/>

<xsl:variable name="author">Teun Duynstee</xsl:variable>
...
<xsl:copy-of select="$author"/>
```

The copy-of element is a convenient way to insert the value of a variable into the output document.

A variable can be used both as a top-level element (*child* of the stylesheet element) and at template level (*descendant* of a template element). As a top-level element, the variable can be used from any place in the document. Within the template, the variable can be seen by all elements following the declaration (and their descendants).

In conclusion, the variable element doesn't really live up to its name, because it cannot change. There is no way to change the content. This is done by design. The XSLT specification does not want to specify any order for the evaluation of different nodes. By introducing changing values, it would become relevant for the result whether a certain action is performed *before* or *after* the change.

param

The param element works very much like the variable element. The param element has a name attribute and a select attribute, but the select attribute on the param element is only a default value. If a value is passed, this replaces the value in the select attribute.

Passing a Parameter to a Template

If a template has a parameter defined, a value can be passed when the template is executed (by apply-templates or call-template). Suppose you have this template:

```
<xsl:template name="numbered-item">
<xsl:param name="format" select="1. "/>
  <xsl:number format="{$format}"/>
<xsl:apply-templates/>
</xsl:template>
```

If you call it using call-template, its index number would be formatted numerically (1.). But we could also have the same template output the number in another format using the parameter format (which is used in the attribute value template in the number element):

```
<xsl:template match="OL/LI">
<xsl:call-template name="numbered-item">
  <xsl:if test="@count = 'alpha'">
    <xsl:with-param name="format" select="'a. '"/>
  </xsl:if>
</xsl:call-template>
</xsl:template>
```

This template will match on LI elements that have an OL parent. The transformation of these elements is implemented in the template 'numbered-item'. Only if the matched element has a count attribute with value 'alpha' does the template get called with a passed parameter value. This will cause the called template to output the number of the element in another format.

The with-param element can be used as a child of call-template and apply-templates. The name must be specified; the value can also be specified with the content of the element (just like the variable and param elements can).

Passing a Parameter to a Stylesheet

Although the XSLT specification defines a way to declare global parameters, nothing is mentioned about passing a parameter to the stylesheet. This depends on the implementation of the library you use. The SAXON and XT implementations both allow passing parameters on the command line. In the developers preview of MSXML, you can set a parameter to a stylesheet only by using the special XMLDOMXSLProcessor object. This object is new in the MSXML library and is intended to cache compiled stylesheets to improve performance for repeated transforms with the same stylesheet. If your stylesheet contains a parameter called $x, the following code could be used to make the transformation:

```
Dim oDoc as new MSXML2.DOMDocument
Dim oXSLT as new MSXML2.DOMDocument
Dim oResult as new MSXML2.DOMDocument
Dim oTemplate as new MSXML2.XSLTemplate
Dim oXMLDOMXSLProcessor as new MSXML2.XMLDOMXSLProcessor

oDoc.async = false
oXSLT.async = false

oDoc.load "http://www.comp.com/sourceDocument.xml"
oXSLT.load "http://www.comp.com/stylesheet.xsl"

Set oTemplate.stylesheet = oXSLT.documentElement

Set oXMLDOMXSLProcessor = oTemplate.createProcessor
Set oXMLDOMXSLProcessor.input = oDoc
Set oXMLDOMXSLProcessor.output = oResult

oXMLDOMXSLProcessor.addParameter("x", "Value we want to pass in")
oXMLDOMXSLProcessor.transform
```

There are quite a lot of objects that we need here, three DOMDocument objects for starters. One of them may be empty. It is the target for the transform (oResult). The second one contains the source document (oDoc) and the third one contains the stylesheet (oXSLT). oXSLT is used to build the right template object. This template is used to create an XMLDOMXSLProcessor object. We inform the processor about the input and output documents, and then finally add our parameter value and let it transform. As this library is by no means stable at the time of writing – it is only a preview after all – it is very possible (so indicates the preliminary documentation) that the syntax will be different in the final release. In any case, the functionality of passing parameters *will* be included in that release.

Top Level Settings

The top-level settings are a set of elements that can only be used at the top level of an XSLT document, and hold settings that specify how the stylesheet should be used. They specify the behavior of the processor on a few points.

output

The output element is a bag of attributes that indicate settings about the style of output that is generated. The main setting is defined in the method attribute. The possible values are xml, html and text.

xml

If the method is set to xml, the output document will be an XML document. What this means depends largely on the other attributes of the output element:

❑ The version attribute specifies which version of XML should be used – we only have version 1.0 now, but that will probably change in the future. This number will also appear in the XML declaration if one is generated. The default version is 1.0.

❑ The encoding attribute sets the preferred encoding for the destination document. If it is not specified, XSLT processors will use UTF-8 or UTF-16. If an XML declaration is generated, this will contain the encoding string specified.

❑ The indent attribute can be set to yes to allow the processor to include additional whitespace in the destination document. This can improve readability. The default setting is no.

❑ The attribute cdata-section-elements tells the processor when to use CDATA sections in the destination and when to escape illegal characters by using entity references. The value can hold a whitespace-separated list of element names. Text nodes that have a parent node in this list will be output as CDATA sections. All others will be escaped (characters like < will be replaced by entities like <).

❑ omit-xml-declaration can be set to yes to leave out the XML declaration. By default, XSLT will include one, reflecting the settings of encoding and version. Also, if the standalone attribute has any value, this value will show up in the XML declaration.

❑ With the doctype-system and doctype-public attributes, the validation rules for the destination document can be set. If you use only doctype-system, the processor will include a <!DOCTYPE fragment just before the first element. The doctype will be the name of the root element. The system identifier (URL of the DTD) is the value of the doctype-system attribute. If you also specify a doctype-public attribute, the output will contain a doctype declaration referring to a public DOCTYPE, with the value of doctype-system as its URL. If only doctype-public is used, it will be ignored.

❑ Finally, the media-type attribute can be used to specify a MIME-type for the result. By default this is text/xml, but some XML-based document types may have their own MIME types installed.

html

If the method attribute on the output element is set to html, the results of some of the other attributes change a bit compared to the xml method.

❑ The version attribute now refers to the version of HTML, with a default value of 4.0. The processor will try to make the output conform to the HTML specification.

❑ Empty elements in the destination document will be outputted without a closing tag. Think of HTML elements like BR, HR, IMG, INPUT, LINK, META and PARAM.

❑ Textual content of the script and style elements will not be escaped. So if the XSLT document contains this literal fragment:

```
<script>if (a &gt; b) doSomething()</script>
```

This will be output as:

```
<script>if (a > b) doSomething()</script>
```

❑ If any non-ASCII characters are used, the processor should try to use HTML escaping in the output (ë instead of ë).

❑ If an encoding is specified, the processor will try to add a META element to the HEAD of the document. This will also contain the value for media-type (default is text/html).

```
<HEAD>
<META http-equiv="Content-Type" content="text/html; charset=EUC-JP">
. . .
```

text

If the method attribute is set to text, the output will be restricted to only the string value of every node. The media-type defaults to text/plain, but you can use other MIME types. Think of generating RTF documents from an XML source document. These have no XML mark up, so the most appropriate method is text, with media-type set to application/msword. The encoding attribute can still be used, but the default value is system dependent (on most Windows PCs it will be ISO-8859-1).

Let's have a look at an example. The following stylesheet is used:

```
<?xml version="1.0" encoding="ISO-8859-1"?>
<xsl:stylesheet xmlns:xsl="http://www.w3.org/1999/XSL/Transform">
<xsl:output method="text" indent="yes"/>
<xsl:template match="/">
  <HTML><BODY>
    <TEST>
      This is literal text with an ëxtended character
      <BR/>
      <TABLE>
        <TR><TD>Cell data</TD>
        <TD>Second cell</TD></TR>
      </TABLE>
    </TEST>
  </BODY></HTML>
</xsl:template>
</xsl:stylesheet>
```

We use this stylesheet on an arbitrary, valid XML document. Note that the output will always be the same literal XML tree. We will now only change the output method and have a look at the result. First the result for the xml method:

```
<?xml version="1.0" encoding="utf-8"?>
<HTML>
<BODY>
<TEST>This is literal text with an ëxtended character
    <BR/>
<TABLE>
<TR>
<TD>Cell data</TD>
<TD>Second cell</TD>
</TR>
</TABLE>
</TEST>
</BODY>
</HTML>
```

Note that every element starts on a new line. This is the result of the `indent="yes"` attribute. If this had not been specified, all content would be concatenated on one line. This XSLT processor has defaulted its output to encoding UTF-8. UTF-8 supports the extended character ë, so this is not escaped.

Setting the method to `html` would generate:

```
<HTML>
<BODY>
<TEST>This is literal text with an &euml;xtended character
    <BR>
<TABLE>
<TR>
<TD>Cell data</TD><TD>Second cell</TD>
</TR>
</TABLE>
</TEST>
</BODY>
</HTML>
```

Note that the XML declaration has disappeared and the processor appears to have decided on a slightly different formatting around the TD elements. The processor has been assigned to indenting the resulting document, but in `html` mode, this may only be done in places that cannot influence the appearance of the document in a browser. Also, the ë character cannot be used in HTML, so it is escaped using the preferred HTML entity `&euml;` (not the numeric XML entity).

Using the `text` method, the result would be:

```
This is literal text with an ëxtended character
    Cell dataSecond cell
```

Only the string values of the nodes have been printed. The specified encoding is used, so the special character is no problem. Note that no whitespace appears between the values of the two TD elements. We will see more on whitespace in the next sections.

strip-space and preserve-space

What exactly happens to the whitespace in a document and in the XSLT document itself? This is one of the subjects that often puzzle XML developers. Spaces, tabs and linefeeds seem to emerge and disappear at random. And then there are the XSLT elements to influence them: `strip-space`, `preserve-space` and the `indent` attribute on the `output` element. Let's take a closer look.

During a transformation, there are basically two moments when whitespace can appear or vanish:

- When parsing the source and stylesheet documents and constructing a tree
- Encoding a generated XML tree to the destination document

Before any processing occurs, the XSLT processor loads the source and stylesheet into memory and starts to strip unnecessary whitespace. The parser removes all text nodes that:

- Consist entirely of whitespace characters
- Have no ancestor node with the `xml:space` attribute set to `preserve`
- Are not children of a whitespace-preserving element

For the stylesheet, the only whitespace-preserving parent element is `xsl:text`. For the source element, the list of whitespace-preserving elements can be set using the `strip-space` and `preserve-space` elements from the stylesheet. By default, all elements in the source document preserve whitespace. With the `elements` attribute of `strip-space`, you can specify which elements should not preserve whitespace. Adding elements to the list of elements that have their whitespace preserved is done with `preserve-space`. The `elements` attributes accept a list of XPath expressions. If an element in the source matches multiple expressions, the conflict is resolved following the rules for conflicts between matching templates.

So if a stylesheet contained these whitespace elements:

```
<xsl:strip-space elements="*"/>
<xsl:preserve-space elements="PRE CODE"/>
```

the processor would strip all text nodes in the source document, except for those inside a PRE element or a CODE element.

After stripping space from the source and stylesheet documents, the processing occurs. The generated tree of nodes is then persisted to a string or file. By default, no new whitespace is added to the result document, except if the `output` element has its `indent` attribute set to `yes`.

attribute-set

On the document level, it is possible to define certain groups of attributes that you need to include in many elements together. By grouping them, the XSLT document can be smaller and easier to maintain:

```
<xsl:template match="chapter/heading">
  <font xsl:use-attribute-sets="title-style">
    <xsl:apply-templates/>
  </font>
```

```
  </xsl:template>

  <xsl:attribute-set name="title-style">
    <xsl:attribute name="size">3</xsl:attribute>
    <xsl:attribute name="face">Arial</xsl:attribute>
  </xsl:attribute-set>
```

Here the `attribute-set` element defines a group of two attributes that are often used together. In the template for chapter headings, the `attribute-set` is applied to a literal element, but `use-attribute-set` can also be used on `element`, `copy` and `attribute-set` elements. Be careful not to use `use-attribute-set` by itself (directly or indirectly), as this would generate an error.

namespace-alias

The `namespace-alias` element is used in very special cases, especially when transforming a source document to an XSLT document. In this case, you want the destination document to hold the XSLT namespace and lots of literal XSLT elements, but you don't want these to interfere with the transformation process. See the problem? You are shooting yourself in the foot there.

Using `namespace-alias`, you can use another namespace in the stylesheet, but have the declaration for that namespace show up in the destination document with another URI:

```
<xsl:stylesheet version="1.0" xmlns:xsl="http://www.w3.org/1999/XSL/Transform"
xmlns:axsl="http://www.w3.org/1999/XSL/TransformAlias">

<xsl:namespace-alias stylesheet-prefix="axsl" result-prefix="xsl"/>

<xsl:template match="/">
  <axsl:stylesheet>
    <xsl:apply-templates/>
  </axsl:stylesheet>
</xsl:template>
...
</xsl:stylesheet>
```

Instead of declaring the literal XSLT output elements in their real namespace, they have a fake namespace in this document. In the destination document, the same prefixes will be used, but they will refer to another URI:

```
<?xml version="1.0" encoding="utf-8"?>
<axsl:stylesheet xmlns:axsl="http://www.w3.org/1999/XSL/Transform">
...
</axsl:stylesheet>
```

key

The `key` element is a very special one. It will take a little time to discover its full potential. It is more or less analogous to creating an index on a table in a relational database. It allows you to access a set of nodes in a document directly with the `key()` function, using an identifier of that node that you specify. Let's describe an example. We could, using the `key` element, define that the key `person-by-name` gives us access to PERSON elements by passing the value of their name attribute. If the `key` is set up correctly, we would use `key('person-by-name', 'Teun')` to get a result set of PERSON elements that have their name attribute set to 'Teun'.

To set this key, you would have used the element like this:

```
<xsl:key name="person-by-name" match="PERSON" use="@name"/>
```

Try to see what each of the attributes name, match and use specifies. The name attribute is simple: it just serves to refer to a specific key of which there may be many. The match attribute holds a pattern that nodes must match to be indexed by this key; this pattern is identical to the template match attribute. It is not a problem if the same node is indexed by multiple keys. For each node in the selected set, the XPath expression in the use attribute is evaluated. The string value of the result of this expression is used to retrieve the indexed node. Multiple nodes can have the same result when evaluating use in their context. When the key function is called with this value, it will return a result set holding all nodes that had this result. The result can be a node set. In this case, each of the nodes will be converted to a string and each of these strings can be used to retrieve the selected node.

Don't worry if you can't see the point of this yet. We will do an extensive example on this. Suppose we have this XML document:

```
<?xml version="1.0"?>
<FAMILY>
  <TRADITIONAL_NAMES>
    <NAME>Peter</NAME>
    <NAME>Mary</NAME>
  </TRADITIONAL_NAMES>
  <PERSON name="Peter">
    <CHILDREN>
      <PERSON name="Peter"/>
      <PERSON name="Archie"/>
    </CHILDREN>
  </PERSON>
</FAMILY>
```

We are transforming the XML source with an XSLT document that starts like this:

```
<?xml version="1.0" encoding="ISO-8859-1"?>
<xsl:stylesheet  version="1.0"  xmlns:xsl="http://www.w3.org/1999/XSL/Transform" >

<xsl:key name="all-names" match="PERSON" use="@name"/>
<xsl:key name="parents-names" match="PERSON[CHILDREN/PERSON]" use="@name"/>
...
```

If we now use the key() function, our results will be:

Expression Used in key()	Result
key('all-names', 'Peter')	Both PERSON elements with name="Peter"
key('parent-names', 'Peter')	Only the Peter that has children
key('all-names', /FAMILY/TRADITIONAL_NAMES/NAME)	Both Peters, because Peter is one of the traditional names in the family

Now what are the cases where using a key is a good idea? Think of situations where XML elements often refer to each other using some sort of ID, but without using the validation rules for IDs (because these are sometimes too rigid). The key construct can:

❏   Keep your code more readable.

❏   Depend on the implementation, which may help performance. The XSLT processor can keep a hash-table structure in memory of all key references in the source document. If these references are often used, performance gains can be substantial.

Built-in Functions

XSLT has defined a set of built-in functions that can be used in expressions. These are complementary to the functions already available through XPath. These XPath functions include string functions like starts-with(), numeric functions like sum() and others like id(). These have been covered earlier in this chapter. We will not describe all available XSLT functions here; we will just select a few. You can find all functions in Appendix D.

format-number(number, string, string)

The format-number function converts the numeric first argument to a string. To do this, it uses the second argument as a format specifier and the third (optional) argument as a reference to a decimal-format element. First, we will look how the function behaves if we do not specify our own decimal formats. Say we leave the third parameter out. The format that we can pass to the second parameter can hold two formats at a time: one for positive numbers, one for negative numbers. They are separated by the semicolon. The format is built up from these special characters:

Symbol	Meaning
0	digit
#	digit, hides leading and trailing zeroes
.	decimal separator
,	grouping separator
–	negative prefix
%	multiply by 100 and show as percentage
‰	multiply by 1000 and show per mille
X	any other character can serve as prefix or suffix

So using this function would give the following results:

Numeric Value	Format	Result String
2	DM .00	DM 2.00
2	DM ##.00	DM 2.00

Numeric Value	Format	Result String
12.3456	000.00	012.35
12.3456	.##	12.35
123.456	##,##.##	1,23.46
0.456	##.##%	45.6%

Different countries use different characters for separating the decimal part of a floating-point number from the integer part and for grouping the digits. That's why XSLT allows you to change the special characters to other symbols. This can be done by including an xsl:decimal-format element as a top level element in your document. The format-number function can refer to this decimal format by name. Consider this example:

```
<xsl:decimal-format
  name = qname
  decimal-separator = char
  grouping-separator = char
  infinity = string
  minus-sign = char
  NaN = string
  percent = char
  per-mille = char
  zero-digit = char
  digit = char
  pattern-separator = char />
```

The name attribute is for referring to the format from a format-number function. All other attributes are for overruling the default character. This new character must be used in specifying the format string and will also be the output character:

```
<xsl:stylesheet version="1.0"  xmlns:xsl="http://www.w3.org/1999/XSL/Transform" >

<xsl:decimal-format name="numfrmt" decimal-separator="," grouping-separator="." />

<xsl:template match="/">
<xsl:value-of select="format-number(1567.8, '#.###,00', 'numfrmt')"/>
</xsl:template>

</xsl:stylesheet>
```

The output of this stylesheet will be 1.567,80.

current()

The current() function returns the current context. This can be very useful inside subqueries in XPath expressions. It allows you to make constructs in an XPath expression that are similar to SQL inner joins, combining and comparing values from different contexts. Suppose we have this XML document:

```
<?xml version="1.0"?>
<Music>
  <Song>
    <title>Dancing in the street</title>
    <artist>David Bowie</artist>
    <artist>Mick Jagger</artist>
  </Song>
  <Song>
    <title>State of shock</title>
    <artist>Michael Jackson</artist>
    <artist>Mick Jagger</artist>
  </Song>
...
```

We want to generate a list of all songs in the collection with their artists, but for every artist we want to include a link to the other songs in the collection that the artist performs. We will make the list in HTML, creating links from the artist's songs to the entry of that song. To do this, we use a template for the artist element like this:

```
<xsl:template match="artist">
  <xsl:for-each
    select="//Song[artist/text() = current()/text()]
            [title != current()/ancestor::Song/title]
            ">
    <a>
      <xsl:attribute name="href">#Song<xsl:number/></xsl:attribute>
      <xsl:value-of select="title"/>
    </a><br/>
  </xsl:for-each>
</xsl:template>
```

It generates a piece of XML looking like this:

```
<a href="#Song3">Under pressure</a>
<br>
<a href="#Song4">Knock on wood</a>
<br>
```

The essential part here is the XPath expression in the for-each element. It selects the set of all song elements and filters the set by introducing two predicates.

The first predicate: [artist/text() = current()/text()] checks if the text of the artist element (relative to the selected song element) is equal to the text of the current context. The current context is the context of the for-each element, not the context of the predicate. This will select those song elements that have an artist element with the same name as the current artist. This will include the current song (which obviously has the same title as the current song).

The second predicate: [title != current()/ancestor::Song/title] checks if the title of the predicate's context (a song element) is equal to the title of our current context's song ancestor. The element is included in the filtered set if the titles are not equal. The function of this predicate is to remove the song itself from the list of references to other songs. The complete stylesheet, called artist.xsl, can be downloaded from the Wrox web site.

document(object, node-set)

The document() function is specified to combine information from several documents into one destination document. Suppose you have a directory with a load of articles in XML format. All have references to other documents in the same directory. The part that defines the references to other articles looks like:

```
<Article>
  <Authors>
    <Author>Teun Duynstee </Author>
  </Authors>
  <Title>An interesting article </Title>
  <Intro> ... </Intro>
  <Body> ... </Body>
  <Related>
    <Item type="URL" loc="http://www.asptoday.com/art2">Some other article</Item>
    <Item type="local" loc="2"/>
  </Related>
</Article>
```

As you can see, there are two kinds of references; references by URL and local references. The local references point to other articles of the same format in the same directory. The files are called art1.xml, art2.xml, etc... The local reference in the example refers to art2.xml (indicated by loc="2").

What we would like to do now is to generate HTML documents that display a styled version of the XML article. The referenced articles are particularly tricky. We want them to appear like this:

❑ Some other article [external]

❑ A great article (by: James Britt)

Note how the first article is displayed using only content from within the source document, while the second reference displays data about the referenced document that is not available in the source (the title and author). How is this done?

```
<xsl:template match="Item">
  <xsl:if test="@type='URL'">
    <a href="{@loc}"><xsl:value-of select="."/></a>
  </xsl:if>
  <xsl:if test="@type='local'">
    <a href="art{@loc}.xml"><xsl:value-of select="document(concat('art', @loc,
    '.xml'))/Article/Title"/></a>
    (by: <xsl:apply-templates select="document(concat('art', @loc,
    '.xml'))/Article/Authors/Author"/>)
  </xsl:if>
  <br/>
</xsl:template>
```

The template for Item elements is split into two parts. The first part is executed if an Item has type='URL'. This generated an HTML link with the loc attribute as its href attribute and the contained text as its title. This is simple – we've done this before. Note the use of an attribute value template in the literal element a.

The second part of the template is more interesting. If the type of the reference is `local`, then the `href` is constructed in a specific way, concatenating a string together. Now for the title of the referred document: from the `select` attribute of a `value-of` element, we call the `document` function, passing it the relative URL and a small XPath expression, indicating the fragment that is referred to. The result is that the `value-of` action is executed on the title of the referred document, effectively outputting the content of the `title` element. After that, you see the `apply-templates` being used with a remote fragment.

In this example, we used only one parameter, a string value. It is also possible to pass in a node set. If you do so, the `document()` function will convert all nodes to their string values and use these as URIs. The `document()` function then returns a node set of external documents. The second, optional, parameter indicates the base URI to use for relative URI references.

generate-id(node-set)

The `generate-id()` function does just what you would expect: it generates a unique identifier. The identifier is always a string of alphanumeric characters, making sure that it can be used as an XML qualified name (think of filling an ID type attribute). The identifier depends on the first element in the passed node set. If no node set is passed, the context node is used. The implementation is free to choose any convenient way to generate a unique string, as long as it is always the same string for the same node.

Simplified Syntax

For very simple stylesheets that consist of only one template matching the root, a special simplified syntax is specified. In this simplified syntax, the whole document is the content of the template. The stylesheets that can use this simplified syntax are often doing transformations, mostly consisting of literals defining a template document. Only a few values from the source document are entered in specific locations.

The XML documents defining an article's content could be transformed by this stylesheet:

```
<HTML xmlns:xsl="http://www.w3.org/1999/XSL/Transform">
<BODY>
<H1><xsl:value-of select="/Article/Title"/></H1>
<p><b><xsl:value-of select="/Article/Intro"/></b></p>
<p><xsl:value-of select="/Article/Body"/></p>
</BODY></HTML>
```

XSLT Language Extensions

XSLT processor vendors are free to add their own private extensions to the language. The XSLT specification even specifies how they should indicate if an extension element or extension function is supported by their implementation.

In the stylesheet, certain namespaces can be specified to be XSLT extension namespaces with the `xsl:extension-element-prefixes` attribute on the `stylesheet` element. Elements in those namespaces will be processed using the extensions of the used processor.

If the stylesheet author wants to know if the processor supports a certain extension element, the function `element-available()` can be called with the element name as the parameter. If the processor supports this element, the function should return true.

The same information can be retrieved about extension functions using the `function-available()` function.

The IE5 Implementation

When Microsoft released Internet Explorer 5.0, it wanted to ship with it an XML parser that conformed as much as possible to all XML-related standards at that time. XSLT was at that time still a part of the XSL working draft. The XSLT support in IE5 is based on the transformations chapter in the working draft of December 1998. They did quite a good job, but the specification moved on, split itself in two, and by now the MSXML implementation is a very weak and non-compliant version of the now final recommendation of XSLT 1.0. This IE5 implementation of MSXML is version 2.0.

Microsoft has announced that the full specification will be supported in a next release. At the time of printing this book, at least a developers preview is available (called MSXML 2.6). This preview implements the standards much better, but still a lot remains to be done. More information can be found from http://msdn.microsoft.com/downloads/webtechnology/xml/msxml.asp.

The new implementation will support both the W3C XSLT 1.0 recommendation as well as the MSXML 2.0 implementation. Which implementation is used depends on the namespace of the `stylesheet` elements. The MSXML 2.0 implementation uses the namespace:

```
xmlns:xsl="http://www.w3.org/TR/WD-xsl
```

In Appendix D, you can see for each element if it is supported in IE5 (the MSXML 2.0 library). Here we will try to give you a notion of what is unsupported, what is ill-supported and what works fine.

Complete Implementation

MSXML 2.0 does a good job on:

- ❑ Literal elements and attributes
- ❑ The `element` element, the `attribute` element, the `comment` element
- ❑ The `choose`, `when` and `otherwise` elements
- ❑ The `for-each` element
- ❑ The `if` element

Partially Implemented

Some elements can be used in most cases, but fail to support more complex uses or certain attributes. These include:

- ❑ `apply-templates`: you cannot use the mode attribute.
- ❑ `template`: you cannot use the name attribute and the mode attribute. The priority rules are not implemented (see the section entitled '*What if Several Templates Match?*').

❑   `processing-instruction`: is called pi in MSXML 2.0.

❑   `stylesheet`: IE5 does not support any of the attributes for the `stylesheet` element. Note that the `version` attribute is defined as required in XSLT.

❑   `value-of`: `disable-output-escaping` is not supported. See below for undocumented tricks to do this anyway.

The XPath expressions that can be used in lots of places in XSLT are only partially implemented. Basically only the shorthand notation is supported. For details, see the XPath section earlier in this chapter.

Unsupported

The following elements are not supported in MSXML 2.0:

❑   `apply-imports`, `import`, `include`

❑   `attribute-set` (and the related attributes)

❑   `call-template`

❑   `copy-of`

❑   `key`

❑   `number`

❑   `param`, `with-param`, `variable`

❑   `sort` (MSXML 2.0 has implemented attributes on some elements to allow sorting)

❑   `text` (MSXML 2.0 has an undocumented `cdata` element that does more or less the same)

❑   `transform` (which is the same thing as `stylesheet` anyway)

❑   and a whole bunch of top level elements

Although this is a fairly long list, most of these unimplemented elements are the kind you will rarely use anyway. Some of them, however, are dearly missed.

Most of the specified *additional* functions that can be used in XSLT are unsupported in IE5. At the same time, MSXML 2.0 features some functions that can be very useful in overcoming these shortcomings.

There are some unsupported standard functions:

❑   `document()`

❑   `key()`

❑   `generate-id()`:MSXML 2.0 has a function available called `uniqueID()` that can do the same

❑   `format-number()`

MSXML 2.0 has a `formatNumber()` function that works almost identically, except for localization using a `decimal-format` element

❑   current():

> IE5 has a very powerful context() function. This can be used to do the same. context(-1) is equivalent to current().

Tricks for using MSXML 2.0

Although MSXML 2.0 has some limitations compared to the full XSLT specification, it is still a very useful transformation tool. When using it, there are some problems that all developers stumble into. The developer community has been looking for solutions and work-arounds for almost two years now. These are a few of the most important ones.

Output Escaping Off

If you have an XML document containing a piece of text that should appear literally in the output, you can run into trouble. The XML parser and XSLT processor will replace some characters with XML entities, to keep the output well-formed. That is fine, but sometimes we don't care whether the output is well-formed, we just want that exact string to appear in the output. The output is not supposed to be XML anyway – it might be HTML. XSLT allows us to do so by using the disable-output-escaping on the value-of and text elements. IE5 does not support disable-output-escaping, but it does allow the use of an undocumented attribute: no-entities='true' on the eval element. We can use this to generate unescaped content, for example, using the following code:

```
<Author>Teun <![CDATA[<BR>]]> Duynstee </Author>
```

with the following template:

```
<xsl:template match="Author/text()">
  <xsl:eval no-entities='true'>this.nodeValue</xsl:eval>
</xsl:template>
```

This would generate this output:

```
Teun <BR> Duynstee
```

Note that this is not well-formed XML, but that was exactly what we where trying to do. But this also means that we must be very careful using this feature. Note also that this feature is undocumented, so Microsoft might remove it from future versions just when you least expect it.

Local Templates

IE5 does not support modes and calling templates by name, but it does allow something else: **locally scoped templates**. These can be included as a child element of an apply-templates element and the processor will try to use this template before any of the globally scoped templates. Look at this sample:

```
<xsl:template match="Author">
  <b><xsl.value of/></b>
</xsl:template>

<xsl:template match="/">
```

```
<xsl:apply-templates select="//Author"/>
<xsl:apply-templates select="//Author">
  <xsl:template match="Author">
    <i><xsl:value-of/></i>
  </xsl:template>
</xsl:apply-templates>
</xsl:template>
```

The stylesheet has a template defined for use with `Author` elements. It generates a b element with the `Author` element's content in it. The root template performs two `apply-template` actions on all authors in the source document. The first one will match on the template for `Author` elements and output the following:

```
<b>Teun Duynstee</b>
```

The second `apply-templates` element has a template defined locally. This local template also matches the selected nodes, so the second `apply-templates` element will generate:

```
<i>Teun Duynstee</i>
```

XSLT Examples

Let's have a look at some more examples to demonstrate the use of XSLT. In the last part of this section, we will look at using XSLT to style an XML document in HTML. There will be more examples there. Here we will cover examples that are not HTML-related, but targeted to converting one XML dialect into another. This will be a very common case in business-to-business e-commerce, where XML documents containing orders, inventories, product descriptions, etc., are sent automatically and converted on the fly to a format that is suitable for the target system.

Product Information Import

Think of a system that retrieves product descriptions from several suppliers to present users in the organization with a coherent view of all available products. Some of these suppliers will have their product range available in an XML format. In an ideal world, an agreement could be made with all suppliers about the format used for delivering the data. Unfortunately, in the real world suppliers will not be willing to do that, the user will have to settle for what he can get. Some will conform to an industry standard but, in the end, transformation from some other format to that which is required will be necessary.

The format that can be natively imported by our application looks like this:

```
<?xml version="1.0"?>
<Product>
  <ID>21456</ID>
  <Name>
    Nail clipper
  </Name>
  <Product_category>Personal care</Product_category>
  <Supplier>
    <Name>Clippers Inc.</Name>
    <Address>
```

```
        <Street_address>
        234, Wood lane
        Humblestown, MA
        </Street_address>
        <Country>USA</Country>
      </Address>
      <Contact>Macy Marble</Contact>
    </Supplier>
  </Product>
```

The XML descriptions we receive from Clippers Inc look like this:

```
<Clipper product-reference="21456">
  <FullName>Solid quality nail clipper, San Juanito steel</FullName>
  <Short>Nail clipper</Short>
</Clipper>
```

We want to transform this delivered format into our native format using XSLT. We could create a stylesheet for the transformation like this:

```
<xsl:stylesheet xmlns:xsl="http://www.w3.org/1999/XSL/Transform">

  <xsl:template match="/">
    <Product>
      <ID><xsl:value-of select="Clipper/@product-reference"/></ID>
      <Name>
        <xsl:value-of select="Clipper/short"/>
      </Name>
      <Product_category>Personal care</Product_category>
      <xsl:copy-of
        select="document('http://ourserver/supplier_lookup.xml')/suppliers/supplier
        [Name = 'Clippers Inc.']"/>
    </Product>
  </xsl:template>

</xsl:stylesheet>
```

Let's have a look at the sample little by little. There is only one template, matching the root. This template contains a framework for the output document. The Product element and its ID child element are inserted as literals. The value of the ID element is fetched from the source document, by inserting the value of the product-reference attribute from the source. The same thing is done for the name. We create a name element with literals and insert a value from the source document in it. Note that we chose to use the short name from the source and discard the long name. The Product_category element is hard-coded. We expect only products in this category from this supplier.

Now comes the hard part. The supplier information is not provided in this case. Some suppliers will, some will not. We could choose to hard-code the supplier information in the stylesheet. But that would force us to update the stylesheet every time the supplier changes its address or we get a new contact person. We decided to store all supplier information in our own format in one file. While transforming the document, the processor does a lookup in the supplier_lookup.xml document and copies a whole fragment from that document to the destination document using copy-of.

Author Summary

Our second example is for a publishing company; all books are stored in a giant XML document (in fact it is stored in a database, but this database allows access to the data as if it were an XML document). A fragment of this document looks like:

```
<publisher>
  <books>
    <book>
      <title>Stranger in a strange land</title>
      <ISBN>0441788386</ISBN>
      <author-ref ref="rh"/>
      <sold>2300000</sold>
    </book>

    <book>
      <title>Starman Jones</title>
      <ISBN>0345328116 </ISBN>
      <author-ref ref="rh"/>
      <author-ref ref="jldr"/>
      <sold>80000</sold>
    </book>
    ...

  </books>
  <authors>
    <author id="rh">
      <first_name>Robert</first_name>
      <last_name>Heinlein</last_name>
    </author>
    <author id="jldr">
      <first_name>Judy-Lyn</first_name>
      <last_name>Del Rey</last_name>
    </author>
  </authors>
</publisher>
```

Note how the second book has several authors. For making an overview of the most successful authors, the publisher wants to transform this huge books file to something like this:

```
<author>
  <name>Heinlein, Robert</name>
  <total_publications>67</total_publications>
  <total_sold>7343990</total_sold>
  <rank>1</rank>
</author>
```

Authors will be ranked by the total number of copies of books sold, and this should also determine their position in the document. So, the best selling author in the books document should be the highest on the list. This can be accomplished by this stylesheet:

```
<xsl:stylesheet xmlns:xsl="http://www.w3.org/1999/XSL/Transform">

<xsl:template match="/">
<bestsellers-list>
  <xsl:apply-templates select="/publisher/authors/author">
    <xsl:sort select="sum(/publisher/books/book
                            [author- ref/@ref=current()/@id]/sold)"/>
    <xsl:sort select="last_name"/>
  </xsl:apply-templates>
</bestsellers-list>
</xsl:template>

<xsl:template match="author">
  <copy>
    <name><xsl:value-of select="last_name"/>,
    <xsl:value-of select="first_name"/></name>
    <total_publications>
      <xsl:value-of select="count(/publisher/books/book[author-
        ref/@ref=current()/@id])"/>
    </total_publications>
    <total_sold>
      <xsl:value-of select="sum(/publisher/books/book[author-
        ref/@ref=current()/@id]/sold)"/>
    </total_sold>
    <rank><xsl:value-of select="position()"/></rank>
  </copy>
</xsl:template>

</xsl:stylesheet>
```

Some things in this stylesheet are worthy of further comment. First, note how the sum() and count() functions are used, both in the author template for calculating the number of publications and total number sold for each author, and in the sort element within the apply-templates element. Note how the current() function is used to match the author-ref elements to the author elements they refer to. An interesting thing to note is that the current() function within the apply-templates element refers to the current context *after* selecting the new set.

If the source document is large, this stylesheet will probably take a long time to process. Many calculations are done in counting and summing the nodes. In these counting actions, a lot of searching is done on books that have an author-ref element with a certain ref attribute. We could also implement this using a key. If the processor is optimized for using keys, this will speed things up significantly (but I don't know of any such processor at the time of writing). Even if it doesn't give us a performance gain (it still might in the future), our code becomes somewhat cleaner. Then the stylesheet would look like this. See if you can figure it out.

```
<xsl:stylesheet xmlns:xsl="http://www.w3.org/1999/XSL/Transform" version="1.0">

<xsl:key match="/publisher/books/book" use="author-ref/@ref"
                                       name="books-by-author"/>

<xsl:template match="/"><bestsellers-list>
  <xsl:apply-templates select="/publisher/authors/author">
```

```
        <xsl:sort select="sum(key('books-by-author', @id)/sold)"/>
        <xsl:sort select="last_name"/>
    </xsl:apply-templates>
  </bestsellers-list></xsl:template>

  <xsl:template match="author">
    <copy>
      <name>
        <xsl:value-of select="last_name"/>,
        <xsl:value-of select="first_name"/>
      </name>
      <total_publications>
        <xsl:value-of select="count(key('books-by-author', @id))"/>
      </total_publications>
      <total_sold>
        <xsl:value-of select="sum(key('books-by-author', @id)/sold)"/>
      </total_sold>
      <rank>
        <xsl:value-of select="position()"/>
      </rank>
    </copy>
  </xsl:template>

</xsl:stylesheet>
```

At the beginning of the document, we added an `xsl:key` element. It is called 'books-by-author'. The key will give us direct access to a set of nodes from the source document. With the `match` attribute we specify which nodes we want to be able to access. In our case, we want access through the key to all `book` elements in the document (`match="/publisher/books/book"`). With the `use` attribute we specify the key value we want to use to access a `book` element. This is apparently the `ref` attribute on the `author-ref` child element(s) of the book (`use="author-ref/@ref"`).

Now if we use the `key()` function anywhere in the stylesheet like this:

```
key('books-by-author', 'rh')
```

This will return a node set containing all `book` elements that have an `author-ref` child element with `ref="rh"`. Effectively these are all books by Robert Heinlein. Using this, we could simplify some of the expressions in the stylesheet significantly.

Giving Style to XML

With XML only consisting of data content, there is a clear need for ways to display this content. This is commonly referred to as 'styling the content'. At the time of writing, there are two W3C standard stylesheet languages: CSS (Cascading Stylesheets) and XSLT. Both can be used to assign certain looks to specific element types in an XML document.

Until now we have seen how XSLT can be used to transform XML documents from one format to another. The original goal for specifying XSLT was its use as a styling mechanism. But before we try to use XSLT to transform to HTML documents, we'll first have a look at the Cascading Stylesheets.

Using CSS in HTML

You have probably seen CSS before in an HTML context. It is a syntax for specifying the appearance of elements in an HTML document in a structured way. It allows for associating one stylesheet with many content documents, thus centralizing the common layout in one place. The 'Cascading' part of the name refers to the feature of overriding a global property locally by redefining and inheriting properties from parent elements in the document. CSS strikes a fine balance between centralization and developer flexibility.

The current recommendation of the W3C is at version 2. The most important difference between versions 1 and 2 is that support for other media-types was included (printing documents) and more complex selectors were introduced (a selector in CSS2 can be compared with the match attribute in an XSLT template). CSS properties on elements can specify:

- ❑ Font size, family, color, variant (for example smallcaps), style (for example italic)
- ❑ Color, background color, background image (including tiling and positioning)
- ❑ Line, word and letter spacing
- ❑ Alignment, underlining, overlining
- ❑ The margins, borders, etc. of boxes (boxes are TABLE elements, but also P and BODY elements)
- ❑ List styles (square bullets, etc.), display (not displayed, as block, inline)
- ❑ Very detailed positioning and units (inches, cm, pixels, points)

Some simple uses of CSS in HTML are shown here before we head on to styling XML.

```
<P style="text-align:center;text-decoration:underline">This is text</P>
```

The above code would be displayed like this:

This is text

The same would be accomplished by inserting this code at the beginning of the HTML document:

```
<STYLE>
P {
   text-align:center;
text-decoration:underline;
}
</STYLE>
```

Or by associating the HTML document with an external stylesheet by doing this:

```
<LINK href="mystyle.css" rel="style sheet" type="text/css">
```

while a file is present in the same directory, called mystyle.css and with this content:

```
P {
  text-align:center;
  text-decoration:underline;
}
```

There is a lot more to using CSS from HTML, especially when you programmatically change the styles during display. We will not cover the use of classes and more complex concepts in CSS here.

Using CSS in XML

Using CSS to style an XML document is very simple if you know the way it works with HTML. The way of referencing the stylesheet is different, using the processing instruction `xml-stylesheet` instead of the `LINK` element. Inline stylesheets are not possible. Let's look at an example:

```
<?xml version="1.0" encoding="iso-8859-1"?>
<?xml-stylesheet type="text/css" href="article.css"?>
<Article>
  <Authors>
    <Author>James Britt</Author>
    <Author>Teun Duynstee</Author>
  </Authors>

  <Title>A cool article</Title>
  <Intro>An introductory text here ... </Intro>
  <Body>The body text of the article comes here ... </Body>
  <Related>
    <Item type="URL" loc="http://www.asptoday.com/art2">Some other article</Item>
    <Item type="local" loc="2"/>
  </Related>
</Article>
```

This example refers to a cascading stylesheet with a relative URL. The `type` attribute contains a MIME type indicating the kind of stylesheet. Using a different MIME type, we can also use this syntax to associate an XSLT stylesheet with the document – more on that later.

If we leave the `article.css` stylesheet document empty, all text nodes will be displayed flowing over the whole page. What we want is the title to appear larger and have everything aligned, more like how we would expect an article to look, just like this:

The most important thing to realize is that the elements in our document have no style whatsoever. Normally in HTML styling, the P element (paragraph) has some properties set by default. For example: the P element, but also the H1 to H6 elements all have their display attribute set to 'block'. This indicates that the element requires its own line in the document. In XML, the CSS processor assumes nothing. So let's start styling the title of the article:

❑　It should appear on its own line

❑　It should be a little larger than the rest of the text

❑　It should be centered and underlined

❑　We want to use a sans-serif font

Converting this into a CSS statement, we would get:

```
Title {
   display:block;
   text-align:center;
   text-decoration;underline;
   font-size:14pt;
   font-family:helvetica
}
```

Doing this for all elements in the article document, we could come up with a stylesheet like this:

```
BODY {
   color:black;
   display:block;
   width:80%;
   margin-left:20%;
}
Intro {
   color:black;
   font-weight:bold;
   display:block;
   line-height:150%;
   width:80%;
   margin-left:20%;
}
Author {
   text-align:right;
   font-size:8pt;
   display:block;
   text-decoration:italic;
}
TITLE {
   display:block;
   text-align:center;
   text-decoration:underline;
   font-size:14pt;
   font-family:helvetica
}
```

```
Related {
   display: none;
}
```

The good thing is that it is a standard and it works. The bad thing is that it is a bit limited in areas other than the visible style, for example:

❑   Reordering and sorting of elements is not possible

❑   Generation of text is hard. It can be done using the before and after pseudo-elements, but for more than the really basic additions, it's too difficult and besides, these are not implemented in most browsers.

❑   Adding functionality, such as creating a link from certain content elements, is not possible.

Some documents are suitable for styling this way. They have a content that is already in the order of reading and don't need much extra functionality beyond the formatting of the content. Often, the data in XML documents needs some more rigorous form of styling. In these cases, XSLT can be used.

Good points of CSS include:

❑   Many web developers are familiar with the language

❑   Good performance

Using XSLT for Adding Style

We have seen quite a lot of XSLT in this chapter. We saw that it is a language for converting one XML-based document into another. HTML looks very much like an XML-based syntax, only the rules to determine if the document is well-formed are less strict. If we use XSLT to transform XML to an HTML page, the result must always be valid XML. This means that you cannot create just any kind of HTML from XML with XSLT, but for any valid HTML document it is possible to create an HTML document that looks the same and can be created from XML. So if you want text displayed as:

Text **text** *text* text

the HTML you would normally use would look like this:

```
Text <B>text <I>text</B> text</I>
```

However, to be valid *XML*, it would have to be rewritten as:

```
Text <B>text <I>text</I></B><I> text</I>
```

Recently, the W3C specified **XHTML**. XHTML is the same as HTML, but must always be a valid XML document. DTDs for XHTML have been published. You can find the specification, including the associated DTDs, at www.w3.org/TR/xhtml1/. Any XHTML document can be generated from a source using XSLT. However, be careful – if you use these DTDs to validate your XHTML document, you must use HTML in lowercase. In most of the examples in this book, we use uppercase HTML elements (I think this makes the stylesheet elements and the literal HTML elements easier to distinguish). So, the examples do not generate valid XHTML.

As you may remember, the XSLT `output` element allowed us to choose the method `html` for outputting HTML instead of XML. If you do this, you can be sure that XML specifics such as processing instructions and closed empty elements like `<BR/>` will not confuse HTML browsers. But if you do so, you must also be aware of the fact that your output is not valid XML anymore and therefore also not valid XHTML.

So basically anything that can be shown in a browser can be the styled representation of an XML document using XSLT, and this was actually one of the main purposes of developing XSLT in the first place. Using it for transforming into formats other than HTML was only added later. We have already seen a lot of XSLT in this chapter. We will just have a look at some examples and common techniques.

Styling the Article

We'll take the same source documents that we used to show the use of CSS on XML. The documents contain the text of an article and include some references to both remote and other local articles. A sample article looks like this:

```xml
<?xml version="1.0" encoding="iso-8859-1"?>
<Article>
  <Authors>
    <Author>James Britt</Author>
    <Author>Teun Duynstee</Author>
  </Authors>

  <Title>A cool article</Title>
  <Intro>An introductory text here ... </Intro>
  <Body>The body text of the article comes here ... </Body>
  <Related>
    <Item type="URL" loc="http://www.asptoday.com/art2">Some other article</Item>
    <Item type="local" loc="2"/>
  </Related>
</Article>
```

Now, we want to use XSLT to go beyond the styling that CSS made possible. We will include a link for each of the related articles. We will display the remote references with the title in our source document, but for the local references, we will look up the details of those referred articles and include that information in our styled document.

```xml
<?xml version="1.0"?>
<xsl:stylesheet xmlns:xsl="http://www.w3.org/1999/XSL/Transform" version="1.0">

<xsl:template match="Article">
<HTML><BODY>
<xsl:apply-templates select="Title"/>
<xsl:apply-templates select="Intro"/>
<xsl:apply-templates select="Body"/>
<xsl:apply-templates select="Authors"/>
<xsl:apply-templates select="Related"/>
</BODY></HTML>
</xsl:template>

<xsl:template match="Title"><H1><xsl:apply-templates/></H1></xsl:template>
```

```
<xsl:template match="Intro">
  <p style="width:80%;font-weight:bold"><xsl:apply-templates/></p>
</xsl:template>

<xsl:template match="Body">
  <p style="width:80%"><xsl:apply-templates/></p>
</xsl:template>

<xsl:template match="Authors">
  <p>Author(s): <xsl:apply-templates select="Author"/></p>
</xsl:template>

<xsl:template match="Author">
  <xsl:apply-templates/>
  <xsl:if test="position() != last()">, </xsl:if>
</xsl:template>

<xsl:template match="Related">
  <p>Related items:<br/><xsl:apply-templates/></p>
</xsl:template>

<xsl:template match="Item">
  <xsl:if test="@type='URL'">
    <a href="{@loc}"><xsl:value-of select="."/></a>
  </xsl:if>
  <xsl:if test="@type='local'">
    <a href="art{@loc}.xml">
    <xsl:value-of select="document(concat('art', @loc, '.xml'))/Article/Title"/>
    </a>(
    <xsl:apply-templates select=
              "document(concat('art', @loc, '.xml'))/Article/Authors/Author"/>
    )
  </xsl:if>
  <br/>
</xsl:template>

</xsl:stylesheet>
```

Except for the part that generates the HTML for the related articles, everything is fairly simple in the above document. The template that matches on the document element Article, reorders several items in the required order, starting with the title and placing the authors and related articles at the end. The job of specifying how each of these items should look is delegated to other templates. The templates for Title, Intro and Body elements do nothing special. They just output a bit of extra formatting code around the content.

The Author template is a bit more interesting. It is designed to create a comma-separated list in the output. This is done by placing if tags around the literal comma. The test attribute checks if the current author happens to be the last one in the current node set. If so, it doesn't generate the comma.

Then we have the related articles. The template for Item generates a link to these articles. There are two kinds of article references. Some are external, referring to some URL on the web. These have a text node as their content. This is the title of the article, which we want to show as link text. The other type is a local reference. It refers to other articles in the same directory, written in the same XML format as this one. These articles have a title in them and we know where to find the title when we need it, so there is no need for storing the titles of these related articles along with the reference.

The Item template really consists of two parts, one for remote links and one for local links. The remote one is simple. It generates the HTML code for a link, using the href attribute as an attribute value template. The content of the Item element becomes the content of the A element in HTML.

The local references are more complicated. How are we going to get hold of the title from these other files in the same directory? By using the document() function! This is demonstrated twice, once from the value-of element, and once from the apply-templates. In the first case, the processor just opens the other document, finds the title element in the indicated spot and outputs this to the destination document. The second case (fetching a list of authors from the referenced document) uses the apply-templates element. Instead of passing a node set of local nodes to the processor to let it find appropriate templates for them, in this case we hand a set of nodes from another document. The processor does exactly the same. It uses the author template that was already used for creating a comma-separated list of authors of the article itself, but it is now used to create an author list for the referenced document.

Creating Internal Links on Shakespeare

The next example is an XSLT stylesheet that styles the play of Macbeth (and other plays in the same format). Apart from creating a readable layout and highlighting the stage directions, we want to create a sort of navigational structure that allows the reader to jump from the beginning of an act to the beginning of the next or previous act. To do this, we will have to introduce internal links in the HTML document.

An example XML document has the following structure:

```xml
<?xml version="1.0"?>
<!DOCTYPE PLAY SYSTEM "play.dtd">
<PLAY>
<TITLE>The Tragedy of Macbeth</TITLE>

<PERSONAE>
<TITLE>Dramatis Personae</TITLE>
<PERSONA>DUNCAN, king of Scotland.</PERSONA>
<PGROUP>
    <PERSONA>MALCOLM</PERSONA>
    <PERSONA>DONALBAIN</PERSONA>
    <GRPDESCR>his sons.</GRPDESCR>
</PGROUP>
...
</PERSONAE>

<ACT><TITLE>ACT I</TITLE>

<SCENE>
    <TITLE>SCENE I.  A desert place.</TITLE>
    <STAGEDIR>Thunder and lightning. Enter three Witches</STAGEDIR>

    <SPEECH>
        <SPEAKER>First Witch</SPEAKER>
        <LINE>When shall we three meet again</LINE>
        <LINE>In thunder, lightning, or in rain?</LINE>
    </SPEECH>
</SCENE>
</ACT>
</PLAY>
```

A SPEECH element always has a SPEAKER child element and at least one LINE child element. SPEECH and STAGEDIR elements are children of SCENE elements; SCENE elements are children of ACT elements, which are children of the root PLAY element. Phew!

The corresponding stylesheet is called play.xsl and is part of the code download. It is rather big, and so has not been listed in full. Most of this stylesheet is dedicated to the visible layout of several of the content elements; however some of the templates deserve a closer look. For example the SPEECH template creates the speech in a table with the speaker's name on the first line:

```
<xsl:template match="SPEECH">
  <TR><TD style="font-weight:bold">
    <xsl:apply-templates select="SPEAKER"/>
  </TD><TD><xsl:value-of select="LINE[1]"/></TD></TR>
  <xsl:apply-templates select="LINE"/>
</xsl:template>

...

<xsl:template match="LINE">
  <xsl:if test="position() > 1">
  <TR><TD></TD><TD>
    <xsl:value-of select="."/>
  </TD></TR>
  </xsl:if>
</xsl:template>
```

Note how the SPEECH template creates a row in the table, holding both the SPEAKER and the first LINE element. To prevent the line from showing up twice, the LINE template only creates output for LINE elements that have a position higher than 1.

The most interesting part of the stylesheet is the part that generates internal links forward and backward. We will have a look at the templates for ACT elements, one part at a time. First let's look at the part that generates the act title as an internal link target:

```
<A>
  <xsl:attribute name="name">
    <xsl:value-of select="generate-id()"/>
  </xsl:attribute>
  <xsl:value-of select="TITLE"/>
</A>
```

This fragment creates an A element, with the content of the TITLE child element contained within. On this element, a name attribute is generated. The value of this attribute is determined by the function generate-id() without passing a parameter. This causes the function to use the context node (the ACT element) to generate a unique identifier. How the identifier looks is processor-specific.

The links forward and backward are also generated using the generate-id() function, but now by passing the next or previous ACT element to it:

```
<xsl:if test="following-sibling::ACT">
  <A>
    <xsl:attribute name="href">
      <xsl:text>#</xsl:text>
```

```
        <xsl:value-of select="generate-id(following-sibling::ACT[1])"/>
        </xsl:attribute>
        &gt;
    </A>
  </xsl:if>
```

Using the `if` element, we make sure that the 'next' link is only generated if there is any ACT element to link to. If so, an A element is generated, bearing an `href` attribute with an internal link. The # is hardcoded, but the rest of the string is generated by the `generate-id()` function. We use the `following-sibling` axis, constrained by the ACT element name, and select the first node from the resulting set. This node is the next ACT element. Later in the destination document, this node will be used to generate the full text of the next act and create a link target at the spot of the act title. This way, we make sure that the target name of the next act is the same string as used in the `href` attribute of this link.

A third technique that should be noticed is the use of a parameter in the transformation of a PERSONA element in the PERSONAE part. A PERSONA can appear as a direct child of the PERSONAE element or inside a PGROUP. If a PERSONA is inside a PGROUP, we want the name to appear indented. We use the same template for all PERSONA elements, but when called from within a PGROUP, we pass the parameter `indented="yes"` to it.

```
<xsl:template match="PERSONA">
  <xsl:param name="indented">no</xsl:param>
  <TR><TD>
    .<xsl:if test="$indented = 'yes'">
      <xsl:attribute name="style">padding-left:20</xsl:attribute>
    </xsl:if>
    <xsl:value-of select="."/>
  </TD></TR>
</xsl:template>
```

Client Side XSLT Styling

There is one more way to style XML documents with an XSLT stylesheet. It can be done by the browser application. In this scenario, the web server sends a raw (without layout) XML document to the client, but containing a processing instruction that tells the browser which stylesheet to use. This processing instruction uses the same syntax we saw used for attaching a Cascading Stylesheet to an XML document. An example of this is as follows:

```
<?xml version="1.0" ?>
<?xml-stylesheet href="transformation.xsl" type="text/xsl"?>
<CONTENT>
</CONTENT>
```

A web browser that supports XSLT will download the referred stylesheet (`transformation.xsl`) and transform the XML document with that stylesheet before showing it to the user. This technique can take a large part of the processing load from the server to the client machine.

If you have little control over the browser application used (as in most Internet scenarios), you will have to check on the server if the user uses an XSLT supporting browser and transform the content to HTML on the server if not.

Summary

Now that you have come this far, you have seen all the basic techniques you need to start programming and using XML in your Visual Basic applications. The next chapter will introduce you to the linking of XML documents to each other, but that technology is still very premature. So, we've now seen all the subjects that are ready for use.

In this chapter, we have learned a lot:

XPath

❏ We learned how to use XPath to query a very specific subset of nodes from a loaded XML document.

❏ We learned to create sub-queries using predicates on our XPath expressions.

❏ We looked at the built-in functions of XPath.

❏ We covered the limited support of XPath in Internet Explorer 5.0 and the more complete support in the developers preview MSXML 2.6.

XSLT

❏ We learned how XSLT works and which processors can be used to try it out yourself.

❏ We had a long and intensive look at all of the elements and functions supported in XSLT 1.0.

❏ We looked at the level of implementation of XSLT in both IE5 (MSXML 2.0) and MSXML 2.6.

❏ We looked at some examples that used XSLT to transform an XML source into another XML format, converting from one schema to another schema.

Styling

❏ We learned how you can give style to an XML document using Cascading Stylesheets.

❏ We learned how to use XSLT to transform an XML document into an HTML document to display it.

❏ We looked at some uses of XSLT to add functionality (internal navigation, external content) to a document when transforming.

❏ We saw how to use client-side XSLT processing capabilities to let users browse XML documents without first transforming them on the server.

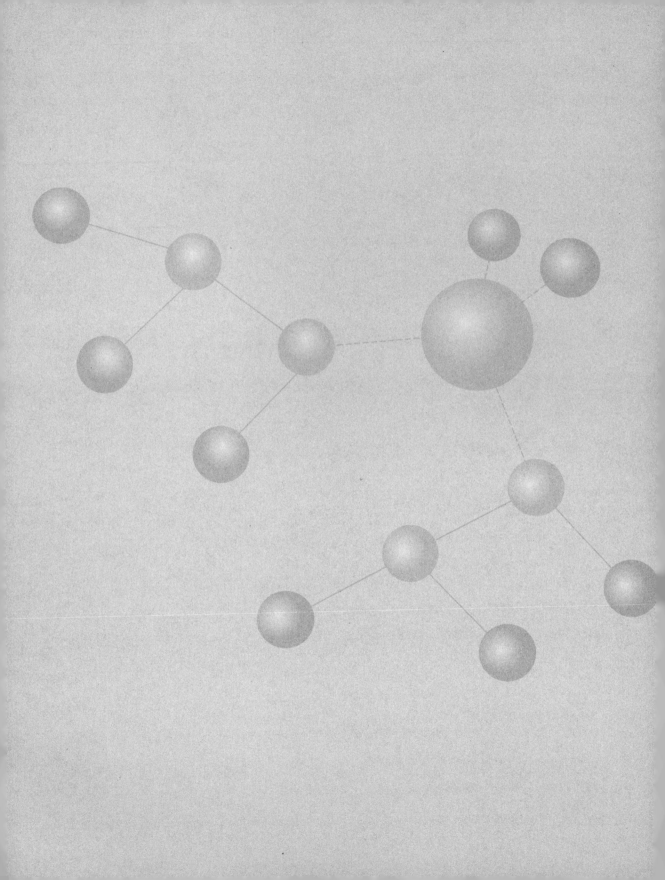

Linking with XPointer and XLink

One of the key features of many online documents is that they contain references to other available online resources. The **hyperlink** is a key feature of the Web. In the previous chapter we saw XML documents that contained reference information. We also saw XSLT being used to transform this information into HTML hyperlinks.

When XML was conceived, one of the first spin-off projects to be started was the specification of a standardized way to include references to other resources in an XML document (both inside the document and external resources). Hence, the requirements for the **XLink** specification were drafted. It was clear that the possibilities of interlinking documents were gravely under-used in HTML, so the target for XLink was set pretty high.

For some reason, XLink is still in draft status. Yet it is undisputed that if a standardized linking syntax is to be recommended, it will be an incarnation of XLink. It will probably be combined with the **XPointer** specification for identifying a part of a document to link to. Although you cannot do anything right now with the knowledge that is presented in this chapter, it is good to know the direction in which XML technology is going.

> Before diving into this chapter, a note of caution: the XPointer and XLink specifications are both still under construction. The W3C specifically states that the working drafts can be changed without notice in the next version. There are currently no real implementations available. Because of the lack of implementations, there will be no real world, hands-on examples in this chapter.

For extended and out-of-line links, it is not expected that stable implementations will be around anytime soon (I would guess at least a year). Still, it can be valuable to have some knowledge of the concepts in both specifications. This chapter is based on the December 1999 version of XPointer and the January 2000 version of XLink.

Restrictions of Linking in HTML

Because HTML linking is a well-known concept, we will compare HTML linking with XLink and XPointer linking. So what does an HTML link look like? An HTML link always links two points in documents (or within the same document). When following a link, the browser moves from the *origin* of the link to the *destination* of the link. The origin of the link is defined by the location of the A tag, the destination of the link is defined by the HREF attribute of the A tag, for example:

```
This is a <A HREF="target_doc.htm#location" TARGET="content">Link title</A>
```

In this sample, four distinct pieces of information can be discerned:

- ❑ The origin of the link, defined by the location of the A element in the origin document (directly after the text 'This is a')

- ❑ The destination of the link, defined by the HREF attribute

- ❑ The behavior of the link (what will happen with the content of the destination), defined by the TARGET attribute

- ❑ The representation of the link in the source document, defined by the content of the A element

All of this is encoded within the content of the source document (actually, part of the destination definition is defined in the destination document, in the name attribute on an A element). If you are very accustomed to HTML this will probably not even strike you as a problem. The XLink Working Group hopes that the following limitations of HTML linking can be overcome using XLink:

- ❑ An HTML link connects only two resources.

- ❑ An HTML link works one way only.

- ❑ To create an HTML link you must have editing permissions in the source document.

- ❑ HTML links get mixed up with the content of the source document.

- ❑ HTML links only link to *entire* documents. Although the link does not necessarily point to the top of the document, you always have to retrieve the full target document.

You may be thinking "Well, yes, that's what a link is, isn't it?" Many people do. But think of the following scenario. You are doing research on a subject. On this subject, many resources are available on-line. You cannot edit most of these resources (articles, specifications, etc). It would be very convenient if you could attach your own comments to specific locations in the articles or make cross-references between the articles. This is basically linking – keeping a set of resources together. But you cannot insert links into the articles without having editing permissions on the resource. After all, not everybody is interested in your comments.

It is for this kind of scenario that the XLink Working Group has been trying to specify the linking of XML documents in a far more generic way than in HTML.

Note that the A element is not the only linking element in HTML. The IMG element is also a link connecting an external resource to a document. The same could be said about the LINK element (for referring to a stylesheet), the APPLET, OBJECT, EMBED or FRAME elements or the `<meta http-equiv="refresh" content="30; url=page2.htm">` *syntax.*

The Link: Concept and Representation

Before getting into the definition of XPointer and XLink, we have to discuss the difference between a link and the *visual representation* of a link. In most HTML browsers today, the user gets a more or less standardized visual representation of the text that is the starting point of a link. It is normally in a different color from the rest of the text, often underlined, and the mouse cursor may change shape when moved over the link.

Still, these representations are not specified by the HTML specification. The only thing defined there is what the target of the link is, and which part of the source document is attached to the link. Most browser vendors have conformed to a *de facto* standard representation, but implementations exist that look very different (for example lynx) but which are still perfectly good HTML browsers.

In HTML, many people do not notice the slight distinction between the link and its representation. In XML, though, this awareness is more important for the developer, because nothing of the rendering and behavior of an XML document is specified. If you build an application that displays XML documents or parts of documents, you will have to think about how the link should be represented.

What Should an XML Browser Do?

The XLink specification only deals with the conceptual side of linking. How the link will appear to the user is entirely up to the displaying application. What does this mean? It depends on the kind of application. For a general purpose XML browser, the task is different than for a specific application used to process only one type of XML documents.

The General XML Browser

XML browsers that can display arbitrary XML documents normally use some styling technique for specifying the appearance of XML elements. In the previous chapter we saw two ways for styling XML documents in XML browsers: CSS and XSLT. When browsers support XLink, the features of displaying links will have to be merged into the existing styling mechanism.

❑ The simplest case is when you use CSS to style your document. If a document contains XLink information, the browser will probably show these links as HTML links, more or less, or at least the simple ones. The more complicated link types don't have very obvious user interfaces and neither XLink nor CSS have ways to allow the behavior of the link to be specified. So you depend on what the browser vendor thinks is the right user interface. Links with several destinations might show a pop-up menu with the different options if you click them.

❑ If you use XSLT to style your documents on the browser, the situation is more complex. Transformations and XLink do not mix nicely. The point is that when you style your XML document by transforming it to HTML, the document you display is not an XML document anymore – it is HTML, and HTML does not support XLink. Therefore it would be better only to use XLink to define links, and implement their behavior in the XML parser yourself during the transformation. If you do this, you will basically make an XLink implementation in XSLT. We will demonstrate making a partial XLink implementation using XSLT and server side VB components in Chapter 10.

The Specific XML Application

If you are building a system including a front-end application, you are in charge of both the XML syntax used and the part of it that is shown to the end user. If you need the functionality of linking resources together, you could use the syntax of XLink. After all, it has already been pondered on by many minds, so why would you do it differently?

XLink does not force you to do anything. You can use the information in the document to let your application 'navigate' to another document. Maybe future releases of XML object models (like MSXML) will include information methods on XLink information contained in a document, or functionality that causes the object model to 'follow' a link. But this is speculation at the moment.

XPointer

Because XML linking should be able to link parts of documents to each other, we have a need for a way to specify *which* part of the document. This is what **XPointer** was made for. It is a syntax to point to a *fragment* or a set of fragments in a document. A fragment may be a node, but may also be a part of a node. Luckily, the syntax is pretty much identical to XPath, which we covered in Chapter 4. XPointer defines a few extensions and additions to XPath. So, if you are comfortable with XPath then using XPointer will not be a problem for you.

Standard XPointer Syntax

The general syntax for using XPointer is to append it to a URL:

```
http://www.mycomp.com/docs/doc.xml#xpointer()
```

Like specifying a location in an HTML document, we can append an XPointer expression by first appending a # to the URL of the full document, and then the string `xpointer`, followed by the XPointer expression in parentheses (the expression itself is left out in the above example). The part after the # specifies the part of the desination document we are linking to. There are also a few shorthand notations where the full `xpointer()` syntax is not necessary.

Shorthand Notations

The first and most common shorthand for the `xpointer()` syntax is for referring to an element in the document by ID. This is just like the way you use `name` attributes in anchors in HTML. The reference then looks like:

```
http://www.mycomp.com/docs/doc.xml#someID
```

This refers to an element in the XML document that bears an attribute of type ID (assigned by the DTD or Schema) that has the value of `someID`. Just like in HTML, creating the link to this element is very easy, but for creating the anchor point in the destination document, we have to edit it (unless, of course, somebody else already defined it). In the XML case, making the destination document ready for linking to it by ID has even more impact than with HTML. In XML, an attribute can only serve as an ID if this is specified in the validation rules. This way of referring to elements is typically done when the destination documents already use validation rules. For example, if you maintain your content in XHTML documents, you could refer to any element in the document using the `id` attribute of that element (in XHTML, any element can carry an `id` attribute that is of type `ID`).

The XPointer Working Group chose to include this shorthand because they wanted to support the use of references by ID. Referencing by ID is considered to be more robust than using a structural reference. Even if the order or structure of a document is changed, the ID of a certain piece of information will probably not change.

The second shorthand syntax in XPointer uses the child numbers of elements as the only identifier. An example would be:

```
http://www.mycomp.com/docs/doc.xml#/1/4/2
```

The meaning of this XPointer would be: the second child of the fourth child of the document element. Only elements can be referenced this way. The appended path must always start with /1, because an XML document can have only one document element. Obviously, this can only be used for very static documents, because the child number of a certain piece of information in the document can change very easily, when new elements are inserted. For linking to documents that readily undergo changes, you should not use this syntax.

Examples of Using XPath in XPointer

The simplest way to select a fragment with XPointer is using a plain XPath expression. It can be placed directly inside the parentheses of the xpointer() syntax. If you are referring to the first chapter element in a document called book.xml, you might use an XPointer reference like this:

```
book.xml#xpointer(//chapter[1])
```

Note that the XPath expression uses the // notation to indicate the use of the descendant axis. Using /chapter[1] would refer to the first chapter element that is a direct child of the document root.

If the element representing chapter 1 of book.xml has an ID of chap1, this can be selected like this:

```
book.xml#chap1
```

This can also be expressed as:

```
book.xml#xpointer(id('chap1'))
```

This next expression links to all par elements containing a descendant whose value contains the string 'linkset'. It is a reference you would expect in the index of a book:

```
book.xml#xpointer(/descendant::par [descendant::*[contains(text(), 'linkset')]])
```

A link to the last chapter in the book that contains at least one image child element would look like this:

```
book.xml#xpointer(/descendant::chapter[descendant::image] [position() = last()])
```

Extensions to XPath

Recall that an XPath expression returns a node or a set of nodes. This is not enough when we come to use XPointer. XPointer should be able to refer to a part of a document in a broader sense. It should be able to point to a specific letter in an attribute but it should also be able to refer to a large part of the document, stretching from one arbitrary point to another. It is clear that XPath does not allow these things, so XPointer defines a few extensions to XPath.

An XPointer expression returns a **location** or a set of locations (compare to a node and a set of nodes that can be returned by an XPath expression). A location can be:

❑ A node

❑ A point, a very specific position in a document (with granularity to the single character)

❑ A range, a fragment of a document, stretching from one point to another

We will take a closer look at the last two concepts. They will also play an important role in the next incarnation of the DOM (Level 2), but that will not be covered here.

Points

A **point** is a very precisely defined location in a document. When used in an XPointer expression, a point is often defined relative to the start of a specific node or relative to a string occurrence. The following example specifies the point directly after the occurrence of the string 'Moby Dick' in the element with ID 'chap1':

```
book.xml#xpointer(end-point(string-range(id('chap1'), "Moby Dick")))
```

A point can always be specified by the combination of its **container** (a node in the document) and an **index** (a non-negative integer). Points can have two forms:

Form	Description	Container	Index
Node point	A location just before or after a single node in the document tree.	Any node in the document that can have child nodes.	The child number of the child node just before the point. If the index is 0, then the point is located before the first child.
Character point	A location just before or after a single character in a text string in the document.	Any node in the document that has a string value, but cannot have child nodes (text nodes and attributes).	The character number in the string value of the character just before the point. So if the string value is 'Pro VB XML' and the index is 5, the point is located just after the V (the fifth character).

An XML fragment like this contains 15 points:

```
<book>
  <chap>
    <title number="1">Hope</title>
  </chap>
</book>
```

The point numbers have been inserted into the source to indicate the location of the points in the source:

```
[1]<book>[2]
  <chap>[3]
    <title number-"[4]1[5]">
[6][7]H[8]o[9]p[10]e[11][12]
    </title>[13]
  </chap>[14]
</book>[15]
```

Note that points can be located at any place inside text strings (though never 'on' a character, but always before or after one). They are a bit like the cursor location in a word processor. You cannot have a point inside a tag name.

The node point labeled 3 has the chap element as its container and an index of 0. The character point 9 has the text node inside the title element as its container and an index of 2. Note how points 6 and 7 appear to be the same, and the same goes for points 11 and 12. The confusion is caused because the text node that holds the string Hope is not really visible in the source document. Between points 6 and 7 is the start of the text node and between points 11 and 12 is the end of the text node.

When finding a location within a string, the string values are first stripped of extra whitespace. All sequences of multiple whitespaces (space, tab, return, linefeed) are converted to one space (this could include several blank lines). Then the search for the specified character starts.

The XPointer specification itself does not specify what the selected location could be used for, but it is easy to imagine. A point will normally be used to either jump to or refer to. It has no real content. The main use of the point is for defining a range, by using two points.

Ranges

A **range** is basically a part of a document, consisting of consecutive characters. Imagine a user of a word processor that drags with his mouse to select a part of the text. That is exactly what defining a range is like. It defines everything between a start point (mouse down) and an end point (mouse up). If you are an experienced user of a word processor, you will recognize the usefulness of the concept of a range, but you will also have experienced some of the limitations. One important limitation of ranges is that they are bound to the order of information in the document. For one consecutive piece of uniform text, this is no problem. But what if the order on screen does not really match the order in the document. Think of footnotes, information in tables. In XML we can also have problems of this kind. If a document contains metadata, together with viewable content, some information will be made invisible to the editor. If the editor makes a selection of any part of the document, he is never sure exactly what information he has selected. Because it was stored in a specific order in the document doesn't mean that the selection is as it seems. With transformed documents (using XSLT) the situation is made even worse. A range in a source document can be unrecognizably scattered all over the destination document after the transformation.

But apart from these caveats, a range is an extremely powerful concept. In XPointer, we define a range with the following syntax:

```
xpointer(expr1 to expr2)
```

The first expression (expr1) defines the starting point of the range or ranges. The second expression (expr2) is evaluated with the result of the first expression as its context node. Have a look at this example:

```
xpointer(//book/chapter to descendant::image)
```

This XPointer expression will return a *set* of ranges. Each range starts at a chapter element that is a child of a book element. The ranges end at the first image element that is a descendant of the chapter. The ranges have been highlighted in the following sample document.

```
<?xml version="1.0"?>
<publisher>
  <book>
    <chapter>
      Text text text text <image/> text text text
      Text text <image/> text text text text text
    </chapter>
    <chapter>
      Text text text text text text text
      Text text <image/> text text text text text
    </chapter>
  </book>
  <book>
    <chapter>
      <paragraph>
        Text text text text <image/> text text text
        Text text <image/> text text text text text
      </paragraph>
    </chapter>
  </book>
</ publisher>
```

If one or both of the locations in the expression is a node instead of a point, the node is converted to a range. For the starting point, the first location is used, for the ending point the second one. To put into normal English, nodes that exist between the start and end points are included within the range. For instance, in the above example, you can see that the image elements are included in the ranges.

A few combinations of points are not acceptable as starting and ending points of a range:

❑ The starting point must come before the ending point in document order.

❑ If the container node of the starting point is anything but an element, text node or the root, the ending node should have the same container node. This means that a range cannot start inside an attribute and end outside that attribute.

XPointer Functions

To define points and ranges, XPointer comes with its own set of functions. We will briefly describe them here. Most of these functions use the type `location-set`. Remember that a location is the superset of nodes, points and ranges.

location-set string-range(location-set, string, number, number)

The `string-range` function searches the passed context for occurrences of the specified substring. It returns a set of ranges of those occurrences.

```
xpointer(string-range(//book/summary, 'war'))
```

This XPointer expression will return all occurrences of the word 'war' in the summaries of books in the document. If the third and fourth (optional) arguments are used, they indicate the starting point and length of the range. By default, the starting point is the start of the string and the length is the length of the matched string. Look at the following example:

```
xpointer(string-range(/, 'password:', 10, 16)
```

This will return a range set of the 16 letters that come after all occurrences of the string 'password:' in the whole document. The number 10, passed as the third argument, sets the starting point just before the tenth character (which is right after the colon from `password:`).

location-set range(location-set)

This function converts a set of locations to a set of ranges that cover the passed locations. Remember that a location can be a point, a range or a node. For covering ranges, the following rules apply:

- ❑ If the location is a range, the covering range is the range itself.
- ❑ If the location is a point, the covering range has the point itself as its starting and ending point. So that would be a range that starts and ends on the same point.
- ❑ For a node, the range stretches from the point just before the node's start tag to the point just after the node's end tag. So, the node itself is included.

location-set range-inside(location-set)

This converts the locations in the passed set to ranges, like the `range()` function. The difference is in the behavior when a node is passed. The `range()` function would convert this to a range running from the beginning of the node to the end of the node. The `range-inside()` function will return a range that covers only the content of the node, but not the node itself.

location-set start-point(location-set)

This returns the starting point for each range in the passed location set. If a node is used, it is first converted to a range.

location-set end-point(location-set)

This returns the ending point for each range in the passed location set. If a node is used, it is first converted to a range.

location-set here()

This returns the location of the XPointer itself. If the XPointer is contained in some sort of XML document, the function returns the element that holds the XPointer as a text value or as one of its attributes.

location-set origin()

The origin() function is only meaningful when XPointer is used in the context of linking. It returns the place from where the link is pointing. This seems very much like the here() function, but it is not necessarily the same thing. In the context of XLink, for example, the origin of a link does not have to be the place where the link is defined in a document.

XLink supports external documents with links connecting other documents to each other. So you can have a document A that contains a link from a location in document B which links to a location in document C. That is, document B links to documents A and C at the same point. In this situation, and from document A's point of view, here() would return the link-defining element in document A, while origin() would return the place in document B that is defined as the origin of the link.

boolean unique()

The unique() function returns true if the context holds only one item. It is thus exactly identical to the XPath expression count() = 1. It is included in the XPointer specification, because checking the uniqueness of a pointer is considered a common task.

Examples

This would return ranges covering the four letters of every occurrence of the name 'Teun' within a person element:

```
xpointer(string-range(/descendant::person, "Teun"))
```

This would return only the first range, in document order, covering the four letters of every occurrence of the name 'Teun' within a person element:

```
xpointer(string-range(/descendant::person, "Teun")[position() = 1])
```

This would return ranges covering the content of all person elements (but not the element itself) whose string values contain the string 'Teun'.

```
xpointer(range-inside(/descendant::person[contains(text(), "Teun")]))
```

This would return the title element that is the child of the next chap element. This would be used, for example, in an attribute on a chap element (defining the chapter of a book). The attribute would point to the title of the next chapter.

```
xpointer(here()/following-sibling::chap[1]/child::title)
```

Empty Result Sets

Unlike XPath, in XPointer it is considered an error if the expression returns no results at all. This makes some sense; XPath is meant to be a querying language, asking questions like: "*return me all cases that are like X*". This can sometimes be a non-existant condition.

The concept of an XPointer is more like: "*I am referring to this exact piece of information: X. If you want it, go get it*". Considering this hidden message, it is indeed an error if you follow the reference and find nothing there – it's a dead link!

It is very easy to create an XPointer that refers to relevant information now, but that refers to nothing after a revision. There are a few ways to prevent these errors from occurring:

- ❑ Refer as much as possible to IDs. When the content of a document is revised, normally the ID of a piece of information remains the same. The XPointer shorthand for referring to IDs was introduced exactly to promote the use of IDs in references.

- ❑ Use a fallback XPointer. You can concatenate a series of XPointer expressions to one large expression. If the first one returns a result, then that is used, but if nothing is found, the next expression is tried. This way you can first refer very precisely, adding additional pointing information just in case.

This example refers to the 23rd `title` element in the `book.xml` document:

```
book.xml#xpointer(//title[23])xpointer(//title[last()])xpointer(/)
```

If that element does not exist – maybe a few chapters have been removed – it refers to the last `title` element to be found in the document. If even that cannot be found (the element name for titles has changed), the XPointer defaults to the start of the document.

XLink

Now that we've seen how to refer to parts of XML documents using ranges and points in XPointer, we'll have a closer look at XLink for tying certain documents (or fragments) together.

Who Implements the Behavior?

XLink specifies only a syntax, conforming to XML and XML namespaces. The implementation of these links must still be done. After all, we say 'link', but what do we mean? Sometimes we may mean to say 'blue-colored piece of text that takes us to another document when clicked', but in many cases that is not what we mean. It is largely application dependent.

One can imagine XLink/XPointer compliant parsers that automatically include or replace elements by their linked counterparts, or parsers that can give the application programmer a list of links that are found in the document and leave implementation of the links to the application programmer. These are issues that are still unresolved and we'll have to wait for these tools to emerge. For now, we can look at the specifications, learn from the issues raised there and maybe use the proposed ideas in our applications. In Chapter 10, we will show how to create a very basic XPointer/XLink implementation using XSLT and some server-side processing.

Recognizing an Element as a Link

If your application is designed to handle documents that contain XLink information, it must first of all be able to identify which parts of the document are XLink nodes. This is (of course) done using a special namespace. The namespace for XLink is:

```
http://www.w3.org/1999/xlink/namespace/
```

Any node in the document carrying a prefix for this namespace will be interpreted as an XLink node. The XLink specification defines only attributes. The key attribute of these is the `xlink:type` attribute. Any element carrying the `xlink:type` attribute turns into a linking element. The value of this attribute determines the kind of linking element. Available types are:

- simple
- extended
- locator
- arc
- resource
- title

Most of these elements need additional attributes to define their exact meaning. The available attributes are:

xlink:href	To specify a location
xlink:role	To identify the content of a location for a processing application
xlink:title	To identify the content of a location for a human user
xlink:show	Specifies what happens when a link is followed
xlink:actuate	Specifies when a link is followed
xlink:to	Specifies the origin of a link
xlink:from	Specifies the destination of a link

Not all attributes can be used in combination with all values for `xlink:type`. At the very end of this chapter you'll find a table indicating which attributes can be used together on one element. You can also refer to Appendix E for a complete xlink/xpointer reference

Have a look at this example of a linking element. You don't have to understand the full meaning of all attributes, but concentrate on how the custom element is turned into a linking element by adding attributes to it.

```
<someElement xmlns:xlink="http://www.w3.org/1999/xlink/namespace/"
  xlink:type="simple"
  xlink:href="books.xml"
  xlink:show="replace"
```

```
    xlink:actuate="onRequest">
  Other books by the author
  </someElement>
```

The several attributes specify what kind of link it is. In this chapter we will always use the prefix `xlink` for attributes in the XLink namespace. This could of course be any arbitrary name, as long as the namespace has been declared with the right URI.

Basically, there are two kinds of links: simple and extended. The simple link comes alone, while an extended link is a combination of many linking elements. Elements with `xlink:type="simple"` specify a simple link. All other types are used to specify an extended link.

Simple Link

The **simple link** is the easiest to work with, because it is very much like an HTML link. Although it is not as complex and powerful as the extended link, it already offers some possibilities beyond the hyperlinking in HTML and is very easy to use.

To make a simple link in XLink, you add an `xlink:type` attribute to an element and give it the value `simple`. Now the element links between its own location and the target of the link. To specify the target of the link we must add the required attribute `xlink:href` to the element.

So we can create a link like this:

```
<W xlink:type="simple" xlink:href=http://www.macaw.nl/>
```

These attributes make the `W` element into a simple link to a web site.

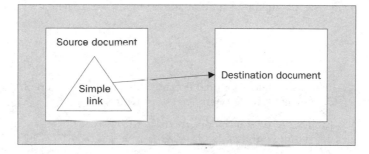

Apart from making a linking element from any normal element, there are some extra attributes that can be used on a simple link to further specify its behavior. The first two are for describing the referenced resource.

xlink:title

The `xlink:title` attribute is added to a link to describe the remote resource in a human readable fashion. It is purely for cosmetic purposes, but if it is used on a simple link, it should describe the resource that it is linked to. The `xlink:title` attribute might be used by applications dealing with links to show what a link is about before it is followed, for example, showing a tool tip with the title when hovering the content of the link.

It is also possible to add an xlink:type attribute with value title to one of the children of the element describing the resource. This has the same effect.

xlink:role

The xlink:role attribute is a bit like the xlink:title attribute. It describes the function of the resource being linked to. However, the xlink:role attribute is meant to be read by machines. The value should always be an XML name, so no whitespace is allowed. The xlink:role attribute is necessary for defining extended links (as we will see later), but it can also be specified for a simple link. It can be thought of as the name of the linked resource. XLink does not specify what it should be used for in simple links.

Here's a small sample of using the xlink:title and xlink:role attributes:

```
<person name="Teun" xmlns:xlink="http://www.w3.org/1999/xlink/namespace/">
  <relative xlink:type="simple"
        href="brother.xml"
        xlink:title="Information about my brother Bart"
        xlink:role="brother_info"/>
</person>
```

The next two attributes are for describing what to do with the referenced resource.

xlink:show

The simple link can be used to link the current document (or location in the document) to another resource. What remains unspecified is what should be done with the other resource. The xlink:show and xlink:actuate attributes give some details on this.

With the xlink:show attribute, the author can specify where the referenced content will appear. Should it replace the current document? Should it appear in a separate window? The possible values for xlink:show are:

Value	Meaning
replace	This is the default setting. It causes the application to replace the current document with the referenced document.
embed	Embed the referenced document in the current document at the location of the starting point of the link.
new	Retrieve the referenced document. Create a new window to show it in. The referring document remains visible and unchanged. This is a feature of HTML links that is used on some sites by setting the target attribute on an A element to _new. Remember that this can be irritating to a user.
undefined	The behavior is not specified and should be determined by the application.

Note that HTML uses these same features, but they cannot be set using an attribute. The A element normally uses the replace action. The IMG, APPLET and EMBED elements are always embedded in the linking document. Showing content by default in a new window is not a method used by any HTML element.

xlink:actuate

The xlink:actuate attribute defines *when* the link will be followed. In HTML, a standard link is followed when it is clicked. Other links are immediately followed, such as the LINK element and FRAME elements. Interestingly, most HTML browsers allow users to choose the show behavior of the IMG element. This allows users to browse only the text on the pages without loading the bandwidth-consuming graphics.

The xlink:actuate attribute can have two values, or it can be undefined:

Value	Meaning
onRequest	The linked resource will only be retrieved after the user has requested this. How the user should do this is not specified. In most cases it will be by clicking on a link or selecting an option.
onLoad	The link is followed immediately after the download of the referring document is complete.
Undefined	The behavior is not specified and should be determined by the application.

The combination of xlink:show and xlink:actuate on a simple link in XLink defines a set of behaviors that we are more or less familiar with. Some examples are shown in the table below:

xlink:show	xlink:actuate	Behavior
new	onRequest	Opens up a new page in a new window. The annoying behavior of some portals that don't want the user to leave to go to another place. When used modestly, this can be a nice feature though.
new	onLoad	The even more irritating behavior of some sites that lets banners pop up in windows when you come to their site. A civilized use of this feature could be popping up a site map.
embed	onLoad	This is what HTML browsers do with images and applets. As soon as the page is loaded, the content of associated resources is also retrieved and displayed inline. It really is a pity that HTML does not allow inserting HTML fragments in this fashion.
replace	onLoad	A strange behavior, that is sometimes used on web sites that have changed URLs. For example, "*You are now being automatically redirected.*"

Examples of Simple Links

Example1:

```
<friends>
  <friend xlink:type="simple"
    xlink:href="http://www.joey.com"
```

```
      xlink:actuate="onRequest"
      xlink:show="replace">Joey</friend>
  </friends>
```

This looks like a simple link to a friends homepage. In HTML it would look like:

```
  <A HREF="http://www.joey.com">Joey</A>
```

Example 2:

This is an example that would be hard to do in HTML (though probably not impossible, as the bounds of HTML prove to be very flexible):

```
<bmgroup>
  <bmgroup xlink:type="simple"
    xlink:show="embed"
    xlink:actuate="onRequest"
    xlink:role="deeper_linkset"
    xlink:href="links.asp?from=15">
    More links
  </bmgroup>
  <bookmark
    xlink:type="simple"
    xlink:href="http://www.duynstee.com">
    Teun Duynstee
  </bookmark>
  <bookmark
    xlink:type="simple"
    xlink:href="http://www.microsoft.com">
    Microsoft
  </bookmark>
</bmgroup>
```

So what is happening here? The root element (at least of this fragment) is a `bmgroup` element. It contains both `bookmark` elements and other `bmgroup` elements. Let's first focus on the `bookmark` elements. They define a simple link in XLink syntax. No `actuate` or `show` information is specified, so this is up to the application to define.

The `bookmark` elements are organized into `bmgroup` elements. Such a `bmgroup` element can be defined as a link to further bookmark information. The nested `bmgroup` element of the above code sample refers to a URL on the server. The resource that can be retrieved from this URL will be embedded into the current document (`xlink:show="embed"`). This way, a potentially huge set of hierarchically ordered bookmarks can be retrieved on demand from the server. Another editor might even maintain part of the bookmark information on another server, but the bookmarks page will appear to the user as a single set of data.

Example 3:

Finally, we'll have a look at a sample of defining accompanying binary images for an XML document using XLink. A fragment in an XML document could be:

```
  <image
    xlink:type="simple"
```

```
      xlink:href="img/graph.jpg"
      xlink:actuate="onLoad"
      xlink:show="embed"
 />
```

In HTML this would simply be:

```
<IMG SRC="img/graph.jpg">
```

Using XSLT, you could create a template that does the transition from this particular XLink usage to the intended HTML functionality.

```
<xsl:template match="image[
  namespace-uri(@*:type) = 'http://www.w3.org/1999/xlink/namespace/'
  ]">
  <IMG>
    <xsl:attribute name="SRC">
      <xsl:value-of select="@*:href[
        namespace-uri() ='http://www.w3.org/1999/xlink/namespace/'
        ]"/>
    </xsl:attribute>
  </IMG>
</xsl:template>
```

This XSLT template can be used (according to the match attribute) for transforming image elements that carry a type attribute in the XLink namespace. We cannot be sure of the prefix that will be used for the XLink namespace (we use xlink: in this chapter, but another prefix could just as well be used). The IMG element is created with a SRC attribute on it. The value of the xlink:href attribute is again determined using the namespace-uri() function.

Extended Link

Extended links are like simple links, but they can link to more than one location. The link element that carries the xlink:type attribute with value 'extended' serves just as a container for the link elements that define the resources linked to and from.

The locator Element

Within every extended link, you will find child elements of the type locator. A locator element defines a remote resource, just like the simple link does, but does not specify what to do with it or what its role in linking is. A piece of XML defining a set of resources that participate in an extended link might look like this:

```
<friends xlink:type="extended">
  <friend
    xlink:type="locator"
    xlink:href="http://www.jooy.com">Joey
  </friend>
  <friend
    xlink:type="locator"
```

```
      xlink:href="http://www.people.com/jenny">Jenny
   </friend>
   <friend
      xlink:type="locator"
      xlink:href="http://www.people.com/angela">Angela
   </friend>
</friends>
```

We can see here how arbitrary elements (friends and friend) are used as linking elements by adding attributes in the XLink namespace to them. The friends element is the full link. The friend elements it contains are the locators that describe the link. They refer to three different resources. Remember that in a simple link, the location of the description of the link was implicitly the origin of the link. In the case of extended links, the location of the link description means nothing. It might be used by the application, but it may not.

The link essentially defines six links, one from each of the resources to each of the other resources. As you can see, the link in this figure is drawn apart from any of the three resources. This is done intentionally. The link *defines* connections between the three resources referred to, but is not necessarily part of one of these resources itself. The document that contains the code we saw before (with the friend elements) can be a fourth document called, for example, relations.xml. We will see more of this concept in the section titled "*Out-of-Line Links*".

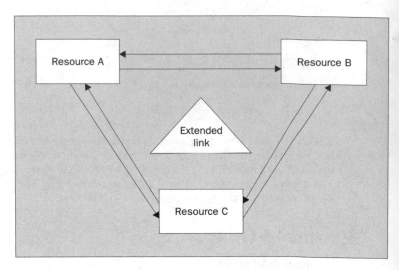

Let's think about how this link would look in a user interface. Suppose that we are viewing one of the three resources and suppose that the linking elements are part of this resource. Our current location is resource A (which refers to joey), so we should display user interface elements representing two links: the link A-B and the link A-C. It would not be appropriate to display information now for the other four links that we are aware of (B-A, B-C, C-A and C-B). After all, these links do not originate at our current location, so we should not be able to follow them. When they should be displayed is unclear and not defined by the XLink specification. You could imagine constructing some kind of site map (site web actually) from the information in the link.

So, we'll try to show the two links that should be visible in our current location. How would they look? This obviously depends on the styling of the bearing elements. But if the friend(s) elements would normally be displayed as:

- ❑ Joey
- ❑ Jenny
- ❑ Angela

we would now expect something like:

- ❑ Joey
- ❑ <u>Jenny</u>
- ❑ Ange<u>la</u>

The first friend element does not generate a link, because this resource is our current location and the link does not define a link from the resources to itself.

The resource Element

All resources linked to by locator elements are known as **remote** resources, even if they are in the same document; they are remote from the linking element. XLink also provides **local** resources, which are the content enclosed by the linking element. This is done by assigning the value resource to the xlink:type attribute of an element. Everything enclosed by this resource element is the local resource.

Note that the linking element of type resource is not the only way to refer to a resource. The locator type also defines a resource. We will show an example of using local resources in the next section.

The arc Element

By combining an arbitrary number of resources into one link, we can now combine multiple documents into one set. If you are viewing one of the documents, you can jump to any of the other documents. This is a very powerful concept, but as with most powerful concepts, there is a downside. Links with many resources will tend to overwhelm the user with related resources, while normally only a few directions of traversal make sense.

Imagine a set of documents, each holding a chapter of a book and one holding the index and table of contents. There are basically only a few normal directions to follow links through the book:

- ❑ Moving to the next chapter
- ❑ Moving to the previous chapter (less obvious, but still useful)
- ❑ Moving from any chapter to the index or table of contents
- ❑ Moving from the table of contents to any chapter
- ❑ Moving from the index to a specific point in a chapter

So what we really want to do is remove all other links from the extended link. In most cases, nobody is interested in jumping from Chapter 7 to Chapter 12 directly. The presence of so many links only confuses the user and distracts from the obvious important links.

> *Interestingly, I know of one book that has multiple orders of chapters. "Rayuela" by the Argentinian author Julio Cortázar (translated into English as "Hopscotch") is really two books. One starts at Chapter 1 and tells a chronological story, suddenly ending at Chapter 56, somewhere in the middle of the book. The other one starts right in the middle and is read by following the number at the end of each chapter to the next chapter. The reader is sent to and fro through the book, very much like clicking around on the web. The book was written in 1963 and is considered one of the masterpieces of Latin American literature.*

The solution of XLink to the multitude of links in an extended link is the `arc` element. The `arc` element is used like this:

```
<friends xlink:type="extended">
  <friend
    xlink:role="joey"
    xlink:type="locator"
    xlink:href="http://www.joey.com">Joey
  </friend>
  <friend
    xlink:role="jenny"
    xlink:type="locator"
    xlink:href="http://www.people.com/jenny">Jenny
  </friend>
  <friend
    xlink:role="angela"
    xlink:type="locator"
    xlink:href="http://www.people.com/angela" >Angela
  </friend>
  <dummy xlink:type="arc"
    xlink:to="jenny"
    xlink:from="joey"/>
  <dummy xlink:type="arc"
    xlink:to="angela"
    xlink:from="jenny"/>
  <dummy xlink:type="arc"
    xlink:to="joey"
    xlink:from="angela"/>
</friends>
```

We have added roles to all locators (and resources if there were any), to allow us to refer to the `locator` elements from the `arc` elements. Every `arc` element specifies a link and bears an `xlink:to` and an `xlink:from` attribute. Both must contain a `role` that is used in the link. If an extended link has any `arc` elements, all implicit links (that automatically appeared when we had no `arc`s defined) are dropped. So this example would result in the following situation:

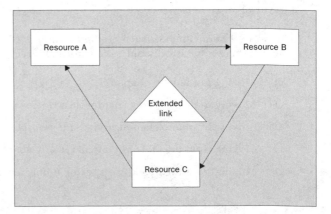

An interesting feature is that the role of a resource (be it local or remote) is not necessarily unique. If several `locator` elements have the same `role` value, an `arc` referring to this role refers to all of these locators. Consider this link, connecting information about all students in a class and a document containing the lesson schedule for that class:

```
<dummy xlink:type="extended">
  <dummy xlink:type="locator" href="students/s12324.xml"
    xlink:role="class5A_student"/>
  <dummy xlink:type="locator" href="students/s82394.xml"
    xlink:role="class5A_student"/>
  <dummy xlink:type="locator" href="students/s52624.xml"
    xlink:role="class5A_student"/>
  <dummy xlink:type="locator" href="schedule.xml"
    xlink:role="class5A_schedule"/>

  <dummy xlink:type="arc" xlink:from="class5A_student"
    xlink:to="class5A_schedule"/>
  <dummy xlink:type="arc" xlink:from="class5A_schedule"
    xlink:to="class5A_student"/>
</dummy>
```

In this extended link, `locators` refer to the students and the schedule. The `locator` for the schedule has `role="class5A_schedule"` while all `locators` referring to information about the students have `role="class5A_student"`.

Links between the `locators` are created with the two `arc` elements, one pointing from `role` `class5A_student` to `class5A_schedule` and one going the other way. This results in six links: three from each of the students to the schedule, and three from the schedule to each of the students in the class. Using this technique, you can define large numbers of links between the same kinds of resources using only a few `arcs`.

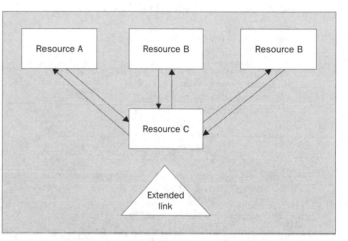

If you have a document containing the contents of a book, you could use this technique to create a table of contents. Imagine a document like the following, which contains no linking information:

```
<book>
  <chapter>
    <title>Tell me why</title>
    <par>We used to sing...</par>
    ...
  </chapter>
  <chapter>
    <title>An idea is born</title>
```

```
      <par>Charles Darwin did not set...</par>
      ...
   </chapter>
   <chapter>
      <title>Universal Acid</title>
      <par>Darwin began his explanation...</par>
      ...
   </chapter>
   ...
</book>
```

This is a fairly simple document, containing a lot of text in a clear structure of chapters, titles and paragraphs. What we need to complete the work is the ability to navigate through it and to get a clear view of the available contents. Somewhere in the beginning of the document we would expect a list of all available chapters, together with some indication of how to get there. In printed books, such a list is called a "Table of Contents" and the navigational support is given by adding a page number. In electronic documents such support would normally be some sort of hyperlink but, in essence, that is not relevant. What we want to include in our document is: "these are the points the Table of Contents should refer to". How this works out in the viewer (be it paper or an HTML browser or something unthought of yet) is not the task of XLink. We will make the whole document into one extended link, defining all of the chapters as internal resources. That way we can easily refer to all chapters from the Table of Contents. All chapters should have the same `xlink:role` attribute. By adding an element to the document that will work as a placeholder for the Table of Contents, we have all our starting and ending points complete. Then, we only have to include the necessary `arcs` to define the direction of the links. We use dummy elements to do that.

The new document would look like this:

```
<book xmlns:xlink="http://www.w3.org/1999/xlink/namespace/"
   xlink:type="extended" >
   <dummy xlink:type="arc"
      xlink:from="toc"
      xlink:to="chapter"/>
   <dummy xlink:type="arc"
      xlink:from="chapter"
      xlink:to="toc"/>
   <placeholder xlink:type="resource"
      xlink:role="toc"/>
   <chapter xlink:type="resource"
      xlink:role="chapter">
      <title>Tell me why</title>
      <par>We used to sing...</par>
      ...
   </chapter>
   <chapter xlink:type="resource"
      xlink:role="chapter">
      <title>An idea is born</title>
      <par>Charles Darwin did not set...</par>
      ...
   </chapter>
   <chapter xlink:type="resource"
      xlink:role="chapter">
```

```
        <title>Universal Acid</title>
        <par>Darwin began his explanation...</par>
        ...
    </chapter>
    ...
</book>
```

Again, how this will look depends on the implementation of XLink. The implementation should in some way allow users to navigate directly from the starting points to the defined ending points of all links.

Out-of-Line Links

Now that we've seen all the varieties of linking options, you may have noticed that some links are very vaguely described regarding how they should work in practice. Consider for example the extended links. They define several resources, some of which may be remote. Then they define links between these resources. If the user is viewing document A, containing an extended link between the documents A, B and C, what should the application do with information about a link from B to C? Should it neglect it? Should it remember the link and then, when the user is viewing document B, display the link (that is not part of document B)? The specification does not (yet) say how a general purpose XLink application should handle these links.

The name for such links is **out-of-line links** (i.e. links that originate from a document other than the document containing the link). They are exactly what you need in order to do some of the things that XLink was designed for – creating annotations, remarks or references for a document that you cannot edit.

Still, even when it is not clear how XLink-enabled browser software would handle out-of-line links, we can use the functionality that *is* clear enough to do the same. An extended link is created that describes all remote resources, both the document we want to annotate (the XLink working draft will be used in this example) and the references and annotations. The xlink:show attribute is used on the locator for the annotated document to embed it into the link document (to which we *do* have edit privileges).

```
<annotations xmlns:xlink="http://www.w3.org/1999/xlink/namespaces/">
  <annoted_doc xlink:type="simple"
    xlink:href="http://www.w3.org/TR/xlink"
    xlink:role="doc"
    xlink:actuate="onLoad"
    xlink:show="embed" />
  <remarks xlink:type="extended" >

    <commented xlink:type="locator"
      xlink:role="orig1"
      xlink:href="xpointer( /annotations/annoted_doc/descendant::A[@name=
                              'Integrating XLink Usage with Other Markup'])"
    />

    <comment xlink:type="resource"
      xlink:role="target1">
      Interestingly, this point ...
    </comment>
```

```
      <commented xlink:type="locator"
        xlink:role="orig2"
        xlink:href="xpointer(/annotations/annoted_doc/descendant::A[@name=
                                 'XLink Processing and Conformance'])"
      />

      <comment xlink:type="resource"
        xlink:role="target2">
        Compare this with XSLT 1.0 Par 4.6.7
      </comment>

      <link xlink:type="arc"
        xlink:from="orig1"
        xlink:to="target1"
        xlink:show="new"
        xlink:actuate="onRequest"
      />

      <link xlink:type="arc"
        xlink:from="orig2"
        xlink:to="target2"
        xlink:show="new"
        xlink:actuate="onRequest"
      />
    </remarks>
  </annotations>
```

There is quite a lot to see in this example. First of all, we'll have a look at how the XLink specification is included in the current document. A simple link is used, but with the xlink:actuate attribute set to onLoad and the xlink:show attribute set to embed. This causes the remote document to be included into the document. Now that it is part of our document, the user sees the content of the specification when the document is loaded, and we can create an extended link in the document that refers to parts of the embedded document that can now serve as the origin for a link.

The rest of the example consists of this link description. For each of the links out of the original document to one of the comments, we created three linking elements: a locator defining an external resource (external to the link, not external to the document), a resource element defining a local resource, and an arc element, defining the link between the two. Note that referring to a part of a remote HTML document is not as easy as referring to a remote XML document. In this case we used the existence of anchor elements in the HTML as unique identifiers, but often these don't exist. When referring to an XML document, we can often use structure information (for example, the fourth chapter in the second section).

External Linksets

One common use of out-of-line links is the situation where the connections between a number of resources are stored in a separate document. This document can then be automatically included from all of the content documents using a special XLink syntax.

The syntax for including an **external linkset** uses a special value for the xlink:role attribute:

```
<extendedLink xmlns:xlink="http://www.w3.org/1999/xlink/namespaces/"
    xlink:role="xlink:external-linkset">
  <dummy xlink:type="locator" xlink:href="linkset.xml"/>
</extendedLink>
```

By setting the xlink:role attribute to xlink:external-linkset, all resources specified within that element are retrieved and parsed for linking information. If the starting point of any of the links found in the external documents is the current document, the link will be displayed (in any way the application deems fit).

Placing linking information in a separate file that is referred to by all documents is probably the most practical and easy way to implement the functionality of out-of-line links. It can be used to make links between a number of resources much more maintainable. Think of a web site that consists of five articles and all articles have a small navigation bar that shows links to all other articles. When an extra article is added, the linking information in all of the articles would have to be changed. Using an external linkset, only the links in the link document have to be changed.

Note that the value of the xlink:role attribute carries a namespace prefix. If the defined prefix for XLink is anything other than xlink, the value of the attribute should also be changed to use this prefix.

Elements Overview

By defining only attributes in the specification, XLink allows us to add linking information to an existing document without adding new elements. This concept can be useful, but sometimes it is also confusing. The value of the xlink:type attribute defines which other XLink attributes may be used.

These are the acceptable attributes for all link types:

Attributes	Type					
	Simple	extended	Locator	arc	resource	title
type	X	X	X	X	X	X
href	X		X			
role	X	X	X	X	X	
title	X	X	X	X	X	
show	X	X		X		
actuate	X	X		X		
from				X		
to				X		

Summary

This chapter was about specifications and papers instead of about software solutions, but linking is such an important feature of electronic documents that I figured it would be useful for the reader of this book to have an idea of what to expect in this area in the not too distant future.

Now that I have said this, we'll go back to real world cases and Visual Basic code. However, we will come back to the XLink and XPointer specifications later on in this book, when we will attempt to make an implementation of XLink ourselves in Chapter 10.

Let's look back on what we learned in this chapter:

❑   We introduced the concepts of points and ranges (which will in the future be used not only in XPointer, but also in the next release of the DOM)

❑   We learned how XPointer can be used, once implemented, to specify a part of a (local or remote) document

❑   We learned how XLink can be used to specify links as in HTML

❑   We learned how more complex links between more than two resources can be specified

❑   We learned what 'out-of-line' links and external linksets are

Maximizing Performance of XML Applications

When the XML specification was written, performance and efficiency were not included in the design goals for the working group. We can demonstrate this by comparing the XML-based persistence format for an ADO `Recordset` with a non-XML binary format called ADTG (Advanced Data Table Gram). A `Recordset` is created by doing a simple query on a back-end database, generating, for example, 2000 records each of 9 fields. When this `Recordset` is saved to a file, the ADTG format uses 330 KB of disk space, whereas the XML format uses 700 KB, over twice the size. The explicit design goal for XML was not efficiency nor performance, but *ease of use*: easy to read (for both human and computer), easy to parse, easy to learn.

Does this mean we should be concerned about performance when we're dealing with XML? Well, yes we should. We should always keep in mind that XML is a broadly supported, but not very efficient, encoding standard for data.

Performance has many facets, including parsing speed, transmission speed, and speed of access. Many of these depend on the techniques used; for example, validation while parsing has a significant detrimental effect on parsing performance.

In this chapter, we start out by showing some ways of improving the performance of your XML application:

- ❑ Showing nodes in a treeview 'on demand'
- ❑ Asynchronous loading of large documents
- ❑ Using SAX
- ❑ Accessing nodes by ID

Each of these is then tested with a performance testing application that will be presented later in this chapter. This tool, apart from demonstrating the performance gains of the techniques listed here, is also used to compare the performance of some other common techniques.

Loading Tree Views on Demand

Often, in VB applications, an XML document is loaded from a file or URL and part or all of the content is displayed in a tree view control. This works fine for small documents, but slows down enormously when dealing with large XML files. Sadly, in real life situations, large XML files are often the rule rather than the exception.

Let's first have a look at what is causing the delay. We take the example application `TreeDOM.vbp` (which is in the source code download) and load into it a fairly large XML document called `macbeth.xml` (which is also available in the source code download). Loading this takes about 3 seconds on my PC, though yours will undoubtedly be different – this isn't a problem as it is the *relative* values that matter. We can break up the processing that happens into three parts:

- ❑ Loading the XML file into the Document Object Model
- ❑ Recursively cycling through all levels of elements in the loaded document
- ❑ Creating a node in the tree view for each of the elements (this is the slow step)

As we test performance, it becomes apparent that most of the time is spent inserting all of the nodes into the tree view control – loading and enumerating the XML is relatively light work. A solution to this problem is to load the XML document into memory first, but not add all nodes to the tree view; just add the nodes that are *visible*. Only when a node is expanded (by clicking the little '+' sign), will this event be handled, by inserting the child nodes for this node.

So, instead of adding thousands of nodes to the control before returning to other jobs, such as responding to user actions, only the first level of nodes is now added before returning. This takes very little processing time. After that, some processing will be required every time the user clicks on the + symbol to expand a branch. each of these actions will hardly be noticed, because the number of child nodes is normally low.

Let's look at the code for an application that does just that. In the source code download you'll find `TreeDOM_expand.vbp`, which is the same base application as `TreeDOM.vbp`, but which now loads the nodes on demand. (It contains all of the code presented in this section.) When the user clicks the button for loading the document, the application loads the selected file into a `DOMDocument` object (called `oDoc`). After that, the root element of `oDoc` is passed to a function called `AddNode`, which will add the node to the tree view control:

```
oDoc.async = False
oDoc.Load "file:///" & Text1.Text 'This text box holds the filename we are
                                  ' loading (macbeth.xml)


AddNode oDoc.documentElement
```

The AddNode method called here is defined as follows:

```
Private Sub AddNode(ByRef oElem As IXMLDOMNode, Optional ByRef oTreeNode As Node)
    Dim oNewNode As Node
    Dim oNodeList As IXMLDOMNodeList
    Dim i As Long
    Dim bRoot As Boolean

    If oTreeNode Is Nothing Then
        ' This is the root node
        Set oNewNode = TreeView.Nodes.Add
        oNewNode.Expanded = True
        bRoot = True
    Else
        Set oNewNode = TreeView.Nodes.Add(oTreeNode, tvwChild)
        oNewNode.Expanded = False
    End If

    oNewNode.Text = oElem.nodeName
    Set oNewNode.Tag = oElem

    ' Adding a Dummy node
    If bRoot Then
        AddNodeList oElem.childNodes, oNewNode
    Else
        Set oNewNode = TreeView.Nodes.Add(oNewNode, tvwChild)
        oNewNode.Expanded = False
        oNewNode.Text = "parsing"
        Set oNewNode.Tag = Nothing
    End If

End Sub
```

It adds a node to the tree view as a child of the passed oTreeNode node. This parameter is optional, to allow for adding a node to the *root* of the tree view. The oElem parameter represents the XML node that holds the information to be displayed by this new treeview node.

The implementation of the function is different when no parent node is passed. Let's firstly consider what happens when a node is passed *with* a specified parent node (here we will step through the code up until the comment 'Adding a Dummy node'):

❑   A new treeview node is created as a child of the specified parent treeview node

❑   The Expanded property of the new node is set to False

❑   The Text property of the treeview node is set to the node name of the XML node

❑   The Tag property of the treeview node is set to the XML DOM node itself

If a parent node was not specified, the following occurs:

❑   A new treeview node is created in the root of the tree view

❑ The Expanded property of the new node is set to True (we want to show the children of the root too)

❑ The Text property of the treeview node is set to the node name of the XML node

❑ The Tag property of the treeview node is set to the XML DOM node itself

Ignore the code after the comment 'Adding a dummy node' for the time being – we'll discuss it in a while. Now, if someone clicks the node to expand it, we have code to handle this event, adding all child nodes:

```
Private Sub Treeview_Expand(ByVal Node As MSComctlLib.Node)
    AddNodeList Node.Tag.childNodes, Node
End Sub
```

```
Private Sub AddNodeList(ByRef oElems As IXMLDOMNodeList, ByRef oTreeNode As Node)
    Dim i As Long

    For i = 0 To oElems.length - 1
        AddNode oElems.Item(i), oTreeNode
    Next
End Sub
```

Note that because the Expanded property is set to False, we don't have to worry about possible children of the nodes just added. They will be taken care of only in the event that the node is expanded. This way, no more nodes than strictly necessary are added to the tree view control.

The Tag property of the treeview node was used before to store, with the treeview node, a reference to the corresponding XML DOM node. Now when the treeview node is expanded, the Tag property will be used again, to find out which DOM object will contain the information for the children of the treeview node.

It looks as if this is a good solution, but it still has some rough edges to polish. The biggest problem is that the user cannot expand a node, because the control doesn't show the necessary + sign. As far as the control is concerned, there are no child nodes, so no + icon is shown. There are several ways to solve this problem. First, child nodes can be added one level in advance, that is: once a node shows up because its parent unfolds, start inserting its children, which remain invisible. This strategy is elegant, but the number of sequential inserts can still get very large because a node normally has far more grandchildren than children. The simplest way is by adding a *dummy* child node to every visible but unexpanded node. This causes the + sign to be displayed and, when the node is unfolded, the dummy node is first removed before adding all the children. The Tag property of the node is simply set to Nothing to mark the node as a dummy node.

In the function AddNode, this is done in the last part:

```
' Adding a Dummy node
If bRoot Then
    AddNodeList oElem.childNodes, oNewNode
Else
    Set oNewNode = TreeView.Nodes.Add(oNewNode, tvwChild)
    oNewNode.Expanded = False
```

```
        oNewNode.Text = "parsing"
        Set oNewNode.Tag = Nothing
    End If
```

If the node that was just added is *not* the root node, another child node is added (this is the dummy node), its Expanded property is set to False, it is given the label 'processing' and the Tag property is set to Nothing. For the root element, this isn't done, but instead AddNodeList is called directly. This will cause all of the node's children to be inserted into the tree view (in this case *dummy* nodes are not added, the *real* nodes are).

This is done in the Treeview_Expand event handler:

```
Private Sub Treeview_Expand(ByVal Node As MSComctlLib.Node)
  ' Remove the dummy
  Treeview.Nodes.Remove (Node.Child.Index)
  ' Add the child nodes to the tree view
  AddNodeList Node.Tag.childNodes, Node
End Sub
```

Now there is only one issue left to consider. If a user expands a node and then collapses it again, the child nodes are still there but they are hidden by the tree view control. If the user then decides to expand the node again, then it is not necessary for all the child nodes to be re-inserted. So we need to check if this node has already been previously expanded. This can easily be done by checking that the node's first child has its Tag property set to Nothing (which means it is a dummy node):

```
Private Sub Treeview_Expand(ByVal Node As MSComctlLib.Node)
If Node.children = 1 Then
  ' Check if the single child
  ' is indeed the dummy child
  If Node.Child.Tag Is Nothing Then
    ' Remove the dummy
    Tree view.Nodes.Remove (Node.Child.Index)
    ' Add the child nodes to the tree view
    AddNodeList Node.Tag.childNodes, Node
  End If
End If
End Sub
```

We first check if the number of child nodes equals 1, because we want to prevent a runtime error in cases where no child node exists at all. Then if the Tag property of the only child is indeed Nothing, it is removed and the process of adding all the child nodes begins.

Asynchronous Loading of Large Documents

Even if we are not doing anything time consuming, such as adding all nodes to a tree view control, the loading of a document can still take a lot of time. This can be caused by very large files, that take a long time to read and parse, or by slow connections. In normal situations, when a document is loaded, the application will wait for it to load and parse before attempting to do anything else. This guarantees that the document is fully ready for reading values or manipulation after the load method is called. However, it freezes our application for the time of processing the document. This can take several minutes for a large document over a slow connection. To prevent this problem, the document can be loaded *asynchronously*. This means that the application doesn't have to wait until all of the loading and parsing is done, but can do other things while waiting for the parser.

This way, the user can at least be given a responsive user interface during the loading of the document. Instead of accessing the data in the document directly after the load command, we have to bind to events from the Document object to alert us of a changed state, hopefully a 'COMPLETED' state.

In the source code download, you will find a project named TreeDOM_async.vbp. This is a variation on the TreeDOM.vbp project. It has the same functionality for displaying a loaded document in a tree view, but this program will load the document asynchronously. The code for the handling of the Load button looks like this:

```
Private Sub Command1_Click()
    Set oDoc = New DOMDocument
    oDoc.async = True
    oDoc.Load "file:///" & Text1.Text
    ' At this point, the DOM is not loaded
    ' We have to use events to know when to
    ' Start reading information from the document

End Sub
```

Now that the load method has been called, we can start doing other things. The document has not been loaded yet, but the DOMDocument will alert us of any status changes, by raising an event. To catch these events, we must have declared the DOMDocument object table with the WithEvents keyword:

```
Dim WithEvents oDoc As MSXML.DOMDocument

Private Sub oDoc_onreadystatechange()
    If oDoc.readyState = 4 Then
        Debug.Print "Document totally loaded"
    End If
End Sub
```

In this case, the only thing that is done is to write the new status to the debug window. In real applications, the status change to 4 (meaning COMPLETE) will often trigger the application to start further processing on the data. If you click the 'Display in tree' button after the readyState has changed to 4, the result will be identical to the result when loaded synchronously.

When parsing a document asynchronously, the document goes through several states. The state the document is in determines what can be done with it:

State	Numeric Value	Description
UNINITIALIZED	0	The object has been created, but there is no XML tree and no load in progress. This essentially means that load() or loadXML() has not yet been called.
LOADING	1	The object is preparing for parsing. LOADING does not mean that the object is already loading data.
LOADED	2	The object is beginning to read and parse data. No data can be retrieved from the object yet.
INTERACTIVE	3	Enough data has been read and parsed to expose a part of the data tree through the object model.
COMPLETED	4	The full document has been loaded.

When working synchronously, we wait until the object reaches a readyState value of 4 before we do anything. This is a very safe way of reading the document, because we can be sure that all information belonging to the document is actually at our disposal.

When we are working asynchronously, the object returns the control to us just after passing to the INTERACTIVE state. At this moment, we cannot be sure about anything. Nodes we expect to be present may not have been read yet. The MSXML parser has some extension properties implemented in the Node objects, which are specifically designed to find out if a node can be accessed yet and if it has already been parsed. We will look at an example to clarify the exact function of these properties. Imagine we are working on an XML document (macbeth.xml) that starts like this:

```
<?xml version="1.0"?>
<PLAY>
  <PERSONAE>
    <PERSONA>DUNCAN</PERSONA>

    <PGROUP>
      <PERSONA>MALCOLM</PERSONA>
      <PERSONA>DONALBAIN</PERSONA>
----------------We are here-----------
      <GRPDESCR>his sons.</GRPDESCR>
    </PGROUP>


    ...
  </PERSONAE>
</PLAY>
```

Suppose that our application reads this XML document asynchronously from a web server over a very slow line. At some moment in time, only part of the document has been read. The line highlighted in the XML code sample indicates the last line received. What would we find if we tried to access data from the document at this point?

The MSXML parser assumes that all elements will be closed later and, if you ask the parser for its XML content, it will include the closing tags that it has not yet read. (If it later turns out that the closing tag does not exist in the document, i.e. the document is not well-formed, an error will be raised and the loaded tree of DOM nodes will be removed again.) So if we were to print or save oDoc.xml, the result would be:

```
<?xml version="1.0"?>
<PLAY>
  <PERSONAE>
    <PERSONA>DUNCAN</PERSONA>


    <PGROUP>
      <PERSONA>MALCOLM</PERSONA>
      <PERSONA>DONALBAIN</PERSONA>
    </PGROUP>
  </PERSONAE>
</PLAY>
```

To check if it is possible to safely use the data in a node, we can check its parsed property. The parsed property of a node is set to True once all its descendents are fully parsed. An element is parsed as soon as its closing tag is successfully parsed. With the failure to parse the line:

```
<GRPDESCR>his sons.</GRPDESCR>
```

the information contained in the PLAY, PERSONAE and PGROUP elements is incomplete, hence the parsed = False statements:

```
PLAY element          - parsed = False
 PERSONAE element      - parsed = False
  PERSONA element       - parsed = True
  PGROUP element        - parsed = False
   PERSONA element       - parsed = True
   PERSONA element       - parsed = True
```

Using SAX with Large XML Documents

There is another problem that affects very large XML files. When loading an XML document, the MSXML parser reads all information into memory, instantiating COM objects for all nodes. This uses an amount of memory roughly three times the size of the XML file. That is no problem as long as files do not grow to the size of the available memory of the processing machine; if this happens, the machine will start swapping memory to the hard drive and when even that space is unsufficient, processing stalls. The DOM, with all its objects, is not the right way to access XML data from large streams. In these cases, you should consider using SAX instead of the DOM. We saw how to use SAX in Chapter 3 and, as you will remember, SAX allows us to process an XML stream by catching events from the parser. The parser will not build a tree of nodes for us. This is good because:

❑   No matter how large the document, SAX will just carry on parsing, because it doesn't try to store the structure of the document in memory.

❑ The way SAX works is more efficient when only a part of the document is required. A SAX parser will not spend processor time creating objects for parts of the document that our application isn't even interested in.

The downsides of SAX are:

❑ A SAX parser does not store any information for us in memory. Everything we want to use later on, we have to store ourselves.

❑ There is no structural awareness during parsing. When an event occurs, the parser can only give information on that specific event. Any additional information, such as the place in the structure of the document, has to be derived from the order in which the events occur. For example, when our application receives an event for the start of a certain element, we do not know if this element is contained by another element. If we want to know this, we have to keep track of it ourselves.

Still, in some cases SAX is very convenient. Imagine a document that is so large that it wouldn't even fit in memory. With SAX, we might filter on occurrences of a certain element from this document and we would not waste precious memory space keeping track of the entire structure of the document. Obviously, the performance of a SAX parser is heavily influenced by whether validation is being used. Some SAX parsers support validation, but this means that they must keep track internally of the document's structure.

Here is a little example of how to use SAX to select a small portion of the stream of data in a large file (you can find this in the source code download, named `SAX_Filter.vbp`). The XML would look like this:

```
<?xml version="1.0"?>
<INVENTORY>
  <PRODUCT prodid="2367" LastUpdate="20000303">
    <!-Product details-->
  </PRODUCT>
  <PRODUCT prodid="2487" LastUpdate="19991231">
    <!-Product details-->
  </PRODUCT>
  <PRODUCT prodid="6317" LastUpdate="20000112">
    <!-Product details-->
  </PRODUCT>
  <!-Many, many more PRODUCT elements -->
</INVENTORY>
```

The document contains data on a huge amount of products, but our application is only interested in the products that have changed since we last imported the file. So we filter the PRODUCT elements that have a LastUpdate attribute that is larger than some Long value we already have determined as read from the Registry.

After parsing, we have a collection filled with the ProductIDs of the recently updated products. Let's look at the code:

```
Dim WithEvents oParser As SAXLib.SAXParser
Dim oCollection As Collection
```

```
Dim lLastUpdate As Long

Private Sub Command1_Click()
  lLastUpdate = CLng(Text1.Text)
  Set oParser = New SAXParser
  oParser.parseFile App.Path & "\testdocument.xml"
End Sub

Private Sub oParser_startDocument()
  Set oCollection = New Collection
End Sub

Private Sub oParser_endDocument()
  Dim sIDs As String

  For Each ID In oCollection
    sIDs = sIDs & ID & vbCrLf
  Next
  MsgBox sIDs
End Sub

Private Sub oParser_startElement _
        (ByVal sName As String, _
         ByVal pAttributeList As SAXLib.ISAXAttributeList)

  If sName = "PRODUCT" Then
    If CLng(getValueByName("LastUpdate", pAttributeList)) > lLastUpdate Then
      ' Store it in the collection
      oCollection.Add getValueByName("prodid", pAttributeList)
    End If
  End If
End Sub

Private Function getValueByName _
        (ByVal sName As String, _
         ByVal pAttributeList As SAXLib.ISAXAttributeList) As String
  ' Helper function to access attributes by name
  For i = 0 To pAttributeList.getLength
    If pAttributeList.getName(i) = sName Then
      getValueByName = pAttributeList.getValue(i)
    End If
  Next
End Function
```

For this example, the XML content is read from a file located in the same directory as the application and the value for lLastUpdate is not retrieved from storage, but can be specified using a textbox. But the process of selecting a small subset of the elements in the document is the same. When the button is clicked, the parser is instantiated and started. Then on retrieving the startDocument() event, the collection of product IDs is cleared. At each startElement event, we include code to check if it is a PRODUCT element. If it is, the LastUpdate attribute is compared with our lLastUpdate value. If it is newer, the prodid value is stored in the collection. For accessing an attribute by name, we created a helper function called getValueByName.

When the end of the document is reached, a message box is displayed containing the product IDs currently in the collection.

Accessing Nodes by ID

In cases where we have a loaded validated document with some attribute declared as ID in the DTD or Schema, we can achieve a considerable performance gain when accessing the elements with an ID attribute. This is especially useful when handling XHTML documents. If we want to get hold of an element of type TABLE with the ID property set to tblValues, there are a few strategies to choose from:

- ❑ Use getElementsByTagname to retrieve all TABLE elements and then check their ID property in a loop to find the right one.

- ❑ Use an XPath string with the selectNodes method. The XPath would be something like //TABLE[@ID = 'tblValues'].

- ❑ The third and fastest way is to use the getElementByID method, passing the value of tblValues to the method.

The last two methods don't follow the DOM standardized methods and will only work with MSXML objects. We will look at how to do this for each case and advice will be given as to when to use each technique. We will devise a simple situation on which to apply each of the three methods. Have a look at the simple VB application AccessByID.vbp in the source code download (the directory includes all the necessary document and DTD files). We have loaded an XHTML document with several tables in it and we are looking for one specific table that has a certain ID we know:

```
Dim oDoc As DOMDocument
Dim sFileName As String

Sub Form_Load()
  Set oDoc = New DOMDocument
  sFileName = App.Path & "\XHTMLSample.htm"
  oDoc.async = False
  oDoc.Load (sFileName)

  If Not oDoc.parseError.errorCode = 0 Then
    MsgBox "Error: " & oDoc.parseError.reason
  End If

End Sub
```

getElementsByTagname

When using standard DOM methods, the fastest way to get to a TABLE element with a certain ID attribute is to use getElementsByTagname. This will find all TABLE elements, which can then be looped through to find the right one. In a normal XHTML file, the number of tables will normally not be astronomical, so this can be a feasible approach. The code to do this would look like this:

```
Sub Command1_Click()
    Dim oTableList As MSXML.IXMLDOMNodeList
    Dim oElement As MSXML.IXMLDOMElement

    Set oTableList = oDoc.getElementsByTagName("table")
```

```
      For i = 0 To oTableList.length - 1
          Set oElement = oTableList.Item(i)
          If oElement.getAttribute("id") = "tblValues" Then
              ' Do something with the element oElement
              MsgBox "found"
          End If
      Next

  End Sub
```

We don't check if the attribute is declared as type ID. The MSXML implementation of the `getElementsByTagname` allows us to use more complex constraints than just the tag name, but this is not what the DOM recommendation specifies. Therefore it should not be used if you only want to use standardized code.

selectNodes

If we use the MSXML implementation, we have the luxury of using the `selectNodes` and `selectSingleNode` methods. These are specifically designed to select a set of nodes from the document according to certain criteria. Because the implementation uses smarter search algorithms than we did in the previous section, this method is normally a lot faster at finding a node. The query syntax uses XPath. We could implement the requested functionality like this:

```
  Private Sub Command2_Click()
      Dim oElement As MSXML.IXMLDOMElement

      Set oElement = oDoc.selectSingleNode("//table[@id='tblValues']")
      ' Do something with the element
      If Not oElement Is Nothing Then MsgBox "found"

  End Sub
```

Here, we use the `selectSingleNode` method, because we know that only one element can fit the description – an ID can only occur once in a document.

nodeFromID

A third technique is to use the method `nodeFromID`. This method, like the `selectNodes` and `selectSingleNode` methods, is a Microsoft-specific add-on. If the document is validated, in other words the parser has its `validateOnParse` property set to `True` (see Chapter 3 for details), and the attribute ID is declared as type ID in the DTD or Schema, this method is by far the fastest way to access the specified table element (internally, MSXML keeps an index of the IDs in the document). It looks like this:

```
  Private Sub Command3_Click()
      Dim oElement As MSXML.IXMLDOMElement

      Set oElement = oDoc.nodeFromID("tblValues")
      ' Do something with the element
      If Not oElement Is Nothing Then MsgBox "found"

  End Sub
```

The retrieval by ID works only with attributes declared as type ID; others will be left out, but note that the name doesn't have to be 'ID'. The method does not work when validation is turned off, because without validation, the parser cannot tell which attributes are IDs and which are not.

It is important to note that these three methods do similar things, but they are not identical. The first two methods select an element according to an attribute called 'ID', whereas the last method selects elements that have an ID-typed attribute with *any* name.

Note also that the performance of the first method decreases linearly with the number of matching elements in the first selection. In this example this will normally not be a problem, but if we wanted to select an arbitrary element with a specific ID, we would quickly run into trouble. It would be better to use the third method described above in this case. Cycling through all elements in a large XML file looking for an attribute is a killer for performance.

Making a Custom Index

This kind of functionality is very common in XML processing applications. It happens when we have elements that refer to other elements in the document using ID/IDREF attributes. If we want to use only DOM 1.0 methods, we have to implement our own indexing mechanism. When we have to search for certain elements again and again, it is best to pre-process the document after loading and store the references to these nodes in a Dictionary object. The Dictionary object can hold a collection of items (Variants) that can be retrieved by name. The Dictionary object is part of the Microsoft Scripting Runtime library that comes with Internet Explorer and IIS.

We will approach the same case that we looked at above, but with this new technique (you can find this code in the sample application AccessByID.vbp). Directly after loading the document, all TABLE elements are stored in a Dictionary, indexed by the value of their ID attribute:

```
Dim oDoc2 As DOMDocument        'This one is for building our own index
Dim oNodeMap As Dictionary      ' This will hold the index

Private Sub Command4_Click()
    Dim oTableList As MSXML.IXMLDOMNodeList
    Dim oElement As MSXML.IXMLDOMElement

    Set oNodeMap = New Dictionary
    Set oDoc2 = New DOMDocument
    oDoc2.async = False

    oDoc.Load (App.Path & "\XHTMLSample.htm")

    Set oTableList = oDoc.getElementsByTagName("table")

    For i = 0 To oTableList.length - 1
        Set oElement = oTableList.Item(i)
        If Not oElement.getAttribute("id") = "" Then
            ' If an attribute is not specified and has no
            ' default value, DOM specifies that getAttribute returns
            ' an empty string
            oNodeMap.Add oElement.getAttribute("id"), oElement
        End If
    Next
```

```
        End Sub
```

Now that all these nodes have been stored, it is easy to retrieve all elements with an ID, using something like:

```
    Private Sub Command5_Click()

        If Not oNodeMap.Item("tblValues") Is Nothing Then MsgBox "found"

    End Sub
```

Once all elements have been added to the dictionary, this will work about as fast as the `nodeFromID` method.

If you studied the previous chapters carefully (especially Chapter 3), you may wonder why we don't use the `NamedNodeMap` object from the DOM with this technique (instead of the `Dictionary` object). After all, isn't the `NamedNodeMap` specifically designed for doing things like this? `NamedNodeMap` can hold a set of nodes in no specific order, retrievable by name. It was added to the DOM to hold a set of `Attribute` nodes.

We would like to use the `NamedNodeMap` to store the elements we want to index. We would use the value of the `ID` property as the name, and the element we want to index as the value.

Unfortunately, the `NamedNodeMap` does not allow the nodes to be stored with a name different to their `nodeName` property. This makes perfect sense when considering holding the attributes of an element (the `href` attribute is stored under the name "href"), but makes the object unusable for our purpose. All nodes in our example are called `TABLE`. The editor of the specification realized this, but decided to restrict the use anyway:

> "As the `nodeName` attribute is used to derive the name which the node must be stored under, multiple nodes of certain types (those that have a special string value) cannot be stored, as the names would clash. This is seen as preferable to allowing nodes to be aliased."

We can only respect their decision and use the `Dictionary` object instead.

Performance Tester Application

It is possible to talk at length about the efficiency of different techniques but, in the end, when we're talking performance, we have to carry out tests. Each alternative must be tried, and the time taken to complete the task measured. With the source code, there is a VB project called `PerfTest.vbp`. This application tests the time needed when performing a task with different approaches. It is also an XML-based application, which uses an XML document to hold all descriptions and names of the tested procedures, including the default number of iterations. When you run the application, a simple window will be displayed:

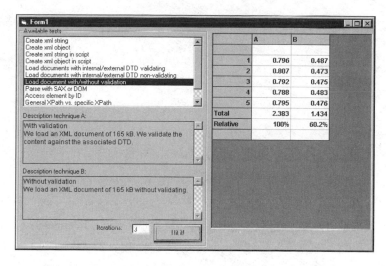

On the left, you can choose one of the available comparison tests. When you select one, the descriptions of both techniques (labeled A and B) will appear in the boxes below it. In the text box control labeled Iterations, the default number of iterations for this test is inserted. If you click Start, the application will start performing the tests. Each test is performed five times. For each of these five times, the tested technique is performed the number of times specified in the Iterations box. For each test, the time taken, in milliseconds, appears in the grid control on the right. After five tests, the measured values are added up (excluding the highest and lowest value, to allow for an anomalous result), and the sums are displayed as relative values, with technique A set to 100%.

This application allows us to measure the time needed to perform a single isolated action. In reality, performance is a much more complex matter. Every application, and certainly a distributed application, consists of a large number of links, each carrying out its own task. Improving the performance of one link will often have no effect on the total performance.

There is also a psychological factor involved in the performance of an application. What matters here is the impression of the end user. A performance improvement is something that allows the end user to wait for a shorter period of time. For example, using a clear UI, or a logical interaction design. Even giving feedback while doing a heavy task (for example showing a gauge with 'percentage ready') can significantly improve the *perceived* performance. All of these are not measured by this application. It is very interesting to look at performance differences at a low level. Just be aware of the fact that the user experience of good performance is not caused by short processing times alone.

Constructing a Simple Document from Scratch

What is the most efficient way to construct a simple XML document from scratch? This is the performance question most frequently asked in newsgroups and mailing lists. Often, you make an application that must pass only a small bit of information, such as the content of a few variables or a small array, to another application, as an XML document.

The first approach (Approach A) is the one taken by most VB developers - just construct a string by hard coding some of the fragments (like the XML declaration) and concatenate all the string fragments to a larger string holding the XML document. Now it can be passed or written to file, which is carried out by this code:

```
Private Sub CheckBuildDocumentA()
    Dim sXML As String
    Dim sContentString As String

    sContentString = "This is some text with a ""quote"" and &'s "
    sXML = "<?xml version=""1.0""?>" & vbCrLf
    sXML = sXML & "<items>"
    For i = 1 To 10
        sXML = sXML & "<item "
        If i > 5 Then
            sXML = sXML & "someAttribute=""" & i & """"
        End If
        sXML = sXML & replaceSpecialChars(sContentString)
        sXML = sXML & "</item>"
    Next
    sXML = sXML & "</items>"

End Sub

'Helper function to escape special characters from text value
Public Function replaceSpecialChars(sPassed As String) As String
    replaceSpecialChars = Replace(sPassed, "&", "&amp;")
    replaceSpecialChars = Replace(replaceSpecialChars, "<", "&lt;")
    replaceSpecialChars = Replace(replaceSpecialChars, ">", "&gt;")
    replaceSpecialChars = Replace(replaceSpecialChars, """", "&quot;")
    replaceSpecialChars = Replace(replaceSpecialChars, "'", "&apos;")
End Function
```

This constructs a very simple document. In a loop we create a set of ten item elements, that all hold an attribute someAttribute with increasing value. To make sure that the XML is well formed, each text value must be processed before appending it to the string. All illegal characters (<, ", &, >, ') must first be replaced by entities (< and others).

The second approach (Approach B) uses the DOM objects to construct a document. The DOMDocument object exposes a whole set of methods to create new nodes. The code for generating a document identical to that created with Approach A would look like this:

```
Private Sub CheckBuildDocumentB()
    Dim sXML As String
    Dim oXML As New DOMDocument
    Dim oRoot As IXMLDOMElement
    Dim oCurrElem As IXMLDOMElement
    Dim sContentString As String

    sContentString = "This is some text with a ""quote"" and &'s "

    Set oRoot = oXML.createElement("items")
    Set oXML.documentElement = oRoot
    oXML.insertBefore _
            oXML.createProcessingInstruction("xml", " version=""1.0"""), oRoot

    For i = 1 To 10
```

```
            Set oCurrElem = oXML.createElement("item")
            oRoot.appendChild oCurrElem
            If i > 5 Then
                oCurrElem.setAttribute "someAttribute", CStr(i)
            End If
            oCurrElem.Text = sContentString
        Next
        sXML = oXML.xml
    End Sub
```

The second approach takes slightly fewer lines of code and is more readable and maintainable. When the generated document is large, this DOM approach will work much better for the developer. It is also easier to break up into subroutines. The developer can rely on the DOM library to create well formed XML (instead of manually replacing illegal characters etc...).

But what about the performance? It is true that the DOM approach carries more overhead – it does not know how simple the content is, so it will check every name and every bit of content for illegal characters. In the process of generating the document, many objects must be instantiated. On the other hand, the MSXML objects were written in C++, a language with a good reputation for high performance programming.

Here are the results from testing with both methods:

Method	Time (ms)	Relative Rating (%)
Create string with concatenation	250	100
Create string with DOM	711	284

It turns out that constructing the string by VB concatenation is nearly three times faster than using the DOM. (The results displayed were measured on a development system with PII 300 MHz 128 MB and Win NT 4 Server installed.) There are many good reasons to use the DOM, but if your documents are very simple and performance of generation is an issue, simple string handling using VB code is clearly faster.

It is important to note that string handling in Visual Basic becomes dramatically slower when you are handling larger strings. When this test was repeated with generation of larger documents (running through the loop 1000 times instead of 10 times), the DOM approach became much faster than string handling.

In the performance tester application provided, a few variations on this test are also included. The test described above compares two methods of creating a string, but what if we want to generate a loaded DOM object tree from scratch? Approach A then has to be extended to include loading a DOMDocument object with the string, whereas Approach B can leave out the last conversion to a String. The results are as follows:

Method	Time (ms)	Relative Rating (%)
Create DOM with concatenation	541	100
Create DOM with DOM	480	89

If the goal of the procedure is a loaded object model, the fastest way to create a new document is using DOM objects.

If you create your document in an ASP page using VBScript, the dilemma is slightly different. String concatenation is very fast in VB, because it is compiled to native machine code when the executable is built. In ASP, code is parsed and interpreted at runtime. Also, all variables are of the `Variant` type. This makes object handling less efficient, because script does not allow direct access to custom COM interfaces. All calls are redirected by COM. This redirecting results in performance loss. VBScript processing will be a lot slower in both techniques. But will it slow down more for string concatenation or for object handling? In the performance tester, scripting performance can be tested using a separate script file that is loaded into a Script Control. The Script Control allows you to run scripts in your VB application using the same scripting engines used by ASP and Windows Scripting Host.

Here are the results for the same operation, but this time performed in script:

Method	Time (ms)	Relative Rating (%)
Create string with concatenation in script	532	100
Create string with DOM in script	1332	250

Method	Time (ms)	Relative Rating (%)
Create DOM with concatenation in script	800	100
Create DOM with DOM in script	1153	144

It turns out that performance loss in generating an XML document is greater for the DOM approach than for string concatenation. When creating a string, both methods lose about the same factor in performance, but for constructing the loaded `Document` object, string concatenation is now faster than using the DOM. So in ASP there is even more reason to use plain string concatenation (at least for small documents). Still, there are good reasons other than performance to stick to the object model.

Parsing With and Without Validation

Parsing XML from a file is relatively easy; XML was designed for that purpose. Implementing all validation rules is a different game. First the parser must read, parse and understand the DTD or Schema syntax. Then every node from the document must be checked for validity. It is obvious that parsing with validation will use more processing time than parsing and just checking whether it is well formed. That's why, in many production environments, validation is not used as the validity has already been checked beforehand. That is also why the MSXML parser can be switched from validating to non-validating by setting the `validateOnParse` property to `False`.

How much slower is it really? The results are given below:

Method	Time (ms)	Relative Rating (%)
Parse the document with validation against a DTD	1653	100
Parse the document without validation	981	59

It turns out that turning off validation makes the MSXML parser about 40% faster. That is not so bad really, considering the extra amount of checks that must be performed for every node in the document. It is however a significant performance loss, significant enough to use non-validating mode in many production environments.

Using an Inline or an External DTD

DTDs specifying the validation rules for a document can be placed within the document or in an external file. So which of these is faster? One would expect the inline DTD to be a bit faster – the parser has to load only one file. The external DTD has to be read in a separate file system operation, which can only be started when the parsing of the document is already on its way. On the other hand, keeping the DTD in a central place and having all documents refer to that one URL is much more manageable.

Of course, performance will depend very heavily on the *bandwidth* of connections to remote hosts. In the performance tester, we look only at external DTDs that come from the file system. In networked scenarios, the performance advantage of the inline syntax gets more and more significant. These are the results:

Method	Time (ms)	Relative Rating (%)
Using an inline DTD	890	100
Using an external DTD	1093	123

So that behaves as expected – accessing two files does cost. But what would happen if we were to turn validation off? The external DTD would not have to be retrieved, while the internal DTD must be parsed anyway. The validation rules will not be applied to the content, but the DTD has to be read and parsed anyway. So we would expect the performance to be better for the document with the external DTD. This turns out to be true:

Method	Time (ms)	Relative Rating (%)
Using an inline DTD	871	100
Using an external DTD	500	57

This conforms exactly to what we expected. Note that the parsing time for this small XML document (about 1 KB in size) hardly decreases when not validated. The task of parsing the text of the DTD weighs a lot more. Note that, to achieve the performance gain associated with not having to read the external DTD when parsing, it is not enough to set `validateOnParse` to `False`. You should also set `resolveExternals` to `False`. If `resolveExternals` is set to `True`, the parser must read the DTD file anyway to check if any entities are declared in it. The entities have implications for whether the document will be well formed or not and are important even if you don't need to validate.

Parsing Using DOM or SAX

As mentioned earlier in this chapter, for parsing really large documents, especially in cases where only a small fragment of the data is required and no modifications to the data are needed, SAX can be a more lightweight API to use, especially when the memory used by DOM can be a problem. For the test, we used a fairly large document (`macbeth.xml`, 165 KB), but not something that causes memory trouble for DOM implementations. The DOM implementation used is MSXML, the SAX implementation used is that produced by Vivid Software. (A trial version can be downloaded from their site at http://www.vivid-creations.com/ – it does not expire, but has a seven seconds delay built in when files larger than 10 KB are parsed.) This delay occurs after the last parsing event, so timing measurement can accurately be done in that last event.

Method	Time (ms)	Relative Rating (%)
Parse the document with SAX	1041	100
Parse the document with DOM	270	26

It turns out that this SAX implementation takes about four times as long as the MSXML DOM. This is a bit of a disappointment, as we would have expected that SAX would parse faster, because it has less internal overhead. It is not so easy to find out why the performance is less than expected. What may cause the slowness is the fact that raising an event to Visual Basic is not as efficient as directly calling a function. Raising events involves the same overhead as calling functions from script. A SAX parser will raise lots of events, so the overhead in the event mechanism is probably to blame here.

Anyway, the SAX model still scales better with larger documents. If documents are larger, eventually the 'load everything into memory' approach of the DOM will cause it to slow down as memory runs low. Doing tests with extremely large documents revealed that the time needed by the SAX parser increases linearly with document size. The footprint (memory used) remains identical, independent of the document size. With a document of 70 MB, the DOM filled the memory on my machine completely (96MB internal memory + 150 MB of swap space). At this point the two implementations took about the same time. For even larger documents, the DOM method just fails because of insufficient memory. So, basically, using this SAX implementation from VB only makes sense if documents are expected to cause the DOM to fail altogether.

Apartment-Threaded Versus Free-Threaded Access

The standard DOMDocument object from the MSXML library uses the **apartment threading model**, which basically means that several clients can access the object, but they must use the object one after another. This synchronization of the calls is done automatically, but it takes a lot of time. This makes the object unfit to be used by many users, or threads, at once. In most applications, that is not an issue, but in specific cases it can be. In an ASP application, for instance, many user requests can be processed simultaneously. Each of these requests has its own thread. These threads share some data in the Application object. If you add a loaded DOMDocument object to the Application object, that will slow the site down significantly when the number of users increases. The same goes for other objects, such as ADO Recordsets (unless you take special measures) and objects built with Visual Basic.

To overcome this problem, Microsoft also developed a *free-threaded* version of the object. It is called DOMFreeThreadedDocument and is functionally identical to DOMDocument. This object can be accessed by many threads at the same time, and implements all the plumbing necessary to be sure that two users will not overwrite and read the value of a node at the same time. Obviously, this takes time and we would expect the performance of the free-threaded object to be less than that of the apartment-threaded object when used by one single user. For multiple users, we expect the free-threaded version to perform better (because the users don't have to wait for each other). Scalability of the free-threaded version will be much better, but scalability testing is beyond the scope of this book.

Going back to our performance testing example, the results of using the free-threaded object with only one user are shown:

Method	Time (ms)	Relative Rating (%)
Parse the document with DOMDocument	181	100
Parse the document with DOMFreeTheadedDocument	190	105

As you see, the decrease in performance by adding the free-threaded capability is very low. We might even consider using the free-threaded version all the time, just to be sure that we will not create bottlenecks later.

So whether to use apartment or free threading is up to you. In this book we do not use the free-threaded document where it isn't needed, because the code looks less clear, and maybe even a bit intimidating, with the long name DOMFreeThreadedDocument in it. Just remember: never store a DOMDocument object in the Application or the Session object in ASP!

Using selectNodes or nodeFromID

In this chapter, we have looked at several ways to access an element in a loaded XML document by its ID attribute. Two extension methods in MSXML were used: selectNodes with the appropriate XPath string and the nodeFromID method, that is specifically for getting to elements using their ID attribute. We can compare these two methods:

Method	Time (ms)	Relative Rating (%)
Accessing nodes with selectNodes	491	100
Parse the document with DOM	70	14

It turns out that using the nodeFromID method is indeed much faster than the more general selectNodes method. Be aware that both methods are not part of the DOM and can only be used with the Microsoft implementation.

General and Specific XPath Queries

When a set of nodes is selected from a loaded document, the time needed for the selection depends very much on the size of the document and the kind of XPath query that was specified. The internal workings of the query processor are not documented and a profiler is not available, so query optimizing is hard and very much a trial and error process. Generally speaking, queries that specify structural relations (a TABLE element that has a BODY element parent) are faster than queries specifying content (any attribute with the value 'Hello World!', for example). When combining these, for example TABLE elements that have a BORDER element with a value of 1, queries are faster when they contain more structural information. The query processor starts with searching all nodes that comply with the structural specification, then it starts checking the content for all elements in that set. If the structural information narrows the set to a small group, finding the ones with the right content is easy.

The example we will test with the performance tester compares two XPath queries for selecting information from macbeth.xml. The first query selects all elements that have content MACBETH, while the second query selects all SPEAKER elements that contain MACBETH and are inside SCENE elements inside ACT elements inside the PLAY element that is the root:

Method	Time (ms)	Relative Rating (%)
Using a very general XPath	1302	100
Using a very specific XPath	220	17

If you want to compare several XPath queries that would all fit your selection, you can use the XPath tester application that was presented in Chapter 4 when we introduced XPath and XSLT.

Transformation by XSLT Versus the DOM

Suppose we have a really simple XML document, something like the family.xml file we saw before, back in Chapter 2. We want to transform it to a very simple HTML document. There are two ways to do this:

❑ Access the information in the XML document using the DOM and concatenate an HTML string from that information

❑ Load an XSLT stylesheet and have family.xml transformed by it

Which of these two techniques would perform best? XSLT is loaded with functionality that will not be used. What's more: XSLT requires the loading of two documents instead of one. On the other hand, all of the processing by the XSLT processor has been coded in C++ and can be expected to be much more efficient than the VB code. Our VB code looks like this:

```
    Dim oDoc As New DOMDocument
    Dim oList As IXMLDOMNodeList
    Dim oElem As IXMLDOMElement
    Dim sResult As String

    oDoc.Load (App.Path & "\..\XMLsources\family.xml")

    sResult = "<HTML><HEAD></HEAD><BODY><UL>"
    'First make a list of persons
    Set oList = oDoc.selectNodes("//PERSON")
    For i = 0 To oList.length - 1
        Set oElem = oList.Item(i)
        sResult = sResult & "<LI><B>" & oElem.getAttribute("name") & "</B></LI>"
    Next

    'Now make a list of the pets
    Set oList = oDoc.selectNodes("//PET")
    For i = 0 To oList.length - 1
        Set oElem = oList.Item(i)
        sResult = sResult & "<LI>" & oElem.getAttribute("name") & " (" & _
                                     oElem.getAttribute("type") & ")</LI>"
    Next

    sResult = sResult & "</UL></BODY></HTML>"
```

The stylesheet that was used to achieve the same effect looks like:

```
<xsl:stylesheet xmlns:xsl="http://www.w3.org/TR/WD-xsl">

<xsl:template match="*"><xsl:apply-templates/></xsl:template>

<xsl:template match="/">
 <HTML><HEAD/><BODY>
   <xsl:apply-templates/>
 </BODY></HTML>
</xsl:template>

<xsl:template match="FAMILY"><UL>
<xsl:apply-templates/>
</UL></xsl:template>

<!--Output: <LI><B>Peter</B></LI>  -->
<xsl:template match="PERSON"><LI>
<B><xsl:value-of select="@name" /></B>
</LI></xsl:template>

<!--Output: <LI>Bonzo (dog) </LI>-->
<xsl:template match="PET"><LI>
<xsl:value-of select="@name" /> (<xsl:value-of select="@type" />)
</LI></xsl:template>

</xsl:stylesheet>
```

Before we look at the performance results, consider the impact each approach has on future changes. What if the layout of the output HTML must be changed or if the rules for the transformation change. The XSLT approach is much more flexible and easy to maintain.

Here are the results:

Method	Time (ms)	Relative Rating (%)
Transform with XSLT	1011	100
Transform with VB and DOM	1552	154

It turns out that the transformation with XSLT is faster, even for a very simple transformation with a small document. This is good news, because it means that XSLT is not only the most flexible and maintainable way to specify a transformation, but also offers the best performance from a VB perspective.

Summary of Performance Issues

Some conclusions that follow from the tests with the performance tester application are:

❑ When it comes to speed, string concatenation is the fastest way to create a document from scratch.

❑ String concatenation is even faster in a scripting environment (ASP, WSH) when compared to a compiled VB program.

❑ Validating takes about as much time as the parsing itself.

❑ SAX is beneficial over the DOM where the size of the document is more than a third of the size of the memory available. Otherwise, MSXML DOM implementation parses faster than tested SAX implementations. (This may change of course, but it seems that doing many callbacks to a VB program is the bottleneck for SAX-based approaches.)

❑ The free-threaded version of the DOMDocument in the MSXML library is not noticeably slower than the apartment threaded implementation on a single user base.

❑ If you use attributes of type ID/IDREF, the nodeFromID method may speed up your application considerably.

❑ XPath queries on the DOM affect performance, even if the same result is obtained. Testing is the only way to determine which query performs best.

❑ Transformation should always be done with XSLT. Extracting data using the DOM and building a new document with that data will always be slower and less flexible for later changes.

Summary

We have covered all of the theory now. However, much of the skills of experienced programmers are not based on thorough knowledge of the theory, but knowledge of many how-to's and practical experience of what kind of solutions will work and what kind will not. Some of these practical facts and how-to's have been covered in this chapter, but it can never beat hands-on experience.

When starting on your first XML project, you will not yet have this experience, but you can rely on many other developers out there. Good places for posting your questions include:

- comp.text.xml
- microsoft.public.xml
- The VBXML mailing list. A very helpful community of VB XML developers: http://www.vbxml.com

In this chapter we learned:

- How to deal with tree view controls for displaying large documents with many nodes
- How to handle large documents using the asynchronous mode of MSXML
- How to handle even larger documents by using SAX
- That sometimes elements in documents can be accessed many times faster by using their ID attribute and the nodeFromID method
- How the performance of many different XML programming techniques compare

In the next chapter we will begin to focus on one large sample application that will use many of the techniques covered in this and previous chapters.

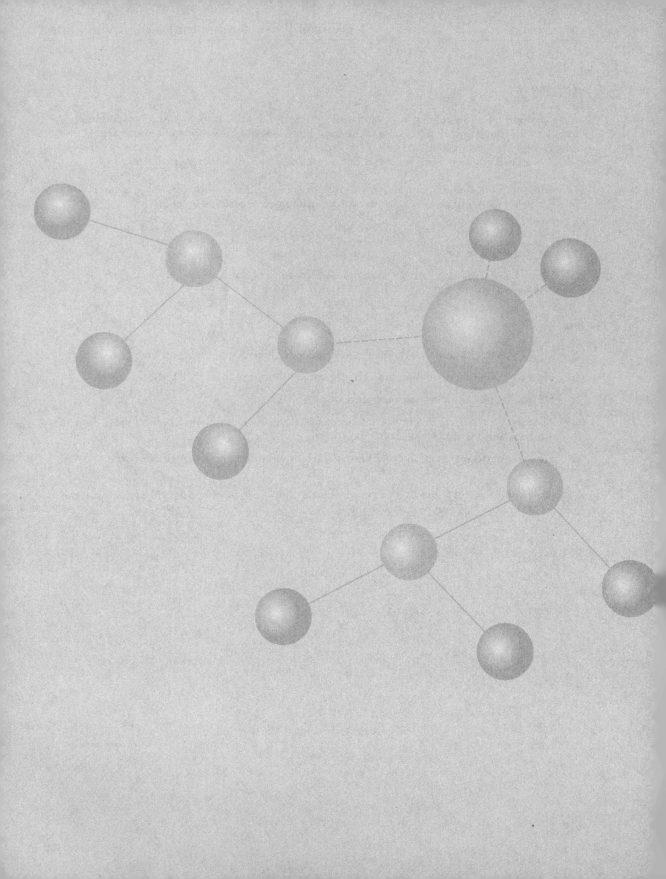

Introducing the Sample Application

Now that you've seen the main parts of the XML family and how they work, we'll get on to building a complete application to see how this all fits together in a practical way. In this chapter we'll *begin* our development of the book's main sample application, a basic e-commerce web site intended to demonstrate the use of Visual Basic with XML in a variety of circumstances. The application will be completed over the next six chapters. As we progress through the chapters, we'll try our hand at different XML technologies, including:

- ❑ Building a SOAP client/server application (this chapter)
- ❑ Writing a basic XML editor (Chapter 8)
- ❑ Handling XML data exchange and storage (Chapter 9)
- ❑ Implementing XML linking in VB (Chapter 10)
- ❑ Using XML and MSMQ for passing object state (Chapter 11)
- ❑ Transforming XML data using XSLT (Chapter 12)

In this chapter we'll discuss the basic framework of the application, consider how distributed components might communicate, and take a detailed look at SOAP, the Simple Object Access Protocol. We'll build a working SOAP client/server program, including some ActiveX DLLs that we will reuse in later chapters as we build the main application.

We'll also look at some current initiatives to define how e-commerce transactions can be encoded as XML, and questions to consider when designing an XML transaction format.

Building a Distributed Application

Our web business will be a simple online store that sells all sorts of things, from books to clothing to lawn maintenance equipment. When a visitor comes to the web site, he or she can look around, do some searching, and view details about products. While some general information about the available products is kept in a database to allow for fast lookup, the details are kept in XML files, which are rendered out to the browser. These files may contain XLink pointers to other data sources, and for that purpose we'll be creating (in Chapter 10) a Visual Basic component that can resolve XLink and XPointer requests for rendering to a browser.

At some point, the user may wish to buy something. The purchase request is sent to the web server, where the purchase transaction is dispatched to a transaction processing object. Requests for items are posted to a message queue, in XML, for later retrieval by a warehouse computer (covered in Chapter 11). A confirmation notice is created and the user is notified that the order is being processed. Meanwhile, the warehouse can ship the order and take care of restocking (part of the transformation process covered in Chapter 12).

Of course, we'll also need to edit our product description files. So in Chapter 8 we'll build a product description file editing tool that includes the ability to edit free-form XML.

Here's a picture of what the overall system will look like:

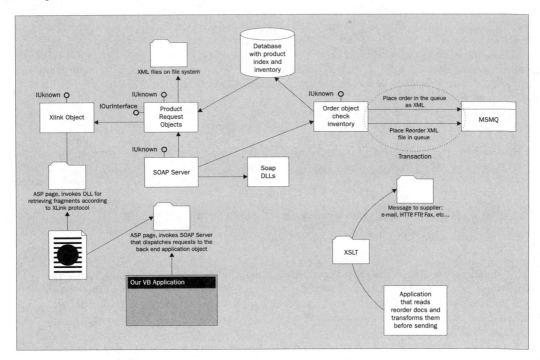

Why XML Files?

A typical product file will look like this:

```
<?xml version="1.0"?>
<PRODUCT ID="103">
  <NAME>
    Fun with metadata
  </NAME>
  <PRICE>
    $10.00
  </PRICE>
  <DESCRIPTION>
    <HEADER>
    </HEADER>
    <BODY>
      Here we allow the description, where we might want to include
      some additional information, such as
      <dimensions>
        <weight unit="kg">
        </weight>
        <height unit="m">
        </height>
      </dimensions>
      for which we do not have a fixed set of elements.
    </BODY>
    <dimensions>
      <weight unit="kg">
      </weight>
      <height unit="m">
      </height>
    </dimensions>
  </DESCRIPTION>
  <CATEGORY>
    Video
  </CATEGORY>
  <RELATEDURLS>
```

Certainly we could have chosen to store all of our product information in a database; there would be a number of benefits of doing this – faster access time for one thing. But databases typically expect to find neat, well-ordered tables and columns. If we decide to add a column, we would need to rebuild our tables. We may decide that a column is needed for only a small number of record entries, but that column will have to exist for *every* record, whether it is used or not.

Our product catalog will hold a great variety of items. There are many columns that apply to all of them (like name or ProductID), but in some cases we want structured information that only makes sense for a particular type of product. For example, our web site might sell books, and we might want the product information to tell us how many pages are in the book. But a numpages field would not make sense for a product such as a desk lamp, where we might instead want a way to describe the light output. A database could have a table for each type of product, but we would have to add a new table every time we wanted to add a new product. We could have hundreds of different products, but very few of any particular type; we might end up with a table for just one item.

So we'll use the database for speed in locating products by general information (such as name, category, or product ID), and XML for the flexibility of storing detailed information with the appropriate metadata.

So, our table will use a reduced schema to hold common, essential information, and a pointer to the XML product description file. We'll be using SQL Server 7; the database will be called `WroxStore`, and the table will be called `Catalog`. The columns are defined like this:

Column Name	SQL Server Data Type	Content
ProdID	int	Unique ID for the product
Name	char	The product name
Category	char	What general category the product belongs to
BriefDesc	char	A short description of the product
Price	money	What the product costs
Inventory	int	How many items we have in inventory
XmlDetails	char	A URL for where to find the XML file containing the product details

Communication and Distributed Applications

Before we get started designing our application, let's consider how the related components will communicate with each other. Among the advantages of building a distributed application are scalability and increased platform options; you can pick the components and operating systems that are best suited for particular tasks. If our application is straining under a heavy load, we can look at where the heavy processing is happening and improve the system by increasing resources at the stress points. For example, we may find that a web site has to deal with more traffic than expected; we can improve performance by adding another web server, and have it talk to the same back-end services. Likewise, our choice of web server should not be tied to our choice of database, or the platform our middle-tier objects require. For example, simply choosing to use Internet Information Server (IIS) should not automatically force us to put all of our code on a Windows system. If we so desire, we could run Stronghold's brand of web server on Linux, while doing middle-tier processing on NT, while talking to one or more databases on any number of platforms.

Of course, for this to work, all of your components need to know how to play well together. Now, you can go and write either CORBA or DCOM for your platforms, but this approach does not lend itself to rapid development. DCOM is a Microsoft standard, which is incredibly easy to implement on Windows, but not so simple on, say, UNIX. And writing CORBA-compliant Visual Basic objects would be impressive, but perhaps this is not what you really want to use VB for. Besides, picking one or the other means that, ultimately, all clients of your services will need to know the same wire protocol. So, rather than get too tied up in either of these, we'll exploit some familiar technologies that ensure cross-platform communication without heavy investments in code. We'll make our services available using HTTP, and to encode our transaction requests, we'll use XML.

XML over the Wire

Inter-object communication requires some means for one object to locate another object, notify that object that it would like to use its services, and receive a response. Information exchanged between the objects needs to be placed in a suitable format that can travel over the wire, and be in a format that both objects can understand.

XML-RPC

In early 1998, Dave Winer, CEO of UserLand, published an article on DaveNet at http://davenet.userland.com, floating the idea of RPC over HTTP via XML. This caught the attention of Bob Atkinson, an architect in the COM group at Microsoft. Winer got invited to Redmond, where he sat down with a group of Microsoft developers. The group worked to develop the syntax and concepts to allow a straightforward means for calling objects via HTTP, using XML to encode the requests and responses. In April 1998 Winer and UserLand took the specification as it stood and released Frontier 5.1. Frontier is an integrated Internet content system, which includes an object database; it uses **XML-RPC** (as the protocol came) to issue requests to objects in the database in order to perform transactions.

Meanwhile, collaboration with Microsoft continued and public attention grew. Whereas Winer had been the focal point of XML-RPC development, requests from other groups for various specifications required more negotiation and management than Winer could provide. Microsoft began to take a more public role in XML-RPC development, and from it developed SOAP, or the Simple Object Access Protocol. We'll look at SOAP later on in this chapter.

What XML-RPC Does

XML-RPC is a client-server technology that uses XML to encode object requests and responses. From the user's point of view, the XML is invisible, in the same way as DCOM hides the underlying marshaling of remote procedure calls. Unless you are *writing* an XML-RPC implementation, you never need to think about XML.

Using an XML-RPC client, you specify a URL, the name of the method to call, and any parameters required. The client transforms this information into an HTTP POST request, and sends the request to an XML-RPC server. On the other side, the server object translates the XML content of the POST and resolves it to a registered object and method call. The request code is run, the response is encoded in XML, then sent back to the client. Finally, the client decodes the XML response into a native format.

The XML-RPC specification, which can be found at http://www.xml-rpc.com/spec, is remarkably brief. It basically defines the format of the HTTP headers, the schema for the request content, and the schema for the reply. Here is a sample XML-RPC request, taken from the specification:

```
POST /RPC2 HTTP/1.0
User-Agent: Frontier/5.1.2 (WinNT)
Host: betty.userland.com
Content-Type: text/xml
Content-length: 181

<?xml version="1.0"?>
<methodCall>
  <methodName>examples.getStateName</methodName>
  <params>
```

```
    <param>
      <value><i4>41</i4></value>
    </param>
  </params>
</methodCall>
```

According to the specification, there are no requirements for the format of the URL in the first line of the HTTP request header. However, a User-Agent and Host must be specified. The Content-Type is always text/xml, and the Content-Length must be correctly specified.

The body of the request is enclosed in the methodCall element, which must have a methodName element indicating the method to call. The specification states that the methodName "may only contain identifier characters, upper and lower-case A-Z, the numeric characters 0-9, underscore, dot, colon and slash". While the above example uses a dot notation similar to VB objects, how the method name string is interpreted is entirely up to the XML-RPC server. These details are determined by the service provider. The method name could just as well be examples_getStateName, or just getStateName, as long as the server code knows how to locate and execute the correct method. If the server were to resolve method requests to COM objects, something like ProgID.MethodName could be used to make dynamic loading of objects a bit easier. We'll see this in just a moment.

The methodCall element uses the params element to hold the parameters we are passing to the method. Each parameter is held in a param element, which in turn holds a value element. The value element holds still more elements, which describe the data type and the actual value. There are scalar data types (single-value items, such as a string or an integer), as well as the array and the struct types. The following tags are used to define a scalar data type:

Tag	Data Type
<i4> or <int>	four-byte signed integer
<boolean>	0 (false) or 1 (true)
<string>	ASCII string
<double>	double-precision signed floating point number
<dateTime.iso8601>	date/time
<base64>	Base64-encoded binary

If no type is indicated, the default type is string.

The array type consists of an array element that has a data element as a child element. The data element in turn holds a series of value elements. Arrays are not limited to holding a single data type; the specification gives this example:

```
<array>
  <data>
    <value><i4>12</i4></value>
    <value><string>Egypt</string></value>
    <value><boolean>0</boolean></value>
```

```
      <value><i4>-31</i4></value>
   </data>
</array>
```

An array's values may contain any of the defined data types, including structs and other arrays.

The struct is somewhat like a Visual Basic Dictionary object. It has member child elements; each member contains a name element and a value element. The name is just that; the name of the item. The value is the same element type used by param and array. Like the array, structs may hold data of different types, including arrays and other structs.

Let's take a look at a function that could be used by an XML-RPC server. (This is just an example to illustrate a point, and is not part of our application. We won't be building an XML-RPC server, so code in this section is intended only to demonstrate some concepts. We will, however, build a SOAP client-server later on in this chapter.) It takes a single XML string as an argument, parses out the relevant data, and uses CallByName to execute the requested method:

```
Public Function HandleRequest(sXML As String) As String
    On Error GoTo ErrHand

    Dim sProgID As String
    Dim sMethod As String
    Dim asArgString() As Variant
    Dim objX As Object
    Dim sResults As String
    Dim objDom As DOMDocument
    Dim objEl As IXMLDOMElement
    Dim nIdx As Integer
    Dim asTemp() As String
    Dim nParamLength As Integer

    Set objDom = New DOMDocument
    If Not (objDom.loadXML(sXML)) Then
        sResults = "<ERROR>XML parsing error:" _
            & objDom.parseError.reason & " </ERROR>"
    Else
        asTemp = _
Split(objDom.getElementsByTagName("methodName").Item(0).childNodes(0).Text, _
        ".")
        sProgID = asTemp(0) & "." & asTemp(1)
        sMethod = asTemp(2)
        nParamLength = objDom.getElementsByTagName("params").length

        If (nParamLength > 0) Then
            ReDim asArgString(nParamLength - 1)
            For nIdx = 0 To nParamLength - 1
                ' A param looks like this
                '   <param>
                '     <value>
                '       <i4>41</i4>
                '     </value>
                '   </param>
```

```
                            ' The value element may contain various data types
                            Set objEl = objDom.getElementsByTagName("param").Item(nIdx)
                        asArgString(nIdx) = GetValue(objEl.childNodes(0))
                    Next
                    Set objX = CreateObject(sProgID)
                    asArgString(0) = ""  'sXML
                    sResults = CallByName(objX, sMethod, VbMethod, asArgString)
                    Set objX = Nothing
                Else
                    ' Some methods may take 0 arguments, and
                    ' trying to pass anything to them will
                    ' cause an error
                    sResults = CallByName(objX, sMethod, VbMethod)
                    Set objX = Nothing
                End If
            End If

    ErrHand:
        If Err.Number <> 0 Then
            sResults = "<ERROR>COM error:" & Err.Description & " </ERROR>"
        End If
        HandleRequest = sResults
    End Function
```

Here's the function that actually parses out argument values:

```
Private Function GetValue(oEl As IXMLDOMElement) As Variant
    Dim sValue As String
    Dim vResult As Variant
    Dim sDataType As String
    Dim sStruct
    Dim avStruct() As Variant
    Dim sArray
    Dim avArray() As Variant
    Dim nItemCount As Integer
    Dim oDOM As DOMDocument

    If (oEl.baseName <> "value") Then
        vResult = "ELEMENT_TYPE_ERROR"
    Else
        sDataType = oEl.childNodes.Item(0).baseName
        ' Should be some datatype
        sValue = oEl.childNodes.Item(1).Text
        ' Should be the text value
        Select Case sDataType
            Case "i4", "int"
                vResult = CInt(sValue)
            Case "boolean"
                vResult = CBool(sValue)
            Case "string"
                vResult = CStr(sValue)
            Case "double"
                vResult = CDbl(sValue)
```

```
            Case "dateTime.iso8601"
                vResult = CDate(sValue)
            Case "base64"
                vResult = b64.Decode(sValue)
            ' This uses the Base64 Encoding Library 2.01,
            ' written by Alvaro Redondo, available at
            ' http://sevillaonline.com/ActiveX/
            Case "array"
                ' An <array> contains a single <data>
                ' element, which can contain
                ' any number of <value>s.
                oDOM.loadXML (oEl.childNodes.Item(1).xml)
                ReDim avArray(oDOM.getElementsByTagName("value").length)
                For nItemCount = _
                        0 To oDOM.getElementsByTagName("value").length - 1
                    avArray(nItemCount) = _
                    GetValue(oDOM.getElementsByTagName("value").Item(nItemCount))
                Next
            Case "struct"
                ' A <struct> contains <member>s and each <member>
                ' contains a <name> and a <value>.
                ' Much more involved. For example, what VB type does this
                ' map to? Dictionary? Collection? Recordset?
                sStruct = oEl.childNodes.Item(1).xml
        End Select
    End If
    GetValue = vResult
End Function
```

There are some problems that need to be thought out. For one thing, when someone passes us a struct value as a parameter, what does it mean? Visual Basic does not have a native type called "struct". Earlier we described it as being like a Dictionary object, but it could also map to an ADO Recordset or a Collection object. This may, however, not be that serious; the fact that we cannot reliably map a struct to a VB object means that we may only write XML-RPC server methods that do not have ambiguous data types. Or, it must be decided in advance that structs are to be considered the functional equivalent of a specific Visual Basic data type. As the provider of the service, we have control over the interface to our services. So, if there is an XML-RPC data type we cannot cleanly convert to a Visual Basic data type, then we are not obligated to use it.

Another, perhaps more germane, question is "how do you pass XML?" There's no 'XML' data type. One approach would exploit the structure of the String type. When checking the contents of a String value, we could check for child nodes other than text. If any exist, we could pull out the XML as a string.

SOAP

SOAP, the **Simple Object Access Protocol**, is a somewhat more complex version of XML-RPC (The "Simple" part of its name comes from comparisons to older RPC protocols, such as CORBA). It does much the same thing, i.e. it marshals object invocation using XML/HTTP as the transport protocol. According to the specification (available at http://msdn.microsoft.com/xml/general/Soapspec-V1.asp), the goals of SOAP are to:

❑ Provide a standard object invocation protocol built on Internet standards, using HTTP as the transport method and XML for data encoding.

❑ Create an extensible protocol and payload format that can evolve.

And, to make clear the purpose of SOAP, the specification of SOAP is *not* intended to:

"Define all aspects of a distributed object system, including the following:

❑ Distributed garbage collection,

❑ Bi-directional HTTP communications,

❑ "Boxcarring" or pipelining of messages,

❑ Objects-by-reference (which requires distributed garbage collection and bi-directional HTTP),

❑ Activation (which requires objects-by-reference)".

Any garbage collection is the responsibility of whoever implements the client and/or server, by whatever means appropriate. There is no prevision for callbacks, nor can you send batch messages. You cannot directly reference a remote object.

So, like XML-RPC, SOAP tries to accomplish a basic task without pretending to turn lead into gold or cure all ills. So what else does SOAP offer?

Namespaces

SOAP gives you the option of using a SOAP XML namespace. This makes it safer to use your own tags at different points without worrying about name collisions. The specification states that, if a SOAP request does use the SOAP namespace, then the SOAP server must be able to correctly process it; and an "Invalid Request" error message must be returned if the namespace is incorrect. (The server has the option of processing requests without the SOAP namespace as if it possessed a correct namespace.)

M-POST

Like XML-RPC, SOAP uses the HTTP POST method. But it also provides for M-POST, an extension to the HTTP specification, to give network administrators more flexibility in deciding how to handle SOAP calls. M-POST requires that the HTTP header contain a few more lines of information that serve a function similar to XML namespaces. Here is an example M-POST header:

```
M-POST /MySite/SomeSoap.asp HTTP/1.1
Content-Type: text/xml-SOAP
Man: urn:schemas-xmlsoap-org:soap.v1; ns=01
01-MessageType: Call
01-MethodName: RunCode
```

The Man: (i.e. mandatory) declaration indicates the namespace for the information that follows; the specification states that it always refers to urn:schemas-xmlsoap-org:soap.v1. ns=*NN* (in this example, *NN* = 01) and specifies the header prefix for the following SOAP header, indicating that the namespace is to be applied to them. (This is similar to having <01:MessageType>Call</01:MessageType> in an XML document.) The MessageType header for a SOAP request is always Call.

A request must always be attempted using the POST method first and, if that fails (indicated by an HTTP status of "405 Method Not Allowed"), retried using the M-POST method. However the SOAP client has the option of not using M-POST if POST fails. This two-tier approach allows network administrators, via firewalls, to restrict SOAP requests to only M-POST, ensuring that the extra information is included in the header.

Making Requests

SOAP request headers should contain the SOAPHeaderName header, followed by the name of the method being called. The format for this value is a URI, plus the "#" character, plus the actual method name. (For this reason, method names may not include the "#" character.) If M-POST is used, then the required additional headers must be included as well. Here's an example request, using POST:

```
POST / HTTP/1.1
Host: www.somebooksite.com
Content-Type: text/xml
Content-Length: 257
SOAPMethodName: www.somebooksite.com#GetLastTradePrice
<SOAP:Envelope xmlns:SOAP="urn:schemas-xmlsoap-org:soap.v1">
    <SOAP:Body>
        <m:GetBookPrice
          xmlns:m="urn:BookStuff.org:BookStuff">
            <isbn>0-937175-64-1</isbn>
        </m:GetBookPrice>
    </SOAP:Body>
</SOAP:Envelope>
```

And here it is using M-POST:

```
M-POST / HTTP/1.1
Host: www.somebooksite.com
Content-Type: text/xml
Content-Length: 257
Man: urn:schemas-xmlsoap-org:soap.v1; ns=01
01-MessageType: Call
01-MethodName: GetLastTradePrice
SOAPMethodName: www.somebooksite.com#GetBookPrice
<SOAP:Envelope xmlns:SOAP="urn:schemas-xmlsoap-org:soap.v1">
    <SOAP:Body>
        <m:GetBookPrice
          xmlns:m="urn:BookStuff.org:BookStuff">
            <isbn>0-937175-64-1</isbn>
        </m:GetBookPrice>
    </SOAP:Body>
</SOAP:Envelope>
```

After the HTTP header information comes the XML document, referred to as the **payload**. The payload uses the SOAP:Envelope root element, with an (optional) namespace declaration. In this case it is followed by the Body element. Note the use of the namespace prefix.

Any of the elements may contain a SOAP:encodingStyle attribute to describe a serialization method (i.e. how the binary data type is translated into an XML string) different from the default SOAP encoding. It applies to the element it appears on, as well as any child elements, unless they have their own SOAP:encodingStyle attribute. Other attributes may be used, but they must be qualified by the appropriate namespace to prevent any possible collision with SOAP attributes.

The payload may contain header information, contained in the optional SOAP:Header element. This element may only appear as the first child of the SOAP:Envelope element. SOAP:Header contains, naturally, header information for the call. More specifically, this is where you would include information that is not directly part of the method request (i.e. it is not a parameter or a method name). For example, you might want to pass along a user ID for the person making the request. Header information elements are described by the element name. If we were to include a user ID, it would look like this:

```
<SOAP:Header>
    <m:UserID
      xmlns:m="urn:BookStuff.org:BookStuff" >
          13
    </m:UserID>
</SOAP:Header>
```

Note that the header markup must be qualified by a namespace.

Header elements may have an optional SOAP:mustUnderstand attribute to indicate that the receiver of the request must either know how to process the header element or fail:

```
<SOAP:Header>
    <m:UserID
      xmlns:m="urn:BookStuff.org:BookStuff"
      SOAP:mustUnderstand="1">
          13
    </m:UserID>
</SOAP:Header>
```

The request payload must then contain the SOAP:Body element, which contains the actual method invocation details:

```
<SOAP:Body>
    <m:GetBookPrice
      xmlns:m="urn:BookStuff.org:BookStuff">
        <isbn>0-937175-64-1</isbn>
    </m:GetBookPrice>
</SOAP:Body>
```

The SOAP:Body element contains an element whose name is the method being called. That element in turn contains elements that name the parameters for the method. The elements take their names from the name of the relevant parameter.

```
<SOAP:Body>
    <m:GetBookPrice
      xmlns:m="urn:BookStuff.org:BookStuff">
            <isbn>0-937175-64-1</isbn>
    </m:GetBookPrice>
</SOAP:Body>
```

The method name element must have a qualifying namespace.

The SOAP HTTP request must also have two other pieces of information. The content type header must be "text/xml" (as opposed to, say, the more typical "text/html" that a web browser would send when requesting a web page). There must also be an additional HTTP header that indicates the target method being called. This header is called SOAPMethodName, and consists of the server URL, followed by the "#" character, followed by the method name:

```
SOAPMethodName: www.somebooksite.com#GetLastTradePrice
```

This leads to the restriction that the method name may not contain the "#" character, since it serves as a demarcation character in the header content.

Getting a Response

The above samples would return something like this:

```
HTTP/1.1 200 OK
Content-Type: text/xml
Content-Length: 255
<SOAP:Envelope xmlns:SOAP="urn:schemas-xmlsoap-org:soap.v1">
    <SOAP:Body>
        <m:GetBookPriceResponse xmlns:m="urn:BookStuff.org:BookStuff">
            <return>50.0</return>
        </m:GetBookPriceResponse>
    </SOAP:Body>
</SOAP:Envelope>
```

(We'll see this for ourselves when we implement our SOAP server later in the chapter.)

The root element type is SOAP:Body. This element contains a response wrapper element that holds the response child elements. These child elements are named after the return parameters for the method. Note that methods may return more than one value, much as a Visual Basic function, that has ByRef arguments, provides a way to return new data in addition to the function return value. The method may have parameters that are also used to return data. A SOAP response body may have more than one element that contains data returned by the request.

Returning Error Information

If the method is returning an error, then the SOAP:Body element must have a SOAP:Fault element, with the first child of the SOAP:Fault element containing error information:

```
<SOAP:Fault>
    <faultcode>300</faultcode>
    <faultstring>Invalid Request</faultstring>
    <runcode>No</runcode>
</SOAP:Fault>
```

SOAP defines these `faultcode` and `faultstring` values:

faultstring value	faultcode value	Meaning
Version Mismatch	100	The call was using an unsupported SOAP version.
Must Understand	200	An XML element was received that contained an element tagged with `mustUnderstand="1"` that was not understood by the receiver.
Invalid Request	300	The receiving application did not process the request because it was incorrectly formed or not supported by the application.
Application Faulted	400	The receiving application faulted when processing the request. The 'detail' element contains the application-specific fault.

The `runcode` value must be an enumerated value; the specification currently defines "Yes", "No", and "Maybe", but the current specification does not define specific numeric values for them. (Version 0.9 of the specification defined them as 2, 1, and 0 respectively).

In the case where the application (meaning the back-end part of your SOAP server implementation that does the actual work for a given request) has faulted, additional information may be given in a `detail` element, which would be placed as another child element of `SOAP:fault`:

```
<SOAP:Fault>
    <faultcode>300</faultcode>
    <faultstring>Invalid Request</faultstring>
    <runcode>No</runcode>
    <detail
        xmlns:e="www.wrox.com/SoapSample"
      xmlns:xsd="W3C-Schemas-URI"
      xsd:type="e:MyFaultType">
      <message>
        The application failed
      </message>
      <errorcode>1001</errorcode>
    </detail>
</SOAP:Fault>
```

The detail element must have a namespace, plus a qualifying XML Schema data type. In the above example, xsd:type indicates that the contents of the detail element conform to a complex data type called MyFaultType, defined by our example namespace, www.wrox.com/SoapSample. (Refer back to Chapter 2, "*XML Validation*" for more information about XML Schemas and data types.)

SOAP Data Types Overview

SOAP relies on XML-Data schemas to define how data types are represented. Bear in mind, though, that XML Schemas are still in the draft stage, and may change. Data types are either simple or compound. A simple value contains only character data; there are no child elements. Compound data consists of named parts (a parent element and its child elements); it is similar to user-defined data. Arrays are considered compound types. According to the SOAP specification, the parameter names (i.e. the names of the element) are referred to as "accessors".

Here is an example of a *simple* data type:

```
<m:GetBookPriceResponse
    xmlns:m="urn:BookStuff.org:BookStuff">
    <return>50.0</return>
</m:GetBookPriceResponse>
```

Here is an example of a *compound* data type:

```
<m:GetBookDetailsResponse
    xmlns:m="urn:BookStuff.org:BookStuff">
    <BookDetails>
        <ISBN>1861003323<ISBN>
        <Publisher>Wrox Press, Ltd.</Publisher>
    </ BookDetails >
</m:GetBookDetailsResponse>
```

In both examples, the definition of the data types would be defined in the corresponding schema, identified by xmlns:m="urn:BookStuff.org:BookStuff".

If further clarification of a data type is required, SOAP allows the use of the xsd:type attribute to explicitly state the intended schema data type:

```
<m:GetBookDetailsResponse
    xmlns:m="urn:BookStuff.org:BookStuff"
    xmlns:xsd=""http://www.w3.org/1999/XMLSchema">
    <BookDetails xsd:type="ExtendedBookDetails">
        <ISBN>1861003323<ISBN>
        <Publisher>Wrox Press, Ltd.</Publisher>
        <PubDate>2000Mar</PubDate>
    </ BookDetails >
</m:GetBookDetailsResponse>
```

Note that if you use the xsd namespace prefix, you must declare it beforehand, either in the element that is using the xsd:type attribute, or in a parent element (which "scopes" the use of the namespace).

SOAP also allows for one element to reference another element, through the use of the SOAP:id and SOAP:href attributes. For example, you may want to send a request that includes address information, such as for an invoice. The parameters may call for both a mailing address and a billing address, though often they are the same. We can use id and href attributes to indicate that one element takes its value from another element:

```
<m:OrderBook
    xmlns:m="urn:BookStuff.org:BookStuff"
    xmlns:xsd=""http://www.w3.org/1999/XMLSchema">
    <MailingAddress SOAP:href='#id-1'/>
    <BillingAddress SOAP:href='#id-1'/>
    <Address SOAP:id='id-1'>
        <Street>123 Main</Street>
        <City>Centreville</City>
        <Postal>12345</Postal>
    </Address>
</m:OrderBook>
```

Bear in mind that both SOAP and XML Schemas are still only drafts. For that reason we are not covering all of the details of SOAP data types and how they are encoded. Updates to the SOAP specification can be found at http://www.develop.com/soap/issues.htm. The current XML Schema draft can be found at http://www.w3.org/TR/xmlschema-1/.

Writing SOAP Client/Server Code

Now it's time to take what we've learned and put it into practice by building our own SOAP client/server application. Our program needs to do the following, depending on its role:

SOAP Client

- ❑ Obtain a SOAP envelope from a calling application
- ❑ Add the appropriate HTTP headers
- ❑ Make a connection to a SOAP server
- ❑ POST the request to a SOAP server
- ❑ Get the response
- ❑ Return the SOAP response to the calling code

SOAP Server

- ❑ Listen for connection requests
- ❑ Receive HTTP POST messages
- ❑ Parse the SOAP envelope and retrieve the request
- ❑ Determine what method has been requested
- ❑ Locate the corresponding code to process the request
- ❑ Run the required back-end code

- ❏ Encode the results as a SOAP response
- ❏ Build the correct HTTP response headers
- ❏ Return the response text to the SOAP client

The Visual Basic Client/Server

We'll build a Visual Basic application that will function as both a small-scale web server and as a simple browser. It will give us an option to either listen on a port (which by default is 80, the standard web server port, though other ports will work too) or send HTTP requests, such as POST or GET, out on port 80.

Our program will use two ActiveX DLLs which we'll build to handle basic HTTP and SOAP activity, plus a third, smaller DLL for managing error information. We'll look at this one first, so that we can use it in the main application.

ErrorUtils.ErrorInfo

First, because DLLs have no visible interface, we need to be very careful when trapping errors. It's considered impolite to have your application throw up a "Run-time error 5" message box because some DLL routine didn't catch an error. Method calls should return meaningful information to indicate that something odd has happened, such as a Boolean False. We need a way to make error information available though, so that a calling application can decide what to do. Often it's just a matter of displaying a message box before continuing. We'll use a DLL to wrap some basic error logging functions, exposing a few methods for setting and getting error information in a few different formats. The ErrorInfo class provides properties for holding error information, methods for setting and clearing this information, and a method for pulling out all of the error details as an XML string. We'll then use this class in our two other utility classes:

```
'************************************************************
' ErrorUtils.ErrorInfo
'************************************************************
Option Explicit

Private m_sErrorLocation As String
Private m_sErrorDescription As String
Private m_lErrorNumber As Long
```

Some private variables are declared for holding error information, which are exposed as class properties:

```
Public Property Get Location() As String
    Location = m_sErrorLocation
End Property

Public Property Let Location(ByVal sLocation As String)
    m_sErrorLocation = sLocation
End Property

Public Property Get Description() As String
    Description = m_sErrorDescription
End Property
```

```
Public Property Let Description(ByVal sDescription As String)
    m_sErrorDescription = sDescription
End Property

Public Property Get Number() As Long
    Number = m_lErrorNumber
End Property

Public Property Let Number(ByVal lNumber As Long)
    m_lErrorNumber = lNumber
End Property
```

This method allows the variables to be set all at once:

```
Public Sub SetErrorInfo(sDesc As String, sLocation As String, lNumber As Long)
    m_sErrorLocation = sDesc
    m_sErrorDescription = sLocation
    m_lErrorNumber = lNumber
End Sub
```

This method clears the values:

```
Public Sub ClearErrorInfo()
    m_sErrorLocation = ""
    m_sErrorDescription = ""
    m_lErrorNumber = 0
End Sub
```

To retrieve the values all at once, this method returns all of the error information as an XML string:

```
Public Function GetErrorInfoXML() As String
    Dim sXML As String
    sXML = ""
    sXML = sXML & "<ERROR>" & Chr(10)
    sXML = sXML & "<LOCATION>" & XmlEncode(m_sErrorLocation) & _
        "</LOCATION>" & Chr(10)
    sXML = sXML & "<DESCRIPTION>" & XmlEncode(m_sErrorDescription) & _
        "</DESCRIPTION>" & Chr(10)
    sXML = sXML & "<NUMBER>" & CStr(m_lErrorNumber) & "</NUMBER>"
    sXML = sXML & "</ERROR>"

    GetErrorInfoXML = sXML
End Function
```

A small function, XmlEncode, is used to make sure any information returned as XML doesn't contain troublesome characters; specifically "&", "<" and ">", which must be replaced by entity references when appearing as XML document content, and the single and double quote characters, so that the function could be used to provide a quoted attribute value:

```
Private Function XmlEncode(sText As String) As String
    sText = Replace(sText, "&", "&amp;")
    sText = Replace(sText, "<", "&lt;")
```

```
        sText = Replace(sText, ">", "&gt;")
        sText = Replace(sText, "'", "&apos;")
        sText = Replace(sText, """", "&quot;")
        XmlEncode = sText
    End Function
```

The HttpUtils.Utils Class

Building and manipulating HTTP headers can be a tedious task, and you don't want the same code littered all over your project, so it has been placed into a separate class, `HttpUtils.Utils`. HTTP headers come in a variety of flavors, depending on what you're doing. Basically, they break down into four categories: general, request, response, and entity.

General headers provide information not specific to either client or server. Typical general headers are `Cache-control`, `Connection`, `Date`, and `Transfer-encoding`. **Request** headers indicate information important to a request method, such as `GET`, `HEAD`, or `POST`. Some request headers are `Accept`, `Cookie`, `Host`, `Referer`, and `User-Agent`. **Server** headers apply to information being sent back from a request. Some typical server headers are `Age` and `Server`. **Entity** headers include `Allow`, `Content-Base`, `Content-Encoding`, `Content-Length`, and `Content-Type`. These refer to the actual content being sent, either as part of a `POST` or as a response.

For the purposes of our SOAP client/server, we're only interested in a small subset of possible HTTP headers, so not all of them are implemented or used in the `Utils` class. It is quite possible to perform `GET`, `POST`, and `HEAD` requests without bothering with all of the details, but you may wish to expand this class to include them.

The class defines a number of private members, then provides `Property Get` and `Let` accessors so you can manipulate them. The idea is to use these properties to construct a proper HTTP header; the code that does the actual header construction only pays attention to a few of the available header properties, and will report an error if anything essential is missing or blank. You may wish to extend this by adding more header types and checking that they have valid values.

```
'***********************************************************
' Class HttpUtils.Utils
' Some functions to help manage HTTP requests and responses
'***********************************************************
Option Explicit

Dim ClassErrors As ErrorUtils.ErrorInfo

Private m_sConnection As String       ' e.g., Keep-alive
Private m_sHttpVersion As String      ' e.g., 0.9, 1.0, or 1.1
Private m_sHttpMethod As String       ' PUT, GET, HEAD,
Private m_sHttpReferer As String      ' Where we came from
Private m_sUserAgent As String        ' Our "browser"
Private m_sContentType As String      ' E.g., text/xml
Private m_sContentBody As String      ' What we're sending
Private m_nContentLength As Integer   ' Byte-length of the body
Private m_sHttpHost As String         ' Who we're calling
Private m_sLastModified As String     ' When our reponse data last changed
Private m_sHttpUri As String          ' The URI we're calling
Private m_sHttpAccept As String       ' Media formats the client can handle
```

```
Private m_nHttpStatusCode As Integer ' e.g. 200, or 404
Private m_sHttpServer As String      ' Name/version of responding server
Private m_sPostData As String        ' What we're sending in the POST
Private m_sSoapMethodHeader As String    ' "SOAPMethodName" header content
```

Here are the property accessor methods. First, the error properties delegate to the `ErrorInfo` class:

```
Public Property Get ErrorDescription() As String
    ErrorDescription = ClassErrors.Description
End Property

Public Property Get ErrorNumber() As Long
    ErrorNumber = ClassErrors.Number
End Property

Public Property Get ErrorLocation() As String
    ErrorLocation = ClassErrors.Location
End Property
```

Access is provided to the HTTP-specific variables:

```
Public Property Get ConnectionType() As String
    ConnectionType = m_sConnection
End Property

Public Property Let ConnectionType(sConnType As String)
    m_sConnection = sConnType
End Property

Public Property Get HttpVersion() As String
    HttpVersion = m_sHttpVersion
End Property

Public Property Let HttpVersion(sVersion As String)
    m_sHttpVersion = sVersion
End Property

Public Property Get HttpMethod() As String
    HttpMethod = m_sHttpMethod
End Property

Public Property Let HttpMethod(sMethod As String)
    m_sHttpMethod = sMethod
End Property

Public Property Get HttpReferer() As String
    HttpReferer = m_sHttpReferer
End Property

Public Property Get UserAgent() As String
    UserAgent = m_sUserAgent
End Property
```

```
Public Property Let UserAgent(sUA As String)
    m_sUserAgent = sUA
End Property

Public Property Get ContentType() As String
    ContentType = m_sContentType
End Property

Public Property Let ContentType(sContType As String)
    m_sContentType = sContType
End Property

Public Property Get ContentLength() As Integer
    ContentLength = m_nContentLength
End Property

Public Property Get HttpHost() As String
    HttpHost = m_sHttpHost
End Property

Public Property Let HttpHost(sHost As String)
    m_sHttpHost = sHost
End Property

Public Property Get LastModified() As String
    LastModified = m_sLastModified
End Property

Public Property Let LastModified(sDate As String)
    m_sLastModified = sDate
End Property

Public Property Get HttpUri() As String
    HttpUri = m_sHttpUri
End Property

Public Property Let HttpUri(sURI As String)
    m_sHttpUri = sURI
End Property

Public Property Get HttpAccept() As String
    HttpAccept = m_sHttpAccept
End Property

Public Property Get HttpServer() As String
    HttpServer = m_sHttpServer
End Property

Public Property Get HttpStatusCode() As Integer
    HttpStatusCode = m_nHttpStatusCode
End Property

Public Property Let HttpStatusCode(sCode As Integer)
    m_nHttpStatusCode = sCode
End Property
```

```
Public Property Get PostData() As String
    PostData = m_sPostData
End Property

Public Property Let PostData(sData As String)
    m_sPostData = sData
End Property

Public Property Get SoapMethodHeader() As String
    SoapMethodHeader = m_sSoapMethodHeader
End Property

Public Property Let SoapMethodHeader(sData As String)
    m_sSoapMethodHeader = sData
End Property
```

Since this is an ActiveX DLL, message boxes cannot realistically be displayed when something goes wrong. Most of the functions return string data, and are not expected to return an empty string. So, error handling is done by returning an empty string when something goes wrong, and setting the error properties of the `ErrorInfo` class. When calling any method that should normally return a non-empty string, you should check the length of the returned data. If it's zero, then inspect the error properties to see if an error was thrown.

> *A note on coding style: typically a VB method will handle errors with either a `Goto` statement (`On Error GoTo SomeLabel`), or will trap errors every place one might expect them. The problem with the first approach is that, if an error occurs, you get thrown to the same place, usually the end of the method, and you have code that must handle all possible errors. This is good for the really odd ones, when you couldn't know in advance what would be a good way to handle it. Trapping errors in-line means you have a lot of "`On Error Resume Next`" statements, and "`If Err.Number <> 0 Then`" code. It's easy to forget to do this. I prefer to write objects that should (ideally) never throw an error. They may fail in what they've been asked to do, but recover gracefully. In a sense, they raise "soft" errors. You have more flexibility in how to respond, and can even ignore the error without the application crashing. So, the main application has fewer extraneous lines of code (all those `On Error Resume Next` statements go away), and the person using the object has more control (he or she can raise an error, if desired).*

BuildMPOSTRequest

The SOAP specification describes the `M-POST` request method for making SOAP requests. This method builds the required HTTP headers, and includes the mandatory `M-POST` information as well:

```
'**************************************************************
' Public Function BuildMPOSTRequest() As String
' Uses the class properties to construct an HTTP POST request.
' If any required information is missing, it sets the Error properties
' and returns an empty string.  So, you can call this with
' If(Len(BuildMPOSTRequest())) then
'    ' OK
' Else
'    ' Error!
' End if
'**************************************************************
```

```
Public Function BuildMPOSTRequest() As String
    On Error GoTo ErrHand
    Dim sRq As String
    Dim sMissingData As String

    Call ClassErrors.ClearErrorInfo
```

Since we're entering a new function, any lingering error information is cleared. The request string is initialized in preparation for building it up, and then a check is made to see that we have all of the required information is available:

```
sRq = ""
sMissingData = ""
If Not Len(m_sHttpUri) Then
    sMissingData = "URI"
ElseIf (Not Len(m_sHttpVersion)) Then
    sMissingData = "HTTP Version"
ElseIf (Not Len(m_sHttpHost)) Then
    sMissingData = "HTTP Host"
ElseIf (Not Len(m_sUserAgent)) Then
    sMissingData = "User Agent"
ElseIf (Not Len(m_sContentType)) Then
    sMissingData = "Content Type"
End If
```

If no data is missing, the request headers are built:

```
If Len(sMissingData) > 0 Then
    sRq = sRq & "POST /" & m_sHttpUri & " HTTP/" & m_sHttpVersion & _
        Chr(10)
    sRq = sRq & "Host: " & m_sHttpHost & Chr(10)
    sRq = sRq & "User-Agent: " & m_sUserAgent & Chr(10)
    sRq = sRq & "Content-Length: " & CStr(Len(m_sPostData)) & Chr(10)
    sRq = sRq & "Content-Type: " & m_sContentType & Chr(10) & Chr(10)
    sRq = sRq & m_sPostData
Else
    sRq = ""
    Call ClassErrors.SetErrorInfo("Missing header information" _
        & sMissingData, -1, "CHTTPUtils.BuildMPOSTRequest")
End If

ErrHand:
    If Err.Number <> 0 Then
        sRq = ""
        Call ClassErrors.SetErrorInfo(Err.Description, _
            Err.Number, "CHTTPUtils.BuildMPOSTRequest")
    End If

    BuildMPOSTRequest = sRq
End Function
```

BuildPOSTRequest

You may prefer to use the more common POST method. This function builds the the POST request, including the required HTTP headers:

```
'*************************************************************
' Public Function BuildPOSTRequest() As String
' Uses the class properties to construct an HTTP POST request.
' If any required information is missing, it sets the Error properties
' and returns an empty string.  So, you can call this with
' If(Len(BuildPOSTRequest())) then
'    ' OK
' Else
'    ' Error!
' End if
'*************************************************************
Public Function BuildPOSTRequest() As String
    On Error GoTo ErrHand
    Dim sRq As String
    Dim sMissingData As String

    Call ClassErrors.ClearErrorInfo
    sRq = ""
    sMissingData = ""

    If Not Len(m_sHttpUri) Then
        sMissingData = "URI"
    ElseIf (Not Len(m_sHttpVersion)) Then
        sMissingData = "HTTP Version"
    ElseIf (Not Len(m_sHttpHost)) Then
        sMissingData = "HTTP Host"
    ElseIf (Not Len(m_sUserAgent)) Then
        sMissingData = "User Agent"
    ElseIf (Not Len(m_sContentType)) Then
        sMissingData = "Content Type"
    End If
```

As in the previous method, a check is made to determine whether the required information exists, and if so, the HTTP header string is built:

```
    If Not Len(sMissingData) Then
        sRq = sRq & "POST /" & m_sHttpUri & " HTTP/" & m_sHttpVersion & _
            Chr(10)
        sRq = sRq & "Host: " & m_sHttpHost & Chr(10)
        sRq = sRq & "User-Agent: " & m_sUserAgent & Chr(10)
        sRq = sRq & "Content-Length: " & CStr(Len(m_sPostData)) & Chr(10)
        sRq = sRq & "Content-Type: " & m_sContentType & Chr(10) & Chr(10)
        sRq = sRq & m_sPostData
```

If anything is missing, an error is reported:

```
    Else
        sRq = ""
        Call ClassErrors.SetErrorInfo("Missing header information: " _
            & sMissingData, -1, "CHTTPUtils.BuildPOSTRequest")
    End If

ErrHand:
    If Err.Number <> 0 Then
        Call ClassErrors.SetErrorInfo(Err.Description, Err.Number, _
            "CHTTPUtils.BuildPOSTRequest")
        BuildPOSTRequest = ""
    End If

    BuildPOSTRequest = sRq
End Function
```

RetrieveHeaderItem

When handling HTTP data, either being received by the server or coming as a response to a request, it can be handy to have a way to simply retrieve header content by name. This function does some simple string manipulation to locate a header of the specified type and return the value:

```
Public Function RetrieveHeaderItem(sHeaderType As String, _
                                   sResponse As String) As String
    Dim nStart As Integer
    Dim nEnd As Integer
    Dim sValue As String
```

Some variables are declared for tracking the position in the string, and a string to hold the results. Any surrounding white space is then trimmed off, before the code looks for the ":" character at the end of the header type string. If it's not there, it is added:

```
    sHeaderType = Trim(sHeaderType)
    If Right(sHeaderType, 1) <> ":" Then
        sHeaderType = sHeaderType & ":"
    End If
```

The entire HTTP response text is checked for the specific header:

```
    nStart = InStr(1, sResponse, sHeaderType)
```

If it is found, the contents of the header are extracted by grabbing all the text from the end of the header type to the end of the line (since each header is on its own line):

```
    If nStart > 0 Then
        nStart = nStart + Len(sHeaderType) + 1
        nEnd = InStr(nStart, sResponse, Chr(10))
        sValue = Trim(Mid(sResponse, nStart, (nEnd - nStart)))
    Else
```

313

Otherwise the response is set to an empty string:

```
        sValue = ""
    End If

    RetrieveHeaderItem = sValue
End Function
```

The `Class_Initialize` method is used to set the default values of the headers:

```
Private Sub Class_Initialize()
    Set ClassErrors = New ErrorInfo
    Call ClassErrors.ClearErrorInfo
    m_sConnection = ""
    m_sHttpVersion = "1.0"
    m_sHttpMethod = ""
    m_sHttpReferer = """"
    m_sUserAgent = "Wrox VB-XML"
    m_sContentType = "text/html"
    m_sContentBody = ""
    m_nContentLength = 0
    m_sHttpHost = ""
    m_sLastModified = ""
    m_sHttpUri = ""
    m_sHttpAccept = "text/*"
    m_nHttpStatusCode = 500
    m_sHttpServer = "Wrox VB-XML/1.0"
End Sub
```

The SOAP Utilities Class

Loading the Correct Object

When a request is sent to a SOAP server, the server receives nothing more than a text string. The SOAP specification does not mandate how that string should be translated into a tangible action. There needs to be some sort of binding between the SOAP XML representation and a tangible piece of binary code (or script). One possibility is to put all of the method calls in the same object, and have the SOAP server coded to always know how to load it. That, however, is pretty restrictive – as the number of methods grows, maintenance becomes a pain. Instead, we'll create a way to describe the relationship between a SOAP request and a physical object. We can use this to get the `ProgID` of the required object and dynamically create it. For this, we'll use an XML "binding file" to hold information that relates SOAP request methods to VB objects and methods.

We'll also need a way to call the method without knowing the name in advance. For this we can use the `CallByName` function. There's one problem though: `CallByName` requires that you know the number of arguments to the method. Ultimately, it seems, any object we call requires some prior knowledge about it. We could restrict all methods to a known number of parameters, but that makes it harder to reuse existing objects. Instead, we'll use a few levels of abstraction to allow a smooth binding from XML representation to any object we want to use.

Here's the plan. Any COM object method we wish to call will have a corresponding wrapper method that handles the translation from SOAP request to binary execution. All wrapper methods are restricted to exactly one `String` argument; this wrapper method can be kept in whatever object we choose. An XML file will be used to hold the bindings between SOAP requests and these wrapper calls. When the SOAP server is started, it loads this XML file and creates a `Dictionary` object to hold the mappings. Requests are parsed out, the correct wrapper object is located, dynamically created, and passed the SOAP request parameters as XML. The wrapper object is then responsible for converting the parameters to the correct data types, calling the actual object, executing it, and translating the results into a SOAP response body. This XML string is then passed back to the SOAP server, which completes the response by adding the correct headers and replying to the client. It looks something like this:

```
Client --> SOAP server --> ExecuteWrapper --> MethodWrapper --> actual method
```

The path is reversed to send the response. This summarizes the process:

1. The client sends SOAP request to server.

2. The SOAP server checks that the request is well-formed and is able to handle it.

3. The SOAP server extracts the request method name and uses the `Dictionary` to locate the corresponding wrapper function details (the `ProgID` and function name for a Visual Basic object).

4. The wrapper class is created (using the `ProgID`) and the SOAP body is passed to the wrapper function using `CallByName`.

5. The wrapper function extracts the parameter values from the SOAP request and passes them to a back-end application object.

6. The back-end object performs the request task, and returns the results to the wrapper function.

7. The wrapper function encodes the results as a SOAP response (or a SOAP fault, if an error is reported).

8. The SOAP server takes the SOAP response from the wrapper function and sends it back to the client.

This may seem a long process, but here is a summary of what it provides for us:

❑ Any existing COM object can be called by SOAP by creating a wrapper for it.

❑ Any object or method explicitly written for SOAP can have whatever number of arguments make sense, passed as a single XML string. These methods do not have to delegate, but can simply do the required work and return the SOAP response body.

❑ Objects can be made available to the SOAP server without touching SOAP code. Nothing in the SOAP server or the SOAP utilities class is hard-coded to a particular method.

❑ Translation from SOAP request to binary execution is isolated to each particular object. You do not need a single, one-size-fits-all class to convert SOAP XML to VB data types and vice-versa.

The SoapUtils.Utils Class

Now on to the SOAP utilities code. This class provides a `Dictionary` object to hold SOAP requests to back-end code bindings. This information is stored in a binding file, which looks like this:

```xml
<?xml version="1.0"?>
<SOAPbindings>
  <binding
        requestMethod="soapStringReverse"
        progID="SoapWrappers.CStringTestWrapper"
        server=""
        objectMethod="soapStringReverse" />
</SOAPbindings>
```

The document root, `SOAPbindings`, holds a series of `binding` elements. The `binding` element has a series of attributes indicating the name of an available SOAP method, the `ProgID` of a COM object, a server name where the object can be found, and the name of a method in the COM object that should be called to perform the requested SOAP method. As the file is parsed, the attributes for each `binding` element are used to construct an entry into the `Dictionary` object. A set of string constants is defined to allow the construction of distinct keys. To retrieve the corresponding information for any SOAP request, the key is constructed by combining the method name with the matching constant. As with the HTTP utilities class, errors have to be handled in a fairly quiet way. These functions return either a `Boolean` value or a `String`. A value of `False` means an error occurred in the method, while an empty string generally means a problem. A set of error properties is used to hold error status. Calls to any of the methods should inspect the return value and then grab the error properties to get more information.

The `SoapUtils` program is a separate ActiveX DLL project with a single class, called `Utils`. The project requires a reference to the `Scripting` library object, a reference to the MSXML parser, and a reference to our `ErrorUtils` object.

We first define the constants, variables and objects we'll need:

```vb
Option Explicit

Const DICT_PROGID_SUFFIX As String = "PROGID"
Const DICT_METHOD_SUFFIX As String = "METHOD"
Const DICT_SERVER_SUFFIX As String = "SERVER"
Const PROGID_STRING As String = "SoapUtils.Utils"


Private m_dictBindings As Scripting.Dictionary
Public ClassErrors As ErrorUtils.ErrorInfo
```

The SOAP specification describes how error information is to be returned. A SOAP:Fault element holds four child elements for the error information: faultcode, faultstring, runcode, and an optional detail element that contains additional user-defined elements. To help manage the construction of SOAP fault response elements, enumerated types for fault codes and run codes will be defined. The fault code describes what category of error occurred. The run code indicates whether or not the requested application code was run, if such information is known. So, for example, if we receive a request but the format is not version 1.0, then we'll reject it with a fault code of 100 (version mismatch), and indicate that we never reached the application code with run code 0. Likewise, if the SOAP request contains a MustUnderstand header that is not recognized, then the fault code is set to 200 (and run code to 0). Request methods that are not implemented will return a fault code of 300; if we do manage to execute the application code, but it raises an error, then the fault code would be 400, and the run code would be 1.

```
Public Enum SOAP_FAULT_CODE
    Version_Mismatch = 100
    Must_Understand = 200
    Invalid_Request = 300
    Application_Faulted = 400
End Enum
```

An enumerated type is defined for SOAP runcodes as well, taking the values from the SOAP 0.9 specification:

```
Public Enum SOAP_RUN_CODE
    Maybe = 0
    No = 1
    Yes = 2
End Enum
```

These types are used when constructing a SOAP:Fault response. Some private member variables are also set up to hold the fault information:

```
Private m_sSoapFaultDescription As String
Private m_sSoapFaultString As String
Private m_nSoapFaultCode As SOAP_FAULT_CODE
Private m_nSoapRunCode As SOAP_RUN_CODE
```

A fault detail element will need to be constructed, and a structure will be used to manage the details:

```
Type udtErrorDetail
    Namespace As String       ' namespace prefix for error detail
    NamespaceURI As String    ' URI of error namespace
    Datatype As String        ' error datatype
    Errorcode As Long         ' error code for error
    Description As String     ' Some useful info
    Location As String        ' Where it happened
End Type

Private Detail As udtErrorDetail
```

LoadMethodBindings

Since a special file is used to track how SOAP requests map to application code, the `LoadMethodBindings` function is included. This takes the path to the bindings file and loads the contents into the `Dictionary` object. It uses the `*_SUFFIX` constants to construct hash keys from the method name. Recall that a binding file has this structure:

```
<?xml version="1.0"?>
<SOAPbindings>
    <binding
        requestMethod = "SomeSoapMethodName"
        ProgId = "Some.ProgID"
        server = "SomeServerNameOrEmpty"
        objectMethod = "SomeMethodFromProgIDClass"
    >
</SOAPbindings>
```

The function's only parameter is a URI that indicates the location of the binding file. If a local file is used, the `"file://"` string needs to be prefixed to the string being passed in.

```
Public Function LoadMethodBindings(sBindingFileURI As String) As Boolean
    On Error GoTo ErrHand

    Dim oDOM As MSXML.DOMDocument
    Dim oEl As MSXML.IXMLDOMElement
    Dim oNodeList As MSXML.IXMLDOMNodeList
    Dim sSoapMethod As String
    Dim nIdx As Integer
```

A `DOMDocument` object is declared to receive the binding file, it is initialized, and the file loaded:

```
    Set oDOM = New DOMDocument

    If oDOM.Load(sBindingFileURI) Then
```

If the load succeeds, the document is parsed to retrieve the binding data. A `NodeList` is used to hold all the binding elements. The code iterates through the elements, and takes the attributes for the dictionary:

```
        Set oNodeList = oDOM.getElementsByTagName("binding")
        For nIdx = 0 To oNodeList.length - 1
            Set oEl = oNodeList.Item(nIdx)
            With oEl.Attributes
                sSoapMethod = .getNamedItem("requestMethod").nodeValue
                m_dictBindings.Add sSoapMethod & DICT_PROGID_SUFFIX, _
                    .getNamedItem("progID").nodeValue
                m_dictBindings.Add sSoapMethod & DICT_METHOD_SUFFIX, _
                    .getNamedItem("objectMethod").nodeValue
                m_dictBindings.Add sSoapMethod & DICT_SERVER_SUFFIX, _
                    .getNamedItem("server").nodeValue
            End With
        Next
```

```
            LoadMethodBindings = True
    Else
```

If the file load fails for any reason, the error values are set with the parser error data, and the response set to `False`:

```
        Call ClassErrors.SetErrorInfo(oDOM.parseError.reason, _
            PROGID_STRING & "LoadMethodBindings", oDOM.parseError.Errorcode)
        LoadMethodBindings = False
    End If
```

Likewise, if a run-time error occurs, the error data and the return value are set:

```
    ErrHand:
        If Err.Number <> 0 Then
            LoadMethodBindings = False
            Call ClassErrors.SetErrorInfo(Err.Description, _
                PROGID_STRING & "LoadMethodBindings", Err.Number)
        End If
    End Function
```

ExecuteRequestWrapper

Here's the workhorse function; it takes the SOAP XML, figures out what method it needs to run, and determines what back-end application object will do the job. It retrieves the object's `ProgID` from the dictionary and uses `CreateObject` to instantiate it. (Note that if we want to use MTS objects, and this SOAP utilities class was itself an MTS object, we would want to call `CreateInstance`. One possibility would be to include an additional attribute in the `binding` element to indicate if the object is in MTS or not, plus a new property for this class to say whether it is in MTS or not. Some simple `If/Then` logic could be used to decide how to create the object. For now, though, everything uses `CreateObject`. We'll be exploring MTS in Chapter 9, "*Storing and Retrieving XML Data*".)

`CallByName` is used to call the matching function, using the function name pulled from the dictionary. The SOAP body XML is passed to it as the single parameter. The return value of this call is expected to be a SOAP-encoded results string, which is then wrapped in the outer `SOAP:body` element. The complete SOAP response is then returned. (This function uses a few helper methods to construct response strings, and we'll cover those after we discuss this method):

```
    Public Function ExecuteRequestWrapper(sSOAPXML As String) As String
        On Error GoTo ErrHand

        Dim objX As Object
        Dim sProgID As String
        Dim sSoapMethodName As String
        Dim sComMethodName As String
        Dim sSoapParamXML As String
        Dim sObjectServer As String
        Dim sResults As String
        Dim sHttpHeader As String
```

A generic `Object` variable is declared, which is used to hold a reference to the specific class that implements the SOAP request wrapper. A `String` is used to hold the SOAP method name (from `sSOAPXML`), and `Strings` to hold the corresponding wrapper class information, which is retrieved from the dictionary. The SOAP version declared in the request is checked by calling `VerifySoapVersion` (which is explained later):

```
If VerifySoapVersion(sSOAPXML) Then
```

If the version is correct, the SOAP method name is extracted from the SOAP XML:

```
sSoapMethodName = RetrieveSoapMethodName(sSOAPXML)
```

`RetrieveSoapMethodName` will return an empty string if it cannot properly locate the method name. If the method name is retrieved, it is used to build keys into the `Dictionary` object, `m_dictBindings`:

```
If Len(sSoapMethodName) Then
    sProgID = m_dictBindings(sSoapMethodName & DICT_PROGID_SUFFIX)
    sComMethodName = m_dictBindings(sSoapMethodName & _
    DICT_METHOD_SUFFIX)
    sObjectServer = m_dictBindings(sSoapMethodName & _
    DICT_SERVER_SUFFIX)
    sSoapParamXML = sSOAPXML
```

If there is no `ProgID` for the request (because there is no matching entry in the dictionary), the SOAP fault data is set, and a `detail` section constructed:

```
If Len(sProgID) < 1 Then
    ' No entry in the Dictionary
    Call SetSoapFault(Invalid_Request, No)
    Call SetDetailInfo("MyFault", _
                       "e", _
                       "Method not supported", _
                       "www.wrox.org/VbSoap", _
                       "ExecuteRequestWrapper", _
                       -1)
```

(The `SetSoapFault` and `SetDetailInfo` helper functions are described later.)

The response value is set:

```
sResults = BuildSoapEnvelopeFault (True)
```

If a `ProgID` is found, then the data from the dictionary is used to create the corresponding object. (The XML file holding the binding information may optionally specify a remote machine for the object.)

```
Else
    If Len(sObjectServer) > 0 Then
        Set objX = CreateObject(sProgID, sObjectServer)
    Else
```

```
                    Set objX = CreateObject(sProgID)
          End If
```

A test is carried out to verify that the object has been created; if so, then the response body can be built and a call made to the back-end object to perform the request:

```
          If Not objX Is Nothing Then
              sResults = _
          "<SOAP:Envelope xmlns:SOAP='urn:schemas-xmlsoap-org:soap.v1' " _
              & Chr(10)
              sResults = sResults & " SOAP:encodingStyle = "
              sResults = sResults & " 'urn:schemas-xmlsoap-"
              sResults = sResults & " org:soap.v1'>" & Chr(10)
              sResults = sResults & "<SOAP:Body>" & Chr(10)
```

The results for the call are added to the response string:

```
              sResults = sResults & _
                  CallByName(objX, sComMethodName, _
                  VbMethod, sSoapParamXML) & Chr(10)
              sResults = sResults & "</SOAP:Body>" & Chr(10)
              sResults = sResults & "</SOAP:Envelope>"
              Set objX = Nothing
```

If the object is not created from the ProgID (perhaps because the binding file had the wrong information, or because the object isn't registered on the machine), a fault response is built:

```
          Else
              Call SetSoapFault(Application_Faulted, No)
              Call SetDetailInfo("MyFault", _
                              "e", _
                              "Failed to create object", _
                              "www.wrox.org/VbSoap", _
                              "ExecuteRequestWrapper", _
                              -1)
              sResults = BuildSoapEvelopeFault(True)
          End If
      End If
  End If
```

If the request specified the wrong version, the fault information is built and the response set:

```
  Else
      Call SetSoapFault(Version_Mismatch, No)
      sResults = BuildSoapEvelopeFault(True)
  End If
```

Finally, if any errors were thrown in the function, a fault response is built to send back:

```
ErrHand:
    If Err.Number <> 0 Then
        Call SetDetailInfo("MyFault", _
                "e", _
                "COM error" & Err.Description, _
                "www.wrox.org/VbSoap", _
                "ExecuteRequestWrapper", _
                Err.Number)
        Call SetSoapFault(Application_Faulted, No)
        sResults = BuildSoapEvelopeFault(True)
        Call ClassErrors.SetErrorInfo(Err.Description, _
                PROGID_STRING & ".ExecuteRequestWrapper ", _
                Err.Number)
    End If
```

Now we have a SOAP response body, and we need to put HTTP headers together before sending the results back to the client:

```
    sHttpHeader = "HTTP/1.1 200 OK" & Chr(10)
    sHttpHeader = sHttpHeader & "Content-Type: text/xml" & Chr(10)
    sHttpHeader = sHttpHeader & "Content -length: "
    sHttpHeader = sHttpHeader & CStr(Len(sResults)) & Chr(10) & Chr(10)
    ExecuteRequestWrapper = sHttpHeader & sResults
End Function
```

SetSoapFault

This method uses several other functions to construct the response if there is a fault: `SetSoapFault`, `BuildSoapEvelopeFault`, `SetDetailInfo`, and `BuildDetailXml`. `SetSoapFault` takes two parameters: the SOAP fault code (which is one of the enumerated types), and a runcode value (another enumerated type). It uses them to set the SOAP fault class variables:

```
'*********************************************************
' Private Sub SetSoapFault(FaultCode As SOAP_FAULT_CODE, _
'                     RunCode As SOAP_RUN_CODE)
' Populate our SOAP fault member variables
'*********************************************************
Private Sub SetSoapFault (FaultCode As SOAP_FAULT_CODE, RunCode As SOAP_RUN_CODE)

    m_nSoapFaultCode = FaultCode
    m_nSoapRunCode = RunCode
```

A `Select` statement is used to set `m_sSoapFaultDescription` so that a more meaningful message string can be added to the response:

```
    Select Case FaultCode
        Case Version_Mismatch:
            m_sSoapFaultDescription = _
```

```
                          "The call was using an unsupported SOAP version."
               m_sSoapFaultString = "Version Mismatch"
           Case Must_Understand:
               m_sSoapFaultDescription = _
               "An XML element was received that contained an element tagged " & _
               "with mustUnderstand='1' that was not understood by the receiver."
               m_sSoapFaultString = "Must_Understand"
           Case Invalid_Request:
               m_sSoapFaultDescription = "The receiving application did not " & _
                           "process the request because it was incorrectly " & _
                           "formed or not supported by the application."
               m_sSoapFaultString = "Invalid Request"
           Case Application_Faulted:
               m_sSoapFaultDescription = "The receiving application faulted " & _
                  when processing the request. The 'detail' element contains " & _
                           "the application-specific fault."/
               m_sSoapFaultString = "Application Faulted"
           Case Else:
               m_sSoapFaultDescription = "Unknown."
               m_sSoapFaultString = "Unknown."
       End Select
   End Sub
```

BuildSoapEnvelopeFault and BuildFaultXml

The following function builds a SOAP:Envelope containing a SOAP:Fault. It takes a single Boolean parameter, to indicate if the fault response is to include a detail element:

```
'***********************************************************
' Private Function BuildSoapEnvelopeFault
'  (bIncludeDetail As Boolean) As String
' Grab the Fault XML and wrap the correct elements around it
'***********************************************************
Private Function BuildSoapEvelopeFault(bIncludeDetail As Boolean) As String
    Dim sRes As String
    sRes = "<SOAP:Envelope xmlns:SOAP='urn:schemas-xmlsoap-org:soap.v1' " & _
        Chr(10)
    sRes = sRes & " SOAP:encodingStyle='urn:schemas-xmlsoap-org:soap.v1'>" & _
        Chr(10)
    sRes = sRes & " <SOAP:Body>" & Chr(10)
    sRes = sRes & BuildFaultXml(bIncludeDetail)
    sRes = sRes & "</SOAP:Body>" & Chr(10)
    sRes = sRes & "</SOAP:Envelope>"

    BuildSoapEvelopeFault = sRes

End Function
```

The function uses BuildFaultXml to put together the SOAP:Fault string. It receives the bIncludeDetail value to decide if it should put a detail structure in the fault. This is an optional parameter, which defaults to False. The code takes the class SOAP fault variables and constructs the XML:

```
Public Function BuildFaultXml(Optional bIncludeDetail As Boolean = False) _
                                    As String
    On Error GoTo ErrHand

    Dim sXML As String
    sXML = ""

    sXML = sXML & "<SOAP:Fault>" & Chr(10)
    sXML = sXML & "<faultcode>" & m_nSoapFaultCode & "</faultcode>" & Chr(10)
    sXML = sXML & "<faultstring>" & m_sSoapFaultString & "</faultstring>" & _
        Chr(10)
    sXML = sXML & "<runcode>" & m_nSoapRunCode & "</runcode>" & Chr(10)
```

If bIncludeDetail is True, BuildDetailXml is called to construct the detail information:

```
    If (IncludeDetail) Then
        sXML = sXML & BuildDetailXml() & Chr(10)
    End If
    sXML = sXML & "</SOAP:Fault>"
```

Finally, there is some runtime error handling code before the result is returned:

```
ErrHand:
    If Err.Number <> 0 Then
        Call ClassErrors.SetErrorInfo(Err.Description, _
                PROGID_STRING & ".BuildFaultXml", _
                Err.Number)
        sXML = ""
    End If
    BuildFaultXml = sXML
End Function
```

SetDetailInfo

The detail element requires a user-defined data type; the data type must contain a namespace prefix, that the information needs to be include, as well as the URI for the namespace schema. Error information is also required: a description of the error, the location of the error, and an error code. These are all members of the Detail class variable. A function is provided to allow all of this information to be set in one pass:

```
Public Sub SetDetailInfo(sDataType As String, _
                         sNamespace As String, _
                         sDesc As String, _
                         sNsURI As String, _
                         sLocation As String, _
                         lErrorcode As Long)
    With Detail
        .Datatype = sDataType
        .Namespace = sNamespace
        .Description = sDesc
        .NamespaceURI = sNsURI
```

```
               .Location = sLocation
               .Errorcode = lErrorcode
        End With
    End Sub
```

BuildDetailXml

When the `detail` XML needs to be created, this function takes the `Detail` class variable and returns the XML string:

```
Public Function BuildDetailXml() As String
    On Error GoTo ErrHand
    Dim sXML As String
    Dim sErrNsAttr As String
    Dim sXsdNsAttr As String
```

A check is made to verify that `Detail` is populated, by calling a small function called `DetailsAreSet`. If no detail data exists, the response XML is set to an empty string:

```
    If Not DetailsAreSet() Then
        sXML = ""
```

Otherwise, the `Detail` members are taken and the XML is constructed:

```
    Else
        sXML = ""
        sXsdNsAttr = "xmlns:xsd='www.w3.org/schemas'"
        With Detail
            sErrNsAttr = "xmlns:" & .Namespace & "='" & .NamespaceURI & _
                    "' xsd:type='" & .Namespace & ":" & .Datatype & "' "
            sXML = sXML & "<detail " & sXsdNsAttr & " " & _
                sErrNsAttr & " >" & Chr(10)
            sXML = sXML & "<message>" & .Description & "</message>" & Chr(10)
            sXML = sXML & "<location>" & .Location & "</location>" & Chr(10)
            sXML = sXML & "<errorcode>" & CStr(.Errorcode) & _
                "</errorcode>" & Chr(10)
            sXML = sXML & "</detail>"
        End With
    End If
```

Again, some error handling code is added at the end:

```
ErrHand:
    If Err.Number <> 0 Then
        Call ClassErrors.SetErrorInfo(Err.Description, _
                PROGID_STRING & ".BuildDetailXml", _
                Err.Number)
        sXML = ""
    End If
    BuildDetailXml = sXML
End Function
```

GetSoapBody

To process the actual SOAP information, the POST data needs to be separated from the total HTTP request. This method takes the HTTP request data and returns the SOAP XML:

```
'*********************************************************
' Public Function GetSoapBody(sPostData As String) As String
' Retrieves the XML from the http post
'*********************************************************
Public Function GetSoapBody(sPostData As String) As String
    Dim asPost() As String
    Dim sXml As String
```

An array is defined for holding separate parts of the POST data, and a String to hold the part that is returned. The HTTP POST should contain a series of HTTP headers, followed by two consecutive linefeed characters. Just in case data has been sent that uses the Windows convention of ending a line with a carriage return and a linefeed combination, such pair are replaced with a single linefeed:

```
    sPostData = Replace(sPostData, vbCrLf, Chr(10))
```

The data is then split, using a double linefeed as the delimiter, and the resulting array placed into asPost. Note that the third parameter to the Split function is being used to specify that no more than two elements are to be returned: everything before the first set of double linefeeds will go into the first array location, and all the remaining text (the actual POST data, which itself might contain double linefeeds) will go into the second element:

```
    asPost = Split(sPostData, Chr(10) & Chr(10), 2)
```

The POST data should contain at least one set of double linefeeds, so the array should have more than one element. If it does, the second element is taken (using zero-based indexing) and it is assigned to the XML string:

```
    If UBound(asPost) > 0 Then
        sXml = asPost(1)
```

If the array has only one element, then the data passed to the function is not a valid POST, so the body cannot be extracted, and an empty string is returned:

```
    Else
        sXml = ""
    End If
    GetSoapBody = sXml
End Function
```

RetrieveSoapMethodName

To work out what back-end application code to call in order to execute the request, the name of the SOAP request method needs to be determined. This function takes the SOAP envelope XML and returns the name of the method being called:

```
Public Function RetrieveSoapMethodName(sXml As String) As String
    Dim oDOM As DOMDocument
    Dim oEl As IXMLDOMElement
    Dim sMethod As String
    Dim asTemp() As String
```

A DOMDocument is declared for parsing the SOAP envelope, an Element for holding the SOAP:Body element, a String to hold the method name, and an array for separating the method-name namespace from the actual method name. After initializing the DOM, the XML is loaded. If the load succeeds, the first (and presumably only) SOAP:Body is found:

```
Set oDOM = New DOMDocument

If oDOM.loadXML(sXml) Then
    Set oEl = oDOM.getElementsByTagName("SOAP:Body").Item(0)
```

A check is made to verify that the element has been retrieved, the name of its first child is obtained, which should (according to the SOAP specification) be the method name element:

```
If Not oEl Is Nothing Then
    sMethod = oEl.childNodes.Item(0).nodeName
```

A split is then carried out on the ":" character to separate the element name from the namespace prefix:

```
If InStr(sMethod, ":") Then
    asTemp = Split(sMethod, ":")
    sMethod = asTemp(1)
```

If there's no ":" character, then the method name element does not have a namespace, so an empty string is returned:

```
Else
    ' No namespace!
    sMethod = ""
End If
```

If the SOAP:Body element could not be retrieved, then an error occurs, and an empty string is returned:

```
Else
    sMethod = ""
End If
```

And if the SOAP XML could not be loaded, then an empty string is returned:

```
Else
    sMethod = ""
End If
RetrieveSoapMethodName = sMethod
Set oDOM = Nothing
End Function
```

VerifySoapMethodHeader

The SOAP request should contain a header specifying the method being called. It must match the information in the SOAP payload. We need a function to check for the header, and verify it:

```
'*************************************************************
' Public Function VerifySoapMethodHeader(sSOAPPayload) As Boolean
' If we receive the HTTP header SOAPMethodName (and we *should*) then
' we need to see that the method name in the payload,
' and its namespace, match.
' Should look something like this:
' SOAPMethodName: http://electrocommerce.org/abc#MyMethod
'*************************************************************
Public Function VerifySoapMethodHeader (sPostData As String) As Boolean
    On Error GoTo ErrHand
    Dim sPayload As String
    Dim nStart As Integer
    Dim nEnd As Integer
    Dim sHeaderValue As String
    Dim asHeaderData() As String
    Dim bOK As Boolean
```

First the POST data is searched to see if it contains the method name HTTP header:

```
        If InStr(1, sPostData, "SOAPMethodName") > 0 Then
```

If it does, then the text that follows the header name is retrieved. First the starting position of the header is found, and the length of the header name string added on to get the starting position of the following text:

```
        nStart = InStr(1, sPostData, "SOAPMethodName:")
        nStart = nStart + Len("SOAPMethodName:") + 1
```

The end position of the text is found by looking for the next linefeed character, and the substring extracted:

```
        nEnd = InStr(nStart, sPostData, Chr(10))
        sHeaderValue = Trim(Mid(sPostData, nStart, (nEnd - nStart)))
```

Finally, the method name is found by splitting the header value on the "#" character into the asHeaderData array:

```
        asHeaderData = Split(sHeaderValue, "#")
```

The value in the SOAPMethodName header is compared to the method name as used in the SOAP body, so RetrieveSoapMethodName is called and its string compared to what was found in the header:

```
        sPayload = GetSoapBody(sPostData)
        If (asHeaderData(1) = RetrieveSoapMethodName(sPayload)) Then
            bOK = True
        Else
```

```
        bOK = False
    End If
```

If the header is missing, then the request is invalid:

```
    Else
        ' No header!
        bOK = False
    End If
```

If the header cannot be found, then a SOAP fault is returned:

```
    If Not bOK Then
        Call SetSoapFault(Invalid_Request, No)
    End If
```

If a runtime error occurs, a fault is returned:

```
ErrHand:
    If Err.Number <> 0 Then
        bOK = False
        Call SetSoapFault(Invalid_Request, No)
        Call ClassErrors.SetErrorInfo(Err.Description, _
                PROGID_STRING & "VerifySoapMethodHeader", _
                Err.Number)
    End If
    VerifySoapMethodHeader = bOK
End Function
```

When the class is first called, a small amount of initialization code is required for the `Dictionary` object:

```
Private Sub Class_Initialize()
    Set m_dictBindings = New Dictionary
End Sub
```

The SOAP Client/Server Application

We'll now take a look at our Visual Basic application, which uses our new DLLs. It's a Visual Basic standard EXE project, with a single form. The project is called `SoapClientServer`, and the form is named `frmMain`.

We'll step through and explain the essential code. The rest of the VB code in the application will not be presented here, because it is self-explanatory and does not teach us anything new or important about using XML with VB, it's simply there to make the application more user friendly. The *complete* code can be downloaded from http://www.wrox.com.

The application provides buttons to initiate connections and requests, as well as text areas for setting the POST data and viewing the results. A web browser was added so we can see rendered HTML.

Here's a list of the controls (all except one of the labels), and what they're used for:

Control Type	Name	Purpose
Text box	txtLocalPort	The socket port we are using
Text box	txtLocalIP	The IP address of the machine we are using
Text box	txtRemoteHost	The IP address of machine to which we are connecting
Text box	txtPage	The web page we requesting (if we are doing a GET or POST)
Option button	optServer	Puts the application in "server" mode
Option button	optClient	Puts the application in "client" mode
Check box	chkKeepAlive	Used to add a "keep-alive" header to a page request
Command button	cmdConnect	Opens a connection to a remote machine
Command button	cmdDisconnect	Closes the socket connection
Command button	cmdPost	Sends a POST request to the remote machine
Command button	cmdGet	Sends a GET request to the remote machine
Command button	cmdListen	Tells the application to listen on the port specified
Command button	cmdExit	Closes the application
Label	lblState	Displays the current state of the socket connection
Text box	txtMessages	Used to display assorted information about events
Winsock OCX	sock	Used for socket communication
Timer	Timer1	Used for polling the state of the socket connection

There's also a tab strip, containing these controls:

Control Type	Name	Tab	Purpose
Text box	`txtPostData`	POST data	The data we are sending in our POST request
Web browser	`wbBrowser`	Rendered HTML	A browser for displaying HTML
Text box	`txtHTTP`	Raw HTTP stuff	The raw HTTP response from the server

Our program will also use the two ActiveX DLLs we've built to encapsulate SOAP and HTTP methods (`HttpUtils.Utils` and `SoapUtils.Utils`), and the `ErrorInfo.Utils` class. It also requires a reference to the Scripting runtime library and the Microsoft XML parser, and uses the Microsoft Internet Transfer control.

This is what the complete form looks like:

We have a multi-line text box to display assorted messages, several buttons for various socket commands (Connect, Disconnect, Post, Get, Listen, plus our application's Exit command), text boxes for local and remote hosts, another text box for the local port to listen on, and yet another text box to specify the page we want to GET or POST to. There is a tab control with three tabs. The first holds a text box for displaying data sent to the server; the second holds a web browser control for rendering any HTML we might get, and the last tab has another text box for entering data to be sent using the POST command.

A frame holds two radio buttons for toggling between client and server roles. There's a label to display the current socket state and a check box for adding a "keep-alive" HTTP header to any POST or GET.

First a few variables need to be declared for our application, so let's look at frmMain:

```
'*************************************************
' SoapClientServer EXE project
' Handles SOAP requests or submits HTTP calls
' frmMain
'*************************************************
Option Explicit

Const MAXTABS As Integer = 3

Dim g_bDataDone As Boolean
Dim g_bListening As Boolean
Dim g_bSendComplete As Boolean
Dim asDataReceived() As String
Dim soapSrvUtils As SoapUtils.Utils
Dim HttpUtils As HttpUtils.Utils
Dim g_sSoapResponse As String
Dim g_bRequestedKeepAlive As Boolean
Dim asSockState(9) As String
```

A few items are initialized when the form loads:

```
'*************************************************
' Private Sub Form_Load()
' Do some initialization stuff
'*************************************************
Private Sub Form_Load()
    Dim nIdx As Integer

    Set HttpUtils = New HttpUtils.Utils
    Set soapSrvUtils = New SoapUtils.Utils
```

We need to load our SOAP request bind file, so a SOAP utility class method is called:

```
    soapSrvUtils.LoadMethodBindings ("c:\SOAPBindings.xml")
```

We also need to give the web browser some content, so that there is a document available for later scripting:

```
    Call RenderHtml
```

We'll examine RenderHtml when we look at how we display any received HTML in the web browser control.

Now the display of the controls contained on the tab strip needs to be set. The controls are first hidden and then the controls are displayed for the first tab only:

```
For nIdx = 0 To MAXTABS - 1
        picTab1(nIdx).Visible = False
        picTab1(nIdx).BackColor = frmMain.BackColor
        picTab1(nIdx).BorderStyle = 0
Next

    picTab1(0).Visible = True
```

An array (asSockState()) is used to hold a set of user-friendly strings for showing the socket state, so a separate method is called to populate the array:

```
    InitSockStateArray
```

Then the timer is enabled and set to run every quarter second:

```
    Timer1.Enabled = True
    Timer1.Interval = 250
```

And the keep-alive flag is set to false:

```
    g_bRequestedKeepAlive = False
End Sub
```

Here's the function for setting the user-friendly socket state strings so the current socket status can be displayed:

```
'***************************************************
' Sub InitSockStateArray()
' Set up an array to make socket state display better.
'***************************************************
Sub InitSockStateArray()
    asSockState(0) = "Closed"
    asSockState(1) = "Open"
    asSockState(2) = "Listening"
    asSockState(3) = "Connection pending"
    asSockState(4) = "Resolving host"
    asSockState(5) = "Host resolved"
    asSockState(6) = "Connecting"
    asSockState(7) = "Connected"
    asSockState(8) = "Closing"
    asSockState(9) = "Error"
End Sub
```

Command Event Handlers and Related Fuctions

Now we'll set up our command event handlers. Some of the commands are basic, so the code is contained within the Click event. Other commands will require more processing logic, and so the code is encapsulated in separate functions.

The `cmdConnect_Click` event simply calls the `Connect` subroutine:

```
'*************************************************
' Private Sub cmdConnect_Click()
' The Connect button
'*************************************************
Private Sub cmdConnect_Click()
    Connect()
End Sub
```

The Connect Function

First, the socket state is checked. If we're busy trying to connect, or already connected, we don't want to try to connect again:

```
    If sock.State = sckConnecting Or sock.State = sckConnected Then
        txtMessages.Text = "Still connecting, or already connected."
```

Otherwise, the socket control is told to connect. The `Connect` method of the Winsock control takes two parameters: the IP address of the remote machine, and a remote port to connect to:

```
    Else
        sock.Protocol = sckTCPProtocol
        sock.Connect txtRemoteHost.Text, "80"
    End If
```

If an error occurs, the socket state label is set, and a message displayed:

```
ErrHand:
    If Err.Number <> 0 Then
        lblStateText.Caption = "Error"
        txtMessages = Err.Description
        MsgBox "Error: " & Err.Description, vbInformation, "Connect Error"
    End If
End Sub
```

Disconnecting is just a matter of telling the socket to close, so the `Click` event on the **Disconnect** button does that:

```
'*************************************************
' Private Sub cmdDisconnect_Click()
' The Disconnect button
'*************************************************
Private Sub cmdDisconnect_Click()
    sock.Close
End Sub
```

The Listen Function

`cmdListen_Click` calls our `Listen` sub-routine. Listening for a connection requires us to bind the socket to a local IP address and port number, and tell the socket to listen. The `g_bDataDone` flag is reset in preparation for receiving data:

```
    Private Sub Listen()
        On Error GoTo ErrHand
```

The socket control is told which protocol is required – we're using TCP. `sckTCPProtocol` is a constant provided by the Winsock control:

```
sock.Protocol = sckTCPProtocol
```

The `g_bListening` flag is set to `True`, and the socket bound to our machine's IP address and the port:

```
g_bListening = True
sock.Bind txtLocalPort.Text, txtLocalIP.Text
```

And then the socket control is told to listen:

```
sock.Listen
```

The "data flag" is set to false in preparation for receiving data:

```
g_bDataDone = False
```

Any runtime errors will be displayed in a message box:

```
ErrHand:
    If Err.Number <> 0 Then
        MsgBox "Error: " & Err.Description, vbInformation, "Listen Error"
    End If
End Sub
```

So, we can now connect to, or disconnect from, a remote machine, or tell our application to listen for a connection request. We're ready to send and receive data.

The WebGET Function

Sending an HTTP GET request requires that we build our HTTP headers and make a socket call, so `cmdGet_Click` will call the `webGET` method to handle it:

```
'*************************************************
' Sub webGET()
' Build the GET request and send it.
'*************************************************
Sub webGET()
    On Error GoTo ErrHand
    Dim sRq As String
```

A local string is defined to hold the request text as it is constructed. The name of the requested page is taken and the first HTTP header is built:

```
sRq = "GET " & Trim$(txtPage.Text) & " HTTP/1.0" & Chr(10)
```

A header is sent to identify the user-agent (i.e. the browser, though it could be a spider or some other web-enabled application):

```
sRq = sRq & "User-Agent: Wrox HTTP/1.0 (WinNT)" & Chr(10)
```

If the "keep-alive" check box has been checked, then a keep-alive header is added as well:

```
If chkKeepAlive.Value Then
    sRq = sNaff & "Connection: keep-alive" & Chr(10)
End If
```

We also want to tell the remote server what type of content we can receive. Here the "*.*" wildcard is used to indicate that anything will be accepted:

```
sRq = sRq & "Accept: *.*" & Chr(10) & Chr(10)
```

A check is made to verify that we are connected, and if so, then the GET request is sent:

```
If sock.State = sckConnected Then
    Call sock.SendData (sRq)
```

Otherwise, a message is displayed:

```
Else
    txtMessages.Text = "Not connected!"
End If
```

If there are any run-time errors, they are caught and displayed in a message box:

```
ErrHand:
    If Err.Number <> 0 Then
        MsgBox "Error: " & Err.Description, vbInformation, "GET Error"
    End If
End Sub
```

For the POST request, the cmdPost_Click event will use a local routine called webPOST that calls a method from the HttpUtils class:

```
'***************************************************
' Sub webPOST()
' Build a POST request using the HttpUtils class
' and send it
'***************************************************
Sub webPOST()
    On Error GoTo ErrHand
    Dim sRq As String
```

A local variable is used to build up the request string, and populate the HTTP header string properties of HttpUtils:

```
With HttpUtils
    .HttpMethod = "POST"
    .HttpUri = txtPage
    .ContentType = "text/xml"
    .HttpVersion = "1.0"
    .HttpHost = txtRemoteHost.Text
    .UserAgent = "Wrox POSTer"
    .PostData = txtPostData.Text
    .SoapMethodHeader = GetSoapMethodName()
    sRq = .BuildPOSTRequest()
End With
```

BuildPOSTRequest returns the full POST request string. (Note that GetSoapMethodName is called, a private function which parses the SOAP envelope that is sent and returns the name of the method. This is required to construct a required SOAP HTTP header.)

If the building of the POST request is successful, the POST string is displayed so we can see just what we're sending, and check that we're connected. If so, then we can send our request:

```
If Len(sRq) > 0 Then
    txtMessages.Text = "Request string:" & vbCrLf & sRq
    If sock.State = sckConnected Then
        Call sock.SendData(sRq)
```

If we're not connected, a message box is displayed:

```
    Else
        MsgBox "Not connected!", vbExclamation, "Socket error"
    End If
```

If BuildPOSTRequest failed and returned an empty string, a message box is displayed, along with the error information from HttpUtils:

```
    Else
        txtMessages.Text = "Request string error: " _
            & vbCrLf & HttpUtils.ErrorDescription
    End If
```

Any runtime errors will be caught and a message box displayed:

```
ErrHand:
    If Err.Number <> 0 Then
        MsgBox "Error: " & Err.Description, vbInformation, "POST Error"
    End If
End Sub
```

GetSoapMethodName

We mentioned that we needed to get the name of the SOAP method being called so we can build an extra HTTP header. (This is the SOAPMethodName header that the SOAP server can use to verify the request.) GetSoapMethodName takes the POST data we are planning to send and locates the SOAP:Body element. The first child must (by definition in the specification) be the method name:

```
Private Function GetSoapMethodName() As String
    On Error GoTo ErrHand

    Dim oDOM As MSXML.DOMDocument
    Dim oEl As IXMLDOMElement
    Dim sMethodName As String
```

A DOMDocument is declared, as well as an Element node for parsing, and a string to hold the results. The DOM is initialized, and the POST data loaded. If there are no load errors, the first (and only) SOAP:Body element is retrieved:

```
    Set oDOM = New DOMDocument
    If oDOM.loadXML(txtPostData) Then
        Set oEl = oDOM.getElementsByTagName("SOAP:Body").Item(0)
```

If the node retrieval works, then the name of its first child is retrieved:

```
        If Not oEl Is Nothing Then
            sMethodName = oEl.firstChild.baseName
```

Otherwise, an empty string is returned:

```
        Else
            sMethodName = ""
        End If
```

If loading the POST data fails, a message box is displayed, and the response is set to an empty string:

```
    Else
        MsgBox "Error parsing POST data: " & oDOM.parseError.reason, _
            vbExclamation, "Parsing error"
        sMethodName = ""
    End If
```

Finally, any runtime errors will display a message box:

```
ErrHand:
    If Err.Number <> 0 Then
        MsgBox "Error finding SOAP method name: " & _
        Err.Description, vbCritical
        sMethodName = ""
    End If

    GetSoapMethodName = sMethodName
End Function
```

Selecting a role for the application will enable or disable certain commands so we don't do anything odd by mistake, like trying to do a GET when we're supposed to be waiting for a connection. This is handy if we're running two copies of the application on the same machine; it helps us keep track of the role of each instance. We use our option buttons to toggle the controls:

```
'**************************************************
' Private Sub optClient_Click()
' Toggle valid commands
'**************************************************
Private Sub optClient_Click()
    If (optClient.Value) Then
        cmdConnect.Enabled = True
        cmdDisconnect.Enabled = True
        cmdGet.Enabled = True
        cmdListen.Enabled = False
        cmdPost.Enabled = True
        txtLocalIP.Enabled = False
        txtLocalPort.Enabled = False
        txtRemoteHost.Enabled = True
        txtPage.Enabled = True
    End If
End Sub
```

```
'**************************************************
' Private Sub optServer_Click()
' Toggle valid commands
'**************************************************
Private Sub optServer_Click()
    If (optServer.Value) Then
        cmdConnect.Enabled = False
        cmdDisconnect.Enabled = True
        cmdGet.Enabled = False
        cmdListen.Enabled = True
        cmdPost.Enabled = False
        txtLocalIP.Enabled = True
        txtLocalPort.Enabled = True
        txtRemoteHost.Enabled = False
        txtPage.Enabled = False
    End If
End Sub
```

Closing the connection just involves calling Close.

```
Private Sub sock_Close()
    sock.Close
End Sub
```

Handling SOAP Requests

If the application is a server, then we want to respond to any connection requests. In particular, we want to handle SOAP requests. (Actually, this is all the server is able to do, so non-SOAP requests will get a SOAP error message.) We reset the g_bDataDone flag to False, and check that the socket is closed before trying to accept a new connection. Accepting the connection will cause the socket to begin accepting data, so we loop until all data has arrived. The DataArrival event handler will take the SOAP request, call the SoapUtils object to process it, and place a response into the g_sSoapResponse global variable, setting g_bDataDone to True. Now we can send the response back to the caller. We then close the connection, pause for a moment to ensure the socket really has closed (and isn't just *saying* it's closed; the Winsock control has a momentary gap between when it reports itself as closed and when the socket has in fact closed. Waiting about two seconds gives it time to finish closing.) Then we begin listening again.

```
'**************************************************
' Private Sub sock_ConnectionRequest(ByVal requestID As Long)
' Respond to the request, and do handle SOAP calls
'**************************************************
Private Sub sock_ConnectionRequest(ByVal requestID As Long)
    Dim sSend As String
```

The Winsock control calls ConnectionRequest whenever a connection request comes in. A variable has been declared to hold the response that will be sent back after the request is handled. A connection request is assigned an ID number by the Winsock control to allow tracking of connections; the ID is shown in the messages box.

> *Our application has a single Winsock control and so cannot handle multiple connections. If we wanted to expand the application to allow multiple simultaneous connections, we would have to have a control array of Winsock controls, and we could use the request ID to manage responses to each client.*

```
    txtMessages.Text = "requestID = " & requestID
```

The "data done" flag is reset in preparation for receiving data:

```
    g_bDataDone = False
```

We cannot accept a connection unless the socket is closed, so the socket state is checked, then closed if it hasn't already been, and then the connection is accepted:

```
    If sock.State <> sckClosed Then sock.Close
    sock.Accept requestID
```

The socket response variable is initialized, and then we wait until all data has been received. (Once a connection has been accepted, and data starts to arrive, the Winsock control will call sock_DataArrival, which collects the incoming data, as we'll see.)

```
        sSend = ""
        Do While g_bDataDone = False
            DoEvents
        Loop
```

sock_DataArrival will set the g_bDataDone flag to True once it is done. It will also handle the SOAP request if the application is running as a server, and build a SOAP response.

```
        sSend = g_sSoapResponse
```

The SOAP response is taken, and prepared to send the results back to the client:

```
        g_bSendComplete = False
        sock.SendData sSend

        Do While Not g_bSendComplete
            DoEvents
        Loop
```

sock_SendComplete will be called by the Winsock control when all the data has been sent; it will set g_bSendComplete to True when done, at which point the connection is closed:

```
        sock.Close
```

Now, a check is made to determine whether the program is running as a server. If it is, we wait for the socket to tell us it's closed. ListenAgain is called to tell the socket to wait for another connection:

```
    If optServer.Value Then
        Do While sock.State <> sckClosed
            DoEvents
        Loop
        'then wait 2 seconds and start listening again ...
        Call ListenAgain(2)
    End If
End Sub
```

The ListenAgain Function

The subroutine ListenAgain takes a Double parameter, which specifies how long to wait before telling the socket to listen:

```
'**************************************************
' Sub ListenAgain(dblWaitSeconds As Double)
' Even though the socket state may say "closed".
' we may get errors if we try to listen right away.
' Pause for dblWaitSeconds seconds, then listen.
'**************************************************
Sub ListenAgain(dblWaitSeconds As Double)
    Dim datLater As Date
    datLater = DateAdd("s", dblWaitSeconds, Now)
```

```
      Do While datLater > Now()
          DoEvents
      Loop
      Call Listen
  End Sub
```

The arrival of any data will set off a few actions, depending on the role of the application. If this is a client, the data will simply be displayed, which should be the result of the GET or POST. If it is running as a server, it will be assumed that this a SOAP request and an attempt will be made to process it.

```
  Private Sub sock_DataArrival(ByVal bytesTotal As Long)
      Dim sData As String

      sock.GetData sData, vbString, bytesTotal
```

After declaring a variable to hold the incoming data, the Winsock control is told to get the data, and then any carriage return characters are removed. The standard end-of-line marker for HTTP headers is the linefeed character, and our HTTP and SOAP utility classes are designed for this. Extraneous carriage returns will throw off the parsing of the HTTP request.

> If you've ever moved text files between Windows and UNIX, you may have noticed how the presentation of the file can appear peculiar: Windows uses a combination of carriage return and line feed to end a line, while UNIX uses just the line feed. Many FTP transfer programs will strip carriage returns from a text file if the file is being sent to a UNIX machine.

```
      txtHTTP.Text = Replace(sData, Chr(10), vbCrLf)
      asDataReceived = Split(sData, Chr(10))
```

If the application is running as a server, the received data is passed to the DoSoap method:

```
      If optServer Then
          g_sSoapResponse = DoSoap(sData)
      End If
```

The global g_sSoapResponse variable to the SOAP response and the "data done" flag are reset before exiting:

```
      g_bDataDone = True
  End Sub
```

The DoSoap Function

DoSoap uses the GetSoapBody method of the SOAP utilities class to get the SOAP envelope from the HTTP POST request and sends it on ExecuteRequestWrapper. This is the method from the SOAP class that dispatches the SOAP request to the correct back-end request handler.

```
  Function DoSoap(sData As String) As String
      Dim sXml As String
      Dim sResults As String
```

```
    sXml = soapSrvUtils.GetSoapBody(sData)
        If Len(sXml) Then
            Debug.Print "DoSoap: " & sXml
            sResults = soapSrvUtils.ExecuteRequestWrapper(sXml)
            DoSoap = sResults
        Else
            sResults = "DoSoap error: " & sData
        End If
        DoSoap = sResults
    End Function
```

When the socket control has finished sending the data, either as an HTTP request or as a response, it calls SendComplete, which sets the g_bSendComplete flag:

```
Private Sub sock_SendComplete()
    g_bSendComplete = True
End Sub
```

Finally, if there are any socket errors along the way, they will be displayed in the message box:

```
Private Sub sock_Error(ByVal Number As Integer, Description As String, _
                ByVal sCode As Long, ByVal Source As String, _
                ByVal HelpFile As String, ByVal HelpContext As Long, _
                CancelDisplay As Boolean)
    txtMessages.Text = "Socket error " & CStr(Number) & _
        "; Desc: " & Description
End Sub
```

The Tab Control

The tab control (tabCtrls) is used to hold data we intend to send, and to display the response that comes back from the server. When a user clicks on one of the tabs, the tabCtrls Click routine is run. It hides all of the controls contained on the tab, and then displays the controls for the selected tab.

```
Private Sub tabCtrls_Click()
    Dim nIdx As Integer
    For nIdx = 0 To MAXTABS - 1
```

The controls for each tab are contained in an array of picture boxes (picTab1()), so changing the visibility of a picture changes what is displayed:

```
        picTab1(nIdx).Visible = False
    Next
    picTab1(tabCtrls.SelectedItem.Index - 1).Visible = True
    If (tabCtrls.SelectedItem.Index = 2) Then
        Call RenderHtml
    End If
End Sub
```

If the middle tab is selected, we want to take the HTTP data we received and render it in the web browser control. We can script the contents of the web browser to dynamically set the HTML, but only if the browser contains a document. Internet Explorer provides some default web pages to show under various circumstances, such as when a page cannot be found. The "Page Not Found" page is loaded from the SHDOCLC.DLL file (part of the IE installation), and then modified the document contents. A Win32 API call is used, which is declared in a project module, to find the correct path for the DLL:

```
Declare Function GetSystemDirectoryA Lib "Kernel32" _
    (ByVal lpBuffer As String, ByVal nSize As Long) As Long
```

RenderHtml

This RenderHtml function is used to initialize the web browser contents, and display any available HTML:

```
Private Sub RenderHtml()
    On Error GoTo ErrHand

    Dim sHTML As String
    Dim sBuf As String
    Dim lSize As Long
    Dim lRetval As Long
```

The variables are declared to be used with GetSystemDirectoryA. It takes two parameters: a String buffer, which it will use to return the path to the system directory, and a Long value to specify the size of the buffer. The function's return value is the size of the string placed into the buffer.

```
    sBuf = String(255, 0)
    lSize = 255
    lRetval = GetSystemDirectoryA(sBuf, lSize)
```

The required data is grabbed using the Left function:

```
    sBuf = Left(sBuf, lRetval)
```

The DLL can now be called, passing in a parameter to indicate what page is required, and we wait until it has finished loading:

```
    wbBrowser.Navigate2 ("res://" & sBuf & "\\SHDOCLC.DLL/dnserror.htm")
    Do While wbBrowser.ReadyState <> READYSTATE_COMPLETE
        DoEvents
    Loop
```

Then the HTTP utility function GetContent is called to give the content from the HTTP response:

```
    sHTML = HttpUtils.GetContent(txtHTTP.Text)
```

If there is no content to display, a simple "No data" message is shown; the existing HTML is then cleared from the browser's document, and the new HTML rendered:

```
      If Len(sHTML) < 1 Then
          sHTML = "<HTML><BODY><H1>No data</H1></BODY></HTML>"
      End If
      wbBrowser.Document.body.innerHTML = ""
      wbBrowser.Document.Write sHTML

ErrHand:
    If Err.Number <> 0 Then
        MsgBox "Error! " & Err.Description, vbCritical
    End If
End Sub
```

The form also holds a timer control to keep the socket status label up-to-date:

```
'*************************************************
' Private Sub Timer1_Timer()
' Display the current state of the socket
'*************************************************
Private Sub Timer1_Timer()
    lblStateText.Caption = asSockState(sock.State)
End Sub
```

That's it. When running as a server, you can select Listen to sit and wait for connection requests. If a connection is requested, it is accepted, and the server receives the data. Once the data has been received, it is sent to the DoSoap function, which in turn calls GetSoapBody to pull out the SOAP XML from the POST data. If the body is successfully retrieved, it is passed on to ExecuteRequestWrapper, which works out what code is needed to run to handle the request, runs that code, and returns the results as an HTTP SOAP response. The SOAP response is then sent back to the connection client.

If we're running as a client, the user can click Connect to open a connection to the server specified in the Remote host field. The Get button will request the page specified in the Page field. The Post button will take the text in the Post data text box and post it to the server. The results will be displayed in the Raw HTTP stuff text box, as well as the web browser control on the second tab.

Trying it Out

What fun is it having a new toy if you can't play with it? Let's write some code that we can call with a SOAP request and see how this works. We'll do something basic: string reversal. To do this, a simple DLL will be created that provides a class with a string reverse function. We'll create an ActiveX DLL project called SoapDest (the destination code for the SOAP request), and give it a single class, CStringTest. The class has one method:

```
Option Explicit

Public Function StringReverse(sText As String) As String
    StringReverse = StrReverse(sText)
End Function
```

It just calls the VB `StrReverse` function and returns the results. Now we need to write a wrapper for this. We create another ActiveX DLL project called `SoapWrappers`, and add a class called `CStringTestWrapper`. The project requires a reference to our `SoapDest.CStringTest` class, as well as to the MSXML object. The wrapper code will be responsible for taking the SOAP method request information and making a call to the destination function, `SoapDest.StringReverse`. It will take the results and construct the SOAP response XML, which will be returned to the SOAP server.

The class has two functions: the main function for handling the request and dispatching the call to the back-end object, and a helper function for extracting namespace information, so we can build the correct response elements. `GetNsStrings` takes an element, extracts the namespace prefix, and builds a string for the `xmlns` attribute. We pass it a reference to the element node we are interested in, and references to two strings to hold the return values. It returns `True` if it all works, and `False` otherwise:

```
Private Function GetNsStrings(oEl As IXMLDOMElement, _
                        sNsPrefix As String, _
                        sNsAttr As String) As Boolean

   On Error GoTo ErrHand
   Dim bResults As Boolean
   Dim asTemp() As String
```

The base name of the node is taken and it is split on the ":" character; the resulting array should have the namespace prefix in the first element:

```
   asTemp = Split(oEl.nodeName, ":")
   sNsPrefix = asTemp(0)
```

The prefix is then used to build the namespace attribute name, and get its value:

```
   sNsAttr = "xmlns:" & sNsPrefix & " = '" & _
       oEl.Attributes.getNamedItem("xmlns:" & sNsPrefix).nodeValue & "'"
   bResults = True

ErrHand:
   If Err.Number <> 0 Then
       bResults = False
   End If
   GetNsStrings = bResults
End Function
```

soapStringReverse

The main function is `soapStringReverse`:

```
'**********************************************************************
' Public Function soapStringReverse(sSoapParams As String) As String
' Wrapper function to take SOAP parameters, decode them into VB types,
' and call the actual VB object to do the work.  The results are then
' encoded as a SOAP XML response.
' The function expects the SOAP Body element (and its children):
'       <SOAP:Body>
'           <m:soapStringReverse xmlns:m='SomeUri'>
```

```
'                <text>Hello, world!</text>
'            </m:soapStringReverse>
'        </SOAP:Body>
'*********************************************************************
Public Function soapStringReverse(sSoapParams As String) As String
    On Error GoTo ErrHand

    Dim soapDestStr As SoapDest.CStringTest
    Dim oDOM As DOMDocument
    Dim oElNode As IXMLDOMElement
    Dim sText As String
    Dim sResults As String
    Dim sNsPrefix As String
    Dim sNsUriAttr As String
    Dim sResponse As String
```

First, the variables are declared, and the DOMDocument initialized. Then the SOAP XML is loaded, and if it parses, a reference to the first child of SOAP:Body is returned, which holds the method name element:

```
Set oDOM = New DOMDocument

If oDOM.loadXML(sSoapParams) Then
    Set oElNode = oDOM.getElementsByTagName("SOAP:Body").Item(0)
    Set oElNode = oElNode.firstChild
```

The namespace information is then retrieved, so the response element can be constructed:

```
If GetNsStrings(oElNode, sNsPrefix, sNsUriAttr) Then
```

If the call returns True, the text parameter is retrieved:

```
Set oElNode = oDOM.getElementsByTagName("text").Item(0)
sText = oElNode.childNodes.Item(0).nodeValue
```

The CStringTest variable is initialized, before StringReverse is called, and the response built:

```
Set soapDestStr = New CStringTest
sResults = soapDestStr.StringReverse(sText)
sResponse = "<" & sNsPrefix & ":soapStringReverseResponse " _
    & sNsUriAttr & " >" & Chr(10)
sResponse = sResponse & "<text>"
sResponse = sResponse & sResults
sResponse = sResponse & "</text>" & Chr(10)
sResponse = sResponse & "</" & sNsPrefix & _
    ":soapStringReverseResponse>"
```

If the namespace information could not be retrieved, a fault is sent back:

```
    Else
        sResponse = sResponse & "<SOAP:Fault>" & Chr(10)
        sResponse = sResponse & "Invalid namespace." & Chr(10)
        sResponse = sResponse & "</SOAP:Fault>"
    End If
```

If the SOAP XML was not properly loaded, a fault is sent back:

```
  Else
      ' DOM parse Error!
      sResponse = sResponse & "<SOAP:Fault>" & Chr(10)
      sResponse = sResponse & "Error parsing parameters: " & Chr(10)
      sResponse = sResponse & oDOM.parseError.reason & Chr(10)
      sResponse = sResponse & "</SOAP:Fault>"
  End If
```

Any runtime errors will return a SOAP fault:

```
  ErrHand:
    If Err.Number <> 0 Then
        sResponse = sResponse & "<SOAP:Fault>" & Chr(10)
        sResponse = sResponse & "COM Error: " & Chr(10)
        sResponse = sResponse & Err.Description & Chr(10)
        sResponse = sResponse & "</SOAP:Fault>"
    End If
```

Finally, the objects are cleared and the response returned:

```
        Set soapDestStr = Nothing
        Set oDOM = Nothing

        soapStringReverse = sResponse
  End Function
```

We need to be sure to compile the DLL; Visual Basic will register it for us when we do this, so it will be available for our test.

Loading SOAP Binding Information

So, how does the SOAP server know to how to call SoapWrappers' soapStringReverse function? We use the binding information. The SOAP server will load our XML file:

```
<?xml version="1.0"?>
<SOAPbindings>
  <binding
      requestMethod="soapStringReverse"
      progID="SoapWrappers.CStringTestWrapper"
      server=""
      objectMethod="soapStringReverse" />
</SOAPbindings>
```

When the SOAP client/server application starts, it loads the binding information. When the program calls `ExecuteRequestWrapper`, it parses out the name of the requested method, locates the corresponding `ProgID` and function name from the `Dictionary`, creates the object, and calls the function using `CallByName`, sending the SOAP request body to `soapStringReverse`. `soapStringReverse`, being a wrapper function, knows how to call the real code to do the work. (Of course, `soapStringReverse` could very well have done the string reverse on its own, and if you're writing code explicitly for SOAP then that would be more efficient. But this demonstration shows that you can use legacy code by simply creating a small wrapper for it.)

To run this, we'll use two instances of the SOAP client/server program. (We need to be sure we don't have a local web server running or it will interfere on port 80. So if IIS or some other web server is running, it will need to be stopped.) We build an executable for our application, run the first instance, and set it to be the server by selecting the "**Server**" option button. We then click the **Listen** button to wait for a connection:

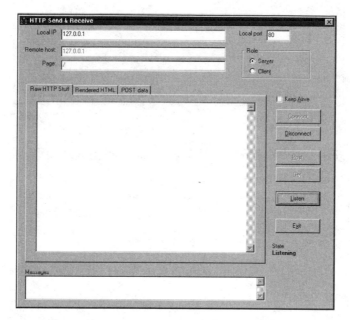

We start another instance, and make it the client. We enter the following SOAP request into the "**POST data**" text box:

```
<SOAP.Envelope
    xmlns:SOAP-"urn:schemas-xmlsoap-org:soap.v1"
    SOAP:encodingStyle="urn:schemas-xmlsoap-org:soap.v1">
 <SOAP:Body>
    <w:soapStringReverse xmlns:w='www.wrox.com/VbXml'>
        <text>Hello, world!</text>
    </w:soapStringReverse>
  </SOAP:Body>
</SOAP:Envelope>
```

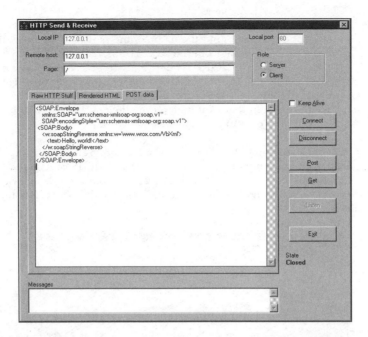

Click Connect on the client, then Post. The server receives the HTTP data as shown here:

This processes the request, sending the SOAP response (with the reversed string) to the client:

How We Use SOAP

No, we're not talking about how to wash ourselves; we now have a way to move data to and from a server, and it doesn't require any weird binary marshaling or secret handshake protocol. We'll go into the details of applying SOAP in Chapter 9, "*Storing and Retrieving XML Data*". We'll see how to build a simpler SOAP client component using the MSXML.HTTPRequest object to talk to Active Server Pages handling SOAP transactions. In Chapter 11, "*Distributed Objects*" we'll use SOAP to allow the web server to communicate with the product database and XML file server, to handle searches and display product information.

Current Efforts to Standardize Web Transactions

We've looked at how distributed objects can communicate with one another for remote function calls, but our application will also need to create an XML document to encode the final purchase transaction by a user. XML-RPC and SOAP describe ways to marshal requests over the wire – the XML is hidden. On the flip-side to this are transaction messages that are in fact XML, such as a purchase order. As XML is becoming more widely known, businesses are keen to take advantage of it to provide ways to encode e-commerce messages. If you're looking to open your web application to outsiders, it becomes very handy to have a standard way to define what a transaction request should look like. We've seen what XML Schemas are, and how they can be used to determine the validity of a document. Even if we don't actually validate any documents, the schema can serve as a public description of what the XML is expected to look like.

One of the important developments in the XML arena is the emergence of independent schema repositories, such as the BizTalk and OASIS initiatives. These repositories allow interested parties to find out what a transaction request should look like so they can properly format their requests. They also serve as an open forum where members of any given business community, such as travel agents or construction firms, can work together to develop a standard exchange format.

BizTalk

BizTalk™ (www.biztalk.org) is an initiative managed by Microsoft to solve two problems. First it is designed to determine how multiple parties, with a common interest, can exchange information (whether they be electronic documents, application data, or something else entirely) without having to cater to each recipient's unique format. Second, it was designed to find out how applications should handle the information received. The BizTalk framework is an attempt to standardize an XML format for documents (however broadly defined) so that creating content and processing the data can be done without reinventing the wheel. It is similar to SOAP in that it defines a high-level outer layer of XML that serves as an envelope for any type of XML document. Like SOAP, BizTalk documents must adhere to a standard format for packaging the data, but allow flexibility regarding how the data is described. You can think of BizTalk as a Federal Express (FedEx) package. On the outside, FedEx requires you to provide certain information in a standard form, but in the package itself you can put almost anything you want.

In addition to the framework specification, BizTalk provides a repository of document schemas intended to serve as a common dialect for particular transactions. For example, suppose you are provider of electronic parts. You deal with several manufacturers on one end, and countless customers on the other. When someone wants to get a price quote from you, they might submit a form describing a particular item. Ideally, you'll be provided with enough information to quickly locate the exact item of interest and have a way to promptly respond to the inquiry. But how is anyone to know just what information is required? Somebody inquiring about a price is likely to be asking other vendors as well. Will each of them have a different format for price inquiries? Maybe, but at the root, each of them will most likely need the same information. Meanwhile, as your stock runs low, you need to contact manufacturers about ordering new components. Again, you'll be dealing will a wide range of companies, but they will all need the same basic information. Life gets much easier when enough people agree on a standard method for doing common tasks. Under the BizTalk approach, a set of transactions could be defined for such things as price inquires, bulk purchases, and individual orders. Anyone looking to do one of these can simply check the BizTalk schema repository to see what format should be used. The receiving parties no longer have to interpret endless variations on a theme, and can use a common body of processing applications for all requests.

All BizTalk framework documents must begin with the `BizTalk` root element. The element must contain a BizTalk namespace declaration:

```
<BizTalk xmlns= "urn:schemas-biztalk-org:BizTalk/biztalk-0.81.xml">
</BizTalk>
```

The root element must also contain a `Body` element as an immediate child. This element serves to indicate that what follows is the real document content of interest. Within the `Body` element is a message type element, which must be qualified by a namespace. The element type describes the message type, for example:

```
<BizTalk xmlns= "urn:schemas-biztalk-org:BizTalk/biztalk-0.81.xml">
  <Body>
    <PriceInquiry xmlns="urn: urn:schemas-biztalk-org:electro-org/inquiry">
    <!--document content -->
    </PriceInquiry>
  </Body>
</BizTalk>
```

BizTalk documents may also contain routing information. The BizTalk framework defines a set of three tags to define where the document came from, and where it should be going. Routing information is optional, but if you decide to include it you must use all three tags. There is the Route tag, and its two child elements, From and To. This example is taken from the "BizTalk Framework XML Tags Specification":

```
<Route>
  <From locationID="111111111" locationType="DUNS"
        process="" path="" handle="3"/>
  <To locationID="222222222" locationType="DUNS"
      process="" path="" handle="23CF15"/>
</Route>
```

According to the specification, "Routing tags are defined to support message delivery using rules-based message delivery agents, such as Microsoft BizTalk Framework Server or other BizTalk Framework-compatible servers" (www.biztalk.org/Resources/tags081.asp). The Route element must be a child of the Body element. A primary goal of the routing information is to allow a processing application to handle the transaction, and determine where to send the response. As the BizTalk document is passed among the different parts of the processing application, the From and To elements may be modified to track the process path. The attributes help define four levels of delivery and processing abstraction: location, application, path and instance:

- ❑ **LocationID:** This attribute indicates a place, perhaps, but not necessarily, a URL. The exact nature of the attribute depends on what process will handle delivery within the BizTalk framework.

- ❑ **LocationType:** This attribute provides additional, qualifying information for the LocationID.

- ❑ **Process:** Much like a SOAP method name, this attribute specifies the process to be invoked.

- ❑ **Path**: This is used as a routing path tracking variable, storing information about what processes have handled the transaction, allowing the route to be reversed.

- ❑ **Handle:** Similar to an ID, this attribute allows the receiving application to distinguish between multiple instances of the same transaction type.

BizTalk Document Content

The message type element of a BizTalk document holds the data the receiving application is ultimately interested in. The BizTalk document design guide states that, beyond using the framework tags to enclose the document, the only other requirement is that a schema exists. The BizTalk web site does offer a style guide for element naming conventions and document structure. It makes some good points about picking names that have clear semantic meaning, e.g. Customer instead of Field1. It recommends the use of what is referred to as "CamelCase" style, described as follows:

> *"If an element reflects a thing (an object, a class or a table name), use* `UpperCamelCase;` *if it is a property, a reference, etc., use* `lowerCamelCase`*"*
> *(www.biztalk.org/Resources/frame081.asp).*

Basically, think of objects or classes as proper nouns that must begin with a capital letter, whereas adjectives and adverbs begin with a lowercase letter.

But nowhere do they mention the use of attributes. The style guide gives an example of a compound element to define a price, with child elements, rather than attributes, to indicate qualifying properties such as currency and quantity. The reasoning behind this is that if something has more than one part, then it will likely need more parts in the future. While this may be true, it completely ignores any concept of semantic differentiation and eliminates the possibility of exploiting qualities unique to attributes, such as default values or implied existence. However, a quick browse through the schema library reveals a number of actual schemas using attributes to define information.

Available Schemas

The BizTalk web site maintains a library of available schemas for a variety of industry groups, such as construction and agriculture. For example, IronSolutions LLC has provided a schema to describe farm equipment inventory, and Timberline Software has a schema for a cost estimate report. The library provides the documentation, sample usage, and the schema itself for downloading.

BizTalk Software

In addition to the schema framework definition, Microsoft is also providing BizTalk software, specifically the BizTalk server. It provides components for delivery of messages by HTTP, HTTPS (secure transmission), SMTP, FTP, DCOM, and through MSMQ (Microsoft Message Queue). It also includes a BizTalk schema editor that allows you to either create a brand new schema, or import an existing schema or DTD and modify it. The BizTalk mapper is a graphical tool for transforming documents from one format to another, using XSL.

The BizTalk Jumpstart kit is available for downloading from the BizTalk web site.

OASIS

An effort similar to BizTalk has been undertaken by **OASIS**, the Organization for the Advancement of Structured Information Standards, to maintain a repository for XML schemas. According to the `XML.org` "Frequently Asked Questions" web page, OASIS is "a non-profit international consortium founded in 1993 to advance the open interchange of documents and structured information objects". Originally focused on SGML, OASIS has evolved to support XML more actively, a subset of SGML designed for easy implementation in commercial and web environments. OASIS, through the XML.org web site, have organized an OASIS registry and repository (www.oasis-open.org/html/rrpublic.htm). Like BizTalk, the idea is to provide a central point for locating and retrieving DTDs and schemas. As their web site points out, increasing numbers of people are asking, "Is there a schema for *such and such*" and, rather than reinvent the same thing over and over again, with the incompatibilities that would inevitably result, the OASIS repository hopes to allow people to use a standard URI to access commonly used schemas. The registry would allow users to query the repository for a DTD or schema that fits their criteria. The results of the query would be some type of pointer or reference to the actual schema or DTD, if it is found.

Somewhat like BizTalk, the schemas are required to follow certain formats. For example, a `driver.dtd` file has been defined that contains entity definitions that point to other DTDs containing more detailed information, such as how the schema or DTD fits a given classification scheme, or the administrative status of the file.

Unlike BizTalk, the OASIS schemas/DTDs are of a broader nature than just describing transaction requests. For example, you may find a DTD for PMML, the Predictive Model Markup Language defined by a company called The Data Mining Group (www.dmg.org). Also, OASIS is, currently at least, attempting to develop a software scaffold to process the DTDs beyond their search and retrieval.

Consensus on Schemas

When writing a web application that uses XML messaging you should take the time to decide if your transaction documents should have a schema, and if so, should the application validate the document or check conformance in some other way? If you decide you want a schema, then perhaps you should see if one already exists that fits your needs. Let's look at these criteria in a little more depth.

What to Use – Schema, DTD, or Neither?

Nothing says you *must* have a schema or DTD, so why bother? If nothing else, taking the time to write out a schema or DTD forces you to think about what you might need before you write any code. This is good, professional programming practice in any case. For example, suppose you are handling hotel reservations. As you write out the schema you can mentally walk through a typical booking scenario, noting such required information as arrival date, departure date, requested room time, requested rate, special requests (smoking or non-smoking? high floor or low floor?), and so on. In many cases, the required information will be driven by the needs of some existing back-end software, such as a central reservation system. But you may want additional information that serves your particular business needs (such as how did the guest hear about the hotel). It's a good exercise, even if you never use it for anything other than a reference document. But by choosing to write this information as a schema or DTD, you naturally fall into using a more precise definition than if you had simply written out an informal design document.

Five Questions to Ask Yourself

1. Do I need to validate?

If you really have no intention of validating your XML, then writing a schema is perhaps a simpler task than writing a DTD. DTD syntax can be somewhat arcane, compared to the XML of a schema. However, if you do think that validation is a possibility, you should think about what XML parser you will be using and whether or not it can validate against a schema. Even then, it may be easier to first write the schema, then convert it into a DTD if required.

Whether you choose to validate or not depends on how you will be receiving and processing the document. For example, you may be receiving XML produced by another piece of your code. If there's a problem with the XML, validation might trap errors, but the real problem is with the code that created the XML to begin with. On the other hand, you may be getting XML from unknown sources. If the use of the XML is an all-or-nothing situation (meaning if any part of it is not valid then the whole document is useless), then validation is a programmatically easy way to check for problems right up front. However, you may get "untrusted" XML that is an aggregate of subdocuments. For example, I may send you a collection of news wire clippings. There may be invalid XML buried inside a particular story, but you might prefer to trap that in your code, keeping what's good and discarding what you can't parse.

There are situations where you may not be able to validate because your application does not know who the recipients of the XML may be. For example, in our sample application, we'll be sending along XML that encodes a transaction request. Part of the XML defines what object will handle the request, but much of the XML is intended for the actual transaction object. Since the framework we're using will allow the dynamic creation of objects, and those objects may each have its own XML requirements, the outer portion of our application cannot use a single schema or DTD for validation. It is easier to trap basic errors in the code and pass the remaining XML to the requested object, where additional error handling can be done.

2. Do I need to agree on a fixed schema with partners (for data exchange), even if I will not validate at runtime?

You need to think about how public your application will be, and what type of interface it will offer. For example, we may decide that we would like any third party to be able to display our products and post purchase requests to our server. For an external web site to do this, it would need to know how to formulate the XML transaction. If there is already a schema that can be used by your application, and which is already in use by other businesses, then it would be reasonable to adopt that schema. You can still choose to ignore validation.

3. What are the data entities that must be included in the document?

If you decide to go with a custom schema or DTD, then you need to begin thinking of "what must be included", "what can be included", and "how open should the DTD/Schema be". What this means is, how strict will do you want to be? You may only need to define some top-level elements, and allow the nested content to be free-form. For example, it may be enough to specify that this is a transaction of a given type:

```
<TRANSACTION  type="Purchase" >
    <!-- data for the order handler -->
<TRANSACTION  >
```

The code for relaying the transaction won't know any details about the destination object that actually processes the order, and we want to keep the XML format completely open. So validation for this type of XML would only want to check that the root element type is TRANSACTION, and that it has the attribute type.

A possible schema would look like this:

```
<Schema xmlns="urn:schemas-microsoft-com:xml-data"
  xmlns:dt="urn:schemas-microsoft-com:datatypes">
  <AttributeType name='type' dt:type='string' required='yes'/>
  <ElementType name='TRANSACTION' content='mixed' model='open' >
  <attribute type='type' />
  </ElementType>
</Schema>
```

Or you may need to ensure that nothing unexpected shows up, and limit everything to specific elements and attributes.

4. Should a certain data entity be stored as an element or as an attribute?

This topic verges on a religious war, and a wide range of opinions can be found. The final choice depends on how the XML is to be handled, by both programs and people reading it. Let's review elements and attributes. Here are some basic comparisons between elements and attributes:

Quality	Element	Attributes
May have default values	No	Yes
May be referenced by index	Yes	No (except through the `NamedNodeMap` interface)
May have child elements	Yes	No
May be repeated	Yes	No
May contain unparsed entities	Yes	No
May have a data type	No	Yes
May have an order	Yes	No

At first glance, it seems that elements have the upper hand, though the attribute's ability to have a data type and a default value are important. But a chart such as this is not able to convey the subtle notions of relationships and, as the example in Chapter 1 (in the section called "*Attributes*") showed, human readability is seriously affected by your choice of structure. The essential point is to express a relationship among the data in such a way that parsing (whether by human eye or machine code) becomes fairly natural. For example, suppose we wanted to build a schema to describe a book purchase transaction. We need to examine what makes up a book, a transaction, what information is required, and how it all relates.

It's useful to build a sample document, since, ultimately, that's what's going to be handled, then work backwards to write the schema. We'll start with a root element:

```
<TRANSACTION>
</TRANSACTION>
```

Now, do we need to indicate what type of transaction this is? Well, do we foresee other transactions besides purchasing? There may be inventory queries, or restock requests, so we should provide some means to distinguish the transaction type. We have a few options for this. We could rename the root element to something like PURCHASE-TRANSACTION, or even BOOK-PURCHASE-TRANSACTION, but somehow this doesn't convey our intentions. It's clear that this could lead to an explosion of document types, and there's no simple way to parse out the difference between, say, BOOK-RESTOCK-TRANSACTION and BOOK-PURCHASE-TRANSACTION, short of string manipulation on the node name. So, we can either use a child element or give TRANSACTION an attribute.

How complex is the transaction type property? Can we simply indicate "purchase", or do we need to represent it with some more detailed, structured data? The transaction type can serve as an indicator of what content is to follow; information that could reside as child elements of a TYPE element can work just as well as children of the TRANSACTION element. The relationship of transaction to type is clearer if the type is an attribute of TRANSACTION:

```
<TRANSACTION type="purchase">
</TRANSACTION>
```

rather than:

```
<TRANSACTION>
  <TYPE>purchase</TYPE>
</TRANSACTION>
```

Furthermore, we can use our schema to restrict the possible values of the type attribute to ensure that we are receiving a transaction we know how to handle. Using a TYPE element means that this is perfectly acceptable:

```
<TRANSACTION>
  <TYPE>gibberish</TYPE>
</TRANSACTION>
```

An application processing transactions can use validation to ensure that it has a valid transaction type; it can then safely pull out the type value and use, say, a SELECT statement to route the transaction to the correct handler.

TRANSACTION may need more metadata as well. You may want to track transactions by a reference number. A refnumber or id can be used to uniquely identify a transaction. Because this is tightly bound to the transaction as a whole, it should be an attribute:

```
<TRANSACTION type="purchase" id="123">
</TRANSACTION>
```

Let's move on to the transaction details. We need some information about the book being purchased, such as the title, ISBN (International Standard Book Number), author, etc. So, once again, do you define an element or an attribute? You need to decide what aspects of the TRANSACTION element are immutable. For example, we can safely say that every transaction will have a type and an ID, but will it always have an ISBN? Should this type of information be tightly bound to the transaction as a whole, or does it serve a purpose as a more independent piece of information? Consider that the document could be used to create an invoice. One rule of thumb for deciding whether something should be an attribute or an element is that data intended for *display* should be in an *element*. Information about the item being purchased is more valuable when bound to that item than when directly tied to the transaction object as a whole. We may also want our processing application to extract the item-specific information from the transaction document and pass it on to yet another part of our code. We may be better served by using an element to represent the purchased item:

```
<TRANSACTION type="purchase" id="123">
  <ITEM ISBN="1-861003-32-3">
  </ITEM>
</TRANSACTION>
```

So, did we jump the gun here? Should ISBN be an attribute of the ITEM element? Assuming that we're always dealing with books then this is fine. It represents an immutable property of the item. Of course, were we trying to design a more generic schema, suitable for a variety of products, then ISBN would be a poor choice for an attribute, and would need to belong to a more focused BOOK element. But let's stick to books as our only product item. The ISBN belongs to the book as a whole, and can serve as a unique identifier. (You may consider calling the attribute something else, such as ID, so that the ITEM element can be referenced by an IDREF attribute.)

Of course, books have other qualities as well. We could also have `author` and `title` attributes, as they are global to the book. But we may also want to make an aesthetic judgment. Attributes with large values can be awkward to read. Besides, there may be more than one author, and the book may credit an editor as well;

```
<TRANSACTION type="purchase" id="123">
  <ITEM ISBN="1-861001-57-6">
    <TITLE>A Survey of American Literature</TITLE>
    <AUTHOR>Jane Doe</AUTHOR>
    <AUTHOR>John Johnson</AUTHOR>
    <EDITOR>Max Revisions</EDITOR>
  </ITEM>
</TRANSACTION>
```

Further refinement is possible, depending on how you intend to use this data. Perhaps you want to track the number of books sold by a given author. In that case, you may want greater structure for the author name:

```
<AUTHOR firstname="Jane" lastname="Doe" middleinitial=""/>
```

Or add more structure to the collection of authors and editors:

```
<CONTRIBUTERS>
  <CONTRIBUTER firstname="Jane" lastname="Doe" MI="" role="author" />
  <CONTRIBUTER firstname="John" lastname="Johnson" MI="J" role="author" />
  <CONTRIBUTER firstname="Max" lastname="Revisions" MI="" role="editor" />
</CONTRIBUTERS>
```

Another option is to omit the details of the specific book entirely, and rely on an external data source to provide this information. You could maintain a database or a set of flat files, indexed by ISBN, to track this instead. Plus, if your web site is tracking a user's shopping cart, it is unlikely to be storing all of the details about each book selected, since the ISBN provides the relevant information. It is more efficient to simply pass along data that can be used (if needed) to reference more information.

Similar thinking must go into the formatting of publisher, price, number of pages, hardbound/paperback, and so on. You need to think about possible uses for the data, how it relates to other parts of the document, and how complex it needs to be. Here's another version:

```
<TRANSACTION type="purchase" id="123">
  <ITEM ISBN="1-861001-57-6" format="pb" language="en">
    <PRICE currency="USD">25.00</PRICE>
    <WEIGHT unit="kg">0.25</WEIGHT>
  </ITEM>
</TRANSACTION>
```

We've removed the book details that can be derived from the ISBN. We've added `language` and `format` attributes to the document because they are intrinsic qualities of a book but are not essential for rendering. We've added `PRICE` and `WEIGHT` elements, instead of attributes, because they require additional qualifiers: a price needs a unit of currency, and a weight needs a unit of measurement.

We need information about the buyer, as well, to describe a delivery address, billing address, payment type, possibly credit card information, and anything else to ensure that we get paid and the customer gets the book.

Things can get more interesting here. How are we handling the financial transaction? Are we doing credit card processing ourselves? Are we going to employ a third party? This is important, because we may want to tailor the customer information for some other application that would receive the extracted billing details.

Let's take a shot this, though, to wrap it up:

```
<PURCHASER type="individual">
  <CONTACTINFO type="contact">
    <NAME first="" last="" MI=""/>
    <ADDRESS>
      <COMPANY></COMPANY>
      <STREET1></STREET1>
      <STREET2></STREET2>
      <CITY></CITY>
      <STATEPROV></STATEPROV>
      <COUNTRY></COUNTRY>
      <POSTAL></POSTAL>
    </ADDRESS>
    <PHONE type="voice"></PHONE>
    <PHONE type="fax"></PHONE>
    <EMAIL></EMAIL>
  </CONTACTINFO>
  <CONTACTINFO type="bill-to">
      <!-- same elements as above -->
  </CONTACTINFO>
  <CONTACTINFO type="ship-to">
      <!-- etc. -->
  </CONTACTINFO>
</PURCHASER>
```

Now, when we first starting designing this layout, we had put all of the address information inside the ADDRESS element as attributes. This made sense, and it reduced the amount of text we would have to move around. But, we realized that we were using rather deliberate text formatting (indentation and white space) to make it readable. This is fine, but the application is unlikely to provide that sort of special arrangement, and trying to read such a document would be just too annoying. Second, we use different elements for the different types of contact information. But by using one element with a qualifying attribute, the schema becomes easier to write and to maintain. If we decide that all of the contact information sections should, say, contain a URL or a cell-phone number, then we would have to be sure to add it to all of them. So, a little planning up front can save us work later.

So, our schema, depending on how we ultimately decided to store and represent the data, might look like this:

```
<?xml version="1.0"?>
<Schema xmlns="schemas-microsoft-com:xml-data">

  <AttributeType name="type" dt:type="string" />
  <AttributeType name="currency" dt:type="string" />
```

```
<AttributeType name="ISBN" dt:type="string" />
<AttributeType name="format" dt:type="string" />
<AttributeType name="language" dt:type="string" />
<AttributeType name="first" dt:type="string" />
<AttributeType name="last" dt:type="string" />
<AttributeType name="MI" dt:type="string" />
<AttributeType name="id" dt:type="idref" required="yes"/>

<ElementType name="PRICE"  content="textOnly" model="closed">
  <attribute type="currency" />
</ElementType>

<ElementType name="WEIGHT"  content="textOnly" model="closed">
  <attribute type="unit" />

</ElementType>

<ElementType name="ITEM"  content="eltOnly" model="closed">
  <attribute type="ISBN" />
  <attribute type="format" />
  <attribute type="language" />
  <element type="PRICE" />
  <element type="WEIGHT" />
</ElementType>

<ElementType name="PHONE" content="textOnly" model="closed">
  <attribute type="type"  />
</ElementType>

<ElementType name="EMAIL" content="textOnly" model="closed">
</ElementType>

<ElementType name="NAME" content="textOnly" model="closed">
  <attribute type="first" />
  <attribute type="last" />
  <attribute type="MI"  />
</ElementType>

<ElementType name="COMPANY" content="textOnly" model="closed">
  <attribute type="type" />
</ElementType>
<ElementType name="STREET1" content="textOnly" model="closed">
  <attribute type="type" />
</ElementType>
<ElementType name="STREET2" content="textOnly" model="closed">
  <attribute type="type" />
</ElementType>
<ElementType name="CITY" content="textOnly" model="closed">
  <attribute type="type" />
</ElementType>
<ElementType name="STATEPROV" content="textOnly" model="closed">
  <attribute type="type" />
</ElementType>
<ElementType name="COUNTRY" content="textOnly" model="closed">
  <attribute type="type" />
</ElementType>
```

```
    <ElementType name="POSTAL" content="textOnly" model="closed">
      <attribute type="type" />
    </ElementType>

    <ElementType name="ADDRESS" content="eltOnly" model="closed">
        <element type="COMPANY" />
        <element type="STREET1" />
        <element type="STREET2" />
        <element type="STATEPROV" />
        <element type="COUNTRY" />
        <element type="POSTAL" />
    </ElementType>

    <ElementType name="CONTACTINFO" content="eltOnly" model="closed">
      <attribute type="type" />
      <element type="NAME" />
      <element type="ADDRESS" />
      <element type="PHONE" />
      <element type="EMAIL" />
    </ElementType>

    <ElementType name="PURCHASER" content="eltOnly" model="closed">
      <attribute type="type" />
      <element type="CONTACTINFO" />
    </ElementType>

    <ElementType name="TRANSACTION" content="eltOnly" model="closed">
      <attribute type="type" />
      <attribute type="id" />
      <element type="ITEM" />
    </ElementType>
  </Schema>
```

Finally, something to consider is the ability of your editing tool to handle attributes, though as tools improve this becomes less of an issue. It may be useful to edit your schema in whatever way your editor makes most convenient, and then transform it to its final form using another tool, though the extra step introduces the chance of errors.

5. Should entities be defined?

Schemas and DTDs are very useful besides validation. They allow you to define entities for use by your document, allowing you to reuse text in numerous places, and help maintain a consistent set of common data. Some examples might be `&disclaimer;`, `&company_address;` or `&copyright;`. For example, your schema may have this:

```
<extEntityDcl name="company_address">
  <systemId href="http://www.somserver.uk/xml/entities/company_address.xml"/>
</extEntityDcl>
```

We may not actually use this in the transaction document until the end of the process when we decide to print an invoice or confirmation, when we might prepare the document for rendering.

If you are defining external entities, you need to be sure that they will be accessible when the document is parsed.

Summary

This chapter presented an introduction to the book's main sample application: a distributed system for a basic e-commerce web site. We saw an overview of the different parts of the application, and what we will build over the next five chapters. The chapter discussed how the various components in a distributed application could communicate, and we looked at using XML and HTTP as a means of executing remote procedure calls. We took a look at two ways of doing this: XML-RPC and SOAP.

XML-RPC introduced the idea of encoding requests as XML, and using HTTP as the transport protocol between client and server. We saw that SOAP was an offshoot of XML-RPC, and implemented a SOAP client/server application to demonstrate how it works. As part of the application, we built two ActiveX DLLs to handle SOAP and HTTP functions, which we'll reuse in later chapters.

The chapter also examined two initiatives to define how business transactions might be encoded as XML: Microsoft's BizTalk, and the OASIS/xml.org Schema repository. We discussed questions that may come up when using XML to encode transactions, such as whether to use an existing format or to design a new one. We then examined some things to consider when designing a transaction format, walked through the construction of a transaction format, and designed a schema to describe it.

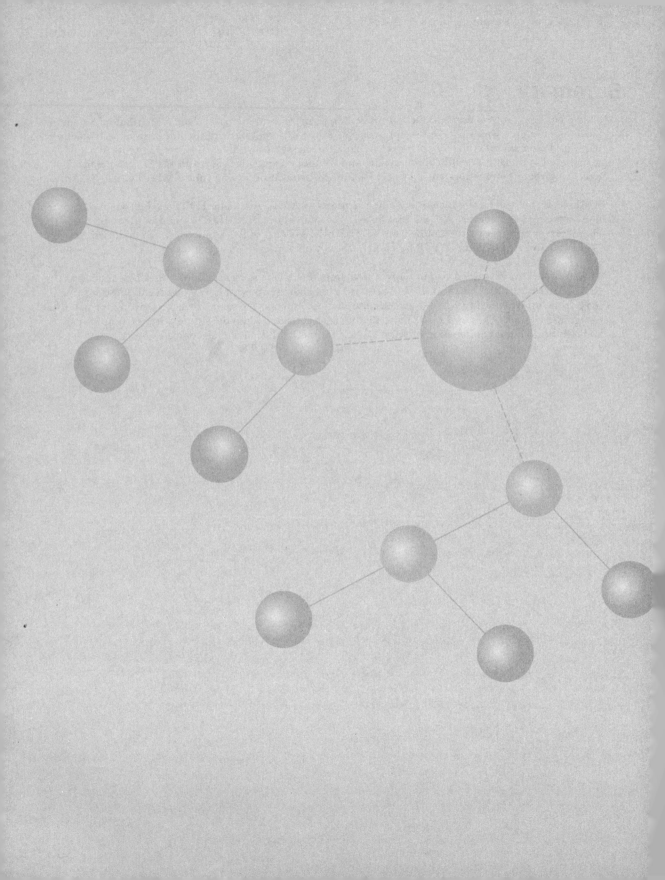

Developing an XML Editor

Our sample application, introduced in the previous chapter, will make use of XML files to store miscellaneous information about the products we're offering for sale through our online store. We need a way to create and edit these files, so in this chapter we'll take a look at developing a VB application to serve as an XML editing tool. This will comprise:

❑ Providing a user interface area for viewing/entering product information

❑ Checking that the information being entered is well-formed XML

❑ Using resource files to reference externally stored information

❑ Saving the newly built/edited files

Data Entry and Parsing

For the most part, the product information file uses a fixed structure to hold basic data, so our editor can use a simple form to hide the fact that an XML document is being edited. But one of the nice things about XML is that we can, if we choose, use a format that allows for some arbitrary structure. For example, our products *require* that certain information be included in the file, but we're also willing to accept *additional* elements because we don't have just one single type of product. Let's take a look at an example product information file and see how this works:

```
<PRODUCT ID-'000000'>
  <NAME>Sample</NAME>
  <DESCRIPTION>
    <HEADER></HEADER>
```

```
   <BODY>
     Here we allow the description, where we might want
     to include some additional information, such as
     <WEIGHT unit='KG'>12</WEIGHT>
     for which we do not have a fixed set of elements.
   </BODY>
 </DESCRIPTION>
 <CATEGORY>PDAs</CATEGORY>
 <RELATEDURLS>
   <URL href='www.wrox.com' />
 </RELATEDURLS>
 <RELATEDPRODUCTS>
   <PRODUCT name='Cat jeep'/>
   <PRODUCT name='Atomic wool'/>
 </RELATEDPRODUCTS>
</PRODUCT>
```

By and large, we can create and edit this data using a simple Visual Basic form, with some single-line text boxes and list controls. But, since the DESCRIPTION element may hold *any* well-formed XML, we need, at least, a multi-line text box. However, it would be nice to have something that gives the user a little help, something smart enough to know when the text is not well-formed, or perhaps clever enough to prevent the entry of malformed XML. Doesn't that sound good? Sure it does but, as yet, Visual Basic doesn't provide an XML edit control, so we'll just have to write our own.

Building an ActiveX XML Text Box

Basically, what we want to do is take a standard text box control and merge it with the parsing functions of the MSXML object. We start by creating a new ActiveX Control project, which we'll call XmlText. (The full source code for this project may be downloaded from the Wrox web site: www.wrox.com; we'll discuss the *interesting* parts in this chapter.) The project requires a reference to the Microsoft XML parser.

Creating a new project will give us a default user control, which we name XmlTextbox. We build the user interface by placing a text box control on the user control. The text box has MultiLine set to True, ScrollBars set to Vertical, and the default Text is set to an empty string. We'll call the text box txtXml. The control looks like this:

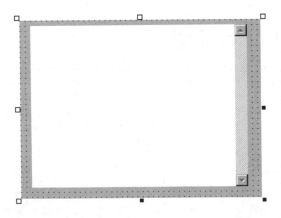

That's all we need for the user interface; the real fun happens behind the scenes. Since our control is a text box, we need to map the text box's properties to the exposed properties of the user control. Using the ActiveX Control Interface Wizard, this is quite straightforward. This Wizard presents a series of dialog boxes that offer a selection of properties, events, and methods that the control might use:

❑ The first dialog box allows us to select the items we want for our control, such as the MouseDown event or SelText (selected text) property.

❑ The next dialog box allows us to add custom properties, events, and methods. For example, our control will have a ParseError event; so we use this dialog box to add this name and define it as an event.

❑ The third dialog box allows us to map the events exposed by the user control to any constituent controls (such as our text box). For example, we want the user control to allow the selection of text in the text box control. So, we map the SelText public property of the user control to the SelText property of the text box control, txtXml.

❑ The fourth dialog box lets us set attributes on any unmapped control members. Our control will have a property called DTD, and it is here that we can define it as read/write, and of type String.

❑ The fifth and final dialog box gives us the option of generating a report before automatically adding the interface code to the project.

We're mainly interested in access to the Text property, as well as SelStart, since, as we'll see later, we want to allow the automatic insertion of text at a given point. In addition, we want to offer the usual text box properties, such as font, size, color, and so on. Using the Interface Wizard, we need to see what properties have been pre-selected, and add the others that we need.

We also need a few custom properties and methods. So, on the **Create Custom Interface Method** panel, we add AutoCheck, NoUserElements, ParseErrorReason, ParseErrorPosition, and ParseErrorSource – these are all properties. We also want two custom events, called ParseError and ParseOK, and a WellFormedCheck function.

Now we need to set the mappings. We map all of the text box-related properties to the text box control – ignoring the custom properties for now. Then we move on to **Set Attributes**. The following table shows the settings for all the properties, methods and events after we have finished:

Name/Type	Data Type	Design Time	Run Time	Description
Property AutoCheck	Boolean	Read/write	Read/write	Automatically checks the XML on each change
Property NoUserElements	Boolean	Read/write	Read/write	Prevents the entry of '<' and '>'
Property ParseErrorReason	String	N/A	Read-only	Parsing error description
Property ParseErrorPosition	Integer	N/A	Read-only	Character position of the error in the XML
Property ParseErrorSource	String	N/A	Read-only	The XML that failed to parse

Name/Type	Data Type	Design Time	Run Time	Description
Property DTD	String	Read/write	Read/write	Holds an optional DTD
Event ParseError	N/A	N/A	N/A	Raised when WellFormedCheck finds an error in the XML
Event ParseOK	N/A	N/A	N/A	Raised when WellFormedCheck finds no errors in the XML
Sub WellFormedCheck	None	N/A	N/A	Checks the XML

Now, we want to provide some special XML behavior, so we'll add code to some of the text box event handlers and determine how the control responds, depending on how the custom properties are set. We're providing two properties to regulate the behavior: the first is AutoCheck. When this is set to True, we want the control to parse the XML any time the contents of the text box change. (This event occurs as the change actually takes place.) So, let's add a txtXml_Change event:

```
Private Sub txtXml_Change()
    RaiseEvent Change
    ' Clear error info since we don't know the
    ' current error state
    m_ParseErrorReason = ""
    m_ParseErrorPosition = 0
    m_ParseErrorSource = ""
    If AutoCheck Then
        Call WellFormedCheck
    End If
End Sub
```

The code propagates the txtXmlChange event back out through the user control, so it can be caught by the host application if required. For our purposes, we want the parsing error properties to be reset to a clean state, then check to see if the control is set to AutoCheck. If it is, then WellFormedCheck is called:

```
Public Sub WellFormedCheck()
    Dim nIdx As Integer
    Dim s As String
```

The code first looks to see if a DTD is loaded. If one is, then we want a temporary XML document to be constructed, that combines the DTD with the text in the XML control:

```
If (Len(m_DTD) > 0) Then
    s = m_DTD & txtXml
```

An attempt is then made to load the new document. If it fails, SetParseErrors is called, which will take the current DOMDocument error information and assign it to the control's error properties:

```
If Not (m_oDOM.loadXML(s)) Then
    Call SetParseErrors
    RaiseEvent ParseError
```

The ParseError event is also raised, to notify the parent application. If there were no parsing errors, then the error properties are cleared:

```
Else
    m_ParseErrorReason = ""
    m_ParseErrorPosition = 0
    m_ParseErrorSource = ""
    RaiseEvent ParseOK
End If
```

If there is no DTD, then the code just loads the text in the control. If there are any errors, they are handled in the same way:

```
ElseIf Not (m_oDOM.loadXML(txtXml)) Then
    Call SetParseErrors
    RaiseEvent ParseError
Else
    m_ParseErrorReason = ""
    m_ParseErrorPosition = 0
    m_ParseErrorSource = ""
    RaiseEvent ParseOK
End If
End Sub
```

The next behavior is to restrict the user from directly entering elements. This is done by catching the KeyUp event of the text box:

```
Private Sub txtXml_KeyUp(KeyCode As Integer, Shift As Integer)
    If m_NoUserElements Then
        If ((KeyCode = 190) Or (KeyCode = 188)) And Shift > 0 Then
            SendKeys "{Bksp}"
            DoEvents
        End If
    End If
End Sub
```

If the user has entered either a "less than" or "greater than" character ("<" and ">", specified by the key codes 190 and 188 respectively), and NoUserElements is True, then we'll simply send our own backspace key to undo the entry. You may wish to add a Beep statement as well, to alert the user, but the visual effect of this code is to delete the offending characters immediately after they appear, which should be sufficient to get the user's attention.)

We also want to track when text is assigned to the text box, so the Let Text property accessor is modified:

```
Public Property Let Text(ByVal New_Text As String)
    txtXml.Text = New_Text
    PropertyChanged "Text"
End Property
```

Setting the text will cause the txtXML Change event to fire, invoking WellFormedCheck if AutoCheck is True.

Since the ParseError property is regularly being set, this is a simple private Sub to simplify the code:

```
Private Sub SetParseErrors()
    With m_oDOM.ParseError
        m_ParseErrorReason = .reason
        m_ParseErrorSource = .srcText
        m_ParseErrorPosition = .filepos
    End With
End Sub
```

We've covered the *essential* code of the control, but will not cover the rest. (If you download the code, you can see the numerous lines of code containing Property Let and Get, and control initialization.) To sum up, we have a text box that feeds an XML parser behind the scenes. Depending on how the properties are set, entries to the text box will raise a custom event if any parsing errors occur. The host application can catch this event and display the error message. We'll see a practical example of the control later when it's used in our product file editor.

Dynamic Resource Files

Now we just need to build our user control so that we can use it in the product information editor. But before that we need to take a look at two areas of Visual Basic that will play a part in our code: resource files and interfaces.

Resource files are a way to hold data that can be used by an application. A typical use for a resource file is to prepare an application for distribution to different countries. Control label strings, in multiple languages, are kept in the resource file. At run time, the application can load the appropriate text depending on what language the application is configured for. Resource files can hold binary data as well as text.

Our product editor will have a web browser form to let us look at our product XML file, transformed using XSLT, as HTML. A resource file is a good place to keep this, rather than trying to build a lengthy string in the program itself.

However, when we add a resource file to a project, and compile our application or DLL, the resource file becomes part of the resulting binary object. If we want to change the resource file, then we need to recompile the application code. If we don't foresee having to change the resource file, except for periodic updates when we would ship a new version of the application, then this not a problem. But if we want to have *dynamic* resource files, then we need to find an alternative approach. Using Visual Basic, we can dynamically load a DLL at run time. Unfortunately, Visual Basic will not let us create a DLL that holds nothing but a resource file. The DLL must have some code. So, we're going to use an approach to resource files that allow us to dynamically load an external DLL that holds the resources we want and provides public methods for getting to it. To do this, we need to take a look at implementing interfaces.

What is an **interface** and why bother implementing it? Well, one of the fundamental concepts of COM is that of interface-based programming. When we interact with an object, we should not know or care how its methods work, only that they do, and always will. The idea of a public interface (the methods and properties that are available outside of the object's code) is that of a contract: when we release an object to the world, we're making an agreement that, whatever we may decide in the future to do to the DLL's internals, the outside world will always see the same methods and properties, the methods will always have the same signature (i.e. the number of arguments and their data types will not change), and the methods will always return the same data type. It's quite likely that at some point you've worked on an ActiveX DLL and realized that one or more of the methods needed some different arguments, or a method should have returned a string instead of an integer. If you've set your component to compile with binary compatibility, you end up getting a cranky message from the compiler about breaking compatibility. This is because you've changed the interface. (You may have noticed, though, that you can gleefully add *new* methods without any problem. Technically you're still changing the interface, but because you haven't changed any previously existing methods, older code can still work, oblivious to the existence of the new methods.)

> *Creating an interface class in Visual Basic is somewhat akin to an abstract class in Java. We define a set of methods that the class should have, but we do not actually put any code in them. In fact, we can achieve the same results by creating a type library directly, using MIDL, but we're going to take the easy route here.*

But what's the value in a class that does nothing? Well, it serves as a template for other classes that *will* do the actual work, and the presence of the type library allows us to set a reference to the basic type, gaining the advantages of early binding, without having to specify a specific binary object in advance.

The interface class for our resource file is defined like this:

```
' Interface class IResFile.ILoadRes
Option Explicit

Public Function LoadResString(nResID As Long) As String
 'Interface only
End Function

Public Function LoadResData(vResID As Variant, vResType As Variant) As Variant
 'Interface only
End Function

Public Function LoadResPicture(vResID As Variant, vResType As _
              LoadResConstants) As IPictureDisp
 'Interface only
End Function
```

It simply defines methods that correspond to the regular Visual Basic methods for retrieving resource file data. So, we create a project called `IResFile`, give it a single class, called `ILoadRes`, and compile it.

Once we have the interface class, we can create a real class that provides the same interface as the abstract class by using the `Implements` keyword. We start a new ActiveX DLL project called `WroxEditorRes`, and add a class called `LoadRes`:

```
Option Explicit

Implements IResFile.IloadRes
```

We set a reference in our project to `IResFile.IloadRes` and use the `Implements` keyword to declare that this class will provide the same methods as `IloadRes`. The IDE will automatically create "shell" functions corresponding to the method names from `IloadRes`. Code now needs to be added to these methods:

```
Private Function ILoadRes_LoadResData(vResID As Variant, _
            vResType As Variant) As Variant
    On Error GoTo ErrHand
    Dim vRes As Variant

    vRes = LoadResData(vResID, vResType)

ErrHand:
    If Err.Number <> 0 Then
        vRes = ""
    End If

    ILoadRes_LoadResData = vRes
End Function
```

```
Private Function ILoadRes_LoadResPicture(vResID As Variant, _
            vResType As LoadResConstants) As stdole.Picture
    On Error GoTo ErrHand
    Dim res As stdole.Picture

    Set res = LoadResPicture(vResID, vResType)

ErrHand:
    If Err.Number <> 0 Then
        Set res = Nothing
    End If
    Set ILoadRes_LoadResPicture = res
End Function
```

```
Private Function ILoadRes_LoadResString(nResID As Long) As String
    On Error GoTo ErrHand
    Dim s As String
    s = LoadResString(nResID)
```

```
ErrHand:
    If Err.Number <> 0 Then
        s = ""
    End If

    ILoadRes_LoadResString = s
End Function
```

We've simply delegated the method calls to the corresponding built-in VB functions for retrieving resource file data. Notice that the functions are all declared as `Private`. Do not change this: the methods will be exposed as `Public` by the DLL's interface, and mapped back to the private members.

Now we add a resource file to the project. Visual Basic ships with a Resource Editor add-in. (If you haven't installed it, you can add it using the Add-in Manager.) From the Project menu select "Add New Resource File" and create a new file in the project directory. The resource file will be added under a "Related Documents" category in the project explorer of the IDE. We then add the following string table resources.

The first one is somewhat lengthy; it's the XSLT that will be used to render the product description file. It looks like this:

```
<xsl:stylesheet xmlns:xsl="http://www.w3.org/TR/WD-xsl">
  <xsl:template>
    <xsl:apply-templates />
  </xsl:template>
  <xsl:template match="text()">
    <xsl:value-of select="." />
  </xsl:template>
  <xsl:template match="text()|@*">
    <xsl:value-of select="." />
  </xsl:template>
  <xsl:template match="PRODUCT">
    <HTML>
      <head>
      </head>
      <body>
        <table border="0" cellspacing="4" cellpadding="3" width="450">
          <tr>
            <td colspan="2" bgcolor="#FF9966" align="center">
              <h3>Product Details File</h3>
            </td>
          </tr>
          <xsl:for-each select="*">
            <tr>
              <td bgcolor="#FFCC00" width="25%">
                <xsl:node-name />
              </td>
              <td bgcolor="#33CCFF">
                <xsl:value-of select="." />
              </td>
            </tr>
          </xsl:for-each>
        </table>
```

```
        </body>
      </HTML>
    </xsl:template>
  </xsl:stylesheet>
```

Since large string table resources can be difficult to manage, we want to add this as a custom resource. We edit the XSL in a text editor, and save it to our project directory. The resource editor has a toolbar button that looks like this:

This is for adding a custom resource. Select this button, which gives the "Open a Custom Resource" dialog box. We locate our XSL file, and select it. The file is now added to the resource file. Note that it will be stored as a binary string; in the main application a conversion function will be used to turn it into regular text.

The new XSL resource will be added into the "CUSTOM" section of the resource file. We want to change the ID, though, to something more meaningful. Double-click on the new resource, and get a properties dialog box. Then change the ID to "PREVIEWXSL". (Custom resources can have string identifiers. String table resources may only have numeric IDs.)

Now we can add the remaining resources into the string table:

ID	Purpose	Contents
101	Product categories	`Art Utensils|Do-it-yourself heaven|Electronics|PDAs|Toys|Video`
102	XML description editor elements	`DESCRIPTION|BODY|PARA|HEADING|SUMMARY`
103	Related products	`Sample|Foo|Bar|Something`

104	Default XML for the description XML edit box	`<DESCRIPTION>`
		`<HEADING></HEADING>`
		`<BODY></BODY>`
		`</DESCRIPTION>`

We can now build the DLL. When we discuss the code for the product information editor, we'll see how the DLL is loaded and the resources retrieved.

The Product Information Editor Application

Now that we've built our own little XML text box control, let's go on to build the main editor. Again, the complete code is available from the Wrox web site; we're going to cover the bulk of the code here.

Here's what the main form will look like:

We start by creating a standard executable project, and adding a few controls and object references. (The project in the download is called XMLEditor). We need references to the Microsoft XML parser and the Scripting runtime library. The project has a single form, frmMain, which holds a tabbed dialog control (an SSTab control and a Common Dialog control) to contain a few editing fields, a web browser control to allow us to preview our product file as HTML, and our text box control, XmlTextbox.

The tabbed dialog control is placed on the left-hand side, and has four tabs, labelled Product Essentials, Product Description, Related Products, and Related URLs. The web browser control will go on the right-hand side.

Creating the Tab Control

Now let's build up the tab control. Each of the four tabs needs controls for entering the different types of product information. We'll first see what they look like and then summarize the controls to be added to each tab.

Product Essentials

The first tab, Product Essentials, looks like this:

It contains text boxes and labels for the product ID, product name, manufacturer's ID, and retail price. There's also a label and list box for product category. Now one of the things to consider is, where do product IDs come from? Does the user enter them, or are they assigned automatically by the main data application? Well, they need to be unique, and should probably follow some sort of sequential numbering convention. So, we'll insist that only the main application can assign IDs and disable editing of this control. We're setting the value to all zeros so that when we submit the file to the data server it can be identified as a new file. We'll go into that in detail later when we discuss interaction with the remote server, in Chapter 9.

Product Description

The next tab is for Product Description. It looks like this:

This tab contains a drop-down combo box that we'll use to hold a list of available XML elements that the user can insert into the description text box. The text box is actually our XML text box control; below it is a standard text box, which we'll use to display any parsing error messages.

Related Products

The third tab is for Related Products:

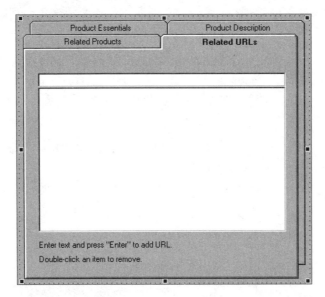

This tab contains a list box control to hold a list of product names, plus a second list box to hold the products selected from the first list. There are some labels as well, to guide the user.

Related URLs

Finally, we have the Related URLs tab:

This tab contains a combo box to allow the entry of any URLs that are relevant to the product.

Here is the complete list of the controls contained on the tabs of the tab control:

Tab Panel	Control Name	Control Type	Purpose
Product Essentials	lblProdID	Label	Label for product ID field
	txtProductID	Text box	Text for product ID
	lblProdName	Label	Label for product name field
	txtProductName	Text box	Text for product name
	lblMftID	Label	Label for manufacturer's ID field
	txtMftID	Text box	Text for manufacturer's ID
	lblPrice	Label	Label for retail price field
	txtPrice	Text box	Text for retail price
	lblProdCategory	Label	Label for category field
	lstProductCategory	List box	List of product categories
Product Description	lblElements	Label	Label for elements drop-down list
	cmbElements	Combo box	List of elements for XML control
	xmlTxtProductDesc	XML Text box	Product description XML
	lblXmlErrors	Label	Label for XML errors field
	txtMessages	Text box	XML parser error messages
Related Products	lblPickAvailProds	Label	Label for available related products list
	lstPickAvailProds	List box	List of available related products
	lblRelProds	Label	Label for selected related products
	lstRelatedProducts	List box	List of selected related products
	lblRemoveRelProd	Label	Brief instructions
Related URLs	cmbUrls	Combo box	Used to enter URLs related to the product
	lblUrslHelp1	Label	Short help
	lblUrlHelp2	Label	Short help

Setting Up frmMain

`frmMain` contains declarations for two global variables, and a variable to reference the `IloadRes` class:

```
'*****************************************************************
' Product Information XML Editor
'*****************************************************************
Option Explicit

Dim g_bLoadComplete As Boolean
Dim g_nSelTextLocation As Integer

Private oWroxRes As IResFile.IloadRes
```

Declares.bas

The project has a Module file, called `Declares.bas`. It holds the constants for referring to the resource file data:

```
Option Explicit

    ' RES file constants
    Global Const RES_CATEGORY_LIST As Integer = 101
    Global Const RES_ELEMENT_LIST As Integer = 102
    Global Const RES_RELPROD_LIST As Integer = 103
    Global Const RES_DESC_DEFAULT_XML As Integer = 104
    Global Const RES_PREVIEW_XSL As String = "PreviewXsl"
```

Coding the Data Entry Fields

Product Essentials

Now we need to add some code to make the application work. Product Essentials is reasonably simple. There are a few text box controls that the user can edit, except for the disabled Product ID field. However, the Product category list needs to be populated. Ideally, the list of valid categories should come from a central location, in other words the data server. But we haven't worked out how to talk to the server yet, so for now, the list contents will come from a resource file. We could just as well have the list populated from a local file, but using a resource file prevents users from tampering with it. The use of our resource DLL also means we can swap the resource without recompiling.

Now, resource items get numeric identifiers, which can make using them in code a bit cumbersome, so constants for the numeric IDs are defined in `Declares.bas`.

Now we need something to populate the category list, so here is a small function to handle this:

```
Private Sub PopulateCategoryList()
    Dim sListItems As String
    Dim asItems() As String
    Dim varItem  As Variant

    sListItems = oWroxRes.LoadResString(RES_CATEGORY_LIST)
    asItems = Split(sListItems, "|")
```

```
        For Each varItem In asItems()
            lstProductCategory.AddItem (varItem)
        Next

    End Sub
```

The function uses the oWroxRes object, which has been declared as type IResFile.IloadRes, the interface class. It uses the LoadResString method to retrieve the list of product categories. It then splits the list into an array, and adds each array element to the product category list.

Product Description

For the Product Description tab, we need to connect the behavior of the three contained controls. We want any XML parsing errors to appear in the text box just below the XML text box control, and we want any item selected from the Elements list to be inserted into the XML text. So, here is a function that displays parse error details to the message field:

```
Private Sub xmlTxtProductDesc_ParseError()
    txtMessages = xmlTxtProductDesc.ParseErrorReason
    xmlTxtProductDesc.SelStart = xmlTxtProductDesc.ParseErrorPosition
End Sub
```

What this does is simply catch the ParseError event and put the error information into the message box. It also moves the selection point to the location in the text where the error was found.

Likewise, the ParseOK event clears any error messages when the XML is correct:

```
Private Sub xmlTxtProductDesc_ParseOK()
    txtMessages = ""
End Sub
```

We also want to be able to insert elements from the drop-down list. The user should be able to place the cursor at some insertion point, then select an item from the list. The problem is that when focus is changed to another control, the text box selection point is lost. So we need to store the cursor location (i.e., the location of the specific character where the cursor was last placed) when the XML text box loses focus:

```
Private Sub xmlTxtProductDesc_LostFocus()
    g_nSelTextLocation = xmlTxtProductDesc.SelStart
End Sub
```

The global variable g_nSelTextLocation is being used here so that the information is available to other methods.

Now, here is the code for the list selection:

```
Private Sub cmbElements_Click()
    Dim sEl As String
    xmlTxtProductDesc.SelStart = g_nSelTextLocation
    sEl = cmbElements.List(cmbElements.ListIndex)
    xmlTxtProductDesc.SelText = "<" & sEl & "></" & sEl & ">"
End Sub
```

When the user clicks on an item in the combo box control, the insertion point is grabbed from g_nSelTextLocation, and used to set the SelStart property of the XML text box, where the text is then inserted.

To initialize the list of elements, we use this function to load the data from the resource file, which is called in Form_Load:

```
Private Sub PopulateElementList()
    Dim sListItems As String
    Dim asItems() As String
    Dim varItem  As Variant

    sListItems = oWroxRes.LoadResString(RES_ELEMENT_LIST)
    asItems = Split(sListItems, "|")
    For Each varItem In asItems()
        cmbElements.AddItem (varItem)
    Next

End Sub
```

Related Products

The Related Products tab uses two list boxes to manage the set of products. The top list is, like the Product category list we saw previously, populated from the resource file. The constant is used for the resource ID, and this function is called in Form_Load to populate it:

```
Function PopulatePickRelatedProductsList() As Boolean
    Dim sListItems As String
    Dim asItems() As String
    Dim varItem  As Variant

    sListItems = oWroxRes.LoadResString(RES_RELPROD_LIST)
    asItems = Split(sListItems, "|")
    For Each varItem In asItems()
        lstPickAvailProds.AddItem (varItem)
    Next
End Function
```

We'll use double-clicking to manage adding and removing items from the list of selected related products. When an item in the top list is double-clicked, it gets removed from the top list, and added to the bottom list. Likewise, when an item in the bottom list is double-clicked, it gets removed from the bottom list, and added to the top list.

Here's the double-click behavior for the top list of available products:

```
Private Sub lstPickAvailProds_DblClick()
    lstRelatedProducts.AddItem _
                    (lstPickAvailProds.List(lstPickAvailProds.ListIndex))
    lstPickAvailProds.RemoveItem (lstPickAvailProds.ListIndex)
End Sub
```

This is how double clicks on the bottom list of selected products are handled:

```
Private Sub lstRelatedProducts_DblClick()
    lstPickAvailProds.AddItem _
                        (lstRelatedProducts.List(lstRelatedProducts.ListIndex))
    lstRelatedProducts.RemoveItem (lstRelatedProducts.ListIndex)
End Sub
```

Related URLs

The Related URLs tab uses a combo box for storing URLs. Text entered into the entry field at the top of the control is added to the list of items when the users presses *Enter* or *Return*. Double-clicking an item in the list removes it.

To add a URL, this code is used:

```
Private Sub cmbUrls_KeyDown(KeyCode As Integer, Shift As Integer)
    If KeyCode = Asc(vbCr) Then
        cmbUrls.AddItem (cmbUrls.Text)
    End If
End Sub
```

And to remove a URL, this code is used:

```
Private Sub cmbUrls_DblClick()
    cmbUrls.RemoveItem (cmbUrls.ListIndex)
End Sub
```

When the application first starts, some initialization work is needed:

```
Private Sub Form_Load()
```

The resource class variable is set to the specific resource DLL we want to use by default:

```
    Set oWroxRes = CreateObject("WroxEditorRes.LoadRes")
```

Then the various lists are populated:

```
    Call PopulateCategoryList
    Call PopulateElementList
    Call PopulatePickRelatedProductsList
```

Some default XML is loaded into the XML text box:

```
    Call SetXmlDefault
```

The editing options are set:

```
    xmlTxtProductDesc.AutoCheck = True
    xmlTxtProductDesc.NoUserElements = True
```

SetXmlDefault uses the resource DLL to load the XML text box:

```
Private Sub SetXmlDefault()
    Dim sXML As String
    sXML = oWroxRes.LoadResString(RES_DESC_DEFAULT_XML)
    sXML = Replace(sXML, vbLf, vbCrLf)
    xmlTxtProductDesc.Text = sXML
End Sub
```

Coding the Menu

Our application needs some menu items as well, for such things as loading and saving documents, and setting the behavior of the XML text box.

We'll create five top-level menu items: Local, Web, Editing Options, Preview and Exit. Using the menu editor, the menu entries should look like this:

The Local Menu

Here's the code for the two items under the Local menu:

```
Private Sub mnuLocalOpen_Click()
    Call OpenLocalFile
End Sub

Private Sub mnuLocalSave_Click()
    Call SaveLocalFile
End Sub
```

Opening a File

Opening a file requires that the user is prompted to select a local file, and then the contents of the file are moved into the correct form locations:

```
'******************************************************************
' Private Sub OpenLocalFile()
' Read in a file from the local file system and parse it into
' the form.  Check that the XML is well-formed, or complain.
'******************************************************************
Private Sub OpenLocalFile()
    On Error GoTo ErrHand
    Dim strFilefilter  As String
    Dim strFilename As String
    Dim objDOM As MSXML.DOMDocument
```

Variables are declared for handling the File Open dialog box, and a DOMDocument for loading the requested file. The DOM object is initialized and then the dialog box is prepared:

```
    Set objDOM = New MSXML.DOMDocument
    strFilefilter = "XML Files (*.xml)|*.xml|All Files (*.*)|*.*"
    strFilename = ""

    With dlgOpen
        .FileName = ""
        .CancelError = True
        .Filter = strFilefilter
        .ShowOpen
    End With
```

We have code to display the dialog box and retrieve the file name:

```
    strFilename = dlgOpen.FileName
```

It also checks that the user has in fact selected something. Note that if the user has clicked Cancel on the dialog box, the dialog box will close and return an empty string:

```
    If (Len(strFilename) > 0) Then
```

If a file name is available, the code tries to load the file into the DOM object:

```
        If Not objDOM.Load("file://" & strFilename) Then
```

If the load fails, a message box is displayed containing the error:

```
            MsgBox "Error loading XML document: " & _
                objDOM.parseError.reason, vbExclamation, "XML load error"
            strFilename = ""
```

Otherwise, our code enables the "Save" menu items:

```
        Else
            mnuLocalSave.Enabled = True
            mnuWebSave.Enabled = True
```

It tries to load the DOM contents into the form. If loading the XML into the form fails, the user is informed with a message box:

```
            If Not ParseDomIntoForm(objDOM) Then
                MsgBox "Error parsing data file into form", vbCritical
            End If
        End If
    End If
```

If any run-time errors are encountered, these also result in a message box:

```
ErrHand:
    If (Err.Number <> 0) And (Err.Number <> cdlCancel) Then
        MsgBox "Error: " & Err.Description, vbExclamation, "Error opening file"
    End If

    Set objDOM = Nothing
End Sub
```

Note that the form requires a `CommonDialog` control, `dlgOpen`, and that the `CancelError` property is set to `True`. If the user cancels the operation, the dialog control will throw an error. That is caught down at the end of the function, and if the error number matches the number given for cancelation, the function is exited. (Note the use of the `CommonDialog` constant `cdlCancel`, which, for the curious, equals 32755.)

`ParseDomIntoForm` takes a `DOMDocument` as an argument, and steps through the contents, putting the values into the form controls:

```
'**********************************************************************
' Private Function ParseDomIntoForm(oDOM As DOMDocument) As Boolean
' We want to take the contents of the DOM and put the data into the
' correct form elements.
'**********************************************************************
Private Function ParseDomIntoForm(oDOM As DOMDocument) As Boolean
    On Error GoTo ErrHand
    Dim oEl As IXMLDOMElement
    Dim oNodeList As IXMLDOMNodeList
    Dim sTemp As String
    Dim nIdx As Integer
```

We also set up some variables to work with. `Element` and a `NodeList` objects are needed to hold parts of the DOM. In addition, a temporary string is used for holding intermediate values, and an index counter for iterating through items.

Now the code steps through the DOM, pulling out the parts we need. First we want to get the product ID, held as an attribute in the root element of the document. (The element should look like this: `<PRODUCT ID='000000'>`.)

```
With oDOM
    sTemp = ""
    Set oEl = .childNodes(0)
    txtProductID = oEl.Attributes.getNamedItem("ID").nodeValue
```

The next step is to grab the `NAME` element and pull out the value from its `Text` node child elements:

```
Set oEl = .getElementsByTagName("NAME").Item(0)
For nIdx = 0 To oEl.childNodes.length - 1
    sTemp = sTemp & oEl.childNodes.Item(nIdx).nodeValue
Next
txtProductName = sTemp
```

More than likely the element will have a single `Text` node child, but it's possible there will be more than one.

By the way, we're not doing any robust error detection here. If the document does not contain a NAME element then this code will raise a run-time error, which will simply take us to the ErrHand label without providing any useful information about why it happened. Something to consider when manipulating DOM objects like this is just how likely are certain errors, and what would be a useful response. Generally, if the XML is being created programmatically, where there are strict controls on how the XML is put together, then we can have some confidence that the file will be well-formed. If a malformed file is found, then chances are there is a problem with the code that created it. Trying to catch and report on all possible errors that might arise from parsing our product files would be overkill for our demonstration purposes.

We now retrieve the description information. We use `getElementsByTagName` to pull out all of the XML that belongs to the `DESCRIPTION` element:

```
Set oEl = .getElementsByTagName("DESCRIPTION").Item(0)
xmlTxtProductDesc.Text = oEl.xml
```

Now it's time to get the category of the product. First, the temporary string is cleared, then the `CATEGORY` element is grabbed, and the text nodes are pulled out:

```
sTemp = ""
Set oEl = .getElementsByTagName("CATEGORY").Item(0)
For nIdx = 0 To oEl.childNodes.length - 1
    sTemp = sTemp & oEl.childNodes.Item(nIdx).nodeValue
Next
```

However, we're not just going to populate a text box; we need to locate the item in a list, and set the list index if a match is found:

```
For nIdx = 0 To lstProductCategory.ListCount - 1
    If lstProductCategory.List(nIdx) = sTemp Then
        lstProductCategory.ListIndex = nIdx
    End If
Next
```

Moving on to the related URL list, a `NodeList` of URL elements is pulled out. In the interest of simplicity, we are going to exploit a Microsoft extension, `selectNodes`:

```
Set oNodeList = .selectNodes("//RELATEDURLS/URL")
For nIdx = 0 To oNodeList.length - 1
    cmbUrls.AddItem _
    (oNodeList.Item(nIdx).Attributes.getNamedItem("href").nodeValue)
Next
```

Each URL retrieved gets added to the URL listbox control. The same thing is done to get the list of related products:

```
Set oNodeList = .selectNodes("//RELATEDPRODUCTS/PRODUCT")
For nIdx = 0 To oNodeList.length - 1
    lstRelatedProducts.AddItem _
    (oNodeList.Item(nIdx).Attributes.getNamedItem("name").nodeValue)
Next
```

And that should do it. The code ends by closing the `With` statement, setting the return value to true, and gliding past the error number check:

```
    End With 'oDOM
    ParseDomIntoForm = True

ErrHand:
    If Err.Number <> 0 Then
        ParseDomIntoForm = False
    End If
End Function
```

Saving a File

To save our information to a local file, we perform a similar operation, but in reverse. We need to visit each of our controls, pull out the data, and build an XML file. The `BuildDocument` function does this for us:

```
Private Function BuildDocument() As String
    On Error GoTo ErrHand
    Dim sDescription As String
    Dim nIdx As Integer
    Dim sXML As String

    sXML = ""

    sXML = sXML & "<PRODUCT ID='" & txtProductID & "'>" & vbCrLf
    sXML = sXML & "<NAME>" & txtProductName & "</NAME>" & vbCrLf
    sXML = sXML & "<PRICE>" & txtPrice & "</PRICE>" & vbCrLf
    sXML = sXML & xmlTxtProductDesc.Text & vbCrLf
    sXML = sXML & "<CATEGORY>" & _
        lstProductCategory.List(lstProductCategory.ListIndex) & _
        "</CATEGORY>" & vbCrLf
    sXML = sXML & "<RELATEDURLS>" & vbCrLf
    For nIdx = 0 To cmbUrls.ListCount - 1
```

```
            sXML = sXML & "<URL href='" & cmbUrls.List(nIdx) & "' />" & vbCrLf
    Next
    sXML = sXML & "</RELATEDURLS>" & vbCrLf
    sXML = sXML & "<RELATEDPRODUCTS>" & vbCrLf
    For nIdx = 0 To lstRelatedProducts.ListCount - 1
        sXML = sXML & _
        "<PRODUCT name='" & lstRelatedProducts.List(nIdx) & "'/>" & vbCrLf
    Next
    sXML = sXML & "</RELATEDPRODUCTS>" & vbCrLf
    sXML = sXML & "</PRODUCT>"
```

It visits each control and wraps XML tags around the values. If there is a run-time error, a message box is displayed:

```
ErrHand:
    If Err.Number <> 0 Then
        MsgBox "Error! " & Err.Description, vbCritical, "Error in " & Err.Source
        sXML = ""
    End If
    BuildDocument = sXML
End Function
```

Next we come on to the `SaveLocalFile` routine. It prompts the user with the <u>S</u>ave dialog, builds the document XML string, and saves it to a file. The project will need a reference to the Microsoft Scripting Runtime object so the `FileSystemObject` and `TextStream` can be used.

```
Sub SaveLocalFile()
    On Error GoTo ErrHand
    Dim strFilename  As String
    Dim fsoSave As Scripting.FileSystemObject
    Dim tsSave As Scripting.TextStream
    Dim strFilefilter  As String
    Dim sXML As String
    Dim nSaveQuery As Integer

    Set fsoSave = New FileSystemObject
    strFilefilter = "XML Files (*.xml)|*.xml|All Files (*.*)|*.*"
    strFilename = ""

    With dlgOpen
        .FileName = ""
        .CancelError = True
        .Filter = strFilefilter
        .ShowSave
    End With

    strFilename = dlgOpen.FileName
```

Just like the `OpenLocalFile` method, a dialog box is used to prompt for a file name. If one is obtained, `BuildDocument` is called to create the XML:

```
    If (Len(strFilename) > 0) Then
        sXML = BuildDocument()
        If Len(sXML) < 0 Then
```

```
            MsgBox "Error building file data"
            strFilename = ""
        Else
```

A check is made that the file exists, and if it does, the user is asked if the file may be overwritten:

```
        If fsoSave.FileExists(strFilename) Then
            nSaveQuery = MsgBox("File exists. Overwrite?", _
    vbYesNoCancel, "Save local file")
            Select Case nSaveQuery
                Case vbYes
                    ' GO overwrite and quite
                    Set tsSave = fsoSave.OpenTextFile(strFilename, _
              ForWriting, False)
                        tsSave.Write (sXML)
                        tsSave.Close
                Case vbNo
                    Call SaveLocalFile
                    ' Redisplay the Save dialog
                Case vbCancel
                    ' Forget it and quit
            End Select
```

If the user selects "Yes", the file is written. If the user selects "No", SaveLocalFile is called again to begin the save process from the start. If the user clicks "Cancel", the cancel error will be thrown, which is caught at the end of the method.

If the file does not exist we go ahead and write it:

```
        Else
            Set tsSave = fsoSave.OpenTextFile(strFilename, _
                    ForWriting, True)
            tsSave.Write (sXML)
            tsSave.Close
        End If
    End If
  End If

ErrHand:
    If (Err.Number <> 0) And (Err.Number <> cdlCancel) Then
        MsgBox "Error: " & Err.Description, vbExclamation, "Error saving file"
    End If

    Set fsoSave = Nothing
    Set tsSave = Nothing

End Sub
```

Previewing a File

This is the code for taking the form data and rendering it as HTML in the browser control invoked by selecting the <u>P</u>review menu item:

```
Private Sub mnuPreview_Click()
    Call PreviewDocument
End Sub


Private Sub PreviewDocument()
    On Error GoTo ErrHand

    Dim sProdXml As String
    Dim sXSL As String
    Dim sHTML As String
    Dim oDomXsl  As MSXML.DOMDocument
    Dim objDOM As MSXML.DOMDocument

    ' Build the document
    sProdXml = BuildDocument()
    Set objDOM = New DOMDocument

    If Not objDOM.loadXML(sProdXml) Then
        wbPreview.Navigate2 "about:<HTML><BODY><H1>Error</H1></BODY></HTML>"
    Else
```

The XML is built and loaded into a DOMDocument. If the load fails, an error message is displayed in the browser control. Notice how we're getting the HTML message into the browser: we use the "about://" protocol. This is what Microsoft refers to as a "pluggable" protocol. Internet Explorer 4 and higher, in addition to understanding the more conventional protocols (such as http or ftp), is able to resolve resource locations based on custom protocols. Describing how to build a custom protocol is outside of the scope of our project, but essentially they are COM objects that Explorer can use to resolve special URLs. The about:// protocol allows text entered as part of the URL to be directly loaded into the browser. (You can learn more about pluggable protocols at http://msdn.microsoft.com/library/periodic/period99/cutting0199.htm.)

If the XML did load without errors, then a second DOMDocument is initialized to hold the XSLT:

```
        Set oDomXsl = New DOMDocument
```

The XSLT is retrieved from the resource file; note that because it was stored as a custom resource it needs to be converted to plain text before it is used, and this is done using the ConvertToAnsi method (described below):

```
        sXSL = ConvertToAnsi(oWroxRes.LoadResData(RES_PREVIEW_XSL, "CUSTOM"))
```

The XSLT is loaded; if there is a parsing error, the error message is displayed in the browser:

```
        If Not oDomXsl.loadXML(sXSL) Then
            wbPreview.Navigate2 "about: " & _
                <HTML><BODY><H1>Error</H1></BODY></HTML>"
            MsgBox "XSL Error: " & oDomXsl.parseError.reason
```

Otherwise the transformation is performed and the HTML is displayed:

```
        Else
            sHTML = objDOM.transformNode(oDomXsl)
            wbPreview.Navigate2 "about:" & sHTML
        End If
    End If
```

Any run-time errors will show the user a message box:

```
ErrHand:
    If Err.Number <> 0 Then
        MsgBox "Error previewing document." & _
            Err.Description, vbCritical, "Preview Error"
    End If
    Set objDOM = Nothing
    Set oDomXsl = Nothing
End Sub
```

To convert from a custom resource to text `ConvertToAnsi` is used:

```
Private Function ConvertToAnsi(ByVal vData As Variant) As String
    On Error GoTo ErrHand
    Dim nIdx As Integer
    Dim sTxt As String
    sTxt = ""
```

Each double-byte character is converted:

```
    For nIdx = 1 To LenB(vData)
        sTxt = sTxt & Chr(AscB(MidB(vData, nIdx, 1)))
    Next

ErrHand:
    If Err.Number <> 0 Then
        MsgBox "Error converting custom resource", vbExclamation
        sTxt = ""
    End If
    ConvertToAnsi = sTxt
End Function
```

The Editing Options Menu

We're going to skip the Web menu item for now; it will be covered later, in Chapter 9. We'll move on to the Editing Options menu. This has three sub-menu items: Disable < and >, and Auto-validate; they serve as toggles for properties of the XML text box control, and Load resource, which allows the user to load a resource file. The first two are concerned with how the XML text box behaves by toggling options on the XML control:

```
Private Sub mnuDisableAngles_Click()
    mnuDisableAngles.Checked = Not mnuDisableAngles.Checked
    xmlTxtProductDesc.NoUserElements = mnuDisableAngles.Checked
End Sub
```

```
Private Sub mnuAutoCheck_Click()
    mnuAutoCheck.Checked = Not mnuAutoCheck.Checked
    xmlTxtProductDesc.AutoCheck = mnuAutoCheck.Checked
End Sub
```

The third sub-menu item allows the user to load a new resource file, containing the data for the various form list boxes and the default XML for the XML control:

```
Private Sub mnuLoadRes_Click()
    Call LoadRes
End Sub
```

LoadRes prompts the user with a "**File Open**" dialog box, and checks to see if a file was selected:

```
Private Sub LoadRes()
    On Error GoTo ErrHand

    Dim sDllName As String
    Dim strFilefilter  As String
    Dim strFilename As String
    Dim asTemp() As String
    Dim sLastEl As Integer

    strFilefilter = "DLL Files (*.dll)|*.dll|All Files (*.*)|*.*"
    strFilename = ""

    With dlgOpen
        .FileName = ""
        .CancelError = True
        .Filter = strFilefilter
        .ShowOpen
    End With

    strFilename = dlgOpen.FileName
    If Len(strFilename) > 0 Then
```

If a file name is present, the string is split on the "\" delimiter to break the full file path into its constituent parts:

```
        asTemp = Split(Trim(strFilename), "\")
```

The name of the DLL will be in the last array element, so the code obtains the upper bound value for the temporary array, and the DLL name without the file extension:

```
        sLastEl = UBound(asTemp)
        sDllName = Left(asTemp(sLastEl), Len(asTemp(sLastEl)) - 4)
```

A reference is then created to the selected DLL. (Note that this requires that the selected DLL contains a class called LoadRes that implements the ILoadRes interface, and that the DLL has been registered.)

```
        Set oWroxRes = CreateObject(sDllName & ".LoadRes")
```

The existing lists must be cleared before adding the new items, so a method named `ClearAllLists` is called before populating the controls:

```
        Call ClearAllLists
        Call PopulateCategoryList
        Call PopulateElementList
        Call PopulatePickRelatedProductsList
        Call SetXmlDefault
    End If
```

If there is an error (which may happen if the user clicks Cancel on the dialog box), it is caught at the end of the subroutine as was done in `OpenLocalFile`:

```
ErrHand:
    If (Err.Number <> 0) And (Err.Number <> cdlCancel) Then
        MsgBox "Error: " & Err.Description, vbExclamation, "Error opening file"
    End If

End Sub
```

`ClearAllLists` iterates through each list and removes items while any remain:

```
Private Sub ClearAllLists()
    Do While lstProductCategory.ListCount > 0
        lstProductCategory.RemoveItem 0
    Loop

    Do While cmbElements.ListCount > 0
        cmbElements.RemoveItem 0
    Loop

    Do While lstPickAvailProds.ListCount > 0
        lstPickAvailProds.RemoveItem 0
    Loop
End Sub
```

The Final Outcome

After building the application, and entering some values into the form fields, we can preview the product information, and see something like this:

So there we go. Our application will allow us to create and edit our XML product information files, loading from, and saving to, a local file. We're still missing a crucial ingredient, which is the ability to interact with the server application. We'll tackle that in the next chapter, "*Storing and Retrieving XML Data*".

Summary

This chapter showed how to create an ActiveX control for editing XML. We saw how we can combine the properties of a standard text box control with the functions of the Microsoft XML parser. The chapter then used this control in a VB application to edit our web store product information files. The program allowed for the creation of new files, and saving and loading files to disk.

We used XSLT to transform the product XML into HTML so we could preview it in a browser control. We stored the XSLT in a resource file, and saw how to build a dynamic resource DLL that allows us to change resource files without having to recompile the entire application.

In the next chapter we'll see how to extend the editor to communicate with a remote server.

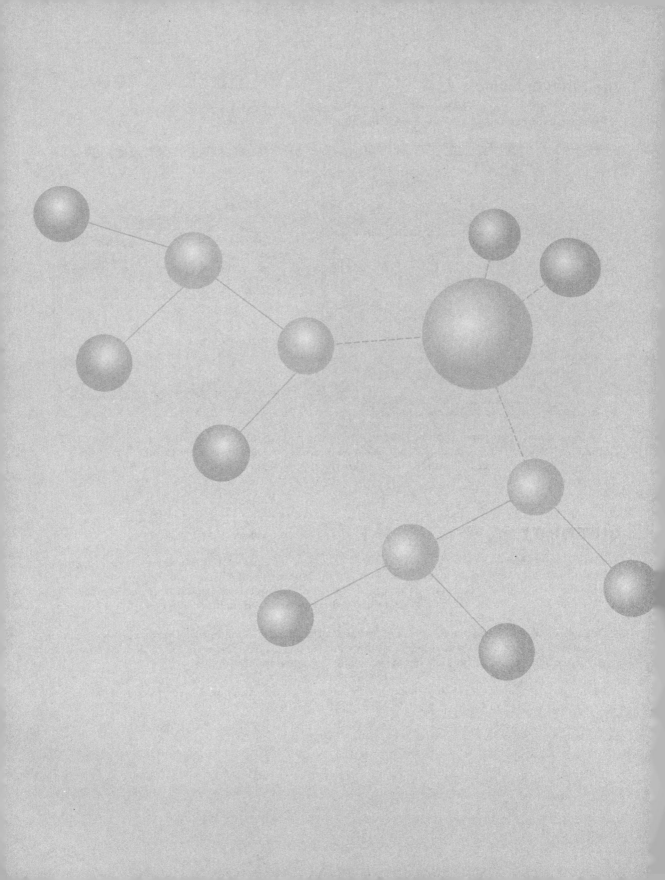

Storing and Retrieving XML Data

In Chapter 7, "*Introducing the Sample Application*", we saw an overview of a distributed e-commerce web site, and saw how we can use SOAP to make remote procedure calls. In Chapter 8, "*Developing an XML Editor*", we took a look at building a VB application for creating and editing product information XML files. This chapter will build on what we've covered so far by describing how the XML files can be stored and retrieved from the product database and product information file server, and by extending the product information editor so that it can interact with a remote server.

To briefly recap, we are developing a web site that allows users to search for products and select items to purchase. The primary information about the products (for example, name and category) is stored in a SQL Server database called `WebProducts`, in a table called `Catalog`; the product details are kept in XML files, with a column in the `Catalog` table holding a URL to the file location.

Now we will build a web front-end that provides an interface to the database and XML file server. We will use an ASP-based SOAP server to handle requests. The SOAP server will dispatch requests to back-end application objects that will take care of database operations and file storage and retrieval.

Once we have a means to interact with the stored product information, we will add remote communication functions to the product information editor, allowing it to fetch and save product information through the SOAP server.

Building Web Objects in VB

What about WebClasses?

Before we begin developing our code, we'll take a look at WebClasses and consider the advantages and disadvantages of using them. We won't actually be using WebClasses in our project but you may find it interesting to hear why not. WebClasses were introduced in Visual Basic 6 (the "New Project" option in the Visual Basic IDE refers to them as an "IIS Application") to help address the needs of web developers looking for a better way to build and debug ASP code.

> *ASP, or Active Server Pages, allows us to add server-side logic to our web site. For example, using ASP, you can validate form data that has been submitted by the user and initiate some additional processing, such as running a query on a database, before building a response to send back to the user.*

If you've spent any time coding ASP sites, you'll probably have developed techniques for separating business logic from display code. This often takes the form of placing your scripting code in a particular part of the page, perhaps right at the top or the bottom, or wrapping chunks of server-side script in functions or sub routines and limiting the display coding to some short method calls. This makes it easier to focus on each given part without getting tangled up in a mass of <% and %> tags. Later on, you might have learned how to place your code into external files and use the #INCLUDE directive to pull in scripting code. This gives the extra value of being able to reuse the logic in multiple pages.

Of course, ASP code is *script*, which means that it will be interpreted each and every time the page is loaded, which brings a performance cost. In addition, as the code grows larger, maintaining and debugging it gets harder. So there comes a time when you might decide that all the code really belongs in a DLL. Now the code runs faster, and debugging gets easier. You can use the VB IDE to build your application logic and catch compiler errors. If you're running IIS and Visual Basic on the same machine, you can set break points in the DLL code and start it, connect to the web page on the local machine, and step through the code in the Visual Basic IDE. Of course, you still need to handle the user interface through the web page.

WebClasses are Visual Basic components that allow us to combine our business logic and user interface generation in a DLL. A WebClass DLL provides access to the built-in ASP Application, Session, Response, and Request objects. When we create a WebClass, an Active Server Page is created for us as an entry point for the DLL. Our class provides the code to respond to events and to generate additional pages.

However, WebClasses were designed to be compatible with both IIS 3 and 4. IIS 4 offered integration with MTS (Microsoft Transaction Server), but IIS 3 does not, hence WebClasses were not designed to be used with MTS. Whether this is a critical factor depends on what you want to do with your object. If you're using the class primarily for the user interface, then you're fine. However, if you want to do any database transactions, you really should be putting that code in another object to keep your application design clean. But it goes a little deeper than that; here are some disadvantages to WebClasses:

❑   WebClasses run in the same process space as IIS; if the WebClass crashes, so does IIS.

❑   WebClasses do not provide the same scalability as MTS components.

❑   Because the code is in a WebClass, and not a standard DLL, the object's functions can't be reused from another DLL or executable. So, any general business logic would need to go into a separate object. Essentially, WebClasses serve as compiled ASP user-interface code.

Of course, there's a little more to it than that: WebClasses allow the use of HTML templates for generation of the rendered pages, which can make the design and maintenance of a site easier.

If we still want our Visual Basic code to have access to the ASP intrinsic objects, but don't want to use WebClasses, there's a simple alternative. By setting a reference in our project to the Active Server Pages type library, we can grab all of the ASP objects in our code. We'll also need to have a reference to the MTS type library, which we will discuss next.

Building for MTS

A complete explanation of Microsoft Transaction Server, or MTS, is outside the scope of this book. For a detailed study, take a look at *"Professional MTS & MSMQ Programming with VB and ASP"* by Alex Homer and David Sussman, from Wrox Press (ISBN 1-861001-46-0). We will present just enough information here to allow us to use MTS. MTS is a run time environment for distributed objects. The name is something of a misnomer, as it does more than simply manage transactions, and in Windows 2000 it is referred to as **Microsoft Component Services**, or **COM+**. While it does provide transaction services, it is also valuable for running objects that do not use them. MTS provides an execution environment for COM objects, handling the details of connection pooling, context management, and thread management. By writing a component for MTS, we focus on the business application logic, without having to worry about how the object could be used concurrently by several applications.

Making an Object Ready for MTS

MTS allows us to deploy our objects in **packages** (these are referred to as *applications* in COM+). There are two types of package: **library** and **server**. A server package runs our objects in a surrogate process space, initiated by MTS, which is isolated from the calling application. Using a server package allows us to define specific security settings. On the other hand, a library package does not run in a separate process space, and objects in a library package are loaded into the same address space as the calling client application. A library does not have its own security settings. Setting a package as a library allows us to run the MTS objects outside of the mtx.exe application. An advantage to running our objects in a server package is that, if the object crashes, it will not take down the base client. The advantage of using a library is that there are no cross-process calls.

When we activate an MTS object, we are not talking to it directly. A call is made to the **Service Control Manager** (**SCM**) on the client's machine, which passes the request to the SCM of the machine where the MTS object lives. The server-side SCM makes a local activation using the CLSID (a string used to identify the class) that has been passed along from the client-side SCM. However, the object is not created directly, but instead, an instance of the MTS package is located, and the SCM arranges for the creation of a new MTS object. If there is no current instance, the SCM launches mts.exe and a new MTS object is activated. Because this is an out-of-process call, a proxy/stub layer exists between the client and the object. In a sense, the client believes it is talking to a local instance of the requested object; this is the **proxy**. MTS provides a **stub**, which passes data in and out of the server-side object.

The **MTS run time** (or MTS Executive) provides the context for all objects running inside of it. Calls going in and out of the MTS objects are mediated by the run time through the context wrapper. When a method call is made on an MTS object, it is received by the context wrapper, which sits between the stub and the MTS object. When the call is completed, control passes back through the context wrapper to the stub. This little bit of interception allows MTS to perform its own pre- and post-processing of method calls.

Creating an object for MTS means that the project should have a reference to the MTS server type library, `mtxas.dll`. The object should also have the following statement, at the top of the project along with your declarations:

```
Implements ObjectControl
```

When a standard ActiveX DLL is run, the `Class_Initialize` subroutine is called when the object is first created. It is here that we would normally place some initialization code, such as setting default values for our global variables or initiating other objects. However, when an object is running under MTS, there is no guarantee that this `Sub` will be run each time a client initializes a reference to the object. The `Initialize` code runs before an object is activated. Objects in MTS may have already been created and used, then placed in a pending state prior to deactivation (known as pooling). A subsequent call to create an object may be grabbing an activated object that will not run the code in the `Initialize` routine. However, implementing `ObjectControl` gives us three additional routines that are called on either the first call to a method (`ObjectControl_Activate`), when an object loses context (`ObjectControl_Deactivate`), or after deactivation, but just prior to being destroyed (`ObjectControl_CanBePooled`).

`CanBePooled` should always return false, as MTS 2.0 does not support object pooling. COM+ does support pooling, but as yet does not support pooling for objects created with Visual Basic. We can use the other two events to perform the same actions we would normally put into `Activate` and `Deactivate`.

Another important aspect of MTS and its use of the context wrapper is how one MTS object goes about creating another MTS object. Typically, we would use the `New` operator or `CreateObject` to instantiate an object. However, doing so inside an MTS object means we are making a call through the SCM. If we are trying to create another MTS object, the SCM will follow the usual routine and contact MTS, but MTS will have no idea that this new object belongs in the same activity as the calling object, and will place the object in a separate activity. Now our two MTS objects must communicate across a proxy/stub layer, which degrades performance. Instead, we want to take advantage of the current object context, and use it to create the new object. So, rather than calling `CreateObject`, we call the `CreateInstance` method of the `ObjectContext` object.

To do this, we need to define an `ObjectContext` variable, and set it to the current context:

```
Dim oCtx as ObjectContext
Set oCtx = GetObjectContext()

Dim oObj as MyOtherMtsClass
Set oObj = oCtx.CreateInstance("MyServer.MyOtherMtsClass")
```

Designing the Request Handlers

As we saw in Chapter 7, our application will consist of several parts, which might not reside on the same machine (though the code *will* run if placed on the same machine). For example, we need to use a database (SQL Server 7.0), a web server for the public web pages (IIS 4.0), MTS, a message queue (MSMQ) and an XML file server. Some of the requests will require coordination among the various parts. For example, adding, changing, or deleting an XML file will require updating the database, whereas searching for and retrieving product information means running a query against the database and retrieving the corresponding XML file. Let's start by listing the likely required functions:

❑ Create a new product description

❑ Retrieve a product description for editing

❑ Update a product description

❑ Delete a product description

❑ Process a purchase order

Let's also take a look at a possible hardware layout for the application. We'll put SQL Server and the public web server on separate machines. The warehouse server is on yet another machine, possibly located in a separate building. We might also want to put our SOAP server on another server to balance process load. However, in our implementation here we will try to keep things simple (as well as affordable) by keeping the number of distinct pieces of hardware to a minimum. But in coding our objects we must always keep in mind that no assumptions can be made about location. Still, for testing and demonstration purposes, the code can all run on the same machine.

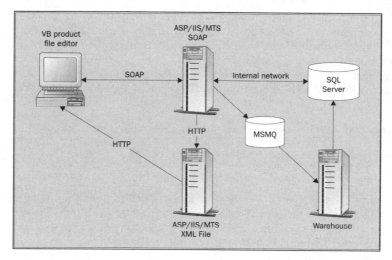

First, we create product descriptions, which means we define our database tables. This is relatively simple – we define the main fields (the ones we want to have fast searching on), and a field for a pointer to the XML documents holding the remaining product data. So, we create a database called WebProducts, with a table called Catalog:

ID	Column Name	Data Type	Size	Nulls	Default	Comments
Yes	ProdID	int	4	No	Auto-increment	This is an identity field, the unique product ID.
No	Name	char	128	Yes	Empty string	What the product is called.
No	Category	char	128	Yes	Empty string	How we classify the product.

Table Continued on Following Page

ID	Column Name	Data Type	Size	Nulls	Default	Comments
No	BriefDesc	char	256	Yes	Empty string	A short description of the product.
No	Price	money	8	Yes	zero	The retail cost of the product.
No	XmlDetails	char	128	Yes	Empty string	A URI to the XML product description file.

We could think of other fields as well, but this is fine for getting started. It allows us to grab enough data to display a basic catalog web page without having to dig into the XML.

We'll use SOAP transactions to manipulate the product description data. This will involve making changes to the contents of the Catalog table as well as storing the XML files on the file server. To retrieve XML files, the file editor will use a SOAP transaction to obtain a list of available products, and an HTTP GET request to get the XML data. The SOAP server will run as an IIS/ASP application. We'll need to build a number of new objects, as well as modify our SOAP utilities class to run under MTS. In addition, we'll need to add a few features to the file editor application so it can handle SOAP transactions.

The new objects that we'll need break down into these groups:

❑ A data services class to manage the database requests.

❑ A class for performing the file operations on the file server web site.

❑ A set of SOAP wrapper classes for product information transactions. These will take the SOAP requests and delegate them to a set of application methods. These methods will also take advantage of utility functions that will handle routine operations, such as writing files to the file server, or running queries against the database.

Data Services

Since some of our objects will be required to communicate with the database, we'll start with the data services object. This requires MTS to be installed on the machine where the ASP/IIS SOAP server is located, since we'll use it to host the object. Its purpose is to isolate calls to the database and to provide connection pooling. The connection to the database is made once and then the connection handle is placed in a pool for possible later reuse. Subsequent connection to the database will not require log-in and authentication, thereby improving performance.

In addition to handling connections to the database, the data services class will provide a few methods for executing SQL queries, and for returning the results of a SQL SELECT as an XML string. The class makes use of our ErrorUtils class from Chapter 7 to manage error information.

The project is an ActiveX DLL called WroxDataAccess. It has a single class, called DataServices. The project requires references to the ActiveX Data Objects 2.1 library, the Microsoft Transaction Server type library, the Microsoft XML parser, and the ErrorUtils DLL. (Once again, the complete code in this chapter is available from the Wrox web site.)

Declaring Properties

We start by declaring some properties needed for our database calls and for returning error information:

```
'******************************************************************
' Data services component to manage our product database.
'******************************************************************
Option Explicit
Implements ObjectControl

Const PROGID As String = "WroxDataAccess.DataServices"
```

This will be an MTS object, so we've used the `Implements ObjectControl` statement. The class should have the `MTSTransactionMode` property set to "3 - UsesTransactions".

```
Dim oRs As ADODB.Recordset
Dim oConn As ADODB.Connection
Dim oError As ErrorUtils.ErrorInfo
Dim oCtx As ObjectContext
```

The data access objects, are declared as well as an error manager object, and an `ObjectContext` object so that this object may interact with ASP objects. A private member is also declared for the connection string, and property accessors for the connection string and error information:

```
Private m_sConnectionString As String

Public Property Get ConnectionString() As String
    ConnectionString = m_sConnectionString
End Property

Public Property Let ConnectionString(sConnStr As String)
    m_sConnectionString = sConnStr
End Property

Public Property Get ErrorDescription() As String
    ErrorDescription = oError.Description
End Property

Public Property Get ErrorLocation() As String
    ErrorLocation = oError.Location
End Property

Public Property Get ErrorNumber() As Long
    ErrorNumber = oError.Number
End Property

Public Function GetErrorInfoXML() As String
    GetErrorInfoXML = oError.GetErrorInfoXML
End Function
```

Converting an ADO Recordset to XML

The results of any SELECT queries will be returned as an XML string. A method is used that takes an ADO Recordset and converts it to XML:

```
'*****************************************************************
' Private Function ConvertRsToXml(oRs As ADODB.Recordset) As String
'*****************************************************************
Private Function ConvertRsToXml(oRs As ADODB.Recordset) As String
    On Error GoTo ErrHand
    Dim sXML As String
    Dim fld As ADODB.Field
    Dim sVal As String


    Call oError.ClearErrorInfo
```

A variable is declared to hold the final XML, a Field variable for iterating through recordset fields, and a String to hold field values. The function takes an ADO Recordset as a parameter, and loops through it to get the row data:

```
    sXML ="<DATA>" & vbCrLf
    Do While Not oRs.EOF
        sXML = sXML & "<Row "
        For Each fld In oRs.Fields
            sVal = ConvertDataToXmlString(fld.Value)
            If oError.Number <> 0 Then
                sXML = sXML & fld.Name & "='ERROR_CONVERTING_TO_XML' "
            Else
                sXML = sXML & fld.Name & "='" & Trim(sVal) & "' "
            End If
        Next
        sXML = sXML & " />" & vbCrLf
        oRs.MoveNext
    Loop
    sXML = sXML & "</DATA>" & vbCrLf
```

If there are any run time errors they are caught here:

```
ErrHand:
    If Err.Number <> 0 Then
        sXML = ""
        Call oError.SetErrorInfo(Err.Description, _
            PROGID & ".ConvertRsToXml", Err.Number)
    End If
    ConvertRsToXml = sXML
End Function
```

The results of this call will look something like this (without the indentation, which is added for readability):

```
<DATA>
  <Row ProdID="12"
    Name="Foo"
    Category="Bar"
    BriefDesc="Something or other"
    Price="10.00"
    XmlDetails="http://127.0.0.1/WroxFileServer/ProductFiles/12.xml"/>
        <!-- more data -->
</DATA>
```

The method calls a helper function, ConvertDataToXmlString, to convert problem characters, such as "&", to entity references, before including them in the XML:

```
Private Function ConvertDataToXmlString(vData As Variant) As String
    On Error GoTo ErrHand
    Call oError.ClearErrorInfo

    Dim sXML As String
    If IsNull(vData) Then
        sXML = "NULL"
    ElseIf TypeName(vData) = "String" Then
        sXML = XmlEncode(vData)
    Else
        sXML = XmlEncode(CStr(vData))
    End If

ErrHand:
    If Err.Number <> 0 Then
        sXML = ""
        Call oError.SetErrorInfo(Err.Description, _
            PROGID & ".ConvertDataToXmlString", Err.Number)
    End If

    ConvertDataToXmlString = sXML
End Function
```

Executing SQL

We use wrapper functions for SQL statements to aid in error handling and reporting. This next method, ExecuteSQL, is used for any SQL statement that does not need to return data, such as UPDATE or INSERT. The SQL statement is passed in via the sSQL parameter. It returns True if all went well, and False otherwise:

```
Public Function ExecuteSQL(ByVal sSQL As String) As Boolean
    On Error GoTo ErrHand
    Dim bResults As Boolean
    Call oError.ClearErrorInfo

    If (Len(m_sConnectionString) > 0) Then
        If oConn.State <> adStateClosed Then
            oConn.Close
        End If
        oConn.Open (m_sConnectionString)
        Set oRs = oConn.Execute(sSQL)
        Set oRs.ActiveConnection = Nothing
        oConn.Close
        bResults = True
```

```
        Else
            bResults = False
            Call oError.SetErrorInfo("No connection string", _
                        PROGID & ".ExecuteSQL", -1)
        End If

ErrHand:
    If Err.Number <> 0 Then
        bResults = False
        Call oError.SetErrorInfo(Err.Description & "SQL = " & sSQL, _
                    PROGID & ".ExecuteSQL", Err.Number)
    End If
    ExecuteSQL = bResults
End Function
```

Executing a SELECT

The `ExecuteSelectXml` method is used to perform SELECTs, returning the results as an XML string:

```
'****************************************************************
' Public ExecuteSelectXml(sSQL As String) As String
'****************************************************************
Public Function ExecuteSelectXml(sSQL As String) As String
    On Error GoTo ErrHand
    Dim sResults As String
    Dim sXML As String

    Call oError.ClearErrorInfo

    If (Len(m_sConnectionString) > 0) Then
        Set oConn = New Connection
        oConn.Open (m_sConnectionString)
        Set oRs = oConn.Execute(sSQL)
        sXML = ConvertRsToXml(oRs)
        If Len(sXML) < 1 Then
            ' Error information should have been set in ConvertRsToXml
            sResults = ""
        Else
            sResults = sXML
        End If
    Else
        Call oError.SetErrorInfo("No connection string", _
                    PROGID & ".ExecuteSelectXml", -1)
        sResults = ""
    End If

ErrHand:
    If Err.Number <> 0 Then
        Call oError.SetErrorInfo(Err.Description, _
                    PROGID & ".ExecuteSelectXml", Err.Number)
        sResults = ""
    End If

    ExecuteSelectXml = sResults
End Function
```

Once again, a simple helper method, `XmlEncode`, is provided for replacing special characters with entity references:

```
Private Function XmlEncode(sText) As String
    Dim s As String
    s = Replace(sText, "&", "&amp;")
    s = Replace(s, "<", "&lt;")
    s = Replace(s, ">", "&gt;")
    s = Replace(s, "'", "&apos;")
    s = Replace(s, """", "&quot;")
    XmlEncode = s
End Function
```

Finally, set up and clean up code is provided in the `ObjectControl` events:

```
Private Sub ObjectControl_Activate()
    m_sConnectionString = ""
    Set oConn = New Connection
    Set oError = New ErrorUtils.ErrorInfo
    Set oCtx = GetObjectContext()
    oError.ClearErrorInfo
End Sub

Private Function ObjectControl_CanBePooled() As Boolean
    ObjectControl_CanBePooled = False
End Function

Private Sub ObjectControl_Deactivate()
    Set oError = Nothing
    Set oConn = Nothing
    Set oCtx = Nothing
End Sub
```

We now need to build our project, and place it in MTS.

The XML File Server

The XML file server is an ASP application running on IIS. It receives product description files through POST requests – the document is contained in the POST data, and the file name is sent as a parameter in the query string. The site consists of a single page, `PutFile.asp`.

The `global.asa` file sets up a single `Application` variable:

```
<SCRIPT LANGUAGE=VBScript RUNAT=Server>
Sub Application_OnStart
    Application("ProdFileDir") = "ProductFiles"
End Sub
</SCRIPT>
```

We set up the `PutFile.asp` page response by turning on buffering to ensure that the results of the POST get sent back as a single stream, which makes it easier to call this page from our own client code without having to implement any sophisticated handling of segmented responses. (Without buffering, the web server may return data in a sequence of chunks. The client then needs to check the HTTP `content-length` header and continue to collect and concatenate pieces of the response until the total number of characters is received.) We also set the response content type to `text/xml` so that the receiving user agent knows how to process it:

```
<%@ Language=VBScript %>
<%
  Response.Buffer = true
  Response.ContentType = "text/xml"
```

A number of object variables are declared: an MSXML DOMDocument for parsing the sent document; an instance of the XmlFileUtils class (which we'll discuss in a moment) to take care of writing the file to disk; and the handy ErrorUtils for nicely formatting any error information we may want to return:

```
  Dim oDOM, oXmlFileUtils, oErr
  Dim sXML, sResults, sFileDir, sURL
  Dim sSavedToURL, sPath, sFilename, sHref
  Dim sUrl, UrlParts()

  Set oDOM = Server.CreateObject("Microsoft.XMLDOM")

  Set oXmlFileUtils = Server.CreateObject("WroxFileServer.XmlFileUtils")
  Set oErr = Server.CreateObject("ErrorUtils.ErrorInfo")
  sFileDir = Application ("ProdFileDir")
  sPath = Server.MapPath("ProductFiles")
  sFilename = Request.QueryString("file")
  nParsed = 0

  Session("ProdFileDir") = "ProductFiles"
```

Some variables are set up for the assorted pieces of data we'll be using. The file destination directory is pulled out of the Application variable, and the physical path is retrieved by calling Server.MapPath. There needs to be a URL that points to where the file can be retrieved through the web server. This is done by grabbing the SERVER_NAME and URL server variables, splitting the URL into its path parts, and taking just the root web application path. The application path is then merged with the server name (the www.yoursite.com part) and the name of the directory where we store the XML files. Finally, the code tacks on the name of the file we're saving. We want this to be sent back to the client if the save was successful:

```
  If( oDOM.load(Request)) Then
    sXML = oDOM.xml
    If (oXmlFileUtils.WriteFile( sXML, sPath, sFilename)) Then
      sUrl =  Request.ServerVariables("URL")
      UrlParts = Split(sUrl, "/")
      sHref= Request.ServerVariables("SERVER_NAME") &  "/" & UrlParts(1)
      sSavedToURL = "http://" & sHref + "/" & sFileDir & "/" + sFilename
      sResults = "<results><OK href='" & sSavedToURL & "'  /></results>"
```

If the save is not successful, error information will be returned:

```
  Else
    sResults = oXmlFileUtils.GetErrorInofXml()
  End if
```

Likewise, if the page was sent XML that could not be parsed, an error message is prepared:

```
  Else
    Call oErr.SetErrorInfo("Failed to parse XML" , _
            Request.ServerVariables("URL"),  -1)
    sResults = oErr.GetErrorInfoXML()
    sResults = "<ERROR>Failed to parse the given document</ERROR>"
  End if

  Response.Write sResults
%>
```

Writing Files to Disk

The ASP code uses the `WroxFileServer.XmlFileUtils` class to write the results to disk. The project for this is an ActiveX DLL. It uses references to the Scripting run time library, the Microsoft XML parser, the `ErrorUtils` DLL, and the MTS type library. The `MTSTransactionMode` is set to "1 – No Transactions".

The project has one class, `XmlFileUtils`. The class has one main function, `WriteFile`, used to do the disk I/O. We will also expose `GetErrorInfoXml` from the error utilities class so that we can return any error information.

First the variables are declared and the `Implements ObjectControl` statement:

```
'*************************************************************
' WroxFileServer.XmlFileUtils
' MTS object to handle putting product description files
' on the web server
'*************************************************************
Option Explicit
Implements ObjectControl
'
Const PROGID As String = "WroxFileServer.XmlFileUtils"
```

A constant has been defined to help set the error information. Next the `ErrorUtils` object is declared:

```
Dim oError As ErrorUtils.ErrorInfo
```

`GetErrorInfoXml` simply wraps the `ErrorUtils` method for returning error information as an XML string:

```
'*************************************************************
' Public Function GetErrorInfoXml()
' Return the error information as an XML string
'*************************************************************
Public Function GetErrorInfoXml()
    GetErrorInfoXml = oError.GetErrorInfoXML
End Function
```

Writing the XML File

The function for writing the file takes the XML file as a string, the path to where we want to save it, and the file name. It also takes an optional parameter to flag whether or not it's OK to overwrite an existing file. This is True by default:

```
Public Function WriteFile(sXML As String, _
                          sFilepath As String, _
                          sFilename As String, _
                          Optional bOverWrite as Boolean = True
                          ) As Boolean
On Error GoTo ErrHand

Dim bResults As Boolean
Dim fso As Scripting.FileSystemObject
Dim tso As Scripting.TextStream
Dim sDetails As String
```

A variable has been declared to hold the results, plus a FileSystemObject for directory and file operations, and a TextStream object for doing the actual file writing. The sDetails variable will be used if the need arises to set some lengthy error information, should the file write fail. Any current error information is cleared, and a check is done to verify that there is a file path and a file name to use:

```
Call oError.ClearErrorInfo

If (Len(sFilepath) > 0) Then
    If (Len(sFilename) > 0) Then
```

If there is a file path and name to use, the FileSystemObject is initialized, and any backslashes are replaced with forward slashes. We do this so that the code can check if the file path already contains a trailing slash. If there isn't one, it is added:

```
Set fso = New FileSystemObject
sFilepath = Replace(sFilepath, "\", "/")
If (Right(sFilepath, 1) <> "/") Then
    sFilepath = sFilepath & "/"
End If
```

A check is done to see if the file already exists. If it does, and bOverWrite is true, then the file is overwritten:

```
If fso.FileExists(sFilepath & sFilename) Then
    If bOverWrite Then
        Set tso = fso.OpenTextFile(sFilepath & sFilename, _
                ForWriting, True)
        tso.Write (sXML)
        tso.Close
        Set tso = Nothing
        Set fso = Nothing
        bResults = True
```

Otherwise, error information is set:

```
        Else
            bResults = False
            Call _
                oError.SetErrorInfo("File exists, overwrite is False.", _
                    PROGID & ".WriteFile", -1)
        End If
```

If the file does not exist then it is created:

```
        Else
            Set tso = fso.OpenTextFile(sFilepath & sFilename, _
                    ForWriting, True)
            tso.Write (sXML)
            tso.Close
            Set tso = Nothing
            Set fso = Nothing
            bResults = True
        End If
```

If there is no file name or file path, error information is set:

```
        Else
            bResults = False
            Call oError.SetErrorInfo("No file name.", _
                    PROGID & ".WriteFile", -1)
        End If
    Else
        bResults = False
        Call oError.SetErrorInfo("No file path.", _
                PROGID & ".WriteFile", -1)
    End If
```

Run time errors are caught at the end of the method:

```
ErrHand:
    If Err.Number <> 0 Then
        sDetails = " - Path=" & sFilepath & "; File name=" & sFilename
        Call oError.SetErrorInfo(Err.Description & sDetails, _
                PROGID & ".WriteFile", Err.Number)
        bResults = False
    End If

    WriteFile = bResults
End Function
```

And, of course, we have `ObjectControl` initialization and clean-up:

```
Private Sub ObjectControl_Activate()
    Set oError = New ErrorUtils.ErrorInfo
    Call oError.ClearErrorInfo
End Sub

Private Function ObjectControl_CanBePooled() As Boolean
    ObjectControl_CanBePooled = False
End Function

Private Sub ObjectControl_Deactivate()
    Set oError = Nothing
End Sub
```

Finally, the project must be compiled and registered in MTS.

Changes to the SoapUtils Class

Our original SOAP utilities class (from Chapter 7) was written to work with a stand-alone executable. However, to make it work well with IIS and ASP, we need to make a few changes. We will create a new project, called `SoapUtilsMts`, which is essentially the same code as the original. We will have to add some additional references. First, to have the DLL run under MTS, the project needs a reference to the MTS type library. Second, to have access to ASP intrinsic objects, the project needs a reference to the Active Server Pages object library.

First, we set the project as an MTS object with the `MTSTransactionMode` set to "1 – No Transactions".

The original `SoapUtils` class used a `Dictionary` object to hold the binding information that mapped a SOAP request to an application handler class. The DLL would read a local file and populate the `Dictionary`. This was fine when the DLL was only loaded once for the duration of the application's use. But in the ASP version, each new request would require the DLL to reload the binding data. Rather than holding this information in the DLL, we can use ASP application variables instead. This allows the data to be loaded once and remain available to the SOAP DLL. We need to add a reference to the ASP `Application` object. At the top of the utilities class code, we make these changes:

```
Option Explicit

Implements ObjectControl

Const DICT_PROGID_SUFFIX As String = "PROGID"
Const DICT_METHOD_SUFFIX As String = "METHOD"
Const DICT_SERVER_SUFFIX As String = "SERVER"
Const PROGID_STRING As String = "SoapUtils.Utils"
Private oCtx As ObjectContext                          ' Add

' Private m_dictBindings As Scripting.Dictionary        ' Remove or comment out
Private oApplication As Application                    ' Add
```

We've added an `ObjectContext` object variable, commented out the reference to the `Dictionary`, and added an ASP `Application` object variable.

In `ObjectControl_Activate` we get the `ObjectContext` reference and initialize the ASP `Application` object:

```
Private Sub ObjectControl_Activate()
    ' Set m_dictBindings = New Dictionary      ' Remove or comment out
    Set ClassErrors = New ErrorUtils.ErrorInfo
    Set oCtx = GetObjectContext()              ' Add
    Detail.Errorcode = 0
    Detail.Description = ""
    Detail.Location = ""

    Set oApplication = oCtx.Item("Application") ' Add
    Call ClassErrors.ClearErrorInfo

End Sub
```

We've also commented out the reference to the `Dictionary` object.

Likewise, we change:

```
Private Sub ObjectControl_Deactivate()
    ' Set m_dictBindings = Nothing         ' Remove or comment out
    Set ClassErrors = Nothing
    Set oApplication = Nothing             ' Add
End Sub
```

Since we will now use ASP `Application` variables, we need to change how the binding information is loaded. This happens in `LoadMethodBindings`. We replace references to the `Dictionary` object with code that sets ASP `Application` values:

```
Public Function LoadMethodBindings(sBindingFile As String) As Boolean
' ...
    If oDOM.Load(sBindingFile) Then
        Set oNodeList = oDOM.getElementsByTagName("binding")
        For nIdx = 0 To oNodeList.length - 1
            Set oEl = oNodeList.Item(nIdx)
            With oEl.Attributes
                sSoapMethod = .getNamedItem("requestMethod").nodeValue
                oApplication(sSoapMethod & DICT_PROGID_SUFFIX) = _
                    .getNamedItem("progID").nodeValue
                oApplication(sSoapMethod & DICT_METHOD_SUFFIX) = _
                    .getNamedItem("objectMethod").nodeValue
                oApplication(sSoapMethod & DICT_SERVER_SUFFIX) = _
                    .getNamedItem("server").nodeValue
            End With
        Next
' ...
End Function
```

Second, since the object will be called from ASP, and IIS will handle the response headers, we need to remove a few lines from the ExecuteRequestWrapper method. First, we retrieve binding information from the ASP Application variable:

```
Public Function ExecuteRequestWrapper(sSOAPXML As String) As String
    ' Declarations go here ...
    ' ... original code ...
    If VerifySoapVersion(sSOAPXML) Then
        sSoapMethodName = RetrieveSoapMethodName(sSOAPXML)
        If Len(sSoapMethodName) Then
            ' Remove or comment out
              ' sProgID = m_dictBindings(sSoapMethodName & _
              '           DICT_PROGID_SUFFIX) ' Remove or comment out
            ' Add this:
              sProgID = oApplication(sSoapMethodName & DICT_PROGID_SUFFIX)
            ' Remove or comment out
              ' sComMethodName = m_dictBindings(sSoapMethodName & _
              '           DICT_METHOD_SUFFIX) CHANGE
            ' Add this:
              sComMethodName = oApplication(sSoapMethodName & DICT_METHOD_SUFFIX)
            ' Remove or comment out
              ' sObjectServer = m_dictBindings(sSoapMethodName & _
              '           DICT_SERVER_SUFFIX) CHANGE
            ' Add this:
              sObjectServer = oApplication(sSoapMethodName & DICT_SERVER_SUFFIX)
            ' ...
```

A little further on, the function built HTTP headers for the response. This will now be done by IIS, so we remove or comment out the following lines:

```
'sHttpHeader = "HTTP/1.1 200 OK" & Chr(10)
'sHttpHeader = sHttpHeader & "Content-Type: text/xml" & Chr(10)
'sHttpHeader = sHttpHeader & "Content-length: " & _
'                            CStr(Len(sResults)) & Chr(10) & Chr(10)
```

The binding information will now be loaded in the global.asa file of the SOAP ASP application. We use Application_OnStart to initialize Application variables for a database connection (to connect to the WebProducts database), the URL for the XML file server, and the name of the resource DLL used to hold XSLT; some SOAP methods will transform database results prior to returning a response:

```
<SCRIPT LANGUAGE=VBScript RUNAT=Server>
Sub Application_OnStart
  Application("ConnString") = _
                  "DRIVER=SQL Server;SERVER=YourServerName;UID=ServerUserID;" &_
                  "WSID=WorkstationID;User Id=DBUserID;PASSWORD=DBPassword;"
  Application("XmlServerURL") = _
                  "http://XmlServerName/WroxFileServer/PutFile.asp"
  Application("ProductTxResDataObject") = "WroxProdTxRes.ResData"
```

The code also creates an instance of the SOAP utilities class and calls LoadMethodBindings to set the application variables. The SOAP request binding information file is kept in a sub directory of the ASP application:

```
      Dim sBindingDataFile
      Dim oSoapUtils
      Set oSoapUtils = Server.CreateObject("SoapUtilsMts.Utils")
      sBindingDataFile = Server.MapPath("config/soapBindings.xml")
      Application("sBindingDataFile") = sBindingDataFile
      oSoapUtils.LoadMethodBindings CStr(sBindingDataFile)

   End Sub
   </SCRIPT>
```

A page called `SoapSrv.asp` is used to receive the SOAP requests. In `SoapSrv.asp`, we set `Response.Buffer = true` so that the SOAP response is sent back in one piece, avoiding possible problems with clients that do not implement a full web browser. We also set the content type to `text/xml` to announce our MIME type. The configuration variables are set from the `Session` values, and an instance of the SOAP utilities object created. The site keeps the SOAP method binding file in a subdirectory, which is loaded using the SOAP utilities `LoadMethodBindings` method. The `SoapSrv.asp` page starts like this:

```
<%@ Language=VBScript %>
<%
   Response.Buffer = true
   Response.ContentType = "text/xml"

   Dim oSoapUtils
   Dim oSoapXml
   Dim sSoapRes
   Dim sBindingDataFile

   Set oSoapUtils = Server.CreateObject("SoapUtilsMts.Utils")
   Set oSoapXml =  Server.CreateObject("Microsoft.XMLDOM")
   sBindingDataFile = Server.MapPath("config/soapBindings.xml")
```

After initializing the SOAP utilities object, and a DOM `Document` object to hold the `POST` data, the DOM object is set to load the data synchronously so that execution waits until all data is loaded:

```
   oSoapXml.async = false
   If Not oSoapXml.load(Request)Then
```

If the `POST`ed data cannot be loaded correctly, a SOAP fault, with the details of the parsing error, is built for the response:

```
      oSoapUtils.SetDetailInfo "MyFault", "e", _
               "Failed to parse request",  "www.wrox.org/VbSoap", _
               "SoapSrv.asp",   1
      oSoapUtils.SetSoapFault 400, 0
      oSoapUtils.BuildFaultXml true
      sSoapRes = oSoapUtils.BuildSoapEvelopeFault(CBool(bIncludeDetail))
```

If the request is correctly loaded into the DOM, then the XML is passed on to the SOAP object to process the request:

```
   Else
      sSoapRes = oSoapUtils.ExecuteRequestWrapper (oSoapXml.xml)
   End If
```

The results in either case are sent back to the client:

```
    Response.Write sSoapRes
%>
```

SOAP Transactions

Request sent to the SOAP utilities object will be dispatched to code in another class containing the back-end request handlers. Our SOAP request handling code is broken down into three parts:

❑ SOAP request wrapper methods, which always take a single String parameter and return a SOAP response body

❑ Back-end application methods that perform the actual work for the SOAP request

❑ A collection of transaction utilities to minimize code replication

All of the code is kept in a single ActiveX DLL project, called WebProducts, in three classes. These are called ProdTxUtils, ProductDescriptionTx, and SoapWrappers. All three are MTS objects. The project requires these references:

❑ Microsoft Transaction Server type library

❑ Microsoft XML parser

❑ ErrorUtils

❑ WroxDataAccess

❑ Microsoft Scripting run time library

❑ Microsoft Active Server Pages object library

❑ SoapUtilsMts

The Web Transaction Utilities Class

Since there are a few operations that are shared across multiple transaction methods, they have been put into the ProdTxUtils utilities class. They handle such functions as talking to the database, or communicating with the XML web server. This class uses the WroxDataAccess.DataServices class, as well as the ErrorUtils.ErrorInfo class. It also defines an enumerated type for specifying a SQL statement, and a user-defined data type for holding the primary product details information:

```
'*****************************************************************
' WebProducts.ProdTxUtils
' Assorted routines to aid product description transactions
' This code is intended to run under MTS on the web server that
' handles SOAP requests.
'*****************************************************************
Option Explicit
Implements ObjectControl

Const PROGID As String = "WebProducts.ProdTxUtils"
```

```
Public Type dbInfo
    ProdID As String
    Name As String
    Category As String
    BriefDesc As String
    XmlDetails As String
    Inventory As Integer
    Price As String
End Type

Enum QUERY_TYPE
    SQL_INSERT = 1
    SQL_UPDATE = 2
    SQL_DELETE = 3
    SQL_SELECT = 4
    SQL_SELECT_DISTINCT_CATEGORY = 5
    SQL_SELECT_PRODUCTS_BY_ID = 65
End Enum
```

A constant has been defined to hold the name of the class to use when setting error information. A user-defined structure exists to hold the product information that goes into the database. Using this makes it easier to pass the data to functions. An enumerated type has also been defined for different kinds of SQL statements that will be used with a function for creating our SQL calls.

We also declare the error information object, the data services object, and a reference for object context:

```
Dim oError As ErrorUtils.ErrorInfo
Dim oWds As WroxDataAccess.DataServices
Dim oCtx As ObjectContext
```

Some properties have been set up to hold such information as an error flag, the database connection string, error information returned from the data services class, and the location of the XML web server:

```
Private m_ErrorOcurred As Boolean
Private m_sConnString As String
Private m_sDataErrorXML As String
Private m_sFileUri As String

Property Get ErrorOccured() As Boolean
    ErrorOccured = m_ErrorOcurred
End Property

Property Let ConnectionString(sConnString As String)
    m_sConnString = sConnString
End Property

Property Get DataErrorXML() As String
    DataErrorXML = m_sDataErrorXML
End Property

Property Let FileUri(sURI As String)
    m_sFileUri = sURI
End Property
```

Constructing SQL Statements

We have a method for constructing SQL statements to make it easier in our main transaction code to build database commands. It takes a QUERY_TYPE parameter to indicate what kind of statement we want, and a dbInfo structure holding the main product information. This makes it easier to pass in several variables at once:

```
Public Function BuildSQL(QueryType As QUERY_TYPE, _
                    ByRef dbInfo As dbInfo) As String
    On Error GoTo ErrHand
    Dim sSQL As String

    Call oError.ClearErrorInfo
    m_ErrorOcurred = False
```

The code looks at the type of statement to construct, and uses the information in dbInfo to build the corresponding SQL string:

```
        Select Case QueryType
            Case SQL_UPDATE:
                With dbInfo
                    sSQL = "UPDATE Catalog Set  Name='" & .Name & _
                        "', Category='" & .Category & _
                        "', Price=" & CCur(.Price) & _
                        ", Inverntory=" & .Inventory & _
                        ", BriefDesc='" & .BriefDesc & _
                        "', XmlDetails='" & .XmlDetails & _
                        "' Where (ProdID = " & .ProdID & ")"
                End With

            Case SQL_INSERT:
                With dbInfo
                    sSQL = "INSERT INTO Catalog " & _
                        "(Name, Category, Price, BriefDesc, Inventory, XmlDetails)"
                    sSQL = sSQL & "VALUES ('" & .Name & "', '" & _
                        .Category & "', " & CCur(.Price) & ", '" _
                        & .BriefDesc & "', " & .Inventory & ", '" _
                        & .XmlDetails & "')"
                End With

            Case SQL_DELETE:
                    sSQL = "DELETE FROM Catalog WHERE ProdID='" & dbInfo.ProdID & "' "

            Case SQL_SELECT:
                With dbInfo
                    If Len(.ProdID) > 0 Then
                        sSQL = sSQL & " AND ProdID='" & .ProdID & "' "
                    End If
                    If Len(.Name) > 0 Then
                        sSQL = sSQL & " AND Name='" & .Name & "' "
                    End If
                    If Len(.Category) > 0 Then
                        sSQL = sSQL & " AND Category='" & .Category & "' "
                    End If
                     If Len(.BriefDesc) > 0 Then
                        sSQL = sSQL & " AND BriefDesc='" & .BriefDesc & "' "
```

```
                    End If
                    If Len(.XmlDetails) > 0 Then
                        sSQL = sSQL & " AND XmlDetails='" & .XmlDetails & "' "
                    End If
                    If Len(.Price) > 0 Then
                        sSQL = sSQL & " AND Price='" & .Price & "' "
                    End If

                End With
```

A specific type of query has been included that will be used when the Wrox web store is built in Chapter 11:

```
            Case SQL_SELECT_DISTINCT_CATEGORY:
                    sSQL = "SELECT DISTINCT Category FROM Catalog "
                sSQL = " & " WHERE Inventory > 0"
```

If the function has been asked to build a SQL string which it does not recognize or which has not been implemented then it returns an empty string:

```
            Case Else
                    sSQL = ""
        End Select
```

Run time errors are caught at the end of the function:

```
    ErrHand:
        If Err.Number <> 0 Then
            Call oError.SetErrorInfo(Err.Description, _
                        PROG_ID & ".BuildSQL", Err.Number)
            m_ErrorOcurred = True
            sSQL = ""
        End If
        BuildSQL = sSQL
    End Function
```

It is also handy to have a method for clearing the contents of a dbInfo structure, since some of the methods attempt to populate or alter the data, and which will return an empty structure when there is an error:

```
    Public Sub ClearMainInfo(ByRef dbi As dbInfo)
        With dbi
            .BriefDesc = ""
            .Category = ""
            .Name = ""
            .ProdID = ""
            .XmlDetails = ""
            .Inventory = 0
            .Price = ""
        End With
    End Sub
```

Creating the File URI

Depending on how and where we save the details file, we may need to construct a complete file path, using the product ID to construct the file name; this information is stored in the XMLDetails column of the Catalog table:

```
Public Function CreateFileUri(sProdID As String) As String
    Dim sTemp As String
    sTemp = m_sFileUri & "/" & sProdID & ".xml"
    CreateFileUri = sTemp
End Function
```

When we run SELECT queries against a database we want to return XML. This is done using the ExecuteSelectXml method in the data services class. If there's an error, then we want to set the error information and return an empty string. Applications using this function need to verify that the call succeeded by checking the length of the return value:

```
Public Function ExecuteSelect(ByVal sSQL As String) As String
    On Error GoTo ErrHand
    Dim sResults As String
```

If the connection string has been set, the code sets the ConnectionString property on the data services class, and passes it the SQL for execution:

```
    If Len(ConnectionString) > 0 Then
        oWds.ConnectionString = ConnectionString
        sResults = oWds.ExecuteSelectXml(sSQL)
```

If there is no connection string, then the function sets the error information:

```
    Else
        Call oError.SetErrorInfo(oWds.ErrorDescription, _
                    oWds.ErrorLocation, oWds.ErrorNumber)
        m_ErrorOcurred = True
        sResults = ""
    End If
```

Run time errors are trapped at the end of the method:

```
ErrHand:
    If Err.Number <> 0 Then
        Call oError.SetErrorInfo(Err.Description, _
                    PROGID & ".ExecuteSelect", Err.Number)
        m_ErrorOcurred = True
        sResults = ""
    End If
    ExecuteSelect = sResults
End Function
```

Returning Error Details

The method for returning error details, GetErrorInfoXml, wraps a call to the ErrorUtils object:

```
Public Function GetErrorInfoXml() As String
    GetErrorInfoXml = oError.GetErrorInfoXml
End Function
```

Inserting a New Product

When we want to insert a new product, we need to get a product ID, and use that ID to update the XML file before storing it on the XML server. The ID is an auto-incremented field in the table; to get the next value, we insert the product information that we have, which will assign a value to the `ProdID` column. We need to locate this new record and retrieve the assigned ID, so that we may update the `XmlDetails` field with the exact location information. We need some unique field value for this, and since we aren't explicitly setting the product ID, we do not yet know what it is. We create this unique ID in the `XmlDetails` field by creating a temporary value based on a time stamp.

Along the way we check that the various database calls succeeded. If everything works, the new ID is returned. If there was an error an empty string is returned.

```
Public Function AddNextProdToDB(dbiData As dbInfo) As String
    On Error GoTo ErrHand

    Dim sSQL As String
    Dim sDate As String
    Dim bRes As Boolean
    Dim sXML As String
    Dim oDOM As DOMDocument
    Dim oEl As IXMLDOMElement
    Dim sProdID As String
```

If the connection has been set, the code sets the data services `ConnectionString` property and creates a time stamp for the `XMLDetails` field:

```
If Len(m_sConnString) > 0 Then
        oWds.ConnectionString = m_sConnString
        sDate = CStr(Now())
        dbiData.ProdID = ""
        dbiData.XmlDetails = sDate
```

The `INSERT` statement is constructed, and sent to the data services class for execution:

```
sSQL = BuildSQL(SQL_INSERT, dbiData)
        If oWds.ExecuteSQL(sSQL) Then
```

If the `INSERT` worked, then the product ID is retrieved, by using the `XmlDetails` field as a unique key:

```
sSQL = "SELECT ProdID FROM Catalog WHERE XmlDetails='" & sDate & "' "
        sXML = oWds.ExecuteSelectXml(sSQL)
        If Len(sXML) > 0 Then   ' Parse out the ProdID:
```

The code takes the results, loads it into the `DOMDocument` object, and extracts the `ProdID` value. If there is an error, the error information is set and an empty response prepared:

```
Set oDOM = New DOMDocument
            If oDOM.loadXML(sXML) Then
                Set oEl = oDOM.getElementsByTagName("Row").Item(0)
                If Not oEl Is Nothing Then
                    sProdID = oEl.Attributes.getNamedItem("ProdID").nodeValue
                    Set oDOM = Nothing
```

```
            Else
                sProdID = ""
                oError.SetErrorInfo "Failed to locate DATA element: " & _
                        oDOM.xml, _
                            PROG_ID & ".AddNextProdToDB", -1
                m_ErrorOcurred = True
            End If
```

If the query results could not be parsed, error data is set, and an empty response prepared:

```
            Else        ' Error parsing results
                sProdID = ""
                Call oError.SetErrorInfo("Error parsing results: " & _
                        oDOM.parseError.reason, _
                            PROG_ID & ".AddNextProdToDB", -1)
                m_ErrorOcurred = True
            End If
```

Likewise, if the INSERT or the subsequent query failed:

```
          Else        ' Error retrieving record
              sProdID = ""
              Call oError.SetErrorInfo("Error retrieving record", _
                      PROG_ID & ".AddNextProdToDB", -1)
              m_sDataErrorXML = oWds.GetErrorInfoXml()
              m_ErrorOcurred = True
          End If
      Else            ' The INSERT failed
          sProdID = ""
          Call oError.SetErrorInfo("Error calling ExecuteSQL", _
                  PROG_ID & ".AddNextProdToDB", -1)
          m_sDataErrorXML = oWds.GetErrorInfoXml()
          m_ErrorOcurred = True
      End If
  Else                ' No connection string
      Call oError.SetErrorInfo("No connection string.", _
              PROG_ID & ".AddNextProdToDB", -1)
      m_ErrorOcurred = True
      sProdID = ""
  End If
```

Run time errors are handled at the end of the method:

```
ErrHand:
    If Err.Number <> 0 Then
        Call oError.SetErrorInfo(Err.Description, _
                PROG_ID & ".AddNextProdToDB", Err.Number)
        m_ErrorOcurred = True
        sProdID = ""
    End If

    AddNextProdToDB = sProdID
End Function
```

Inserting a new product, as previously mentioned, requires a bit of coordinated action. This method performs the addition by inserting whatever product information is available and obtaining the new product ID. The new product ID is used to update the product information XML. The new ID is also used to create the name for the XML file. The code issues a POST request to the XML server; the response from the file server is parsed for the final URL to the file, which is then combined with the product information. The database is then updated with the altered information to complete the addition. This collection of events is done by InsertNewProduct, which takes as parameters the primary database information (in a dbInfo structure), and the XML details:

```
Public Function InsertNewProduct(dbi As dbInfo, sXmlDoc As String) As String
    On Error GoTo ErrHand

    Dim sResults As String
    Dim sSQL As String
    Dim sProdID As String
    Dim sURI As String
    Dim sFilename As String
    Dim sWriteFileResults As String

    Call oError.ClearErrorInfo
    m_ErrorOcurred = False
```

The code calls AddNextProdToDB to add the product information to the database, retrieving the new product ID:

```
    sProdID = AddNextProdToDB(dbi)

    If Len(sProdID) > 0 Then
        dbi.ProdID = sProdID
        sResults = UpdateXmlProdID(sXmlDoc, dbi.ProdID)
```

The product details XML is updated with the new product ID, and the response value set to the new XML; if there was an error, UpdateXmlProdID returns an empty string, so the response value is set:

```
        If Len(sResults) < 1 Then
        ' Error info was set in UpdateXmlProdID
            m_ErrorOcurred = True
            sResults = ""
```

Otherwise, an attempt is made to write the modified XML file to the file server:

```
        Else
            sURI = m_sFileUri
            sFilename = sProdID & ".xml"
            If Not (WriteXmlFileToServer(sResults, sURI, sFilename, dbi)) Then
```

If the write fails, the newly inserted product information must be deleted from the database:

```
                sResults = ""
                m_ErrorOcurred = True
                sSQL = BuildSQL(SQL_DELETE, dbi)
                Call oWds.ExecuteSQL(sSQL)
```

If the file write succeeds, the database entry needs to be updated with the XMLDetails location:

```
            Else
                If Not UpdateDbInfo(dbi) Then
                    ' Leave the error information set by UpdateDbInfo
                    sResults = ""
                    m_ErrorOcurred = True
                Else
                ' Success. sResults should have the update XML already,
                ' so clear the error flag
                    m_ErrorOcurred = False
                End If
            End If
        End If
```

If AddNextProdToDB failed, then the response is set to an empty string:

```
    Else ' Could not getnext prodid
        ' Leave the error information set by GetNextProdID
        m_ErrorOcurred = True
        sResults = ""
    End If
```

Run time errors are caught with the ErrHand label:

```
ErrHand:
    If Err.Number <> 0 Then
        Call oError.SetErrorInfo(Err.Description, _
                    PROG_ID & ".InsertNewProduct", _
                    Err.Number)
        m_ErrorOcurred = True
        sResults = ""
    End If

    InsertNewProduct = sResults
End Function
```

To populate the dbInfo structure with the primary product information we need to parse the details from the XML document. This method goes through the XML string, pulling out the items, and returns a new dbInfo value:

```
Public Function SetMainInfo(sXML) As dbInfo
    On Error GoTo ErrHand
    Dim dbiTemp As dbInfo
    Dim sTemp As String
    Dim oEl As IXMLDOMElement
    Dim oDOM As DOMDocument

    Call oError.ClearErrorInfo
    m_ErrorOcurred = False

    Set oDOM = New DOMDocument

    If Not oDOM.loadXML(sXML) Then
        Call ClearMainInfo(dbiTemp)
        Call oError.SetErrorInfo("Parse Errror: " & oDOM.parseError.reason, _
                    PROGID & ".SetMainInfo", oDOM.parseError.errorCode)
        m_ErrorOcurred = True
```

```
        Else
            Set oEl = oDOM.documentElement
            dbiTemp.ProdID = oEl.Attributes.getNamedItem("ID").nodeValue
            dbiTemp.Name = oDOM.getElementsByTagName("NAME").Item(0).Text
            Set oEl = oDOM.selectSingleNode("//DESCRIPTION/HEADER")
            If Not oEl Is Nothing Then
                dbiTemp.BriefDesc = oEl.Text
            End If
            dbiTemp.Category = oDOM.getElementsByTagName("CATEGORY").Item(0).Text
            dbiTemp.XmlDetails = ""
        End If

ErrHand:
    If Err.Number <> 0 Then
        Call ClearMainInfo(dbiTemp)
        Call oError.SetErrorInfo(Err.Description, _
                    PROGID & ".SetMainInfo", _
                    Err.Number)
        m_ErrorOcurred = True
    End If
    SetMainInfo = dbiTemp
End Function
```

Updating the Database

Once we have changed the main product information for our file, we need to update the database with the final URL for the XML file, which was obtained by sending the file to the XML file server. The UpdateDBInfo method takes a dbInfo structure and runs an UPDATE on the database:

```
'*********************************************************************
' Private Function UpdateDbInfo(dbi As dbInfo) As Boolean
' use this to update the product catalog database with new information,
' such as a new XmlDetails entry.
'*********************************************************************
Private Function UpdateDbInfo(dbi As dbInfo) As Boolean
    On Error GoTo ErrHand
    Dim bResults As Boolean
    Dim sSQL As String

    ' Create SQL for the UPDATE
    sSQL = BuildSQL(SQL_UPDATE, dbi)

    oWds.ConnectionString = m_sConnString
    ' Need to call an UPDATE method on the data services object
    If Not oWds.ExecuteSQL(sSQL) Then
        Call oError.SetErrorInfo("Failed to update database" & _
                    oWds.GetErrorInfoXml, PROGID & ".UpdateDbInfo", -1)
        m_ErrorOcurred = True
        bResults = False
    Else
        m_ErrorOcurred = False
        bResults = True
    End If

ErrHand:
    If Err.Number <> 0 Then
        Call oError.SetErrorInfo(Err.Description, _
                    PROGID & ".UpdateDbInfo", Err.Number)
```

```
            m_ErrorOcurred = True
            bResults = False
        End If

    UpdateDbInfo = bResults
End Function
```

Just as adding a new product required multiple calls, so updating an entry means running a SQL command against the database and sending the file to the XML server. We don't have to deal with the database unless the file POST works, so we do that first, and only afterwards update the database:

```
'*********************************************************************
' Public Function UpdateProduct(sXML As String, dbInfo As dbInfo) As String
' we want to try to write the file to the XML file server, and if that
' works, we'll update the SQL Server.
' We return the XML document if successful, or an empty string on failure.
'*********************************************************************
Public Function UpdateProduct(sXML As String, dbi As dbInfo) As String
    On Error GoTo ErrHand

    Dim sSQL As String
    Dim sProdID As String
    Dim sURI As String
    Dim sFilename As String
    Dim sWriteFileResults As String

    Call oError.ClearErrorInfo
    m_ErrorOcurred = False

    sURI = m_sFileUri
    sFilename = dbi.ProdID & ".xml"
    If Not (WriteXmlFileToServer(sXML, sURI, sFilename, dbi)) Then
        sXML = ""
        m_ErrorOcurred = True
    Else
        ' Now that we have the final URI, based on where the file
        ' was written to, let's update the database
        If Not UpdateDbInfo(dbi) Then
        ' Leave the error stuff set by UpdateDbInfo
            sXML = ""
            m_ErrorOcurred = True
        Else
            ' Success. Set the results flag
            m_ErrorOcurred = False
        End If
    End If

ErrHand:
    If Err.Number <> 0 Then
        Call oError.SetErrorInfo(Err.Description, _
                    PROGID & ".UpdateProduct", _
                    Err.Number)
        m_ErrorOcurred = True
        sXML = ""
    End If

    UpdateProduct = sXML

End Function
```

When we have a new product file, the ID attribute of the PRODUCT element should be zero. Once we've obtained a valid ID from the database, we need to go into the XML and change the ID. The UpdateXmlProdID method takes the XML, locates the ID attribute, and sets it to the new value. It returns the updated document:

```
'**********************************************************************
' Private Function UpdateXmlProdID(sXMl As String, sNewProdID as String)
' As Boolean
' Takes the XML file, locates the ID attribute on the root element,
' and changes it to the new value
'**********************************************************************
Private Function UpdateXmlProdID(sXML As String, sNewProdID As String) As String
    On Error GoTo ErrHand

    Dim oDOM As DOMDocument
    Dim oEl As IXMLDOMElement
    Dim sResults As String

    Call oError.ClearErrorInfo
    m_ErrorOcurred = False

    Set oDOM = New DOMDocument
    If Not oDOM.loadXML(sXML) Then
        Call oError.SetErrorInfo("Parse error: " & _
                    oDOM.parseError.reason, PROGID & ".UpdateXmlProdID", _
                    Err.Number)
        m_ErrorOcurred = True
        sResults = ""
    Else    ' Change ID
        Set oEl = oDOM.documentElement
        oEl.Attributes.getNamedItem("ID").nodeValue = sNewProdID
        sResults = oDOM.xml
    End If

ErrHand:
    If Err.Number <> 0 Then
        Call oError.SetErrorInfo(Err.Description, _
                    PROGID & ".UpdateXmlProdID", Err.Number)
        m_ErrorOcurred = True
        sResults = ""
    End If

    UpdateXmlProdID = sResults

End Function
```

Writing to the File Server

To get an XML file to the file server, we need to know a few things. For our purposes, the XML server is a web site that receives data via a POST request. But we may at some point want to save the file to disk, or use FTP. This method takes the XML document, the URI for where files get saved, the file name (which is created from the product ID), and a reference to a dbInfo structure holding the product details. The code parses the URI protocol; it must contain a prefix, either file:// or http://. The protocol determines how we'll store the XML. The file:// protocol will have the XML written to a local file. For HTTP requests we'll use the MSXML.XMLHTTPRequest object to talk to our web server. If we succeed in saving the file, we update the dbInfo structure with the new URI. (Note that this only changes when the data is POSTed to the web site.)

```
Private Function WriteXmlFileToServer(ByVal sXML As String, _
                                      ByVal sURI As String, _
                                      ByVal sFilename As String, _
                                      ByRef dbiProd As dbInfo _
                                      ) As Boolean
     On Error GoTo ErrHand
     Dim sUriType As String
     Dim sFullFilePath As String
     Dim asUriParts() As String
     Dim oXmlHttp As MSXML.XMLHTTPRequest
     Dim oDOM As DOMDocument
     Dim oEl As IXMLDOMElement
     Dim fso As Scripting.FileSystemObject
     Dim tso As Scripting.TextStream
     Dim sFinalURI  As String
     Dim bResults As Boolean

     m_ErrorOcurred = False
     Call oError.ClearErrorInfo
```

The code splits the URI to put the protocol into the first array element. If there is no protocol, the response is set to False:

```
     asUriParts = Split(sURI, "://")

     If UBound(asUriParts) < 1 Then
         ' No protocol!
         m_ErrorOcurred = True
         bResults = False
         Call oError.SetErrorInfo("URI does not have a protocol", _
                 PROGID & ".WriteXmlFileToServer", -1)
```

Otherwise the protocol is used to determine how to save the file:

```
     Else
         Select Case UCase(asUriParts(0))
             Case "HTTP"
```

If the protocol is HTTP, then the XML is loaded into a DOM object. If there are any parsing errors, the response is set to False and the parsing error information is set in the oError object:

```
             ' The URI should look something like this:
             ' http://TheServer/TheReceivingPage.asp'
             Set oXmlHttp = New XMLHTTPRequest
             Set oDOM = New DOMDocument
             If Not oDOM.loadXML(sXML) Then
                 m_ErrorOcurred = True
                 bResults = False
                 Call oError.SetErrorInfo("Error parsing XML" & _
                     oDOM.parseError.reason, _
                     PROGID & ".WriteXmlFileToServer", -1)
```

If the XML does load, we prepare the XMLHTTPRequest object to POST the XML to the file server. An additional query string parameter is appended to the web page address, to tell the XML file server what name to use for the file:

```
    Else
        oXmlHttp.open "POST", sURI & "?file=" & sFilename, False
        oXmlHttp.send oDOM
```

After sending the POST, the response is placed into the DOM object. A check is made to see that the file server correctly processed the request:

```
    Set oDOM = oXmlHttp.responseXML
    ' Need to check that this worked.
    ' We'll have the web server return errors
    ' in the same format as the ErrorUtils object
    If oDOM.documentElement.nodeName = "ERROR" Then
        m_ErrorOcurred = True
        bResults = False
        Call oError.SetErrorInfo("Server error:" & oDOM.xml, _
                    PROGID & ".WriteXmlFileToServer", -1)
```

If the file server was able to save the XML, it will return a URI pointing to the new file:

```
    Else
        ' Parse out the new URI.  The ASP page that handles
        ' saving files should return:
        '<results><OK href='the new url
        'to fetch the file'/></results>
        Set oEl = oDOM.getElementsByTagName("OK").Item(0)
        sFinalURI = oEl.Attributes.getNamedItem("href").nodeValue
```

A check is done to make sure that the response included an href value. If it did, then a True response is set; if not, error information is recorded:

```
            If (Len(sFinalURI) > 0) Then
                dbiProd.XmlDetails = sFinalURI
                m_ErrorOcurred = False
                bResults = True
            Else
                m_ErrorOcurred = True
                bResults = False
                Call oError.SetErrorInfo("No href in results", _
                        PROGID & ".WriteXmlFileToServer", -1)
            End If
        End If
    End If
```

If the XML is to be saved as a file, a `FileSystem` object is used to save it locally:

```
Case "FILE"
    Set fso = New FileSystemObject
    If (Right(asUriParts(1), 1) <> "/") Then
        asUriParts(1) = asUriParts(1) & "/"
    End If
    Set tso = fso.OpenTextFile(asUriParts(1) & sFilename, _
                ForWriting, True)
    tso.Write sXML
    tso.Close
    Set tso = Nothing
    Set fso = Nothing
    bResults = True
```

Any other type of request will return `False`:

```
Case Else
    m_ErrorOcurred = True
    bResults = False
    Call oError.SetErrorInfo("Unknown protocol: " & _
                asUriParts(0), PROGID & ".WriteXmlFileToServer", -1)
    End Select
End If

ErrHand:
    If Err.Number <> 0 Then
        m_ErrorOcurred = True
        bResults = False
        Call oError.SetErrorInfo("sURI = " & sURI  & ". " & Err.Description, _
                PROGID & ".WriteXmlFileToServer", Err.Number)
    End If
    WriteXmlFileToServer = bResults
End Function
```

Once again we complete the class with the ubiquitous `ObjectControl` methods:

```
Private Sub ObjectControl_Activate()
    Set oError = New ErrorUtils.ErrorInfo
    Set oCtx = GetObjectContext()
    Set oWds = oCtx.CreateInstance("WroxDataAccess.DataServices")
    m_ErrorOcurred = False
    Call oError.ClearErrorInfo
    m_sConnString = ""
End Sub

Private Function ObjectControl_CanBePooled() As Boolean
    ObjectControl_CanBePooled = False
End Function

Private Sub ObjectControl_Deactivate()
    Set oError = Nothing
    Set oWds = Nothing
    Set oCtx = Nothing
End Sub
```

The Back-End Application Class

As we mentioned, the real work is done by the back-end application methods, with some help from the `ProdTxUtils` class. The next class, `ProductDescriptionTx`, begins with the setting up of a few objects for it to use, and include the `Implements ObjectControl` statement:

```
'***********************************************************************
' WebProducts.ProductDescriptionTx
' Methods for handling product description data in the SQL Server
' and product description XML files.
'***********************************************************************
Option Explicit

Implements ObjectControl

Const PROG_ID As String = "WebProducts.ProductDescriptionTx"
Dim oDOM As MSXML.DOMDocument
Dim oErrors  As ErrorUtils.ErrorInfo
Dim TxUtils As ProdTxUtils
Dim oCtx As ObjectContext
```

Since the methods will need to interact with the file server web site and the SQL Server holding our product information table, a simple method is defined to configure a server URL and a connection string. Note that what it really does is pass the information on to the transaction utilities class, which is where it's really needed.

```
'***********************************************************************
' Public Function Configure(sConnStr As String,
'          sFileDestUri As String) As Boolean
'***********************************************************************
Public Function Configure(sConnStr As String, sFileDestUri As String) As Boolean
    TxUtils.FileUri = sFileDestUri
    TxUtils.ConnectionString = sConnStr
End Function
```

Creating a New Product

Here's the method for creating a new product. It needs to take the file and parse out the pertinent information for the database. The code will take that information and create a new entry in the database, and send the XML file to the file server for storage. `CreateNewProduct` takes a single `String` parameter: the product information XML we want to add to the database and the file server. It uses methods from `ProdTxUtils` to accomplish this. The function returns the final URI, which can be used to retrieve the XML file.

You'll see that the code uses a variable of type `dbInfo`. This is a user-defined data type to hold information about our product entry. It is defined in the `ProdTxUtils` class, which we'll look at later, and is a simple structure that makes it easier to pass around a block of data.

```
Public Function CreateNewProduct(ByVal sXmlDoc As String) As String
    On Error GoTo ErrHand

    Dim dbi As dbInfo
    Dim sReturn As String
    Dim sFileURI  As String

    dbi = TxUtils.SetMainInfo(sXmlDoc)
    dbi.Inventory = 1
```

The code populates the `dbi` variable by calling `SetMainInfo`; it also adds a default `Inventory` value, as this information is not kept in the product XML. If any errors occurred in `SetMainInfo`, the code prepares a response:

```
If TxUtils.ErrorOccured Then
    Call oError.SetErrorInfo("Could not set main info", _
                PROG_ID & ".CreateNewProduct", -1)
    sReturn = oError.GetErrorInfoXml()
Else
```

Otherwise, it calls `InsertNewProduct` to add the information to the database and send the XML to the file server; `InsertNewProduct` will return the updated XML if all went well:

```
sReturn = TxUtils.InsertNewProduct(dbi, sXmlDoc)
```

If `SetMainInfo failed`, it will return an empty string, in which case we set error information is set for the response:

```
    If Len(sReturn) < 1 Then
        Call oError.SetErrorInfo("Could not insert new file." & _
                TxUtils.GetErrorInfoXml, _
                PROG_ID & ".CreateNewProduct", -1)
        sReturn = oError.GetErrorInfoXml()
    End If
End If

ErrHand:
    If Err.Number <> 0 Then
        Call oError.SetErrorInfo(Err.Description & "; nLastLine  = " & _
                nLastLine, PROG_ID & ".CreateNewProduct", Err.Number)
        sReturn = oError.GetErrorInfoXml()
    End If

    CreateNewProduct = sReturn
End Function
```

Getting a Product List

A SOAP request for a list of available products is handled by the back-end `GetProductList` method. It's extremely straightforward, as it simply takes advantage of the data services class to get XML data from a SELECT query:

```
Public Function GetProductList() As String
    On Error GoTo ErrHand
    Dim sSQL As String
    Dim sResults As String
    Dim dbi As dbInfo
    sSQL = TxUtils.BuildSQL(SQL_SELECT, dbi)
    sResults = TxUtils.ExecuteSelect(sSQL)
    If Len(sResults) < 1 Then
        sResults = TxUtils.GetErrorInfoXml()
    End IfErrHand:
```

```
        If Err.Number <> 0 Then
            Call oErrors.SetErrorInfo(Err.Description, PROG_ID & _
                         ".CreateNewProduct", Err.Number)
            sResults = oErrors.GetErrorInfoXml()
        End If

        GetProductList = sResults
    End Function
```

Updating the Product File

When a request is made to save a product file, the SOAP wrapper decides if it should be saved as a new product or as an update. This next method, `UpdateProductFile`, handles the update; it's similar to the `CreateNewProduct` method, except that it does not try to obtain a new product ID. Instead, it parses out the main product information from the file, and uses the ID to perform the UPDATE transaction:

```
    Public Function UpdateProductFile(ByVal sXmlDoc As String) As String
        On Error GoTo ErrHand

        Dim dbi As dbInfo
        Dim sReturn As String
        Dim sFileURI  As String

        dbi = TxUtils.SetMainInfo(sXmlDoc)
        If TxUtils.ErrorOccured Then
            Call oError.SetErrorInfo("Could not set main info", _
                         PROG_ID & ".UpdateProductFile", -1)
            sReturn = oError.GetErrorInfoXml()
        Else
            sReturn = TxUtils.UpdateProduct(sXmlDoc, dbi)
            If Len(sReturn) < 1 Then
                Call oError.SetErrorInfo("Could not update file." & _
                         TxUtils.GetErrorInfoXml, PROG_ID _
                         & ".UpdateProductFile", -1)
                sReturn = oError.GetErrorInfoXml()
            End If
        End If

    ErrHand:
        If Err.Number <> 0 Then
            Call oErrors.SetErrorInfo(Err.Description, PROG_ID & _
                         ".UpdateProductFile", Err.Number)
            sReturn = oErrors.GetErrorInfoXml()
        End If
        UpdateProductFile = sReturn
    End Function
```

We use the `ObjectControl` events for initialization, and again use `CreateInstance` to instantiate any objects that are running under MTS:

```
    Private Sub ObjectControl_Activate()
        Set oDOM = New MSXML.DOMDocument
        Set oErrors = New ErrorUtils.ErrorInfo
        Set oCtx = GetObjectContext()
        Set TxUtils = oCtx.CreateInstance("WebProducts.ProdTxUtils")
    End Sub
```

```
Private Function ObjectControl_CanBePooled() As Boolean
    ObjectControl_CanBePooled = False
End Function

Private Sub ObjectControl_Deactivate()
    Set oDOM = Nothing
    Set oErrors = Nothing
    Set TxUtils = Nothing
End Sub
```

The SOAP Wrappers Class

The `SoapWrappers` class holds the methods that map to the SOAP requests. These functions serve to take the parameters sent in the SOAP body, and call into the `ProductDescriptionTx` routines.

We declare objects for the ASP `Application` object and `ObjectContext` object so that we can set the ASP `Application` values. We also declare references to the `ProductDescriptionTx` class, the `SoapUtilsMts` class, and the error utility class. We also have two private members for the database connection string and the URL for the XML file server web site:

```
'***********************************************************************
' WebProducts.SoapWrappers
' Class to hold the wrappers that SOAP will call to run the
' back-end application code.
' Uses a reference to the ASP object library to get configuration
' information.
'***********************************************************************
Option Explicit
Implements ObjectControl

Dim oApplication As ASPTypeLibrary.Application
Dim oCtx As ObjectContext
Dim ProdTx As WebProducts.ProductDescriptionTx
Dim oError As ErrorUtils.ErrorInfo
Dim oSoapUtils As SoapUtilsMts.Utils
Private m_sDbConnString As String
Private m_sFileServerURL As String
```

Once again `ObjectControl_Activate` is used to set up the objects. The code initializes the `oApplication` object to allow access to the ASP application variables where configuration information is stored. It then configures the `ProductDescriptionTx` object with the URL for the XML file server and the connection string for the `WebProducts` database:

```
Private Sub ObjectControl_Activate()
    Set oCtx = GetObjectContext()
    Set oError = New ErrorUtils.ErrorInfo
    Set ProdTx = oCtx.CreateInstance("WebProducts.ProductDescriptionTx")
    Set oSoapUtils = oCtx.CreateInstance("SoapUtilsMts.Utils")

    Set oApplication = oCtx.Item("Application")
    m_sDbConnString = oApplication("ConnString")       ' These were session
    m_sFileServerURL = oApplication("XmlServerURL")
    Call ProdTx.Configure(m_sDbConnString, m_sFileServerURL)
End Sub
```

Saving the Product File

The SOAP wrappers class provides methods for saving product information, and for retrieving a list of existing products. soapWrapSaveProductFile takes the SOAP body which contains the XML we want to save. It looks at the ID attribute in the XML to see if this is a new file or an update. If the file is new, it calls CreateNewProduct. If it is an update, it calls UpdateProductFile:

```
Public Function soapWrapSaveProductFile(sSoapParams As String) As String
    On Error GoTo ErrHand

    Dim sXmlDoc As String
    Dim sResults As String
    Dim sResponse As String
    Dim sDbConnStr As String
    Dim oDOM As DOMDocument
    Dim oElNode As IXMLDOMElement
    Dim sProdID As String


    Set oDOM = New DOMDocument
    ' We need to check the PRODUCT ID attribute. We can't simply
    ' save a document unless it has a valid ID (not 0)
    ' If it is a new document, we'll call CreateNewProduct instead
    ' of UpdateProductFile.
    If oDOM.loadXML(sSoapParams) Then
        ' Get the ID
        Set oElNode = oDOM.getElementsByTagName("PRODUCT").Item(0)
        sProdID = oElNode.Attributes.getNamedItem("ID").nodeValue
        ' Get the product file from the SOAP envelope
        Set oElNode = oDOM.getElementsByTagName("doc").Item(0)
        sXmlDoc = oElNode.childNodes.Item(0).xml
        If CInt(sProdID) = 0 Then
            sResults = ProdTx.CreateNewProduct(sXmlDoc)
        Else
            sResults = ProdTx.UpdateProductFile(sXmlDoc)
        End If
```

After calling the appropriate utility function, the code builds a response:

```
        sResponse = "<w:soapSaveProductFileResponse "
        sResponse = sResponse & " xmlns:w='www.wrox.com/VbXml' >" & vbLf
        sResponse = sResponse & "<doc>"
        sResponse = sResponse & sResults
        sResponse = sResponse & "</doc>" & vbLf
        sResponse = sResponse & "</w:soapSaveProductFileResponse>"
```

If the SOAP XML could not be parsed, an error response is built:

```
    Else
        ' DOM parse Error!
        sResponse = BuildParamParseErrorResponse("soapSaveProductFile", oDOM)
    End If
```

If there is a run time error, an error response is constructed to send back the information:

```
ErrHand:
    If Err.Number <> 0 Then
        sResponse = BuildComErrorResponse(Err)
    End If

    soapWrapSaveProductFile = sResponse
End Function
```

Handling Errors

Building an XML parsing error uses methods from the SOAP utilities class to construct detail and SOAP:Fault elements and wrap them in a SOAP response envelope:

```
Private Function BuildParamParseErrorResponse(sMethod As String, _
               oSoapDom As DOMDocument) As String
    Call oSoapUtils.SetDetailInfo("MyFault", "e", _
             "Error parsing parameters: " & oSoapDom.parseError.reason, _
             "www.wrox.org/VbSoap", _
             sMethod, -1)
    Call oSoapUtils.SetSoapFault(Invalid_Request, 0)
    Call oSoapUtils.BuildFaultXml(True)

    BuildParamParseErrorResponse = oSoapUtils.BuildSoapEvelopeFault(True)
End Function
```

BuildComErrorResponse works in a similar way:

```
Private Function BuildComErrorResponse(oVbErr As ErrObject) As String
    Call oSoapUtils.SetDetailInfo("MyFault", "e", _
             "COM Error: " & oVbErr.Description, _
             "www.wrox.org/VbSoap", _
             "SoapSrv.asp", -1)
    Call oSoapUtils.SetSoapFault(Application_Faulted, 0)
    Call oSoapUtils.BuildFaultXml(True)
    BuildComErrorResponse = oSoapUtils.BuildSoapEvelopeFault(True)
End Function
```

Getting the Product List

In order to edit a file, it would be useful to provide a list of catalog entries. This method wraps a call to a back-end function that queries the Catalog table and returns an XML string with the results. The editor application will use this to provide a list of files that can be downloaded and edited. GetProductList does not use any parameters, so soapWrapGetProductList does not need to extract any information from the SOAP XML:

```
Public Function soapWrapGetProductList(sSoapParams As String) As String
    On Error GoTo ErrHand
    Dim sResults As String
    Dim sResponse  As String

    sResults = ProdTx.GetProductList()
    sResponse = "<w:soapGetProductListResponse "
    sResponse = sResponse & " xmlns:w='www.wrox.com/VbXml' >" & vbLf
    sResponse = sResponse & "<list>"
```

```
        sResponse = sResponse & sResults
        sResponse = sResponse & "</list>" & vbLf
        sResponse = sResponse & "</w: soapGetProductListResponse >"

ErrHand:
    If Err.Number <> 0 Then
        sResponse = BuildComErrorResponse(Err)
    End If
    soapWrapGetProductList = sResponse
End Function
```

The code is rounded off with the remaining `ObjectControl` routines:

```
Private Function ObjectControl_CanBePooled() As Boolean
    ObjectControl_CanBePooled = False
End Function

Private Sub ObjectControl_Deactivate()
    Set oCtx = Nothing
    Set ProdTx = Nothing
    Set oApplication = Nothing
    Set oError = Nothing
    Set oSoapUtils = Nothing
End Sub
```

Additions to the Product File Editor

Now that we have some productive transactions, and a new infrastructure, we can add some new functions to the product description editor (described in Chapter 8) to allow us to save and retrieve XML files over the network. The editor will use SOAP requests to send and retrieve product information. To do this, we need to give the editor HTTP capabilities. We'll build a new ActiveX DLL that provides this.

The project is called `SoapRequest`, and has a single class, `XmlHttp`. It requires a reference to the Microsoft XML parser.

```
'*********************************************************************
' Class SoapRequest.XmlHttp
'*********************************************************************
Option Explicit
Private oHttp As MSXML.XMLHTTPRequest
Private oDOM As MSXML.DOMDocument
Private m_sTransactionNamespace As String
Private m_SoapServer As String
Private m_sErrDesc As String
Private m_lErrNumber As Long
Private m_sErrSource As String
Private m_nTimeoutSeconds As Integer
Const HTTPRQ_COMPLETE As Long = 4
```

Error information is exposed as read-only using `Property` methods:

```
Public Property Get ErrorDescription() As String
    ErrorDescription = m_sErrDesc
End Property

Public Property Get ErrorNumber() As Long
    ErrorNumber = m_lErrNumber
End Property

Public Property Get ErrorSource() As String
    ErrorSource = m_sErrSource
End Property
```

When sending a SOAP request, we need to provide a special HTTP header that provides the SOAP methods being called and the namespace it belongs to; the `TransactionNamespaceURI` property is used to help build this:

```
Public Property Get TransactionNamespaceURI() As String
    TransactionNamespaceURI = m_sTransactionNamespace
End Property

Public Property Let TransactionNamespaceURI(ByVal sNamespaceURI As String)
    m_sTransactionNamespace = sNamespaceURI
End Property
```

The `SoapServer` property holds the URL for the SOAP server:

```
Public Property Get SoapServer() As String
    SoapServer = m_SoapServer
End Property

Public Property Let SoapServerURL(ByVal sServer As String)
    m_SoapServer = sServer
End Property
```

Since HTTP requests may fail, a property is provided for a request timeout when a `POST` is sent to the SOAP server:

```
Public Property Get TimeoutSeconds() As Integer
    TimeoutSeconds = m_nTimeoutSeconds
End Property

Public Property Let TimeoutSeconds(ByVal nTimeoutSeconds As Integer)
    m_nTimeoutSeconds = nTimeoutSeconds
End Property
```

The SOAP specification mandates that the HTTP request includes a special header called `SOAPMethodName`. It includes the namespace for the request and the name of the method being called. `GetMethodName` looks at the SOAP payload that is to be sent, and retrieves the name of the SOAP method:

```
Private Function GetMethodName(sPayload As String) As String
    On Error GoTo ErrHand
    Dim oPayDOM As DOMDocument
    Dim oEl As IXMLDOMElement
    Dim asTemp() As String
    Dim sMethodName As String

    Call ClearErrorInfo
    Set oPayDOM = New DOMDocument

    If oPayDOM.loadXML(sPayload) Then
        Set oEl = _
            oPayDOM.getElementsByTagName("SOAP:Body").Item(0).childNodes.Item(0)
```

The method tries to load the SOAP payload, and if there are no parsing errors, it retrieves the first child of the SOAP:Body element. The code then gets the element name, and splits the value on the ":" delimiter to get the base name without the namespace prefix:

```
If Not oEl Is Nothing Then
    sMethodName = oEl.nodeName        ' baseName
    If InStr(sMethodName, ":") Then
        asTemp = Split(sMethodName, ":")
        sMethodName = asTemp(1)
```

If there is no ":" (and therefore no namespace), the code sets a response of an empty string and registers error information:

```
Else
    sMethodName = ""
    Call SetErrorInfo("Error getting method name.", _
        "SoapRequest.XmlHttp.GetMethodName", -1)
End If
Else
```

If no SOAP:Body element was found, then error information is set as well:

```
sMethodName = ""
Call SetErrorInfo("Error getting method name. No SOAP:Body", _
    "SoapRequest.XmlHttp.GetMethodName", -1)
End If
```

Failing to parse the SAOP payload will also return an empty string:

```
Else
    sMethodName = ""
    Call SetErrorInfo("Error getting method name.", _
        "SoapRequest.XmlHttp.GetMethodName", -1)
End If

ErrHand:
    If Err.Number <> 0 Then
        Call SetErrorInfo("COM error: " & Err.Description, _
            "SoapRequest.XmlHttp.GetMethodName", Err.Number)
        sMethodName = ""
    End If

    GetMethodName = sMethodName
End Function
```

A SOAP request is POSTed by passing the SOAP payload to PostRequest:

```
Public Function PostRequest(sSoapPayload As String) As String
    On Error GoTo ErrHand
    Dim sMethodName As String
    Dim sResults As String
    Dim oDomRsp As DOMDocument
    Dim sDecoded As String
    Dim nIdx As Integer
    Dim datWaitUntil As Date
    Dim sErrorReason As String
    Dim oDOM As MSXML.DOMDocument
    Dim oHttp As MSXML.XMLHTTPRequest
```

An XMLHTTPRequest object is declared (an addition to the Microsoft XML object that performs HTTP requests), and a DOMDocument exists for manipulating the XML being sent and received. First, any existing error information is cleared before the objects are initialized:

```
    Call ClearErrorInfo
    Set oHttp = New XMLHTTPRequest
    Set oDOM = New DOMDocument
```

The code checks that a SOAP server URL and a transaction namespace have been provided. It then tries to load the SOAP payload into a DOM:

```
    If (Len(m_SoapServer) > 0) And (Len(m_sTransactionNamespace) > 0) Then
        If oDOM.loadXML(sSoapPayload) Then
```

If the payload can be loaded, the code retrieves the request method name and begins to set HTTP headers:

```
            sMethodName = GetMethodName(sSoapPayload)
            If Len(sMethodName) Then
                oHttp.open "POST", m_SoapServer, False
                oHttp.setRequestHeader "Content-type:", "text/xml"
                oHttp.setRequestHeader "Content-length:", CStr(Len(sSoapPayload))
                oHttp.setRequestHeader "SOAPMethodName:", _
                                m_sTransactionNamespace & "#" & sMethodName
```

The XMLHTTPRequest object sends the request to the SOAP server; a timed loop is set up to limit how long the code will wait for a response. The code will wait until either the timeout has expired, or until the XMLHTTPRequest readyState property indicates that the response has been received:

```
                oHttp.send oDOM
                ' Set up a timer so we don't wait forever
                ' for a response
                datWaitUntil = DateAdd("s", m_nTimeoutSeconds, Now())
                Do While (oHttp.readyState <> HTTPRQ_COMPLETE) And _
                            (datWaitUntil > Now())
                    DoEvents
                Loop
```

If the ready state is not complete, then the response and error information is set:

```
If (oHttp.readyState <> HTTPRQ_COMPLETE) Then
    sResults = ""
    Call SetErrorInfo("Request timed out", _
        "SoapRequest.XmlHttp.PostRequest", _
        -1)
```

Otherwise, the HTTP response headers and body are collected:

```
Else
    sResults = oHttp.getAllResponseHeaders
    sResults = sResults & oHttp.responseText
End If
```

If any of the required information could be retrieved, error information is registered, and an empty response prepared:

```
        Else
        ' Could not retrieve method name
        ' Error information is set in GetMethodName
            sResults = ""
        End If
    Else
        Call SetErrorInfo("Error parsing request: " & _
            oDOM.parseError.reason & _
            "filepos: " & oDOM.parseError.filepos, _
            "SoapRequest.XmlHttp.PostRequest", oDOM.parseError.errorCode)
        sResults = ErrorDescription
    End If
Else
    ' no server name or no namespace!
    If Len(m_SoapServer) < 1 Then
        sErrorReason = "No remote server was specified."
    Else
        sErrorReason = "No transaction namespace was given."
    End If
    Call SetErrorInfo(sErrorReason, "SoapRequest.XmlHttp.PostRequest", -1)
    sResults = ""
End If
```

Run time errors are trapped at the end of the function:

```
ErrHand:
    If Err.Number <> 0 Then
        Call SetErrorInfo("COM error: " & Err.Description, _
            "SoapRequest.XmlHttp.PostRequest", Err.Number)
        sResults = ""
    End If
    Set oHttp = Nothing
    Set oDOM = Nothing
    PostRequest = sResults
End Function
```

The class uses the `SetErrorInfo` method to set the error information in one call:

```
Private Sub SetErrorInfo(sDesc As String, sSource As String, lNumber As Long)
    m_sErrDesc = sDesc
    m_lErrNumber = lNumber
    m_sErrSource = sSource
End Sub
```

There's also a method to clear the error information:

```
Private Sub ClearErrorInfo()
    m_sErrDesc = ""
    m_lErrNumber = 0
    m_sErrSource = ""
End Sub
```

When the class is first called, the timeout property is given a default value:

```
Private Sub Class_Initialize()
    m_nTimeoutSeconds = 120
End Sub
```

Now we just need to build the project so we can use the class in the product information editor, and add some new functions. We now have a class to send SOAP requests, so next we will add some functions to take advantage of it.

We will add a new class, called `WebTx`, to the product editor project. In addition to sending SOAP requests through the `SoapRequest.XmlHttp` object, it will manage the display of product listings, and configuration of the new web functions. (This requires adding a reference to the `SoapRequest.XmlHttp` class to the editor project. The class has no global declarations, and should simply have `Option Explicit` at the top.)

The WebTx Class

For saving files, we have a method to build SOAP requests. It takes the product information XML as a parameter, and wraps a SOAP envelope around it:

```
Public Function BuildSoapRequestSaveProdFile(sProdXml As String) As String
    Dim sSoap As String

    If Len(sProdXml) > 0 Then
        sSoap = ""
        sSoap = sSoap & "<SOAP:Envelope"
        sSoap = sSoap & " xmlns:SOAP='urn:schemas-xmlsoap-org:soap.v1' "
        sSoap = sSoap & " SOAP:encodingStyle="
        sSoap = sSoap & "'urn:schemas-xmlsoap-org:soap.v1'>" & vbLf
        sSoap = sSoap & " <SOAP:Body>" & vbLf
        sSoap = sSoap & "  <w:soapSaveProductFile "
        sSoap = sSoap & " xmlns:w='www.wrox.com/VbXml'>" & vbLf
        sSoap = sSoap & "   <doc>" & vbLf
        sSoap = sSoap & sProdXml & vbLf
        sSoap = sSoap & "   </doc>" & vbLf
        sSoap = sSoap & "  </w:soapSaveProductFile>" & vbLf
        sSoap = sSoap & " </SOAP:Body>" & vbLf
        sSoap = sSoap & "</SOAP:Envelope>"      Else
        sSoap = ""
    End If
    BuildSoapRequestSaveProdFile = sSoap
End Function
```

Building a Product List

When a user wants to open a product information file from the server, the editor will make a SOAP request to get a list of all products. `BuildSoapRequestGetProductList` creates the XML for a SOAP request to pull back this list:

```
Public Function BuildSoapRequestGetProductList() As String
    Dim sSoap As String
    sSoap = ""
    sSoap = sSoap & "<SOAP:Envelope"
    sSoap = sSoap & " xmlns:SOAP='urn:schemas-xmlsoap-org:soap.v1' "
    sSoap = sSoap & " SOAP:encodingStyle="
    sSoap = sSoap & "'urn:schemas-xmlsoap-org:soap.v1'>" & vbLf
    sSoap = sSoap & " <SOAP:Body>" & vbLf
    sSoap = sSoap & "   <w:soapGetProductList "
    sSoap = sSoap & "xmlns:w='www.wrox.com/VbXml'>" & vbLf
    sSoap = sSoap & "   </w:soapGetProductList>" & vbLf
    sSoap = sSoap & " </SOAP:Body>" & vbLf
    sSoap = sSoap & "</SOAP:Envelope>"

    BuildSoapRequestGetProductList = sSoap
End Function
```

After sending a SOAP request, we need to extract the body from the response:

```
Public Function GetSoapBody(ByVal sPostData As String) As String
    On Error GoTo ErrHand
    Dim asPost() As String
    Dim sXML As String
    ' The data should contain an empty line; actually,
    ' two consecutive vbLf. But it might not.
    sPostData = Replace(sPostData, vbCrLf, vbLf)
    asPost = Split(sPostData, vbLf & vbLf)
    If UBound(asPost) > 0 Then
        sXML = asPost(1)
    Else
        MsgBox "Error extracting SOAP body from response.", _
               vbExclamation, "Error"
    End If

ErrHand:
    If Err.Number <> 0 Then
        MsgBox "Error extracting SOAP body from response:" & _
             '  Err.Description, vbExclamation, "Error"
        sXML = ""
    End If
    GetSoapBody = sXML
End Function
```

Retrieving the Document Contents

This next method, `GetReturnedDoc`, retrieves the contents of the doc element after a file has been saved to the server and the SOAP request has returned:

```
Public Function GetReturnedDoc(sSoapBody As String) As String
    On Error GoTo ErrHand

    Dim oDOM As DOMDocument
    Dim sDoc As String
    Dim oEl As IXMLDOMElement

    Set oDOM = New DOMDocument
    If Not oDOM.loadXML(sSoapBody) Then
        sDoc = ""
    Else
        Set oEl = oDOM.getElementsByTagName("doc").Item(0)
        sDoc = oEl.childNodes(0).xml
    End If

ErrHand:
    If Err.Number <> 0 Then
        sDoc = ""
    End If
    GetReturnedDoc = sDoc
End Function
```

When a SOAP request is made to retrieve a list of products, the response contains a series of Row elements holding the basic product information from the database. To display this list, the code will iterate through the Row elements and pull out the attributes holding the data fields. The function makes use of the `frmWebFileList` form, populating a flex grid control with the product information. (We'll look at the code behind `frmWebFileList` in a moment.) When a user selects a file from the grid and clicks the OK button, an HTTP GET request is made using the URL from the XmlDetails field.

```
Public Function DisplayFileList(sXML As String) As Boolean
    Dim oDOM As DOMDocument
    Dim sItem As String
    Dim oEl As IXMLDOMElement
    Dim oNodeList As IXMLDOMNodeList
    Dim nIdx As Integer
    Dim bResults As Boolean
    Dim sProdID As String
    Dim sCategory As String
    Dim sName As String
    Dim sURI As String

    Set oDOM = New DOMDocument
```

The function takes the SOAP response XML and tries to load it into a DOM. If it successfully loads the XML, it displays `frmWebFileList`. It then gets a NodeList of all Row elements, and for each element, adds an item to the grid control on the form:

```
        If oDOM.loadXML(sXML) Then
            Load frmWebFileList
            Set oNodeList = oDOM.getElementsByTagName("Row")
            For nIdx = 0 To oNodeList.length - 1
                Set oEl = oNodeList.Item(nIdx)
                sProdID = oEl.Attributes.getNamedItem("ProdID").nodeValue
                sCategory = oEl.Attributes.getNamedItem("Category").nodeValue
                If Len(Trim(sCategory)) < 1 Then
                    sCategory = String(10, " ")
                End If
                sName = oEl.Attributes.getNamedItem("Name").nodeValue
                If Len(Trim(sName)) < 1 Then
                    sName = String(10, " ")
                End If
                sURI = oEl.Attributes.getNamedItem("XmlDetails").nodeValue
                sItem = sProdID & vbTab & sName & vbTab & sCategory & vbTab & sURI
                If Not frmWebFileList.AddItem(sItem) Then
                    bResults = False
                End If
            Next
            frmWebFileList.Show
```

If the XML could not be loaded, an error message is displayed:

```
        Else
            bResults = False
            MsgBox "Error displaying list of files", vbExclamation, "Error"
        End If

        DisplayFileList = bResults
    End Function
```

`GetListData` takes the SOAP response body from the request for the product list, and retrieves the list XML:

```
    Public Function GetListData(sSoapBody As String) As String
        Dim oDOM As DOMDocument
        Dim sXML As String
        Dim oEl As IXMLDOMElement

        Set oDOM = New DOMDocument
        If oDOM.loadXML(sSoapBody) Then
            Set oEl = oDOM.getElementsByTagName("list").Item(0)
            sXML = oEl.xml
        Else
            sXML = ""
        End If
        GetListData = sXML
    End Function
```

If a user has selected a product file from the list displayed on frmWebFileList, a request is made to the XML file server. This function performs the GET using the XMLHTTPRequest object and returns the XML response:

```
Public Function RetrieveFile(sURL As String) As String
    On Error GoTo ErrHand
    Dim oHttpRq As MSXML.XMLHTTPRequest
    Dim oDomResponse As DOMDocument
    Dim sXML As String

    Set oDomResponse = New DOMDocument
    Set oHttpRq = New XMLHTTPRequest

    oHttpRq.open "GET", sURL, False
    oHttpRq.send
    Set oDomResponse = oHttpRq.responseXML
    Debug.Print oDomResponse.xml
    RetrieveFile = oDomResponse.xml

ErrHand:
    If Err.Number <> 0 Then
        RetrieveFile = ""
    End If
End Function
```

We need to add a reference to the SoapRequest.XmlHttp class to the editor project (which we had named XMLEditor), and add these declarations in frmMain:

```
Dim oSoapRqst As SoapRequest.XmlHttp  ' SOAP posting DLL
Dim oWebTx As WebTx                   ' Our SOAP request tools
```

Implementing the Web Menu Item

Under the Web menu item, we need to have three submenu items: Open, Save, and Configure. We add these event handlers in frmMain:

```
Private Sub mnuWebConfig_Click()
    Call ConfigureWeb
End Sub

Private Sub mnuWebOpen_Click()
    Call OpenWebFile
End Sub

Private Sub mnuWebSave_Click()
    Call SaveWebFile
End Sub
```

In order to construct and make SOAP requests, the application needs to know the transaction namespace; ConfigureWeb displays a form allowing the user to set this information in the registry:

```
Private Sub ConfigureWeb()
    On Error GoTo ErrHand
    Dim sSoapUrl As String
    Dim sTxNamespace As String
    frmWebConfig.Show vbModal
    Call SaveSetting(APPNAME, "Startup", "SoapUrl", g_sSoapUrl)
    Call SaveSetting(APPNAME, "Startup", "TxNamespace", g_sTxNamespace)

ErrHand:
        If Err.Number <> 0 Then
            MsgBox Err.Description, vbExclamation, "Config error."
        End If
End Sub
```

This displays a new form, `frmWebConfig`, which prompts the user for configuration information:

`frmWebConfig` has two text boxes: `txtSoapUrl` and `txtTxNamespace`, corresponding labels, and OK and Cancel buttons. It verifies that both fields have entries, and puts the data in the registry:

```
'***********************************************************
' frmWebConfig
' Dialog box to handle configuration of web transactions
'***********************************************************
Option Explicit

Private Sub CancelButton_Click()
    Unload Me
End Sub

Private Sub Form_Load()
    txtSoapUrl.Text = g_sSoapUrl
    txtTxNamespace.Text = g_sTxNamespace
End Sub

Private Sub OKButton_Click()
    If Len(txtSoapUrl.Text) < 1 Then
        MsgBox "You must enter a SOAP URL!", vbCritical, "Missing entry."
    Else
        If Len(txtTxNamespace.Text) < 1 Then
            MsgBox "You must enter a transaction namespace!", vbCritical, _
                "Missing entry."
```

```
            Else
                g_sSoapUrl = txtSoapUrl.Text
                g_sTxNamespace = txtTxNamespace.Text
                Unload Me
            End If
        End If
End Sub
```

Some global variables have been added in the `Declares.bas` module to pass the configuration information back to `ConfigureWeb`:

```
' SOAP configuration information added to Declares.bas
Global g_sSoapUrl As String
Global g_sTxNamespace  As String
Global Const APPNAME As String = "Wrox Product Editor"     ' For SOAP settings
                                                           ' in registry
```

Opening a product file from the server calls the `OpenWebFile` function:

```
Public Function OpenWebFile()As Boolean
    Dim sSoapTx As String
    Dim sResults As String
    Dim sSoapBody As String
    Dim sListData As String

    sSoapTx = oWebTx.BuildSoapRequestGetProductList()
    With oSoapRqst
        .SoapServerURL = g_sSoapUrl
        .TransactionNamespaceURI = g_sTxNamespace
        .TimeoutSeconds = 300
        sResults = .PostRequest(sSoapTx)
    End With
    ' Now we need to pull out the response body
    sSoapBody = oWebTx.GetSoapBody(sResults)
    sListData = oWebTx.GetListData(sSoapBody)
    If Len(sListData) > 0 Then
        Call oWebTx.DisplayFileList(sListData)
    Else
        MsgBox "Error getting list data from SOAP response.", vbExclamation, _
               "Error."
    End If
    Debug.Print sListData
End Function
```

It basically calls a method on `oSoapRqst` to build a SOAP request and `POST` the transaction to the SOAP server.

To save a file to the server, the code calls `SaveWebFile`:

```
Private Function SaveWebFile() As Boolean
    On Error GoTo ErrHand

    Dim bRes as Boolean
    Dim sErrMsg As String
    Dim sResults As String
    Dim sSoapTx As String
    Dim sSoapBody As String
    Dim sReturnedDoc As String
    Dim oDomResults As DOMDocument
    Dim sProdXml  As String
```

The function first checks that SOAP configuration information has been provided. If it hasn't, the user is prompted to enter it:

```
If (Len(g_sTxNamespace) < 1) Or (Len(g_sSoapUrl) < 1) Then
    ' Prompt for config info
    Call ConfigureWeb
End If
```

The form data is then turned into an XML string by calling BuildDocument:

```
Screen.MousePointer = vbHourglass
sProdXml = BuildDocument()
```

A SOAP request is constructed for saving the file to the server, and POSTed to the SOAP server:

```
sSoapTx = oWebTx.BuildSoapRequestSaveProdFile(sProdXml)
If Len(sSoapTx) > 0 Then
    With oSoapRqst
        .SoapServerURL = g_sSoapUrl
        .TransactionNamespaceURI = g_sTxNamespace
        .TimeoutSeconds = 300
        sResults = .PostRequest(sSoapTx)
    End With
Else
    MsgBox "Error creating SOAP transaction", _
        vbExclamation, "Web save error."
    SaveWebFile = False
    Exit Function
End If
```

The body of the SOAP response is retrieved; it contains the original XML, plus an updated product ID if this was a new file:

```
sSoapBody = oWebTx.GetSoapBody(sResults)
sReturnedDoc = oWebTx.GetReturnedDoc(sSoapBody)
Set oDomResults = New DOMDocument
If Not oDomResults.loadXML(sReturnedDoc) Then
    MsgBox "File server did not return proper XML:" & _
        oDomResults.parseError.reason, vbCritical, _
        "XML error"
    bRes = False
Else
```

The returned document is then loaded into the application:

```
            If Not ParseDomIntoForm(oDomResults) Then
                MsgBox "Error parsing data file into form", vbCritical
                bRes = False
             Else
                bRes = True
            End If
        End If

ErrHand:
        If Err.Number <> 0 Then
            sErrMsg = "Error saving file to remote server."
            bRes = False
        End if
        SaveWebFile = bRes
        Screen.MousePointer = vbDefault

End Function
```

Displaying the Data

The form for displaying the list of product information is called frmWebFileList. It contains a flex grid control, called grdFiles, and OK and Cancel buttons. It looks like this:

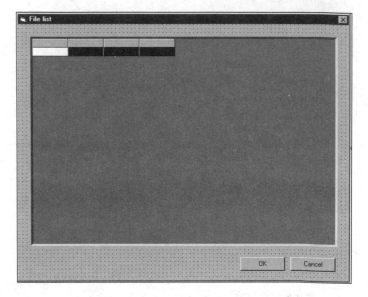

The grid is populated by the DisplayFileList function, which loads the form into memory and calls AddItem for each row of Catalog data. Here is the code for the form:

```
Option Explicit
Const GRIDCOLWIDTH1 As Long = 500
Const GRIDCOLWIDTH2 As Long = 1500
Const GRIDCOLWIDTH3 As Long = 1500
Const SCROLLBARWIDTH As Long = 350

Private g_sPodUrl As String
```

```
Public Function AddItem(sItem As String) As Boolean
    On Error GoTo ErrHand
    grdFiles.AddItem sItemErrHand:
    If Err.Number <> 0 Then
        AddItem = False
    End If
    AddItem = True
End Function

Private Sub CancelButton_Click()
    Unload Me
End Sub

Private Sub Form_Load()
    Dim lGridWidth
    lGridWidth = grdFiles.Width - SCROLLBARWIDTH
    grdFiles.Cols = 4
    grdFiles.ColWidth(0) = GRIDCOLWIDTH1
    grdFiles.ColWidth(1) = GRIDCOLWIDTH2
    grdFiles.ColWidth(2) = GRIDCOLWIDTH3
    grdFiles.ColWidth(3) = lGridWidth-(GRIDCOLWIDTH1+GRIDCOLWIDTH2+GRIDCOLWIDTH3)
End Sub
```

Selecting a row sets a URL variable as follows:

```
Private Sub grdFiles_Click()
    g_sPodUrl = grdFiles.TextMatrix(grdFiles.RowSel, 3)
End Sub
```

This is used to retrieve the file if the user clicks the **OK** button. The retrieved file is sent to the `ParseDomIntoForm` function (part of `frmMain`) to be loaded into the editor:

```
Private Sub OKButton_Click()
    Dim oWebTx As WebTx
    Dim sFileXml As String
    Dim oDOM As DOMDocument

    Set oWebTx = New WebTx
    Set oDOM = New DOMDocument
    sFileXml = oWebTx.RetrieveFile(g_sPodUrl)
    If oDOM.loadXML(sFileXml) Then
        Call frmMain.ParseDomIntoForm(oDOM)
        Unload Me
    Else
        MsgBox "Error loading file into form", vbCritical, "Error"
    End If
End Sub
```

In Chapter 5 we learned about XPointer and XLink; in Chapter 10 we'll see how to implement a VB object to resolve XLinks. We need to make a small change to how we build the product XML before saving it so that relationships among products can be established using XLink. First, the list of related products should display the items with both the product name and ID; a list item will look like this:

```
Sample [200]
```

We then change the `BuildDocument` method by adding two new variables, and some code to insert XLink information into the XML:

```
Private Function BuildDocument() As String
    On Error GoTo ErrHand
    Dim sDescription As String
    Dim nIdx As Integer
    Dim sXML As String

    Dim sRelName As String
    Dim sRelID As String

    sXML = "<PRODUCT ID='" & txtProductID & _
           "' xmlns:xl='http://www.w3.org/1999/xlink/namespaces/'>" & vbCrLf
    sXML = sXML & "<NAME>" & txtProductName & "</NAME>" & vbCrLf
    sXML = sXML & "<PRICE>" & txtPrice & "</PRICE>" & vbCrLf
    sXML = sXML & xmlTxtProductDesc.Text & vbCrLf
    sXML = sXML & "<CATEGORY>" & _
           lstProductCategory.List(lstProductCategory.ListIndex) & _
           "</CATEGORY>" & vbCrLf
    sXML = sXML & "<RELATEDURLS>" & vbCrLf
    For nIdx = 0 To cmbUrls.ListCount - 1
        sXML = sXML & "<URL href='" & cmbUrls.List(nIdx) & "' />" & vbCrLf
    Next
    sXML = sXML & "</RELATEDURLS>" & vbCrLf
    sXML = sXML & "<RELATEDPRODUCTS>" & vbCrLf
    For nIdx = 0 To lstRelatedProducts.ListCount - 1
        Call GetSegments(lstRelatedProducts.List(nIdx), sRelName, sRelID)
        sXML = sXML & _
               "<PRODUCT id='" & sRelID & _
               "' name='" & sRelName & "' xl:type='simple' xl:Show='replace'" & _
               "xl:actuate='onRequest' xl:href='" & sRelID & "'/>" & vbCrLf
    Next
    sXML = sXML & "</RELATEDPRODUCTS>" & vbCrLf
    sXML = sXML & "</PRODUCT>"
```

We also add a new function, `GetSegments`, to extract the product name and ID from the selected **Related Products** list:

```
Private Function GetSegments(sRelProd As String, sName As String, sID As String) _
                        As Boolean
    Dim asTemp() As String

    asTemp = Split(sRelProd, "[")
    sName = Trim(asTemp(0))
    sID = Trim(Replace(asTemp(1), "]", ""))
    If (Len(sName) = 0) Or (Len(sName) = 0) Then
        GetSegments = False
    Else
        GetSegments = True
    End If

End Function
```

Putting this all together, a typical flow of events for editing a file and saving it to the server would go like the diagram on the following page:

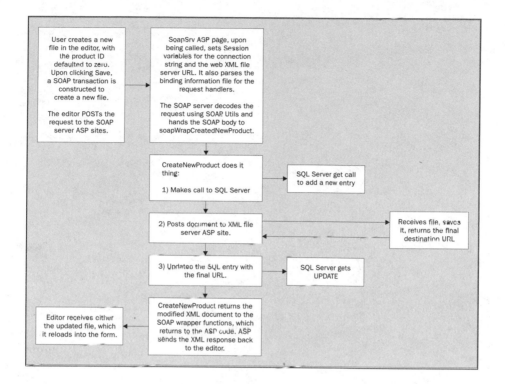

Summary

In this chapter we looked at:

❑ How our product information editor would be able to exchange data with a remote machine

❑ How we can use SOAP requests as the transport medium

❑ The pros and cons of WebClasses, and we decided instead to use ASP pages that called into MTS components

❑ An overview of MTS and how it communicates with client applications

We then did some further work on our sample application and:

❑ Modified the SOAP utility class from Chapter 7 so that it would run under MTS and use ASP variables for storing method information

❑ Built some additional objects to handle SOAP requests

❑ Constructed a class for performing database services

❑ Built an MTS object and web pages for storing XML on a file server

In the next chapter, we'll see how to build a Visual Basic component to implement XLink functions.

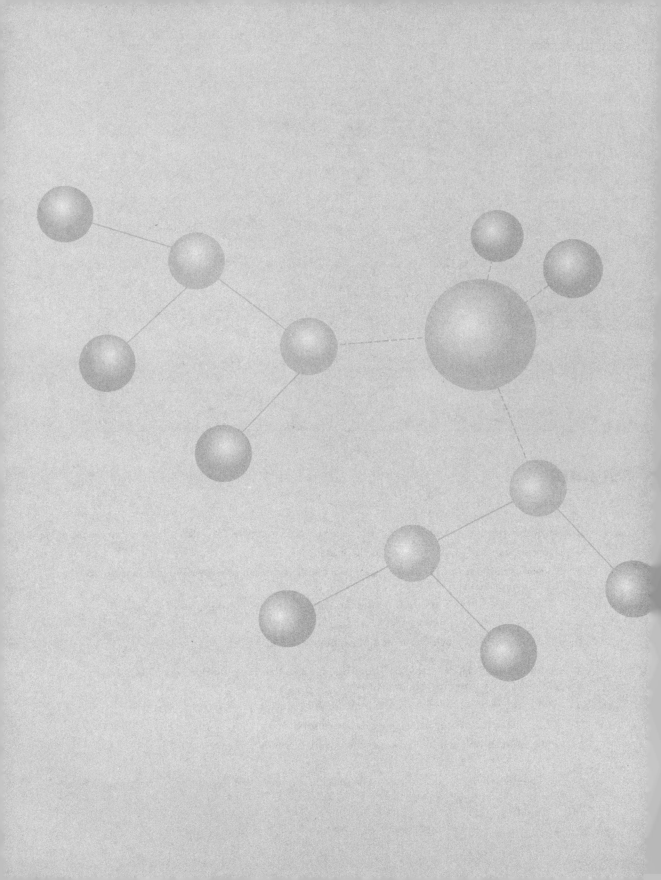

Using a VB Component to Implement Linking

In the previous chapter we saw how to create server side objects that can be used to store and retrieve XML describing the product a user is interested in. To display this to a user, we have several options:

❑ Create a VB application that displays several elements (including information from the database and information that is stored in the XML files) as we want them to appear. This was the approach we took for editing the content. However, the problem with this approach when viewing the application is that there are so many customers and we don't want to ask them to install it on their machines just to view our product descriptions. What is more, they might run machines on another platform (such as Linux) and our VB application would be worthless to them. This situation screams for a web-based solution.

❑ Show the content of our product description files in a web browser that can display XML with CSS. This would work, but only for users with supporting browsers.

❑ Convert our product description to an HTML page that can be displayed in any HTML browser. We can use XSLT (described in Chapter 4) on the server to do the transformation.

In this case, where we want broad reach (that is, we would ideally want any browser to be able to view our product information), we'll go for the last option. However, note that the document on the server not only contains plain descriptions, but also elements with XLink information. These elements refer to related products in the database. An example document would look like this:

```
<PRODUCT>
  <NAME>Casio E-105</NAME>
  <PRICE>$450.00</PRICE>
  <DESCRIPTION>
    <!-Description text here -->
  </DESCRIPTION>
  <CATEGORY>PDAs</CATEGORY>
  <RELATEDURLS>
    <URL href='www.casio.com' />
  </RELATEDURLS>
  <RELATEDPRODUCTS>
    <PRODUCT id='pda2345' name='docking station'
      xl:type="simple"
      xl:show="new"
      xl:actuate="onRequest"
      xl:href="pda2345.xml"
    />
    <PRODUCT name='pda543' name='net adapter'
      xl:type="simple"
      xl:show="new"
      xl:actuate="onRequest"
      xl:href="pda543.xml"
    />
  </RELATEDPRODUCTS>
</PRODUCT>
```

In this example, the XLink elements must be converted to HTML links in order for them to be displayed in the user's browser. This could easily be done using an XSLT stylesheet, because the links are all of a simple type and contain no XPointer expressions attached.

In this chapter we will try to provide more than just a minimum implementation of XLink, which will allow extended use of XLink in the application without changing the entire architecture. For example, you might think of placing all relations between products in a central link base to improve maintainability. The task of this component will be to preprocess more complex XLink information to a format that we can easily handle with an XSLT stylesheet.

But is that the right order of events? XLink was designed to be resolved on the client in the XML browser. So, according to the XLink specification, the correct order of events is:

❑ The browser retrieves XML content, including XLink information.

❑ The XLink information is parsed and some of the linked content (the `actuate=onLoad` links) is immediately downloaded.

❑ If the user clicks any of the links, that resource is also downloaded by the browser.

Compare this with the server side generation of a user interface (which is what we are now trying to do):

- ❑ The generator retrieves XML content, including XLink information.

- ❑ The content is converted to HTML and sent to the browser. It is not possible to leave the XLink information in the document. XLinks often refer to the target location of the link using element names and the position of the target location in the document. During the transformation, this will all change. The only thing you can do is interpret the links during the transformation and try to convert the XLinks to HTML links (where possible).

- ❑ If the user clicks a link, this is handled in the usual way by the HTML browser

We want to use transformation to create the user interface and we want to use XLink on the client for its powerful linking capacities. Once the content is with the browser, the XLink information is lost (HTML just does not allow the complex linking that XLink does). The XLink and XSLT specifications do not give details about how to handle the combination of XLink resources and transforming resources.

So, the best solution would be to create a client-side application that can deal with both specifications, and which shows a transformed document, while remembering which elements are linked to which other resources. Then the source location and the target location of the link can be mapped to the HTML that is created during transformation and the browser could show a link between these two HTML fragments. There would still be some trade-offs to be made, such as what happens if the same XML content shows up at different places within the transformed HTML document, but it would be an acceptable solution. Sadly, the advent of XML browsers supporting this functionality is still a long way off, and so, we'll have to compromise and come up with a solution somewhere in the middle.

Our Chosen Approach

What we will do is:

- ❑ Assume a standard HTML browser.

- ❑ Try to implement link behavior in HTML links.

- ❑ Implement as many features as possible on the server.

- ❑ Combine the generation of the user interface and the creation of the HTML links in a stylesheet.

- ❑ Put the complex tasks in a server side VB component, where parsing xpointer() expressions, and retrieving parts of remote documents wil be carried out.

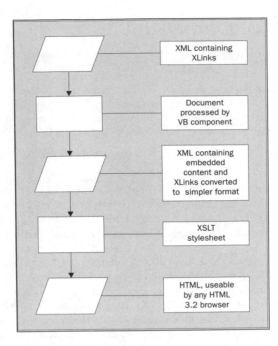

Simple Links

Let's first have a look at some simple links, which might appear in the product description XML files, their desired effect and how they might be implemented in our user interface (check back to Chapter 5 for an explanation of the XLink syntax):

Code	Effect	Implementation in HTML

`<link`
`  xlink:type="simple"`
`  xlink:show="replace"`
`  xlink:actuate="onRequest"`
`/>`
	When the user clicks the link, the remote resource replaces the current document.	Plain `<A HREF="">` tag.

`<link`
`  xlink:type="simple"`
`  xlink:show="new"`
`  xlink:actuate="onRequest"`
`/>`
	When the user clicks the link, the remote resource appears in a new window.	`<A HREF=""`
		`TARGET="_new">`

`<link`
`  xlink:type="simple"`
`  xlink:show="embed"`
`  xlink:actuate="onLoad"`
`/>`
	Remote resource appears as part of the document.	Not easy to implement on the client. It would not be very hard to do this on the server, before sending the document to the client.

Code	Effect	Implementation in HTML
```<link xlink:type="simple" xlink:show="embed" xlink:actuate="onRequest" />```	Remote resource appears as part of the document when the user clicks the link.	Not easy to implement at all. It could be done on the server by embedding the remote resource into the page, but only making it visible when clicked. However, that would not be a smart solution (considering document size etc) We'll try to create another solution, but it will inevitably not be perfect.

The display of most simple links in an HTML browser seems possible. The hard part is determining what the remote resource is. An XLink `href` attribute can hold an XPointer expression, referring to parts of XML documents. So an XLink implementation should not only be able to retrieve a part of a document, but also be capable of parsing and evaluating XPointer expressions. This can not be done by most HTML browsers, because they don't support XML, let alone XPointer. We will create an ASP page that can return a partial document (read further to find out which part of XPointer we will leave unimplemented). For each simple link, we will have to determine on the server what the URL of the remote resource is, converting it to the URL of the ASP page when necessary.

So is the XLink contains a URL like:

```
http://www.somedomain.com/document.xml#xpointer(//para[3])
```

This would be translated to:

```
http://www.ourdomain.com/xpointersolve.asp?fullURL=
http%3A%2F%2Fwww.somedomain.com%2Fdocument.xml%23xpointer%28%2F%2Fpara%5B3%5D%29
```

The URL, including the `xpointer()` expression is passed to this ASP page on the server (as a CGI variable). This page will retrieve the indicated XML document, select the fragment specified by the XPointer expression and return this to the browser.

Extended Links

Extended links seem much more complicated than simple links. Considering that we had a hard time partially implementing simple links, shouldn't we just leave extended links out? Well, not really. If you take a closer look at extended links, you'll see that they are really only a set of simple links. So if we can resolve a simple link to an HTML link, we should also be able to resolve a set of simple links to a set of HTML links. So our approach will be this – try to convert extended links to multiple simple links and then process the simple links and converted extended links together.

The problem with links that are part of an extended link is that you not only have to find out what the target is, but also what the origin is. With simple links that was easy – it was the link element itself. On the other hand, if you can find the target of an XLink, you can also find the origin – in extended links, the same XPointer syntax is used to specify both the origin and the target of a link. How we are going to achieve this will be detailed in the section '*Implementation*'.

But what if the origin of a link is in another document? Remember that in XLink it is possible to describe a link in document A that originates in document B. That's a hard one. XLink says nothing about implementing links from places that are not in your current view. It only describes the conceptual link, not the user interface that would display such a link to the user. In our implementation, we'll just ignore them. Note that this is not in any way limiting for the user; a link originating in another document cannot be followed anyway. XLink specifies it to accommodate applications that show more complex relations between documents. It is not very relevant for browsing information.

External Linksets

What about external linksets? Well, if we can handle internal extended links, the external ones should be no problem. We'll have to retrieve the document containing the linkset and figure out which of these links originate in our current document. Those links will be treated just as internal extended links.

Accepting these limitations, we can build a partial implementation of XLink and XPointer. At the very minimum it will be good enough for generating full product descriptions for our sample application, but we will try to expand our implementation a little a bit further.

What Will be Left Unimplemented?

There are quite a few parts of the XPointer and XLink specifications that we will not be implementing. This is because they are very difficult to code and it doesn't really serve the purpose of this book, which is learning XML programming rather than low-level string handling. And, when push comes to shove, VB wouldn't be the tool to create such software anyway. (Developers building their solutions on top of an implementation of XLink need the best possible performance, which is delivered by C++.)

So what will we leave out?

❑ Points and ranges – this would involve a lot of work, considering that no support currently exists in the XML DOM to do these kinds of operations. So, an XPointer in our model will always refer to a node.

❑ Most of the XPointer extensions to XPath. Functions for setting and changing points and ranges are not implemented. An expression with xpointer(expr) will only work if expr is a valid XPath expression.

Component Functionality

The component we are going to build will have to do quite complex operations on arbitrary XML documents.

❑ It should scan a passed location (URL plus locator string) for XLink information.

❑ It should store all simple links in the document in an internal linkbase.

❑ Any extended links and external linksets present should be converted to simple links and also stored in the linkbase.

For the links that have their origin in the current document:

❏   If they are to be embedded in the current document, retrieve the target and perform all actions above on the fragment as well.

❏   If the target is outside the current document, create a URL that will retrieve the referred fragment when necessary.

❏   For all starting and ending points in the current document, add a special element (in a namespace of its own) to tell the user interface generator where the links and anchors should appear.

Component Output

Let's have a look at how XLink is used to create a more complex link. We have a directory of XML documents describing products. One of these documents might look like this:

```
<PRODUCT ID='pda234' xmlns:xl="http://www.w3.org/1999/xlink/namespaces/">
  <NAME>Casio E-105</NAME>
  <PRICE>$450.00</PRICE>
  <DESCRIPTION>
    <HEADER></HEADER>
    <BODY>
      Here we allow the description, where we might want
      to include some additional information, such as
      <WEIGHT unit='KG'>12</WEIGHT>
      for which we do not have a fixed set of elements.
    </BODY>
  </DESCRIPTION>
  <CATEGORY>PDAs</CATEGORY>
  <RELATEDURLS>
    <URL href='www.casio.com' />
  </RELATEDURLS>
  <RELATEDPRODUCTS>
    <PRODUCT id='pda2345' name='docking station'
      xl:type="simple"
      xl:show="new"
      xl:actuate="onRequest"
      xl:href="pda2345.xml"
    />
    <PRODUCT name='pda543' name='net adapter'
      xl:type="simple"
      xl:show="new"
      xl:actuate="onRequest"
      xl:href="pda543.xml"
    />
  </RELATEDPRODUCTS>
</PRODUCT>
```

This document would typically be named 'pda234.xml' (look at the product ID) and would be found in the products directory. Now, suppose that we wanted to provide an XML document for a specific product that contains only a few fragments from the document stored on the file system, for example selecting only the description and the related products, but leaving out related URLs, price and category. From the information in the database, a mini document could be constructed like this:

```
<PRODUCT ID='pda234'>
  <NAME>Casio E-105</NAME>
  <DESCRIPTION xmlns:xl="http://www.w3.org/1999/xlink/namespaces/"
    xl:type="simple"
    xl:href="/products/pda234.xml#xpointer(//DESCRIPTION)"
    xl:show="embed"
    xl:actuate="onLoad"
  />
  <RELATED_PROD xmlns:xl="http://www.w3.org/1999/xlink/namespaces/"
    xl:type="simple"
    xl:href="/products/pda234.xml#xpointer(//RELATEDPRODUCTS)"
    xl:show="embed"
    xl:actuate="onLoad"
  />
</PRODUCT>
```

Are you getting a feel for where we are heading? We hand the XML that comes from the database over to the XLinker component. The component scans the document for links and embeds any available auto-embed links, which are embedded into the XML document. These embedded nodes are themselves also scanned for links; we will not check for circular references, so we must be sure that these do not occur. This specific embedded XML document (the product details file shown above) will contain two simple links that should appear when the user clicks somewhere. These are the links:

```
<DESCRIPTION xmlns:xl="http://www.w3.org/1999/xlink/namespaces/"
  xl:type="simple"
  xl:href="/products/pda234.xml#xpointer(//DESCRIPTION)"
  xl:show="embed"
  xl:actuate="onLoad"
/>
<RELATED_PROD xmlns:xl="http://www.w3.org/1999/xlink/namespaces/"
  xl:type="simple"
  xl:href="/products/pda234.xml#xpointer(//RELATEDPRODUCTS)"
  xl:show="embed"
  xl:actuate="onLoad"
/>
```

They both point to resources outside the current document, so we will transform them later to links like this:

```
<A HREF="xpointersolve.asp?fullURL=http://doc...#xpointer(... etc)"
TARGET="_new"></A>
```

In the XML document we will include an element to tell the XSLT processor to include some sort of HTML link on that spot. The full XLinked document result would look something like:

```
<PRODUCT ID='pda234'
  xmlns:tl="http://www.wrox.com/ProVBXML/TransformLink"
>
  <NAME>Casio E-105</NAME>
  <DESCRIPTION>
    <HEADER></HEADER>
    <BODY>
      Here we allow the description, where we might want
```

```
      to include some additional information, such as
      <WEIGHT unit='KG'>12</WEIGHT>
      for which we do not have a fixed set of elements.
      </BODY>
    </DESCRIPTION>

    <RELATEDPRODUCTS>
      <tl:link
        type="start"
        show="new"
        actuate="onRequest"
        href="http://www.ourserver/xpointersolve.asp?fullURL=
        http://doc...#xpointer(... etc)"
      />
      <tl:link
        tl:type="start"
        tl:show="new"
        tl:actuate="onRequest"
        href="http://www.ourserver/xpointersolve.asp?fullURL=
        http://doc...#xpointer(... etc)"
      />
    </RELATEDPRODUCTS>
  </PRODUCT>
```

In this document, the content of the DESCRIPTION element is imported from another XML document. The links to related articles are also imported. Note the link elements in the namespace http://www.wrox.com/ProVBXML/TransformLink. Those are the placeholders that we will use later to insert A elements into the document, which happens in an XSLT stylesheet.

Once this XML without XLink-specific content has been generated, we can use XSLT to transform everything to a formatted HTML to be displayed.

The XLink Component

We now know that our component will take XML from the database and appropriately handle any links it finds. Let's look at how this will be achieved. We will have a look at each of the classes now, just describing what each one does. Later we will get into the implementation details.

Object Model Overview

The classes we need to implement XLink on the server side. They are packaged as an ActiveX DLL project. You can find the full project with all code in the source code download. The project is called XLinker.vbp. The object model is fairly simple. Most of the functionality is hidden inside the XLinkedDocument class. This includes the retrieval of resources, resolving relative URLs and embedding links. The other classes implement data holders and minor tools to be used by the XLinkedDocument class. Before looking at the properties and methods of the classes in more detail, we'll list all classes with a short description:

- ❑ Location – refers to a place in a document (which can be either local or remote).

- ❑ XLinkSimple – represents a simple link (as in the XLink specification). Defines a link between an origin location and a destination location.

❑ XLinkExtended – A tool to convert an extended link (as in XLink) to a collection of simple links.

❑ XLinkArc – A data holder to keep two locations together.

❑ XLinkedDocument – This is the big one. It serves to convert an XML document containg XLink information to a document containing simpler linking information, ready to be transformed to HTML links.

Location

First of all we have the Location class. The Location class will be used to refer to the starting and ending points of links. It describes a location in the sense of the XPointer specification. This means it can be a range, a point or a node in any XML document. Well, we decided to drop the support for ranges and points, so the Location object holds a description for a single node in an XML document. This description can have several forms. Sometimes we have a DOM node object that we want to set the Location to (the origin of a simple link); in other cases we only know the URL of the location (with some location path appended to it). The Location class can hold either an object reference or a complex URL.

The Location class also knows how to split up an absolute URL with location path appended into a normal URL and a collection of XPath expressions. For example, you could have a complex URL like this:

http://localhost/document.xml#xpointer(expr1)xpointer(expr2)

The Location object can split it up into the following:

❑ A URL: http://localhost/document.xml

❑ A collection of XPath expressions: expr1 and expr2

If the appended location path has the form of an ID reference or a child-path, then it is converted to XPath expressions:

❑ #someID becomes id('someID')

❑ /1/4/3 becomes /*[1]/*[4]/*[3]

The Location class does not resolve the URL to a node object by itself. To understand why not, consider this example. Document A contains an extended link. One of the links has its origin within document A. The origin of the link is defined using a URL. We want to know which of the nodes in our current document (a loaded DOM document) is specified by the URL we found in the link. To do this, there has to be a reference to the DOMDocument object. The Location class doesn't have this reference, so it is uncapable of resolving the URL. The XLinkedDocument class, which has access to the DOMDocument object and all Location objects, will perform the resolving of the URLs to nodes.

Also, the Location class has two attributes, sRole and sTitle, that you may recognize as XLink attributes. These can be set to a simple link element to describe the linked resource. The definition of the Location class looks like this:

Class name:	Location
Public Interface	
Attributes:	oXMLNode As MSXML2.IXMLDOMNode
	sComplexURL As String
	sURLPart As String
	collXPaths As Collection
	sRole As String
	sTitle As String
	sRelURL As String
	sBaseURL As String
Methods:	SplitURL()
	CombineURLs()

XLinkSimple

The XLinkSimple class represents the simple link from the XLink specification. It always has one starting point and one ending point. Both are Location objects. It also carries two attributes, sShow and sActuate, which are XLink attributes that can be set to the simple link element. Note that we chose to put the role and title attributes on the Location class and the show and actuate attributes on the XLinkSimple element. This is done because role and title attributes provide information that is about the destination location, that is they describe what the link points to. It is appropriate to keep this information in the Location class, while the show and actuate attributes give information about the link itself, that is how the link works and when it works. A summary of the class definition is as follows:

Class name:	XLinkSimple
Public Interface	
Attributes:	FromLocation As Location
	sShow As String
	sActuate As String
	ToLocation As Location

XLinkExtended

The XLinkExtended class does not really represent an extended link, rather it implements a tool to extract extended linking information from a document fragment, building the links structure and converting it into a set of simple links.

When using it, the object exposes one method, buildLinkSet, that expects a node and a string. The string holds the prefix for the XLink namespace. When this method is called, the XLinkExtended object scans the passed node for all contained linking elements. These are used to build a collection of XLinkSimple objects. This collection is exposed as a public property. The class definiton is shown overleaf:

Class name:	**XLinkExtended**
Public Interface	
Attributes:	`collSimpleLinks As Collection`
	`sBaseURL As String`
Methods:	`buildLinkset()`

XLinkArc

`XLinkArc` is a very small helper class that is used by the `XLinkExtended` class to build the collection of links. The `XLinkArc` class represents an XLink arc, connecting two types of locations (or internal resources). The class has four public properties: `sFrom`, `sTo`, `sShow` and `sActuate`. All represent attributes that can be placed on an XLink element of type `arc`. You may notice that the layout of the `XLinkArc` class is very much like the `XLinkSimple` class. The difference is that the `XLinkArc` class holds string values for its 'to' and 'from' values, whereas the `XLinkSimple` class has `Location` objects as 'to' and 'from' values.

`XLinkArc` is used to store the combination of four string values during the process of building the extended link and converting it to simple links. The class definition is as follows:

Class name:	**XLinkArc**
Public Interface	
Attributes:	`sFrom As String`
	`sTo As String`
	`sShow As String`
	`sActuate As String`

XLinkedDocument

This is the big one. The `XLinkedDocument` class serves to make any XML resource containing XLink information ready for display. This means that most of the XLink information is replaced by new application-specific elements that can be interpreted by a front-end application. This front-end can be anything, but in our case, we will use an XSLT stylesheet to convert to HTML.

Two scenarios for the use of `XLinkedDocument` could be:

❑ An application object on the server creates an XML document object in memory and passes it to an instance of the `XLinkedDocument` class on the server. The `XLinkedDocument` object exposes the method `makeLinked()` that modifies the document object. After calling `makeLinked()`, the document contains the fragments that must be included (`onLoad`) as well as simplified linking information.

❑ An application (an ASP page or whatever) passes in a URL, with or without an appended XPointer path. When `makeLinked()` is called, the `XLinkedDocument` object retrieves the resource over HTTP and implements the XLink changes.

When XLinkedDocument encounters an XLink with show="embed" and actuate="onLoad", it creates a new instance of XLinkedDocument to retrieve the new resource.

To tell an XLinkedDocument object which document should be processed, it has an oLocation property of type Location. We can use it to pass in a URL like this:

```
oXLinkedDocument.oLocation.sComplexURL = _
                           "http://www.ourdomain.com/XLinked_document.xml"
oXLinkedDocument.makeLinked
```

But it also allows us to do something else. Suppose that we have found a simple link in our document that must be embedded into the current document (that is, it has attributes show="embed" and actuate="onLoad"). The information about this link is stored in an XLinkSimple object. The XML document fragment that the link refers to can now be retrieved using:

```
Set oXLinkedDocument.oLocation = oXLinkSimple.ToLocation
oXLinkedDocument.makeLinked
```

The target of a link is already stored as a Location object, so this can be passed into the new XLinkedDocument instance.

The Location object that is passed to the XLinkedDocument can have several content states. These influence the actions that XLinkedDocument takes to return the linked document:

State of the Location object	Action of the XLinkedDocument
Location has only the URL loaded, possibly with an XPointer path.	The XLinkedDocument retrieves the referred document, selects the fragment specified by the XPointer path and performs linking operations on this node.
Location has no URL loaded, but it has a node object attached to it.	The node object is used to perform linking operations on.
Both the URL and an XML node object are loaded in the Location object.	The node object is used and the URL is ignored.

Finally here is a summary of the XLinkedDocument class:

Class name:	XLinkedDocument
Public Interface	
Attributes:	oDocNode As MSXML2.IXMLDOMNode
	oLocation As Location
Methods:	makeLinked()

The Implementation

In this sample application (XLinker.vbp), we make extensive use of the MSXML version 2.0 library from Microsoft, which was shipped with Internet Explorer 5.0. The implementation in this version of XSLT and XPath is rather limited (see Chapter 4 and Appendices C and D for more details). The next implementation of the library is expected to be out shortly after the original publication of this book.

In this project we have also been using the developer's preview of the full implementation. The name of the preview library is MSXML2, to allow installing it side-by-side with the existing library (which is called MSXML). The release version of the full implementation will probably be called MSXML again and will be installed over the older implementation.

So, if you see an object declared in the code as:

```
Dim oNode as MSXML2.IXMLDOMNode
```

and you want to use the example with the final release, you'll probably have to change the code to:

```
Dim oNode as MSXML.IXMLDOMNode
```

> *Check on the MSDN site (http://msdn.microsoft.com/xml) or one of the Microsoft XML newsgroups (microsoft.public.xml, microsoft.public.xml.msxml-webrelease) to find out when the new version of MSXML will be finally released.*

Location

The Location class is basically a set of properties:

```
Public oXMLNode As MSXML2.IXMLDOMNode
Public sComplexURL As String
Public sURLPart As String
Private sTrailing As String
Public collXPaths As Collection
Public sRole As String
Public sTitle As String
Public sRelURL As String
Public sBaseURL As String
```

The most important properties are sComplexURL and oXMLNode. They reflect the two ways the class can use to specify a location in a document. The first holds a complex URL (i.e. including an XPointer expression). The second holds a reference to a node in a DOMDocument object. Note that the Location class does not use this node for anything – it just holds it. Other classes can set and retrieve the node from the Location object.

The sComplexURL property is used to indicate the location using an URL with an appended XPointer path. If the client of the Location object does not know the full absolute URL needed for sComplexURL, it can also pass a separate relative URL and a base URL using the properties sRelURL and sBaseURL.

There are two public methods:

- ❏ CombineURLs() combines the base URL and the relative URL into a new full URL.
- ❏ SplitURL() takes the full URL, and splits it into two parts on the hash sign. The part before the # is stored in sURLpart and the part after it in the private variable sTrailing.

CombineURLs()

The CombineURLs method is a simple one, and one that you may use on many occasions. It uses the functionality of the WinInet library, which comes with Internet Explorer, Internet Information Server and basically all other Internet-oriented products on the Windows platform. The declaration of the library function, together with a function that uses the API call in the proper way, is placed in a module called WinInetFunctions.

```
Public Sub CombineURLs()
    'The Internet Combine function needs a base
    If sBaseURL = "" Then Err.Raise 9999, "XLinker::XLinkedDocument", _
        "No base URL specified"
    sComplexURL = ResolveURL(sBaseURL, sRelURL)
End Sub
```

The method CombineURLs doesn't do very much: it checks the sBaseURL variable. If it's empty, the URL cannot be resolved. If the variable has any value, the ResolveURL function in the module is called and its return value is passed back.

So what happens in this ResolveURL function?

```
Declare Function InternetCombineUrl _
    Lib "WinInet.dll" _
    Alias "InternetCombineUrlA" _
        (ByVal sBaseURL As String, _
        ByVal sRelURL As String, _
        ByVal sNewURL As String, _
        ByRef lNewLength As Long, _
        ByVal lFlags As Long) As Long

Public Const UCI_NO_ENCODE = &H20000000
```

Let's take a little time out to look at what is happening here. An API function is declared that is implemented in a DLL called WinInet.dll. The function is called InternetCombineURL and all of the parameters that must be passed are also specified here. So how did we know that this function even existed? Well, you can look it up in the online MSDN documentation (http://msdn.microsoft.com). This function declaration can also be found there. The first three parameters of the InternetCombineURLA function are easy to understand – they are the base URL, the relative URL and the fully resolved URL. You have to pass in a string for the resolved URL, because the return value of API functions is used for returning error codes.

The fourth parameter, lNewLength, must contain the length of the string that was passed in for the full URL. The implementation of strings is different in C and C++ than it is in Visual Basic. In VB, the VB Runtime keeps track of the length of any strings. If we append something to a string, the extra memory that is needed for storing the now larger string is automatically declared. In C, the language that the API libraries are targeting, you have to do that yourself. If you pass a static string to another function, there is no problem – the end of a static string must be identified by a null character that is a byte with a value of zero. But if that other function is going to change the string, we would be in trouble (if we were programming in C, that is). This is why the library function cannot change the length of the string. It must be passed a string that is long enough to contain the result and we must tell the function how much space it may use to write down the result.

The last parameter, lFlags, is used to tell the API function how it should work – whether it should encode any values, or strip out white space, and so on. The constant UCI_NO_ENCODE performs no encoding at all, that is if a '?' character is passed in, it is not encoded to %23.

So, how is this function used?

```
Function ResolveURL(sBaseURL As String, sURL As String)
    Dim sFullURL As String
    Dim lLength As Long
    Dim lResult As Long

    sFullURL = String(1024, "*")
    lLength = Len(sFullURL) - 1
    lResult = InternetCombineUrl(sBaseURL, sURL, sFullURL, lLength,_
            UCI_NO_ENCODE)
    If lResult = 0 Then
        Err.Raise vbError + 1, "XLinkedDocument", _
                "Error solving URL from " _
                & sBaseURL & " to " & sURL
    End If
    sFullURL = Left$(sFullURL, lLength)
    ResolveURL = sFullURL
End Function
```

A long string is first constructed (1024 asterisks long, though you could use any character) to pass to the API function; 1024 characters should be long enough to hold most URLs. If it is not long enough, the API call returns the required length in the lNewLength variable. This example does no recovery for results that are too long. Then the length of the string is calculated, and 1 subtracted from the length returned by the Len function to allow for the terminating null character used by the API function. The API function is then called, passing all parameters, and store the returned Long value. If the return value is not zero, an error is raised.

The API function has written the resolved value of the URL into the string value sFullURL. The length of the new string is stored in lLength. All string content after that point is not relevant, so it is stripped out.

SplitURL()

When the client of the Location class calls SplitURL(), it expects the Location class to do two things – first split the complex URL into a URL part and an XPointer path, and second, convert this path to a set of XPath expressions.

```
Public Sub SplitURL()
    SplitURLonHash
    ConvertHashStringToPaths (sTrailing)
End Sub
```

First we look at the `SplitURLonHash` function. This is very straightforward. The VB string handling functions check for the presence of a # and then the string is split into two parts at that location. Note that wherever the # is located, or even if it is absent, both `sURLPart` and `sTrailing` get overwritten by this function:

```
Private Sub SplitURLonHash()
    Dim lHashLocation As Long
    lHashLocation = InStr(sComplexURL, "#")
    If lHashLocation > 0 Then
        sTrailing = Mid$(sComplexURL, lHashLocation + 1)
        sURLPart = Left$(sComplexURL, lHashLocation - 1)
    Else
        sTrailing = ""
        sURLPart = sComplexURL
    End If
End Sub
```

Now we come to the `ConvertHashStringToPaths` function. This one is rather complex. There are a number of possibilities that must be handled. Let's make a short list:

Value of `sTrailing`	Result
Empty	Empty collection of XPaths.
String starts with "xpointer("	It may be a set of multiple expressions, so we must parse the string for matching parentheses. Once that is done, we assume the expressions to be XPath expressions, so we store them in the collection.
String starts with something other than "xpointer(", but not a "/"	This must be an ID reference. We parse the string for any slashes, because there may be an element path attached. The ID reference is converted to an XPath and stored.
String starts with a slash or after the ID reference a slash is found	The path of form /1/3/5 is converted to an XPath of form /*[1]/*[3]/*[5] .

The code is shown below. The `sTrailing` string is copied into a string called `sWorking` that will be chopped up into fragments, and some initialization is done. An empty collection is created and the variable `collXPaths` set to it:

```
Private Sub ConvertHashStringToPaths(sTrailing As String)
    Dim sWorking As String
    Dim iPathNumber As Integer
    Dim iCharNumber As Integer
    Dim iLastPathStart As Integer
    Dim iNestingLevel As Integer

    sWorking = sTrailing
    iPathNumber = 0
    Set collXPaths = New Collection
```

Now the fun starts. If the first nine characters of the string turn out to be the string "xpointer(", the code start scanning for parentheses. What we really want to find out is where the expression ends. Maybe there are several expressions, so those have to be check for too.

```
If Left(sTrailing, 9) = "xpointer(" Then
    ' Walk the string to match parentheses Literal )'s are
    ' to be escaped as ^) even within quotes
    iCharNumber = 10
    iNestingLevel = 1
    iLastPathStart = iCharNumber
    While iCharNumber <= Len(sWorking)
        If Mid(sWorking, iCharNumber, 1) = ")" Then iNestingLevel _
            = iNestingLevel - 1
        If Mid(sWorking, iCharNumber, 1) = "(" Then iNestingLevel _
            = iNestingLevel + 1
        If Mid(sWorking, iCharNumber, 2) = "^)" Then iCharNumber = _
            iCharNumber + 1
        If Mid(sWorking, iCharNumber, 2) = "^(" Then iCharNumber = _
            iCharNumber + 1
        If Mid(sWorking, iCharNumber, 2) = "^^" Then iCharNumber = _
            iCharNumber + 1
        If iNestingLevel = 0 Then
            collXPaths.Add Mid(sWorking, iLastPathStart, _
             iCharNumber - iLastPathStart)
            If Mid(sWorking, iCharNumber + 1, 9) = "xpointer(" Then
                iNestingLevel = 1
                iCharNumber = iCharNumber + 9
                iLastPathStart = iCharNumber + 1
                iPathNumber = iPathNumber + 1
            Else
                ' Check if no content is left. If there is any: Syntax error
                If Len(Trim(Mid(sWorking, iCharNumber + 1))) > 0 Then
                    Err.Raise 9999, "WROXSample:XLinkSolver", _
                            "Syntax error: unrecognized scheme"
                End If
            End If
        End If
        iCharNumber = iCharNumber + 1
    Wend
```

The code keeps track of the character number and of the nesting level of parentheses. Every time an opening parenthesis is encountered, the nesting level is incremented by one; literal parentheses must be escaped using an ^. When the nesting level reaches 0, the matching parenthesis of the "xpointer(" syntax must have been found. The string between the two points is added to the collection. If the rest of the string starts with "xpointer(", the process starts all over again. If the rest of the string is something else, a syntax error is raised.

Also if we reach the end of the string without reaching nesting level 0, we apparently have unmatched parentheses and raise a syntax error:

```
If iNestingLevel > 0 Then
    'Syntax error
    Err.Raise 9999, "WROXSample:XLinkSolver", "Syntax error"
End If
```

If the string was of the "xpointer(" syntax, this is the end of the function. But there are other options. We may have an ID reference and/or an element path. We first search the string for the first slash and split it there. Both possibilities are converted to XPath expressions and concatenated again to result in one expression. So:

```
#blah/4/3/2
```

results in adding this expression to the collection:

```
id('blah')/*[4]/*[3]/*[2]
```

If the code reaches this point, we have apparently a string appended to the URL, but it doesn't start with the string "xpointer(":

```
    Else
        ' Split the id and possible path
        Dim sIDpart As String
        Dim sPathPart As String
        Dim iSlashPosition As Integer
        Dim sFullPath As String

        iSlashPosition = InStr(1, sWorking, "/", vbTextCompare)
        If iSlashPosition = 0 Then       'No slash found: only an id
            sIDpart = sWorking
            sPathPart = ""
        Else
            sIDpart = Mid(sWorking, 1, iSlashPosition - 1)
            sPathPart = Mid(sWorking, iSlashPosition)
        End If
        ' If any ID expression is found, it is converted to the kind of
        ' XPath expression IE5 understands: blah becomes id('blah')
        If Len(sIDpart) > 0 Then
            sFullPath = "id('" & sIDpart & "')"
        End If

        ' If any path expression is found, it is converted to the kind of
        ' XPath expression IE5 understands: /1/4/2 becomes /*[0]/*[3]/*[1]
        If Len(sPathPart) > 0 Then
            iCharNumber = 2
            While iCharNumber <= Len(sPathPart)
                iSlashPosition = InStr(iCharNumber, sPathPart, "/")
                If iSlashPosition = 0 Then
                    sFullPath = sFullPath & "/*[" & Mid(sPathPart, _
                            iCharNumber) & "]"
                    iCharNumber = Len(sPathPart)
                Else
                    sFullPath = sFullPath & "/*[" & Mid(sPathPart, _
                        iCharNumber, iSlashPosition - iCharNumber) & "]"
                    iCharNumber = iSlashPosition
                End If
                iCharNumber = iCharNumber + 1
            Wend
        End If
        If Len(sFullPath) > 0 Then collXPaths.Add sFullPath
    End If
End Sub
```

A check is made to see if it starts with a slash. If so, it is a child element path (#/1/4/2). Otherwise, it is an ID reference – and maybe a child element path after that. The code starts building the XPath expression with the ID reference (if any) and then appends the child element path if there is one. After that, the XPath expression is added to the collection of XPaths, but only if it is longer than 0.

This leaves us with a class that is capable of holding a reference to a node in an XML document, either by holding a reference to a DOM node or by holding a URL with an XPointer expression appended. In the above class, the tools to create absolute URLs from relative URLs and parse the complex URLs with an XPointer expression to a simple URL and a set of XPath expressions.

XLinkSimple

The `XLinkSimple` class is extremely simple to implement. Now that we have implemented the code that refers to parts of documents – the `Location` class – the simple link is little more than combining two `Location` objects. When I refer to 'little more', I mean that there is the possibility of holding `show` and `actuate` properties for a link with the 'to' and 'from' locations. When scanning a document for linking information, a collection of `XLinkSimple` objects will be created.

```
Public FromLocation As Location
Public ToLocation As Location
Public sShow As String
Public sActuate As String

Private Sub Class_Initialize()
    Set FromLocation = New Location
    Set ToLocation = New Location
End Sub
```

On initialization, new instances for the two locations are created. In this way, we don't have to worry about initializing them when the `XLinkSimple` class is used. Sometimes we will not need this, because we pass the locations in from the outside and unnecessary instantiation of the class will cause some overhead. However, efficiency is not the point in this exercise anyway.

XLinkArc

The `XLinkArc` class is a simple data holder that will be used in the `XLinkExtended` class while converting extended link information to a set of simple links. The public properties reflect possible attributes on a `linking` element of type `arc`.

```
Public sFrom As String
Public sTo As String
Public sShow As String
Public sActuate As String
```

XlinkExtended

The `XLinkExtended` class is really more a tool than a proper class. It knows how to extract extended linking information from an XML document fragment and convert it to a collection of `XLinkSimple` objects. You can pass it a DOM node and tell it to extract the linking information. It will fill a collection of `XLinkSimple` objects that can be retrieved. The `Collection` is implemented as a public property.

```
Public collSimpleLinks As New Collection
Public sBaseURL As String
```

The second public property, sBaseURL, must always be set, because XLinkExtended uses it to resolve URLs from the link. (Remember that the class has no way to determine the original URI of the document.) The only method of note in the class is called buildLinkset and it scans the passed DOM element node for extended linking information, converting it to simple links. The class assumes that the passed element is actually an extended link.

So how are we going to convert all this information to simple links? It is done by first making an inventory of all available resources. A resource can be remote, defined by a linking element with xlink:type="locator" or it can be local, identified by a linking element with xlink:type="resource". Using XPath expressions and the method selectNodes on the passed element, we can easily find all these elements. The information about these resources is stored in a Location object; for some resources the URL is stored, for others, the node itself is stored – the Location class gives this flexibility. The role and title properties of the Location object are set and stored in a collection:

```
Public Sub buildLinkset(oExtendedElement As MSXML2.IXMLDOMElement, _
                    sPrefix As String)

    ' variable declarations not displayed---

    ' First build a set of locators and resources. What the arcs
    ' do is of later concern. We'll store them as locations
    Set oLocatorList = oExtendedElement.selectNodes("descendant::* _
                    [attribute::" & sPrefix & ":type = 'locator']")
    For i = 1 To oLocatorList.length
        Set oLinkElement = oLocatorList.Item(i - 1)
        Set oLoc = New Location
        sTempURL = NullCatcher(oLinkElement.getAttribute(sPrefix & ":href"))
        sTempURL = ResolveURL(sBaseURL, sTempURL)

        oLoc.sComplexURL = sTempURL
        oLoc.SplitURL
        oLoc.sRole = NullCatcher(oLinkElement.getAttribute(sPrefix & ":role"))
        oLoc.sTitle = NullCatcher(oLinkElement.getAttribute(sPrefix & ":title"))
        collResources.Add oLoc
    Next

    ' The locators are stored: now for the resources
    Set oResourceList = oExtendedElement.selectNodes("descendant::*" & _
                    "[attribute::" & sPrefix & ":type = 'resource']")
    For i = 1 To oResourceList.length
        Set oLinkElement = oResourceList.Item(i - 1)

        Set oLoc = New Location
        Set oLoc.oXMLNode = oLinkElement 'reference the content in
                                         ' the local resource link
        oLoc.sRole = oLinkElement.selectSingleNode("attribute::" _
                & sPrefix & ":role").nodeValue
        oLoc.sTitle = oLinkElement.selectSingleNode("attribute::" _
                & sPrefix & ":title").nodeValue
        collResources.Add oLoc
    Next
```

So what we have now is a `Collection` filled with `Location` objects, one for each resource including locator and resource elements. Now a collection is going to be filled with all the `arc` elements in the extended link. The information for each `arc` element is stored in an `XLinkArc` object. The `NullCatcher` function used here is a small helper function that returns the passed parameter, but converts a `Null` value to `""`:

```
'Now we build a list of arcs. This is a collection of XLinkArc objects
Set oArcList = oExtendedElement.selectNodes("descendant::*" & _
        "[attribute::" & sPrefix & ":type = 'arc']")
For i = 1 To oArcList.length
    Set oLinkElement = oArcList.Item(i - 1)

    Set oTmpArc = New XLinkArc
    oTmpArc.sFrom = NullCatcher(oLinkElement.getAttribute(sPrefix & ":from"))
    oTmpArc.sTo = NullCatcher(oLinkElement.getAttribute(sPrefix & ":to"))
    oTmpArc.sActuate = NullCatcher(oLinkElement.getAttribute _
            (sPrefix & ":actuate"))
    oTmpArc.sShow = NullCatcher(oLinkElement.getAttribute(sPrefix & ":show"))

    collArcs.Add oTmpArc
Next
```

Now comes the hardest part – combining all these `resources` and `arcs` into a set of links. This is done in a set of nested loops. The outer loop cycles through all `arcs`. For each `arc`, all `resources` are looped through, comparing the `arc`'s `sTo` attribute with the role of the `resource`. For each matching target, the `resources` are looped through again, this time matching on the `sFrom` attribute of the `arc`. If `resources` are found for both the `sFrom` and `sTo` attributes, an `XLinkSimple` object is created, relevant properties are set for it and the object is added to the publicly accessible collection `collSimpleLinks` which holds all simple links.

```
'Now we loop through the arcs, constructing Simple links
'from the associated locators and resources
For i = 1 To collArcs.Count
    For j = 1 To collResources.Count
        If (collArcs(i).sFrom = "" Or collArcs(i).sFrom = _
          collResources(j).sRole) Then
            For k = 1 To collResources.Count
                If (collArcs(i).sTo = "" Or collArcs(i).sTo = _
                  collResources(k).sRole) Then
                    ' This arc's to and from attributes
                    ' match the roles of 2 resources
                    ' Hurray!
                    Set oTmpLink = New XlinkSimple
                    Set oTmpLink.FromLocation = collResources(j)
                    Set oTmpLink.ToLocation = collResources(k)
                    oTmpLink.sActuate = collArcs(i).sActuate
                    oTmpLink.sShow = collArcs(i).sShow
                    collSimpleLinks.Add oTmpLink
                End If
            Next
        End If
    Next
Next
End Sub
```

XLinkedDocument

Until now, we have created a set of data holders and tools. Now the XLinkedDocument class knows how to use all of these classes to take an XML document, either a URL or a DOM object, parse it for XLink information, import embedded links and external linksets, convert extended links to simple links and add this information in a namespace of its own. The node is copied into an empty DOMDocument object and passed back to the client. How this wrapping takes place depends on the node type of the result:

❑ If the result is an element, the element becomes the root element of the DOMDocument object.

❑ If the result is an attribute, the attribute is set to a dummy element that becomes the root of the DOMDocument object.

❑ If the result is a text node, it becomes the content of a dummy root element.

The public interface of XLinkedDocument is very small. It consists of a public property of type Location (to tell the object which content we want it to transform) and a public method makeLinked that returns a DOMDocument containing the requested resource. The makeLinked function calls quite a long list of private functions. We will look at its implementation later.

```
Private oDocNode As MSXML2.IXMLDOMNode

'This Location object is used to pass in 'the location that must be XLinked
Public oLocation As New Location
Private oLinkBase As New Collection

Public Function makeLinked() As DOMDocument

    Dim lHashLocation As Long
    Dim oTmpDoc As DOMDocument

    ' We don't want to handle a relative URL here
    ' The location object can deal with that
    If oLocation.sComplexURL = "" Then oLocation.CombineURLs

    ' This method will fetch the DOM node referred to by the Location object
    Set oDocNode = getXMLNode(oLocation)

    'If no Node was retrieved, we have to pass back an error message,
    ' but we don't want to break an application if one include cannot be found
    If oDocNode Is Nothing Then
        Set oTmpDoc = New DOMDocument
        oTmpDoc.setProperty "SelectionLanguage", "XPath"
        Set oDocNode = oTmpDoc.createElement("dummy")
        oDocNode.Text = "Resource could not be found"
        Set oTmpDoc = Nothing
    End If

    ' Scan the Node for Link information and build a linkbase
    extractXLinks

    ' If any links in the link base must be embedded onLoad, we do it now
    importEmbeddedLinks
```

```
        ' For all remaining links, we insert new information
        ' into the document to prepare
        processLinks

        ' We make the Node into a Document. This makes it easier to handle,
        ' because you can be more sure of the returned object.
        Select Case oDocNode.nodeType
            Case NODE_DOCUMENT
                Set makeLinked = oDocNode
            Case NODE_ELEMENT
                Set oTmpDoc = New DOMDocument
                Set oTmpDoc.documentElement = oDocNode
                Set makeLinked = oTmpDoc
            Case NODE_ATTRIBUTE
                Set oTmpDoc = New DOMDocument
                Set oTmpDoc.documentElement = oTmpDoc.createElement("dummy")
                oTmpDoc.documentElement.setAttributeNode oDocNode
            Case NODE_TEXT, NODE_CDATA_SECTION, NODE_COMMENT
                Set oTmpDoc = New DOMDocument
                Set oTmpDoc.documentElement = oTmpDoc.createElement("dummy")
                oTmpDoc.documentElement.appendChild (oDocNode)
            Case Else
                Err.Raise 9999, "XLinker::XLinkedDocument", _
                    "Node type " & oDocNode.nodeTypeString & " not supported"
        End Select
End Function
```

The basic sequence of events is not hard to follow. When `makeLinked` is called, the node that must be processed is found, and then all available links in the document are retrieved. If they are to be embedded, that is done right away and the embedded document scanned for link information. After that, all links are processed into a format that can easily be transformed to a pleasing user interface.

Then the node is wrapped in a `DOMDocument` object. This is done to verify which object is returned from the `makeLinked` function. If it is left as a node, it could be any type of node, so the client (especially a script client) would have to test the type to know which methods can be executed against it. Wrapping everything in a `DOMDocument` object makes this easier. It does mean that the code has to do some checking on the type in the class. If it's a `Document`, then it is passed directly. If it's an element, a document is created and the element made the `documentElement` in that document. If it's an attribute or text node, a dummy document element has to be created and the result node made a child of that dummy.

So let's discuss some of the functions called by the `makeLinked` function. The first, `getXMLNode`, loads a remote document for us and passes back the node indicated by a possible XPointer part in the `Location`:

```
Private Function getXMLNode(oLocation As Location) As IXMLDOMNode
    Dim oDoc As New MSXML2.DOMDocument

    'If the location holds a direct reference: return that
    If Not oLocation.oXMLNode Is Nothing Then
        Set getXMLNode = oLocation.oXMLNode
    Else
        If oLocation.sComplexURL = "" Then Err.Raise 9999, _
          "XLinker::XLinkedDocument", "Cannot retrieve resource with unknown URL"
```

```
        ' Just to be sure, we call SplitURL on the Location object to convert
        ' the complex URL into a base URL and a set of XPath expressions
        oLocation.SplitURL

        oDoc.async = False
        oDoc.Load (oLocation.sURLPart)
        oDoc.setProperty "SelectionLanguage", "XPath"
        Set getXMLNode = getNodeFromDocument(oDoc, oLocation)
    End If
End Function
```

If the `Location` object has a loaded DOM node connected to it, this node is used, overruling any other content in the `Location`. If this is not the case, the URL is split into a base URL and the XPointer information by calling `SplitURL` on the `Location` object. The resource at the base URL is loaded into a new `DOMDocument`. This Document object is passed, together with the `Location` object, to the `getNodeFromDocument` function. This function tries to execute all XPaths in the `Location` object against the document until any content is returned:

```
Private Function getNodeFromDocument(oDoc As DOMDocument, _
                     oLocation As Location) As IXMLDOMNode
    Dim i As Long
    Dim oNodeList As IXMLDOMNodeList
    Dim oNode As IXMLDOMNode

    If oLocation.collXPaths.Count = 0 Then
        Set getNodeFromDocument = oDoc.documentElement
    Else
        For i = 1 To oLocation.collXPaths.Count
            Set oNodeList = oDoc.selectNodes(oLocation.collXPaths(i))
            If oNodeList.length > 0 Then
                Set oNode = oNodeList.Item(0)
            End If
            If Not oNode Is Nothing Then
                i = oLocation.collXPaths.Count ' Exit the loop
            End If
        Next
        Set getNodeFromDocument = oNode
    End If
End Function
```

The first node in the returned list is chosen to be the `Location` node. Note that XPointer can return more than one node, but it depends on the application if it is appropriate to use all of them. For instance, how would a document browser jump to ten different places in a document at once? For the sake of convenience and simplicity, only the first hit is used.

So, the location that our client passed to us in a `Location` object has been found, and a `DOMDocument` is loaded the node indicated by our client retrieved. Now it's time for the linking.

The search for links is done by the `extractLinks` function. The full code will not be shown here, because it is quite straightforward – you can look it up in the source code download. What it does is query for nodes of a certain type using `selectNodes` and stores the attributes found in the results in an `XLinkSimple` object. It then adds this to the `oLinkbase` object. Finding the simple links in the fragment is done like this:

```
        Set oElementList = oDocNode.selectNodes("/descendant::*[attribute::* _
                        [local-name() = 'type' and namespace-uri() = '" _
                        & XLINK_NS & "'] = 'simple']")
```

The properties of the XLinkSimple object are set using the attributes of the linking element. The ToLocation and FromLocation are set using the linking node itself (FromLocation) and the href attribute (ToLocation).

Then a similar loop is used for iterating along all extended links. Extracting information from an extended link is done using a separate function, called includeExtendedLink.

```
    For i = 1 To oElementList.length
        includeExtendedLink oElementList(i - 1)
    Next
```

The third thing the function does is to select all external linksets from the document, retrieve those documents, scan them for extended links and pass those to includeExtendedLink:

```
    Set oElementList = oDocNode.selectNodes("/descendant::*" & _
                "[contains(attribute::*[local-name() = 'role'" & _
                "and namespace-uri() = '" & XLINK_NS & "'], 'external-linkset')]")
    For i = 1 To oElementList.length
        Set oLinkElement = oElementList.Item(i - 1)
        Set oDoc = New DOMDocument
        oDoc.async = False
        oDoc.Load (ResolveURL(oLocation.sURLPart, _
                oLinkElement.selectSingleNode("attribute::*[local-name()" & _
                "= 'href' and namespace-uri() = '" & XLINK_NS & "']").nodeValue))
        oDoc.setProperty "SelectionLanguage", "XPath"
        Set oElementList = oDoc.selectNodes("/descendant::*[attribute::*" & _
                "[local-name() = 'type' and namespace-uri() = '" & XLINK_NS _
                & "'] = 'extended']")

        For j = 1 To oElementList.length
            includeExtendedLink oElementList(j - 1)
        Next
    Next
```

So what happens in this includeExtendedLink function? Not much, because most of the functionality was already built in the XLinkExtended class. An XLinkExtended object is created, properties like sBaseURL are set and the linking node and the prefix for the XLink namespace are passed to the buildLinkset method. This method fills a collection of XLinkSimple objects. The only thing we have to do is copy all of these links to the oLinkbase collection of our document.

```
    Private Sub includeExtendedLink(oLinkElement As IXMLDOMElement)
        Dim oExtLink As XLinkExtended
        Dim attr As IXMLDOMAttribute
        Dim j As Long

        Set attr = oLinkElement.selectSingleNode("attribute::*[local-name()" & _
                "= 'type' and namespace-uri() = '" & XLINK_NS & "']")
```

```
        Set oExtLink = New XLinkExtended
        oExtLink.sBaseURL = oLocation.sURLPart
        oExtLink.buildLinkset oLinkElement, attr.prefix

        'Copy all built simple links to our documents linkset
        For j = 1 To oExtLink.collSimpleLinks.Count
            If LCase(oLocation.sURLPart) = _
                LCase(oExtLink.collSimpleLinks(j).FromLocation.sURLPart) Then
                oLinkBase.Add oExtLink.collSimpleLinks(j)
            End If
        Next
End Sub
```

Two steps remain – importing the embedded links and processing the remaining links.

First, let's discuss embedding. This is really a lot easier then you might imagine. We are only interested in embedding links that:

❑ Originate in the current document. This means that the oXMLNode property of the origin of the links must be known (otherwise the application won't know where to embed them).

❑ Have correct values for their sShow and sActuate properties (sShow="embed" and sActuate="onLoad").

Other links will be ignored (if they don't originate in the current document) or processed later (if they are not going to be embedded). If the link is to be embedded, a new XLinkedDocument is instantiated, the oLocation property of the document set to the target property of the link and makeLinked called. Isn't object based programming nice?

Now we just take the document element of the returned document and replace the link's origin with this element. We just have to do some administration in the collection of links afterwards, because the linking element isn't there anymore, so it should also be removed from the link base.

```
Private Sub importEmbeddedLinks()
    Dim i As Long
    Dim j As Long
    Dim oLocTo As Location
    Dim oLocFrom As Location
    Dim oNode As IXMLDOMNode
    Dim oXLinker As XLinkedDocument

    For i = 1 To oLinkBase.Count
        If oLinkBase.Item(i).sShow = "embed" And oLinkBase.Item(i).sActuate _
                        = "onLoad" Then
            Set oLocTo = oLinkBase.Item(i).ToLocation
            Set oLocFrom = oLinkBase.Item(i).FromLocation

            Set oXLinker = New XLinkedDocument
            Set oXLinker.oLocation = oLocTo
            Set oNode = oXLinker.makeLinked.documentElement

            If Not (oNode Is Nothing) And Not (oLocFrom.oXMLNode Is Nothing) Then
```

```
                    oLocFrom.oXMLNode.parentNode.replaceChild _
                  oNode.cloneNode(True), oLocFrom.oXMLNode 'Replace the
                                            ' linking node by the linked node
            End If
        End If
    Next


    ' Just some administration to do
    i = 1
    While i <= oLinkBase.Count
        'We loop through the same links again and remove them
        '(they should be removed from the document now)
        If oLinkBase.Item(i).sShow = "embed" And oLinkBase.Item(i).sActuate _
            = "onLoad" Then
            oLinkBase.Remove (i)
            i = i - 1 'Correction for the change in index numbers
        End If
        i = i + 1
    Wend
End Sub
```

The remaining links will be processed outside the component, for example by an XSLT stylesheet. All information collected from the XLink elements into the document must be encoded in a way that is relatively easy to display. To do this, an XML syntax has to be defined that can be added to any XML document, without being mistaken for other content. If you have paid close attention up till now, you'll be thinking, "namespaces!" Well you're quite right; we need to create a namespace for the information gathered from the links. As you know, the URI used doesn't necessarily have to point to any resource, so for the example, we choose:

http://www.wrox.com/books/XML/ProVBXML/SimpleLink

The linking scheme should be as straightforward as simple links from XLink (the origin of the link is always the linking element itself), but it must be able to point to several other locations, because extended links might indeed do this. The schema will look like this:

```
<someElement
  xmlns:sl=" http://www.wrox.com/books/XML/ProVBXML/SimpleLink"
  sl:id="12345"
  >
  <sl:ext-resource>http://www.mycomp.com</sl:ext-resource>
  <sl:int-resource>23456</sl:int-resource>
</someElement>
```

The int-resource child elements point to other elements in the same document that have an sl:id of the value shown. The ext-resource child elements point to complete remote documents. All elements that are part of a link, either as a target or a starting point, must have an sl:id.

The processLinks function loops through the whole set of links. For each link it first checks if we have an object reference for the 'from' location or only a URL. If we have only a URL, but the base URL of the location is identical to that of the current document, we try to resolve the URL to an object reference.

```vb
Private Sub processLinks()
    Dim i As Long
    Dim oSL As XlinkSimple
    Dim oNode As IXMLDOMElement
    Dim oChildElement As IXMLDOMElement

    For i = 1 To oLinkBase.Count
        Set oSL = oLinkBase(i)

        ' If a location is not an object reference, but the document it refers to
        ' is the current document, we solve the reference to an object
        If oSL.FromLocation.oXMLNode Is Nothing And _
            LCase(oSL.FromLocation.sURLPart) = LCase(oLocation.sURLPart) Then
            Set oSL.FromLocation.oXMLNode = _
              getNodeFromDocument(oDocNode.ownerDocument, oSL.FromLocation)
        End If
        If oSL.ToLocation.oXMLNode Is Nothing And LCase(oSL.ToLocation.sURLPart) _
            = LCase(oLocation.sURLPart) Then
            Set oSL.ToLocation.oXMLNode = _
                getNodeFromDocument(oDocNode.ownerDocument, oSL.ToLocation)
        End If
```

Now, if our origin is a node reference, the `SimpleLink` namespace is set to it and an attribute `sl:id` added to the element. The value of the `sl:id` attribute is calculated with the `UniqueID` function from the code module. The `UniqueID` function returns a unique string for each DOM node passed to it. If the same node is passed twice, it should return the same string, but when the document is loaded again (into a second `DOMDocument` object), the string will be different. It is implemented by using the undocumented `ObjPtr` function that converts the memory location of a certain object to a `Long` value. It is not a pointer, just a number with the same value as a pointer to that object.

```vb
        'For all locations that are a node reference, we create
        'the namespace and set the ID
        If Not oSL.ToLocation.oXMLNode Is Nothing Then
            Set oNode = oSL.ToLocation.oXMLNode
            If oNode.getAttributeNode("xmlns:sl") Is Nothing Then _
                    oNode.setAttribute "xmlns:sl", SIMPLE_LINK_NS
            oNode.setAttribute "sl:id", UniqueID(oNode)
        End If
        If Not oSL.FromLocation.oXMLNode Is Nothing Then
            Set oNode = oSL.FromLocation.oXMLNode
            If oNode.getAttributeNode("xmlns:sl") Is Nothing Then _
                    oNode.setAttribute "xmlns:sl", SIMPLE_LINK_NS
            oNode.setAttribute "sl:id", UniqueID(oNode)
        End If
```

Then internal and external target nodes are added. For the internal ones the `UniqueID` function is used again.

```vb
        'For links that are coming from the current page,
        'we will include child elements
        If Not oSL.FromLocation.oXMLNode Is Nothing Then
            Set oNode = oSL.FromLocation.oXMLNode
            If oSL.ToLocation.oXMLNode Is Nothing Then
```

```
                        'create a child element for external link
                        Set oChildElement = oNode.ownerDocument.createElement _
                              ("sl:ext-target")
                        oChildElement.appendChild _
                           oNode.ownerDocument.createTextNode(oSL.ToLocation.sComplexURL)
                        oChildElement.setAttribute "sl:title", oSL.ToLocation.sTitle
                        oChildElement.setAttribute "sl:show", oSL.sShow
                        oChildElement.setAttribute "sl:actuate", oSL.sActuate
                        oNode.insertBefore oChildElement, oNode.childNodes.Item(0)
                   Else
                        'create a child element for internal link
                        Set oChildElement = oNode.ownerDocument.createElement _
                              ("sl:int-target")
                        oChildElement.appendChild _
                                 oNode.ownerDocument.createTextNode _
                              (UniqueID(oSL.ToLocation.oXMLNode))
                        oNode.insertBefore oChildElement, oNode.childNodes.Item(0)
                   End If
              End If
         Next
    End Sub
```

And that is it! The library is finished and we have looked at most of the code. Please be aware that it is only an example and I wouldn't recommend using this library as it is in a production environment. Error handling is not implemented at all and the XLink logic is not complete, for example:

- ❏ A link from a node in our document to a node in an embedded document will not be resolved as a local link.

- ❏ Many XPointer features remain unimplemented (especially ranges, points and associated functions).

- ❏ We still have to handle displaying it.

The User Interface

The user interface comprises two parts – an HTML page and an ASP page. We also need a stylesheet.

The HTML Page

When a user comes to our web site to view product information, we now have the code in place to retrieve the minimal information about our product from the database. We have the XLinker library that will convert all XLink information to simple link information in its own namespace. But we still have no visible representation of the product information. What we can do now is transform the XML returned by the XLinker component to HTML, using an XSLT stylesheet. This is why we tried to translate the XLink information to a simpler linking syntax in the first place.

So, what would such a page look like and how would we achieve that using XSLT? Of these questions, the first one is really the harder of the two. Lets look at a case – an element in an XML document is linked to two other resources using an extended XLink:

```
<LinkedElement>some textual content</LinkedElement>
```

The XLink information is not visible in this fragment. The link description may be in another document (using an external linkset). Anyway, the LinkedElement element is the origin of two links. Our XLinker component has translated this to the following XML code:

```
<LinkedElement xmlns:tl=" http://www.wrox.com/ProVBXML/TransformLink ">
  <tl:link
    type="start"
    show="new"
    actuate="onRequest"
    href="http://www.ourserver/xpointersolve.asp?fullURL=
    http://doc...#xpointer(... etc)"
  />
  <tl:link
      tl:type="start"
    tl:show="new"
    tl:actuate="onRequest"
    href="http://www.ourserver/xpointersolve.asp?fullURL=
    http://doc...#xpointer(... etc)"
  />
  some textual content
</LinkedElement>
```

The content of the link is still the text "some textual content". The element links to two remote resources. In HTML, we can think of several ways to display this behaviour. We could place the linking element (A in HTML) around the content:

```
<A HREF=" http://www.ourserver/xpointersolve.asp?fullURL=
    http://doc...#xpointer(... etc)">
  <A HREF=" http://www.ourserver/xpointersolve.asp?fullURL=
      http://doc...#xpointer(... etc)">
    some textual content
  </A>
</A>
```

However the above code is invalid; nested A elements are not supported in HTML. Many browsers, faced with code like that above, will either raise an error; others will ignore one of the links. Another solution is shown below. It is not as esthetic, but much more pragmatic. It would place the links separate from the content:

```
<A HREF=" http://www.ourserver/xpointersolve.asp?fullURL=
    http://doc...#xpointer(... etc)">Link 1</A>
<A HREF=" http://www.ourserver/xpointersolve.asp?fullURL=
    http://doc...#xpointer(... etc)">Link 2</A>
some textual content
```

Then only one question remains – which content will appear inside the links? In the example above, the generic texts Link1 and Link2 are inserted, and what we want is to describe what the links points to. This is just what the title attribute in XLink does; it describe the remote resource. So the solution looks like this:

- ❑ Separate the link from the content.
- ❑ Use the title attribute as link content.
- ❑ If no title is available, use a generic text.

Now what will we do with the problem of dynamically embedding content into the document? A rather simple solution can be achieved using a small script and instantiating a DOMDocument on the client that retrieves the new content, copying it out to the HTML document. This solution will work only with IE5 and later, but at least it's an elegant solution.

The Stylesheet

So what would the stylesheet look like? First of all, the namespace would be declared like this:

```
<xsl:stylesheet xmlns:xsl="http://www.w3.org/1999/XSL/Transform"
        xmlns:sl="http://www.wrox.com/books/XML/ProVBXML/SimpleLink" version="1.0">
```

Then a template would have to be implemented that recognizes an element as a linking element:

```
<xsl:template match="*[@sl:id]" priority="2">
  <A><xsl:attribute name="name">
    <xsl:value-of select="@sl:id"/></xsl:attribute>
  </A>
  <xsl:apply-templates select="sl:ext-target|sl:int-target" mode="linkmaking"/>
  <xsl:apply-templates />
</xsl:template>

<xsl:template match="sl:int-target|sl:ext-target"/>
```

Note how the first template overrules all others when an sl:id attribute is encountered; this is because of the high priority of the template. It then first creates an empty anchor element with just the ID of the linking element, and then calls apply-templates for the child nodes in the sl namespace, using a special mode ('linkmaking'). This is done to prevent the standard templates from outputting the hyperlinks in the child nodes as text. The second template makes sure that the sl elements will not produce any output when accidentally encountered by a default template.

So how will we create the links themselves? They are basically all A tags, but with different attributes:

```
<xsl:template match="sl:ext-target" mode="linkmaking">
  <A>
  <xsl:if test="@sl:show !='embed' ">
    <xsl:attribute name="href">
      getXLinkedResource.asp?resURL=<xsl:value-of select="text()"/>
    </xsl:attribute>
    <xsl:if test="@sl:show='new' ">
      <xsl:attribute name="target">_new</xsl:attribute>
    </xsl:if>
  </xsl:if>
  <xsl:if test="@sl:show='embed' ">
    <xsl:attribute
            name="onClick">openHere('getXLinkedResource.asp?resURL=
            <xsl:value-of select="text()"/>', this)
    </xsl:attribute>
  </xsl:if>
  <xsl:if test="count(@sl:title) = 0">
    [link]
  </xsl:if>
  <xsl:value-of select="@sl:title"/><xsl:text> </xsl:text>
  </A>
</xsl:template>
```

Note how we insert a standard text [link] if no title attribute is present. Also note how the URL is not accessed directly, but is passed to the ASP page again. The most interesting part is actually the onClick attribute. It is programmed to call the function openHere, passing the URL and a reference to the element itself. This function is implemented in the HTML page by declaring it in the root template in XSLT (look carefully at how the CDATA section is used; scripts often use & and < symbols.)

```
<xsl:template match="/PRODUCT"><HTML><BODY>
<SCRIPT>
//<![CDATA[
function openHere(url, elm)
{
  var doc = new ActiveXObject("MSXML.DOMDocument");
  doc.async = false;
  doc.load(url);
  if (doc.parseError.errorCode == 0)
  {
    elm.outerHTML = doc.documentElement.xml;
  }
}
//]]>
</SCRIPT>
  <xsl:apply-templates select="NAME"/>
  <xsl:apply-templates select="DESCRIPTION"/>
  <xsl:apply-templates select="RELATEDPRODUCTS"/>
  </BODY></HTML>
</xsl:template>
```

The ASP Page

The ASP page is very simple. It has to get the parameter indicating the desired resource from the client, instantiate an XLinkedDocument object, pass the parameter to it, get the results back and transform them to HTML. For the base URL we have chosen a rather arbitrary one: http://www.some.com. It's not very relevant anyway; you have to pass *absolute* URLs to this ASP page. The base URL is filled in because the XLinkedDocument needs it.

```
<%@ Language=VBScript %>
<%
Option Explicit
Response.ContentType = "text/xml"
Dim oXLinker
Set oXLinker = Server.CreateObject("XLinker.XLinkedDocument")

If (Request("resURL").Count = 0) then
  Response.Write "<ERROR>Error: no resURL passed</ERROR>"
  Response.End
End If

oXLinker.oLocation.sBaseURL = "http://www.some.com"
oXLinker.oLocation.sRelURL = Request("resURL")

Dim oDoc
Dim oStyle
Set oStyle = Server.CreateObject("MSXML2.DOMDocument")
```

```
oStyle.async = False
oStyle.load(Server.MapPath("SimpleLinkStyle.xsl"))

Set oDoc = oXLinker.makeLinked()
Response.Write oDoc.transformNode(oStyle)
%>
```

Summary

One of the reasons that XLink is taking such a long time to reach Recommendation status is that no good reference implementations are available. This makes deciding on the right functionalities a hard task for the W3C Working Group, as feedback on their ideas is scarce. The problems encountered in this chapter while doing only a very basic implementation of XLink serve as an illustration of the implementation problems.

XLink gives a nice and clear description of the connection between several resources (both local and remote), but says nothing about how this should be implemented in a general XLink application. This is left to the implementors and turns out to be a difficult task.

In this chapter we achieved:

❑   Implementing a basic XLink implementation for use on the server

❑   Support for all Xlink features needed for the sample application (embedded fragments and simple links)

❑   Additional support for translating extended links to a set of simpler links

Now that we have a way to show the product details from the database and the XML document merged into one browser interface, we want to offer ordering functionality in the browser. This is what we will do in the next chapter: processing an order request using XML documents holding the order details.

Distributed Objects

In Chapter 9 we saw how the product information for our distributed application would be transmitted and stored. The product information editor (introduced in Chapter 8, and expanded in Chapter 9) would use SOAP to send product information to an ASP-based SOAP server. The SOAP server would in turn populate a database and send the XML to an ASP-based XML file server. Also, in Chapter 10, we learned how to implement XLink functions in a Visual Basic component.

Now it's time to put it all together. We're building a web site for online purchases. There will be some Active Server Page code, of course, though we won't be going into all of the details for a complete, robust site. We'll show the basic pages to allow a user to search for products, get information about the items using XLink, select items to purchase, and submit a purchase order. Along the way we'll see how to integrate code running on different machines, and how to coordinate activity among distributed components.

The Application Architecture

Our system has six main parts:

- ❏ The user's web browser
- ❏ The Wrox store web server
- ❏ An ASP-based SOAP server
- ❏ An XML file server storing the product details
- ❏ A SQL Server database holding basic product information
- ❏ An ordering/restocking system that runs at the warehouse site

The web-based components use MTS to handle various Visual Basic objects for the bulk of the business logic. A diagram of the system looks like this:

A typical sequence of events might be:

1. The user visits the web store and decides to do a search.

2. Form data is posted up to the web server, converted to XML, and passed to an MTS object to perform the search.

3. The MTS object makes a SOAP request to perform the search.

4. The SOAP server queries the database, and basic information for any matching items is returned as an XML string.

5. The XML is transformed to HTML with XSL for rendering in the browser.

6. The returned HTML includes transformed XLink references, so that if the user wants to see more details about a search result, the browser will fetch the related information.

7. The user may select items for purchase. Product IDs for the selected items are posted to the web server. An MTS object sends a SOAP request to get the product information, and to check that the items are still in stock.

8. The user is presented with a purchase form, listing the items selected (and their availability status.) After completing some billing information, the form is submitted to the web server.

9. The web server formats the posted data as an XML string and passes it to an MTS object to handle the submission of purchase orders. A response is returned to the user indicating that the order has been submitted.

10. The purchase order is then placed into a local message queue (MSMQ) for later processing by the warehouse system.

11. The warehouse system is responsible for tracking the order, and checking inventory levels for reordering.

Let's get to the code for the application, see how each part works, and explore some approaches for distributed communication.

Posting Purchase Requests to a Remote Application

Our first task will involve creating an interface – but what exactly is an interface and what is the benefit of using one? An **interface** describes the public functions an object provides. One of the fundamental concepts of COM is that of interface-based programming. When we interact with an object, we don't need to know how its methods work, only that they do, and always will; an object is a "black box" that we can always rely on. The idea of a public interface (that is, one whose methods and properties are freely accessible from outside) is that of a contract: when we release an object to the world, we're making an agreement that, whatever we may decide in the future to do to the code, the outside world will always see the same methods and properties. The methods will always have the same signature (i.e. number of arguments, and their data types will not change), and will always return the same data type. However, it is possible that someone working on an ActiveX DLL might realize that one or more of the methods needs a different argument, or a method should be returning a string instead of an integer. If we've set our component to compile with binary compatibility, we end up getting a cranky message from the compiler about breaking compatibility. This is because the interface has changed. (You may have noticed, though, that you can gleefully add *new* methods without any problem. Technically you're still changing the interface, but because you haven't changed any previously existing methods, older code can still work, oblivious to the existence of the new methods.)

Creating an interface class in Visual Basic is somewhat akin to an abstract class in Java. You define a set of methods that the class should have, but you do not actually put any code in them.

> *In fact, you can achieve the same results by creating a type library directly, using MIDL (Microsoft Interface Definition Language), which resembles the C programming language. This requires editing a MIDL text file and running it through the MIDL compiler; we're going to take an easier route.*

But what's the value of a class that does nothing? Well, it serves as a template for other classes that *will* actually do the work, and the presence of the type library allows us to set a reference to the basic type, gaining the advantages of early binding, without having to specify a binary object in advance.

> *When we declare a reference to a specific object in a Visual Basic project, the information about that object's functions and properties are available to the VB compiler. The compiler can verify that the referenced object exists, and that any methods or properties that are used are specified correctly. This process is referred to as **early binding**. However, if we declare a variable of type* `Object`*, the VB compiler cannot perform the verification because it does not have a specific object to refer to. Instead, the verification process takes place at run time, after the* `Object` *variable has been set to a particular object. This is known as **late binding**; the object's properties and methods are verified each time VB executes a line of code that includes the object. This repeated verification slows down the application.*

The IRemoteTransactions.IProductOrders Interface Class

So, for our product orders object, which will be responsible for somehow getting our user's purchase request some place for processing, we want to define a basic set of methods that will allow us to perform any required configuration, perform the actual order dispatch, and provide any error information in case we suspect foul play. We create a Visual Basic ActiveX DLL project, called `IRemoteTransactions`, and add a single class, `IProductOrders`.

We define a method called `Configure` that takes a single `String` parameter, `sXmlConfigData`, which is an XML string. By using XML, we can avoid the problem of having to know in advance how many actual arguments will be needed. Note that using an XML string is a mixed blessing. Using XML allows us to pass in arbitrarily complex data in a single parameter, but the downside is that you need to know a little something about what that XML should look like. It's not as obvious as using, say, an `Integer` parameter. (It would be handy if we could declare the parameter type by specifying a DTD or Schema, but this is not possible!) But even when using more direct data types we often have to know what the value is intended for and what an acceptable range would be, so in many cases we cannot escape the problem of needing some inside knowledge.

The method is required to return a `Boolean` value to indicate whether or not the configuration succeeded. We can use this method to pass in whatever data is needed to configure the code so that it can commmunicate with a remote machine and exchange data. For example, if we were implementing this in a class in order to do a SOAP request, we might need to set the SOAP server URL. If we were using this to send a message to a remote MSMQ, we would need to pass in information on how to locate the remote queue.

```
Public Function Configure(ByVal sXmlConfigData As String) As Boolean

End Function
```

We now define a method to return any error data as an XML string. Again, making use of this requires some knowledge of what that XML will look like (but that's what documentation is for).

```
Public Function GetErrorInfoXml() As String

End Function
```

Finally, we have a method for actually posting the purchase order. It expects a `String` (the XML purchase order) and returns a `String`:

```
Public Function PostPurchaseOrder(ByVal sPoXml As String) As String

End Function
```

We take this class and compile it.

> Note that we've used the "I" prefix in our object name to indicate that this is an interface class. This is not required, but simply a coding convention to warn potential users that this is an interface.

The compilation will generate a DLL (with no practical code), but it will also create a type library, which is what we really want. We can now build some real classes to do the work. We'll look at two versions. One will use SOAP to post a purchase order to some SOAP server, and the other will use the Microsoft Message Queue.

Moving Information in a Distributed Application

We will show how to provide alternate means for sending a user's product order to the remote warehouse system. But before we do so, it would be useful to consider some issues when sending data in a distributed application. When we write a simple, stand-alone application, we pretty much have complete control over the various parts of our code. We can define our classes and rely on them being there when we need them. If an error occurs, we can generally tell what it is, and decide how to respond to the given circumstances. Errors really shouldn't occur, except under unusual circumstances. With a distributed application, things are very different. We're interacting with code that may live on a machine on another continent, on a completely different platform, using a stateless protocol such as HTTP over a possible shaky connection. The failure rate becomes a more significant issue, and we have to plan accordingly. For one thing, we may initiate a remote request, but never get a response. We're left wondering what happened: should we assume the request went through, and carry on regardless? This could lead to the loss of data and serious problems later on. Should we be pessimistic and assume the worst? This may be more prudent, but unless we have a way to synchronize with the remote objects, we may end up duplicating our request. If you've ever had your PC momentarily lock-up and repeatedly pressed the *Enter* key (believing that your actions were being ignored), you have some idea of what can happen with unintended duplication of events.

Because of these potential risks to data integrity, the concept of transactions was developed. Databases often use transactions to ensure that complex procedures complete correctly, with all parties involved going away happy and assured that what was expected to happen *did* happen. Or, if there was a problem with some part of the transaction, all data is restored to the condition prior to the transaction. For example, we may have a transaction that involves moving financial information among multiple tables. Before changing anything in one table, we want to be sure that a corresponding activity has taken place in another table. From the point of view of each table, the procedure is not complete until the other part has successfully completed. Of course, these events aren't (necessarily) going to happen simultaneously, so some precautions need to be taken. In such a case, each activity is performed in an intermediate process: data may be changed or deleted in a given table, but the information is stored in such a way that the action could be undone (or "rolled back", in database lingo) if there is reason to suspect a failure on the other end. Each part of the transaction will attempt to conduct the requested action, but the transaction as a whole is not complete until all the events have reported back that everything went well. Only then are the requests formally committed.

Part of the routine for determining if all went well may involve some sort of time factor. We may only want to wait so long for the "all OK" response before deciding that something has failed and reverting to our previous state. In the case of distributed applications, we come across the notion of **disconnected applications**. These are applications that do not require persistent connections among all of the components. There may be cases where it is impractical to wait until another event has completed. Because we do not control what's on the other end of a request, and perhaps have no idea just how our request is to be handled, we may not know when a request would complete. Waiting is no longer a real option.

In our web store application, we make requests over HTTP to web servers. We have some idea of what amount of time would be reasonable; in fact, if we think the time is too great to provide service to a user, we would likely change our remote request methods. If a request fails, we are able to maintain some state in our web pages and application variables. It may be an inconvenience to the user, but the data could be re-entered and the request resubmitted. But once the user has issued a purchase request, we move into a transaction that will almost certainly involve more activity and more time.

For us to process a purchase order, several things need to happen: first, we have to retrieve the purchase order. Then we need to verify that we have the requested items in stock. If we do this, we want to decrease the inventory amount and issue a command to go get it and package it up. If we do not have the item, we need to modify the purchase request. In either case we want to prepare something to send to the buyer (either by e-mail or a regular letter) to indicate the status of the order. Finally, if the inventory drops too low, we may want to initiate restocking processes so that we always have plenty of things to sell.

There's also no guarantee that the system responsible for this will be running 24 hours a day, solely dedicated to processing newly-placed orders. The system may perform other tasks; it may get taken down for maintenance. We certainly can't have the user staring at a browser while all this takes place. We need to get the user's order and put it somewhere safe, so that we can give a quick reply. We can then tell the user that the order is being processed, while we wait for the transaction to occur offline.

Earlier, we discussed a class that would handle posting the purchase order to some remote system. We showed two implementations of this: one that sent a SOAP request (presumably to some machine that could take care of all the related details), and one that used the Microsoft Message Queue (MSMQ). The value of using a SOAP transaction is that it provides a platform-neutral way to communicate with another machine. We may want to do our product ordering and managing the inventory on a Unix box; it wouldn't matter. However, SOAP by itself does nothing to ensure safe storage of transmitted data. It is simply a transport and messaging system. We would still have to implement our own system for storing the product orders, and some means for retrieving them. This is not necessarily difficult, and depending on what platform we choose it may be required. But message queues were invented to solve exactly this sort of problem, so we might as well take advantage of them. Note that because we're using XML to describe our messages, we are still free to pass the information to pretty much anywhere we like. We can use MSMQ locally on a machine running NT, and provide an additional transactional interface to it that pulls out messages and instructs the queue to delete messages once we are confident that we have the required information. A message queue will provide, at the least, a secure place to hold our data temporarily.

This brings us to the concept of state in a distributed application. It is a mantra in component development that you should avoid relying on state (i.e. the persistence of instance-specific data over time) when interacting with remote objects. The reason for this is that it is costly to hold an object instance simply for the purpose of storing data. Objects consume memory and execution threads; once we've used an object to perform a certain task, we should take our data and leave, freeing the object and its resources. However, individual parts of a distributed application need the ability to stop what they're doing and hold tight in case other parts of the application stop responding. What's needed are ways to avoid what might be referred to as moments of suspense – those points in our application's activities where it is unclear who owns the data. For example, we may wish to have our application send e-mail. We could open up a socket and attempt to send the mail ourselves, but while the event requirements are being negotiated we have a period of time where both the main application and the socket activities both have a claim to the data. On the other hand, we could write a file to a mail folder, and let the mail system take it from there. There is still the chance of an error occurring, but we are in a much better position to recover without losing the data. Either our main application still has it, or the mail system has it. Likewise, using a message queue allows us to simply drop off the order information and forget about it, something less likely with SOAP.

The main points here are that distributed applications put us at a higher risk for disruption, and that applications need to either quickly dispatch important data, or provide a means to recover from errors and undo any related actions. Using the former approach gives a cleaner, less tightly coupled system with greater ability to scale, with less overhead.

Purchase Order Posting Classes

The first class sends a SOAP request to the warehouse system that processes customer orders. The project is an ActiveX DLL. We will provide the code to implement the `IRemoteTransactions.IProductOrders` interface, plus some private helper functions, but we won't add any additional public methods. The methods provided by implementing `IProductOrders` provide a consistent interface in case we want to swap objects and use a different way to send the purchase orders. When we want to use this class in another application, we can set a reference in the application project to the interface class, and define an object of type `IProductOrders`. We would then use `CreateObject("WroxRemoteTX.ProductOrdersSoap")` to instantiate the specific object type.

WroxRemoteTX.ProductOrdersSoap

We want our classes to run under MTS, so we set a reference in our project to the MTS type library and use the `Implements ObjectControl` statement. But we also set a reference to our new `IRemoteTransactions.IProductOrders` type library, and use the `Implements IRemoteTransactions.IProductOrders` statement:

```
Implements IRemoteTransactions.IProductOrders
```

We define a constant to make constructing error data strings a little easier. Our project will use a reference to our error utilities class, and a reference to our SOAP posting class:

```
Const PROGID As String = "WroxRemoteTX.ProductOrdersSoap"

Private oSoapRq As SoapRequestMts.XmlHttp
Private oError As ErrorUtils.ErrorInfo
Private oCtx As ObjectContext
```

We also set a reference to the `Scripting.Dictionary` object, which we'll use for managing configuration data:

```
Private oConfigDataDict As Scripting.Dictionary
```

Managing SOAP Requests

We'll also define a private method to build our SOAP request. It takes the order information XML and wraps it in a SOAP request envelope:

```
Private Function BuildSoapPostOrder(sOrderInfoXml As String) As String
    Dim sSoapTx As String
    Dim sOrderInfo As String
    Dim oDOM As DOMDocument

    Set oDOM = New DOMDocument

    If oDOM.loadXML(sOrderInfoXml) Then
    sSoapTx = "</SOAP:Body>" & vbLf
        sSoapTx = sSoapTx & " </SOAP:Envelope>"
        sSoapTx = sSoapTx & "<soapPostPurchaseOrder>" & vbLf
        sSoapTx = sSoapTx & "   <w:orderInfo "
```

```
            sSoapTx = sSoapTx & "xmlns:w='www.wrox.com/VbXml'>" & vbLf
            sSoapTx = sSoapTx & sOrderInfoXml & "</w:orderInfo>" & vbLf
            sSoapTx = sSoapTx & "</soapPostPurchaseOrder>" & vbLf
            sSoapTx = sSoapTx & " </SOAP:Body>" & vbLf
            sSoapTx = sSoapTx & "</SOAP:Envelope>"
      Else
            Call oError.SetErrorInfo("Error parsing XML: " & oDOM.parseError.reason, _
                        PROGID & ".BuildSoapPostOrder", oDOM.parseError.errorCode)
            sSoapTx = ""
      End If
      Set oDOM = Nothing
      BuildSoapPostOrder = sSoapTx
   End Function
```

Now, as you may have noticed when you used `Implements ObjectControl`, the `Implements` keyword causes your project to automatically create additional method "shells" corresponding to the public methods defined by the interface class. These are defined as `Private`; however you should not change them to `Public`. Despite the seeming inaccessibility of the method, the magic of vTable lookup will expose these as `Public`, without the leading "`IProductOrders_`" part.

> *It is worth noting here that this process of indirectly locating an object's methods prevents these methods from being used in scripting languages. If you create a class that implements a custom interface, those methods belonging to the custom interface will not be visible. For a detailed explanantion of this, refer to the following MSDN article by Ted Pattison:*
> *http://msdn.microsoft.com/library/periodic/period00/basics0100.htm*

The Configure Function

Let's build our `Configure` code. We use the `Dictionary` object to store name/value pairs taken from the received XML configuration data. The XML should look like this:

```
<Config>
 <Item type='soapServerUrl' value='http://192.168.0.1/soapb2/SoapSrv.asp'/>
 <Item type='transactionNamespace' value='http://www.logicmilestone.com/vbSoap'/>
 <Item type='timeoutSeconds ' value='300'/>
</Config>
```

Our next function walks the node list of items and populates the dictionary. The function returns True if there were no errors, `False` otherwise:

```
Private Function IProductOrders_Configure(ByVal sXmlConfigData As String) _
            As Boolean
   On Error GoTo ErrHand
   Dim oDOM As MSXML.DOMDocument
   Dim bResults As Boolean
   Dim oNodeList As IXMLDOMNodeList
   Dim oEl As IXMLDOMElement
   Dim sKey As String
   Dim sData As String
   Dim nIdx As Integer
```

```
        Set oDOM = New DOMDocument
        If oDOM.loadXML(sXmlConfigData) Then
            Set oNodeList = oDOM.getElementsByTagName("Item")
            For nIdx = 0 To oNodeList.length
                Set oEl = oNodeList.Item(nIdx)
                sKey = oEl.Attributes.getNamedItem("type").nodeValue
                sData = oEl.Attributes.getNamedItem("value").nodeValue
                oConfigDataDict.Add sKey, sData
            Next
            bResults = True
        Else ' Bad XML!
            Call oError.SetErrorInfo("XML error: " & oDOM.parseError.reason, _
                      PROGID & ".Configure", oDOM.parseError.errorCode)
            bResults = False
        End If

ErrHand:
    If Err.Number <> 0 Then
        Call oError.SetErrorInfo("COM error: " & Err.Description, _
            PROGID & ".Configure", Err.Description)
        bResults = False
    End If
End Function
```

Other Functions

For the error information, we'll just subclass the method from the error utilities class:

```
Private Function IProductOrders_GetErrorInfoXml() As String
    IProductOrders_GetErrorInfoXml = oError.GetErrorInfoXML()
End Function
```

Finally, for posting orders, we take the XML passed in, wrap a SOAP request envelope and request body around it, and send it off:

```
'*********************************************************************
' Private Function IProductOrders_PostPurchaseOrder(ByVal sPoXml As String)
' As String
'*********************************************************************
Private Function IProductOrders_PostPurchaseOrder(ByVal sPoXml As String) _
                As String
    On Error GoTo ErrHand

    Dim sResults As String
    Dim sSoap As String

    sSoap = BuildSoapPostOrder(sPoXml)

    With oSoapRq
        .SoapServerURL = oConfigDataDict.Item("soapServerUrl")
        .TransactionNamespaceURI = oConfigDataDict.Item("transactionNamespace")
        .TimeoutSeconds = oConfigDataDict.Item("timeoutSeconds")
        sResults = .PostRequest(sSoap)
        sResults = .GetResponseBody(sResults)
    End With
```

```
        sResults = "<OK/>"

ErrHand:
    If Err.Number <> 0 Then
        Call oError.SetErrorInfo("COM Error: " & Err.Description, _
            PROGID & ".PostPurchaseOrder", -1)
        sResults = oError.GetErrorInfoXML()
    End If

    IProductOrders_PostPurchaseOrder = sResults
End Function
```

We must also implement the `ObjectControl` methods:

```
Private Sub ObjectControl_Activate()
    Set oCtx = GetObjectContext()
    Set oError = New ErrorUtils.ErrorInfo
    Set oSoapRq = oCtx.CreateInstance("SoapRequestMts.XmlHttp")
End Sub

Private Function ObjectControl_CanBePooled() As Boolean
    ObjectControl_CanBePooled = False
End Function

Private Sub ObjectControl_Deactivate()
    Set oError = Nothing
    Set oSoapRq = Nothing
    Set oCtx = Nothing
End Sub
```

There you go. Now we'll create an "identical" class, but using MSMQ instead. (Later on in this chapter we'll see how to configure the web store to dynamically load a particular class to handle the order request.)

WroxRemoteTX.ProductOrdersMsmq

We begin with the expected `Implements` statements:

```
Option Explicit

Implements ObjectControl
Implements IRemoteTransactions.IProductOrders
```

Then we define a few constants for MSMQ:

```
Const PROGID  As String = "WroxRemoteTX.ProductOrdersMsmq"
Const MQ_SEND_ACCESS = 2
Const MQ_DENY_NONE = 0
```

We also declare our MSMQ objects:

```
Private Qinfo As MSMQ.MSMQQueueInfo
Private Q As MSMQ.MSMQQueue
Private Qmsg As MSMQ.MSMQMessage
```

And the additional objects used above:

```
Private oError As ErrorUtils.ErrorInfo
Private oCtx As ObjectContext
Private oConfigDataDict As Scripting.Dictionary
```

The Configure Function

Our configuration function will work the same as it did in the SOAP version. Of course, the XML string will contain different values for the Item attributes. We'll need to pass in the machine name where MSMQ resides, and the name of queue we want to see, like this:

```
<Config>
  <Item type='machineName' value='' />
  <Item type='queueName' value='' />
</Config>

Private Function IProductOrders_Configure(ByVal sXmlConfigData As String) _
              As Boolean
    On Error GoTo ErrHand

    Dim oDOM As MSXML.DOMDocument
    Dim bResults As Boolean
    Dim oNodeList As IXMLDOMNodeList
    Dim oEl As IXMLDOMElement
    Dim sKey As String
    Dim sData As String
    Dim nIdx As Integer

    Call oError.ClearErrorInfo
    Set oDOM = New DOMDocument

    If oDOM.loadXML(sXmlConfigData) Then
        Set oNodeList = oDOM.getElementsByTagName("Item")
        For nIdx = 0 To oNodeList.length - 1
            Set oEl = oNodeList.Item(nIdx)
            sKey = oEl.Attributes.getNamedItem("type").nodeValue
            sData = oEl.Attributes.getNamedItem("value").nodeValue
            oConfigDataDict.Add sKey, sData
        Next
        bResults = True
    Else ' Bad XML!
        Call oError.SetErrorInfo("XML error: " & oDOM.parseError.reason, _
                    PROGID & ".Configure", oDOM.parseError.errorCode)
        bResults = False
    End If

ErrHand:
    If Err.Number <> 0 Then
        Call oError.SetErrorInfo("COM error: " & Err.Description, _
                    PROGID & ".Configure", Err.Number)
        bResults = False
    End If

    IProductOrders_Configure = bResults
End Function
```

Other Functions

Again we subclass the error utilities method:

```
Private Function IProductOrders_GetErrorInfoXml() As String
    IProductOrders_GetErrorInfoXml = oError.GetErrorInfoXML()
End Function
```

For posting purchase orders, we'll create an MSMQ message and drop it off in a queue:

```
Private Function IProductOrders_PostPurchaseOrder(ByVal sPoXml As String) _
            As String
    On Error GoTo ErrHand

    Dim sResults As String
    Dim sMachineName As String
    Dim sQueueName As String

    Call oError.ClearErrorInfo
```

We need to set the queue path:

```
    sMachineName = oConfigDataDict.Item("machineName")
    sQueueName = oConfigDataDict.Item("queueName")
    If Len(sMachineName) > 0 Then
        sMachineName = "\\" & sMachineName & "\"
    End If
    Qinfo.PathName = sMachineName & sQueueName
```

Then open up the queue:

```
    Set Q = Qinfo.Open(MQ_SEND_ACCESS, MQ_DENY_NONE)
```

Then create the message:

```
    Set Qmsg = New MSMQ.MSMQMessage
    Qmsg.Label = "WROXPO_" & Now()      ' Create a unique label
    Qmsg.Body = sPoXml
```

And finally send it:

```
    Qmsg.send Q
```

Then the queue is closed and the results are returned:

```
    'Invoke the Close method
    Q.Close
    sResults = "<OK/>"

ErrHand:
    If Err.Number <> 0 Then
        Call oError.SetErrorInfo("COM error: " & Err.Description & _
                    "Qinfo.PathName = " & Qinfo.PathName, _
                    PROGID & ".PostPurchaseOrder", Err.Number)
        sResults = oError.GetErrorInfoXML()
    End If

    IProductOrders_PostPurchaseOrder = sResults
End Function
```

Our `ObjectControl` code performs some basic initialization and clean up.

The Wrox Store Web Site

The web site serves to collect and display data for the user. The logic for this, and the code for interacting with the other parts of our application, is in an MTS object called `WroxStore.WebTransactions`.

The WroxStore.WebTransactions Object

The object primarily constructs SOAP requests for product data. It also handles some XSL transformations, and makes use of our XLink solver object, described in Chapter 10.

The project is an ActiveX DLL, with references to the MTS type library, the ASP object library, the Microsoft XML parser, our SOAP request posting class (described in Chapter 9), our error utilities class, and the `IProductOrders` interface class we just created.

The code starts out with the usual MTS `Implements ObjectControl` statement, and some object declarations:

```
'*****************************************************************************
' Class WroxStore.WebTransactions
' Methods for performing web store transactions
'*****************************************************************************
Option Explicit

Implements ObjectControl

Const PROGID As String = "WroxStore.WebTransactions"
Private oRemoteOrderTx As IRemoteTransactions.IProductOrders
Private oCtx As ObjectContext
Private oError As ErrorUtils.ErrorInfo
Private oApplication As ASPTypeLibrary.Application
Private oXlinkDoc As Xlinker.XLinkedDocument
Private oSoapRq As SoapRequestMts.XmlHttp

Private m_sSoapUrl As String
```

When our object is first activated, we run some code to initialize our global objects:

```
Private Sub ObjectControl_Activate()
    Set oCtx = GetObjectContext()
    Set oProdTxUtils = oCtx.CreateInstance("WebProducts.ProdTxUtils")
    Set oApplication = oCtx.Item("Application")
    Set oSoapRq = oCtx.CreateInstance("SoapRequestMts.XmlHttp")
    m_sSoapUrl = oApplication("SoapUrl")
    Set oError = New ErrorUtils.ErrorInfo
End Sub
```

Because we'll be constructing a number of SOAP requests, we've set up two methods for building chunks of SOAP envelope code:

```
Private Function AddSoapFoot() As String
    Dim sStr As String
    sStr = " </SOAP:Body>" & VbLf
    sStr = sStr & " </SOAP:Envelope>"
    AddSoapFoot = sStr
End Function
```

```
Private Function AddSoapHead() As String
    Dim sStr As String
    sStr = "<SOAP:Envelope "
    sStr = sStr & "xmlns:SOAP='urn:schemas-xmlsoap-org:soap.v1' "
    sStr = sStr & "SOAP:encodingStyle='urn:schemas-xmlsoap-org:soap.v1'>" & vbLf
    sStr = sStr & "<SOAP:Body>" & vbLf
    AddSoapHead = sStr
End Function
```

We also have some methods for building the specific transactions we'll use:

```
Private Function BuildSoapGetCategoryListTx() As String
    Dim sSoapTx As String
    sSoapTx = AddSoapHead()
    sSoapTx = sSoapTx & "<w:soapGetCategoryList "
    sSoapTx = sSoapTx & "xmlns:w='www.wrox.com/VbXml'>" & vbLf
    sSoapTx = sSoapTx & "</w:soapGetCategoryList>" & vbLf
    sSoapTx = sSoapTx & AddSoapFoot()
    BuildSoapGetCategoryListTx = sSoapTx
End Function
```

The `soapGetCategoryList` request doesn't require any parameters; the server code that handles these just returns a list of unique product categories based on what is in the `Catalog` table of our product database. `BuildSoapGetSelectedProductsTx` creates a SOAP request for retrieving information about items a user has decided to buy. It takes an XML string containing the product IDs and quantities:

```
Private Function BuildSoapGetSelectedProductsTx(ByVal sXmlParams As String) _
            As String
  Dim sSoapTx As String
    sSoapTx = AddSoapHead()
    sSoapTx = sSoapTx & "<w:soapGetSelectedProducts "
    sSoapTx = sSoapTx & "xmlns:w='www.wrox.com/VbXml'>" & vbLf
    sSoapTx = sSoapTx & sXmlParams & vbLf
    sSoapTx = sSoapTx & "</w:soapGetSelectedProducts>" & vbLf
    sSoapTx = sSoapTx & AddSoapFoot()
    BuildSoapGetSelectedProductsTx = sSoapTx
End Function
```

Searching for products requires sending a SOAP request containing the search criteria, a combination of product category and/or a product name. We have a method to build this request:

```
Private Function BuildSoapSearchTx(sName As String, sCategory As String) As String
    Dim sSoapTx As String
    sSoapTx = AddSoapHead()
    sSoapTx = sSoapTx & "<w:soapSearchForProduct "
    sSoapTx = sSoapTx & "xmlns:w='www.wrox.com/VbXml'>" & vbLf
    sSoapTx = sSoapTx & "   <name>" & Trim(sName) & "</name>" & vbLf
    sSoapTx = sSoapTx & "   <category>" & Trim(sCategory) & "</category>" & vbLf
    sSoapTx = sSoapTx & "</w:soapSearchForProduct>" & vbLf
    sSoapTx = sSoapTx & AddSoapFoot()
    BuildSoapSearchTx = sSoapTx
End Function
```

Constructing the SOAP Request

When our web application is started, global.asa (which we will discuss a little further on in the chapter) calls a transaction to retrieve a list of unique product categories based on what is currently in the Catalog table. The method begins with some variable declarations. It will construct a SOAP request, post the request to the SOAP server, parse the response, and transform it into a set of HTML OPTION elements:

```
Public Function GetCategoryList() As String
    On Error GoTo ErrHand

    Dim oDOM As MSXML.DOMDocument
    Dim oSoapDom As MSXML.DOMDocument
    Dim sSoapRq As String
    Dim oEl As MSXML.IXMLDOMElement
    Dim sProdName As String
    Dim sProdCategory As String
    Dim sSoapResp As String
    Dim sResults As String
    Dim sXSL As String
    Dim sXML As String

    Set oDOM = New DOMDocument
    sSoapRq = BuildSoapGetCategoryListTx()
    oSoapResp = PostSoapRq(sSoapRq)
```

We should get back a response that resembles this:

```
<SOAP:Envelope xmlns:SOAP="urn:schemas-xmlsoap-org:soap.v1"
        SOAP:encodingStyle="urn:schemas-xmlsoap-org:soap.v1">
  <SOAP:Body>
    <w:soapGetCategoryListResponse xmlns:w='www.wrox.com/VbXml' >
      <results>
        <DATA>
          <Row Category="foocat" />
          <Row Category="bardog" />
        </DATA>
      </results>
    </w:soapGetCategoryListResponse>
  </SOAP:Body>
</SOAP:Envelope>
```

So the function needs to retrieve the parts we want:

```
        If oDOM.loadXML(sSoapResp) Then
            Set oEl = oDOM.getElementsByTagName("results").Item(0)
            If oEl Is Nothing Then
                Call oError.SetErrorInfo("Failed to get valid results: " & oDOM.xml, _
                            PROGID & ".GetCategoryList", -1)
                sResults = oError.GetErrorInfoXml()
            Else
                sXML = oEl.xml
```

If the code can parse the SOAP results, then we want it to pull some XSL out of the web application to transform the data into an OPTION list:

```
            ' Get the XSL from the web application
            sXSL = oApplication("CategoryListXsl")
            sResults = TransformXml (sSoapResp, sXSL)
        End If
    Else
        Call oError.SetErrorInfo("Failed to parse parameters: " & _
                    oDOM.parseError.reason, PROGID & ".GetCategoryList", -1)
        sResults = ""
    End If

ErrHand:
    If Err.Number <> 0 Then
        Call oError.SetErrorInfo(Err.Description & " XML = " & sSoapResp, _
                    PROGID & ".GetCategoryList", Err.Number)
        sResults = ""
    End If
    GetCategoryList = sResults
End Function
```

To make XSL transformation a little more robust, we put the code into a separate method. It removes the repetitive code for instantiating temporary DOM objects for holding the XML and XSL, running the transformation, checking for errors, and destroying the DOM objects:

```
Public Function TransformXml(ByVal sXML As String, sXSL As String) As String
    On Error GoTo ErrHand

    Dim oXmlDom As MSXML.DOMDocument
    Dim oXslDom As MSXML.DOMDocument
    Dim sResults As String

    Set oXmlDom = New DOMDocument
    Set oXslDom = New DOMDocument

    If oXmlDom.loadXML(sXML) Then
        If oXslDom.loadXML(sXSL) Then
            sResults = oXmlDom.transformNode(oXslDom)
        Else ' Failed to parse XSL
        Call oError.SetErrorInfo("XSL error: " & oXmlDom.parseError.reason, _
                    PROGID & ".TransformXml", oXmlDom.parseError.errorCode)
            sResults = ""
        End If
    Else ' Failed to parse XML
        Call oError.SetErrorInfo("XML error: " & oXmlDom.parseError.reason, _
                    PROGID & ".TransformXml", oXmlDom.parseError.errorCode)
        sResults = ""
    End If

ErrHand:
    If Err.Number <> 0 Then
        Call oError.SetErrorInfo("COM error: " & Err.Description, _
                    PROGID & ".TransformXml", Err.Number)
        sResults = ""
    End If

    Set oXmlDom = Nothing
    Set oXslDom = Nothing

    TransformXml = sResults
End Function
```

The class methods provide for error trapping, in the event that something is amiss. Should we need to pass this (or any other method's errors) back to the calling application, we expose the GetErrorInfoXml method:

```
Public Function GetErrorInfoXml() As String
    GetErrorInfoXml = oError.GetErrorInfoXml()
End Function
```

When a user has picked some items from the search results list, and submits the form to begin the purchasing procedure, Purchase.asp makes a call using GetSelectedProducts to pull back the information. The method makes a SOAP request to get the main data from the database. Before the data is returned it is manipulated to insert an additional attribute for the quantity of items ordered:

```
Public Function GetSelectedProducts(ByVal sXmlParams As String)
    On Error GoTo ErrHand

    Dim oSoapDom As MSXML.DOMDocument
    Dim sSoapRq As String
    Dim sSoapResp  As String
    Dim sResults As String
    Dim sXML As String
    Dim sXSL As String
    Dim oEl As MSXML.IXMLDOMElement
    Dim oXmlDom As MSXML.DOMDocument
    Dim oXslDom As MSXML.DOMDocument

    Set oXmlDom = New DOMDocument
    Set oXslDom = New DOMDocument
```

The code loads the XML parameters, and if there were no parsing errors it passes the XML to BuildSoapGetSelectedProductsTx and sends the SOAP request:

```
If oXmlDom.loadXML(sXmlParams) Then
    sSoapRq = BuildSoapGetSelectedProductsTx(sXmlParams)
    sSoapResp = PostSoapRq(sSoapRq)
```

The SOAP response body is again loaded into the DOM to ensure that it is proper XML, and returned data is extracted:

```
If oXmlDom.loadXML(sSoapResp) Then
    Set oEl = oXmlDom.getElementsByTagName("DATA").Item(0)
    If oEl Is Nothing Then
        Call oError.SetErrorInfo("Failed to get valid results: " & _
                    oXmlDom.xml, PROGID & ".GetSelectedProducts", -1)
        sResults = ""
    Else
        sXML = oEl.xml
```

The data should look like this (here formatted for readability):

```
<DATA>
  <Row ProdID="97"
       Name="Paint"
       Category="Art Utensils"
       BriefDesc="Be creative! Use paint!"
       XmlDetails="http://192.168.0.1/WroxFileServer/ProductFiles/97.xml"
       Price="12" Inventory="120"
       Qty="2"/>
  <Row ProdID="100"
       Name="Cat"
       Category="Toys"
       BriefDesc="Cat description"
       XmlDetails="http://192.168.0.1/WroxFileServer/ProductFiles/100.xml"
       Price="50"
       Inventory="130"
       Qty="2"/>
  <TotalCost>124</TotalCost>
</DATA>
```

We want to transform this into HTML to be sent to the browser. The XSLT is kept in an ASP `Application` variable. It will check the `Inventory` attribute, and if it is "0," it will insert a message that the item is not available:

```
                sXSL = oApplication("SelectedItemsXsl")
                If oXslDom.loadXML(sXSL) Then
                    sResults = oEl.xml
                    sResults = TransformXml(sResults, sXSL)
                Else
                    sResults = ""
                End If
            End If
```

Various errors, such as failing to load any of the XML, will set error information and return an empty string:

```
        Else ' Bad XML in response
            Call oError.SetErrorInfo("Failed to parse SOAP response: " & _
                    oXmlDom.parseError.reason, PROGID _
                    & ".GetSelectedProducts", -1)
            sResults = ""
        End If
    Else
        Call oError.SetErrorInfo("Failed to parse XML params: " & _
                oXmlDom.parseError.reason, PROGID & ".GetSelectedProducts", _
                oXmlDom.parseError.errorCode)
        sResults = ""
    End If
```

```
ErrHand:
    If Err.Number <> 0 Then
        Call oError.SetErrorInfo("COM error: " & _
                    Err.Description, PROGID & ".GetSelectedProducts", Err.Number)
        sResults = ""
    End If

    GetSelectedProducts = sResults
End Function
```

The XSL, kept in the web application variable `SelectedItemsXsl`, looks like this:

```
<xsl:stylesheet xmlns:xsl="http://www.w3.org/TR/WD-xsl" >
<xsl:template><xsl:apply-templates/></xsl:template>
<xsl:template match="text()"><xsl:value-of select="."/></xsl:template>

<xsl:template match="text()|@*">
 <xsl:value-of select="."/>
</xsl:template>

<xsl:template match="*"><xsl:apply-templates/></xsl:template>
<xsl:template match="text()"></xsl:template>

<xsl:template match="DATA">
 <TABLE border="0" cellpadding="3" cellspacing="5" width="100%">
  <TR>
    <TD class="ResultsHeader">Name</TD>
    <TD class="ResultsHeader">Category</TD>
    <TD class="ResultsHeader">Desc</TD>
    <TD class="ResultsHeader">Price</TD>
    <TD class="ResultsHeader">Qty</TD>
  </TR>
  <xsl:for-each select="Row">
  <TR>
    <TD class="ResultsBody"><xsl:value-of select="@Name" /></TD>
    <TD class="ResultsBody"><xsl:value-of select="@Category" /></TD>
    <TD class="ResultsBody"><xsl:value-of select="@BriefDesc" /></TD>
    <TD class="ResultsBody">
    <xsl:choose>
      <xsl:when test="Inventory[. = '0']">
        This item is not currently available
      </xsl:when>
      <xsl:otherwise>$<xsl:value-of select="@Price" />
      </xsl:otherwise>
      </xsl:choose>
    </TD>
    <TD class="ResultsBody">
    <xsl:value-of select="@Qty" />
    </TD>
  </TR>
</xsl:for-each>
<TR>
 <TD colspan="3"> </TD>
 <TD class="ResultsBody">$<xsl:value-of select="TotalCost"/>
 </TD>
 </TR>
</table>
```

The resulting HTML will be inserted into an HTML page created by the ASP code. The page includes a form for submitting the final order; a hidden form field is used to store the products being ordered. The XSLT only selects those items where the inventory is not zero:

```
    <INPUT type="hidden" name="PRODUCTS">
    <xsl:attribute name="value"><xsl:for-each select="Item[Inventory != '0']">
        <PRODUCT><xsl:value-of select="PRODUCT/@ID" /></PRODUCT></xsl:for-each>
    </xsl:attribute>
    </input>
  </xsl:template>
</xsl:stylesheet>
```

Committing a Purchase Order

Once a user has decided to hand over some hard-earned money, the CommitPurchase.asp code passes the user data to PostPurchaseOrder, our class that implements the IProductOrders interface. The code retrieves the ProgID for the object to handle the actual product ordering, and uses the ProgID to create an instance of the object. Configuration data for the object is kept in a file on the web server and loaded into an application variable. The ASP code calls the object's PostPurchaseOrder method, passing it the XML created in the ASP code. It checks the results of the call, and returns either thumbs up or thumbs down:

```
Public Function PostPurchaseOrder(ByVal sPoDataXml As String) As String
    On Error GoTo ErrHand

    Dim sResults As String
    Dim sRemProdTxProgID As String
    Dim sConfigData As String
    Dim sPostResults As String
    Dim vRes As Variant

    sRemProdTxProgID = oApplication.Value("RemoteProdOrderTxProgID")
    sConfigData = oApplication.Value("RemoteProdOrderTxConfig")
    Set oRemoteOrderTx = oCtx.CreateInstance(sRemProdTxProgID)

    If (oRemoteOrderTx.Configure(sConfigData)) Then
        sPostResults = oRemoteOrderTx.PostPurchaseOrder(sPoDataXml)
        If (InStr(sPostResults, "OK")) Then
            sResults = "<OK/>"
        Else ' remote post ruined our day ...
            Call oError.SetErrorInfo("Post to remote machine failed!", _
                        PROGID & ".", -1)
            sResults = oRemoteOrderTx.GetErrorInfoXml()
        End If
    Else ' config data has bad mojo
        Call oError.SetErrorInfo("Configuration of remote poster class failed.", _
                    PROGID & ".", -1)
            sResults = oError.GetErrorInfoXml()
    End If

ErrHand:
    If Err.Number <> 0 Then
        Call oError.SetErrorInfo("COM error: " & Err.Description, _
                    PROGID & ".PostPurchaseOrder", Err.Number)
        sResults = oError.GetErrorInfoXml()
    End If

    PostPurchaseOrder = sResults
End Function
```

All of our SOAP requests are dispatched using the `PostSoapRq` method. It uses our SOAP posting object (`SoapRequest.XmlHttp`) to create the correct request headers and send the request to the SOAP server, returning the results of the request. The code pulls the SOAP configuration data from the application variables:

```
Private Function PostSoapRq(sSoap As String) As String
    On Error GoTo ErrHand

    Dim oDOM  As MSXML.DOMDocument
    Dim sResults As String

    Set oDOM = New DOMDocument
```

The URL for the SOAP server is taken from an ASP `Application` variable, the required HTTP header information prepared, and the request is sent off (refer to Chapter 9 for the details of the `SoapRequest.XmlHttp` object):

```
    m_sSoapUrl = oApplication.Value("SoapUrl")

    If Len(m_sSoapUrl) < 1 Then
        Call oError.SetErrorInfo("No SOAP URL", _
                    PROGID & "PostSoapRq", -1)
        sResults = oError.GetErrorInfoXml()
    Else
        If oDOM.loadXML(sSoap) Then
            ' Set up parameters for SOAP request
            With oSoapRq
                .SoapServerURL = oApplication.Value("SoapURL")
                .TransactionNamespaceURI = _
                    oApplication.Value("SoapTransactionNamespaceURI")
                .TimeoutSeconds = oApplication.Value("SoapTimeout")
                sResults = .PostRequest(sSoap)
                sResults = .GetResponseBody(sResults)
            End With
        Else
            Call oError.SetErrorInfo("Failed to parse SOAP request: " & _
                    oDOM.parseError.reason, PROGID & "PostSoapRq", -1)
            sResults = oError.GetErrorInfoXml()
        End If
    End If

ErrHand:
    If Err.Number <> 0 Then
        Call oError.SetErrorInfo("COM error: " & _
                    Err.Description, PROGID & ".PostSoapRq", Err.Number)
        sResults = oError.GetErrorInfoXml()
    End If

    PostSoapRq = sResults
End Function
```

When a user submits the search criteria from the search web page, `SearchResults.asp` takes the form data and passes it on (as XML) to the `SearchForProducts` method. It makes a SOAP request to retrieve a set of matching products:

```
Public Function SearchForProducts(ByVal sXmlParams As String) As String
    On Error GoTo ErrHand

    Dim oDOM As MSXML.DOMDocument
    Dim oSoapDom As MSXML.DOMDocument
    Dim sSoapRq As String
    Dim oEl As MSXML.IXMLDOMElement
    Dim sProdName As String
    Dim sProdCategory As String
    Dim sSoapResp As String
    Dim sResults As String
    Dim sSQL As String
    Dim sXSL As String
    Dim sXML As String

    Set oDOM = New DOMDocument
    If oDOM.loadXML(sXmlParams) Then
        ' Parse out the parameters
        Set oEl = oDOM.documentElement
        sProdName = oEl.Attributes.getNamedItem("name").nodeValue
        sProdCategory = oEl.Attributes.getNamedItem("category").nodeValue
        sSoapRq = BuildSoapSearchTx(sProdName, sProdCategory)
        ' POST the request
        sSoapResp = PostSoapRq(sSoapRq)
```

The SOAP call should return a response similar to this:

```
<SOAP:Envelope xmlns:SOAP="urn:schemas-xmlsoap-org:soap.v1"
        SOAP:encodingStyle="urn:schemas-xmlsoap-org:soap.v1">
  <SOAP:Body>
   <w:soapSearchForProductResponse xmlns:w='www.wrox.com/VbXml'>
      <results>
          <DATA>
            <Row ProdID="20" Name="Foo"
                Category="foocat" BriefDesc="bloog"
                XmlDetails="http://127.0.0.1/ProdFiles/20.xml"/>
            <Row ProdID="21" Name="Bar"
                Category="foocat" BriefDesc="flig"
                XmlDetails=" http://127.0.0.1/ProdFiles/21.xml"/>
          </DATA>
      </results>
   </w:soapSearchForProductResponse>
  </SOAP:Body>
</SOAP:Body>
```

So, we snip out the parts we want from the SOAP body, format it with XSL taken from a web application variable, and return the results. The formatting includes changing the `XmlDetails` URL into a link to display the complete product information.

```
            If oDOM.loadXML(sSoapResp) Then
                Set oEl = oDOM.getElementsByTagName("results").Item(0)
                sXML = oEl.xml
            Else
                Call oError.SetErrorInfo("Failed to parse parameters: " _
                        & oDOM.parseError.reason, PROGID _
                        & ".SearchForProducts", -1)
                sResults = ""
            End If
            ' Get the XSL
            sXSL = oApplication("SearchResultsXsl")
            sResults = TransformXml(sSoapResp, sXSL)
        Else    ' Failed to load XML
            Call oError.SetErrorInfo("Failed to parse parameters: " _
                        & oDOM.parseError.reason, PROGID _
                        & ".SearchForProducts", -1)
            sResults = ""
        End If

ErrHand:
    If Err.Number <> 0 Then
        Call oError.SetErrorInfo(Err.Description, _
                    PROGID & ".SearchForProducts", Err.Number)
        sResults = ""
    End If

    SearchForProducts = sResults
End Function
```

Finally, we complete the remaining `ObjectControl` methods:

```
Private Function ObjectControl_CanBePooled() As Boolean
    ObjectControl_CanBePooled = False
End Function
```

```
Private Sub ObjectControl_Deactivate()
    Set oApplication = Nothing
    Set oSoapRq = Nothing
    Set oProdTxUtils = Nothing
    Set oError = Nothing
End Sub
```

Designing the Web Site

The Wrox web store is not an extremely complex site. For example, there's no shopping cart, no sophisticated queries, no slick graphics. There is just enough to demonstrate the basic operations, from search to purchase.

The action begins in the `global.asa` file. Pretty much every Active Server Page application has a file with this name, and it serves a special purpose, similar to the `OnLoad` event for a Visual Basic application form. When a user visits a web site processing ASP, the first call to any file with the `.asp` extension causes the application to load and parse the `global.asa` file. The file allows for subroutines to handle up to four events: `Application_OnStart`, `Application_OnEnd`, `Session_OnStart`, and `Session_OnEnd`. If this is the first time anyone has called an ASP page, then the `Application_OnStart` event is fired. Any code associated with this event will then be processed. So, for example, our `global.asa` file might have something like this:

```
<SCRIPT LANGUAGE=VBScript RUNAT=Server>
    Sub Application_OnStart
      Application(MyApplicationVariable) = "Some Value. "
      resolvelink.htc
    End Sub
</SCRIPT>
```

In this basic example, the start of the application causes the creation of a variable called `MyApplicationVariable`, with the value `"Some Value. "`. `Application` variables are available to all ASP code, for any user, as long as the application is running.

An `Application` ends when the web server is shut down (properly, rather than crashing). We may, for example, want to keep a log of our application's duration, and have some code to write to a file whenever the application is shut down. So, we could do something like this:

```
<SCRIPT LANGUAGE=VBScript RUNAT=Server>
    Sub Application_OnStart
      Application("MyApplicationVariable") = "Some Value."
    End Sub

    Sub Application_OnEnd
      ' Some code to append to a log file
    End Sub

</SCRIPT>
```

(Bear in mind, though, that if the application crashes, the `OnEnd` code will not get run.)

We may have also chosen to have some session-specific bit of code:

```
<SCRIPT LANGUAGE=VBScript RUNAT=Server>
    Sub Application_OnStart
      Application("MyApplicationVariable") = "Some Value."
    End Sub

    Sub Application_OnEnd
      ' Some code to append to a log file
    End Sub

    Sub Session_OnStart
      Session ("MySessionVariable") = "Some Other Value."
    End Sub
</SCRIPT>
```

This creates a `Session` variable called `MySessionVariable`, with the value `"Some Other Value."`. This value is available to all ASP code for the *specific* session begun by the user's first call to an ASP page. When the session ends (either because of the lack of activity over a certain period of time, or because some ASP code explicitly ends it), the `Session` variable disappears.

Typically, `Application` events are used for setting variables that will be needed regardless of who the user is, such as defining an ADO connection string. `Session` variables are used to track user-specific information, such as might be used in a shopping cart application.

Configuring global.asa

So, we can use the `global.asa` file to initialize a number of items that we'll need for our application:

```
<SCRIPT LANGUAGE=VBScript RUNAT=Server>
Option Explicit
```

The file defines a subroutine, `LoadConfigData`, which is used to read in a local file and assign the contents to an `Application` variable:

```
Sub LoadConfigData(sServerPath, sVarName)
  Dim sFname
  Dim fso
  Dim tso

  sFname = Server.MapPath(sServerPath)
  Set fso = Server.CreateObject("Scripting.FileSystemObject")
  If fso.FileExists(sFname) Then
    Set tso = fso.OpenTextFile(sFname, 1, False)
    Application(sVarName) = tso.ReadAll()
  Else
    Application(sVarName) = ""
  End if
  Set fso = Nothing
  Set tso = Nothing
End Sub
```

`Application_OnStart`, after defining some local variables, initializes some `Application` variables to hold configuration data for the SOAP server. We need to tell the web store ASP code where to find the server (the URL), the namespace our SOAP transactions will use, and a timeout value so that we aren't held up by a slow server. We've set it to 120 seconds, or two minutes, which should be plenty of time to get a response.

```
Sub Application_OnStart

  Dim sXslFile        ' Path to XSL file
  Dim oWebTx          ' Wrox store web transaction class
  Dim sPoPosterConfig ' XML string for configuring the
                      ' class for posting purchase orders

  ' SOAP server config data
  Application("SoapURL") = "http://192.168.0.1/soapb2/SoapSrv.asp"
  Application("SoapTransactionNamespaceURI") = _
            "http://www.logicmilestone.com/vbSoap"
  Application("SoapTimeout") = 120 ' Seconds we wait for a response
```

When a user makes a purchase, the purchase order information needs to be sent to the warehouse computer. We're going to use MSMQ for this, but the actual method is contained in a separate DLL that implements a specific interface. This allows the web site to be configured to use a different method (such as BizTalk, or a SOAP request) without having to recompile the main web site code. We define an `Application` variable to hold the `ProgID` for an object to handle purchase order requests:

```
Application("RemoteProdOrderTXProgID") = "WroxRemoteTX.ProductOrdersMsmq"
```

The `WroxRemoteTX.ProductOrdersMsmq` object requires some configuration data (such as the name of the MSMQ server) that is kept in an XML file in the config subdirectory. `LoadConfigData` stores this in an `Application` variable:

```
LoadConfigData "config/RemotePosterConfigMsmq.xml", "RemoteProdOrderTxConfig"
```

The Visual Basic object for the site uses some XSLT files, kept in the style subdirectory of the web application. `LoadConfigData` is used to store the contents:

```
LoadConfigData "style/SearchResultsXLink.xsl", "SearchResultsXsl"
LoadConfigData "style/CategoryList.xsl", "CategoryListXsl"
LoadConfigData "style/SelectedItems.xsl", "SelectedItemsXsl"
LoadConfigData "style/Product.xsl", "ProductXsl"
```

When the user goes to the search page, an option list is presented showing product categories. To ensure that the list is current, a call is made to the `WebTransactions` class to query the database and return a list of categories:

```
Set oWebTx = Server.CreateObject("WroxStore.WebTransactions")

Application("CategoryOptions") =  "<OPTION> " & oWebTx.GetCategoryList()
If (Len(Application("CategoryOptions")) = 0) Then
  Application("CategoryOptions") = "<OPTION>Error"
End if

Set oWebTx = Nothing
End Sub
</SCRIPT>
```

The Default Page

Like any good ASP application, our site has a default home page, called (surprise!) `Default.asp`. It doesn't really do anything except display a link for searching, but because it's an ASP file it will trigger the processing of `global.asa`. So, when a user comes to the site, he or she will be greeted by this eye-catching page:

Well, it's not much but it serves our purpose.

The Search Page

When the user clicks the Search link, the Search.asp page is loaded:

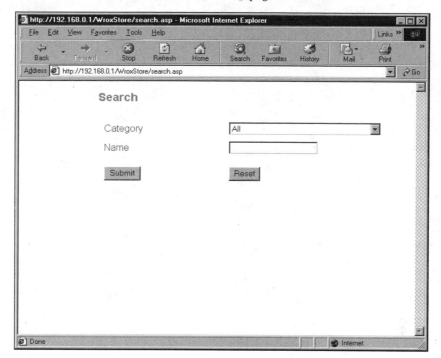

This code is marginally more complex than that of the default page:

```
<%@ Language=VBScript %>
<%
  ' Search.asp
  Option Explicit
%>
<HTML>
<HEAD> <TITLE> Wrox Store Search</TITLE>
<LINK rel=stylesheet type="text/css" href="style/wrox.css">
</HEAD>
<BODY>
<TABLE width=650 border=0 cellSpacing=1 cellPadding=1>
  <TR>
    <TD width=120> </TD>
    <TD><H1>Search</H1></TD>
    <TD></TD>
  </TR>
  <TR>
    <TD></TD>
    <TD>
    <FORM name="search" method="post" action="SearchResultsVb.asp" >
    <TABLE width="100%" border=0 cellSpacing=10 cellPadding=0>
    <TR>
```

```
      <TD width="200">Category</TD>
      <TD>
        <SELECT id="category" name="category" >
             <OPTION selected value="">All</OPTION>
             <%=Application("CategoryOptions") %>
          </SELECT>
          </TD>
  </TR>
  <TR>
    <TD>Name</TD>
    <TD>
      <INPUT id="name" name="name">
    </TD>
  </TR>
  <TR>
    <TD></TD>
    <TD></TD>
  </TR>
  <TR>
    <TD><INPUT id=submit1 name=submit1 type=submit value=Submit></TD>
    <TD><INPUT id=reset1 name=reset1 type=reset value=Reset></TD>
  </TR>
  </TABLE>
  </FORM>
  </TD>
  <TD></TD>
  </TR>
</TABLE>
</BODY>
</HTML>
```

It's a basic form with a dropdown list for the available categories, but the list of options is pulled from the session variable created in global.asa.

The Search Results Page

So, suppose the user decides to search for something, and simply selects a category from the list, and submits the form. The data is sent to SearchResults.asp, which initiates events for locating matching products:

```
<%@ Language=VBScript %>
<%
  Option Explicit
  Dim oWebTx
  Dim sXmlParams
  Dim sName
  Dim sCategory
  Dim sResults
  Dim sErr

  Set oWebTx = Server.CreateObject("WroxStore.WebTransactions")
  sName = Request.Item("name")
  sCategory = Request.Item("category")
  sXmlParams = "<Params name='" & sName & "' category='" & sCategory & "' />"
  sResults =  oWebTx.SearchForProducts(sXmlParams)
  sErr = oWebTx.GetErrorInfoXml()
```

```
%>
<HTML>
<HEAD><TITLE>Wrox Store Search Results</TITLE>
  <LINK rel=stylesheet type="text/css" href="style/wrox.css">
</HEAD>
<BODY>
<H3>Search Results</H3>
<FORM name="Purchase" action="PurchaseVb.asp" method="get">
<%=sResults%>
<TABLE border="0" cellpadding="5">
  <TR>
    <TD><INPUT type="submit" value="Click to purchase!"></TD>
    <TD><INPUT type="reset" value="Reset" ></TD>
  </TR>
</TABLE>
</FORM>
</BODY>
</HTML>
```

The server-side VBScript takes the form values and constructs an XML string, which is passed to the
SearchForProducts method of the WroxStore.WebTransactions MTS object.
SearchForProducts returns matching products in an HTML table:

Resolving XLinks

The items in the table of matching products contain links to display the product details. The details are
shown in a new page, created by getXLinkedResource.asp, which also contains links for related
products. Related product information is kept in the product information XML file as XLink references.

getXLinkedResource.asp creates an instance of the XLinker.XlinkedDocument object described in Chapter 10, "*Using a VB Component to Implement Linking*". The code sets a base URL and relative URLs, and calls makeLinked to fetch the requested details file. (Refer to Chapter 10 for more details on how the object works.) The file to display is passed in a query string parameter called resURL.

```
<%@ Language=VBScript %>
<%
Option Explicit

Dim oXLinker
Set oXLinker = Server.CreateObject("XLinker.XLinkedDocument")

If (Request("resURL").Count = 0) Then
      Response.Write "<ERROR>Error: no resURL passed</ERROR>"
      Response.End
End If

oXLinker.oLocation.sBaseURL = "http://192.168.0.1/wroxstore/"
oXLinker.oLocation.sRelURL = "http://192.168.0.1/WroxFileServer/ProductFiles/" _
                  & Request("resURL") & ".xml"

Dim oDoc
Dim oDoc2
Dim oStyle

Set oStyle = Server.CreateObject("MSXML2.DOMDocument")
oStyle.async = False
oStyle.load(Server.MapPath("style/SimpleLinkStyle.xsl"))

Set oDoc2 = Server.CreateObject("MSXML2.DOMDocument")
Set oDoc = oXLinker.makeLinked()
```

The XML returned by makeLinked is transformed into HTML by XSLT kept in the style subdirectory of the ASP application, and is sent to the browser:

```
If oDoc2.loadXML(oDoc.xml) Then
      Response.Write oDoc2.transformNode(oStyle)
Else
      Response.Write "<H3>Error retrieving product file</H3>"
End if

%>
```

The results look like this:

Purchasing Items

After conducting a search, the user has the option to purchase items by entering a quantity in the Qty column and clicking the Submit button. The form data, including the selected product IDs and quantities, is sent off to Purchase.asp. This page takes the form data and constructs an XML string, which is passed on to the `GetSelectedProducts` method of `WroxStore.WebTransactions`. This method in turn will handle a SOAP request to check that the selected items are still in stock, and to pull back the details. The page displays the product information, including a special message should any item be out of stock. The page also contains a form for the user to provide billing information. (Note that this is a sample application, and in order to focus on the main concepts behind transforming and exchanging XML, certain details have been omitted. In a real application, you would probably want to include separate name and address fields for billing and mailing, options for the user to save personal information, calculations of tax and shipping charges, and so on.)

Let's look at the code for this:

```
<%@ Language=VBScript %>
<%
Option Explicit
  Response.Buffer = true

  Dim oWebTx, asItems, asItemValues, sProdIdXml
  Dim asItemData, nIdx, sNoItems, sSelProds, sErrInfo
```

After declaring our variables, we create an instance of the `WebTransactions` class, which will be used to send the form data to the message queue. A flag is set to determine if the user did not select any items to purchase:

```
Set oWebTx = Server.CreateObject("WroxStore.WebTransactions")
sNoItems = "FALSE"
sProdIdXml = "<Products>" & vbLf
```

The code goes through each item in the query string, building an XML string to be placed in a hidden form field. The query string would look something like this:

```
http://192.168.0.1/WroxStore/Purchase.asp?128=3&129=&127=1&97=&100=&104=&105=&106=
```

Each item specifies a product item and the quantity being ordered. Only where the user entered a quantity will a product ID have a value. The loop checks the length of the query string item value to see if the product has been requested before adding it to the XML:

```
For nIdx = 1 to Request.QueryString.Count
  If Len(Request.QueryString.Item(nIdx)) > 0 Then
    sProdIdXml = sProdIdXml & "<id qty='"
    sProdIdXml = sProdIdXml & Request.QueryString.Item(nIdx) & "'>"
    sProdIdXml = sProdIdXml & Request.QueryString.Key(nIdx)
    sProdIdXml = sProdIdXml & "</id>" & vbLf
  End If
```

The code then checks the XML string to see if any items were ordered:

```
    If (sProdIdXml = "<Products>" & vbLf) Then
      sNoItems = "TRUE"
    End If
  Next
  sProdIdXml = sProdIdXml & "</Products>" & vbLf
%>

<HTML>
 <HEAD><TITLE>Wrox Store Purchase</TITLE>
 <LINK rel=stylesheet type="text/css" href="style/wrox.css">
 </HEAD>
 <BODY>
 <%
 If(sNoItems = "FALSE") Then
     sSelProds = oWebTx.GetSelectedProducts(sProdIdXml)
%>
```

If the user did order items, the page calls `GetSelectedProducts` to retrieve information about what is being ordered, so that it may be displayed in the page, and builds the billing information form:

```
    <FORM name="purchase" action="CommitPurchase.asp" method="post" >
    <H3>Selected items:</H3>
    <%=sSelProds%><P>
    <INPUT type="hidden" name="PRODUCTS" value="<%=sProdIdXml%>"><P>
    <TABLE border="0" cellPadding="3" cellSpacing="2" width="650" >
     <TR>
      <TD>
        <TABLE border=0 cellPadding=1 cellSpacing=1 width="100%">
          <TR>
            <TD>First name</TD>
            <TD><INPUT id=FIRSTNAME name=FIRSTNAME maxlength=50 size=50></TD>
            <TD></TD></TR>
          <TR>
```

```
            <TD>Last name</TD>
            <TD><INPUT id=LASTNAME name=LASTNAME maxlength=50 size=50></TD>
            <TD></TD></TR>
        <TR>
            <TD>Address</TD>
            <TD><INPUT id=ADDR1 name=ADDR1 maxlength=50 size=50></TD>
            <TD></TD></TR>
        <TR>
            <TD>Address</TD>
            <TD><INPUT id=ADDR2 name=ADDR2 maxlength=50 size=50></TD>
            <TD></TD></TR>
        <TR>
            <TD>City</TD>
            <TD><INPUT id=CITY name=CITY maxlength=30 size=30></TD>
            <TD></TD></TR>
        <TR>
            <TD>State</TD>
            <TD><INPUT id=STATE name=STATE maxlength=4 size=4></TD>
            <TD></TD></TR>
        <TR>
            <TD>Postal</TD>
            <TD><INPUT id=POSTAL name=POSTAL maxlength=12 size=12></TD>
            <TD></TD></TR>
        <TR>
            <TD>Credit card type</TD>
            <TD>
              <SELECT id=CCTYPE name=CCTYPE>
               <OPTION   selected value="VI">Visa</OPTION>
               <OPTION   value="MC">MasterCard</OPTION>
               <OPTION   value="AX">AmEx</OPTION>
              </SELECT>
            </TD>
            <TD></TD></TR>
        <TR>
            <TD>Credit card number</TD>
            <TD><INPUT id=CCNUM name=CCNUM></TD>
            <TD></TD></TR>
        <TR>
            <TD><INPUT id=submit1 name=submit1 type=submit value=Submit></TD>
            <TD><INPUT id=reset1 name=reset1 type=reset value=Reset></TD>
            <TD></TD>
        </TR>
      </TABLE>
    </TD>
  <TR></TR>
 </TABLE>
</FORM></P>
```

If no quantities for any items were given, the user is shown a brief, functional message:

```
    <%
    Else
    %>
      <H3>You did not pick anything!</H3>
    <%
    End If
    %>
    </BODY>
</HTML>
```

The user then completes the form, and submits it back to the server to `CommitPurchase.asp`.

Once again, the ASP code wraps the form data in XML, and it is sent to another method of `WebTransactions`, `PostPurchaseOrder`. The user is then told that the order has been submitted:

```
<%@ Language=VBScript %>
<%
Option Explicit
' Take the posted data, format the XML for sending to
' the remote warehouse computer.

    Dim oWebTx, sResults
    Dim sXML, sPRODUCTS, sFIRSTNAME, sLASTNAME
    Dim sADDR1, sADDR2, sCITY, sSTATE, sPOSTAL
    Dim sCCNUM, sCCTYPE

    Set oWebTx = Server.CreateObject("WroxStore.WebTransactions")
    sPRODUCTS = Request.Item("PRODUCTS")
    sFIRSTNAME = Request.Item("FIRSTNAME")
    sLASTNAME = Request.Item("LASTNAME")
    sADDR1 = Request.Item("ADDR1")
    sADDR2 = Request.Item("ADDR2")
    sCITY = Request.Item("CITY")
    sSTATE = Request.Item("POSTAL")
    sPOSTAL = Request.Item("POSTAL")
    sCCNUM = Request.Item("CCNUM")
    sCCTYPE =Request.Item("CCTYPE")

    sXML = "<PurchaseOrder>" & vbLf
    sXML = sXML &  sPRODUCTS
    sXML = sXML &  "<CustomerData>" & vbLf
    sXML = sXML &  "<Address>" & vbLf
    sXML = sXML &  "<Addr1>" +  sADDR1 + "</Addr1>" & vbLf
    sXML = sXML &  "<Addr2>" +  sADDR2 + "</Addr2>" & vbLf
    sXML = sXML &  "<City>" +  sCITY + "</City>" & vbLf
    sXML = sXML &  "<State>" +  sSTATE + "</State>" & vbLf
    sXML = sXML &  "<Postal>" +  sPOSTAL + "</Postal>" & vbLf
    sXML = sXML &  "</Address>" & vbLf
    sXML = sXML &  "<PaymentData>" & vbLf
    sXML = sXML &  "<CCnum>" +  sCCNUM + "</CCnum>" & vbLf
    sXML = sXML &  "<CCtype>" +  sCCTYPE + "</CCtype>" & vbLf
    sXML = sXML &  "</PaymentData>" & vbLf
    sXML = sXML &  "</CustomerData>"
    sXML = sXML &  "</PurchaseOrder>" & vbLf
    sResults = oWebTx.PostPurchaseOrder(sXML)
%>
<HTML>
<HEAD>
 <TITLE>Order Sent</TITLE>
 <LINK rel=stylesheet type="text/css" href="style/wrox.css">
</HEAD>
<BODY>
    <H3>Your order has been submitted</H3>
    <%=sResults%>
</BODY>
</HTML>
```

That's the web site finished. It provides some basic forms for searching and ordering products, and uses server-side script to interact with MTS Visual Basic objects.

The SOAP Server

The web site makes use of SOAP requests to get data from our database and file server. As far as the web site is concerned, this is all magic – it need not know anything about where the database or file server is, or if they even exist. Wrapping the requests in SOAP means that we can distribute our application to any number of machines, on any number of platforms, and the details are hidden from view. Our file server is running on NT using IIS, but that's a mere detail. It could just as well be running on Linux using Apache. In fact, because we're using HTTP for our application protocol, we could change web servers and no one would be any the wiser (except for the server administrator, who may get a slight shock!).

The Soap Wrappers Class

Our SOAP requests are primarily front-end wrappers for more complex application functions. We have a class called `WebProducts.SoapWrappers` that contains methods called in response to SOAP requests, but which delegates to other functions in another class, `WebProducts.ProductDescriptionTx`. We've already seen some of the SOAP wrapper and back-end application code when we looked at how our product details file editor interacted with the remote system, in Chapter 9. Now let's see the new code specific to the web store. (This code is added to the existing `WebProducts.SoapWrappers` class.)

Getting Product Categories

The `soapWrapGetCategoryList` method calls into the `ProductDescriptionTx` class to perform a search for a list of unique product categories, formatting the results as a SOAP response:

```
Public Function soapWrapGetCategoryList(sSoapParams As String) As String
    On Error GoTo ErrHand

    Dim oDOM As MSXML.DOMDocument
    Dim oEl As IXMLDOMElement
    Dim sName As String
    Dim sCategory As String
    Dim sResponse As String

    Set oDOM = New DOMDocument
    sResponse = ""
```

`ProductDescriptionTx` requires some information about the product database and the location of the file server; this data is defined in the SOAP web server and stored in application variables. (Some classes are initialized and configured in `ObjectControl_Activate`.)

The application code doesn't require any parameters, so we just call `GetCategoryList` and format the response:

```
If oDOM.loadXML(sSoapParams) Then
    sResponse = sResponse & "<w:soapGetCategoryListResponse "
    sResponse = sResponse & " xmlns:w='www.wrox.com/VbXml' >" & vbLf
    sResponse = sResponse & "<results>" & vbLf
    sResponse = sResponse & ProdTx.GetCategoryList() & vbLf
    sResponse = sResponse & "</results>" & vbLf
    sResponse = sResponse & "</w:soapGetCategoryListResponse>"
```

```
        Else
            sResponse = BuildParamParseErrorResponse("soapGetCategoryListResponse",_
                    oDOM)
        End If

    ErrHand:
        If Err.Number <> 0 Then
            sResponse = BuildComErrorResponse(Err)
        End If

        soapWrapGetCategoryList = sResponse
    End Function
```

(Refer to Chapter 9 for a description of the `BuildComErrorResponse` and `BuildParamParseErrorResponse` functions.)

Searching for a Product

When a user goes to search for a product, a SOAP request is sent, containing a product name and/or a product category. The wrapper passes this to `SearchForProduct` and receives a list of matching products:

```
Public Function soapWrapSearchForProduct(ByVal sSoapParams As String) As String
    On Error GoTo ErrHand

    Dim oDOM As MSXML.DOMDocument
    Dim sName As String
    Dim sCategory As String
    Dim sResponse As String

    Set oDOM = New DOMDocument
    sResponse = ""

    If oDOM.loadXML(sSoapParams) Then
        sName = oDOM.getElementsByTagName("name").Item(0).Text
        sCategory = oDOM.getElementsByTagName("category").Item(0).Text
        sResponse = sResponse & "<w:soapSearchForProductResponse "
        sResponse = sResponse & " xmlns:w='www.wrox.com/VbXml' >" & vbLf
        sResponse = sResponse & "<results>" & vbLf
        sResponse = sResponse & ProdTx.SearchForProduct(sName, sCategory) & vbLf
        sResponse = sResponse & "</results>" & vbLf
        sResponse = sResponse & "</w:soapSearchForProductResponse>"
    Else
        sResponse = BuildParamParseErrorResponse("soapWrapCreateNewProduct", oDOM)
    End If

ErrHand:
    If Err.Number <> 0 Then
        sResponse = BuildComErrorResponse(Err)
    End If

    soapWrapSearchForProduct = sResponse
End Function
```

Getting Selected Products

Once a search has been made, and the user chooses some items to purchase, the selected items are pulled from the database using `soapWrapSelectedProducts`:

```
Public Function soapWrapSelectedProducts(ByVal sSoapParams As String) As String
    On Error GoTo ErrHand

    Dim sXmlDoc As String
    Dim sResults As String
    Dim sResponse As String
    Dim oDOM As DOMDocument
    Dim oEl As IXMLDOMElement
    Dim sProdID As String
```

The code parses the list of IDs, and passes the XML string to `GetSelectedProducts`:

```
    Set oDOM = New DOMDocument

    If oDOM.loadXML(sSoapParams) Then
        Set oEl = oDOM.getElementsByTagName("Products").Item(0)
        sResults = ProdTx.GetSelectedProducts(oEl.xml)
        sResponse = "<w:soapGetSelectedProductsResponse "
        sResponse = sResponse & " xmlns:w='www.wrox.com/VbXml' >" & vbLf
        sResponse = sResponse & sResults & vbLf
        sResponse = sResponse & "</w:soapGetSelectedProductsResponse>"
    Else ' Failed to parse SOAP body
        sResponse = BuildParamParseErrorResponse("soapWrapSelectedProducts", oDOM)
    End If

ErrHand:
    If Err.Number <> 0 Then
        sResponse = BuildComErrorResponse(Err)
    End If

    soapWrapSelectedProducts = sResponse
End Function
```

Additions to the WebProducts.ProductDescriptionTx Class

`WebProducts.ProductDescriptionTx` receives calls from the SOAP wrapper methods to perform the back-end application logic. To handle the new SOAP requests coming from the web site, we now add some methods to the `ProductDescriptionTx` class. The `WebProducts` project will require a reference to the `WroxXml.CDomFunctions` class described in Chapter 3.

Getting the Category List

`soapWrapGetCategoryList` calls `GetCategoryList` to retrieve a list of categories. We define a SQL statement to perform a `DISTINCT` selection and return the XML results. We use a helper method from the utilities class to build the SQL:

```
Public Function GetCategoryList() As String
    On Error GoTo ErrHand
    Dim sSQL As String
    Dim sResults As String
```

```
    Dim dbi As dbInfo

    ' We need to connect to the database, pull back all of the
    ' product information, and return an XML string encoding this.
    sSQL = TxUtils.BuildSQL(SQL_SELECT_DISTINCT_CATEGORY, dbi)
```

(Note that BuildSQL requires two arguments: one to indicate the type of SQL to construct, and a dbInfo user-defined type (described in Chapter 9) which, ordinarily, holds a product's basic information. The code to construct the DISTINCT Category SQL does not use the second parameter; so we've passed an empty dbInfo structure.)

```
    sResults = TxUtils.ExecuteSelect(sSQL)
    If Len(sResults) < 1 Then
        sResults = TxUtils.GetErrorInfoXml()
    End If

ErrHand:
    If Err.Number <> 0 Then
        Call oError.SetErrorInfo(Err.Description, PROG_ID _
                & ".GetCategoryList", Err.Number)
        sResults = oError.GetErrorInfoXml()
    End If

    GetCategoryList = sResults
End Function
```

Getting Selected Products

When the user has finally selected some products for purchase, a SOAP request is sent to retrieve the product data. It receives the XML defining the requested products, and the quantities required:

```
Public Function GetSelectedProducts(ByVal sXmlIdList As String) As String
    On Error GoTo ErrHand
    Dim oXmlDom As MSXML.DOMDocument
    Dim oXslDom As MSXML.DOMDocument
    Dim oNodeList As IXMLDOMNodeList
    Dim sSQL As String
    Dim sXsl As String
    Dim sResults As String
    Dim nIdx As Integer

    Set oXmlDom = New DOMDocument
    Set oXslDom = New DOMDocument

    sSQL = "SELECT * FROM Catalog WHERE "

    If oXmlDom.loadXML(sXmlIdList) Then
        Set oNodeList = oXmlDom.getElementsByTagName("id")
```

The code builds the SQL in-line:

```
        For nIdx = 1 To oNodeList.length - 1
            sSQL = sSQL & " (ProdID = " & oNodeList.Item(nIdx).Text & ") OR "
        Next
        sSQL = sSQL & " (ProdID = " & oNodeList.Item(0).Text & ") "
```

And executes it:

```
        sResults = TxUtils.ExecuteSelect(sSQL)
```

We want to add an additional attribute to the XML before returning it. For rendering in the browser, and calculating the total cost of the order, we add a "qty" attribute. The XML passed to `GetSelectedProducts` looks like this:

```
<Products>
    <id qty="2">128</id>
    <id qty="5">129</id>
    <id qty="1">104</id>
</Products>
```

The result of the SQL query looks like this (formatting has been added to make the XML easier to read):

```
<DATA>
  <Row ProdID='104' Name='COBOL &amp; XML'
      Category='Video' BriefDesc='The future'
      XmlDetails='http://192.168.0.1/WroxFileServer/ProductFiles/104.xml'
      Price='10' Inventory='100'  />
  <Row ProdID='128' Name='Scouting'
      Category='Video' BriefDesc='How to scout'
      XmlDetails='http://192.168.0.1/WroxFileServer/ProductFiles/128.xml'
      Price='22.5' Inventory='1'  />
  <Row ProdID='129' Name='Celtic Fiddle'
      Category='Video' BriefDesc='Playing fiddle'
      XmlDetails='http://192.168.0.1/WroxFileServer/ProductFiles/129.xml'
      Price='30.99' Inventory='1'  />
</DATA>
```

If the SQL query was successful, the query results XML and the selected products XML is passed to `AddQty`, which performs the attribute addition:

```
        If Len(sResults) > 0 Then
            sResults = AddQty(sResults, sXmlIdList)
        End If
```

If there are errors the code returns an empty string:

```
    Else
        Call oError.SetErrorInfo("Failed to parse XML ID list: " & _
                oDOM.parseError.reason, PROG_ID & ".GetSelectedProducts", _
                Err.Number)
        sResults = ""
    End If

ErrHand:
    If Err.Number <> 0 Then
        Call oError.SetErrorInfo(Err.Description, PROG_ID & _
                    ".GetSelectedProducts", Err.Number)
        sResults = ""
    End If
    GetSelectedProducts = sResults
End Function
```

AddQty takes two XML strings as arguments: the first is the XML returned by the selected products SQL query, and the second is the original XML that specified what products and quantities the user requested. It takes the quantity values given by the user and adds them as an attribute to the SQL results data. It uses the WroxXml.CDomFunctions class from Chapter 3 to add the attribute:

```
Private Function AddQty(sXmlData As String, sXmlIdList As String) As String
    On Error GoTo ErrHand

    Dim oDomData As DOMDocument
    Dim oDomId As MSXML.DOMDocument
    Dim oNodeList As IXMLDOMNodeList
    Dim oElData As IXMLDOMElement
    Dim oElId As IXMLDOMElement
    Dim oWroxDw As WroxXml.CDomFunctions
    Dim sResults As String
    Dim nIdx As Integer
    Dim sProdID  As String
    Dim sQtyVal As String
    Dim dblTotal As Double
    Dim sPrice As String

    dblTotal = 0

    Set oDomData = New DOMDocument
    Set oDomId = New DOMDocument
    Set oWroxDw = New WroxXml.CDomFunctions
```

If there are problems loading either of the XML strings passed in, the function sets the error information and exits:

```
    If Not oDomData.loadXML(sXmlData) Then
        Call oError.SetErrorInfo("oDomData.loadXML erorr = " & _
                    oDomData.parseError.reason, PROG_ID & _
                    ".AddQty", -1)
        sResults = ""
        Exit Function
    End If

    If Not oDomId.loadXML(sXmlIdList) Then
        Call oError.SetErrorInfo("oDomId.loadXML erorr = " & _
                    oDomId.parseError.reason, PROG_ID & _
                    ".AddQty", -1)
        sResults = ""
        Exit Function
    End If
```

Otherwise, the code creates a NodeList of all the Row elements in the SQL results XML:

```
    Set oNodeList = oDomData.getElementsByTagName("Row")
```

For each element in the `NodeList`, the code extracts the `ProdID` attribute value and uses it to find the corresponding element in the selected products XML:

```
For nIdx = 0 To oNodeList.length - 1
    Set oElData = oNodeList.Item(nIdx)
    sProdID = oElData.Attributes.getNamedItem("ProdID").nodeValue
    Set oElId = oDomId.selectSingleNode("Products/id[.=" & sProdID & "]")
```

The quantity is taken from the selected product element, and used to add an attribute on the SQL results element:

```
    sQtyVal = oElId.Attributes.getNamedItem("qty").nodeValue
    Call oWroxDw.AddAttribute(oDomData, oElData, "Qty", sQtyVal)
```

A running total of the product cost is kept, which will be used to add an additional element to the end of the SQL results XML, which will be used to display the total cost when rendered in the browser:

```
    sPrice = oElData.Attributes.getNamedItem("Price").nodeValue
    dblTotal = dblTotal + CDbl(sQtyVal) * CDbl(sPrice)
Next
```

The extra element is added as a child of the `DATA` element:

```
Set oElData = oDomData.getElementsByTagName("DATA").Item(0)
If Not oWroxDw.AddElement(oDomData, oElData, _
            "TotalCost", CStr(dblTotal)) Then
    Call oError.SetErrorInfo("AddElement failed.", PROG_ID & ".AddQty", -1)
    sResults = ""
Else
    sResults = oDomData.xml
End If
```

Any run time errors are caught at the end of the method. Before returning, the code releases the objects used:

```
ErrHand:
    If Err.Number <> 0 Then
        Call oError.SetErrorInfo(Err.Description, PROG_ID & _
                    ".AddQty", Err.Number)
        sResults = ""
    End If
    Set oDomData = Nothing
    Set oDomId = Nothing
    Set oNodeList = Nothing
    Set oElData = Nothing
    Set oElId = Nothing
    Set oWroxDw = Nothing

    AddQty = sResults
End Function
```

Searching for Products

The SOAP request for product searching calls out to `SearchForProduct`, which takes the name and category entered by the user and performs a SQL query to obtain the matching products. It's pretty simple, relying on the utilities class to do the real work:

```
Public Function SearchForProduct(ByVal sName, ByVal sCategory) As String
    On Error GoTo ErrHand
    Dim dbi As dbInfo
    Dim sSQL As String
    Dim sResults As String

    dbi.Name = sName
    dbi.Category = sCategory
    sSQL = TxUtils.BuildSQL(SQL_SELECT, dbi)

    sResults = TxUtils.ExecuteSelect(sSQL)
    If Len(sResults) < 1 Then
        sResults = TxUtils.DataErrorXML()
    End If

ErrHand:
    If Err.Number <> 0 Then
        Call oError.SetErrorInfo(Err.Description, PROG_ID & ".SearchForProduct", _
                    Err.Number)
        sResults = oError.GetErrorInfoXml()
    End If

    SearchForProduct = sResults
End Function
```

Additions to the WebProducts.ProdTxUtils Class

We first looked at `WebProducts.ProdTxUtils` when we were discussing how to get our product detail files from the XML editor to the file server, in Chapter 9. We've added a few more methods to help out with the web store transactions.

We've extended our `QUERY_TYPE` enumerator to include queries needed by some new transactions:

```
Enum QUERY_TYPE
    SQL_INSERT = 1
    SQL_UPDATE = 2
    SQL_DELETE = 3
    SQL_SELECT = 4
    SQL_SELECT_DISTINCT_CATEGORY = 5
End Enum
```

We've then modified the `BuildSQL` function to include these new queries:

```
    Select Case QueryType

' existing Case statements ...

        Case SQL_SELECT_DISTINCT_CATEGORY:
                sSQL = "SELECT DISTINCT Category  FROM Catalog" & _
                       "WHERE Inventory > 0"
        Case Else
            sSQL = ""
    End Select
```

Summary

In this chapter we introduced more points of data exchange to the main sample application: a web server (and corresponding web browsers), and a message queue (Microsoft's MSMQ). The chapter focused on the development of the Wrox web store site, an Active Server Page application on IIS that uses MTS objects, making SOAP requests to communicate with the product database and XML file server. We created a new Visual Basic object to handle the web site business logic, and discussed how the final purchase request could be sent to a warehouse computer for further processing.

The chapter also discussed some concepts relating to moving information in a distributed application, and we saw how to create a dynamically loaded class that implements a specific interface, allowing us to configure the web site to use different objects to transmit the purchase order, without having to recompile primary application code.

We saw how to use the Visual Basic XLink solver object from Chapter 10 to display related product data to the user. We also added new SOAP request methods to the classes introduced in Chapter 9 and then completed the web site.

In the next chapter, we'll wrap up the application. We'll see how the purchase order is retrieved by the warehouse system, and describe the use of XSLT for transforming the purchase order into different display formats suitable for each of our suppliers.

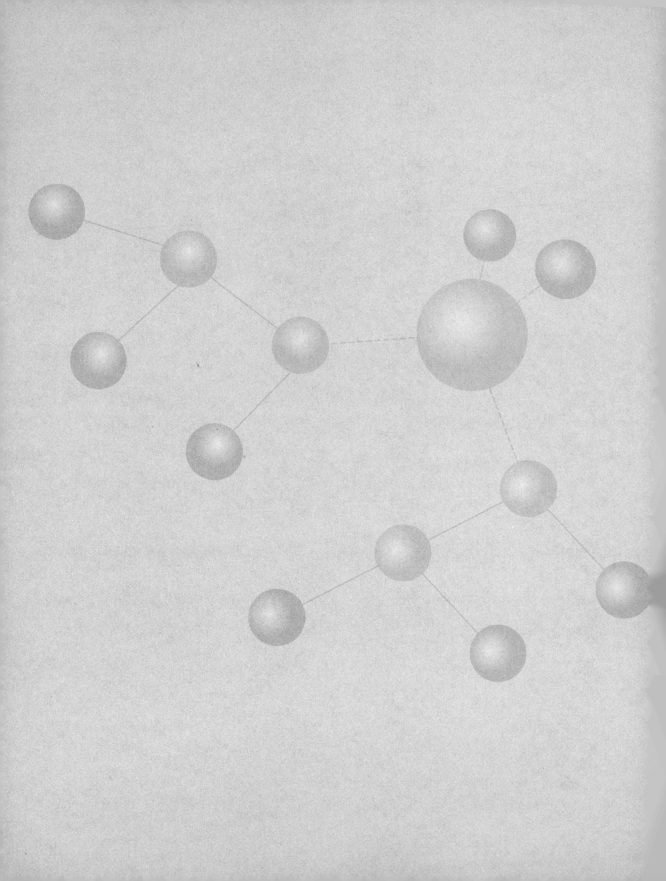

Transforming and Transmitting the Data

One of the important features of XML is its platform independency. Being plain text, it can be passed around using practically any protocol. Probably the most widely available of these are, at the moment, HTTP and SMTP. Both can be used for transmitting XML and we will use these protocols in this chapter to send reorder request to all our suppliers using their preferred transport mechanism.

In this chapter we're going to complete our sample application. Previously, the interactive web site application has committed an order request to the Message Queue. The last part of our sample application deals with acting upon the requested order and fulfilling the request.

This fulfillment can be divided into two parts. First, there is the shipping of the order and the notification of the warehouse. Second, we may want to act on the new stock level, and reorder if the level has reached a predefined point. This reordering is the part we will focus on in this chapter and we'll leave out the first part as it will teach us nothing about XML.

The reordering process is rather complex. For each of the products in our store we have a supplier. If the stock level falls below a certain level (which can be set separately for each product), we want to notify the supplier. The way we communicate with each of these suppliers can vary significantly. Some suppliers have automated their order entry systems to expect some sort of XML feed to be sent to them over HTTP; others can only manually handle faxed orders containing a nice note ('Dear Mr. X...'). So we have different procedures for different suppliers and their different platforms – some highly automated and some very basic. The procedures have two characteristics: the structure of the message (XML, comma separated values, nice letter) and the transport mechanism (HTTP, SOAP, SMTP mail).

Outline of the Solution

So how would we set this up? First of all, we have to write an application that reads messages out of the Message Queue. It has to do some processing on them and check and update the inventory. Then, if necessary, a reorder message has to go out to the supplier. The task of sending messages containing the same *content* but wildly differing *formats* is typical of what can be achieved with XSLT. The process to be followed is shown in the flowsheet:

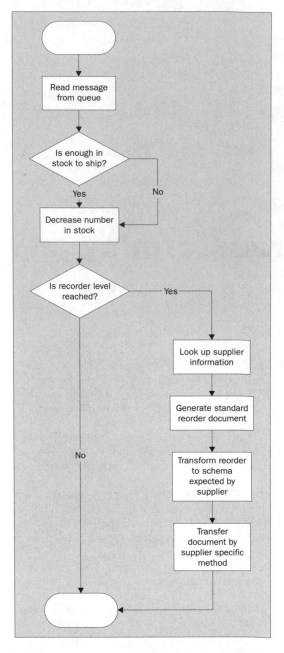

Let's talk through this model. First of all, our application reads a message from the queue. The message body contains an XML document placed in the queue by the web application. The message is parsed and the requested products compared with the database to check for availability. If all products are available in stock, we proceed to decrease the stock in the database and place a shipping order in the database.

What happens if there is not enough in stock to fulfill the shipment? This is an interesting question, but we will not really solve this problem here, as it is hardly XML related. We will only take note of the problem and keep decreasing the stock as if nothing happened. When there is insufficient stock, our system will just decrease the stock level, causing the value to become a negative number. We could in these cases alert the customer that shipment may take a while.

We will also not cover the shipping and handling here, and will assume that the warehouse has some way to check for current shipping orders in the database and remove them after fulfilling them.

Once we have decreased the stock level, we check if the set reorder level for this product has been reached. This is where the interesting part starts. If the reorder level is reached, we look up the supplier information. This contains information about the supplier itself (address, name, etc.), but also details of the expected format and the transmission method for the supplier.

Next, a standard reorder document is generated, containing information about the product and amount ordered, as well as information about the supplier. This document is first read from the Message Queue, then transformed to the *format* expected by the supplier's system, before transferred to them using the *transfer method* which is supported.

The whole thing, from reading the message down to sending the reorder request, should be done in one transaction. So if the reordering process does not work, the entire process will be rolled back. The message should then remain in the queue.

For implementing different transfer methods we will create an abstract interface, `IReorderTransfer`, for COM objects that will be implemented several times. (An abstract interface is a like a template for a class; implementation is done in another class, but only using the methods and properties of the interface). This way, we can transparently isolate the implementation of the data transfer from the application logic. The `ProgID` of the object that is to be used is retrieved from the database. To store this information (both about our suppliers and about their preferred transfer method), we will have to make a few changes to the data model.

The Basic Application

For creating and sending the reorder form we will need some extra information from the database. Therefore we should change the database model to have the following structure:

539

You don't have to do this; the data model in the source code download is already of this form.

We have added some fields to the `Catalog` table to store the values of `Reorder_threshold`, `Reorder_amount` and the 'already ordered' amount (`Reorder_submitted`). To store information about each of the suppliers a new table has been added: `Supplier`. In this table, which is fully explained in the section entitled '*Create a Default Reorder Document*', fields have been added called `Name`, `DestinationDetails`, `ReorderFormat` (the filename of an XSLT document to perform transformation to the format the supplier expects), and `TransportMethod` (the `ProgID` for the COM object that performs the actual transport).

Reading the Message

The basic application for processing messages should ideally be an NT system service, responding whenever a message ends up in the queue. An NT system service runs in the background (i.e. has no user interface) and can be installed to start up automatically. However, we have chosen to use a very simple GUI application instead, to allow for easier interactive testing. You can find the full code for this application and the COM library (an ActiveX DLL) that does the actual processing in the source code download. The ActiveX DLL project is called `OrderProcessing.vbp`, the small GUI test application is called `ReorderTestGUI.vbp`. The application has one form with a text box to specify the name of the queue, which will be used to retrieve orders posted by the web application.

With the button labeled '**Process a message**', the application can be used to read a message from the queue and process it (to facilitate testing, there is a second button, labeled '**Place Message**', to post a dummy order document to the queue). All of this – the reading of the message, the updating of the database and sending of any messages, must happen inside a COM object, because we want all of these actions to behave as one single transaction. So the code behind the command button that starts the processing is extremely simple:

```
Private Sub btnProc_Click()
    Dim oMsg As MSMQMessage
    Dim oQueue As MSMQQueue
    Dim oInfo As New MSMQQueueInfo
    Dim oProcessor As New OrderProcessing.MessageProcessor

    oInfo.PathName = lstQueues.List(lstQueues.ListIndex)
    Set oQueue = oInfo.Open(MQ_RECEIVE_ACCESS, MQ_DENY_NONE)

    If oProcessor.processMessage(oQueue) = False Then
        MsgBox "Error occurred"
    End If
End Sub
```

The COM object `OrderProcessing.MessageProcessor` that is created by the GUI application has its `MTSTransactionMode` property set to `RequiresTransaction`. This means that the object will always run as part of a transaction (when running inside MTS, that is). If its caller is not part of a transaction, a new transaction is created, otherwise it will participate in the existing transaction. In our case it will have to create a new transaction.

The `processMessage` method starts by retrieving a handle (oCtx) to the `ObjectContext`. This object reference can later be used to call `SetAbort` or `SetComplete` to rollback or commit the transaction. Calling `rollBack` in this `ObjectContext` will cause MTS to roll back all changes in the enlisted resources; in this case, the enlisted resources are the message read from the queue and the database connection.

An `MSMQMessage` (oMsg) object is read from the `MSMQQueue` (oQueue) object that is passed in from the application. We state specifically that we want this operation (the reading of the message) to be part of an MTS transaction. The Message Queue can also organize its own transactions, but these cannot be combined with other MTS transactions, such as database operations.

```
Dim oDoc as MSXML.DOMDocument

Public Function processMessage(oQueue As MSMQQueue) As Boolean
    Dim oMsg As MSMQMessage
    Dim oCtx As MTxAS.ObjectContext
    Dim oList As IXMLDOMNodeList
    Dim oElem As IXMLDOMElement

    On Error GoTo processMessage_Handler

    Set oCtx = GetObjectContext()
    Set oMsg = oQueue.Receive(ReceiveTimeout:=1000, _
        Transaction:=MQ_MTS_TRANSACTION)
    If oMsg Is Nothing Then Exit Function

    readBody (oMsg.Body)

    Set oList = oDoc.selectNodes("//Products/Product")
    For i = 0 To oList.length - 1
        Set oElem = oList.Item(i)
        lCurrentProdID = oElem.selectSingleNode("ID/text()").nodeValue
        lCurrentAmount = oElem.selectSingleNode("Amount/text()").nodeValue

        checkStock
        decreaseStock
        checkReorderLevel
    Next
    processMessage = True
    oCtx.SetComplete
End Function

processMessage_Handler:
    processMessage = False
    oCtx.SetAbort

End Function
```

```
Private Sub readBody(sMessage As String)
    Set oDoc = New DOMDocument
    oDoc.async = False
    oDoc.loadXML (sMessage)
    If Not oDoc.parseError.errorCode = 0 Then
        Err.Raise 9999, "MessageProcessor", "Problem parsing the XML: " & _
            oDoc.parseError.reason
    End If
End Sub
```

The XML content in the message is loaded into a DOMDocument object (in the readBody sub) and inspected for product orders. For each ordered product, a set of operations is performed:

❑ Checking stock

❑ Changing the inventory level

❑ Checking reorder requirements

❑ Performing the reordering procedure

Checking Stock

For each product in the order, the ordered amount is compared with the stock as indicated in the database. If the amount in stock is lower than the ordered amount, nothing extraordinary will be done. In a normal business environment, you would want to notify the customer of this problem and take action to make sure that the stock could be restored as soon as possible. But implementing this will teach nothing about XML, so we will just note the fact and continue on.

```
Private Sub checkStock()
    Dim sSQL As String
    Dim rsResult As Recordset

    Set rsResult = oConnection.Execute("SELECT Inventory from Catalog" & _
            " where ProdID = " & lCurrentProdID)
    If rsResult.EOF Then Err.Raise 9999, "MessageProcessor", "No such Product ID"
    If rsResult("Inventory").Value < lCurrentAmount Then
        'Take appropriate action. For simplicity, we will do nothing
    End If
End Sub
```

Changing Inventory Level

The inventory level must be decreased by the amount ordered. This is carried out whatever the circumstances, and the stock level will be allowed to become negative, so the code for this is simple enough:

```
Private Sub decreaseStock()
    Dim sSQL As String
    sSQL = "UPDATE Catalog SET Inventory = Inventory - " & lCurrentAmount & _
        " WHERE ProdID = " & lCurrentProdID

    oConnection.Execute sSQL
End Sub
```

Checking Reorder Requirements

When checking for the need to reorder, a SELECT query is carried out on the Catalog table and the values of the Inventory, Reorder_submitted and Reorder_threshold fields compared. If the sum of Inventory and Reorder_submitted is smaller than the threshold value, a reorder must be submitted to the supplier.

If a reorder is submitted, this is also written to the database, by increasing the value of Reorder_submitted by the value in Reorder_amount. Normally, we would assume that another application would be used in the warehouse to increase the Inventory value and decrease the Reorder_submitted value when new shipments arrive. For the sake of simplicity, this won't be implemented here.

```
Private Sub checkReorderLevel()
    Dim sSQL As String
    Dim rsResult As Recordset
    Dim oReorder As DOMDocument

    Set rsResult = New Recordset
    rsResult.CursorLocation = adUseClient
    rsResult.Open "SELECT * from Catalog where ProdID = " & lCurrentProdID, _
            oConnection
    Set rsResult.ActiveConnection = Nothing
    If rsResult("Inventory").Value + rsResult("Reorder_submitted").Value < _
            rsResult("Reorder_threshold").Value Then
        'We have to make a reorder
        'First we process the reorder in our own database
        sSQL = "UPDATE Catalog SET " & _
            " Reorder_submitted = Reorder_submitted + Reorder_amount " & _
            " WHERE ProdID = " & lCurrentProdID
        oConnection.Execute sSQL

        Set oReorder = createDefaultReorder(rsResult("Name").Value, _
            rsResult("SupplID").Value)

        transportMessage oReorder
    End If
End Sub
```

After updating the database for the reordering, a reorder document is created and sent to the supplier. We will now look at the nuts and bolts of that part of the procedure.

Transforming the Reorder Information

Creating a Default Reorder Document

Once we have established that a reorder message is necessary, we start to formulate this reorder into an XML document, using the schema that suits us best. A document will be created from scratch using the DOM. A typical reorder document would look like this:

```
<REORDER>
  <PRODUCT>
    <ID>2</ID>
```

```
      <Amount>2</Amount>
      <Name>Arm chair</Name>
   </PRODUCT>
   <SUPPLIER>
     <Name>Furniture Inc</Name>
     <Destination_Details>
     <URL>
        <BASE>http://www.supplier.com/b2b/incoming.asp</BASE>
        <METHOD>POST</METHOD>
        <PARAMS>
          <PARAM type="content">body</PARAM>
        </PARAMS>
     </URL>
     </Destination_Details>
     <Supplier_Format>default.xsl</Supplier_Format>
        <Transport_Method>OrderProcessing.DummyTransfer</Transport_Method>
   </SUPPLIER>
</REORDER>
```

Building a document like this with the DOM is quite easy:

```
Set oReorder = New DOMDocument
Set oReorder.documentElement = oReorder.createElement("REORDER")

Set oElem = oReorder.createElement("PRODUCT")
oReorder.documentElement.appendChild oElem
Set oChildElem = oReorder.createElement("ID")
oElem.appendChild oChildElem
oChildElem.appendChild oReorder.createTextNode(lCurrentProdID)
Set oChildElem = oReorder.createElement("Amount")
oElem.appendChild oChildElem
oChildElem.appendChild oReorder.createTextNode(lCurrentAmount)
Set oChildElem = oReorder.createElement("Name")
oElem.appendChild oChildElem
oChildElem.appendChild

... Etc, etc,
```

The only hard part is where we want to include the destination details in the document. Because the method of transportation can be different for each supplier, so too can be the form of the destination address. For example, suppliers who want their orders faxed to them will have a fax number as their destination, while others may have an e-mail address or a URL to post information to. To accommodate for this flexibility, we store the destination in the database as an XML fragment. A supplier that wants to be faxed would have a destination description like:

```
<FAXNUMBER>
  <CTRY>31</CTRY>
  <AREA>23</AREA>
  <LOCAL>56 93939</LOCAL>
</FAXNUMBER>
```

while a supplier that has an HTTP-based gateway set up that we can post the information to would have a description like this:

```
<URL>
  <BASE>http://www.supplier.com/b2b/incoming.asp</BASE>
  <METHOD>POST</METHOD>
  <PARAMS>
   <PARAM type="content">body</PARAM>
  </PARAMS>
</URL>
```

The problem now is that we want this information inside our standard reorder document. In the database, this information is stored as a string. If an attempt is made to set the textValue of an element to this value, the DOM implementation will escape all occurrences of < to <, effectively taking all the structure out of the information and turning it into a string. However, we are not interested in the string value, but in the structured information that it represents (not '<PARAM type="content">body</PARAM>', but a PARAM element with type set to 'content' and text value 'body'). So we have to parse it before adding it to the reorder document. A second document is created for this purpose and the string loaded into it. The parsed content can then be added to the document.

```
Set oElem = oReorder.createElement("SUPPLIER")
oReorder.documentElement.appendChild oElem
Set oChildElem = oReorder.createElement("Name")
oElem.appendChild oChildElem
oChildElem.appendChild oReorder.createTextNode(rsResult("Name").Value)

'Now we want to include the xml fragment in the field DestinationDetails
Set oTmp = New DOMDocument
oTmp.loadXML (rsResult("DestinationDetails"))
Set oChildElem = oReorder.createElement("Destination_Details")
oElem.appendChild oChildElem
oChildElem.appendChild oTmp.documentElement.cloneNode(True)
```

So we created a document containing all the information for making a reorder. But now we have to convert it to the format that our supplier expects. Of course, converting XML information to another form is a typical task for an XSLT stylesheet. We will look at a few examples of conversions that would be interesting to use.

Transforming to Another Schema

The most obvious kind of transformation would be to turn our XML information to another form of XML using a different schema. The schema a supplier expects will not hold the destination information and the full description of the supplier, but the rest of the data will probably be expected in some way in the document, regardless of the schema.

Let's create an XSLT stylesheet for making such a transformation. Suppose that the supplier prefers a document with the following structure:

```
<ORDER>
  <FROM>OnlinePurchase Inc.</FROM>
  <ORDERLINE SKU="2" NR="2"/>
  <ORDERLINE SKU="432" NR="10"/>
  <ORDERLINE SKU="8" NR="12"/>
</ORDER>
```

The main differences between this format and the standard reorder document we have created are that our supplier is not interested in all the information about himself (he already knows that) and expects a line indicating the identity of the customer (in other words, us). Their schema uses a SKU attribute where we use an ID element, an NR attribute where we use an Amount element, and an ORDERLINE element where we use a PRODUCT element. These are easy enough to transform.

```
<?xml version="1.0"?>
<xsl:stylesheet xmlns:xsl="http://www.w3.org/1999/XSL/Transform" version="1.0">
<xsl:template match="/">
  <ORDER>
    <!--The FROM element is hardcoded-->
    <FROM>OnlinePurchase Inc.</FROM>
    <xsl:apply-templates select="//PRODUCT"/>
  </ORDER>
</xsl:template>

<xsl:template match="PRODUCT">
  <ORDERLINE>
    <xsl:attribute name="SKU">
      <xsl:value-of select="ID"/>
    </xsl:attribute>
    <xsl:attribute name="NR">
      <xsl:value-of select="Amount"/>
    </xsl:attribute>
  </ORDERLINE>
</xsl:template>
</xsl:stylesheet>
```

Note how we have hardcoded the FROM element into the stylesheet. We had to do this, because the sender information is not part of the source document. We could alternatively pass the sender name into the transformation as a parameter.

> *The comment just before the FROM element will not show up in the result. As a comment, it is ignored when parsing the stylesheet. If you wanted comments in the destination document, you would have to use the xsl:processing-instruction element.*

Transforming to CSV

Suppose a supplier has set up some way of automatically reordering when stocks are low, but this system does not work with XML, and instead, works with comma separated values in an ASCII file. That should not pose a serious problem to our system – generating plain text should be perfectly possible using XSLT.

The easiest way to generate a plain table of values is by setting up a stylesheet with a for-each block for iterating all the lines, using a value-of element for each value. Quotes, commas and carriage returns can be inserted as literals.

Using the IE5 version of XSLT, it can be very hard to specify to the processor when to output white space, including new lines, and when not to. In creating CSV (comma separated values) files, this is a serious problem. The only way to prevent this with IE5 is by stripping all whitespace from the stylesheet.

```xml
<?xml version="1.0"?>
<xsl:stylesheet xmlns:xsl="http://www.w3.org/TR/WD-xsl">

<xsl:template match="/"><xsl:for-each select="//PRODUCT"><xsl:value-of
select="ID/text()"/>,<xsl:value-of select="Name/text()"/>,<xsl:value-of
select="Amount/text()"/></xsl:for-each>
</xsl:template>

</xsl:stylesheet>
```

If we can use the complete implementation of XSLT, we have lots of ways to specify exactly how and where we want whitespace to be stripped and where to preserve it. At the time of writing, support in the developers preview of MSXML for these features was still limited, but using full-blown XSLT, generating CSV data would work like this:

```xml
<?xml version="1.0"?>
<xsl:output method="text"/>
<xsl:stylesheet xmlns:xsl="http://www.w3.org/1999/XSL/Transform" version="1.0">
<xsl:template match="/">
  <xsl:for-each select="//PRODUCT">
    <xsl:value-of select="ID"/><xsl:text>,</xsl:text>
    <xsl:value-of select="Name"/><xsl:text>,</xsl:text>
    <xsl:value-of select="Amount"/><xsl:text>&#10;</xsl:text>
  </xsl:for-each>
</xsl:template>
</xsl:stylesheet>
```

According to the XSLT specification, all white space gets stripped, unless indicated otherwise (using xsl:preserve-space). The xsl:text element is the only one that preserves whitespace by default. So, if xsl:text elements are used for adding whitespace, everything works just fine. The entity reference
 inserts a new line.

Setting the output method to 'text' will ensure that no XML declaration ('<?xml version...?>') will be output.

Transforming to Human Readable Format

The least automated kind of supplier does not expect any kind of machine readable format, he just wants a nicely formatted order sheet, containing the product name and amount, but also a piece of text explaining that this is an order from us.

There are a few ways to format such a letter. One way would be to create an XHTML document that displays the content. This could be sent by e-mail, either as an HTML mail message or as an attachment. You could also choose to create a simple plain text letter and use this, for example as the body of a mail message.

In this example an HTML message will be created to be sent by e-mail:

```
<xsl:stylesheet xmlns:xsl="http://www.w3.org/1999/XSL/Transform" version="1.0">

<xsl:template match="/" xml:space="preserve">
  Dear Sir/Madam,

  We would like to place a new order with you.
  <xsl:for-each select="//PRODUCT">  Product:<xsl:value-of select="Name" />
  Amount:<xsl:value-of select="Amount"/>
  </xsl:for-each>

  With kind regards,
  OnlinePurchase Inc.
</xsl:template>
</xsl:stylesheet>
```

This will create the following message:

```
Dear Sir/Madam,

We would like to place a new order with you.

Product:Arm chair

Amount:2

With kind regards,

OnlinePurchase Inc.
```

However, there is one problem that we cannot solve in this way. In one day of order processing, several products from one supplier may reach the critical level and be reordered. The way the system is set up, these products will all be reordered separately. For an automated order entry system, this is no problem, but a supplier that handles the orders manually will get separate faxes for each reordered product, rather than one fax containing all the data. We will not solve this obvious flaw here. After all, our goal is not to show how to build a logistics management application, but rather to emphasize the use of XML and XSLT to facilitate parts of the solution to the logistics management problem.

Transferring Information

To allow the use of several ways of transferring the information to our suppliers, our application uses an abstract interface (achieved by creating a class without any implementation in it) and has this interface implemented by several classes. Three classes have been implemented here: DummyTransfer, MailTransfer and HTTPTransfer, but the model is extensible. So, in our project, a class has been included called IReorderTransfer (it is common to start names of interfaces with a capital I). This class contains the methods needed to transfer any sort of content, independent of the tranformations that have occurred. The methods have no implementation whatsoever, they are just names and placeholders. In the transfer classes these methods are implemented. The class to implement the IReorderTransfer interface is specified by starting the code in the classes with the following line:

```
Implements IReorderTransfer
```

The code for the empty specification of the interface is very short:

```
Public Sub Transfer(sMsg As String, oMsg As DOMDocument)
End Sub
```

Before transformation, a string is passed into the transfer object holding the full message and a reference to the original XML document. This document holds (among many other things) the address details for the transfer. The implementation will have to know how to retrieve the addressing information from the standard reorder message as this addressing can have different forms for different transfer methods.

The Dummy Transfer

The test transfer object is a class to test our system without having any remote supplier to receive our message. The `DummyTransfer` class implements the `IReorderTransfer` interface, but if it is called, it will just call `MsgBox` to display the whole content of the message string on the screen. The DOM reference is not used because an address is not needed:

```
Implements IReorderTransfer

Private Sub IReorderTransfer_Transfer(sMsg As String, oMsg As MSXML.DOMDocument)
    MsgBox sMsg
End Sub
```

Transfer Using HTTP

Posting the content to a script on the web server of our supplier is more complicated in VB than would be expected. VB comes with a very handy control for downloading and uploading all kinds of information using HTTP, FTP, etc. (it is called the Internet Transfer Control). But the problem of a control is that it must reside on a form and our COM object is not a form.

There are probably several ways to solve the problem, but here I chose to make direct calls to the WinInet API (contained in `wininet.dll`, which comes with basically everything shipped by Microsoft in the last few years).

This DLL contains no COM object, which we prefer to use from VB, but only compiled functions that must be declared in VB using the `Declare` keyword. The DLL contains functions to handle operations on URLs (like escaping characters), open Internet sessions, perform an HTTP request and receive the resulting data. I will not discuss the exact method of calling these functions, because it is rather complex and not specifically XML related. It is a delicate task and when done wrongly can result in serious crashes of your VB environment. If you are interested in this kind of programming, have a look at the code in the module called `WinInet.bas` or read the Wrox publication 'Visual Basic 6 Win32 API tutorial' (ISBN 1-861002-43-2).

For the purpose of our class, the WinInet module contains two public functions: `URLEscape` and `PostData`. `URLEscape` returns a 'URLEscaped' string for the passed input string. If you pass in 'This & That' it returns 'This%20%26%20That'. This function is required to escape the body of the posted content. For the actual posting, `PostData` is created. It can be passed a server name, script name (the path of the script on the server) and a content string. The function posts the content to the indicated script on the server, and returns an integer holding the HTTP status code of the request. If any result is returned other than 200 (which means 'OK' in HTTP), an error will be raised and all operations rolled back.

If the WinInet module is in place, the actual `HTTPTransfer` class doesn't do anything special:

```
Implements IReorderTransfer

Private Sub IReorderTransfer_Transfer(sMsg As String, oMsg As _
        MSXML.IXMLDOMDocument)
    Dim sServer As String
    Dim sPath As String
    Dim sPostBody As String
    Dim lResult As Long

    sServer = oMsg.selectSingleNode("/REORDER/SUPPLIER//URL/SERVER").Text
    sPath = oMsg.selectSingleNode("/REORDER/SUPPLIER//URL/PATH").Text
    sPostBody = _
        URLEscape(oMsg.selectSingleNode("/REORDER/SUPPLIER//URL/PARAMS/PARAM _
        [@type='content']").Text)
    sPostBody = sPostBody & "=" & URLEscape(sMsg)

    lResult = PostData(sServer, sPath, sPostBody)

    If Not lResult = 200 Then          'HTTP Status is not OK
        Err.Raise 9999, "HTTPTransfer", "HTTP error: " & lResult
    End If

End Sub
```

The `selectSingleNode` function is used on the passed reorder document object (the untransformed one) to fetch the server name and script location from the message.

Transfer Using e-mail

If the transfer method is set to e-mail using the `ProgID 'OrderProcessing.MailTransfer'`, the message string is the full body of the message. The information in the passed document is used just to find the destination e-mail address:

```
Implements IReorderTransfer

Private Sub IReorderTransfer_Transfer(sMsg As String, oMsg As _
                MSXML.IXMLDOMDocument)
    Dim oMail As New CDONTS.NewMail
    oMail.Subject = "Order"
    oMail.From = "procurement@onlinesales.com"
    oMail.To = oMsg.selectSingleNode("/REORDER/SUPPLIER//MAIL_ADDRESS").Text
    oMail.Body = sMsg
    oMail.Send
End Sub
```

This will only work if you have CDO for NT 1.2 (CDONTS) set up on your system (and set a reference to the library CDO for NT). This is an SMTP service that gets installed with the typical installation of IIS 4.0. In the References dialog, you will find it listed as "Microsoft CDO for NTS 1.2 Library". It is a lightweight version of the full CDO (Collaborative Data Objects), which can be used to working with Exchange folders from VB.

If we want to send fancier mail, we can also send HTML mail. Transforming to well formatted HTML is of course a breeze. Sending HTML mail can be done easily using:

```
objMail.BodyFormat = cdoBodyFormatHTML
```

Summary

In this chapter we really saw the flexibility of XML at work. We wrote code for creating one kind of reorder document and used it for a set of different users by applying different stylesheets to the document. This technique is very interesting for content publishers and content syndicators. The same core information can be made available for high end HTML browsers, small screen PDA browsers and WAP enabled cellular phones.

❏ We learned how to retrieve a message from a Message Queue and process it within a transaction.

❏ We learned how to deal with different end users expecting different electronic documents, ranging from differently shaped XML documents to human readable text documents.

That brings us to the end of our main sample application. We covered all the major, interesting features of the code, and left some room for you to improve and modify the more routine VB functionality.

In our final chapter we will look at a problem encountered by many VB developers – how to convert proprietary data files (in this case Microsoft Word documents) into XML.

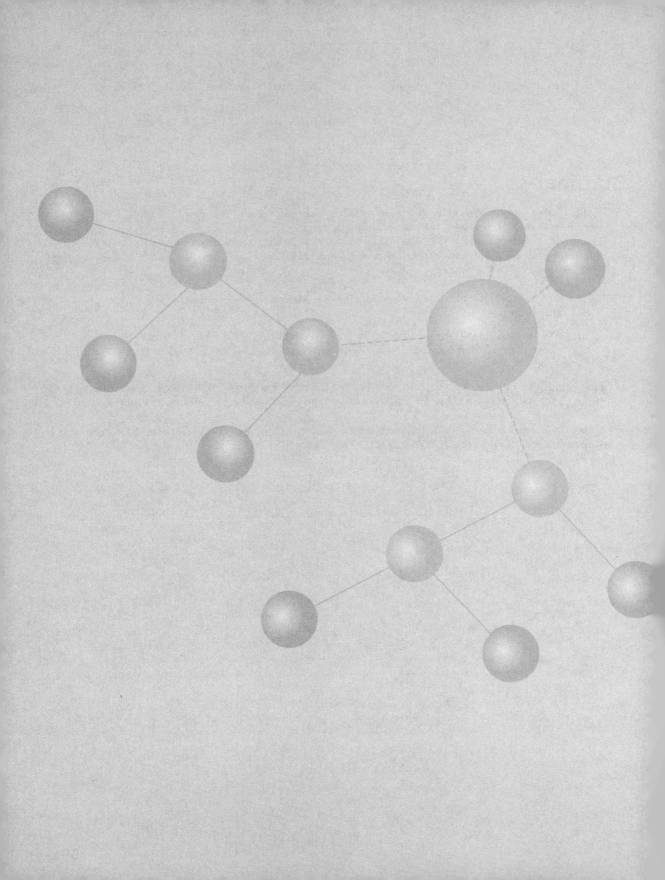

Converting Word To XML

This chapter is a mini-case study, and is quite separate from the sample application that we've developed throughout the book. It aims to answer one of the key questions VB developers may ask – namely, how to convert a document created in a proprietory package, such as Microsoft Excel or Word, into an XML document, which can then be shared with other applications on other platforms.

Here we will just look at one example of such a conversion (Microsoft Word) but the principles and techniques will be similar no matter what package you want to use as the source for files to be converted into XML, provided you have access to the document's formatting data.

Introduction

One of the benefits of using XML is the ability to exchange documents in a non-proprietary format. Word processing software, such as Microsoft's Word, typically saves documents as binary data. While other editing applications may be able to convert the file, it requires sophisticated code and detailed knowledge of the format. Often, the conversion is flawed, and some degree of formatting is lost.

Some progress was made when word processors were able to save documents as HTML. This increased portability, but the limitations of HTML resulted in a loss of control over presentation details, and certain standard document features, such as embedded comments, do not have a natural counterpart in HTML.

Microsoft, with the release of the Office 2000 suite, made significant enhancements to how documents were saved as HTML by the use of CSS (Cascading Style Sheets) and embedded islands of XML data. The result is that a Word document saved as HTML will appear almost exactly in a browser as it does in Word. The catch, though, is that the enhanced HTML is only understood by Internet Explorer 4 or better.

If you look at the generated HTML, it appears to be XML, which would certainly be a step towards application independence. The content is readable in any text editor, and conversion to another format could be performed by XSLT. However, although it looks like XML, there are flaws. When Word creates the HTML, it often inserts incorrectly nested tags, and fails to quote all attributes. Here's an example of what Word places near the top of the HTML document:

```
<meta http-equiv=Content-Type content="text/html; charset=windows-1252">
<meta name=ProgId content=Word.Document>
<meta name=Generator content="Microsoft Word 9">
<meta name=Originator content="Microsoft Word 9">
```

It seems that quotes are only used when an attribute value contains white space. Another problem with the HTML is the immense amount of formatting information included in the document. A simple document one line in length can produce an HTML file of over 200 lines, because of the inclusion of style definitions that are not even used.

There are tools available, such as "tidy" (obtainable free from www.w3c.org), that will go through an HTML document and attempt to convert it to XML. However, such programs will need to make assumptions about what is the best way to correct formatting problems, and the result may not always be what is wanted. For example, if an element is missing a closing tag, the program may not realize this until the end of the document, and decide to append it there.

One possible solution to the conversion problem is to do it yourself. We will take a look here at using Visual Basic and Microsoft Word to convert a Word document to XML. However, note that this is *not* a complete application; converting every possible item in a Word document (such as drawings or embedded comments) is a highly involved task. We will, though, provide code for an ActiveX DLL that can perform the conversion of most Word content, and which can provide the foundation for a more comprehensive application.

Scripting Word

Microsoft has done a tremendous job in developing the suite of Office applications as scriptable objects. Without even launching an application, you can create a reference to the Application object, and manipulate it. This is the basis for how our code will work. We'll take advantage of the extensive properties and methods exposed by the Word Document object. The Word Application object holds a collection of Document objects; one of them, the ActiveDocument, is the document that receives the scripting events by default, and this is one of the objects that will be used in our code.

We will not go into great detail about the Word object model, which is quite complex. For more information refer to the Microsoft Office 2000 Developer Object Model Guide, at http://msdn.microsoft.com/library/officedev/odeomg/deovrobjectmodelguide.htm.

However, you can learn much about Word and how it works by letting it create code for you. For example:

❑ Open up Word, type in some text, and select a section.

❑ Select the Tools menu item, then choose Macro, and then Record New Macro. A dialog box will appear.

❑ Simply click OK. A small, square, floating toolbar will appear.

❏ Click the toolbar button for "bold" text, and stop the macro recorder by clicking the "Stop" button on the floating toolbar.

❏ Word has a built-in Visual Basic for Applications (VBA) IDE; VBA is essentially Visual Basic, though you cannot compile the code. From Tools | Macros, select Visual Basic Editor. The IDE will open up; it looks very similar to the regular VB editor. The project explorer will list your document as a project, and it will contain a Modules folder. This folder will have an item called NewMacros, which should be open in the editor by default. Your new macro should look something like this:

```
Sub Macro1()
'
' Macro1 Macro
' Macro recorded 3/7/00 by James
'
    Selection.Font.Bold - wdToggle
End Sub
```

So, now we can see an example of how the Selection object is used to apply formatting. (We'll be using the Selection object frequently in our code.) Rather than first learning about the Word object model and trying to figure out how to perform an action, it is much easier to first record some actions and see how Word chooses to do it. Of course, you should still take the time to understand the finer points of the object model, but it can be much clearer after you've let Word create some VBA examples for you. You might also want to refer to the "Word VBA Programmer's Reference" publication (ISBN 1-861002-55-6) from Wrox Press.

Word-XML Conversion Application

We will convert Word documents into XML by using a DLL to handle the content conversion. The DLL will be called by a macro in a Word template; we'll look at creating this later, after we have coded the DLL. Much of the code for the DLL came directly from macros recorded in Word; though some changes had to be made to compensate for idiosyncrasies in how Word elected to implement certain actions, and to guard against unwanted operations on special hidden characters.

The WordXml DLL

The project is an ActiveX DLL called WordXML, with a single class, called Convert. It requires references to the Microsoft Word object library and the Scripting run time library. Not all of the code will be shown here, just enough to give a good idea of how to go about exploiting Word's built-in methods. The complete code is available from the Wrox web site.

The code starts with some declarations: we define a structure to hold information about table cells, which will be used when converting tables into XML:

```
Private Type CellAttributes
    Shading As Boolean
    Texture As Long
    BackPatternColor As Long
    ForePatternColor As Long
    Text As String
End Type
```

We also use a flag to determine if the DLL has been given a reference to a Word Application object to work with:

```
    Private g_mbAppAssigned As Boolean
```

We also have variables for Word objects, and a Dictionary object to hold table background color information:

```
    Private g_wdDoc As Word.Document
    Private g_wdApp As Application
    Private g_dictColors As Scripting.Dictionary
```

The first function is used to receive a reference to the Word Application object. The function takes the Application reference, and the name of the document to work on:

```
    Public Function AssignDocument(wdNewApp As Application, _
                                   sNewDoc As String) As Boolean
        On Error GoTo ErrHand
        Dim bResults As Boolean
```

The code sets the global Word Application variable, and activates the specified document. Note that, by default, any scripting we do will be performed on the *active* document.

```
        Set g_wdApp = wdNewApp
        g_wdApp.Windows(sNewDoc).Activate
```

The code then gets a reference to the active document, and checks for errors:

```
        Set g_wdDoc = g_wdApp.ActiveDocument
        bResults = True
        g_mbAppAssigned = True

    ErrHand:
        If Err.Number <> 0 Then
            bResults = False
            g_mbAppAssigned = False
        End If
        AssignDocument = bResults
    End Function
```

The next function, ConvertToXml, is the main one. It uses the reference to the Word document and calls helper routines to perform the required document preparation and conversion. First, these variables are declared:

```
    Public Function ConvertToXML() As Boolean
        On Error GoTo ErrHand

        Dim arrStyles() As String
        Dim nStyCount As Integer
        Dim sMsg As String
```

```
Dim bMoreToDo As Boolean
Dim nStyIdx  As Integer
Dim nIdx As Integer
Dim nSwitch As Integer
Dim sID As String
```

The code then checks that it has a reference to a Word document. If not, it exits right away:

```
If Not g_mbAppAssigned Then
    ConvertToXML = False
    Exit Function
End If
```

An array of document styles is then created. The code will use this to wrap tags around text, based on the style used in the original document.

```
ReDim arrStyles(g_wdApp.ActiveDocument.Styles.Count)
```

Certain script operations (such as moving the text selection point) will not work properly if the document is not in Normal view, so this code ensures the right view is selected:

```
g_wdApp.ActiveDocument.ActiveWindow.View.Type = wdNormalView
```

The code for adding markup and removing the corresponding Word styles (in preparation for saving the document as a text file once the conversion is done) needs to work as well as possible for any document. There are, however, cases where the presence of certain hidden formatting commands (such as section breaks) can confuse the code, so the document needs to be "prepared" before the conversion. A separate method, PrepareDoc (which we'll discuss further down), is called here:

```
' Fix up the content that may confuse e.g. some automatic formatting
If Not PrepareDoc() Then
    ConvertToXML = False
    Exit Function
End If
```

Before trying to turn Word styles into XML elements, we want to get a list of only those styles that are actually in use. The code iterates through the list of document styles (which holds the names of all available styles) and looks at the InUse property to build an array of styles used:

```
nStyCount = 0
For nIdx = 1 To g_wdApp.ActiveDocument.Styles.Count
    If (ActiveDocument.Styles.Item(nIdx).InUse) And _
                    (ActiveDocument.Styles.Item(nIdx) _
            <> "Default Paragraph Font") _
            And (ActiveDocument.Styles.Item(nIdx) _
            <> "Normal") And _
            (ActiveDocument.Styles.Item(nIdx) _
            <> "Normal,Normal.dot") Then
        arrStyles(nStyCount) = g_wdApp.ActiveDocument.Styles.Item(nIdx)
        nStyCount = nStyCount + 1
        sMsg = sMsg & " " & g_wdApp.ActiveDocument.Styles.Item(nIdx) & "."
    End If
Next
```

Since XML disallows the use of certain characters as document content, the code calls a separate method to replace these with suitable entity references:

```
ReplaceSpecialChars    ' Change "&", "<", etc. into &amp;, &lt;, etc.
```

Now the function can really get working on the conversion. It goes through the array of styles in use, locates each chunk of text that has that particular style, and replaces the formatting with the appropriate XML markup. First it configures the `Find` options:

```
For nStyIdx = 0 To nStyCount - 1
    DoEvents
    sMsg = arrStyles(nStyIdx)
    g_wdApp.Selection.Find.ClearFormatting
    g_wdApp.Selection.Find.Style = g_wdApp.ActiveDocument.Styles(sMsg)
    g_wdApp.Selection.HomeKey Unit:=wdStory  ' sets cursor to top of doc
    With g_wdApp.Selection.Find
        .Text = ""
        .Replacement.Text = ""
        .Forward = True
        .Wrap = wdFindContinue
        .Format = True
        .MatchCase = False
        .MatchWholeWord = False
        .MatchWildcards = False
        .MatchSoundsLike = False
        .MatchAllWordForms = False
    End With
End With
```

Note the use of the `ClearFormatting` function. This is called to make sure that the `Find` command will only look for the formatting we are specifying, and does not have any residual configuration from a previous search.

Now the code loops while there are still instances of the given style in use. If any text has "Default Paragraph Font" formatting applied, it is replaced with "normal" formatting:

```
bMoreToDo = True
Do While bMoreToDo = True
    DoEvents
    bMoreToDo = g_wdApp.Selection.Find.Execute
    If bMoreToDo = True Then
        g_wdApp.Selection.Range.Style = _
            g_wdApp.ActiveDocument.Styles("Default Paragraph Font")
        g_wdApp.Selection.Range.Style = _
            g_wdApp.ActiveDocument.Styles(wdStyleNormal)
```

Note that the conversion of even a moderate-sized document may take some time, as there is a lot of searching and replacing and deleting operations going on. The `DoEvents` statement is inserted in many of the program's loops to prevent the program from monoplizing all application processing. This way, the Word document that will use our DLL will still respond to mouse and keyboard events.

If the text selected by `Find` is not empty, the name of the style is used to create tags. Special consideration is taken in case the selection is a form-feed or carriage return (which may themselves be formatted). The `Extend` parameter tells the `Selection` object that we want to increase the selected area, as opposed to just moving the selection point:

```
                If Selection.Text <> "" Then
                    Do While (vbCr = Right(Selection.Text, 1))
                        g_wdApp.Selection.MoveLeft _
                         Unit:=wdCharacter, Count:=1, Extend:=wdExtend
                        DoEvents
                    Loop
                    If (Selection.Text <> vbFormFeed) _
                                And (Selection.Text <> vbCr) Then
                        g_wdApp.Selection.Copy
                        g_wdApp.Selection.Cut
                        sMsg = Replace(sMsg, " ", "-")
                        g_wdApp.Selection.TypeText Text:="<" & sMsg & ">"
                        g_wdApp.Selection.Paste
                        g_wdApp.Selection.TypeText Text:="</" & sMsg & ">"
                    End If
                End If
            End If
        Loop
    Next nStyIdx
```

The code then calls methods to handle specific types of character formatting, which are not included in the list of `Document` styles:

```
    Call TagBold
    Call TagItalics
    Call TagUnderLine
```

After creating tags for each of the styles, there may be adjacent sections of text that can be combined, for example, `<p></p>` can be changed to `<p/>`. The `TightenTags` function is called to do this, but skips any "List" or "Bullet" styles that may require distinct markup to delineate the tagged items:

```
    For nStyIdx = 0 To nStyCount - 1
        DoEvents
        g_wdApp.Selection.HomeKey Unit:=wdStory    'moves cursor to top of doc
        sMsg = Replace(arrStyles(nStyIdx), " ", "-")
        If ((InStr(sMsg, "List") = 0) And (InStr(sMsg, "Bullet") = 0)) Then
            Call TightenTags(sMsg)
        End If
    Next
```

Next, line breaks are replaced with "`<br/>`" markup by calling `TagLineBreaks`:

```
    Call TagLineBreaks
```

Word bookmarks are a useful way to identify text without applying any formatting. BookmarkTags (which is explained later) goes through the document's bookmark collection and creates elements based on the bookmark name:

```
Call BookmarkTags
```

The code now sets the cursor to the top of the document, and calls AddRoot to insert the XML declaration, a root document element, metadata containing the document's built-in properties (such as Title, Subject, Author) and any custom properties defined by the author of the document:

```
g_wdApp.Selection.HomeKey Unit:=wdStory
AddRoot
```

Finally, another function (explained in a later section) is called to convert any tables in the document:

```
DoAllTables
```

Any errors are trapped at the end of the function, followed by some clean-up code:

```
ErrHand:
    If Err.Number <> 0 Then
        ConvertToXML = False
    Else
        ConvertToXML = True
    End If
    If Not g_wdApp Is Nothing Then Set g_wdApp = Nothing
    If Not g_wdDoc Is Nothing Then Set g_wdDoc = Nothing
    g_mbAppAssigned = False
End Function
```

The Helper Functions

Now let's take look at the assorted helper functions. PrepareDoc simply wraps a series of calls to specific methods for removing potential problems. Each of these locates specific objects or hidden characters (pictures, page breaks, borders, section breaks, carriage returns), and either removes them or replaces them with some alternative text. (We won't show all of the functions here as there are a lot of them. They all use fairly similar techniques.)

```
Private Function PrepareDoc() As Boolean

    If Not g_mbAppAssigned Then
        PrepareDoc = False
        Exit Function
    End If

    If Not RemoveAllPictures() Then
        PrepareDoc = False
        Exit Function
    End If
```

```
        DoEvents
        If Not PrepareManualPageBreaks() Then
            PrepareDoc = False
            Exit Function
        End If

        DoEvents
        If Not RemoveAllBorders() Then
            PrepareDoc = False
            Exit Function
        End If

        DoEvents
        If Not PrepareSectionBreaks Then
            PrepareDoc = False
            Exit Function
        End If

        DoEvents
        If Not MakeNormalSoloCr Then
            PrepareDoc = False
            Exit Function
        End If

        PrepareDoc = True
End Function
```

Removing Graphics

RemoveAllPictures uses the special Word search string ^g to locate graphics, and replaces them with text:

```
Private Function RemoveAllPictures() As Boolean
    On Error GoTo ErrHand

    Selection.HomeKey Unit:=wdStory

    ' We do not want the new text have any formatting that may have been left
    ' over from a previous find/replace, so the code calls ClearFormatting
    Selection.Find.ClearFormatting
    Selection.Find.Replacement.ClearFormatting

    With Selection.Find
        .Text = "^g"
        .Replacement.Text = "GRAPHICS"
        .Forward = True
        .Wrap = wdFindContinue
        .Format = False
        .MatchCase = False
        .MatchWholeWord = False
        .MatchWildcards = False
        .MatchSoundsLike = False
        .MatchAllWordForms = False
    End With
    Selection.Find.Execute Replace:=wdReplaceAll
```

```
ErrHand:
    If Err.Number <> 0 Then
        RemoveAllPictures = False
    Else
        RemoveAllPictures = True
    End If
End Function
```

Note that the wdReplaceAll constant specifies that Find should continue running until all matched text in the document is replaced.

Formatting Tables

ConvertToXml called a function named DoAllTables. It calls a function, AssignColorHash, which populates a Dictionary object with Word color constants and corresponding strings (such as those used in HTML). It then calls another function, TagTable, which actually converts the table into XML. Word keeps a list of all tables in the document. As the TagTable function does its job, it removes the table from the document, so the loop always calls the first table in the list until there are no more tables.

```
Private Function DoAllTables() As Boolean
    On Error GoTo ErrHand
    Call AssignColorHash
    Do While g_wdApp.ActiveDocument.Tables.Count > 0
        Call TagTable(1)
    Loop

ErrHand:
    If Err.Number <> 0 Then
        DoAllTables = False
    Else
        DoAllTables = True
    End If
End Function
```

TagTable takes an integer that is used to index into the document's collection of tables. It uses the Rows and Columns properties of the table to construct the markup. The code selects the specified table, and retrieves the number of rows and columns:

```
Private Function TagTable(nTable As Integer) As Boolean
    On Error GoTo ErrHand

    Dim caCellInfo() As CellAttributes
    Dim nRows As Integer
    Dim nCols As Integer
    Dim asContent() As String
    Dim nX As Integer
    Dim nY As Integer
    Dim sTableBookmark As String
    Dim oDoc As Document

    Set oDoc = g_wdApp.ActiveDocument
```

```
oDoc.Tables(nTable).Select
nRows = oDoc.Tables(nTable).Rows.Count
nCols = oDoc.Tables(nTable).Columns.Count
```

It also looks to see if the table is part of a bookmark. If it is, a variable will be set, so that the markup can contain a "NAME" attribute based on the bookmark name:

```
If g_wdApp.Selection.Bookmarks.Count > 0 Then
    sTableBookmark = g_wdApp.Selection.Bookmarks(1).Name
End If
```

The function then loops through each cell, collecting the cell attributes:

```
ReDim caCellInfo(1 To nRows, 1 To nCols)
For nY = 1 To nCols
    For nX = 1 To nRows
        caCellInfo(nX, nY).Text = _
                    oDoc.Tables(nTable).Cell(nX, nY).Range.Text
        caCellInfo(nX, nY).Text = Left(caCellInfo(nX, nY).Text, _
                Len(caCellInfo(nX, nY).Text) - 2)
        caCellInfo(nX, nY).BackPatternColor = _
                oDoc.Tables(nTable).Cell(nX, _
                nY).Shading.BackgroundPatternColorIndex
        caCellInfo(nX, nY).ForePatternColor = _
                oDoc.Tables(nTable).Cell(nX,_
                nY).Shading.ForegroundPatternColorIndex
    Next nX
Next nY
```

The table is then deleted, and an XML version is constructed in its place. Cell colors are applied by retrieving values from the Dictionary object:

```
oDoc.Tables(nTable).Delete
g_wdApp.Selection.InsertAfter "<TABLE  NAME = " & Chr(34) & _
                sTableBookmark & Chr(34) & " >" & vbCr
For nX = 1 To nRows
    g_wdApp.Selection.InsertAfter vbTab & "<TR>" & vbCr
        For nY = 1 To nCols
            g_wdApp.Selection.InsertAfter vbTab & vbTab & _
                " <TD BGCOLOR='" & _
                g_dictColors.Item(caCellInfo(nX, nY).BackPatternColor) _
                & "'"
            g_wdApp.Selection.InsertAfter "> <FONT COLOR='" & _
                g_dictColors.Item(caCellInfo(nX, _
                nY).ForePatternColor) _
                & "'>" & _
                caCellInfo(nX, nY).Text & "</FONT></TD>" & vbCr
        Next nY
    g_wdApp.Selection.InsertAfter vbTab & "</TR>" & vbCr
Next nX
g_wdApp.Selection.InsertAfter "</TABLE>" & vbCr
```

Any run time errors are caught at the end of the function:

```
ErrHand:
    If Err.Number <> 0 Then
        TagTable = False
    Else
        TagTable = True
    End If
End Function
```

Formatting Bookmarks

The `Document` object contains a list of all bookmarks. `BookmarkTags` goes through the list and wraps tags around the bookmarked text, using the bookmark name for the element name. In Word, whenever you use the menu items to go to a bookmark, the entire bookmark text is selected; bookmark navigation is a function of the `Selection` object. We take advantage of that to locate the start and end of the bookmark text, and insert the appropriate tags:

```
Private Sub BookmarkTags()
    Dim nIdx As Integer
    Dim sTag As String

    Dim oBkMarks As Bookmarks
    Set oBkMarks = ActiveDocument.Bookmarks

    For nIdx = 1 To oBkMarks.Count
        sTag = oBkMarks.Item(nIdx).Name
        With ActiveDocument.Bookmarks
            .DefaultSorting = wdSortByName
            .ShowHidden = False
        End With

        Selection.GoTo What:=wdGoToBookmark, Name:=sTag
        Selection.MoveLeft Unit:=wdCharacter, Count:=1
        Selection.TypeText Text:="<" & sTag & ">"
        Selection.GoTo What:=wdGoToBookmark, Name:=sTag
        With ActiveDocument.Bookmarks
            .DefaultSorting = wdSortByName
            .ShowHidden = False
        End With
        Selection.MoveRight Unit:=wdCharacter, Count:=1
        Selection.TypeText Text:="</" & sTag & ">"
    Next
End Sub
```

Adding MetaData

The `AddRoot` function gives the final document a root element and an XML declaration. It also inserts metadata elements with the document properties:

```
Private Function AddRoot() As Boolean
    Dim sHead As String

    sHead = "<?xml version=" & Chr(34) & "1.0" & Chr(34) & "?>" & Chr(10)
    sHead = sHead & "<WordDoc>" & Chr(10)
```

```
        sHead = sHead & GetDocProperties
        sHead = sHead & GetCustomProperties
    With Selection
          .InsertBefore sHead
          .Collapse Direction:=wdCollapseEnd
    End With
    Selection.EndKey Unit:=wdStory
    With Selection
          .InsertAfter "</WordDoc>"
          .Collapse Direction:=wdCollapseEnd
    End With
End Function
```

The regular document properties are obtained by calling `GetDocProperties`, which simply iterates through the `ActiveDocument`'s set of built-in properties:

```
Private Function GetDocProperties() As String
    Dim sXML As String
    Dim nIdx As Integer
    Dim kDocProps As Object           ' DocumentProperties
    Dim oDocProp As Object            ' DocumentProperty
    Dim sName As String
    Dim sValue As String
    sXML = ""
    Set kDocProps = ActiveDocument.BuiltInDocumentProperties
    For nIdx = 1 To kDocProps.Count
        sName = kDocProps.Item(nIdx).Name
```

The code has to trap a possible error here. If the document has never been printed, accessing the `DateLastPrinted` property throws a run time error:

```
        On Error Resume Next
        sValue = kDocProps.Item(nIdx).Value
        If sValue <> "" Then
            sXML = sXML & "<meta type='builtin' name='" & _
                   sName & "' value='" & sValue & "' />" & vbCrLf
        End If
        sValue = ""
    Next

    GetDocProperties = sXML
End Function
```

The user-defined properties are obtained in the same way, except that we use the `CustomDocumentProperties` collection:

```
Private Function GetCustomProperties() As String
    Dim sXML As String
    Dim nIdx As Integer
    Dim kDocProps As Object           ' DocumentProperties
    Dim oDocProp As Object            ' DocumentProperty
    Dim sName As String
    Dim sValue As String
```

```
        sXML = ""
        Set kDocProps = ActiveDocument.CustomDocumentProperties
        For nIdx = 1 To kDocProps.Count
            sName = kDocProps.Item(nIdx).Name
            On Error Resume Next
            sValue = kDocProps.Item(nIdx).Value
            If sValue <> "" Then
                sXML = sXML & "<meta type='custom' name='" & _
                        sName & "' value='" & sValue & "' />" & vbCrLf
            End If
            sValue = ""
        Next
        GetCustomProperties = sXML
    End Function
```

The Word Template

That's it for the Visual Basic code we'll show. We'll look now at the Word template and create a macro to use our DLL. We open up Word, and select File | New. We're creating a template, so in the New dialog box we select the "template" option (under Create New, in the lower right-hand corner). A new document appears when we click OK. We create a new macro by using the macro recorder; it doesn't matter what we record, as we'll be replacing the text later. We call the macro "ConvertToXml" and specify that it is to be saved in the new template, not in the "normal.dot" template.

Now we open the VBA editor, locate the macro and remove any code inside it. On the IDE toolbar, we select Tools | References… which allows us to add a reference to an ActiveX DLL, just as in the standard Visual Basic editor. We add a reference to WordXML.Convert.

In the editor, we add these lines to ConvertToXml:

```
Sub ConvertToXml()
    Dim oWordXml As WordXml.Convert
    Set oWordXml = New WordXml.Convert
    oWordXml.AssignDocument Application, Application.ActiveDocument.Name
    bRes = oWordXML.ConvertToXml

    If Not oWordXML.ConvertToXml Then
        MsgBox "Error converting to XML"
    End If
    Set oWordXML = Nothing
End Sub
```

We save our work, naming the template "ConvertToXml.dot".

Test Document

To test that the application works, we now create a new document based on the new template. We enter some text, apply some formatting, and add a bookmark:

Text	Formatting
Test Document	Heading 1 style
This is some test text.	Italics
This line contains a bookmark	Insert bookmark

Then, we select the `ConvertToXml` macro from the <u>T</u>ools | <u>M</u>acro | <u>M</u>acros menu, and run it.

This is the result:

```
<?xml version="1.0"?>
<WordDoc>
<meta type='builtin' name='Title' value='Convert To Xml' />
<meta type='builtin' name='Author' value='James' />
<meta type='builtin' name='Template' value='ConvertToXml.dot' />
<meta type='builtin' name='Revision number' value='1' />
<meta type='builtin' name='Application name' value='Microsoft Word 9.0' />
<meta type='builtin' name='Creation date' value='3/7/00 1:51:00 AM' />
<meta type='builtin' name='Total editing time' value='1' />
<meta type='builtin' name='Number of pages' value='1' />
<meta type='builtin' name='Number of words' value='15' />
<meta type='builtin' name='Number of characters' value='121' />
<meta type='builtin' name='Security' value='0' />
<meta type='builtin' name='Company' value=' ' />
<meta type='builtin' name='Number of bytes' value='11181' />
<meta type='builtin' name='Number of lines' value='4' />
<meta type='builtin' name='Number of paragraphs' value='4' />
<meta type='builtin' name='Number of characters (with spaces)' value='132' />
<Heading-1> Test Document</Heading-1>
<i> This is some test text.<br/>
</i>
This line <MyBookmark>contains</MyBookmark> a bookmark<br/>
</WordDoc>
```

Feel free to test more complex documents with different formatting styles applied.

Summary

We saw that Microsoft Word exposes an object model that can be scripted using Visual Basic. Much can be learned about how Word performs certain tasks by using the Word macro recorder and examining the generated code. That same code can be placed in a DLL, with some modifications, and used to manipulate a Word `Application` object reference.

Scripting Word with Visual Basic allows us to take the document formatting and properties, and create our own markup. Certain features are harder to convert than others, but with some restrictions most documents can be turned into XML.

Links and References

The XML 1.0 specification: http://www.w3.org/TR/1998/REC-xml-19980210

Tutorial on XML and DTD:
http://wdvl.internet.com/Authoring/Languages/XML/Tutorials/Intro/toc.html

The May 1998 Note on XML-Data, on which the MS Schema is based:
http://www.w3.org/TR/1998/NOTE-XML-data-0105/

Information on the MS Schema implementation on MSDN:
http://msdn.microsoft.com/xml/c-frame.htm?945101468859#/xml/xmlguide/schema-overview.asp

The most recent versions of XML Schema:
http://www.w3.org/TR/xmlschema-1/ and http://www.w3.org/TR/xmlschema-2/

Good coverage on the standardization process of XML Schema:
http://www.xml.com

Repositories of schemas (DTDs and MS Schemas):
http://www.oasis-open.org
http://www.biztalk.org
http://www.schema.net

A Final Word

So now we have come to the end of the book. I'm sure that the content of this book and the example applications have shown just how flexible and versatile XML is, and how Visual Basic is an ideal programming tool to exploit all of its features. Happy programming!

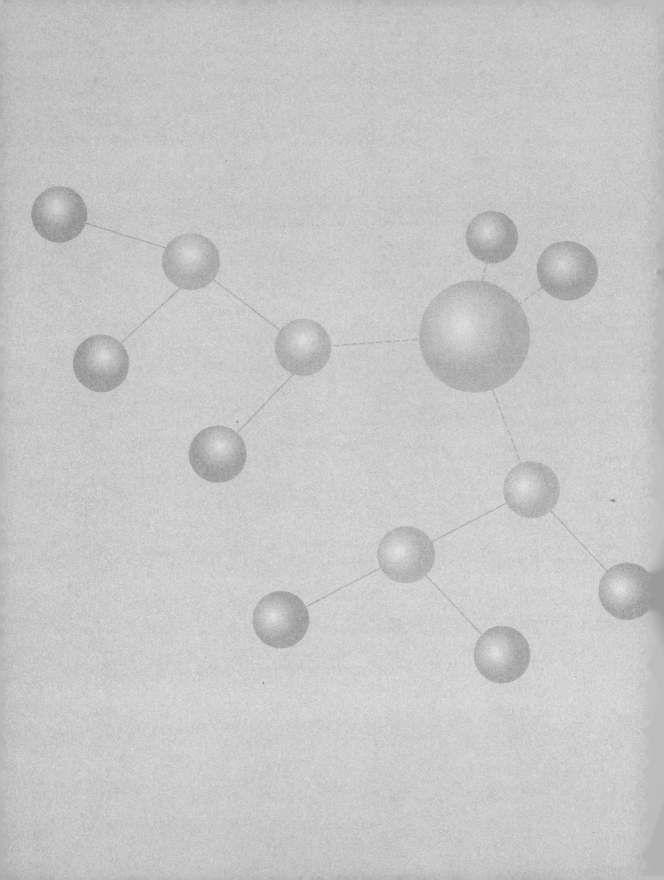

XML Document Object Model

The DOM was discussed in Chapter 3; this appendix contains a complete reference to the XML Document Object Model as supported in Internet Explorer 5. This includes full support for the W3C version 1.0 DOM Recommendations, plus extensions specific to IE5 (indicated by '**Ext**' in the tables below). The appendix is divided into four sections, each arranged alphabetically for ease of access:

❑ The Base DOM Objects

❑ The High-Level DOM Objects

❑ IE5-Specific Parser Objects

❑ The DOM NodeTypes

The Base DOM Objects

In Internet Explorer 5 all the nodes that appear in an XML document, with a couple of minor exceptions, are based on the IXMLDOMNode object. This represents the base node object from which the specialist node objects, such as Element, Attribute, Comment, etc., inherit. There are two other base objects as well; the full list is:

❑ NamedNodeMap (the IXMLDOMNamedNodeMap object)

❑ Node (the IXMLDOMNode object)

❑ NodeList (the IXMLDOMNodeList object)

NamedNodeMap (IXMLDOMNamedNodeMap) Object

This object provides a collection of node objects that allows access by name as well as by index. This collection is typically used with `Attribute` objects rather than elements or other node types, and is 'live', meaning that changes to the document are mirrored in the list immediately. The IE5 extensions add support for namespaces, and iteration through the collection of attribute nodes. This base object is implemented as `IDOMNamedNodeMap` by Microsoft.

NamedNodeMap Property

Name	Description
length	Returns the number of nodes in the named node map.

NamedNodeMap Methods

Name		Description
getNamedItem(name)		Retrieves the node object with the specified name. Typically used to retrieve attributes from an element.
getQualifiedItem(base_name, namespace_uri)	Ext	Returns the node object with the specified base_name and namespace_uri values.
item(index)		Returns the node at position index in the named node map, where the first node is indexed zero.
nextNode()	Ext	Returns the next node object in the named node map, or null if there are no more nodes.
removeNamedItem(name)		Removes the node object with the specified name from the named node map. Typically used to remove attributes from an element.
removeQualifiedItem (base_name, namespace_uri)	Ext	Removes the node object with the specified base_name and namespace_uri values from the named node map.
reset()	Ext	Resets the internal pointer to the point before the first node in the node list. Prepares the list for iteration with the nextNode() method.
setNamedItem (new_node)		Inserts the node object new_node into the named node map, updating the XML document. Any existing node with the same name is replaced with the new node. Typically used to update attribute values for an element.

Node (IXMLDOMNode) Object

The IE5 IXMLDOMNode object extends the W3C DOM recommendations (which Microsoft implements as the IDOMNode object) by adding support for data types, namespaces, DTDs, and XML Schemas.

Node Properties

Name		Description
attributes		Returns a collection of the Attribute (or Attr) objects for this node as a NamedNodeMap object.
baseName	Ext	Returns the node name with any namespace removed. For example, in a node declared as <nspace:elemname> it returns the elemname part.
childNodes		Returns a NodeList containing all the child nodes of this node, for nodes that can have child nodes.
dataType	Ext	Sets or returns the data type for this node.
definition	Ext	For EntityReference nodes, returns the entry in the DTD or schema containing the definition for the entity, i.e. <!ENTITY entityname 'entity value'>. For other nodes, returns null.
firstChild		Returns a reference to the first child node of this node.
lastChild		Returns a reference to the last child node of this node.
namespaceURI	Ext	Returns the URI for the namespace as a string. For example, in the namespace declaration xmlns:name="uri" it returns the uri part.
nextSibling		Returns a reference to the next sibling node of this node, i.e. the next node in the source data file at the same level of the hierarchy.
nodeName		Returns the name of the node, which will depend on the node type. See the list of *Node Types* at the end of this appendix for more details.
nodeTypeString	Ext	Returns the node type as a string. See the list of *Node Types* at the end of this appendix for more details.
nodeType		Returns the node type as a number. See the list of *Node Types* at the end of this appendix for more details.
nodeTypedValue	Ext	Sets or returns the strongly typed value of the node, expressed in its defined data type. If no data type has been defined for the node, its nodeValue is returned.
nodeValue		Sets or returns the value of the node as plain text.

Name		Description
parentNode		Returns the parent node of this node, for nodes that can have parents.
parsed	**Ext**	Returns true if this node and all its descendants have been parsed and instantiated.
prefix	**Ext**	Returns the element namespace prefix as a string. For example, in a node declared as `<nspace:elemname>` it returns the nspace part.
previousSibling		Returns a reference to the previous sibling node of this node, i.e. the previous node in the source file at the same level of the hierarchy.
specified	**Ext**	Indicates whether the node value is explicitly specified or derived from a default value in the DTD or schema. Normally only used with attribute nodes.
text	**Ext**	Sets or returns the entire text content of this node and all its descendant nodes.
xml	**Ext**	Returns the entire XML content of this node and all its descendant nodes.

Node Methods

Name	Description
appendChild (new_node)	Appends the node object new_node to the end of the list of child nodes for this node.
cloneNode (recurse_ children)	Creates a new node object that is an exact clone of this node, including all descendant nodes of this node if recurse_children is set to true.
hasChildNodes()	Returns true if this node has any child nodes.
insertBefore (new_node, this_node)	Inserts a new node object new_node into the list of child nodes for this node, to the left of the node object this_node or at the end of the list if this_node is omitted.
removeChild (this_node)	Removes the child node this_node from the list of child nodes for this node, and returns it.
replaceChild (new_node, old_node)	Replaces the child node old_node with the new child node object new_node, and returns the old child node.

Name		Description
selectSingleNode (pattern)	**Ext**	Applies a specified pattern to this node's context and returns just the first Node object that matches. The string pattern specifies the XSL pattern-matching operation to be used.
transformNode (stylesheet)	**Ext**	Processes this node and its children using an XSL stylesheet specified in the stylesheet argument, and returns the resulting transformation. The stylesheet must be either a Document node object, in which case the document is assumed to be an XSL stylesheet, or a Node object in the xsl namespace, in which case this node is treated as a standalone stylesheet fragment.

NodeList (IXMLDOMNodeList) Object

This object represents a collection (or list) of Node objects. The object list is 'live' like the NamedNodeMap object. The IE5 extensions support iteration through the list in addition to indexed access. (The base NodeList object is implemented in IE5 as IDOMNodeList).

NodeList Property

Name	Description
length	Returns the number of nodes in the node list.

NodeList Methods

Name		Description
item(index)		Returns the node at position index in the node list, where the first node is indexed zero.
nextNode()	**Ext**	Returns the next node object in the node list, or null if there are no more nodes.
reset()	**Ext**	Resets the internal pointer to the point before the first node in the node list. Prepares the list for iteration with the nextNode() method.

The High-Level DOM Objects

Because each type of node in an XML document differs in both obvious and subtle ways, specific objects are available for different types of nodes. Most inherit the properties and methods of the base Node (IXMLDOMNode) object, and add the specific properties and methods required for best tailoring the object to its own purpose.

The specific objects are:

- ❑ Attribute or Attr (the IXMLDOMAttribute object)

- ❑ CDATASection (the IXMLDOMCDATASection object)

- ❑ CharacterData (the IXMLDOMCharacterData object)

- ❑ Comment (the IXMLDOMComment object)

- ❑ Document (the IXMLDOMDocument object)

- ❑ DocumentFragment (the IXMLDOMDocumentFragment object)

- ❑ DocumentType (the IXMLDOMDocumentType object)

- ❑ Element (the IXMLDOMElement object)

- ❑ Entity (the IXMLDOMEntity object)

- ❑ EntityReference (the IXMLDOMEntityReference object)

- ❑ Implementation (the IXMLDOMImplementation object)

- ❑ Notation (the IXMLDOMNotation object)

- ❑ ProcessingInstruction (the IXMLDOMProcessingInstruction object)

- ❑ Text (the IXMLDOMText object)

In addition to these, there are interfaces called IDOMDocument, IDOMDocumentType etc., which implement the W3C Recommendation, without the Microsoft extensions. These inherit from IDOMNode, which is the Microsoft implementation of the W3C Node object. The following tables repeat the base properties and methods, and add the node-specific ones. This provides a complete reference, with no need to check elsewhere which extra properties and methods the base objects provide in addition.

Attribute or Attr (IXMLDOMAttribute) Object

This object represents an attribute of an Element object. In the W3C DOM recommendations, the object name is Attr rather than Attribute, to avoid clashing with existing interface definition languages. An Attribute node has a name and a value, and attributes are normally manipulated through a NamedNodeMap object. Microsoft implements the unextended object as IDOMAttribute.

Attribute Properties

Name		Description
attributes		Returns a collection of the Attribute (or Attr) objects for this node as a NamedNodeMap object.
baseName	**Ext**	Returns the node name with any namespace removed. For example, in a node declared as <nspace:elemname> it returns the elemname part.

Name		Description
dataType	**Ext**	Sets or returns the data type for this node.
definition	**Ext**	For `EntityReference` nodes, returns the entry in the DTD or schema containing the definition for the entity, i.e. `<!ENTITY entityname 'entity value'>`. For other nodes, returns null.
firstChild		Returns a reference to the first child node of this node.
lastChild		Returns a reference to the last child node of this node.
name		Sets or returns the name of the attribute.
namespaceURI	**Ext**	Returns the URI for the namespace as a string. For example, in the namespace declaration `xmlns:name="uri"` it returns the uri part.
nextSibling		Returns a reference to the next sibling node of this node, i.e. the next node in the source data file at the same level of the hierarchy.
nodeName		Returns the name of the node, which will depend on the node type. See the list of *Node Types* at the end of this appendix for more details.
nodeTypeString	**Ext**	Returns the node type as a string, depending on the node type. See the list of *Node Types* at the end of this appendix for more details.
nodeType		Returns the node type as a number. See the list of *Node Types* at the end of this appendix for more details.
nodeTypedValue	**Ext**	Sets or returns the strongly typed value of the node, expressed in its defined data type. If no data type has been defined for the node, its `nodeValue` is returned.
nodeValue		Sets or returns the value of the node as plain text.
ownerDocument		Returns the root node of the document that contains the node.
parentNode		Returns the parent node of this node, for nodes that can have parents.
parsed	**Ext**	Returns true if this node and all its descendants have been parsed and instantiated.
prefix	**Ext**	Returns the element namespace prefix as a string. For example, in a node declared as `<nspace:elemname>` it returns the nspace part.
previousSibling		Returns a reference to the previous sibling node of this node, i.e. the previous node in the source file at the same level of the hierarchy.

Name		Description
tagName		Returns the name of the element that contains this attribute.
text	**Ext**	Sets or returns the entire text content of this node and all its descendant nodes.
xml	**Ext**	Returns the entire XML content of this node and all its descendant nodes.
value		Sets or returns the value of the attribute.

Attribute Methods

Name		Description
appendChild(new_node)		Appends the node object new_node to the end of the list of child nodes for this node.
cloneNode(recurse_ children)		Creates a new node object that is an exact clone of this node, including all descendant nodes of this node if recurse_children is set to true.
hasChildNodes()		Returns true if this node has any child nodes.
insertBefore (new_node, this_node)		Inserts a new node object new_node into the list of child nodes for this node, to the left of the node object this_node or at the end of the list if this_node is omitted.
removeChild (this_node)		Removes the child node this_node from the list of child nodes for this node, and returns it.
replaceChild (new_node, old_node)		Replaces the child node old_node with the new child node object new_node, and returns the old child node.
selectNodes (pattern)	**Ext**	Applies a specified pattern to this node's context and returns a node list object containing matching nodes. The string pattern specifies the XSL pattern-matching operation to be used.
selectSingleNode (pattern)	**Ext**	Applies a specified pattern to this node's context and returns just the first node object that matches. The string pattern specifies the XSL pattern-matching operation to be used.
transformNode (stylesheet)	**Ext**	Processes this node and its children using an XSL stylesheet specified in the stylesheet argument, and returns the resulting transformation. The stylesheet must be either a Document node object, in which case the document is assumed to be an XSL stylesheet, or a Node object in the xsl namespace, in which case this node is treated as a standalone stylesheet fragment.

CDATASection (IXMLDOMCDATASection) Object

CDATA sections in a DTD or schema are used to 'escape' blocks of text that are not designed to be interpreted as markup. They are declared in the DTD using a `<!CDATA...>` element. The `IXMLDOMCDATASection` interface is inherited from the `IXMLDOMText` interface, and adds no extra methods or properties. IE5 implements the unextended W3C object as the `IDOMCDATASection` object.

CDATASection Properties

Name		Description
attributes		Returns collection of the `Attribute` (or `Attr`) objects for this node as a `NamedNodeMap` object.
baseName	**Ext**	Returns the node name with any namespace removed. For example, in a node declared as `<nspace:elemname>` it returns the elemname part.
childNodes		Returns a `NodeList` containing all the child nodes of this node, for nodes that can have child nodes.
data		Contains this node's value, which depends on the node type.
dataType	**Ext**	Sets or returns the data type for this node.
definition	**Ext**	For `EntityReference` nodes, returns the entry in the DTD or schema containing the definition for the entity, i.e. `<!ENTITY entityname 'entity value'>`. For other nodes, returns null.
firstChild		Returns a reference to the first child node of this node.
lastChild		Returns a reference to the last child node of this node.
length		Returns the number of characters for the data, i.e. the string length.
namespaceURI	**Ext**	Returns the URI for the namespace as a string. For example, in the namespace declaration `xmlns:name="uri"` it returns the uri part.
nextSibling		Returns a reference to the next sibling node of this node, i.e. the next node in the source data file at the same level of the hierarchy.
nodeName		Returns the name of the node, which will depend on the node type. See the list of *Node Types* at the end of this appendix for more details.
nodeTypeString	**Ext**	Returns the node type as a string, depending on the node type. See the list of *Node Types* at the end of this appendix for more details.
nodeType		Returns the node type as a number. See the list of *Node Types* at the end of this appendix for more details.

Name		Description
nodeTypedValue	**Ext**	Sets or returns the strongly typed value of the node, expressed in its defined data type. If no data type has been defined for the node, its nodeValue is returned.
nodeValue		Sets or returns the value of the node as plain text.
ownerDocument		Returns the root node of the document that contains the node.
parentNode		Returns the parent node of this node, for nodes that can have parents.
parsed	**Ext**	Returns true if this node and all its descendants have been parsed and instantiated.
prefix	**Ext**	Returns the element namespace prefix as a string. For example, in a node declared as <nspace:elemname> it returns the nspace part.
previousSibling		Returns a reference to the previous sibling node of this node, i.e. the previous node in the source file at the same level of the hierarchy.
specified	**Ext**	Indicates whether the node value is explicitly specified or derived from a default value in the DTD or schema. Normally only used with attribute nodes.
text	**Ext**	Sets or returns the entire text content of this node and all its descendant nodes.
xml	**Ext**	Returns the entire XML content of this node and all its descendant nodes.

CDATASection Methods

Name	Description
appendChild(new_node)	Appends the node object new_node to the end of the list of child nodes for this node.
appendData(text)	Appends the string in the text argument to the existing string data.
cloneNode(recurse_children)	Creates a new node object that is an exact clone of this node, including all descendant nodes of this node if recurse_children is set to true.
deleteData(char_offset, num_chars)	Deletes a substring from the string data of the node, starting at char_offset and continuing for num_chars.
hasChildNodes()	Returns true if this node has any child nodes.

Name		Description
insertBefore(new_node, this_node)		Inserts a new node object new_node into the list of child nodes for this node, to the left of the node object this_node or at the end of the list if this_node is omitted.
insertData(char_offset, text)		Inserts the string in the text argument at the specified character offset within the data contained by the node.
removeChild(this_child)		Removes the child node this_node from the list of child nodes for this node, and returns it.
replaceChild(new_node, old_node)		Replaces the child node old_node with the new child node object new_node, and returns the old child node.
replaceData(char_offset, num_chars, text)		Replaces the specified number of characters in the existing string data of the node, starting at the specified character offset, with the string in the text argument.
selectNodes(pattern)	Ext	Applies a specified pattern to this node's context and returns a node list object containing matching nodes. The string pattern specifies the XSL pattern-matching operation to be used.
selectSingleNode(pattern)	Ext	Applies a specified pattern to this node's context and returns just the first node object that matches. The string pattern specifies the XSL pattern-matching operation to be used.
splitText(char_offset)		Splits the node into two separate nodes at the specified character offset, then inserts the new node into the XML as a sibling that immediately follows this node.
substringData(char_offset, num_chars)		Returns as a string the specified number of characters, starting at the specified character offset, from the data contained in the node.
transformNode(stylesheet)	Ext	Processes this node and its children using an XSL stylesheet specified in the stylesheet argument, and returns the resulting transformation. The stylesheet must be either a Document node object, in which case the document is assumed to be an XSL stylesheet, or a Node object in the xsl namespace, in which case this node is treated as a standalone stylesheet fragment.

CharacterData (IXMLDOMCharacterData) Object

This object is the base for several higher-level objects including Text, CDATASection (which is inherited from the Text object) and Comment. It provides text information properties like length, and a range of text manipulation methods like substringData() that are used by these objects. The IE5 implementation of CharacterData follows the W3C recommendations for character data manipulation in the appropriate elements with the exception of those properties and methods marked with '**Ext**' in the following tables. The unextended W3C CharacterData object is implemented in IE5 by the IDOMCharacterData object.

CharacterData Properties

Name		Description
attributes		Returns a collection of the Attribute (or Attr) objects for this node as a NamedNodeMap object.
baseName	**Ext**	Returns the node name with any namespace removed. For example, in a node declared as <nspace:elemname> it returns the elemname part.
childNodes		Returns a NodeList containing all the child nodes of this node, for nodes that can have child nodes.
data		Contains this node's value, which depends on the node type.
dataType	**Ext**	Sets or returns the data type for this node.
definition	**Ext**	For EntityReference nodes, returns the entry in the DTD or schema containing the definition for the entity, i.e. <!ENTITY entityname 'entity value'>. For other nodes, returns null.
firstChild		Returns a reference to the first child node of this node.
lastChild		Returns a reference to the last child node of this node.
length		Returns the number of characters for the data, i.e. the string length.
namespaceURI	**Ext**	Returns the URI for the namespace as a string. For example, in the namespace declaration xmlns:name="uri" it returns the uri part.
nextSibling		Returns a reference to the next sibling node of this node, i.e. the next node in the source data file at the same level of the hierarchy.
nodeName		Returns the name of the node, which will depend on the node type. See the list of *Node Types* at the end of this appendix for more details.
nodeTypeString	**Ext**	Returns the node type as a string. See the list of *Node Types* at the end of this appendix for more details.

Name		Description
nodeType		Returns the node type as a number. See the list of *Node Types* at the end of this appendix for more details.
nodeTypedValue	**Ext**	Sets or returns the strongly typed value of the node, expressed in its defined data type. If no data type has been defined for the node, its nodeValue is returned.
nodeValue		Sets or returns the value of the node as plain text.
ownerDocument		Returns the root node of the document that contains the node.
parentNode		Returns the parent node of this node, for nodes that can have parents.
parsed	**Ext**	Returns true if this node and all its descendants have been parsed and instantiated.
prefix	**Ext**	Returns the element namespace prefix as a string. For example, in a node declared as <nspace:elemname> it returns the nspace part.
previousSibling		Returns a reference to the previous sibling node of this node, i.e. the previous node in the source file at the same level of the hierarchy.
specified	**Ext**	Indicates whether the node value is explicitly specified or derived from a default value in the DTD or schema. Normally only used with attribute nodes.
text	**Ext**	Sets or returns the entire text content of this node and all its descendant nodes.
xml	**Ext**	Returns the entire XML content of this node and all its descendant nodes.

CharacterData Methods

Name	Description
appendChild(new_node)	Appends the node object new_node to the end of the list of child nodes for this node.
appendData(text)	Appends the string in the text argument to the existing string data.
cloneNode(recurse_children)	Creates a new node object that is an exact clone of this node, including all descendant nodes of this node if recurse_children is set to true.
deleteData(char_offset, num_chars)	Deletes a substring from the string data of the node, starting at char_offset and continuing for num_chars.

Name		Description
hasChildNodes()		Returns true if this node has any child nodes.
insertBefore(new_node, this_node)		Inserts a new node object new_node into the list of child nodes for this node, to the left of the node object this_node or at the end of the list if this_node is omitted.
insertData(char_offset, text)		Inserts the string in the text argument at the specified character offset within the data contained by the node.
removeChild(this_child)		Removes the child node this_node from the list of child nodes for this node, and returns it.
replaceChild(new_node, old_node)		Replaces the child node old_node with the new child node object new_node, and returns the old child node.
replaceData(char_offset, num_chars, text)		Replaces the specified number of characters in the existing string data of the node, starting at the specified character offset, with the string in the text argument.
selectNodes(pattern)	**Ext**	Applies a specified pattern to this node's context and returns a NodeList object containing matching nodes. The string pattern specifies the XSL pattern-matching operation to be used.
selectSingleNode (pattern)	**Ext**	Applies a specified pattern to this node's context and returns just the first node object that matches. The string pattern specifies the XSL pattern-matching operation to be used.
substringData(char_offset, num_chars)		Returns as a string the specified number of characters, starting at the specified character offset, from the data contained in the node.
transformNode (stylesheet)	**Ext**	Processes this node and its children using an XSL stylesheet specified in the stylesheet argument, and returns the resulting transformation. The stylesheet must be either a Document node object, in which case the document is assumed to be an XSL stylesheet, or a Node object in the xsl namespace, in which case this node is treated as a standalone stylesheet fragment.

Comment (IXMLDOMComment) Object

Represents the content of an XML comment element. This object is derived from the
`IXMLDOMCharacterData` object. The unextended W3C `Comment` object is implemented in IE5 by the
`IDOMComment` interface.

Comment Properties

Name		Description
attributes		Returns a collection of the `Attribute` (or `Attr`) objects for this node as a `NamedNodeMap` object.
BaseName	**Ext**	Returns the node name with any namespace removed. For example, in a node declared as `<nspace:elemname>` it returns the elemname part.
childNodes		Returns a `NodeList` containing all the child nodes of this node, for nodes that can have child nodes.
Data		Contains this node's value, which depends on the node type.
DataType	**Ext**	Sets or returns the data type for this node.
definition	**Ext**	For `EntityReference` nodes, returns the entry in the DTD or schema containing the definition for the entity, i.e. `<!ENTITY entityname 'entity value'>`. For other nodes, returns null.
firstChild		Returns a reference to the first child node of this node.
lastChild		Returns a reference to the last child node of this node.
length		Returns the number of characters for the data, i.e. the string length.
namespaceURI	**Ext**	Returns the URI for the namespace as a string. For example, in the namespace declaration `xmlns:name="uri"` it returns the uri part.
nextSibling		Returns a reference to the next sibling node of this node, i.e. the next node in the source data file at the same level of the hierarchy.
nodeName		Returns the name of the node, which will depend on the node type. See the list of *Node Types* at the end of this appendix for more details.
nodeTypeString	**Ext**	Returns the node type as a string, depending on the node type. See the list of *Node Types* at the end of this appendix for more details.
nodeType		Returns the node type as a number. See the list of *Node Types* at the end of this appendix for more details.

Name		Description
nodeTypedValue	**Ext**	Sets or returns the strongly typed value of the node, expressed in its defined data type. If no data type has been defined for the node, its nodeValue is returned.
nodeValue		Sets or returns the value of the node as plain text.
ownerDocument		Returns the root node of the document that contains the node.
parentNode		Returns the parent node of this node, for nodes that can have parents.
parsed	**Ext**	Returns true if this node and all its descendants have been parsed and instantiated.
prefix	**Ext**	Returns the element namespace prefix as a string. For example, in a node declared as <nspace:elemname> it returns the nspace part.
previousSibling		Returns a reference to the previous sibling node of this node, i.e. the previous node in the source file at the same level of the hierarchy.
specified	**Ext**	Indicates whether the node value is explicitly specified or derived from a default value in the DTD or schema. Normally only used with attribute nodes.
text	**Ext**	Sets or returns the entire text content of this node and all its descendant nodes.
xml	**Ext**	Returns the entire XML content of this node and all its descendant nodes.

Comment Methods

Name	Description
appendChild(new_node)	Appends the node object new_node to the end of the list of child nodes for this node.
appendData(text)	Appends the string in the text argument to the existing string data.
cloneNode(recurse_children)	Creates a new node object that is an exact clone of this node, including all descendant nodes of this node if recurse_children is set to true.
deleteData(char_offset, num_chars)	Deletes a substring from the string data of the node, starting at char_offset and continuing for num_chars.
hasChildNodes()	Returns true if this node has any child nodes.

Name		Description
insertBefore(new_node, this_node)		Inserts a new node object new_node into the list of child nodes for this node, to the left of the node object this_node or at the end of the list if this_node is omitted.
insertData(char_offset, text)		Inserts the string in the text argument at the specified character offset within the data contained by the node.
removeChild(this_child)		Removes the child node this_node from the list of child nodes for this node, and returns it.
replaceChild(new_node, old_node)		Replaces the child node old_node with the new child node object new_node, and returns the old child node.
replaceData(char_offset, num_chars, text)		Replaces the specified number of characters in the existing string data of the node, starting at the specified character offset, with the string in the text argument.
selectNodes(pattern)	**Ext**	Applies a specified pattern to this node's context and returns a NodeList object containing matching nodes. The string pattern specifies the XSL pattern-matching operation to be used.
selectSingleNode(pattern)	**Ext**	Applies a specified pattern to this node's context and returns just the first node object that matches. The string pattern specifies the XSL pattern-matching operation to be used.
substringData(char_offset, num_chars)		Returns as a string the specified number of characters, starting at the specified character offsct, from the data contained in the node.
transformNode(stylesheet)	**Ext**	Processes this node and its children using an XSL stylesheet specified in the stylesheet argument, and returns the resulting transformation. The stylesheet must be either a Document node object, in which case the document is assumed to be an XSL stylesheet, or a Node object in the xsl namespace, in which case this node is treated as a standalone stylesheet fragment.

Document (IXMLDOMDocument)

The Document object is the root object for an XML document. In IE5, it is the object that is instantiated by creating a new ActiveX object with the identifier "Microsoft.XMLDOM".

The IE5 IXMLDOMDocument object extends the base DOM document interface (implemented in IE5 by the IDOMDocument object) to include parser-specific functions. These include the ability to load documents asynchronously and control validation. The IXMLDOMDocument object also provides access to other IE5-specific objects such as parseError.

Document Properties

Name		Description
async	**Ext**	Sets or returns whether asynchronous download of the XML data is permitted. Values are true (the default) or false.
attributes		Returns a collection of the Attribute (or Attr) objects for this node as a NamedNodeMap object.
baseName	**Ext**	Returns the node name with any namespace removed. For example, in a node declared as <nspace:elemname> it returns the elemname part.
childNodes		Returns a NodeList containing all the child nodes of this node, for nodes that can have child nodes.
dataType	**Ext**	Sets or returns the data type for this node.
definition	**Ext**	For EntityReference nodes, returns the entry in the DTD or schema containing the definition for the entity, i.e. <!ENTITY entityname 'entity value'>. For other nodes, returns null.
doctype		Returns a reference to the DocumentType node specifying the DTD or schema for this document.
documentElement		Returns a reference to the outermost element of the document.
firstChild		Returns a reference to the first child node of this node.
implementation		Returns a reference to the Implementation object for the document. This object provides methods that are application-specific and document object model implementation-independent.
lastChild		Returns a reference to the last child node of this node.
namespaceURI	**Ext**	Returns the URI for the namespace as a string. For example, in the namespace declaration xmlns:name="uri" it returns the uri part.
nextSibling		Returns a reference to the next sibling node of this node, i.e. the next node in the source data file at the same level of the hierarchy.

Name		Description
nodeName		Returns the name of the node, which will depend on the node type. See the list of *Node Types* at the end of this appendix for more details.
nodeTypeString	**Ext**	Returns the node type as a string. See the list of *Node Types* at the end of this appendix for more details.
nodeType		Returns the node type as a number. See the list of *Node Types* at the end of this appendix for more details.
nodeTypedValue	**Ext**	Sets or returns the strongly typed value of the node, expressed in its defined data type. If no data type has been defined for the node, its nodeValue is returned.
nodeValue		Sets or returns the value of the node as plain text.
ownerDocument		Returns the root node of the document that contains the node.
parentNode		Returns the parent node of this node, for nodes that can have parents.
parsed	**Ext**	Returns true if this node and all its descendants have been parsed and instantiated.
parseError	**Ext**	Returns a reference to the ParseError object that contains information about any errors encountered while parsing the document.
prefix	**Ext**	Returns the element namespace prefix as a string. For example, in a node declared as <nspace:elemname> it returns the nspace part.
preserveWhiteSpace	**Ext**	Specifies whether whitespace should be preserved. The default is false.
previousSibling		Returns a reference to the previous sibling node of this node, i.e. the previous node in the source file at the same level of the hierarchy.
readyState	**Ext**	Indicates the current state of the XML document:
		0 ("uninitialized") - the object has been created but the load() has not yet been executed.
		1 ("loading") - the load() method is executing.
		2 ("loaded") - loading is complete and parsing is taking place.
		3 ("interactive") - some data has been read and parsed and the object model is now available. The data set is only partially retrieved and is read-only.
		4 ("completed") - document has been completely loaded. If successful the data is available as read/write, if not the error information is available.

Name		Description
resolveExternals	**Ext**	Indicates whether external entities are resolved and the document is validated against external DTDs or schemas. The default is false.
specified	**Ext**	Indicates whether the node value is explicitly specified or derived from a default value in the DTD or schema. Normally only used with attribute nodes.
text	**Ext**	Sets or returns the entire text content of this node and all its descendant nodes.
url	**Ext**	Returns the URL of the last successfully loaded document, or null if the document was built from scratch in memory.
validateOnParse	**Ext**	Sets or returns whether the parser should validate the document. Takes the value true to validate or false (the default) to check if the XML is well-formed.
xml	**Ext**	Returns the entire XML content of this node and all its descendant nodes.

Document Methods

Name		Description
abort()	**Ext**	Aborts a currently executing asynchronous download.
appendChild(new_node)		Appends the node object new_node to the end of the list of child nodes for this node.
cloneNode(recurse_children)		Creates a new node object that is an exact clone of this node, including all descendant nodes of this node if recurse_children is set to true.
createAttribute(attr_name)		Creates an Attribute node with the specified name.
createCDATASection(text)		Creates a CDATASection node containing text.
createComment(text)		Creates a Comment node containing text as the comment between the <!-- and --> delimiters.
createDocument_Fragment()		Creates an empty DocumentFragment node that can be used to build independent sections of a document.
createElement(tag_name)		Creates an Element node with the specified name.
createEntityReference(ref_name)		Creates an EntityReference node with the supplied name for the reference.

Name		Description
createNode (node_type, node_name, namespace_uri)	**Ext**	Creates any type of node using the specified node_type, node_name, and namespace_uri parameters.
createProcessing_ Instruction(target, text)		Creates a ProcessingInstruction node containing the specified target and data.
createTextNode (text_data)		Creates a Text node containing the specified text data.
getElementsByTagName (tag_name)		Returns a NodeList of elements that have the specified tag name. If tag_name is "*" it returns all elements.
hasChildNodes()		Returns true if this node has any child nodes.
insertBefore(new_node, this_node)		Inserts a new node object new_node into the list of child nodes for this node, to the left of the node object this_node or at the end of the list if this_node is omitted.
load(url)	**Ext**	Loads an XML document from the location in url.
loadXML(string)	**Ext**	Loads a string that is a representation of an XML document.
nodeFromID(id_value)	**Ext**	Returns the node object whose ID attribute matches the supplied value.
removeChild(this_node)		Removes the child node this_node from the list of child nodes for this node, and returns it.
replaceChild(new_ node, old_node)		Replaces the child node old_node with the new child node object new_node, and returns the old child node.
save(destination)	**Ext**	Saves the document to the specified destination, assuming the appropriate permissions are granted.
selectNodes(pattern)	**Ext**	Applies a specified pattern to this node's context and returns a NodeList object containing matching nodes. The string pattern specifies the XSL pattern-matching operation to be used.
selectSingleNode (pattern)	**Ext**	Applies a specified pattern to this node's context and returns just the first node object that matches. The string pattern specifies the XSL pattern-matching operation to be used.

Name		Description
transformNode (stylesheet)	Ext	Processes this node and its children using an XSL stylesheet specified in the stylesheet argument, and returns the resulting transformation. The stylesheet must be either a Document node object, in which case the document is assumed to be an XSL stylesheet, or a Node object in the xsl namespace, in which case this node is treated as a standalone stylesheet fragment.

Document Events

Name		Description
ondataavailable	Ext	The ondataavailable event occurs when data becomes available. When an asynchronous data load is in progress it allows processing in parallel with the download. The readyState property changes through several states to indicate the current status of the download.
onreadystatechange	Ext	The onreadystatechange event occurs when the value of the readyState property changes. This provides an alternative way to monitor the arrival of XML data when asynchronous loading is not used.
ontransformnode	Ext	The ontransformnode event is fired when a node is transformed through the transformNode() method of the Node object using an XSL stylesheet.

DocumentFragment (IXMLDOMDocumentFragment) Object

A document fragment is a lightweight object that is useful for tree insert operations. A new document fragment can be created and elements added to it, then the entire fragment can be added to an existing document. It is also useful for storing sections of a document temporarily, such as when cutting and pasting blocks of elements. This object adds no new methods or properties to the base IXMLDOMNode object. The unextended object is implemented in IE5 by the IDOMDocumentFragment object.

DocumentFragment Properties

Name		Description
attributes		Returns a collection of the Attribute (or Attr) objects for this node as a NamedNodeMap object.
baseName	Ext	Returns the node name with any namespace removed. For example, in a node declared as <nspace:elemname> it returns the elemname part.
childNodes		Returns a NodeList containing all the child nodes of this node, for nodes that can have child nodes.

Name		Description
dataType	**Ext**	Sets or returns the data type for this node.
definition	**Ext**	For `EntityReference` nodes, returns the entry in the DTD or schema containing the definition for the entity, i.e. `<!ENTITY entityname 'entity value'>`. For other nodes, returns null.
firstChild		Returns a reference to the first child node of this node.
lastChild		Returns a reference to the last child node of this node.
namespaceURI	**Ext**	Returns the URI for the namespace as a string. For example, in the namespace declaration `xmlns:name="uri"` it returns the uri part.
nextSibling		Returns a reference to the next sibling node of this node, i.e. the next node in the source data file at the same level of the hierarchy.
nodeName		Returns the name of the node, which will depend on the node type. See the list of *Node Types* at the end of this appendix for more details.
nodeTypeString	**Ext**	Returns the node type as a string, depending on the node type. See the list of *Node Types* at the end of this appendix for more details.
nodeType		Returns the node type as a number. See the list of *Node Types* at the end of this appendix for more details.
nodeTypedValue	**Ext**	Sets or returns the strongly typed value of the node, expressed in its defined data type. If no data type has been defined for the node, its `nodeValue` is returned.
nodeValue		Sets or returns the value of the node as plain text.
ownerDocument		Returns the root node of the document that contains the node.
parentNode		Returns the parent node of this node, for nodes that can have parents.
parsed	**Ext**	Returns true if this node and all its descendants have been parsed and instantiated.
prefix	**Ext**	Returns the element namespace prefix as a string. For example, in a node declared as `<nspace:elemname>` it returns the nspace part.
previousSibling		Returns a reference to the previous sibling node of this node, i.e. the previous node in the source file at the same level of the hierarchy.

Name		Description
specified	**Ext**	Indicates whether the node value is explicitly specified or derived from a default value in the DTD or schema. Normally only used with attribute nodes.
text	**Ext**	Sets or returns the entire text content of this node and all its descendant nodes.
xml	**Ext**	Returns the entire XML content of this node and all its descendant nodes.

DocumentFragment Methods

Name		Description
appendChild(new_node)		Appends the node object new_node to the end of the list of child nodes for this node.
cloneNode(recurse_children)		Creates a new node object that is an exact clone of this node, including all descendant nodes of this node if recurse_children is set to true.
hasChildNodes()		Returns true if this node has any child nodes.
insertBefore(new_node, this_node)		Inserts a new node object new_node into the list of child nodes for this node, to the left of the node object this_node or at the end of the list if this_node is omitted.
removeChild(this_node)		Removes the child node this_node from the list of child nodes for this node, and returns it.
replaceChild(new_node, old_node)		Replaces the child node old_node with the new child node object new_node, and returns the old child node.
selectNodes(pattern)	**Ext**	Applies a specified pattern to this node's context and returns a node list object containing matching nodes. The string pattern specifies the XSL pattern-matching operation to be used.
selectSingleNode(pattern)	**Ext**	Applies a specified pattern to this node's context and returns just the first node object that matches. The string pattern specifies the XSL pattern-matching operation to be used.
transformNode(stylesheet)	**Ext**	Processes this node and its children using an XSL stylesheet specified in the stylesheet argument, and returns the resulting transformation. The stylesheet must be either a Document node object, in which case the document is assumed to be an XSL stylesheet, or a Node object in the xsl namespace, in which case this node is treated as a standalone stylesheet fragment.

DocumentType (IXMLDOMDocumentType) Object

This object contains information about the document type declaration or schema for the document. It is the equivalent of the `<!DOCTYPE>` node. IE5 implements this base object as `IDOMDocumentType`.

DocumentType Properties

Name		Description
attributes		Returns a collection of the `Attribute` (or `Attr`) objects for this node as a `NamedNodeMap` object.
baseName	**Ext**	Returns the node name with any namespace removed. For example, in a node declared as `<nspace:elemname>` it returns the elemname part.
childNodes		Returns a `NodeList` containing all the child nodes of this node, for nodes that can have child nodes.
dataType	**Ext**	Sets or returns the data type for this node.
definition	**Ext**	For `EntityReference` nodes, returns the entry in the DTD or schema containing the definition for the entity, i.e. `<!ENTITY entityname 'entity value'>`. For other nodes, returns null.
entities		Returns a node list containing references to the `Entity` objects declared in the document type declaration.
firstChild		Returns a reference to the first child node of this node.
lastChild		Returns a reference to the last child node of this node.
name		Returns the name of the document type (`!DOCTYPE`) for this document.
namespaceURI	**Ext**	Returns the URI for the namespace as a string. For example, in the namespace declaration `xmlns:name="uri"` it returns the uri part.
nextSibling		Returns a reference to the next sibling node of this node, i.e. the next node in the source data file at the same level of the hierarchy.
nodeName		Returns the name of the node, which will depend on the node type. See the list of *Node Types* at the end of this appendix for more details.
nodeTypeString	**Ext**	Returns the node type as a string, depending on the node type. See the list of *Node Types* at the end of this appendix for more details.
nodeType		Returns the node type as a number. See the list of *Node Types* at the end of this appendix for more details.

Name		Description
nodeTypedValue	Ext	Sets or returns the strongly typed value of the node, expressed in its defined data type. If no data type has been defined for the node, its nodeValue is returned.
nodeValue		Sets or returns the value of the node as plain text.
notations		Returns a node list containing references to the Notation objects present in the document type declaration.
ownerDocument		Returns the root node of the document that contains the node.
parentNode		Returns the parent node of this node, for nodes that can have parents.
parsed	Ext	Returns true if this node and all its descendants have been parsed and instantiated.
prefix	Ext	Returns the element namespace prefix as a string. For example, in a node declared as <nspace:elemname> it returns the nspace part.
previousSibling		Returns a reference to the previous sibling node of this node, i.e. the previous node in the source file at the same level of the hierarchy.
specified	Ext	Indicates whether the node value is explicitly specified or derived from a default value in the DTD or schema. Normally only used with attribute nodes.
text	Ext	Sets or returns the entire text content of this node and all its descendant nodes.
xml	Ext	Returns the entire XML content of this node and all its descendant nodes.

DocumentType Methods

Name	Description
appendChild (new_node)	Appends the node object new_node to the end of the list of child nodes for this node.
cloneNode(recurse_ children)	Creates a new node object that is an exact clone of this node, including all descendant nodes of this node if recurse_children is set to true.
hasChildNodes()	Returns true if this node has any child nodes.
insertBefore(new _node, this_node)	Inserts a new node object new_node into the list of child nodes for this node, to the left of the node object this_node or at the end of the list if this_node is omitted.

Name		Description
removeChild (this_node)		Removes the child node this_node from the list of child nodes for this node, and returns it.
replaceChild (new_node, old_ node)		Replaces the child node old_node with the new child node object new_node, and returns the old child node.
selectNodes (pattern)	Ext	Applies a specified pattern to this node's context and returns a NodeList object containing matching nodes. The string pattern specifies the XSL pattern-matching operation to be used.
selectSingleNode (pattern)	Ext	Applies a specified pattern to this node's context and returns just the first node object that matches. The string pattern specifies the XSL pattern-matching operation to be used.
transformNode (stylesheet)	Ext	Processes this node and its children using an XSL stylesheet specified in the stylesheet argument, and returns the resulting transformation. The stylesheet must be either a Document node object, in which case the document is assumed to be an XSL stylesheet, or a Node object in the xsl namespace, in which case this node is treated as a standalone stylesheet fragment.

Element (IXMLDOMElement) Object

This object represents the elements in the document, and together with the Attribute and Text nodes, is likely to be one of the most common. Note that the text content of an Element node is stored in a child Text node. An Element node always has a nodeValue of null. IE5 implements the unextended object through the IDOMElement interface.

Element Properties

Name		Description
attributes		Returns a collection of the Attribute (or Attr) objects for this node as a NamedNodeMap object.
baseName	Ext	Returns the node name with any namespace removed. For example, in a node declared as <nspace:elemname> it returns the elemname part.
childNodes		Returns a NodeList containing all the child nodes of this node, for nodes that can have child nodes.
dataType	Ext	Sets or returns the data type for this node.

Name		Description
definition	Ext	For EntityReference nodes, returns the entry in the DTD or schema containing the definition for the entity, i.e. <!ENTITY entityname 'entity value'>. For other nodes, returns null.
firstChild		Returns a reference to the first child node of this node.
lastChild		Returns a reference to the last child node of this node.
namespaceURI	Ext	Returns the URI for the namespace as a string. For example, in the namespace declaration xmlns:name="uri" it returns the uri part.
nextSibling		Returns a reference to the next sibling node of this node, i.e. the next node in the source data file at the same level of the hierarchy.
nodeName		Returns the name of the node, which will depend on the node type. See the list of *Node Types* at the end of this appendix for more details.
nodeTypeString	Ext	Returns the node type as a string, depending on the node type. See the list of *Node Types* at the end of this appendix for more details.
nodeType		Returns the node type as a number. See the list of *Node Types* at the end of this appendix for more details.
nodeTypedValue	Ext	Sets or returns the strongly typed value of the node, expressed in its defined data type. If no data type has been defined for the node, its nodeValue is returned.
nodeValue		Sets or returns the value of the node as plain text.
ownerDocument		Returns the root node of the document that contains the node.
parentNode		Returns the parent node of this node, for nodes that can have parents.
parsed	Ext	Returns true if this node and all its descendants have been parsed and instantiated.
prefix	Ext	Returns the element namespace prefix as a string. For example, in a node declared as <nspace:elemname> it returns the nspace part.
previousSibling		Returns a reference to the previous sibling node of this node, i.e. the previous node in the source file at the same level of the hierarchy.
specified	Ext	Indicates whether the node value is explicitly specified or derived from a default value in the DTD or schema. Normally only used with attribute nodes.

Name		Description
tagName		Sets or returns the name of the element node; i.e. the text name that appears within the tag.
text	**Ext**	Sets or returns the entire text content of this node and all its descendant nodes.
xml	**Ext**	Returns the entire XML content of this node and all its descendant nodes.

Element Methods

Name	Description
appendChild(new node)	Appends the node object new_node to the end of the list of child nodes for this node.
cloneNode(recurse_ children)	Creates a new node object that is an exact clone of this node, including all descendant nodes of this node if recurse children is set to true.
getAttribute(attr_name)	Returns the value of the attribute with the specified name.
getAttributeNode(attr_ name)	Returns the attribute node with the specified name as an object.
getElementsByTagName (name)	Returns a node list of all descendant elements matching the specified name.
hasChildNodes()	Returns true if this node has any child nodes.
insertBefore(new_node, this_node)	Inserts a new node object new_node into the list of child nodes for this node, to the left of the node object this_node or at the end of the list if this_node is omitted.
normalize()	Combines all adjacent text nodes into one unified text node for all descendant element nodes.
removeAttribute(attr_ name)	Removes the value of the attribute with the specified name, or replaces it with the default value.
removeAttributeNode (attr_node)	Removes the specified attribute node from the element and returns it. If the attribute has a default value in the DTD or schema, a new attribute node is automatically created with that default value and the specified property is updated.
removeChild(this_node)	Removes the child node this_node from the list of child nodes for this node, and returns it.

Name		Description
replaceChild(new_node, old_node)		Replaces the child node old_node with the new child node object new_node, and returns the old child node.
selectNodes (pattern)	**Ext**	Applies a specified pattern to this node's context and returns a NodeList object containing matching nodes. The string pattern specifies the XSL pattern-matching operation to be used.
selectSingleNode (pattern)	**Ext**	Applies a specified pattern to this node's context and returns just the first Node object that matches. The string pattern specifies the XSL pattern-matching operation to be used.
setAttribute(attr_ name, value)		Sets the value of the attribute with the specified name.
setAttributeNode (attr_node)		Adds the new attribute node to the element. If an attribute with the same name exists, it is replaced and the old attribute node is returned.
transformNode (stylesheet)	**Ext**	Processes this node and its children using an XSL stylesheet specified in the stylesheet argument, and returns the resulting transformation. The stylesheet must be either a Document node object, in which case the document is assumed to be an XSL stylesheet, or a Node object in the xsl namespace, in which case this node is treated as a standalone stylesheet fragment.

Entity (IXMLDOMEntity) Object

This object represents a parsed or unparsed entity as declared with an <!ENTITY...> element in the DTD. However, it does not provide a reference to the entity declaration. The W3C DOM recommendation does not define an object in version 1.0 that models the declaration of entities. In IE5 the unextended object is implemented by the IDOMEntity object.

Entity Properties

Name		Description
attributes		Returns a collection of the Attribute (or Attr) objects for this node as a NamedNodeMap object.
baseName	**Ext**	Returns the node name with any namespace removed. For example, in a node declared as <nspace:elemname> it returns the elemname part.
childNodes		Returns a NodeList containing all the child nodes of this node, for nodes that can have child nodes.

Name		Description
dataType	**Ext**	Sets or returns the data type for this node.
definition	**Ext**	For EntityReference nodes, returns the entry in the DTD or schema containing the definition for the entity, i.e. <!ENTITY entityname 'entity value'>. For other nodes, returns null.
firstChild		Returns a reference to the first child node of this node.
lastChild		Returns a reference to the last child node of this node.
namespaceURI	**Ext**	Returns the URI for the namespace as a string. For example, in the namespace declaration xmlns:name="uri" it returns the uri part.
nextSibling		Returns a reference to the next sibling node of this node, i.e. the next node in the source data file at the same level of the hierarchy.
nodeName		Returns the name of the node, which will depend on the node type. See the list of *Node Types* at the end of this appendix for more details.
nodeTypeString	**Ext**	Returns the node type as a string, depending on the node type. See the list of *Node Types* at the end of this appendix for more details.
nodeType		Returns the node type as a number. See the list of *Node Types* at the end of this appendix for more details.
nodeTypedValue	**Ext**	Sets or returns the strongly typed value of the node, expressed in its defined data type. If no data type has been defined for the node, its nodeValue is returned.
nodeValue		Sets or returns the value of the node as plain text.
notationName	**Ext**	Returns the name of the notation linked to the entity.
ownerDocument		Returns the root node of the document that contains the node.
parentNode		Returns the parent node of this node, for nodes that can have parents.
parsed	**Ext**	Returns true if this node and all its descendants have been parsed and instantiated.
prefix	**Ext**	Returns the element namespace prefix as a string. For example, in a node declared as <nspace:elemname> it returns the nspace part.
previousSibling		Returns a reference to the previous sibling node of this node, i.e. the previous node in the source file at the same level of the hierarchy.

Name		Description
publicId		Sets or returns the PUBLIC identifier value for this entity node.
specified	**Ext**	Indicates whether the node value is explicitly specified or derived from a default value in the DTD or schema. Normally only used with attribute nodes.
systemId		Sets or returns the SYSTEM identifier value for this entity node.
text	**Ext**	Sets or returns the entire text content of this node and all its descendant nodes.
xml	**Ext**	Returns the entire XML content of this node and all its descendant nodes.

Entity Methods

Name		Description
appendChild(new_node)		Appends the node object new_node to the end of the list of child nodes for this node.
cloneNode(recurse_children)		Creates a new node object that is an exact clone of this node, including all descendant nodes of this node if recurse_children is set to true.
hasChildNodes()		Returns true if this node has any child nodes.
insertBefore(new_node, this_node)		Inserts a new node object new_node into the list of child nodes for this node, to the left of the node object this_node or at the end of the list if this_node is omitted.
removeChild(this_node)		Removes the child node this_node from the list of child nodes for this node, and returns it.
replaceChild(new_node, old_node)		Replaces the child node old_node with the new child node object new_node, and returns the old child node.
selectNodes(pattern)	**Ext**	Applies a specified pattern to this node's context and returns a node list object containing matching nodes. The string pattern specifies the XSL pattern-matching operation to be used.
selectSingleNode (pattern)	**Ext**	Applies a specified pattern to this node's context and returns just the first node object that matches. The string pattern specifies the XSL pattern-matching operation to be used.

Name		Description
transformNode (stylesheet)	Ext	Processes this node and its children using an XSL stylesheet specified in the stylesheet argument, and returns the resulting transformation. The stylesheet must be either a Document node object, in which case the document is assumed to be an XSL stylesheet, or a Node object in the xsl namespace, in which case this node is treated as a standalone stylesheet fragment.

EntityReference (IXMLDOMEntityReference) Object

This object represents an entity reference node within the XML document. If the XML processor expands entity references while building the structure model, it's possible that no entity reference objects will appear in the tree, being replaced by the replacement text of the entity. The object is implemented without extensions by Microsoft as the IDOMEntityReference object.

EntityReference Properties

Name		Description
attributes		Returns a collection of the Attribute (or Attr) objects for this node as a NamedNodeMap object.
baseName	Ext	Returns the node name with any namespace removed. For example, in a node declared as <nspace:elemname> it returns the elemname part.
childNodes		Returns a NodeList containing all the child nodes of this node, for nodes that can have child nodes.
dataType	Ext	Sets or returns the data type for this node.
definition	Ext	For EntityReference nodes, returns the entry in the DTD or schema containing the definition for the entity, i.e. <!ENTITY entityname 'entity value'>. For other nodes, returns null.
firstChild		Returns a reference to the first child node of this node.
lastChild		Returns a reference to the last child node of this node.
namespaceURI	Ext	Returns the URI for the namespace as a string. For example, in the namespace declaration xmlns:name="uri" it returns the uri part.
nextSibling		Returns a reference to the next sibling node of this node, i.e. the next node in the source data file at the same level of the hierarchy.
nodeName		Returns the name of the node, which will depend on the node type. See the list of *Node Types* at the end of this appendix for more details.

Name		Description
nodeTypeString	**Ext**	Returns the node type as a string, depending on the node type. See the list of *Node Types* at the end of this appendix for more details.
nodeType		Returns the node type as a number. See the list of *Node Types* at the end of this appendix for more details.
nodeTypedValue	**Ext**	Sets or returns the strongly typed value of the node, expressed in its defined data type. If no data type has been defined for the node, its nodeValue is returned.
nodeValue		Sets or returns the value of the node as plain text.
ownerDocument		Returns the root node of the document that contains the node.
parentNode		Returns the parent node of this node, for nodes that can have parents.
parsed	**Ext**	Returns true if this node and all its descendants have been parsed and instantiated.
prefix	**Ext**	Returns the element namespace prefix as a string. For example, in a node declared as <nspace:elemname> it returns the nspace part.
previousSibling		Returns a reference to the previous sibling node of this node, i.e. the previous node in the source file at the same level of the hierarchy.
specified	**Ext**	Indicates whether the node value is explicitly specified or derived from a default value in the DTD or schema. Normally only used with attribute nodes.
text	**Ext**	Sets or returns the entire text content of this node and all its descendant nodes.
xml	**Ext**	Returns the entire XML content of this node and all its descendant nodes.

EntityReference Methods

Name	Description
appendChild (new_node)	Appends the node object new_node to the end of the list of child nodes for this node.
cloneNode(recurse_ children)	Creates a new node object that is an exact clone of this node, including all descendant nodes of this node if recurse_children is set to true.
hasChildNodes()	Returns true if this node has any child nodes.

Name		Description
insertBefore(new_node, this_node)		Inserts a new node object new_node into the list of child nodes for this node, to the left of the node object this_node or at the end of the list if this_node is omitted.
removeChild(this_node)		Removes the child node this_node from the list of child nodes for this node, and returns it.
replaceChild(new_node, old_node)		Replaces the child node old_node with the new child node object new_node, and returns the old child node.
selectNodes(pattern)	**Ext**	Applies a specified pattern to this node's context and returns a node list object containing matching nodes. The string pattern specifies the XSL pattern-matching operation to be used.
selectSingleNode(pattern)	**Ext**	Applies a specified pattern to this node's context and returns just the first node object that matches. The string pattern specifies the XSL pattern-matching operation to be used.
transformNode(stylesheet)	**Ext**	Processes this node and its children using an XSL stylesheet specified in the stylesheet argument, and returns the resulting transformation. The stylesheet must be either a Document node object, in which case the document is assumed to be an XSL stylesheet, or a Node object in the xsl namespace, in which case this node is treated as a standalone stylesheet fragment.

Implementation (IXMLDOMImplementation) Object

This object provides access to methods that are application-specific and independent of any particular instance of the document object model. It is a child of the Document object.

Implementation Method

Name	Description
hasFeature(feature, version)	Returns true if the specified version of the implementation supports the specified feature.

Notation (IXMLDOMNotation) Object

This object represents a notation declared in the DTD or schema with a <!NOTATION...> element. The unextended object is implemented as the IDOMNotation object in IE5.

Notation Properties

Name		Description
Attributes		Returns a collection of the `Attribute` (or `Attr`) objects for this node as a `NamedNodeMap` object.
BaseName	**Ext**	Returns the node name with any namespace removed. For example, in a node declared as `<nspace:elemname>` it returns the elemname part.
ChildNodes		Returns a `NodeList` containing all the child nodes of this node, for nodes that can have child nodes.
DataType	**Ext**	Sets or returns the data type for this node.
Definition	**Ext**	For `EntityReference` nodes, returns the entry in the DTD or schema containing the definition for the entity, i.e. `<!ENTITY entityname 'entity value'>`. For other nodes, returns null.
FirstChild		Returns a reference to the first child node of this node.
LastChild		Returns a reference to the last child node of this node.
NamespaceURI	**Ext**	Returns the URI for the namespace as a string. For example, in the namespace declaration `xmlns:name="uri"` it returns the uri part.
NextSibling		Returns a reference to the next sibling node of this node, i.e. the next node in the source data file at the same level of the hierarchy.
NodeName		Returns the name of the node, which will depend on the node type. See the list of *Node Types* at the end of this appendix for more details.
NodeTypeString	**Ext**	Returns the node type as a string, depending on the node type. See the list of *Node Types* at the end of this appendix for more details.
NodeType		Returns the node type as a number. See the list of *Node Types* at the end of this appendix for more details.
NodeTypedValue	**Ext**	Sets or returns the strongly typed value of the node, expressed in its defined data type. If no data type has been defined for the node, its `nodeValue` is returned.
NodeValue		Sets or returns the value of the node as plain text.
OwnerDocument		Returns the root node of the document that contains the node.
ParentNode		Returns the parent node of this node, for nodes that can have parents.
parsed	**Ext**	Returns true if this node and all its descendants have been parsed and instantiated.

Name		Description
prefix	**Ext**	Returns the element namespace prefix as a string. For example, in a node declared as `<nspace:elemname>` it returns the nspace part.
previousSibling		Returns a reference to the previous sibling node of this node, i.e. the previous node in the source file at the same level of the hierarchy.
publicId		Sets or returns the PUBLIC identifier value for this entity node.
specified	**Ext**	Indicates whether the node value is explicitly specified or derived from a default value in the DTD or schema. Normally only used with attribute nodes.
systemId		Sets or returns the SYSTEM identifier value for this entity node.
text	**Ext**	Sets or returns the entire text content of this node and all its descendant nodes.
xml	**Ext**	Returns the entire XML content of this node and all its descendant nodes.

Notation Methods

Name		Description
appendChild (new_node)		Appends the node object new_node to the end of the list of child nodes for this node.
cloneNode (recurse_ children)		Creates a new node object that is an exact clone of this node, including all descendant nodes of this node if `recurse_children` is set to true.
hasChildNodes()		Returns true if this node has any child nodes.
insertBefore (new_node, this_node)		Inserts a new node object new_node into the list of child nodes for this node, to the left of the node object `this_node` or at the end of the list if `this_node` is omitted.
removeChild (this_node)		Removes the child node this_node from the list of child nodes for this node, and returns it.
replaceChild (new_node, old_node)		Replaces the child node old_node with the new child node object new_node, and returns the old child node.
selectNodes (pattern)	**Ext**	Applies a specified pattern to this node's context and returns a node list object containing matching nodes. The string pattern specifies the XSL pattern-matching operation to be used.

Name		Description
selectSingleNode (pattern)	**Ext**	Applies a specified pattern to this node's context and returns just the first node object that matches. The string pattern specifies the XSL pattern-matching operation to be used.
transformNode (stylesheet)	**Ext**	Processes this node and its children using an XSL style sheet specified in the stylesheet argument, and returns the resulting transformation. The stylesheet must be either a Document node object, in which case the document is assumed to be an XSL stylesheet, or a Node object in the xsl namespace, in which case this node is treated as a standalone stylesheet fragment.

ProcessingInstruction (IXMLDOMProcessingInstruction) Object

This element represents an instruction embedded in the XML within the '<?' and '?>' delimiters. It provides a way of storing processor-specific information within an XML document. The text content of the node is usually subdivided into the target (the text after the '<?' and up to the first whitespace character) and the data content (the remainder up to the closing '?>'). The W3C Recommendation for this object is implemented in IE5 by the IDOMProcessingInstruction object.

ProcessingInstruction Properties

Name		Description
attributes		Returns a collection of the Attribute (or Attr) objects for this node as a NamedNodeMap object.
BaseName	**Ext**	Returns the node name with any namespace removed. For example, in a node declared as <nspace:elemname> it returns the elemname part.
ChildNodes		Returns a NodeList containing all the child nodes of this node, for nodes that can have child nodes.
Data		Contains this node's value, which depends on the node type.
DataType	**Ext**	Sets or returns the data type for this node.
Definition	**Ext**	For EntityReference nodes, returns the entry in the DTD or schema containing the definition for the entity, i.e. <!ENTITY entityname 'entity value'>. For other nodes, returns null.
FirstChild		Returns a reference to the first child node of this node.
LastChild		Returns a reference to the last child node of this node.

Name		Description
length		Returns the number of characters for the data, i.e. the string length.
namespaceURI	**Ext**	Returns the URI for the namespace as a string. For example, in the namespace declaration xmlns:name="uri" it returns the uri part.
nextSibling		Returns a reference to the next sibling node of this node, i.e. the next node in the source data file at the same level of the hierarchy.
nodeName		Returns the name of the node, which will depend on the node type. See the list of *Node Types* at the end of this appendix for more details.
nodeTypeString	**Ext**	Returns the node type as a string, depending on the node type. See the list of *Node Types* at the end of this appendix for more details.
nodeType		Returns the node type as a number. See the list of *Node Types* at the end of this appendix for more details.
nodeTypedValue	**Ext**	Sets or returns the strongly typed value of the node, expressed in its defined data type. If no data type has been defined for the node, its nodeValue is returned.
nodeValue		Sets or returns the value of the node as plain text.
ownerDocument		Returns the root node of the document that contains the node.
parentNode		Returns the parent node of this node, for nodes that can have parents.
parsed	**Ext**	Returns true if this node and all its descendants have been parsed and instantiated.
prefix	**Ext**	Returns the element namespace prefix as a string. For example, in a node declared as <nspace:elemname> it returns the nspace part.
previousSibling		Returns a reference to the previous sibling node of this node, i.e. the previous node in the source file at the same level of the hierarchy.
specified	**Ext**	Indicates whether the node value is explicitly specified or derived from a default value in the DTD or schema. Normally only used with attribute nodes.
target		Specifies the application to which this processing instruction is directed. This is the text up to the first whitespace character in the node content.
text	**Ext**	Sets or returns the entire text content of this node and all its descendant nodes.
xml	**Ext**	Returns the entire XML content of this node and all its descendant nodes.

ProcessingInstruction Methods

Name		Description
appendChild(new_node)		Appends the node object new_node to the end of the list of child nodes for this node.
cloneNode(recurse_ children)		Creates a new node object that is an exact clone of this node, including all descendant nodes of this node if recurse_children is set to true.
hasChildNodes()		Returns true if this node has any child nodes.
insertBefore(new_node, this_node)		Inserts a new node object new_node into the list of child nodes for this node, to the left of the node object this_node or at the end of the list if this_node is omitted.
removeChild(this_child)		Removes the child node this_node from the list of child nodes for this node, and returns it.
replaceChild(new_node, old_node)		Replaces the child node old_node with the new child node object new_node, and returns the old child node.
selectNodes(pattern)	**Ext**	Applies a specified pattern to this node's context and returns a node list object containing matching nodes. The string pattern specifies the XSL pattern-matching operation to be used.
selectSingleNode (pattern)	**Ext**	Applies a specified pattern to this node's context and returns just the first node object that matches. The string pattern specifies the XSL pattern-matching operation to be used.
transformNode (stylesheet)	**Ext**	Processes this node and its children using an XSL stylesheet specified in the stylesheet argument, and returns the resulting transformation. The stylesheet must be either a Document node object, in which case the document is assumed to be an XSL stylesheet, or a Node object in the xsl namespace, in which case this node is treated as a standalone stylesheet fragment.

Text (IXMLDOMText) Object

This object represents the text content of an element node or an attribute node. It is derived from the CharacterData object, and the CDATASection object is in turn inherited from it. The W3C CDATASection object is implemented in IE5 by the IDOMText object.

Text Properties

Name		Description
attributes		Returns a collection of the Attribute (or Attr) objects for this node as a NamedNodeMap object.
baseName	Ext	Returns the node name with any namespace removed. For example, in a node declared as <nspace:elemname> it returns the elemname part.
childNodes		Returns a NodeList containing all the child nodes of this node, for nodes that can have child nodes.
data		Contains this node's value, which depends on the node type.
dataType	Ext	Sets or returns the data type for this node.
definition	Ext	For EntityReference nodes, returns the entry in the DTD or schema containing the definition for the entity, i.e. <!ENTITY entityname 'entity value'>. For other nodes, returns null.
firstChild		Returns a reference to the first child node of this node.
lastChild		Returns a reference to the last child node of this node.
length		Returns the number of characters for the data, i.e. the string length.
namespaceURI	Ext	Returns the URI for the namespace as a string. For example, in the namespace declaration xmlns:name="uri" it returns the uri part.
nextSibling		Returns a reference to the next sibling node of this node, i.e. the next node in the source data file at the same level of the hierarchy.
nodeName		Returns the name of the node, which will depend on the node type. See the list of *Node Types* at the end of this appendix for more details.
nodeTypeString	Ext	Returns the node type as a string, depending on the node type. See the list of *Node Types* at the end of this appendix for more details.
nodeType		Returns the node type as a number. See the list of *Node Types* at the end of this appendix for more details.
nodeTypedValue	Ext	Sets or returns the strongly typed value of the node, expressed in its defined data type. If no data type has been defined for the node, its nodeValue is returned.
nodeValue		Sets or returns the value of the node as plain text.
ownerDocument		Returns the root node of the document that contains the node.

Name		Description
parentNode		Returns the parent node of this node, for nodes that can have parents.
parsed	**Ext**	Returns true if this node and all its descendants have been parsed and instantiated.
prefix	**Ext**	Returns the element namespace prefix as a string. For example, in a node declared as <nspace:elemname> it returns the nspace part.
previousSibling		Returns a reference to the previous sibling node of this node, i.e. the previous node in the source file at the same level of the hierarchy.
specified	**Ext**	Indicates whether the node value is explicitly specified or derived from a default value in the DTD or schema. Normally only used with attribute nodes.
text	**Ext**	Sets or returns the entire text content of this node and all its descendant nodes.
xml	**Ext**	Returns the entire XML content of this node and all its descendant nodes.

Text Methods

Name	Description
appendChild(new_node)	Appends the node object new_node to the end of the list of child nodes for this node.
appendData(text)	Appends the string in the text argument to the existing string data.
cloneNode(recurse_children)	Creates a new node object that is an exact clone of this node, including all descendant nodes of this node if recurse_children is set to true.
deleteData(char_offset, num_chars)	Deletes a substring from the string data of the node, starting at char_offset and continuing for num_chars.
hasChildNodes()	Returns true if this node has any child nodes.
insertBefore(new_node, this_node)	Inserts a new node object new_node into the list of child nodes for this node, to the left of the node object this_node or at the end of the list if this_node is omitted.
insertData(char_offset, text)	Inserts the string in the text argument at the specified character offset within the data contained by the node.

Name		Description
`removeChild(this_child)`		Removes the child node `this_node` from the list of child nodes for this node, and returns it.
`replaceChild(new_node, old_node)`		Replaces the child node `old_node` with the new child node object `new_node`, and returns the old child node.
`replaceData(char_offset, num_chars, text)`		Replaces the specified number of characters in the existing string data of the node, starting at the specified character offset, with the string in the `text` argument.
`selectNodes(pattern)`	**Ext**	Applies a specified pattern to this node's context and returns a `NodeList` object containing matching nodes. The string `pattern` specifies the XSL pattern-matching operation to be used.
`selectSingleNode(pattern)`	**Ext**	Applies a specified pattern to this node's context and returns just the first node object that matches. The string `pattern` specifies the XSL pattern matching operation to be used.
`splitText(char_offset)`		Splits the node into two separate nodes at the specified character offset, then inserts the new node into the XML as a sibling that immediately follows this node.
`substringData(char_offset, num_chars)`		Returns as a string the specified number of characters, starting at the specified character offset, from the data contained in the node.
`transformNode(stylesheet)`	**Ext**	Processes this node and its children using an XSL stylesheet specified in the `stylesheet` argument, and returns the resulting transformation. The stylesheet must be either a `Document` node object, in which case the document is assumed to be an XSL stylesheet, or a `Node` object in the `xsl` namespace, in which case this node is treated as a standalone stylesheet fragment.

IE5-Specific XML Parser Objects

While the document object is quite tightly standardized as far as the structure of the document is concerned, there are other peripheral activities that any XML application must handle. This includes managing and reporting errors, originating and handling HTTP requests, and interfacing with stylesheets. These are all application-specific tasks, and in IE5 are managed by three subsidiary objects:

- ❑ `HttpRequest` (the `IXMLHttpRequest` object)
- ❑ `ParseError` (the `IDOMParseError` object)
- ❑ `Runtime` (the `IXTLRuntime` object)

In the following tables, all are marked '**Ext**' to indicate that the W3C recommendations do not cover this area of the DOM.

HttpRequest (IXMLHttpRequest) Object

This object provides client-side protocol support for communication with HTTP servers. A client can use the `HttpRequest` object to send an arbitrary HTTP request, receive the response, and have the IE5 DOM parse that response.

HttpRequest Properties

Name		Description
readyState	**Ext**	Indicates the current state of the XML document being loaded:
		0 ("uninitialized") - the object has been created but the load() has not yet been executed.
		1 ("loading") - the load() method is executing.
		2 ("loaded") - loading is complete and parsing is taking place.
		3 ("interactive") - some data has been read and parsed and the object model is now available. The data set is only partially retrieved and is read-only.
		4 ("completed") - document has been completely loaded. If successful the data is available as read/write, if not the error information is available.
responseBody	**Ext**	Returns the response as an array of unsigned bytes.
responseStream	**Ext**	Returns the response as an IStream object.
responseText	**Ext**	Returns the response as an ordinary text string.
responseXML	**Ext**	Returns the response as an XML document. For security reasons, validation is turned off during this process to prevent the parser from attempting to download a linked DTD or other definition file.
status	**Ext**	Returns the status code sent back from the server as a long integer.
statusText	**Ext**	Returns the status text sent back from the server as a string.

HttpRequest Methods

Name		Description
abort()	**Ext**	Cancels a current HTTP request.
getAllResponseHeaders()	**Ext**	Returns all the HTTP headers as name/value pairs delimited by the carriage return-linefeed combination.

Name		Description
getResponseHeader (header_name)	**Ext**	Returns the value of an individual HTTP header from the response body as specified by the header name.
open(method, url, async, userid, password)	**Ext**	Initializes a request, specifying the HTTP method, the URL, whether the response is to be asynchronous, and authentication information for the request.
send()	**Ext**	Sends an HTTP request to the server and waits to receive a response.
setRequestHeader (header_name, value)	**Ext**	Specifies an HTTP header to send to the server.

ParseError (IDOMParseError) Object

The properties of this object return detailed information about the last error that occurred while loading and parsing a document. This includes the line number, character position, and a text description.

ParseError Properties

Name		Description
errorCode	**Ext**	Returns the error number or error code as a decimal integer.
filepos	**Ext**	Returns the absolute character position in the file where the error occurred.
line	**Ext**	Returns the number of the line in the document that contains the error.
linepos	**Ext**	Returns the character position of the error within the line in which it occurred.
reason	**Ext**	Returns a text description of the source and reason for the error, and can also include the URL of the DTD or schema and the node within it that corresponds to the error.
srcText	**Ext**	Returns the full text of the line that contains the error or an empty string if the error cannot be assigned to a specific line.
url	**Ext**	Returns the URL of the most recent XML document that contained an error.

Runtime (IXTLRuntime) Object

This object implements a series of properties and methods that are available within XSL stylesheets.

Runtime Properties

Name		Description
attributes	**Ext**	Returns a collection of the Attribute (or Attr) objects for this node as a NamedNodeMap object.
baseName	**Ext**	Returns the node name with any namespace removed. For example, in a node declared as <nspace:elemname> it returns the elemname part.
childNodes	**Ext**	Returns a NodeList containing all the child nodes of this node, for nodes that can have child nodes.
dataType	**Ext**	Sets or returns the data type for this node.
definition	**Ext**	For EntityReference nodes, returns the entry in the DTD or schema containing the definition for the entity, i.e. <!ENTITY entityname 'entity value'>. For other nodes, returns null.
firstChild	**Ext**	Returns a reference to the first child node of this node.
lastChild	**Ext**	Returns a reference to the last child node of this node.
namespaceURI	**Ext**	Returns the URI for the namespace as a string. For example, in the namespace declaration xmlns:name="uri" it returns the uri part.
nextSibling	**Ext**	Returns a reference to the next sibling node of this node, i.e. the next node in the source data file at the same level of the hierarchy.
nodeName	**Ext**	Returns the name of the node, which will depend on the node type. See the list of *Node Types* at the end of this appendix for more details.
nodeTypeString	**Ext**	Returns the node type as a string. See the list of *Node Types* at the end of this appendix for more details.
nodeType	**Ext**	Returns the node type as a number. See the list of *Node Types* at the end of this appendix for more details.
nodeTypedValue	**Ext**	Sets or returns the strongly typed value of the node, expressed in its defined data type. If no data type has been defined for the node, its nodeValue is returned.
nodeValue	**Ext**	Sets or returns the value of the node as plain text.
ownerDocument	**Ext**	Returns the root node of the document that contains the node.

Name		Description
parentNode	Ext	Returns the parent node of this node, for nodes that can have parents.
parsed	Ext	Returns true if this node and all its descendants have been parsed and instantiated.
prefix	Ext	Returns the element namespace prefix as a string. For example, in a node declared as <nspace:elemname> it returns the nspace part.
previousSibling	Ext	Returns a reference to the previous sibling node of this node, i.e. the previous node in the source file at the same level of the hierarchy.
specified	Ext	Indicates whether the node value is explicitly specified or derived from a default value in the DTD or schema. Normally only used with attribute nodes.
text	Ext	Sets or returns the entire text content of this node and all its descendant nodes.
xml	Ext	Returns the entire XML of this node and all descendant nodes of this node.

Runtime Methods

Name		Description
absoluteChildNumber (this_node)	Ext	Returns the index of a specified node within its parent's childNodes list. Values start from "1".
ancestorChild Number (node_ name, this_node)	Ext	Finds the first ancestor node of a specified node that has the specified name, and returns the index of that node within its parent's childNodes list. Values start from "1". Returns null if there is no ancestor.
appendChild (new_ node)	Ext	Appends the node object new_node to the end of the list of child nodes for this node.
childNumber (this_node)	Ext	Finds the first node with the same name as the specified node within the specified node's parent's childNodes list (i.e. its siblings). Returns the index of that node or null if not found. Values start from "1".
cloneNode (recurse_ children)	Ext	Creates a new node object that is an exact clone of this node, including all descendant nodes of this node if recurse_children is set to true.
depth(start_node)	Ext	Returns the depth or level within the document tree at which the specified node appears. The documentElement or root node is at level 0.

Name		Description
elementIndex_ List(this_ node, node_name)	**Ext**	Returns an array of node index numbers for the specified node and all its ancestors up to and including the document root node, indicating each node's position within their parent's `childNodes` list. The ordering of the array starts from the root document node.
		When the node_name parameter is not supplied, the method returns an array of integers that indicates the index of the specified node with respect to all of its siblings, the index of that node's parent with respect to all of its siblings, and so on until the document root is reached.
		When the node_name parameter is specified, the returned array contains entries only for nodes of the specified name, and the indices are evaluated relative to siblings with the specified name. Zero is supplied for levels in the tree that do not have children with the supplied name.
		Although this method is included in the Microsoft documentation, it was not supported by IE5 at the time of writing.
formatDate (date, format, locale)	**Ext**	Formats the value in the date parameter using the specified formatting options. The following format codes are supported:
		m - Month (1-12)
		mm - Month (01-12)
		mmm - Month (Jan-Dec)
		mmmm - Month (January-December)
		mmmmm - Month as the first letter of the month
		d - Day (1-31)
		dd - Day (01-31)
		ddd - Day (Sun-Sat)
		dddd - Day (Sunday-Saturday)
		yy -Year (00-99)
		yyyy - Year (1900-9999)
		The locale is used in determining the correct sequence of values in the date. If omitted the sequence month-day-year is used.

Name		Description
formatIndex (number, format)	**Ext**	Formats the integer number using the specified numerical system.
		1 - Standard numbering system
		01 - Standard numbering with leading zeroes
		A - Uppercase letter sequence "A" to "Z" then "AA" to"ZZ".
		a - Lowercase letter sequence "a" to "z" then "aa" to "zz".
		I - Uppercase Roman numerals: "I", "II", "III", "IV", etc.
		i - Lowercase Roman numerals: "i", "ii", "iii", "iv", etc.
formatNumber (number, format)	**Ext**	Formats the value number using the specified format. Zero or more of the following values can be present in the format string:
		# (pound) – Display only significant digits and omit insignificant zeros.
		0 (zero) – Display insignificant zeros in these positions.
		? (question) – Adds spaces for insignificant zeros on either side of the decimal point, so that decimal points align with a fixed-point font. You can also use this symbol for fractions that have varying numbers of digits.
		. (period) – Indicates the position of the decimal point.
		, (comma) – Display a thousands separator or scale a number by a multiple of one thousand.
		% (percent) – Display number as a percentage.
		E or e – Display number in scientific (exponential) format. If format contains a zero or # (hash) to the right of an exponent code, display the number in scientific format and inserts an "E" or "e". The number of 0 or # characters to the right determines the number of digits in the exponent.
		E- or e- Place a minus sign by negative exponents.
		E+ or e+ Place a minus sign by negative exponents and a plus sign by positive exponents.

Name		Description
formatTime (time, format, locale)	Ext	Formats the value in the time parameter using the specified formatting options. The following format codes are supported:
		h - Hours (0-23)
		hh - Hours (00-23)
		m - Minutes (0-59)
		mm - Minutes (00-59)
		s - Seconds (0-59)
		ss - Seconds (00-59)
		AM/PM - Add "AM" or "PM" and display in 12 hour format
		am/pm - Add "am" or "pm" and display in 12 hour format
		A/P - Add "A" or "P" and display in 12 hour format
		a/p - Add "a" or "p" and display in 12 hour format
		[h]:mm – Display elapsed time in hours, i.e. "25.02"
		[mm]:ss - Display elapsed time in minutes, i.e. "63:46"
		[ss] - Display elapsed time in seconds
		ss.00 - Display fractions of a second
		The locale is used to determine the correct separator characters.
hasChildNodes()	Ext	Returns true if this node has any child nodes.
insertBefore (new_node, this_node)	Ext	Inserts a new node object new_node into the list of child nodes for this node, to the left of the node object this_node or at the end of the list if this_node is omitted.
removeChild (this_node)	Ext	Removes the child node this_node from the list of child nodes for this node, and returns it.
replaceChild (new_node, old_node)	Ext	Replaces the child node old_node with the new child node object new_node, and returns the old child node.
selectNodes (pattern)	Ext	Applies a specified pattern to this node's context and returns a NodeList object containing matching nodes. The string pattern specifies the XSL pattern-matching operation to be used.

Name		Description
selectSingleNode (pattern)	Ext	Applies a specified pattern to this node's context and returns just the first node object that matches. The string pattern specifies the XSL pattern-matching operation to be used.
transformNode (stylesheet)	Ext	Processes this node and its children using an XSL stylesheet specified in the stylesheet argument, and returns the resulting transformation. The stylesheet must be either a Document node object, in which case the document is assumed to be an XSL stylesheet, or a Node object in the xsl namespace, in which case this node is treated as a standalone stylesheet fragment.
uniqueID (this_node)	Ext	Returns the unique identifier for the specified node.

The DOM NodeTypes

Each node exposes its type through the nodeType property. In IE5, there is also a nodeTypeString property, which exposes the node type as a named string rather than an integer. This saves having to explicitly convert it each time. Each node type also has a named constant. These make up the IDOMNodeType enumeration.

IDOMNodeType Enumeration

The IDOMNodeType enumeration specifies the valid settings for particular DOM node types. This includes the range and type of values that the node can contain, whether the node can have child nodes, etc. Note that default string and numeric entities (such as &) are exposed as text nodes, rather than as entity nodes.

Named Constant	nodeType	nodeName	nodeValue	nodeType String(IE5)
NODE_ ELEMENT	1	tagName property	null	"element"

NODE_ELEMENT can be the child of a Document, DocumentFragment, EntityReference, Element node. It can have child nodes of type Element, Text, Comment, ProcessingInstruction, CDATASection, EntityReference.

NODE_ATTRIBUTE	2	name property	value property	"attribute"

NODE_ATTRIBUTE cannot be the child of any other node type. It only appears in other nodes' attributes node lists. It can, however, have child nodes of type Text, EntityReference.

NODE_TEXT	3	"#text"	content of node	"text"

NODE_TEXT can be the child of an Attribute, DocumentFragment, Element, EntityReference node. It cannot have any child nodes.

NODE_CDATA_ SECTION	4	"#cdata section"	content of node	"cdata section"

NODE_CDATA_SECTION can be the child of a DocumentFragment, EntityReference, Element node. It cannot have any child nodes.

NODE_ENTITY_ REFERENCE	5	entity reference name	null	"entity reference"

NODE_ENTITY_REFERENCE can be the child of an Attribute, DocumentFragment, Element, EntityReference node. It can also have child nodes of type Element, ProcessingInstruction, Comment, Text, CDATASection, EntityReference.

NODE_ENTITY	6	entity name	null	"entity"

NODE_ENTITY can be the child of a DocumentType node. It can have child nodes that represent the expanded entity, that is Text, EntityReference.

NODE_PROCESSING_ INSTRUCTION	7	target property	content of node excluding target	"processing instruction"

NODE_PROCESSING_INSTRUCTION can be the child of a Document, DocumentFragment, Element, EntityReference node. It cannot have any child nodes.

NODE_COMMENT	8	"#comment"	comment text	"comment"

NODE_COMMENT can be the child of a Document, DocumentFragment, Element, EntityReference node. It cannot have any child nodes.

NODE_DOCUMENT	9	"#document"	null	"document"

NODE_DOCUMENT represents the root of the document so cannot be a child node. It can have a maximum of one `Element` child node, and other child nodes of type `Comment`, `DocumentType`, `ProcessingInstruction`.

NODE_DOCUMENT_TYPE	10	doctype name	null	"document type"

NODE_DOCUMENT_TYPE can be the child of the `Document` node only. It can have child nodes of type `Notation`, `Entity`.

NODE_DOCUMENT_FRAGMENT	11	"#document-fragment"	null	"document fragment"

NODE_DOCUMENT_FRAGMENT represents an unconnected document fragment, so cannot be the child of any node type. It can have child nodes of type `Element`, `ProcessingInstruction`, `Comment`, `Text`, `CDATASection`, `EntityReference`.

NODE_NOTATION	12	notation name	null	"notation"

NODE_NOTATION can be the child of a `DocumentType` node only. It cannot have any child nodes.

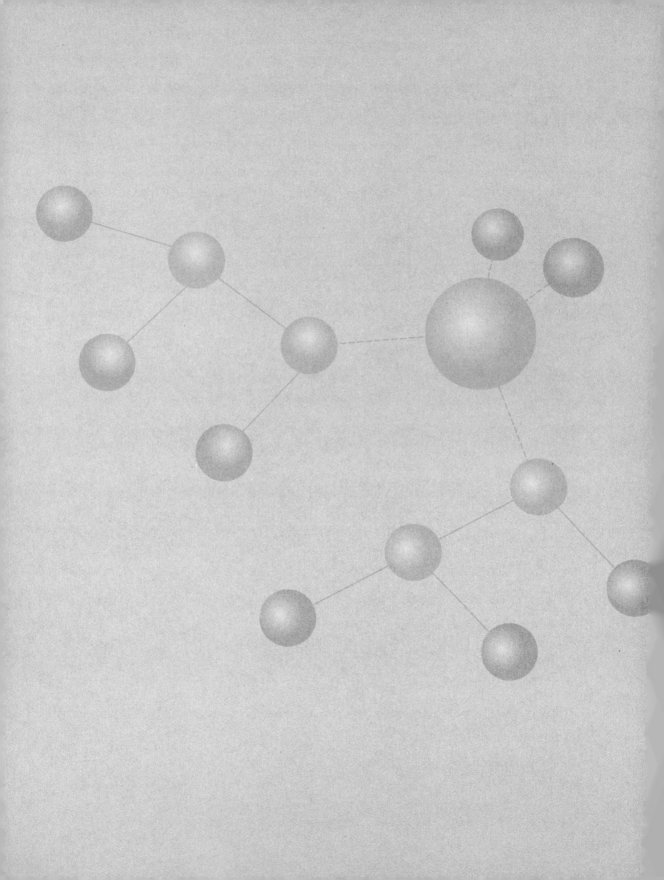

SAX 1.0: The Simple API for XML

This appendix contains the specification of the SAX interface. It is taken largely verbatim from the definitive specification to be found on http://www.megginson.com/sax/, with editorial comments added in italics.

The classes and interfaces are described in alphabetical order; within each class, the methods are also listed alphabetically.

The SAX specification is in the public domain: see the web site quoted above for a statement of policy on copyright. Essentially the policy is: do what you like with it, copy it as you wish, but no-one accepts any liability for errors or omissions.

The SAX distribution also includes three "helper classes":

❏ AttributeListImpl is an implementation of the AttributeList interface

❏ LocatorImpl is an implementation of the Locator interface

❏ ParserFactory is a class that enables you to load a parser identified by a parameter at run-time.

The documentation of these helper classes is not included here. For this, and for SAX sample applications, see the SAX distribution available from http://www.megginson.com.

Class Hierarchy

```
class java.lang.Object
    interface org.xml.sax.AttributeList
    class org.xml.sax.helpers.AttributeListImpl
        (implements org.xml.sax.AttributeList)
    interface org.xml.sax.DTDHandler
    interface org.xml.sax.DocumentHandler
    interface org.xml.sax.EntityResolver
    interface org.xml.sax.ErrorHandler
    class org.xml.sax.HandlerBase
        (implements org.xml.sax.EntityResolver,
                    org.xml.sax.DTDHandler,
                    org.xml.sax.DocumentHandler,
                    org.xml.sax.ErrorHandler)
    class org.xml.sax.InputSource
    interface org.xml.sax.Locator
    class org.xml.sax.helpers.LocatorImpl
        (implements org.xml.sax.Locator)
    interface org.xml.sax.Parser
    class org.xml.sax.helpers.ParserFactory
class java.lang.Throwable (implements java.io.Serializable)
    class java.lang.Exception
    class org.xml.sax.SAXException
    class org.xml.sax.SAXParseException
```

Interface org.xml.sax.AttributeList

An AttributeList is a collection of attributes appearing on a particular start tag. The Parser supplies the DocumentHandler with an AttributeList as part of the information available on the startElement event. The AttributeList is essentially a set of name-value pairs for the supplied attributes; if the parser has analyzed the DTD it may also provide information about the type of each attribute.

Interface for an Element's Attribute Specifications

The SAX parser implements this interface and passes an instance to the SAX application as the second argument of each startElement event.

The instance provided will return valid results only during the scope of the startElement invocation (to save it for future use, the application must make a copy: the AttributeListImpl helper class provides a convenient constructor for doing so).

An AttributeList includes only attributes that have been specified or defaulted: #IMPLIED attributes will not be included.

There are two ways for the SAX application to obtain information from the AttributeList. First, it can iterate through the entire list:

```
public void startElement (String name, AttributeList atts) {
    for (int i = 0; i < atts.getLength(); i++) {
        String name = atts.getName(i);
```

```
          String type = atts.getType(i);
          String value - atts.getValue(i);
          [...]
      }
  }
```

(Note that the result of getLength() will be zero if there are no attributes.)

As an alternative, the application can request the value or type of specific attributes:

```
  public void startElement (String name, AttributeList atts) {
     String identifier = atts.getValue("id");
     String label = atts.getValue("label");
     [...]
  }
```

The AttributeListImpl helper class provides a convenience implementation for use by parser or application writers.

Method Name	Description
getLength()	The SAX parser may provide attributes in any arbitrary order, regardless of the order in which they were declared or specified. The number of attributes may be zero. Returns the number of attributes in this list.
getName(index)	The names must be unique: the SAX parser shall not include the same attribute twice. Attributes without values (those declared #IMPLIED without a value specified in the start tag) will be omitted from the list. Returns the name of an attribute in this list (by position). If the attribute name has a namespace prefix, the prefix will still be attached. Parameter: the index of the attribute in the list starting at zero (int).
getType(index)	The attribute type is one of the strings "CDATA", "ID", "IDREF", "IDREFS", "NMTOKEN", "NMTOKENS", "ENTITY", "ENTITIES", or "NOTATION" (always in upper case). If the parser has not read a declaration for the attribute, or if the parser does not report attribute types, then it must return the value "CDATA" as stated in the XML 1.0 Recommendation (clause 3.3.3, "Attribute-Value Normalization"). For an enumerated attribute that is not a notation, the parser will report the type as "NMTOKEN". Returns the type of an attribute in the list (by position). Parameter: the index of the attribute in the list starting at zero (int).

Table Continued on Following Page

Method Name	Description
getType(name)	The return value is the same as the return value for getType(index). If the attribute name has a namespace prefix in the document, the application must include the prefix here. Returns the type of an attribute in the list (by name). Parameter: the name of the attribute (String).
getValue(index)	If the attribute value is a list of tokens (IDREFS, ENTITIES, or NMTOKENS), the tokens will be concatenated into a single string separated by whitespace. Returns the value of an attribute in the list (by position). Parameter: the index of the attribute in the list starting at zero (int).
getValue(name)	The return value is the same as the return value for getValue(index). If the attribute name has a namespace prefix in the document, the application must include the prefix here. Returns the value of an attribute in the list (by name). Parameter: the name of the attribute (String).

Interface org.xml.sax.DocumentHandler

Every SAX application is likely to include a class that implements this interface, either directly or by subclassing the supplied class HandlerBase.

Receive Notification of General Document Events

This is the main interface that most SAX applications implement: if the application needs to be informed of basic parsing events, it implements this interface and registers an instance with the SAX parser using the setDocumentHandler method. The parser uses the instance to report basic document-related events like the start and end of elements and character data.

The order of events in this interface is very important, and mirrors the order of information in the document itself. For example, all of an element's content (character data, processing instructions, and/or subelements) will appear, in order, between the startElement event and the corresponding endElement event.

Application writers who do not want to implement the entire interface can derive a class from HandlerBase, which implements the default functionality; parser writers can instantiate HandlerBase to obtain a default handler. The application can find the location of any document event using the Locator interface supplied by the parser through the setDocumentLocator method.

Method Name	Description

`characters(ch[], start, length)`
 	
`throws SAXException`
	Receives notification of character data. The parser will call this method to report each chunk of character data. SAX parsers may return all contiguous character data in a single chunk, or they may split it into several chunks; however, all of the characters in any single event must come from the same external entity, so that the `Locator` provides useful information.
	
	The application must not attempt to read from the array outside of the specified range *and must not attempt to write to the array.* Note that some parsers will report whitespace using the `ignorableWhitespace()` method rather than this one (validating parsers must do so).
	
	Parameters:
	`ch` – the characters from the XML document (`char` array)
	`start` – the start position in the array (`int`)
	`length` – the number of characters to read from the array (`int`).
	
	Throws: `SAXException` – any SAX exception, possibly wrapping another exception.

`endDocument()`
 	
`throws SAXException`
	Receives notification of the end of a document. The SAX parser will invoke this method only once *for each document*, and it will be the last method invoked during the parse. The parser shall not invoke this method until it has either abandoned parsing (because of an unrecoverable error) or reached the end of input.
	
	Throws: `SAXException` – any SAX exception, possibly wrapping another exception.

`endElement(name)`
 	
`throws SAXException`
	Receives notification of the end of an element. The SAX parser will invoke this method at the end of every element in the XML document; there will be a corresponding `startElement()` event for every `endElement()` event (even when the element is empty).
	
	If the element name has a namespace prefix, the prefix will still be attached to the name.
	
	Parameter: the element type name (`String`)
	
	Throws: `SAXException` – any SAX exception, possibly wrapping another exception.

Table Continued on Following Page

Method Name	Description

`ignorableWhitespace (ch[], start, length)`
 	
`throws SAXException`
	Receives notification of ignorable whitespace in element content. Validating parsers must use this method to report each chunk of ignorable whitespace (see the W3C XML 1.0 recommendation, section 2.10). Non-validating parsers may also use this method if they are capable of parsing and using content models.
	
	SAX parsers may return all contiguous whitespace in a single chunk, or they may split it into several chunks; however, all of the characters in any single event must come from the same external entity, so that the `Locator` provides useful information. The application must not attempt to read from the array outside of the specified range.
	
	Parameters:
	`ch` – The characters from the XML document (`char` array).
	`start` – The start position in the array (`int`).
	`length` – The number of characters to read from the array (`int`).
	
	Throws: `SAXException` – any SAX exception, possibly wrapping another exception.

`processingInstruction (target, data)`
 	
`throws SAXException`
	Receives notification of a processing instruction. The parser will invoke this method once for each processing instruction found: note that processing instructions may occur before or after the main document element.
	
	A SAX parser should never report an XML declaration (XML 1.0, section 2.8) or a text declaration (XML 1.0, section 4.3.1) using this method.
	
	Parameters:
	`target` – The processing instruction target (`String`).
	`data` – The processing instruction data, or null if none was supplied (`String`).
	
	Throws: `SAXException` – any SAX exception, possibly wrapping another exception.

Method Name	Description
setDocumentLocator (locator)	Receives an object for locating the origin of SAX document events. A SAX parser is strongly encouraged (though not absolutely required) to supply a locator. If it does so, it must supply the locator to the application by invoking this method before invoking any of the other methods in the DocumentHandler interface. The locator allows the application to determine the end position of any document-related event, even if the parser is not reporting an error. Typically, the application will use this information for reporting its own errors (such as character content that does not match an application's business rules). The information returned by the locator is probably not sufficient for use with a search engine. In practice, some implementations report the start position of the event (e.g. the column number where a tag starts) rather than the end position. Note that the locator will return correct information only during the invocation of the events in this interface. The application should not attempt to use it at any other time. Parameter: locator – An object that can return the location of any SAX document event (of type Locator).
startDocument () throws SAXException	Receives notification of the beginning of a document. The SAX parser will invoke this method only once *for each document*, before any other methods in this interface or in DTDHandler (except for setDocumentLocator). Throws: SAXException– any SAX exception, possibly wrapping another exception.
startElement (name, atts) throws SAXException	Receives notification of the beginning of an element. The parser will invoke this method at the beginning of every element in the XML document; there will be a corresponding endElement () event for every startElement () event (even when the element is empty). All of the element's content will be reported, in order, before the corresponding endElement () event. If the element name has a namespace prefix, the prefix will still be attached. Note that the attribute list provided will contain only attributes with explicit values (specified or defaulted): #IMPLIED attributes will be omitted. Parameters: name – The element type name (String). atts The attributes attached to the element (of type AttributeList). Throws: SAXException – any SAX exception, possibly wrapping another exception.

Interface org.xml.sax.DTDHandler

This interface should be implemented by the application, if it wants to receive notification of events related to the DTD. SAX does not provide full details of the DTD, but this interface is available because without it, it would be impossible to access notations and unparsed entities referenced in the body of the document.

Notations and unparsed entities are rather specialized facilities in XML, so most SAX applications will not need to use this interface.

Receive Notification of Basic DTD-Related Events

If a SAX application needs information about notations and unparsed entities, then the application implements this interface and registers an instance with the SAX parser using the parser's `setDTDHandler` method. The parser uses the instance to report notation and unparsed entity declarations to the application.

The SAX parser may report these events in any order, regardless of the order in which the notations and unparsed entities were declared; however, all DTD events must be reported after the document handler's `startDocument` event, and before the first `startElement` event.

It is up to the application to store the information for future use (perhaps in a hash table or object tree). If the application encounters attributes of type "NOTATION", "ENTITY", or "ENTITIES", it can use the information that it obtained through this interface to find the entity and/or notation corresponding with the attribute value.

The `HandlerBase` class provides a default implementation of this interface, which simply ignores the events.

Method Name	Description

`notationDecl(name, publicId, systemId)`
 	
 `throws SAXException`
	Receives notification of a notation declaration event. It is up to the application to record the notation for later reference, if necessary. If a system identifier is present, and it is a URL, the SAX parser must resolve it fully before passing it to the application.
	
	 Parameters:
	 `name` – The notation name (`String`).
	 `publicId` – The notation's public identifier, or null if none was given (`String`).
	 `systemId` – The notation's system identifier, or null if none was given (`String`).
	
	 Throws: `SAXException` – any SAX exception, possibly wrapping another exception.

Method Name	Description
unparsedEntityDecl(name, publicId, systemId, notationName) throws SAXException	Receives notification of an unparsed entity declaration event. Note that the notation name corresponds to a notation reported by the notationDecl() event. It is up to the application to record the entity for later reference, if necessary. If the system identifier is a URL, the parser must resolve it fully before passing it to the application. Parameters: name – The unparsed entity's name (String). publicId – The entity's public identifier, or null if none was given (String). systemId – The entity's system identifier (it must always have one) (String). notationName – The name of the associated notation (String). Throws: SAXException – any SAX exception, possibly wrapping another exception.

Interface org.xml.sax.EntityResolver

When the XML document contains references to external entities, the URL will normally be automatically analyzed by the parser. The relevant file will be located and parsed where appropriate. This interface allows an application to override this behavior. This might be needed, for example, if you want to retrieve a different version of the entity from a local server, or if the entities are cached in memory on stored in a database, or if the entity is really a reference to variable information such as the current date.

When the parser needs to obtain an entity, it calls this interface, which can respond by supplying any InputSource object.

Basic Interface for Resolving Entities

If a SAX application needs to implement customized handling for external entities, it must implement this interface and register an instance with the SAX parser using the parser's setEntityResolver method.

The parser will then allow the application to intercept any external entities (including the external DTD subset and external parameter entities, if any) before including them.

Many SAX applications will not need to implement this interface, but it will be especially useful for applications that build XML documents from databases or other specialized input sources, or for applications that use URI types other than URLs.

The following resolver would provide the application with a special character stream for the entity with the system identifier "http://www.myhost.com/today":

```
import org.xml.sax.EntityResolver;
import org.xml.sax.InputSource;

public class MyResolver implements EntityResolver {
    public InputSource resolveEntity (String publicId, String systemId)
    {
            if (systemId.equals("http://www.myhost.com/today")) {
                // return a special input source
              MyReader reader = new MyReader();
              return new InputSource(reader);
            } else {
                // use the default behaviour
              return null;
            }
    }
}
```

The application can also use this interface to redirect system identifiers to local URIs or to look up replacements in a catalog (possibly by using the public identifier).

The `HandlerBase` class implements the default behavior for this interface, which is simply always to return null (to request that the parser use the default system identifier).

Method Name	Description
resolveEntity (publicId, systemId) throws SAXException, IOException	Allows the application to resolve external entities. The parser will call this method before opening any external entity except the top-level document entity (including the external DTD subset, external entities referenced within the DTD, and external entities referenced within the document element): the application may request that the parser resolve the entity itself, that it use an alternative URI, or that it use an entirely different input source. Application writers can use this method to redirect external system identifiers to secure and/or local URIs, to look up public identifiers in a catalogue, or to read an entity from a database or other input source (including, for example, a dialog box). If the system identifier is a URL, the SAX parser must resolve it fully before reporting it to the application. Returns an `InputSource` object describing the new input source, or null to request that the parser open a regular URI connection to the system identifier. Parameters: `publicId` – The public identifier of the external entity being referenced, or null if none was supplied (`String`). `systemId` – The system identifier of the external entity being referenced (`String`). Throws: `SAXException` – any SAX exception, possibly wrapping another exception Throws: `IOException` – a Java-specific IO exception, possibly the result of creating a new `InputStream` or reader for the `InputSource`.

Interface org.xml.sax.ErrorHandler

You may implement this interface in your application if you want to take special action to handle errors. There is a default implementation provided within the HandlerBase *class.*

Basic Interface for SAX Error Handlers

If a SAX application needs to implement customized error handling, it must implement this interface and then register an instance with the SAX parser using the parser's setErrorHandler method. The parser will then report all errors and warnings through this interface.

The parser shall use this interface instead of throwing an exception: it is up to the application whether to throw an exception for different types of errors and warnings. Note, however, that there is no requirement that the parser continue to provide useful information after a call to fatalError (in other words, a SAX driver class could catch an exception and report a fatalError).

The HandlerBase class provides a default implementation of this interface, ignoring warnings and recoverable errors and throwing a SAXParseException for fatal errors. An application may extend that class rather than implementing the complete interface itself.

Method Name	Description
error(exception) throws SAXException	Receives notification of a recoverable error. This corresponds to the definition of "error" in section 1.2 of the W3C XML 1.0 Recommendation. For example, a validating parser would use this callback to report the violation of a validity constraint. The default behavior is to take no action. The SAX parser must continue to provide normal parsing events after invoking this method; it should still be possible for the application to process the document through to the end. If the application cannot do so, then the parser should report a fatal error even if the XML 1.0 recommendation does not require it to do so. Parameter: exception – the error information encapsulated in a SAXParseExeption. Throws: SAXException – any SAX exception, possibly wrapping another exception.

Table Continued on Following Page

635

Method Name	Description

`fatalError(exception)`
 	
`throws SAXException`
	Receive notification of a non-recoverable error. This corresponds to the definition of "fatal error" in section 1.2 of the W3C XML 1.0 Recommendation. For example, a parser would use this callback to report the violation of a well-formedness constraint.
	
	The application must assume that the document is unusable after the parser has invoked this method, and should continue (if at all) only for the sake of collecting additional error messages: in fact, SAX parsers are free to stop reporting any other events once this method has been invoked.
	
	Parameter: `exception` – the error information encapsulated in a `SAXParseExeption`.
	
	Throws: `SAXException` – any SAX exception, possibly wrapping another exception.

`warning(exception)`
 	
`throws SAXException`
	Receives notification of a warning. SAX parsers will use this method to report conditions that are not errors or fatal errors as defined by the XML 1.0 recommendation. The default behavior is to take no action.
	
	The SAX parser must continue to provide normal parsing events after invoking this method: it should still be possible for the application to process the document through to the end.
	
	Parameter: `exception` – the error information encapsulated in a `SAXParseExeption`.
	
	Throws: `SAXException` – any SAX exception, possibly wrapping another exception.

Class org.xml.sax.HandlerBase

This class is supplied with SAX itself: it provides default implementations of most of the methods that would otherwise need to be implemented by the application. If you write classes in your application as subclasses of `HandlerBase`, *you need only code those methods where you want something other than the default behavior.*

Default Base Class for Handlers

This class implements the default behavior for four SAX interfaces: `EntityResolver`, `DTDHandler`, `DocumentHandler`, and `ErrorHandler`.

Application writers can extend this class when they need to implement only part of an interface; parser writers can instantiate this class to provide default handlers when the application has not supplied its own.

Note that the use of this class is optional.

In the description below, only the behavior of each method is described. For the parameters and return values, see the corresponding interface definition.

Method Name	Description

`characters(ch[], start, length)`
 	
`throws SAXException`
	By default, do nothing. Application writers may override this method to take specific actions for each chunk of character data (such as adding the data to a node or buffer, or printing it to a file).

`endDocument()`
 	
`throws SAXException`
	Receives notification of the end of the document.
	
	By default, do nothing. Application writers may override this method in a subclass to take specific actions at the beginning of a document (such as finalizing a tree or closing an output file).

`endElement(name)`
 	
`throws SAXException`
	By default, do nothing. Application writers may override this method in a subclass to take specific actions at the end of each element (such as finalizing a tree node or writing output to a file).

`error(exception)`
 	
`throws SAXException`
	The default implementation does nothing. Application writers may override this method in a subclass to take specific actions for each error, such as inserting the message in a log file or printing it to the console.

`fatalError(exception)`
 	
`throws SAXException`
	The default implementation throws a `SAXParseException`. Application writers may override this method in a subclass if they need to take specific actions for each fatal error (such as collecting all of the errors into a single report): in any case, the application must stop all regular processing when this method is invoked, since the document is no longer reliable, and the parser may no longer report parsing events.

`ignorableWhitespace(ch[], start, length)`
 	
`throws SAXException`
	By default, do nothing. Application writers may override this method to take specific actions for each chunk of ignorable whitespace (such as adding data to a node or buffer, or printing it to a file).

`notationDecl(name, publicId, systemId)`	By default, do nothing. Application writers may override this method in a subclass if they wish to keep track of the notations declared in a document.

Method Name	Description

`processingInstruction(target, data)`
 	
`throws SAXException`
	By default, do nothing. Application writers may override this method in a subclass to take specific actions for each processing instruction, such as setting status variables or invoking other methods.

`resolveEntity(publicId, systemId)`
 	
`throws SAXException`
	Always return null, so that the parser will use the system identifier provided in the XML document. This method implements the SAX default behavior: application writers can override it in a subclass to do special translations such as catalog lookups or URI redirection.

`setDocumentLocator(locator)`	By default, do nothing. Application writers may override this method in a subclass if they wish to store the locator for use with other document events.

`startDocument()`
 	
`throws SAXException`
	By default, do nothing. Application writers may override this method in a subclass to take specific actions at the beginning of a document (such as allocating the root node of a tree or creating an output file).

`startElement(name, attributes)`
 	
`throws SAXException`
	By default, do nothing. Application writers may override this method in a subclass to take specific actions at the start of each element (such as allocating a new tree node or writing output to a file).

`unparsedEntityDecl(name, publicId, systemId, notationName)`	By default, do nothing. Application writers may override this method in a subclass to keep track of the unparsed entities declared in a document.

`warning(exception)`
 	
`throws SAXException`
	The default implementation does nothing. Application writers may override this method in a subclass to take specific actions for each warning, such as inserting the message in a log file or printing it to the console.

Class org.xml.sax.InputSource

An InputSource object represents a container for the XML document or any of the external entities it references (technically, the main document is itself an entity). The InputSource class is supplied with SAX: generally the application instantiates an InputSource and updates it to say where the input is coming from, and the parser interrogates it to find out where to read the input from.

The InputSource object provides three ways of supplying input to the parser: a system identifier (or URL), a reader (which delivers a stream of Unicode characters), or an InputStream (which delivers a stream of uninterpreted bytes).

A Single Input Source for an XML Entity

This class allows a SAX application to encapsulate information about an input source in a single object, which may include a public identifier, a system identifier, a byte stream (possibly with a specified encoding), and/or a character stream.

There are two places that the application will deliver this input source to the parser: as the argument to the Parser.parse method, or as the return value of the EntityResolver.resolveEntity method.

The SAX parser will use the InputSource object to determine how to read XML input. If there is a character stream available, the parser will read that stream directly; if not, the parser will use a byte stream, if available. If neither a character stream nor a byte stream is available, the parser will attempt to open a URI connection to the resource identified by the system identifier.

An InputSource object belongs to the application: the SAX parser shall never modify it in any way (it may modify a copy if necessary).

If you supply input in the form of a Reader or InputStream, it may be useful to supply a system identifier as well. If you do this, the URI will not be used to obtain the actual XML input, but it will be used in diagnostics, and more importantly to resolve any relative URIs within the document, for example entity references.

Method Name	Description
InputSource()	Zero-argument default constructor.
InputSource (systemId)	Creates a new input source with a system identifier.
	Applications may use setPublicId to include a public identifier as well, or setEncoding to specify the character encoding, if known. If the system identifier is a URL, it must be full resolved.
	Parameter: systemId – the system identifier (String).
InputSource (byteStream)	Creates a new input source with a byte stream.
	Application writers may use setSystemId to provide a base for resolving relative URIs, setPublicId to include a public identifier, and/or setEncoding to specify the object's character encoding.
	Parameter: byteStream – the raw byte stream containing the document, of type InputStream.
InputSource (characterStream)	Creates a new input source with a character stream.
	Application writers may use setSystemId to provide a base for resolving relative URIs, and setPublicId to include a public identifier. The character stream should not include a byte order mark.
	Parameter: characterStream the character stream containing the document, of type Reader

Table Continued on Following Page

639

Method Name	Description
`setPublicId (publicId)`	Sets the public identifier for this input source. The public identifier is always optional: if the application writer includes one, it will be provided as part of the location information. Parameters: `publicId` – the public identifier as a `String`.
`getPublicId()`	Gets the public identifier for this input source. Returns the public identifier (`String`), or `null` if none was supplied.
`setSystemId (systemId)`	Sets the system identifier for this input source. The system identifier is optional if there is a byte stream or a character stream, but it is still useful to provide one, since the application can use it to resolve relative URIs and can include it in error messages and warnings. (The parser will attempt to open a connection to the URI only if there is no byte stream or character stream specified.) If the application knows the character encoding of the object pointed to by the system identifier, it can register the encoding using the `setEncoding` method. If the system ID is a URL, it must be fully resolved. Parameter: `systemId` – the system identifier as a `String`.
`getSystemId()`	Gets the system identifier for this input source. The `getEncoding` method will return the character encoding of the object pointed to, or null if unknown. If the system ID is a URL, it will be fully resolved. Returns the system identifier as a `String`.
`setByteStream (byteStream)`	Sets the byte stream for this input source. The SAX parser will ignore this if there is also a character stream specified, but it will use a byte stream in preference to opening a URI connection itself. If the application knows the character encoding of the byte stream, it should set it with the `setEncoding` method. Parameter: `byteStream` – a byte stream containing an XML document or other entity, of type `InputStream`.
`getByteStream()`	Gets the byte stream for this input source. The `getEncoding` method will return the character encoding for this byte stream, or null if unknown. Returns the byte stream (as an `InputStream` object), or `null` if none was supplied.

Method Name	Description
setEncoding (encoding)	Sets the character encoding, if known. The encoding must be a string acceptable for an XML encoding declaration (see section 4.3.3 of the XML 1.0 recommendation). This method has no effect when the application provides a character stream. Parameter: encoding – a string describing the character encoding.
getEncoding()	Gets the character encoding for a byte stream or URI. Returns the encoding as a String, or null if none was supplied.
setCharacterStream(ch aracterStream)	Sets the character stream for this input source. If there is a character stream specified, the SAX parser will ignore any byte stream and will not attempt to open a URI connection to the system identifier. Parameter: characterStream – The character stream containing the XML document or other entity, of type Reader.
getCharacterStream()	Gets the character stream for this input source. Returns the character stream (as a Reader object), or null if none was supplied.

Interface org.xml.sax.Locator

This interface provides methods that the application can use to determine the current position in the source XML document.

Interface for Associating a SAX Event with a Document Location

If a SAX parser provides location information to the SAX application, it does so by implementing this interface and then passing an instance to the application using the document handler's setDocumentLocator method. The application can use the object to obtain the location of any other document handler event in the XML source document.

Note that the results returned by the object will be valid only during the scope of each document handler method: the application will receive unpredictable results if it attempts to use the locator at any other time.

SAX parsers are not required to supply a locator, but they are very strongly encouraged to do so. If the parser supplies a locator, it must do so before reporting any other document events. If no locator has been set by the time the application receives the startDocument event, the application should assume that a locator is not available.

Method Name	Description
getPublicId()	Returns the public identifier for the current document event as a String, or null if none is available.
getSystemId()	Returns the system identifier for the current document event as a String, or null if none is available.

If the system identifier is a URL, the parser must resolve it fully before passing it to the application. |
| getLineNumber() | Returns the line number where the current document event ends or -1 if none is available.

In practice some parsers report the line number and column number where the event starts. Note that this is the line position of the first character after the text associated with the document event. |
| getColumnNumber() | Return the column number where the current document event ends, or -1 if none is available.

Note that this is the column number of the first character after the text associated with the document event. The first column in a line is position 1. |

Interface org.xml.sax.Parser

Every SAX parser must implement this interface. An application parses an XML document by creating an instance of a parser (that is, a class that implements this interface) and calling one of its parse() methods.

Basic Interface for SAX (Simple API for XML) Parsers.

All SAX parsers must implement this basic interface: it allows applications to register handlers for different types of events and to initiate a parse from a URI, or a character stream.

All SAX parsers must also implement a zero-argument constructor (though other constructors are also allowed).

SAX parsers are reusable but not re-entrant: the application may reuse a parser object (possibly with a different input source) once the first parse has completed successfully, but it may not invoke the parse() methods recursively within a parse.

Method Name	Description

`parse(source)`
 	
`throws`
`SAXException,`
`IOException`
	Parses an XML document.
	
	The application can use this method to instruct the SAX parser to begin parsing an XML document from any valid input source (a character stream, a byte stream, or a URI).
	
	Applications may not invoke this method while a parse is in progress (they should create a new `Parser` object instead for each additional XML document). Once a parse is complete, an application may reuse the same `Parser` object, possibly with a different input source.
	
	Parameter: `source` – the input source for the top level of the XML document, of type `InputSource`.
	
	Throws: `SAXException` – any SAX exception, possibly wrapping another exception.
	
	Throws: `IOException` – an IO exception from the parser, possibly from a byte stream or character stream supplied by the application.

`parse(systemId)`
 	
`throws`
`SAXException,`
`IOException`
	Parses an XML document from a system identifier (URI).
	
	This method is a shortcut for the common case of reading a document from a system identifier. It is the exact equivalent of the following syntax:
	
	`parse(new InputSource(systemId));`
	
	If the system identifier is a URL, it must be fully resolved by the application before it is passed to the parser.
	
	Parameter: `systemId` – The system identifier as a `String`.
	
	Throws: `SAXException` – any SAX exception, possibly wrapping another exception.
	
	Throws: `IOException` – an IO exception from the parser, possibly from a byte stream or character stream supplied by the application.

Table Continued on Following Page

Method Name	Description
`setDocumentHandler (handler)`	Allows an application to register a document event handler.
	If the application does not register a document handler, all document events reported by the SAX parser will be silently ignored (this is the default behavior implemented by `HandlerBase`).
	Applications may register a new or different handler in the middle of a parse, and the SAX parser must begin using the new handler immediately.
	Parameter: `handler` – The document handler, of type `DocumentHandler`.
`setDTDHandler (handler)`	Allows an application to register a DTD event handler.
	If the application does not register a DTD handler, all DTD events reported by the SAX parser will be silently ignored (this is the default behavior implemented by `HandlerBase`).
	Applications may register a new or different handler in the middle of a parse, and the SAX parser must begin using the new handler immediately.
	Parameter: handler – The DTD handler, of type `DTDHandler`.
`setEntityResolver (resolver)`	Allows an application to register a custom entity resolver.
	If the application does not register an entity resolver, the SAX parser will resolve system identifiers and open connections to entities itself (this is the default behavior implemented in `HandlerBase`).
	Applications may register a new or different entity resolver in the middle of a parse, and the SAX parser must begin using the new resolver immediately.
	Parameter: resolver – The object for resolving entities, of type `EntityResolver`.

Method Name	Description
setErrorHandler (handler)	Allows an application to register an error event handler. If the application does not register an error event handler, all error events reported by the SAX parser will be silently ignored, except for fatalError, which will throw a SAXException (this is the default behavior implemented by HandlerBase). Applications may register a new or different handler in the middle of a parse, and the SAX parser must begin using the new handler immediately. Parameter: handler – the error handler, of type ErrorHandler.
setLocale(locale) throws SAXException	Allows an application to request a locale for errors and warnings. SAX parsers are not required to provide localization for errors and warnings; if they cannot support the requested locale, however, they must throw a SAX exception. Applications may not request a locale change in the middle of a parse. Parameter: locale – a Java Locale object. Throws: SAXException – throws an exception (using the previous or default locale) if the requested locale is not supported.

Class org.xml.sax.SAXException

This class is used to represent an error detected during processing either by the parser or by the application.

Encapsulate a General SAX Error or Warning

This class can contain basic error or warning information from either the XML parser or the application: a parser writer or application writer can subclass it to provide additional functionality. SAX handlers may throw this exception or any exception subclassed from it.

If the application needs to pass through other types of exceptions, it must wrap those exceptions in a SAXException or an exception derived from a SAXException.

If the parser or application needs to include information about a specific location in an XML document, it should use the SAXParseException subclass.

Method Name	Description
getMessage()	Returns a detailed error or warning message for this exception as a String. If there is a embedded exception, and if the SAXException has no detail message of its own, this method will return the detail message from the embedded exception.
getException()	Returns the embedded exception, or null if there is none.
toString()	Converts the exception to a string.

Class org.xml.sax.SAXParseException

This exception class represents an error or warning condition detected by the parser or by the application. In addition to the basic capability of SAXException, a SAXParseException allow information to be retained about the location in the source document where the error occurred. For an application-detected error, this information might be obtained from the Locator object.

Encapsulate an XML parse error or warning

This exception will include information for locating the error in the original XML document. Note that although the application will receive a SAXParseException as the argument to the handlers in the ErrorHandler interface, the application is not actually required to throw the exception; instead, it can simply read the information in it and take a different action.

Since this exception is a subclass of SAXException, it inherits the ability to wrap another exception.

Method Name	Description
SAXParseException(message, locator)	Creates a new SAXParseException from a message and a locator. This constructor is especially useful when an application is creating its own exception from within a DocumentHandler callback. Parameters: message – The error or warning message as a String. locator – The locator object for the error or warning, of type Locator.

Method Name	Description
SAXParseException(message, locator, e)	Wraps an existing exception in a SAXParseException. This constructor is especially useful when an application is creating its own exception from within a DocumentHandler callback, and needs to wrap an existing exception that is not a subclass of SAXException. Parameters: message – The error or warning message as a String, or null to use the message from the embedded exception. locator – The locator object for the error or warning, of type Locator. e – any exception
SAXParseException(message, publicId, systemId, lineNumber, columnNumber)	Creates a new SAXParseException. This constructor is most useful for parser writers. If the system identifier is a URL, the parser must resolve it fully before creating the exception. Parameters: message – The error or warning message. publicId – The public identifier of the entity that generated the error or warning. systemId – The system identifier of the entity that generated the error or warning. The first three parameters are all Strings. lineNumber – The line number of the end of the text that caused the error or warning. columnNumber – The column number of the end of the text that cause the error or warning. These last two parameters are integers.

Table Continued on Following Page

Method Name	Description
SAXParseException(message, publicId, systemId, lineNumber, columnNumber, e)	Creates a new SAXParseException with an embedded exception. This constructor is most useful for parser writers who need to wrap an exception that is not a subclass of SAXException. If the system identifier is a URL, the parser must resolve it fully before creating the exception. Parameters: message – The error or warning message, or null to use the message from the embedded exception. publicId – The public identifier of the entity that generated the error or warning. systemId – The system identifier of the entity that generated the error or warning. The first three parameters are all Strings. lineNumber – The line number of the end of the text that caused the error or warning. columnNumber – The column number of the end of the text that cause the error or warning. These two parameters are integers. e – another exception to embed in this one.
getPublicId()	Gets a string containing the public identifier of the entity where the exception occurred, or null if none is available.
getSystemId()	Gets a string containing the system identifier of the entity where the exception occurred, or null if none is available. If the system identifier is a URL, it will be resolved fully.
getLineNumber()	Gets the line number of the end of the text where the exception occurred, or -1 if none is available.
getColumnNumber()	Gets the column number of the end of the text where the exception occurred, or -1 if none is available. The first column in a line is position 1.

XPath Reference

General Introduction

An XPath expression contains one or more "location steps", separated by slashes. Each location step has the following form:

```
axis-name::node-test [predicate]*
```

In other words, there is an axis name, then two colons, then a node test and finally zero or more predicates in square brackets. A predicate is an expression. Consisting of values, operators and other XPath expressions. We will show a list of valid axes and a list of valid node tests in this appendix.

The XPath axis contains a part of the document, defined from the perspective of the "context node". The node test makes a selection from the nodes on that axis. By adding predicates, it is possible to select a subset from these nodes. If the expression in the predicate returns true, the node remains in the selected set, otherwise it is removed. XPath defines a set of functions for use in predicates. These are listed in the appendix as well.

Axes

ancestor

Contains the parent node, the parent's parent node etc., all the way up to the document root.

Primary node type:	element
Implemented:	W3C 1.0 specification, MSXML 2.6 (preview).

ancestor-or-self

This is identical to the ancestor axis, but includes the context node itself.

Primary node type:	element
Implemented:	W3C 1.0 specification, MSXML 2.6 (preview).

attribute

Contains all attributes on the context node.

Primary node type:	attribute
Implemented:	W3C 1.0 specification, MSXML 2.6 (preview).

child

Contains all direct children of the context node.

Primary node type:	element
Shorthand:	(default axis)
Implemented:	W3C 1.0 specification, MSXML 2.6 (preview), MSXML 2.0 (IE5 shorthand syntax only).

descendent

This refers to all children of the context node, including all children's children recursively.

Primary node type:	element
Shorthand:	//
Implemented:	W3C 1.0 specification, MSXML 2.6 (preview), MSXML 2.0 (IE5 shorthand syntax only).

descendent-or-self

This is identical to the descendant axis, but includes the context node itself.

Primary node type:	element
Implemented:	W3C 1.0 specification, MSXML 2.6 (preview).

following

Contains all nodes that come after the context node in the document order.

Primary node type:	element
Implemented:	W3C 1.0 specification.

following-sibling

Contain all siblings (that is, children of the same parent node) of the context node that come after the context, node in document order.

Primary node type:	element
Implemented:	W3C 1.0 specification, MSXML 2.6 (preview).

namespace

Contains all valid namespaces that can be used on the context node. This includes the default namespace and the XML namespace, which are automatically declared in any document.

Primary node type:	namespace
Implemented:	W3C 1.0 specification, MSXML 2.6 (preview).

parent

Contains only the direct parent node of the context node.

Primary node type:	element
Shorthand:	. .
Implemented:	W3C 1.0 specification, MSXML 2.6 (preview), MSXML 2.0 (IE5 shorthand syntax only).

preceding

Contains all nodes that come before the context node in the document order.

Primary node type:	element
Implemented:	W3C 1.0 specification.

preceding-sibling

Contains all siblings (that is, children of the same parent node) of the context node that come before the context node, in document order.

Primary node type:	element
Implemented:	W3C 1.0 specification, MSXML 2.6 (preview).

self

Contains only the context node itself.

Primary node type:	element
Shorthand:	.
Implemented:	W3C 1.0 specification, MSXML 2.6 (preview), MSXML 2.0 (IE5 shorthand syntax only).

Node Tests

*

Returns true for all nodes of the primary type of the axis.

Implemented:	W3C 1.0 specification, MSXML 2.6 (preview), MSXML 2.0 (IE5).

comment()

Returns true for all comment nodes.

Implemented:	W3C 1.0 specification, MSXML 2.6 (preview), MSXML 2.0 (IE5).

literal-name()

Returns true for all nodes of that name. If the node test is 'PERSON', it returns true for all nodes of name 'PERSON'.

Implemented:	W3C 1.0 specification, MSXML 2.6 (preview), MSXML 2.0 (IE5).

node()

Returns true for all nodes, except attributes and namespaces.

Implemented:	W3C 1.0 specification, MSXML 2.6 (preview), MSXML 2.0 (IE5).

processing-instruction(name?)

Returns true for all processing instruction nodes. If a name is passed, returns true only for processing instruction nodes of that name.

Implemented·	W3C 1.0 specification, MSXML 2.6 (preview), MSXML 2.0 (IE5). The test is called pi() in MSXML 2.0.

text()

Returns true for all text nodes.

Implemented:	W3C 1.0 specification, MSXML 2.6 (preview), MSXML 2.0 (IE5).

Functions

boolean boolean(object)

Converts anything passed to it into a Boolean value (true or false).

Parameter: object	Numbers are true if they are not zero or NaN (not a number). Strings are true if their length is non-zero. Node sets return true if they are not empty.
Implemented:	W3C 1.0 specification, MSXML 2.6 (preview).

number ceiling(number)

Rounds a passed number up to the nearest integer, for example 2.2 becomes 3.

Parameter: number	The number to be rounded.
Implemented:	W3C 1.0 specification.

string concat(string, string+)

Concatenates all strings passed.

Parameter 1: string	The first string.
Parameters 2+: string	All subsequent strings.
Implemented:	W3C 1.0 specification, MSXML 2.6 (preview).

boolean contains(string, string)

Returns true if the first passed string contains the second passed string.

Parameter 1: string	The string to be searched.
Parameter 2: string	The search string.
Implemented:	W3C 1.0 specification, MSXML 2.6 (preview).

number count(node-set)

Returns the number of nodes in the passed node set.

Parameter: node-set	The node set that is to be counted.
Implemented:	W3C 1.0 specification, MSXML 2.6 (preview).

boolean false()

Only returns false.

Implemented:	W3C 1.0 specification, MSXML 2.6 (preview).

number floor(number)

Rounds a passed number down to the nearest integer, for example 2.8 becomes 2.

Parameter: number	The number to be rounded.
Implemented:	W3C 1.0 specification.

node-set id(string)

Returns the element, identified by the passed identifier. Note that this will only work in validated documents.

Parameter: string	The ID value.
Implemented:	W3C 1.0 specification, MSXML 2.6 (preview), MSXML 2.0 (IE5).

boolean lang(string)

Returns true if the language of the context node is the same as the passed language identifier. The language of the context node can be set using the xml:lang on it or any of its ancestors.

Parameter: string	Language identifier. lang('en') returns true for English language nodes.
Implemented:	W3C 1.0 specification.

number last()

Returns the index number of the last node in the current context node set.

Implemented:	W3C 1.0 specification, MSXML 2.6 (preview), MSXML 2.0 (IE5). The function is called end() in MSXML 2.0.

string local-name(node-set?)

Returns the local part of the name of the first node (in document order) in the passed node set. The local part of an xsl:value-of element is 'value-of'.

Parameter (opt): node-set	If no node set is specified, the current context node is used.
Implemented:	W3C 1.0 specification, MSXML 2.6 (preview).

string name(node-set?)

Returns the name of the passed node. This is the fully qualified name, including the namespace prefix.

Parameter (opt): node-set	If no node set is specified, the current context node is used.
Implemented:	W3C 1.0 specification, MSXML 2.6 (preview).

string namespace-uri(node-set?)

Returns the full URI that defines the namespace of the passed node.

Parameter (opt): node-set	If no node set is specified, the current context node is used.
Implemented:	W3C 1.0 specification, MSXML 2.6 (preview).

string normalize-space(string?)

Returns the whitespace-normalized version of the passed string. This means that all leading and trailing whitespace gets stripped and all sequences of whitespace get combined to one single space.

Parameter (opt): string	If no string is passed, the current node is converted to a string.
Implemented:	W3C 1.0 specification, MSXML 2.6 (preview).

boolean not(boolean)

Returns the inverse from the passed value (that is true becomes false and visa versa).

Parameter: boolean	true or false.
Implemented:	W3C 1.0 specification, MSXML 2.6 (preview).

number number(object?)

Converts the passed value to a number. String values are converted according to the IEE 754 standard, Boolean values are converted to 1 or 0, node sets are first converted to string values and then to the numerical equivalent.

Parameter (opt): object	If nothing is passed, the current context node is used.
Implemented:	W3C 1.0 specification, MSXML 2.6 (preview).

number position()

Returns the position of the current context node in the current context node set.

Implemented:	W3C 1.0 specification, MSXML 2.6 (preview).

number round(number)

Rounds a passed number to the nearest integer (up or down), i.e. 2.5 becomes 3 and 2.4 becomes 2.

Parameter: number	The number to be rounded.
Implemented:	W3C 1.0 specification.

boolean starts-with(string, string)

Returns true if the first passed string starts with the second passed string.

Parameter 1: string	The string to be checked.
Parameter 2: string	The substring that must be searched.
Implemented:	W3C 1.0 specification, MSXML 2.6 (preview).

string string(object?)

Converts the passed object to a string value.

Parameter (opt): object	If nothing is passed, the result is an empty string.
Implemented:	W3C 1.0 specification, MSXML 2.6 (preview).

number string-length(string?)

Returns the number of characters in the passed string.

Parameter: object	If nothing is passed, the current context is converted to a string.
Implemented:	W3C 1.0 specification, MSXML 2.6 (preview).

string substring(string, number, number?)

Returns the substring from the passed string starting at the first numeric value, with the length specified by the second numeric value. If no length is passed, the substring runs to the end of the passed string.

Parameter 1: string	The string that will be used as the source for the substring.
Parameter 2: number	Start location of the substring.
Parameter 3 (opt): number	Length of the substring.
Implemented:	W3C 1.0 specification, MSXML 2.6 (preview).

string substring-after(string, string)

Returns the string following the first occurrence of the second passed string inside the first passed string. The return value of substring-after('2000/2/22', '/') would be '2/22'.

Parameter 1: string	The string that serves as the source.
Parameter 2: string	The string that is searched in the source string.
Implemented:	W3C 1.0 specification, MSXML 2.6 (preview).

string substring-before(string, string)

Returns the string part preceding the first occurrence of the second passed string inside the first passed string. The return value of substring-before('2000/2/22', '/') would be '2000'.

Parameter 1: string	The string that serves as the source.
Parameter 2: string	The string that is searched in the source string.
Implemented:	W3C 1.0 specification, MSXML 2.6 (preview).

number sum(node-set)

Sums the values of all nodes in the set when converted to a number.

Parameter: node-set	The node set containing all values to be summed.
Implemented:	W3C 1.0 specification.

string translate(string, string, string)

Translates characters in a string to other characters. The strings to translate from and to are specified by the second and third parameters respectively. So `translate('A Space Odissei', 'i', 'y')` would result in 'A Space Odyssey', and `translate('abcdefg', 'aceg', 'ACE')` results in 'AbCdEf'. The final g gets translated to nothing, because the third string has no corresponding character to the g in the second string.

Parameter 1: `string`	String to be translated character by character.
Parameter 2: `string`	String defining which characters must be translated.
Parameter 3: `string`	String defining what the characters from the second string should be translated to.
Implemented:	W3C 1.0 specification, MSXML 2.6 (preview).

boolean true()

Always returns `true`.

Implemented:	W3C 1.0 specification, MSXML 2.6 (preview).

A Few Examples of XPath Expressions

Select all descendent elements from the root:

```
/descendent::*
```

Select ancestor elements of the context node that are named `Chapter`:

```
ancestor::Chapter
```

Select nodes that have more than two direct children with the name `Skip`:

```
/descendant::node()[count(child::Skip) < 2]
```

Select all `Student` elements whose name attribute starts with an `A` (using shorthand notation):

```
//Student[starts-with(@name, 'A']
```

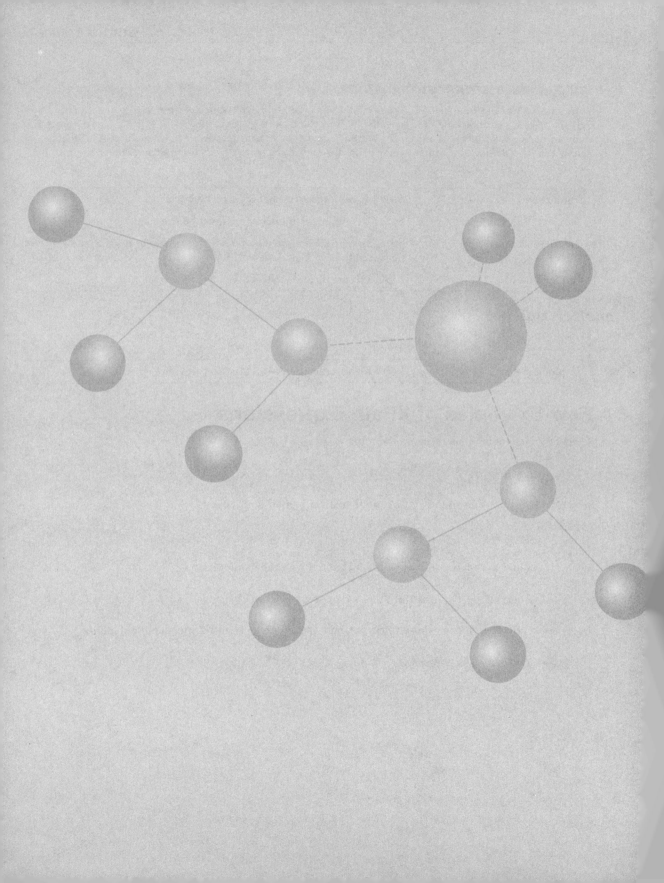

XSLT Reference

This reference appendix describes the elements and functions which can be used with XSLT (which was covered in Chapter 4.)

Elements

xsl:apply-imports

Used to call a template from an imported stylesheet that was overruled by the stylesheet that imported it. This is normally used if you want to add functionality to a standard template that you imported using `xsl:import`.

Implemented:	W3C 1.0 specification.
Can contain:	N/A
Can be contained by:	`xsl:attribute xsl:comment xsl:copy xsl:element xsl:fallback xsl:for-each xsl:if xsl:message xsl:otherwise xsl:param xsl:processing-instruction xsl:template xsl:variable xsl:when`

xsl:apply-templates

Used to pass the context on to another template. The `select` attribute specifies which nodes should be transformed now, and the processor decides which templates will be used.

Attribute: `select`	Type: `node-set-expression`
Attribute: `mode`	Type: `qname`
Implemented:	W3C 1.0 specification, MSXML 2.6 (preview), MSXML2.0 (IE5)
Can contain:	`xsl:sort xsl:with-param`
Can be contained by:	`xsl:attribute xsl:comment xsl:copy xsl:element xsl:fallback xsl:for-each xsl:if xsl:message xsl:otherwise xsl:param xsl:processing-instruction xsl:template xsl:variable xsl:when`

xsl:attribute

Generates an attribute in the destination document. It should be used in the context of an element (either a literal, `xsl:element` or some other element that generates an element in the output). It must occur before any text or element content is generated.

Attribute: `name`	Attribute Value: `Template` Type: `qname`
Attribute: `namespace`	Attribute Value: `Template` Type: `uri-reference`
Implemented:	W3C 1.0 specification, MSXML 2.6 (preview), MSXML2.0 (IE5)
Can contain:	`xsl:apply-imports xsl:apply-templates xsl:call-template xsl:choose xsl:copy xsl:copy-of xsl:fallback xsl:for-each xsl:if xsl:message xsl:number xsl:text xsl:value-of xsl:variable`
Can be contained by:	`xsl:attribute-set xsl:copy xsl:element xsl:fallback xsl:for-each xsl:if xsl:message xsl:otherwise xsl:param xsl:template xsl:variable xsl:when`

xsl:attribute-set

For defining a set of attributes that can be added to an element as a group by specifying the `attribute-set` name in the `use-attribute-sets` attribute on the `xsl:element` element.

Attribute: `name`	Type: `qname`
Attribute: `use-attribute-sets`	Type: `qnames`
Implemented:	W3C 1.0 specification.
Can contain:	`xsl:attribute`
Can be contained by:	`xsl:stylesheet xsl:transform`

xsl:call-template

Calling a template by name. Causes no context switch (change of context node) as `apply-templates` and `for-each` do. The template you call by name will still be processing the same context node as your current template. This element can be used to reuse the same functionality in several templates.

Attribute: `name`	Type: qname
Implemented:	W3C 1.0 specification.
Can contain:	`xsl:with-param`
Can be contained by:	`xsl:attribute xsl:comment xsl:copy xsl:element xsl:fallback xsl:for-each xsl:if xsl:message xsl:otherwise xsl:param xsl:processing-instruction xsl:template xsl:variable xsl:when`

xsl:choose

For implementing the choose/when/otherwise construct. Compare to Select/Case in Visual Basic.

Implemented:	W3C 1.0 specification, MSXML 2.6 (preview), MSXML2.0 (IE5)
Can contain:	`xsl:otherwise xsl:when`
Can be contained by:	`xsl:attribute xsl:comment xsl:copy xsl:element xsl:fallback xsl:for-each xsl:if xsl:message xsl:otherwise xsl:param xsl:processing-instruction xsl:template xsl:variable xsl:when`

xsl:comment

For generating a comment node in the destination document.

Implemented:	W3C 1.0 specification, MSXML 2.6 (preview), MSXML2.0 (IE5)
Can contain:	`xsl:apply-imports xsl:apply-templates xsl:call-template xsl:choose xsl:copy xsl:copy-of xsl:fallback xsl:for-each xsl:if xsl:message xsl:number xsl:text xsl:value-of xsl:variable`
Can be contained by:	`xsl:copy xsl:element xsl:fallback xsl:for-each xsl:if xsl:message xsl:otherwise xsl:param xsl:template xsl:variable xsl:when`

xsl:copy

Generates a copy of the context node in the destination document. Does not copy any children or attributes.

Attribute: `use-attribute-sets`	Type: qnames
Implemented:	W3C 1.0 specification, MSXML 2.6 (preview), MSXML2.0 (IE5)

Can contain:	`xsl:apply-imports xsl:apply-templates`
	`xsl:attribute xsl:call-template xsl:choose`
	`xsl:comment xsl:copy xsl:copy-of xsl:element`
	`xsl:fallback xsl:for-each xsl:if xsl:message`
	`xsl:number xsl:processing-instruction`
	`xsl:text xsl:value-of xsl:variable`

Can be contained by:	`xsl:attribute xsl:comment xsl:copy`
	`xsl:element xsl:fallback xsl:for-each xsl:if`
	`xsl:message xsl:otherwise xsl:param`
	`xsl:processing-instruction xsl:template`
	`xsl:variable xsl:when`

xsl:copy-of

Copies a full tree, including children and attributes, to the destination document. If multiple nodes are matched by the `select` attribute, they are all copied.

Attribute: `select`	Type: expression
Implemented:	W3C 1.0 specification, MSXML 2.6 (preview).
Can contain:	N/A

Can be contained by:	`xsl:attribute xsl:comment xsl:copy xsl:element`
	`xsl:fallback xsl:for-each xsl:if xsl:message`
	`xsl:otherwise xsl:param  xsl:processing-instruction`
	`xsl:template xsl:variable xsl:when`

xsl:decimal-format

Top-level element for defining settings for conversion to numeric values.

Attribute: `name`	Type: qname
Attribute: `decimal-separator`	Type: char
Attribute: `grouping-separator`	Type: char
Attribute: `infinity`	Type: string
Attribute: `minus-sign`	Type: char
Attribute: `NaN`	Type: string
Attribute: `percent`	Type: char

Attribute: `per-mille`	Type: `char`
Attribute: `zero-digit`	Type: `char`
Attribute: `digit`	Type: `char`
Attribute: `pattern-separator`	Type: `char`
Implemented:	W3C 1.0 specification, MSXML 2.6 (preview).
Can contain:	N/A
Can be contained by:	`xsl:stylesheet xsl:transform`

xsl:element

Generates an element with the specified name in the destination document.

Attribute: `name`	Attribute Value: `Template` Type: `qname`
Attribute: `namespace`	Attribute Value: `Template` Type: `uri-reference`
Attribute: `use-attribute-sets`	Type: `qnames`
Implemented:	W3C 1.0 specification, MSXML 2.6 (preview), MSXML 2.0 (IE5)
Can contain:	`xsl:apply-imports xsl:apply-templates xsl:attribute xsl:call-template xsl:choose xsl:comment xsl:copy xsl:copy-of xsl:element xsl:fallback xsl:for-each xsl:if xsl:message xsl:number xsl:processing-instruction xsl:text xsl:value-of xsl:variable`
Can be contained by:	`xsl:copy xsl:element xsl:fallback xsl:for-each xsl:if xsl:message xsl:otherwise xsl:param xsl:template xsl:variable xsl:when`

xsl:fallback

Can be used to specify actions to be executed if the action of its parent element is not supported by the processor.

Implemented:	W3C 1.0 specification.
Can contain:	`xsl:apply-imports xsl:apply-templates xsl:attribute xsl:call-template xsl:choose xsl:comment xsl:copy xsl:copy-of xsl:element xsl:fallback xsl:for-each xsl:if xsl:message xsl:number xsl:processing-instruction xsl:text xsl:value-of xsl:variable`
Can be contained by:	`xsl:attribute xsl:comment xsl:copy xsl:element xsl:fallback xsl:for-each xsl:if xsl:message xsl:otherwise xsl:param xsl:processing-instruction xsl:template xsl:variable xsl:when`

xsl:for-each

For repeatedly processing a series of XSLT elements. The context is shifted to the current node in the loop.

Attribute: `select`	Type: `node-set-expression`
Implemented:	W3C 1.0 specification, MSXML 2.6 (preview), MSXML2.0 (IE5)
Can contain:	`xsl:apply-imports xsl:apply-templates xsl:attribute xsl:call-template xsl:choose xsl:comment xsl:copy xsl:copy-of xsl:element xsl:fallback xsl:for-each xsl:if xsl:message xsl:number xsl:processing-instruction xsl:text xsl:value-of xsl:variable`
Can be contained by:	`xsl:attribute xsl:comment xsl:copy xsl:element xsl:fallback xsl:for-each xsl:if xsl:message xsl:otherwise xsl:param xsl:processing-instruction xsl:template xsl:variable xsl:when`

xsl:if

Executes the contained elements only if the test expression returns true (or a filled node set).

Attribute: `test`	Type: `boolean-expression`
Implemented:	W3C 1.0 specification, MSXML 2.6 (preview), MSXML2.0 (IE5)
Can contain:	`xsl:apply-imports xsl:apply-templates xsl:attribute xsl:call-template xsl:choose xsl:comment xsl:copy xsl:copy-of xsl:element xsl:fallback xsl:for-each xsl:if xsl:message xsl:number xsl:processing-instruction xsl:text xsl:value-of xsl:variable`
Can be contained by:	`xsl:attribute xsl:comment xsl:copy xsl:element xsl:fallback xsl:for-each xsl:if xsl:message xsl:otherwise xsl:param xsl:processing-instruction xsl:template xsl:variable xsl:when`

xsl:import

Imports the templates from an external stylesheet document into the current document. The priority of these imported templates is very low, so if a template is implemented for the same pattern, it will always prevail over the imported template. The imported template can be called from the overriding template using `xsl:apply-imports`.

Attribute: `href`	Type: `uri-reference`
Implemented:	W3C 1.0 specification.
Can contain:	N/A
Can be contained by:	`xsl:stylesheet xsl:transform`

xsl:include

Includes templates from an external document as if they were part of the importing document.

Attribute: href	Type: uri-reference
Implemented:	W3C 1.0 specification, MSXML 2.6 (preview).
Can contain:	N/A
Can be contained by:	xsl:stylesheet xsl:transform

xsl:key

Can be used to create index-like structures that can be queried from the key function. It basically is a way to describe name/value pairs inside the source document (like a Dictionary object in VB or an associative array in Perl). Only in XSLT, more than one value can be found for one key and the same value can be accessed by multiple keys.

Attribute: name	Type: qname
	The name that can be used to refer to this key.
Attribute: match	Type: pattern
	The pattern defines which nodes in the source document can be accessed using this key. In the name/value pair analogy, this would be the definition of the value.
Attribute: use	Type: expression
	This expression defines what the key for accessing each value would be, for example: if an element PERSON is matched by the match attribute and the use attribute equals "@name", the key function can be used to find this specific PERSON element by passing the value of its name attribute.
Implemented:	W3C 1.0 specification.
Can contain:	N/A
Can be contained by:	xsl:stylesheet xsl:transform

xsl:message

To issue error messages or warnings. The content is the message.

Attribute: terminate	Type: yes/no
Implemented:	W3C 1.0 specification.
Can contain:	xsl:apply-imports xsl:apply-templates xsl:attribute xsl:call-template xsl:choose xsl:comment xsl:copy xsl:copy-of xsl:element xsl:fallback xsl:for-each xsl:if xsl:message xsl:number xsl:processing-instruction xsl:text xsl:value-of xsl:variable
Can be contained by:	xsl:attribute xsl:comment xsl:copy xsl:element xsl:fallback xsl:for-each xsl:if xsl:message xsl:otherwise xsl:param xsl:processing-instruction xsl:template xsl:variable xsl:when

xsl:namespace-alias

Used to make a certain namespace appear in the destination document without using that namespace in the stylesheet. The main use of this element is in generating new XSLT stylesheets.

Attribute: `stylesheet-prefix`	Type: `prefix|#default`
	The prefix for the namespace that is used in the stylesheet.
Attribute: `result-prefix`	Type: `prefix|#default`
	The prefix for the namespace that must replace the aliased namespace in the destination document.
Implemented:	W3C 1.0 specification.
Can contain:	N/A
Can be contained by:	`xsl:stylesheet xsl:transform`

xsl:number

For outputting the number of a paragraph or chapter in a specified format. Has very flexible features, to allow for different numbering rules.

Attribute: `level`	Type: `single|multiple|any`
	The value 'single' counts the location of the nearest node matched by the count attribute (along the ancestor axis) relative to its preceding siblings of the same name. Typical output: chapter number. The value 'multiple' will count the location of the all nodes matched by the count attribute (along the ancestor axis) relative to their preceding siblings of the same name. Typical output: paragraph number of form 4.5.3. The value 'any' will count the location of the nearest node matched by the count attribute (along the ancestor axis) relative to their preceding nodes (not only siblings) of the same name. Typical output: bookmark number.
Attribute: `count`	Type: `pattern`
	Specifies the type of node that is to be counted.
Attribute: `from`	Type: `pattern`
	Specifies the starting point for counting.
Attribute: `value`	Type: `number-expression`
	Used to specify the numeric value directly instead of using 'level', 'count' and 'from'.
Attribute: `format`	Attribute Value: `Template` Type: `string`
	How to format the numeric value to a string (1 becomes 1, 2, 3, ...; a becomes a, b, c, ...)

Attribute: `lang`	Attribute Value: `Template` Type: `nmtoken`
	Language used for alphabetic numbering.
Attribute: `letter-value`	Attribute Value: `Template` Type: `alphabetic|traditional`
	Some languages have traditional orders of letters specifically for numbering. These orders are often different from the alphabetic order.
Attribute: `grouping-separator`	Attribute Value: `Template` Type: `char`
	Character to be used for group separation.
Attribute: `grouping-size`	Attribute Value: `Template` Type: `number`
	Number of digits to be separated. `grouping-separator=";"` and `grouping-size="3"` causes: 1;000;000.
Implemented:	W3C 1.0 specification.
Can contain:	N/A
Can be contained by:	`xsl:attribute xsl:comment xsl:copy xsl:element xsl:fallback xsl:for-each xsl:if xsl:message xsl:otherwise xsl:param xsl:processing-instruction xsl:template xsl:variable xsl:when`

xsl:otherwise

Content is executed if none of the `xsl:when` elements is matched.

Implemented:	W3C 1.0 specification, MSXML 2.6 (preview), MSXML2.0 (IE5)
Can contain:	`xsl:apply-imports xsl:apply-templates xsl:attribute xsl:call-template xsl:choose xsl:comment xsl:copy xsl:copy-of xsl:element xsl:fallback xsl:for-each xsl:if xsl:message xsl:number xsl:processing-instruction xsl:text xsl:value-of xsl:variable`
Can be contained by:	`xsl:choose`

xsl:output

Top level element for setting properties regarding the output style of the destination document. The xsl:output element basically describes how the translation from a created XML tree to a character array (string) happens.

Attribute: method	Type: xml|html|text|qname-but-not-ncname
	xml is default, html will create empty elements like and use HTML entities like à. text will cause no output escaping to happen at all (no entity references in output.)
Attribute: version	Type: nmtoken
Attribute: encoding	Type: string
Attribute: omit-xml-declaration	Type: yes/no
Attribute: standalone	Type: yes/no
Attribute: doctype-public	Type: string
Attribute: doctype-system	Type: string
Attribute: cdata-section-elements	Type: qnames
	Specifies a list of elements that should have their content escaped by using a CDATA section instead of entities.
Attribute: indent	Type: yes/no
	Specifies the addition of extra whitespace for readability.
Attribute: media-type	Type: string
	To specify a specific MIME type while writing out content.
Implemented:	W3C 1.0 specification, MSXML 2.6 (preview).
Can contain:	N/A
Can be contained by:	xsl:stylesheet xsl:transform

xsl:param

Defines a parameter in an xsl:template or xsl:stylesheet.

Attribute: name	Type: qname
Attribute: select	Type: expression
	Specifies the default value for the parameter.
Implemented:	W3C 1.0 specification, MSXML 2.6 (preview).

Can contain:	xsl:apply-imports xsl:apply-templates xsl:attribute xsl:call-template xsl:choose xsl:comment xsl:copy xsl:copy-of xsl:element xsl:fallback xsl:for-each xsl:if xsl:message xsl:number xsl:processing-instruction xsl:text xsl:value-of xsl:variable
Can be contained by:	xsl:stylesheet xsl:transform

xsl:preserve-space

Allows you to define which elements in the source document should have their whitespace content preserved. See xsl:strip-space.

Attribute: elements	Type: tokens
Implemented:	W3C 1.0 specification.
Can contain:	N/A
Can be contained by:	xsl:stylesheet xsl:transform

xsl:processing-instruction

Generates a processing instruction in the destination document.

Attribute: name	Attribute Value: Template Type: ncname
Implemented:	W3C 1.0 specification, MSXML 2.6 (preview), MSXML2.0 (IE5). Note that this element is called xsl:pi in IE5.
Can contain:	xsl:apply-imports xsl:apply-templates xsl:call-template xsl:choose xsl:copy xsl:copy-of xsl:fallback xsl:for-each xsl:if xsl:message xsl:number xsl:text xsl:value-of xsl:variable
Can be contained by:	xsl:copy xsl:element xsl:fallback xsl:for-each xsl:if xsl:message xsl:otherwise xsl:param xsl:template xsl:variable xsl:when

xsl:sort

Allows specifying a sort order for xsl:apply-templates and xsl:for-each elements. Multiple sort elements can be specified for primary and secondary sorting keys.

Attribute: select	Type: string-expression
Attribute: lang	Attribute Value: Template Type: nmtoken
Attribute: data-type	Attribute Value: Template Type: text/number/qname-but-not-ncname
Attribute: order	Attribute Value: Template Type: ascending/descending

Attribute: case-order	Attribute Value: Template Type: upper-first/lower-first
	Note that case insensitive sorting is not supported.
Implemented:	W3C 1.0 specification, MSXML 2.6 (preview).
Can contain:	N/A
Can be contained by:	xsl:apply-templates

xsl:strip-space

Allows you to define which elements in the source document should have their whitespace content stripped. See xsl:preserve-space.

Attribute: elements	Type: tokens
Implemented:	W3C 1.0 specification, MSXML 2.6 (preview).
Can contain:	N/A
Can be contained by:	xsl:stylesheet xsl:transform

xsl:stylesheet

The root element for a stylesheet. Synonym to xsl:transform.

Attribute: id	Type: id
Attribute: extension-element-prefixes	Type: tokens
	Allows you to specify which namespace prefixes are XSLT extension namespaces (like msxml).
Attribute: exclude-result-prefixes	Type: tokens
	Namespaces that are only relevant in the stylesheet or in the source document, but not in the result document, can be removed from the output by specifying them here.
Attribute: version	Type: number
Implemented:	W3C 1.0 specification, MSXML 2.6 (preview), MSXML2.0 (IE5)
Can contain:	xsl:attribute-set xsl:decimal-format xsl:import xsl:include xsl:key xsl:namespace-alias xsl:output xsl:param xsl:preserve-space xsl:strip-space xsl:template xsl:variable
Can be contained by:	N/A

xsl:template

Defines a transformation rule. Some templates are built-in and don't have to be defined.

Attribute: `match`	Type: `pattern`
Attribute: `name`	Type: `qname`
Attribute: `priority`	Type: `number`
Attribute: `mode`	Type: `qname`
Implemented:	W3C 1.0 specification, MSXML 2.6 (preview), MSXML2.0 (IE5)
Can contain:	`xsl:apply-imports xsl:apply-templates xsl:attribute xsl:call-template xsl:choose xsl:comment xsl:copy xsl:copy-of xsl:element xsl:fallback xsl:for-each xsl:if xsl:message xsl:number xsl:processing-instruction xsl:text xsl:value-of xsl:variable`
Can be contained by:	`xsl:stylesheet xsl:transform`

xsl:text

Generates a text string from its content. Whitespace is never stripped from a text element.

Attribute: `disable-output-escaping`	Type: yes/no
Implemented:	W3C 1.0 specification, MSXML 2.6 (preview), MSXML2.0 (IE5)
Can contain:	N/A
Can be contained by:	`xsl:attribute xsl:comment xsl:copy xsl:element xsl:fallback xsl:for-each xsl:if xsl:message xsl:otherwise xsl:param xsl:processing-instruction xsl:template xsl:variable xsl:when`

xsl:transform

Identical to `xsl:stylesheet`.

Attribute: `id`	Type: `id`
Attribute: `extension-element-prefixes`	Type: `tokens`
Attribute: `exclude-result-prefixes`	Type: `tokens`
Attribute: `version`	Type: `number`
Implemented:	W3C 1.0 specification.
Can contain:	`xsl:attribute-set xsl:decimal-format xsl:import xsl:include xsl:key xsl:namespace-alias xsl:output xsl:param xsl:preserve-space xsl:strip-space xsl:template xsl:variable`
Can be contained by:	N/A

xsl:value-of

Generates a text string with the value of the `select` expression.

Attribute: `select`	Type: `string-expression`
Attribute: `disable-output-escaping`	Type: `yes/no`
	You can use this to output < instead of < to the destination document. Note that this will cause your destination to become invalid XML. Normally used to generate HTML or text files.
Implemented:	W3C 1.0 specification, MSXML 2.6 (preview), MSXML2.0 (IE5)
Can contain:	N/A
Can be contained by:	`xsl:attribute xsl:comment xsl:copy xsl:element xsl:fallback xsl:for-each xsl:if xsl:message xsl:otherwise xsl:param xsl:processing-instruction xsl:template xsl:variable xsl:when`

xsl:variable

Defines a variable with a value. A variable really is not variable, but constant.

Attribute: `name`	Type: `qname`
Attribute: `select`	Type: `expression`
Implemented:	W3C 1.0 specification, MSXML 2.6 (preview).
Can contain:	`xsl:apply-imports xsl:apply-templates xsl:attribute xsl:call-template xsl:choose xsl:comment xsl:copy xsl:copy-of xsl:element xsl:fallback xsl:for-each xsl:if xsl:message xsl:number xsl:processing-instruction xsl:text xsl:value-of xsl:variable`
Can be contained by:	`xsl:attribute xsl:comment xsl:copy xsl:element xsl:fallback xsl:for-each xsl:if xsl:message xsl:otherwise xsl:param xsl:processing-instruction xsl:stylesheet xsl:template xsl:transform xsl:variable xsl:when`

xsl:when

Represents one of the options for execution in an `xsl:choose` block.

Attribute: `test`	Type: `boolean-expression`
Implemented:	W3C 1.0 specification, MSXML 2.6 (preview), MSXML2.0 (IE5)
Can contain:	`xsl:apply-imports xsl:apply-templates xsl:attribute xsl:call-template xsl:choose xsl:comment xsl:copy xsl:copy-of xsl:element xsl:fallback xsl:for-each xsl:if xsl:message xsl:number xsl:processing-instruction xsl:text xsl:value-of xsl:variable`
Can be contained by:	`xsl:choose`

xsl:with-param

Defines a parameter on an xsl:template or xsl:stylesheet. Also specifies a default value.

Attribute: name	Type: qname
Attribute: select	Type: expression
Implemented:	W3C 1.0 specification, MSXML 2.6 (preview).
Can contain:	N/A
Can be contained by:	xsl:apply-templates xsl:call-template

msxml:script

Contains a script block with functions that can be called from expressions (i.e. from xsl:value-of). Note that this is a Microsoft extension to the XSLT specification.

Attribute: language	Type: language-name
Attribute: implements-prefix	Type: namespace-prefix
Implemented:	MSXML 2.6 (preview), MSXML 2.0 (IE5) (Called xsl:script).
Can contain:	N/A
Can be contained by:	N/A

Functions

The functions are listed, with a brief description and a list of parameters. (A question mark after the parameter signifies that it is optional). All of these functions are implemented in W3C 1.0 unless specified otherwise.

node-set current()

Implemented in MSXML 2.6 (preview only). Returns the current context, outside the current expression. For MSXML 2.0 you can use the context() function as a workaround. context(-1) is synonymous to current().

node-set document(object, node-set?)

Allows a reference to be obtained to an external source document.

Parameter 1: object	If an object of type string, the URL of the document to be retrieved. If a node-set, all nodes are converted to strings and all these URLs are retrieved in a node-set.
Parameter 2: node-set	Represents the base URL from where relative URLs are resolved.

boolean element-available(string)

To query availability of a certain extension element.

Parameter: `string`	Name of the extension element.

string format-number(number, string, string?)

Formats a numeric value into a formatted and localized string.

Parameter 1: `number`	The numeric value to be represented.
Parameter 2: `string`	The format string that should be used for the formatting.
Parameter 3: `string`	Reference to an `xsl:decimal-format` element to indicate localization parameters.

boolean function-available(string)

To query availability of a certain extension function.

Parameter: `string`	Name of the extension function.

node-set generate-id(node-set?)

Generates a unique identifier for the specified node. Each node will cause a different ID, but the same node will always generate the same ID. You cannot be sure that the IDs generated for a document during multiple transformations will remain identical.

Parameter: `node-set`	The first node of the passed node-set is used. If no node-set is passed, the current context is used.

node-set key(string, object)

Allows the retrieval of a reference to a node using the specified `xsl:key`.

Parameter 1: `string`	The name of the referenced `xsl:key`.
Parameter 2: `object`	If of type string, the index string for the key. If of type node-set, all nodes are converted to strings and all are used to get nodes back from the key.

object system-property(string)

Allows the retrieval of certain system properties from the processor.

Parameter: string	The name of the system property. Properties that are always available are xsl:version, xsl:vendor and xsl:vendor-url.

node-set unparsed-entity-url(string)

Returns the URI of the unparsed entity with the passed name.

Parameter 1: string	Name of the unparsed entity.

Inherited XPath Functions

Check the XPath reference (Appendix C) for information on these functions. The following can all be used in XSLT: boolean, ceiling, concat, contains, count, false, floor, id, lang, last, local-name, name, namespace-uri, normalize-space, not, number, position, round, starts-with, string, string-length, substring, substring-after, substring-before, sum, translate and true.

XSLT Types

boolean	Can have values true and false.
char	A single character.
expression	A string value, containing an XPath expression.
id	A string value. Must be an XML name. The string value can be used only once as an id in any document.
language-name	A string containing one of the defined language identifiers. American English = EN-US
name	A string value that conforms to the name conventions of XML. That means: no whitespace, should start with either a letter or an _.
names	Multiple name values separated by whitespace.
namespace-prefix	Any string that is defined as a prefix for a namespace.
ncname	A name value that does not contain a colon.
node	A node in an XML document. Can be of several types, including: element, attribute, comment, processing instruction, text node, etc...
node-set	A set of nodes in a specific order. Can be of any length.
node-set-expression	A string value, containing an XPath expression that returns nodes.

`number`	A numeric value. Can be both floating point or integer.
`object`	Anything. Can be a string, a node, a node-set, anything.
`qname`	Qualified name: the full name of a node. Made up of two parts: the local name and the namespace identifier.
`qnames`	A set of qname values, separated by whitespace.
`string`	A string value.
`token`	A string value that contains no whitespace.
`tokens`	Multiple token values separated by whitespace.
`uri-reference`	Any string that conforms to the URI specification.

XLink/XPointer Reference

This reference appendix describes the various elements and attributes in the XLink namespace and the syntax for XPointer (both topics were covered in Chapter 5).

XLink

Namespace

The namespace for XLink is:

http://www.w3.org/1999/xlink

Simple Links

The following section describes all of the attributes necessary to describe simple links, and how elements with these attributes must be associated together.

xlink:type = "simple"

Required. An element must be declared with this attribute to indicate the presence of a simple link. The element with this attribute should be rendered as the linked element by the rendering engine.

Attribute: `href`	Optional. The URI of the remote resource. For simple links, this URI is the "destination" of the link.
Attribute: `role`	Optional. Used to describe the function of a remote resource in a machine-readable fashion. It may be qualified with a namespace. For simple links, this attribute is descriptive only.
Attribute: `title`	Optional. Used to provide a human-readable description of a remote resource's function. A rendering engine might use this value to indicate a link to other information.
Attribute: `show`	Optional. Used to define *how* the rendering engine should show the content of the remote resource. Legal values are: `new` – Creates a new context in which the remote resource is to be rendered (by, for example, opening a new browser window). `replace` – Renders the content in place of the resource being navigated from. `embed` – Embed the content of the remote resource at the location of the link in the current resource. `undefined` – The rendering engine may choose how the remote resource is to be rendered.
Attribute: `actuate`	Optional. Indicates *when* the remote resource is to be rendered. Legal values are: `onLoad` – The remote resource should be navigated to when the current resource is loaded and its contents rendered immediately. `onRequest` – The remote resource should be navigated to only when the user requests that the navigation should happen. `undefined` – The rendering engine may decide when the remote resource's content is to be actuated.

Extended Links

The following section describes all of the attributes necessary to describe extended links, and how elements with these attributes must be associated together.

xlink:type = "extended"

Required. An element must be declared with this attribute to indicate the presence of an extended link. The element with this attribute should be rendered as the linked element by the rendering engine.

Attribute: role	Optional. Used to describe the function of a link in a machine-readable fashion. It may be qualified with a namespace. For extended links, this attribute is descriptive only.
Attribute: title	Optional. Used to provide a human-readable description of an extended link's function. A rendering engine might use this value to control the way the extended link is rendered.

xlink:type = "locator"

Optional. An element declared with this type must be a child of an element with xlink:type = extended. This element type describes a remote resource that participates in the extended link.

Attribute: href	Required. The URI of the remote resource that is participating in the link.
Attribute: role	Optional. Used to describe the function of a remote resource in a machine-readable fashion. It may be qualified with a namespace. For remote resources, this attribute is also used to govern the definition of arcs between linked resources – see the xlink:type = "arc" element for more information.
Attribute: title	Optional. Used to provide a human-readable description of a remote resource's function. A rendering engine might use this value to control the way the extended link is rendered.

xlink:type = "arc"

Optional. An element declared with this type must be a child of an element with xlink:type = "extended". This element type describes traversal rules between the resources that participate in the extended link.

Attribute: role	Optional. Used to describe the function of a traversal path in a machine-readable fashion. It may be qualified with a namespace. For arcs, this information is descriptive only.
Attribute: title	Optional. Used to provide a human-readable description of a traversal path. A rendering engine might use this value to control the way the extended link is rendered.

Attribute: show	Optional. Used to define *how* the rendering engine should show the content of the target resource when the link is traversed. Legal values are:
	new – Creates a new context in which the target resource is to be rendered (by, for example, opening a new browser window).
	replace – Renders the content in place of the resource being navigated from.
	embed – Embeds the content of the target resource at the location of the link in the current resource.
	undefined – The rendering engine may choose how the target resource is to be rendered.
Attribute: actuate	Optional. Indicates *when* the target resource is to be rendered. Legal values are:
	onLoad – The target resource should be navigated to when the current resource is loaded and its contents rendered immediately.
	onRequest – The target resource should be navigated to only when the user requests that the navigation should happen.
	undefined – The rendering engine may decide when the target resource's content is to be actuated.
Attribute: from	Optional. Indicates the role of the starting resource. Any resource participating in the extended link with a role matching the role specified in the from attribute of this arc will be treated as a starting resource for traversal using this arc's definition. If this attribute is not supplied, all participating resources are assumed to be valid starting resources for this arc.
Attribute: to	Optional. Indicates the role of the target resource. Any resource participating in the extended link with a role matching the role specified in the to attribute of this arc will be treated as a target resource for traversal using this arc's definition. If this attribute is not supplied, all participating resources are assumed to be valid target resources for this arc.

xlink:type = "resource"

Optional. An element declared with this type must be a child of an element with xlink:type = "extended". This element type describes a local resource that participates in the extended link.

Attribute: role	Optional. Used to describe the function of a local resource in a machine-readable fashion. It may be qualified with a namespace. For local resources, this attribute is also used to govern the definition of arcs between linked resources – see the xlink:type = "arc" element for more information.
Attribute: title	Optional. Used to provide a human-readable description of a local resource. A rendering engine might use this value to control the way the extended link is rendered.

xlink:type = "title"

Optional. An element declared with this type must be a child of an element with xlink:type = "extended", xlink:type = "arc", or xlink:type = "locator". This element type describes additional title information about the link, arc, or locator. It has no attributes.

XPointer

Syntax

XPointers may be defined using full XPointer syntax or "bare" syntax.

The full syntax for XPointer is:

```
Full_document_URL#xpointer(XPath_expression)
```

The "bare" syntax for XPointer allows an ID to be specified without the XPointer prefix. So, the XPointer:

```
#chapter1
```

is equivalent to:

```
#xpointer(id("chapter1"))
```

More than one XPointer expression may be included – each one is evaluated, from left to right, and if any succeed for a node, then that node is included in the result. For example:

```
#xpointer(id("chapter1"))xpointer(id("chapter2"))
```

will include both chapter1 and chapter2.

See Appendix C for more information on XPath expressions.

XPointer Extensions to XPath

The point Location Type

XPath defines a new type of location, called a point. It does not necessarily correspond directly to a node; rather, it defines a location within the document. It may represent the location preceding any individual character in text content, or preceding or following any node in the document.

The range Location Type

XPath defines another new type of location, called a range. A range is defined as all of the structure and content between two points (see the definition of the point location type, above).

New Node Tests

`point()`	Matches any location in the location set (analogous to a node set for pure XPath) that is a point.
`range()`	Matches any location in the location set that is a range.

New Operators

`to`	Returns a range between the start point of the covering range of the first operand and the end point of the covering range of the second operand.

New Functions

`location-set string-range (location-set string number? number?)`	Returns a set of range locations for each non-overlapping incidence of the `string` argument found in the string values of the members of the `location-set` argument. If the third argument is provided, it is the position of the start point of the range relative to the location of the matched string. If the fourth argument is provided, it is the number of characters to be returned in each range (if not provided, only the matched string is returned in the range).
`location-set range(location-set)`	Returns a set of ranges that are covering ranges for each location specified in the argument `location-set`.
`location-set range-inside(location-set)`	Returns a set of ranges that are covering ranges for the contents of each location specified in the argument `location-set` (but not necessarily the location itself).
`location-set start-point(location-set)`	Returns a set of points that correspond to the start point of the covering ranges, for each location in the argument `location-set`.
`location-set end-point(location-set)`	Returns a set of points that correspond to the end point of the covering ranges, for each location in the argument `location-set`.

`location-set here()`	Returns a location set containing a single element node that contains or bears the XPointer itself.
`location-set origin()`	Returns a location set corresponding to the source link of a traversal. This function is only meaningful if XPointer is being used in conjunction with some link traversal mechanism such as XLink.
`boolean unique()`	Returns `true` if the current context size is 1.

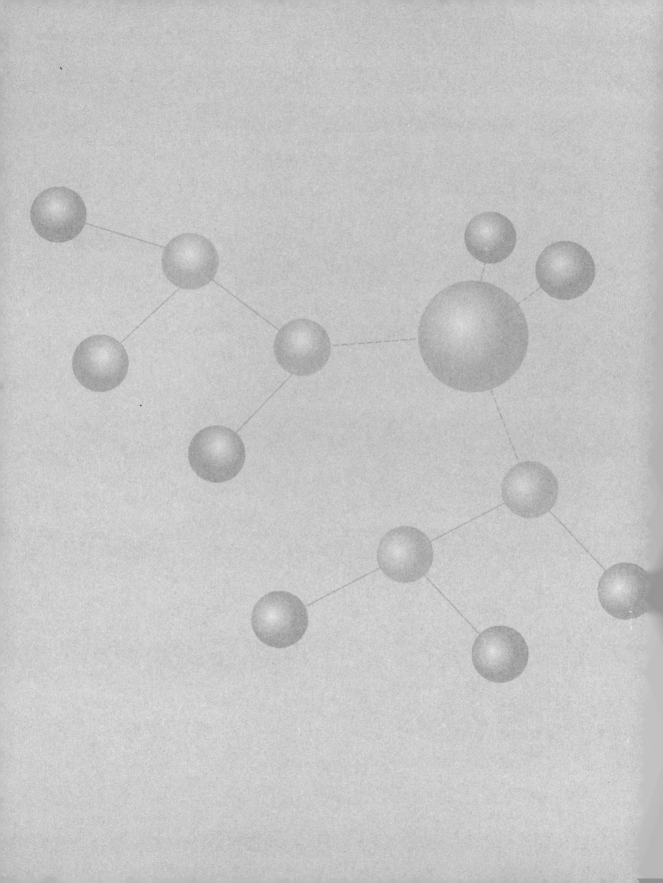

F

Support and Errata

One of the most irritating things about any programming book is when you find that bit of code you've just spent an hour typing simply doesn't work. You check it a hundred times to see if you've set it up correctly and then you notice the spelling mistake in the variable name on the book page. Of course, you can blame the authors for not taking enough care and testing the code, the editors for not doing their job properly, or the proofreaders for not being eagle-eyed enough, but this doesn't get around the fact that mistakes do happen.

We try hard to ensure no mistakes sneak out into the real world, but we can't promise that this book is 100% error free. What we can do is offer the next best thing by providing you with immediate support and feedback from experts who have worked on the book, and try to ensure that future editions eliminate these gremlins. The following section will take you step by step through the process of posting errata to our web site to get that help. The sections that follow, therefore, are:

- ❑ Wrox Developers Membership
- ❑ Finding a list of existing errata on the web site
- ❑ Adding your own errata to the existing list
- ❑ What happens to your errata once you've posted it (why doesn't it appear immediately)?

There is also a section covering how to e-mail a question for technical support. This comprises:

- ❑ What your e-mail should include
- ❑ What happens to your e-mail once it has been received by us

So that you only need view information relevant to yourself, we ask that you register as a Wrox Developer Member. This is a quick and easy process, that will save you time in the long-run. If you are already a member, just update membership to include this book.

Wrox Developer's Membership

To get your FREE Wrox Developer's Membership click on Membership in the top navigation bar of our home site – http://www.wrox.com. This is shown in the following screenshot:

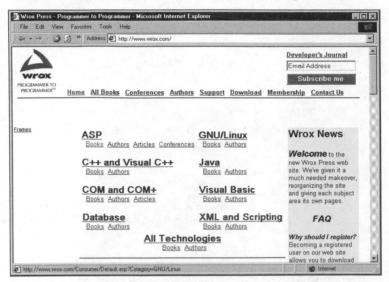

Then, on the next screen (not shown), click on New User. This will display a form. Fill in the details on the form and submit the details using the Register button at the bottom. Before you can say 'The best read books come in Wrox Red' you will get the following screen:

Type in your password once again and click Log On. The following page allows you to change your details if you need to, but now you're logged on, you have access to all the source code downloads and errata for the entire Wrox range of books.

Finding an Erratum on the Web Site

Before you send in a query, you might be able to save time by finding the answer to your problem on our web site – http:\\www.wrox.com.

Each book we publish has its own page and its own errata sheet. You can get to any book's page by clicking on Support from the top navigation bar.

Halfway down the main support page is a drop down box called Title Support. Simply scroll down the list until you see Professional Visual Basic 6.0 XML. Select it and then hit Errata.

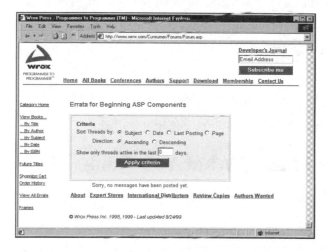

This will take you to the errata page for the book. Select the criteria by which you want to view the errata, and click the Apply criteria button. This will provide you with links to specific errata. For an initial search, you are advised to view the errata by page numbers. If you have looked for an error previously, then you may wish to limit your search using dates. We update these pages regularly to ensure that you have the latest information on bugs and errors.

Add an Erratum : E-mail Support

If you wish to point out an erratum to put up on the web site, or directly query a problem in the book page with an expert who knows the book in detail, then e-mail support@wrox.com, with the title of the book and the last four numbers of the ISBN in the subject field of the e-mail. A typical e-mail should include the following things:

❑ The name, last four digits of the ISBN and page number of the problem in the subject field

❑ Your name, contact information and the problem in the body of the message

We won't send you junk mail. We need the details to save your time and ours. If we need to replace a disk or CD we'll be able to get it to you straight away. When you send an e-mail it will go through the following chain of support:

Customer Support

Your message is delivered to one of our customer support staff who are the first people to read it. They have files on most frequently asked questions and will answer anything general immediately. They can answer general questions about the book and the web site.

Editorial

Deeper queries are forwarded to the technical editor responsible for that book. They have experience with the programming language or particular product and are able to answer detailed technical questions on the subject. Once an issue has been resolved, the editor can post the errata to the web site.

The Authors

Finally, in the unlikely event that the editor can't answer your problem, s/he will forward the request to the author. We try to protect the author from any distractions from writing. However, we are quite happy to forward specific requests to them. All Wrox authors help with the support on their books. They'll mail the customer and the editor with their response, and again all readers should benefit.

What We Can't Answer

Obviously with an ever growing range of books and an ever-changing technology base, there is an increasing volume of data requiring support. While we endeavor to answer all questions about the book, we can't answer bugs in your own programs that you've adapted from our code. But do tell us if you're especially pleased with the routine you developed with our help.

How to Tell Us Exactly What You Think

We understand that errors can destroy the enjoyment of a book and can cause many wasted and frustrated hours, so we seek to minimize the distress that they can cause.

You might just wish to tell us how much you liked or loathed the book in question. Or you might have ideas about how this whole process could be improved. In which case you should e-mail feedback@wrox.com. You'll always find a sympathetic ear, no matter what the problem is. Above all you should remember that we do care about what you have to say and we will do our utmost to act upon it.

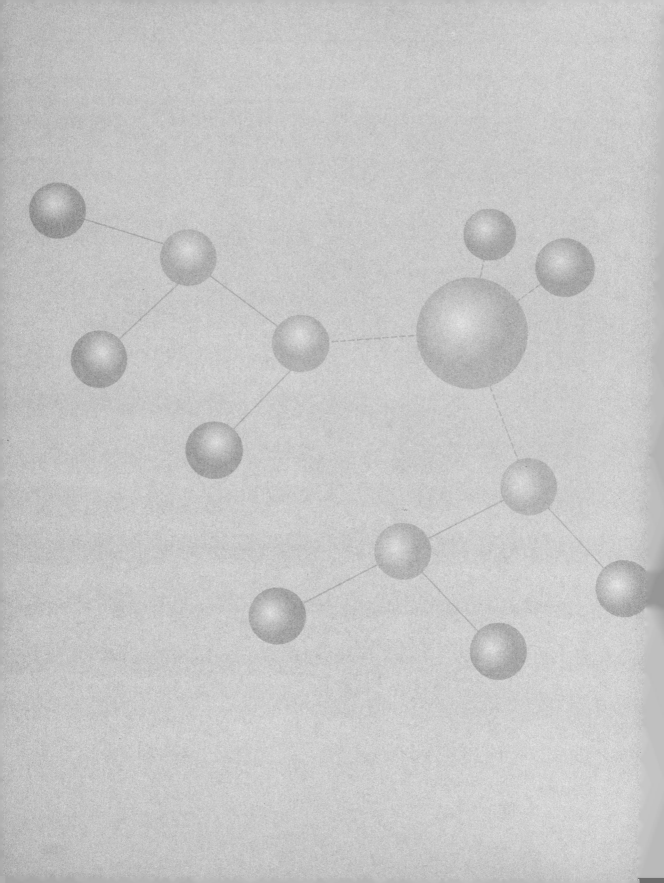

Index

Symbols

!=
  operators, 168
#IMPLIED default value
  ATLIST declaration, 50
#PCDATA
  ELEMENT declaration
    CONTENT, 46
Ӓ
  general entities, 54
覫
  general entities, 54
&
  general entities, 54
'
  general entities, 54
>
  general entities, 54
<
  general entities, 54
"
  general entities, 54
*
  description, 164
| (vertical bar)
  operators, 168
+, -, *
  operators, 168
<, <=, >, >=
  operators, 168
=
  operators, 168

A

A tag
  HREF attribute, 236
accessing nodes by ID
  nodeFromID method, 274
  performance, maximizing, 273
  selectNodes method
    XPath query syntax, 274
  selectSingleNode method
    XPath query syntax, 274

ActiveDocument object
  GetDocProperties, 565
  receives scripting events by default, 554
ActiveX DLLs
  conversion of Word content to XML
    create, 554
  Word-XML conversion application, 555
    adding metaData, 564
    Convert class, 555
    formatting bookmarks, 564
    formatting tables, 562
    helper functions, 560
    removing graphics, 561
    test document
      create macro, 567
    Word template, 566
      create macro, 566
  SOAP
    client/server program, 289
ActiveX XML test box
  building, 366
  properties, methods and events
    table, 367
AddElement function
  Element node, adding a new
    appendChild method, 103
    node interface, 103
AddNode function
  DOM, 130
  frmAddNode form
    CDomFunctions class, 148
AddNode method
  parent node not specified, 265
  parent node specified, 265
  XML applications
    performance, 265
AddNodeList method
  XML applications
    performance, 267
AddRoot method
  Word-XML conversion application, 560, 564
ADO
  XML will not replace, 17
ADO recordset
  converting to XML, 404
    ConvertDataToXmlString helper function, 405
    run time errors, 404

Index

Allowed child nodes
Node types
table, 99
ancestor
description, 163
ancestor-or-self
description, 163
and
operators, 168
ANY
ELEMENT declaration
CONTENT, 46
Apache Xerces, 34
apartment-threaded model
DOMDocument object, 283
free-threaded access
comparison, 283
appendChild method
createCDATASection
class function, add
CDATA function, 93
Element node, adding a new
Comment node
createComment method, 108
node interface, 102
Element node, adding a new, 103
AddAttribute method, 106
AddElement function
validating Element tag name, 104
Comment node, add, 108
error trapping, 107
PI, add, 107
wrapper method, 103
AddElement function, 103
HIERARCHY_REQUEST_ERR exception, 102
NO_MODIFICATION_ERR exception, 102
WRONG_DOCUMENT_ERR exception, 102
appendData method
CharacterData interface, 124
NO_MODIFICATION_ALLOWED_ERR
DOMException, 124
application
create and send reorder form, 539
change database model, 539
create database, 401
diagram, 401
new objects required
class for performing file operations, 402
data service class, 402
SOAP wrapper classes, 402
required functions, 400
SOAP transactions
using, 402
application architecture, 491
diagram of system, 492
typical sequence of events, 492
Application_OnEnd
global.asa
allows subroutines to handle up to four events, 513

Application_OnStart
global.asa
allows subroutines to handle up to four events, 513
array type
data element as child element, 294
ASP
adds server side logic, 398
code is script, 398
performance cost, 398
ASP Application object
declare, 434
ASP/IIS SOAP server
MTS
needs to be on same machine, 402
asynchronous loading of large documents
DOMDocument object
WithEvents keyword, 268
performance, maximizing, 268
state of document
readyState value 4, 268
table, 268
ATLIST declaration
XE, 50
element type, 48
NMTOKENS attribute
default values, 50
ID method, 50
IDREF method, 50
NOTATION attribute, 50
Attr
ATTRIBUTE_NODE, 100
Attr interface
attributes of Elements, 116
Boolean specified method, 116
String name method, 116
String value method, 117
attribute and AttributeType
to be merged, 74
ATTRIBUTE_NODE
Attr, 100
attributes
description, 163
name/value pair assigned to elements, 21
names
case sensitive, 21
must be unique, 21
not to be repeated inside of tag, 21
Node attributes, 102
value must be enclosed in quotes, 21
entity references
to be used when both types of quotes are present, 21
attributes for all link types
table, 259
attributeType element
child elements
dataType, 68
descriptionType, 68
default attribute, 68

ElementType element
  default attribute element, 68
  required attribute element, 68
  type attribute element, 68
  name attribute, 68
  required attribute, 68
axis
  ancestor, 163
  ancestor-or-self, 163
  attribute, 163
  child, 163
  descendant, 163
  descendant-or-self, 163
  description, 162
  diagram, 163
  following, 163
  following-sibling, 163
  namespace, 163
  parent, 163
    description, 163
  preceding, 163
  preceding-sibling, 163
  self, 163
  table, 162

B

back-end application class, 431
  creating a new product, 431
    CreateNewProduct method, 431
  getting a product list
    GetProductList method, 432
  product file
    updating, 433
  UpdateProductFile method, 433
bin.base64
  extension types, 62
bin.hex
  extension types, 62
BizTalk
  available schemas, 354
  CamelCase style, 353
  document content, 353
    style guide for naming conventions, 353
  goals
    standardization of XML format, 352
  repository of document schemas, 352
  software, 354
BizTalk framework
  BizTalk root element, must start with
    BizTalk namespace declaration, 352
  BizTalk root element, must start with, 352
  Route tag
    child element
      Handle attribute, 353
      LocationID attribute, 353
      LocationType attribute, 353

    Path attribute, 353
    Process attribute, 353
    From child element, 353
    To child element, 353
BookmarkTags method
  Word-XML conversion application, 560, 564
boolean
  extension types, 62
Boolean specified method
  Attr interface, 116
BuildDocument method
  turns form data into XML string, 449
buildLinkset method
  XLinkExtended class, 465
BuildPOSTRequest function
  SOAP client/server application
    Visual Basic EXE project, 337
BuildSoapEnvelopeFault function
  SOAP response body, 323
  SOAP:Envelope
    SOAP:Fault, 323
BuildSoapRequestGetProductList method
  product list, 443
built in functions
  boolean functions, 172
  node set functions, 169
    count, 169
    id, 169
    last(), 169
    namespace-uri, 170
    position(), 169
  number functions
    number(), 171
    round(), 171
    sum(), 171
  string functions, 170
    starts-with, 170
    string, 170
    translate, 170

C

CallByName function
  loading the correct object, 314
  SOAP request methods, 315
  SoapUtils program, 319
CamelCase style
  BizTalk, 353
Cascading Style Sheets
  see CSS
CDATA
  document interface
    forbidden]]> string
      check for, 93
  syntax, 27
  uses, 27
CDATA attribute
  ATLIST declaration, 48

CDATA node, create
document interface
append to parent node, 93
set response to False, 94
error handling, 94
set response to True, 93
createCDATASection, 93
CDATA sections
document interface
parent node, allows
check for, 93
restrictions on text, 92
CDATA_SECTION_NODE
CDATASection, 100
CDATASection interface, 125
CDATASection object
no methods or attributes, 125
create CDATASection method, 125
Document object, 125
Text object, derived from, 125
CDomFunctions class
frmAddNode form
declare an object, 148
changing inventory level, 542
char
extension types, 62
character data
see also text
see CDATA
character point
specified by its container and index, 240
character references
definition, 26
uses, 26
CharacterData interface, 123
appendData method, 124
NO_MODIFICATION_ALLOWED_ERR
DOMException, 124
data attribute, 123
DOMSTRING_SIZE_ERR exception, 123
NO_MODIFICATION_ALLOWED_ERR
DOMException, 123
deleteData method, 124
INDEX_SIZE_ERR DOMException, 124
NO_MODIFICATION_ALLOWED ERR exception, 124
insertData method, 124
INDEX_SIZE_ERR DOMException, 124
NO_MODIFICATION_ALLOWED ERR exception, 124
length function, 123
replaceData method, 125
INDEX_SIZE_ERR DOMException, 125
NO_MODIFICATION_ALLOWED_ERR exception, 125
substringData method, 123
DOMSTRING_SIZE_ERR exception, 123
INDEX_SIZE_ERR exception, 123
check socket state
SOAP requests
SOAP client/server application
Visual Basic EXE project, 340

checking reorder requirements
SELECT query
Catalog table, 543
checking stock, 542
childnodes
Node attributes, 101
Class Initialize method
Visual Basic application, 314
ClearFormatting method
Word-XML conversion application, 558
clients to perform XML/XSL transformation
IE5, limits users to, 12
cloneNode method
node interface, 111
cmdConnect_Click event
command event handlers, 334
COM object method, any
wrapper method, corresponding, 315
COM+
see also MTS
CombineURLs method
Location class, 464
uses WinInet library, 469
comma seperated value
see CSV
command event handlers
cmdListen_Click event, 334
Comment
COMMENT_NODE, 100
Comment interface
no methods or properties, 123
comment()
description, 164
COMMENT_NODE
Comment, 100
Common Object Request Broker Architecture
see CORBA
complex type declarations, 74
configure function
build, 498
MSMQ, 501
ConnectionRequest function
SOAP requests, 340
Constant name
Node types
table, 99
context node
as starting point for XPath queries, 162
definition, 162
ConvertHashStringToPaths function
SplitURL method, 471
ConvertToXml function
Word-XML conversion application, 556
CORBA
encode method in XML
HTTP port 80, use to get round firewall, 12

CountElements function
frmMain form, 142
CountNodes function
frmMain form, 141
createAttribute method
document interface
String sAttrName parameter, 94
createCDATASection
class function, add
CDATA function
appendChild method, 93
CDATASection interface, 125
document interface, 92
create new CDATA node, 93
creates new CDATASection node
sNodeData parameter, 92
creates new CDATASection node object, 92
HTML DOM object, called on
NOT_SUPPORTED_ERR DOMException, raises, 92
Document object
CDATASection interface, 125
createCDATASection factory method
document interface, 93
createCDATASectiondocument interface
CDATA text invalid
error trapping, 92
createComment method
document interface
creates new comment, 92
creates new comment node object
sNodeData parameter, 92
Element node, adding a new
Comment node
appendChild method, 108
createDocumentFragment method
document interface
creates an empty DocumentFragment object, 91
no parameters, 91
CreateElement method
document interface
creates a new Element object
returns a reference to it, 90
INVALID_CHARACTER_ERR DOMException
raised in case od invalid characters, 90
tagName parameter
element type set by, 90
tagName parameter
case sensitive, 90
createEntityReference method
document interface, 94
EntityReference node object, create
String sEntityRef parameter, 94
INVALID_CHARACTER_ERR
called if name has invalid character, 95
NOT_SUPPORTED_ERR
raised if called on HTML DOM object, 95
CreateObject function
SoapUtils program, 319
createProcessingInstruction node
document interface
String sInstruction parameter, 94
String sTarget parameter, 94

createTextNode method
document interface
creates new Text node object, 92
sNodeData parameter, 92
CSV
one dimensional, 12
custom index
making, 275
CustomDocumentProperties collection
Word-XML conversion application, 565

D

data
DisplayFileList function
populates grid, 450
displaying, 450
transforming and transmitting, 537
data attribute
CharacterData interface, 123
DOMSTRING_SIZE_ERR exception, 123
NO_MODIFICATION_ALLOWED_ERR
DOMException, 123
ProcessingInstruction interface, 130
data entry and parsing, 365
data entry fields, coding
product example, 380
Data services class
declaring properties, 403
MTS objects
declaring, 403
data services object
declare, 417
provides methods for executing SQL queries, 402
database
updating, 425
WebProducts
Catalog, 401
DataChannel XJ Parser, 34
datatype element, 70
Datatypes, 60
extension types
bin.hex, 62
boolean, 62
char, 62
date, 62
dateTime, 62
dateTime.tz, 62
fixed.14.4, 62
float, 62
i1, 63
i2, 63
i4, 63
int, 62
number, 63
r4, 63
r8, 63
time, 63
time.tz, 63
ui1, 63

ui2, 64
ui4, 64
uri, 64
uuid, 64
primitve types
entities, 61
entity, 61
enumeration, 61
idref, 61
idrefs, 61
nmtoken, 61
nmtokens, 61
notation, 61
string, 61
date
extension types, 62
dateTime
extension types, 62
dateTime.tz
extension types, 62
DCOM
encode method in XML
HTTP port 80, use to get round firewall, 12
leaving ports open
security risk, 13
Default.asp
Web site
designing, 516
deleteData method
CharacterData interface, 124
INDEX_SIZE_ERR DOMException, 124
NO_MODIFICATION_ALLOWED ERR exception, 124
descendant
description, 163
descendant-or-self
description, 163
description element, 69
DetailsAreSet function
detail XML, 325
Dictionary object
custom index
DOM
store references, 275
SoapUtils.Utils, 316
Distributed application
advantages
increased platform options, 292
CORBA, 292
DCOM, 292
IIS, 292
scalability, 292
communication, 292
concept of a state, 496
moving information, 495
issues, 495
data integrity, 495
disconnected applications, 495
failure rate, 495
processing a purchase order, 496
SOAP requests, 496

SOAP requests
advantages, 496
online store, 290
diagram, 290
transaction processing object, 290
XML files
product information, stored in, 290
XLink pointers, 290
XPointers, 290
product files
table, 292
XML product description file, 292
XML, why use, 291
Distributed Component Object Model
see DCOM
distributed objects, 491
div
operators, 168
DoAllTables method
Word-XML conversion application, 560, 562
DocmentType interface, 126
entities attribute, 127
NamedNodeMap object interface, 127
name attribute, 127
notations attribute, 127
NamedNodeMap object interface, 127
doctype attribute
document interface, 90
DOCTYPE declaration
external reference, 44
PUBLIC keyword, 44
SYSTEM keyword, 44
root element, 43
two parts, 43
Document
DOCUMENT_NODE, 100
document content retrieving
GetReturnedDoc method, 444
document element
see root element
document interface
CDATA
forbidden]]> string
check for, 93
CDATA node, create
append to parent node, 93
set response to False, 94
error handling, 94
set response to True, 93
createCDATASection, 93
CDATA sections
parent node, allows
check for, 93
restrictions on text, 92
createAttribute method
String sAttrName parameter, 94
createCDATASection, 92
CDATA text invalid
error trapping, 92
create new CDATA node, 93

creates new CDATASection node object, 92
sNodeData parameter, 92
HTML DOM object, called on
NOT_SUPPORTED_ERR DOMException, raises, 92
createCDATASection factory method, 93
createComment, 92
creates new comment node object
sNodeData parameter, 92
createDocumentFragment method
creates an empty DocumentFragment object, 91
no parameters, 91
CreateElement method
creates a new Element object
returns a reference to it, 90
INVALID_CHARACTER_ERR DOMException
raised in case od invalid characters, 90
tagName parameter
element type set by, 90
createEntityReference method, 94
EntityReference node object, create
String sEntityRef parameter, 94
INVALID_CHARACTER_ERR
called if name has invalid character, 95
NOT_SUPORTED_ERR
raised if called on HTML DOM object, 95
createProcessingInstruction node
String sInstruction parameter, 94
String sTarget parameter, 94
createTextNode method
creates new Text node object, 92
sNodeData parameter, 92
doctype attribute, 90
documentElement attribute, 90
getElementsByTagName method, 95
String sTagName parameter
returns a NodeList object containing all element names
with relevant tag, 95
implementation attribute, 90
Document Object Model
see DOM
Document Type Definition
see DTD
DOCUMENT_FRAGMENT_NODE
DocumentFragment, 100
DOCUMENT_NODE
Document, 100
DOCUMENT_TYPE_NODE
DocumentType, 100
documentElement attribute
document interface, 90
DocumentFragment
DOCUMENT_FRAGMENT_NODE, 100
not a complete XML document, 88
DocumentFragment interface
create new nodes under
diagram, 89
document tree
diagram, 89
DocumentFragment object
definition, 88

does not have to be well formed, 88
may have multiple child nodes, 88
temporary parent node, 89
insert new nodes into document
diagram, 89
DocumentFragment object
DocumentFragment interface
definition, 88
does not have to be well formed, 88
temporary parent node, 89
DocumentType
DOCUMENT_TYPE_NODE, 100
DOM
AddNode function, 130
custom index
Dictionary object
store references, 275
making, 275
Element types
read only, 136
search and replace, 135, 136
email example
node diagram, 82
error handling, 135
frmAddNode form, 147
CDomFunctions class
AddNode function, 148
declare an object, 148
frmMain form, 138
CountElements function, 142
CountNodes function, 141
DOM menu, 141
DOM XML method, 141
getElementsByTagName function, 142
GetElementText function, 143
InspectNode function, 145
ListElements function, 143
ListNodes function, 144
LoadDocument function, 140
Nodes menu, 145
ReplaceElementType function, 149
SearchAndReplace function, 149
text boxes, 139
Tree View control
populates, 150
inspecting properties, 138
IsNodeIndexOK function, 131
large XML documents
consider using SAX, 270
limitations
does not cover thread safety, 84
does not define all functionality found in DHTML, 84
does not raise events, 84
internal and external subset has no structure model, 84
no interface definition for XSL rendering, 84
no methods to control access, 84
no validation against a schema, 84

manipulating the, 130, 131, 134, 138
  set error information, 132
node interface
  based on, 79
objects, 84
or SAX
  comparison, 282
programming, 79
querying, 161
replaceChild method, 137
SearchAndReplace function, 132, 134
SearchAndReplaceElementType function, 137
view as a tree of nodes
  branches and leaves, 81
XSLT, not part of, 136
DOM level 2 recommendation
not yet official, 95
DOM menu
frmMain form, 141
DOM objects
node interface
  defines methods and properties, 79
DOM XML method
frmMain form, 141
DOMDocument object
declare, 318
IE5
  save (not part of DOM specification), 96
initialize, 347
loading, 95
MSXML library
  apartment-threaded model
    description, 283
WithEvents keyword
  asynchronous loading of large documents, 268
DOMException enumerated type
defining, 86
DOMException errors
MSXML object
  no node creation methods raise, 92
DOMException interface
DOMSTRING_SIZE_ERR, 85
error information properties, general
  setting, 86
    private methods, add, 87
    public property methods, add, 87
HIERARCHY_REQUEST_ERR, 85
INDEX_SIZE_ERR, 85
INUSE_ATTRIBUTE_ERR, 86
INVALID_CHARACTER_ERR, 85
NO_DATA_ALLOWED_ERR, 85
NO_MODIFICATION_ALLOWED_ERR, 85
NOT_FOUND_ERR, 86
NOT_SUPPORTED_ERR, 86
UNKNOWN
  additional values, 86
WRONG_DOCUMENT_ERR, 85

DOMFreeThreadedDocument object
MSXML library
  free-threaded access
    description, 283
DOMImplementation interface, 87
hasFeature method
  Boolean value returned, 88
  example, 88
  feature parameter, 87
  version parameter, 87
DOMSTRING_SIZE_ERR, 85
DoSoap method
SOAP client/server application, 342
DTD
Ӓ
  general entities, 54
覫
  general entities, 54
'
  general entities, 54
>
  general entities, 54
"
  general entities, 54
all SGML documents require, 9
ATLIST declaration, 48
  #IMPLIED default value, 50
  CDATA attribute, 48
  element type, 48
  ENTITY attribute, 50
  Enumeration attribute, 48
  ID attribute, 48
  IDREF attribute, 48
  IDREFS attribute, 48
  NMTOKEN attribute, 49
  NMTOKENS attribute, 49
DOCTYPE declaration
  external reference, 44
    PUBLIC keyword, 44
    SYSTEM keyword, 44
  root element, 43
  two parts, 43
ELEMENT declaration, 45
  CONTENT, 45
    #PCDATA, 46
    ANY, 46
    EMPTY, 45
  element content, 47
  NAME, 45
    must be valid XML name, 45
entities
  declaration, 54
  reference, 54
external entities
  declaring, 55
external parameter entities
  declaring, 56
general entities, 54
  &, 54
  declaring, 55

have own syntax, 9
    difficult to write, 9
how elements are defined, 20
ID attributes
    value must be unique throughout document, 22
IDREF attributes
    must match an ID attribute, 22
internal declaration notation, 25
neccessary for validation, 30
Notation, 56
Notation declaration, 56
parameter entities, 54
    declaring, 55
syntax elements, 43
validation rules, specifying, 37
validation syntax
    limitations
        cannot specify type of text content, 57
        no free content model, 57
        only ordered child elements, or mixed content model, 57
XML
    also uses, 9
XML parsing tools, 39
XML schema
    all values are string values, 60
DTD declaration
    determines role of ID and IDREF attributes, 22
DTD or schema
    choosing, 75
DummyTransfer class
    transferring information, 549
dynamic resource files, 370

E

early binding
    definition, 493
editing options menu, 392
Element
    ELEMENT_NODE, 100
element and ElementType
    to be merged, 74
ELEMENT declaration
    DTD, 45
Element interface, 117
    getAttribute method, 117
    getAttributeNode method, 117
    getElementsByTagName method, 119
    normalize method, 120
        wrapper function, 121
    removeAttribute method, 117
    removeAttributeNode method, 118
    setAttribute method, 117
    setAttributeNode method, 118
    String tagName method, 117
ELEMENT_NODE
    Element, 100

elements
    attributes, 21
    definition, 20
    may contain other elements, 20
    must be properly nested, 20
    names, 20
    root element, 19
elements and attributes
    comparison, 24
    which to use, 23
ElementType element
    child elements
        attributeType, 67
        datatype, 67
        description, 67
        element, 67
        element element, 67
        group, 67
    content attribute
        eltOnly value, 65
        empty value, 65
        mixed value, 65
        textOnly value, 65
    element element
        maxOcurrs attribute, 67
        minOcurrs attribute, 67
        type attribute, 67
    model attribute, 66
    name attribute, 66
    order attribute
        many value, 66
        one value, 66
        seq value, 66
email example
    node diagram
        root element
            child nodes, 82
EMPTY
    ELEMENT declaration
        CONTENT, 45
encodings
    ASCII characters, 28
        divergence after 128 characters, 28
    code page, 28
    unicode, 28
    UTF-8, 28
entities
    # include directory
        similar to, 25
    begin with ampersand and end with semi colon, 25
    declaration, 54
    different types, 25
        combinations, 25
        examples, 25
    must be declared before being referenced, 25
    predefined, 25
    primitve types, 61
    reference, 54

substituting text
  used for, 25
unparsed
  requires associated notation, 26
entities attribute
  NamedNodeMap object interface
  DocmentType interface, 127
entity
  ENTITY_NODE, 100
  primitve types, 61
Entity interface, 127
  nodeName attribute, 127
  notationName attribute, 128
  publicId attribute, 128
  systemId attribute, 128
entity references
  to be used when both types of quotes are present,
  21
ENTITY_NODE
  Entity, 100
ENTITY_REFERENCE_NODE
  EntityReference, 100
EntityReference
  ENTITY_REFERENCE_NODE, 100
EntityReference interface
  EntityReference node, 128
  wrapper function, 129
enumeration
  primitve types, 61
Enumeration attribute
  ATLIST declaration, 48
error details
  returning, 420
error function
  subclass the method from error utilities, 499
error information
  Application Faulted, 302
  Invalid Request, 302
  Must Understand, 302
  Version Mismatch, 302
error information object
  declare, 417
error information properties, general
  setting
  declare private variables, 86
errorCode property
  parseError object, 98
event flow
  editing file and saving to server
  diagram, 453
ExcuteSQL method
  statements that do not return data
  UPDATE or INSERT, 405
Execute
  ObjectControl events
  SELECT, 407

ExecuteRequestWrapper method
  SOAP envelope, 342
  SoapUtils class
  modify to use ASP variables for storing method
  information, 414
ExecuteSelectXml method
  data services class
  SELECT queries, 420
  SELECT, 406
Extended interfaces, 125
extended link
  arc element, 253
  external linksets, 460
  have to find origin and target, 460
  locator element, 251
  resource element, 253
extensibility
  definition, 11
  XML, 7, 11
Extensible Bookmark Exchange Language
  see XBEL
Extensible Markup Language
  see XML
Extensible Stylesheet Language Transformations
  see XSLT
extension types
  when to use, 64
external entities
  declaring, 55
external linksets
  extended links, 460
external parameter entities
  declaring, 56

F

File server
  writing to, 427
Filepos property
  parseError object, 98
firstChild
  Node attributes, 102
fixed.14.4
  extension types, 62
float
  extension types, 62
following
  description, 163
following-sibling
  description, 163
free-threaded access
  apartment-threaded model
  comparison, 283
frmMain form
  DOM, 138
  Form_Load subroutine, 139

menu, 139
text boxes, 139
Fundamental DOM interfaces
DOMException interface, 85
DOMString type interface, 85

G

general entities
declaring, 55
getAttribute method
Element interface, 117
getAttributeNode method
Element interface, 117
GetCategoryList method
soapWrapGetCategoryList
getting the category list, 528
GetContent function in HTTP class
gives content from HTTP response, 344
getElementsByName method
NodeList object interface, 111
getElementsByTagName method
accessing TABLE elements by ID attribute, 273
document interface, 95
String sTagName parameter
returns a NodeList object containing all element names
with relevant tag, 95
Element interface, 119
frmMain form, 142
used to retrieve list of elements from XML
document, 20
GetElementText function
frmMain form, 143
GetNamedItem method
NamedNodeMap object interface, 112
GetProductList method
does not use parameters, 436
GetReturnedDoc method
retrieves content of document element, 444
GetSoapBody method
DoSoap method
SOAP client/server application
Visual Basic EXE project, 342
GetSoapMethodName function
SOAP:Body element, 338
GetSystemDirectoryA function
SOAP client/server application, 344
getting selected products
SQL in-line, 529
Qty attribute
add, 530
getting the category list
soapWrapGetCategoryList
GetCategoryList method, 528

global.asa
allows subroutines to handle up to four events,
513
Application_OnEnd, 513
Application_OnStart, 513
Session_OnEnd, 513
Session_OnStart, 513
configure, 515
designing
Web site, 513
group element
child elements
description element, 69
element, 69
maxOccurs element, 69
minOccurs element, 69
order element, 69
GUI application
COM object
OrderProcessing.MessageProcessor object, 541
easier interactive testing, 540
processing messages, 540
processMessage method, 541

H

hasChildNodes method
nodes interface, 110
returns true or false, 110
hasFeature method
DOMImplementation
feature parameter, 87
DOMImplementation interface
Boolean value returned, 88
version parameter, 87
HIERARCHY_REQUEST_ERR, 85
HREF attribute
A tag, 236
HTML
CSS
examples, 223
properties, 223
syntax specifying appearance of elements, 223
disadvantages, 8
easy to learn, 8
example, 8
exchange documents
limitations, 553
hypertext linking
good at, 8
limits of, for summarization tools, 9
markup tags
organize content, 12
Netscape and Microsoft
competing object models, 80
W3C created a standard to define the DOM, 80

semantic information, does not provide, 8
using CSS, 223
  description, 223
web page layout
  good at, 8
XLink
  does not support, 237
XML will not replace, 17
HTML links
destination defined by A tag HREF attribute, 236
example, 236
limitations to be overcome by XLink, 236
  connects only two resources, 236
  links get mixed up with content, 236
  links only to entire documents, 236
  must have editing permissions, 236
  works one way only, 236
origin defined by A tag location, 236
restrictions of, 236
visual representation, 237
  not part of specification, 237
HTTP header method
POST data, 328
HTTP headers
Entity, 307
General, 307
HttpUtils.Utils, 307
Request, 307
Response, 307
HTTP port 80, use to get round firewall
encode method in XML, 12
HTTP requests failing
request time out
  property, 438
HTTP-based gateway
default reorder document
  destination details
    reorder information, 545
HTTPTransfer class
transferring information, 549
human readable format
transforming
  email example, 548
  XHTML document
    can be sent as email or attachment, 547
Hyper Text Markup Language
see HTML
hyperlinks
key feature of web, 235

I

i1
extension types, 63
i2
extension types, 63

i4
extension types, 63
IBM xml4j, 34
ID attribute
ATLIST declaration
  DTD, 48
ID method
NMTOKENS attribute
  ATLIST declaration, 50
idref
primitve types, 61
IDREF attribute
ATLIST declaration, 48
IDREF method
NMTOKENS attribute
  ATLIST declaration, 50
idrefs
primitve types, 61
IDREFS attribute
ATLIST declaration, 48
IE5, 33
assessing priority of templates
  bottom up strategy, 198
can perform XML, XSL and CSS processing, 12
conformance
  XPath, 172
URI
  load method, 95
    returns Boolean value for load correct, 95
W3C DOM
  implements, 84
XML string
  loadXML method, 95
    returns Boolean value for load correct, 95
IIS
XML file server runs on, 407
implementation attribute
document interface, 90
INDEX_SIZE_ERR, 85
insert new product, 421
INSERT statement
create, 421
insertBefore method
NO_MODIFICATION_ALLOWED_ERR
exception, 109
node interface, 109
  HIERARCHY_REQUEST_ERR exception, 109
  similar to appendChild method, 109
  WRONG_DOCUMENT_ERR exception, 109
NOT_FOUND_ERR exception, 109
insertData method
CharacterData interface, 124
  INDEX_SIZE_ERR DOMException, 124
  NO_MODIFICATION_ALLOWED ERR exception, 124
InspectNode function
frmMain form, 145

int
extension types, 62
interface
definition, 88
XML editor, 371
interface class
creating in Visual Basic, 493
similar to an abstract class in Java, 493
serves as template, 493
interface-based programming
fundamental COM concept, 493
Internet Explorere 5
see IE5
Internet Transfer Control
transferring information, 549
INUSE_ATTRIBUTE_ERR, 86
INVALID_CHARACTER_ERR, 85
IRemoteTransactions
IProductOrders class
add, 493
IsNodeIndexOK function
DOM, 131
item method
NamedNodeMap object interface, 115
nIndex parameter, 115
NodeList object interface, 111

J

James Clark's Expat, 34

L

lastChild
Node attributes, 102
late binding
definition, 493
leaf nodes
as end points, 99
length function
CharacterData interface, 123
NamedNodeMap object interface, 115
Line property
parseError object, 98
Linepos property
parseError object, 98
link
see XLink
link solution
description, 457
linking
implementation, 468
Location class
set of properties, 468
using a VB component, 455
options, 455

VB component
component functionality, 460
component output, 461
example, 461
ListElements function
frmMain form, 143
Listen function
run as server
Visual Basic EXE project
SOAP client/server application, 345
ListNodes function
frmMain form, 144
LoadDocument function
frmMain form, 140
LoadMethodBindings function
*_SUFFIX constants, 318
Dictionary object, 318
SOAP request bind file, 332
SoapUtils class
modify to use ASP variables for storing method
information, 413
SoapUtils program, 318
local menu, coding, 384
Location class
CombineURLs method, 464
is set of properties, 468
SplitURL method, 464
XLink component
object model overview, 464
table of attributes and methods, 464
Location object
XLinkedDocument class
table of action, 467

M

MailTransfer class
transferring information, 550
makeLinked method
XLinkedDocument class, 467, 477
Markup Languages
discussion of, 8
meta data and content
can be mixed together, 12
SGML, 8
menu, coding, 384
meta data
often outside of data file, 12
Microsoft Component Services
see also MTS
Microsoft Transaction Server
see MTS
mod
operators, 168
module file
create, 380
MS parser
see IE5

MS schema
  advantages
    Datatypes
      support of, 60
  attribute and AttributeType
    to be merged, 74
  attributeType element, 68
    child elements
      dataType, 68
      descriptionType, 68
      ElementType element
        default attribute element, 68
        required attribute element, 68
        type attribute element, 68
      name attribute, 68
      required attribute, 68
  available elements, 64
  datatype element, 70
  Datatype specification, 58
  Datatypes
    extension types
      table, 61
    primitive types
      table, 61
  description element, 69
  element and ElementType
    to be merged, 74
  ElementType element, 65
    child elements, 67
      attributeType, 67
      datatype, 67
      description, 67
      element element, 67
      group, 67
    content attribute, 65
      eltOnly value, 65
      empty value, 65
      mixed value, 65
      textOnly value, 65
    element element
      maxOcurrs attribute, 67
      minOcurrs attribute, 67
      type attribute, 67
    model attribute, 66
    name attribute, 66
  example, 70
    closed content model, 73
    element and namespace declarations, 71
    invalidity messages, 73
  formulated in XML, 58
  group element
    child elements
      description element, 69
      element, 69
      maxOccurs element, 69
      minOccurs element, 69
      order element, 69
  refers to IE5 implementation of XML schema, 58
  schema element
    child elements
      attribute type, 65
      description, 65
      element type, 65
    root element, 65

Structure specification, 58
syntax
  XML Namespaces, 59
XML schema
  compared, 74
MSMQ
  configure function, 501
  declare objects, 500
  define constants, 500
  error utilities method
    set queue path, 502
    subclass, 502
  Implements statements, 500
MSXML 2.0
  tricks
    local templates, 217
      locally scoped templates, 217
    output escaping off, 217
MSXML COM object
  XML processors, 15
MTS
  library packages
    description, 399
  objects deployed in packages, 399
  overview, 399
  provides a stub, 399
  proxy, 399
  proxy/stub layer, 399
  server packages
    description, 399
MTS object
  Data services
  declaring, 403
  SCM
    call made to, 399
MTS run time
  context for objects, 399
MTS transaction
  reading messages, 541
MTS type library
  setting reference to
    ImplementsObjectControl statement
    using, 497

N

name attribute
  DocmentType interface, 127
NamedNodeMap object
  interface
    setNamedItem method
      Attr node, re use, 112
  removeNamedItem method
    Attr node, remove
      NOT_FOUND_ERR exception, 115
NamedNodeMap object interface
  description, 111
  entities attribute
    DocmentType interface, 127

getNamedItem method, 112
item method, 115
  nIndex parameter, 115
length function, 115
notations attribute
  DocmentType interface, 127
removeNamcdItem method, 115
  Attr node, remove, 115
setNamedItem method, 112
  INUSE_ATTRIBUTE_ERR exception, 112
  NO_MODIFICATION_ALLOWED_ERR excetion, 112
  WRONG_DOCUMENT_ERR DOMException, 112
namespace
description, 163
namespace information, retrieve
SOAP client/server application
  Visual Basic EXE project, 347
nextSibling
Node attributes, 102
nmtoken
primitve types, 61
NMTOKEN attribute
ATLIST declaration, 49
nmtokens
piimltve types, 61
NMTOKENS attribute
ATLIST declaration, 49
NO_DATA_ALLOWED_ERR, 85
NO_ERROR
additional values, 86
DOMException interface
  additional values, 86
NO_MODIFICATION_ALLOWED_ERR, 85
node
description, 164
Node attributes
attributes, 102
childnodes, 101
firstChild, 102
lastChild, 102
nextSibling, 102
nodeName, 101
nodeType, 101
nodeValue, 101
ownerDocument, 102
Parentnode, 101
previousSibling, 102
table, 100
node interface
appendChild method, 102
  Element node, adding a new, 103
  AddAttribute method, 106
  AddElement function
    validating Element tag name, 104
  Comment node, add, 108
  error trapping, 107
  PI, add, 107

  wrapper method, 103
  AddElement function, 103
  HIERARCHY_REQUEST_ERR exception, 102
  NO_MODIFICATION_ERR exccption, 102
  WRONG_DOCUMENT_ERR exception, 102
cloneNode method, 111
insertBefore method, 109
  HIERARCHY_REQUEST_ERR exception, 109
  WRONG_DOCUMENT_ERR exception, 109
removeChild method, 110
  NO_MODIFICATION_ALLOWED_ERR exception, 110
  NOT_FOUND_ERR exception, 110
replaceChild method, 110
  HIERARCHY_REQUEST_ERR exception, 110
  NO_MODIFICATION_ALLOWED_ERR exception, 110
  NOT_FOUND_ERR exception, 110
  WRONG_DOCUMENT_ERR exception, 110
Node interface, 99
node point
specified by its container and index, 240
node test
*, 164
comment, 164
description, 162
node, 164
processing-instruction(), 164
take no arguments, 164
text, 164
Node types
table, 99
nodeFromID method
accessing nodes by ID, 274
selectNodes method
  comparison, 283
using, 283
NodeList object interface, 111
getElementsByName method, 111
item method, 111
length attribute, 111
nodes must be part of the same document, 111
nodeName
Node attributes, 101
nodeName attribute
Entity interface, 127
Notation interface, 127
nodes interface
hasChildNodes method, 110
Nodes menu
frmMain form, 145
nodeType
Node attributes, 101
nodeValue
Node attributes, 101
normalize method
Element interface, 120
  wrapper function, 121
NOT_FOUND_ERR, 86

NOT_SUPPORTED_ERR, 86

notation
primitve types, 61
NOTATION_NODE, 100

Notation interface, 127
nodeName attribute, 127
publicId attribute, 127
systemId attribute, 127
used to define the format of an unparsed entity, 127

NOTATION_NODE
Notation, 100

notationName attribute
Entity interface, 128

notations attribute
DocumentType interface, 127
NamedNodeMap object interface
DocmentType interface, 127

number
extension types, 63

O

OASIS
maintains a repository of XML schemas, 354
schemas/DTD's
broader than just transactactions, 355

object context
reference
declare, 417

object control methods
implement, 500

Office 2000
HTML
exchange documents
flaws, 554
improvements made, 553

ondataavailable event
readyState property, 96
COMPLETED value, 96
INTERACTIVE value, 96
LOADED value, 96
LOADING value, 96
when new data arrives, 96

onreadystatechange event, 96
declare object
WithEvents keyword, 96
loading and saving asynchronously, 96
whenever the readyState property changes, 96

open exchange
XSLT
handles transformations, 13

opening a file, 385, 386, 388

operators
!=, 168
| (vertical bar), 168
+, -, *, 168
<, <=, >, >=, 168
=, 168
and, 168
div, 168
mod, 168
or, 168

or
operators, 168

OrderProcessing.MessageProcessor object
GUI application
COM object, 541

Organization for the Advancement of Structured Information Standards
see OASIS

out-of-line links
definition, 257

ownerDocument
Node attributes, 102

P

packages
see also applications for COM+

parameter entities
declaring, 55

Parentnode
Node attributes, 101

parseError object
errorCode property, 98
Filepos property, 98
Line property, 98
Linepos property, 98
Reason property, 98
SrcText property, 98
url property, 98
W3C DOM specification, not part of, 98

parsing
with and without validation
table, 281
with validation against a DTD, 281
without validation, 281

payload
see also XML document

performance tester application, 276, 277
summary, 286

PI
special tag syntax, use, 29

points
specified by container and index, 240

PostSoapRq method
SOAP requests
all dispatched by, 511

preceding
description, 163

preceding-sibling
description, 163

pre-declared entities
see predefined entities
predefined entities, 25
PrepareDoc method
Word-XML conversion application, 557
previewing a file, 391
previousSibling
Node attributes, 102
primitive types
when to use, 64
processing instructions
see PI
PROCESSING_INSTRUCTION_NODE
ProcessingInstruction, 100
ProcessingInstruction
PROCESSING_INSTRUCTION_NODE, 100
ProcessingInstruction interface, 130
data attribute, 130
target attribute, 130
processing-instruction()
description, 164
processMessage method
GUI application, 541
product editor application, 375
Product file editor
ActiveX DLL
build, 437
additions, 437
create HTTP capabilities, 437
product files
table, 292
reduced schema,, 292
XML product description file, 292
pointers to, 292
product list
building, 443
getting, 436
ProgID attribute
SoapUtils program, 320
programming language
strong typing, 40
weak typing, 40
public interface
concept of contract
methods and properties remain stable, 493
publicId attribute
Entity interface, 128
Notation interface, 127
purchase order
CommitPurchase.asp, 510
passes data to PostPurchaseOrder class, 510
IProductOrders interface, implements, 510
purchase order posting classes, 497
configure function
build, 498
error function
subclass the method from error utilities, 499

first class, 497
MTS type library
setting reference to, 497
object control methods
implement, 500
SOAP requests
managing, 497
purchase requests
posting to a remote application, 493
create interface, 493
purchasing items
Web site
designing, 521
PutFile.asp
XML file server, 407

Q

querying, 161

R

r4
extension types, 63
r8
extension types, 63
readyState value 4
state of document
asynchronous loading of large documents, 268
Reason property
parseError object, 98
referencing by ID
XPointer
shorthand notation, 238
remote procedure calls
see RPCs
removeAttribute method
Element interface, 117
removeAttributeNode method
Element interface, 118
removeChild method
node interface, 110
NO_MODIFICATION_ALLOWED_ERR exception, 110
NOT_FOUND_ERR exception, 110
removeNamedItem method
NamedNodeMap object
Attr node, remove
NOT_FOUND_ERR exception, 115
NamedNodeMap object interface, 115
Attr node, remove, 115
RenderHtml function
SOAP client/server application, 344
Visual Basic EXE project, 332
reorder information
default reorder document
create, 543

destination details, 544
   HTTP-based gateway, 545
   transforming to another schema, 545
  transforming, 543
reordering
  different suppliers, different platforms, 537
   solution, 538
replaceChild method, 137
  node interface, 110
   HIERARCHY_REQUEST_ERR exception, 110
   NO_MODIFICATION_ALLOWED_ERR exception, 110
   NOT_FOUND_ERR exception, 110
   WRONG_DOCUMENT_ERR exception, 110
replaceData method
  CharacterData interface, 125
   INDEX_SIZE_ERR DOMException, 125
   NO_MODIFICATION_ALLOWED_ERR exception, 125
ReplaceElementType function
  frmMain form, 149
request handlers
  designing, 400
resource files
  description:, 370
RetrieveSoapMethodName function
  Dictionary object
   build keys, 320
  SoapUtils program, 320
returning error
  GetErrorInfoXml method
   ErorUtils object, calls, 420

S

SaveWebFile method, 448
saving a file, 388
saving the product file
  SoapWrappers class
   soapWrapSaveProductFile method, 435
SAX
  advantages, 270
   will not build a tree of nodes, 270
    continues parsing, 270
  disadvantages
   does not store information in memory, 271
   no structural awareness during parsing, 271
  example, 271
  large XML documents, 270
  or DOM
   comparison, 282
  when to use, 155
scalar data type
  <base64>, 294
  <boolean>, 294
  <dataTime.iso8601>, 294
  <double>, 294
  <i4>, 294
  <int>, 294
  <string>, 294

schema element
  child elements
   attribute type, 65
   description, 65
   element type, 65
schemas or DTD's
  fixed schema necessary, 356
  should some entities be defined, 362
  validation, 355
  what data entries are necessary, 356
   stored as element or atribute, 356
    table, 357
  what to use, 355
scripting Word, 554
Search.asp
  Web site
   designing, 517
SearchAndReplace function
  DOM, 132, 134
  frmMain form, 149
SearchAndReplaceElementType function, 137
  frmMain form, 149
SearchForProduct method
  searching for a product, 533
  SOAP server
   searching for a product, 527
SearchForProducts method
  SearchResults.asp
   returns matching products in HTML table, 519
  SOAP requests
   SearchResults.asp, 512
searching for a product
  SearchForProduct method, 533
SearchResults.asp
  SearchForProducts method
   returns matching products in HTML table, 519
  Web site
   designing, 518
SELECT
  Execute
   ObjectControl events, 407
  ExecuteSelectXml method, 406
  XmlEncode helper method, 406
SELECT queries
  Catalog table, 543
  ExecuteSelectXml method
   data services class, 420
Selection object
  Extend parameter, 559
selectNodes method
  nodeFromID method
   comparison, 283
  using, 283
  XPath query syntax
   accessing nodes by ID, 274
selectSingleNode method
  XPath query syntax
   accessing nodes by ID, 274

self
  description, 163
sending back faults
  SOAP client/server application
    Visual Basic EXE project, 348
server side user interface
  correct order of events, 457
Service Control Manager
  see SCM
Session_OnEnd
  global.asa
    allows subroutines to handle up to four events, 513
Session_OnStart
  global.asa
    allows subroutines to handle up to four events, 513
setAttribute method
  Element interface, 117
setAttributeNode method
  Element interface, 118
setNamedItem method
  NamedNodeMap object
    interface
      Attr node, re use, 112
      INUSE_ATTRIBUTE_ERR exception, 112
      NO_MODIFICATION_ALLOWED_ERR exception, 112
      WRONG_DOCUMENT_ERR DOMException, 112
SGML
  all documents require
    DTD, 9
  difficult to learn, 9
  DTD created
    provides better use of semantic information, 10
  elements, can define, 9
  example, 9
  invented in 1974, 9
  parsing programs
    adds complexity to, 10
  provides endless options, 8
SGML documents
  must specify validation rules, 39
SGML editor
  DTD
    parse, 9
Simple API for XML
  see SAX
simple link
  table, 458
  XLink, 247
    examples, 250
  xlink:actuate attribute, 249
    onLoad value, 249
    onRequest value, 249
    Undefined value, 249
  xlink:actuate attribute, and xlink:show attribute
    combination
      behaviour, 249
  xlink:role attribute, 248

xlink:show attribute, 248
  embed value, 248
  new value, 248
  replace value, 248
  undefined value, 248
  used to link to another resource, 248
xlink:title attribute, 247
xlink:type attribute, 247
  add to element
    give value simple, 247
SOAP, 289
  client code
    writing, 304
  client/server program, 289
    ActiveX DLLs, 289
  data types
    overview, 303
  definition and function, 13
  error information, 301
    Application Faulted, 302
    Invalid Request, 302
    Must Understand, 302
    table, 302
    Version Mismatch, 302
  getting a response, 301
  goals
    provide evolvable extensible protocol, 298
    provide standard object invocation, 298
  making requests, 299
  M-POST
    gives flexibility, 298
  not intended to
    define all aspects of distributed object system, 298
  payload, 299
  request headers, 299
    M-POST example, 299
    POST example, 299
  server code
    writing, 304
  SOAP XML namespace option, 298
  SOAP:Body element, 300
  SOAP:Envelope element, 300
  SOAP:Header element, 300
  SOAP:mustUnderstand attribute, 300
  XML schemas
    data types
      compound, 303
      simple, 303
    relies on, 303
SOAP ASP application
  binding information held in, 414
SOAP client/server application, 329
  use two instances of, 349
  Visual Basic EXE project, 329
    command event handlers
      Click event, 333
      cmdConnect_Click event, 334
      cmdListen_Click event, 334
      send and receive data, 334, 335
      set up, 333

DLL
  compile, 348
DoSoap method, 342
  GetSoapBody method, 342
Example
  ActiveX DLL, create, 345
  soapStringReverse function, 346
  string reverse function, 345
frmMain form, 332
  loading, 332
GetContent function in HTTP class
  gives content from HTTP response, 344
GetSoapMethodName function
  SOAP:Body element, 338
GetSystemDirectoryA function, 344
HTTP data
  render into web browser, 344
HTTP headers
  build, 335
  keep alive header, add, 336
legacy code
  create wrapper function, 349
LoadMethodBindings function
  SOAP request bind file, 332
namespace information, retrieve, 347
POST request
  cmdPost_Click event, 336
  webPOST, 336
  webPOST function, 336
RenderHtml function, 332, 344
run as server
  Listen function, 345
run two copies of application on same machine, 339
run-time errors
  SOAP fault returned, 348
  sending back faults, 348
SOAP envelope
  ExecuteRequestWrapper function, 342
SOAP requests
  check socket state, 340
  ConnectionRequest function, 340
  handling, 340
  ListenAgain function, 341
  processing, 342
  send results back to client, 341
  socket response variable, initialize, 340
SOAP XML, load, 347
SOAPMethodName header, 338
SoapWrappers
  soapStringReverse function, 348
tab control, 343
  contained in array of picture boxes, 343
  used for, 343
table of controls, 330
tab strip, 331
SOAP fault returned
run-time errors, 348
SOAP request methods
CallByName function, 315
summary, 315
Visual Basic objects and methods
  ProgID, 315
  XML binding file, 314

SOAP requests
create, 505
  declaring variables, 505
managing, 497
parse the response, 505
  transform into HTML OPTION elements, 505
post the request, 505
PostSoapRq method
  all dispatched by, 511
retrieving data from Catalog table, 505
SearchResults.asp
  SearchForProducts method, 512
SOAP response body, 322
SOAP server, 526
getting product categories
  soapWrapGetCategoryList method
    ProductDescriptionTx class, 526
searching for a product, 527
  SearchForProduct method, 527
SOAP requests
  SoapWrappers class, 526
SOAP transactions
references required, 416
request handling code
  back end application methods, 416
  collection of transaction utilities, 416
  kept in ActiveX DLL project, 416
  SOAP request wrapper methods, 416
SOAP:encodingStyle attribute
used to describe serialization method, 300
SOAP:Fault elements
XML parsing error, 436
SOAPbindings
document root, 316
soapStringReverse function
Example, 346
SoapWrappers, 348
SoapUtils class
modify to run under MTS, 412
modify to use ASP variables for storing method information, 412
  ExecuteRequestWrapper method, 414
  LoadMethodBindings method, 413
modify to work with IIS and ASP, 412
modify to work with IIS and ASP
  create new project, 412
SoapUtils program
ActiveX DLL project, separate
  references required, 316
CallByName function, 319
CreateObject function, 319
DOMDocument object
  declare, 318, 327
LoadMethodBindings function, 318
  *_SUFFIX constants, 318
  Dictionary object, 318
ProgID attribute, 320

RetrieveSoapMethodName function, 320
  Dictionary object
    build keys, 320
separating POST data from HTTP request, 326
SOAP request
  header specifying method
    should contain, 328
  POST data
    HTTP header method, 328
SOAP response body, 322
  building, 321
  BuildSoapEnvelopeFault function, 323
  detail element, 324
  detail XML, 325
    DetailsAreSet function, 325
  fault responses, 322
  HTTP headers, 322
SOAP:Body element
  retrieve, 327
SOAP:Fault element, 317
  child elements
    detail element, 317
    faultcode, 317
    faultstring, 317
    runcode, 317
    MustUnderstand header, 317
VerifySoapVersion function, 320
SoapUtils.Utils, 316
  description, 316
  Dictionary object, 316
  SOAPbindings
    attributes, 316
    document root, 316
soapWrapGetCategoryList method
  ProductDescriptionTx class
    getting product categories, 526
soapWrapGetProductList method
  does not need to get information from SOAP
  XML, 436
SoapWrappers class, 434
  ASP Application object
    declare, 434
  ObjectContext object
    declare, 434
  saving the product file, 435
    soapWrapSaveProductFile method, 435
  UpdateProductFile method, 435
soapWrapSaveProductFile method
  SoapWrappers class
    saving the product file, 435
soapWrapSelectedProducts method
  SOAP server
    getting selected products, 528
specific node interfaces, 116
splitText method
  Text interface, 122
    INDEX_SIZE_ERR DOMException, 122
    NO_MODIFICATION_ALLOWED_ERR exception, 122

SplitURL method
  ConvertHashStringToPaths function, 471
    table of possibilities, 471
  Location class, 464
  SplitURLonHash function, 471
SQL
  executing, 405
  wrapper functions, 405
SQL in-line
  getting selected products, 529
SQL statements
  constructing, 418
SrcText property
  parseError object, 98
Standard Generalized Markup Language
  see SGML
string
  primitve types, 61
String name method
  Attr interface, 116
stylesheet
  namespace
    declared, 486
substringData method
  CharacterData interface, 123
    DOMSTRING_SIZE_ERR exception, 123
    INDEX_SIZE_ERR exception, 123
systemId attribute
  Entity interface, 128
  Notation interface, 127

T

tab control, creating, 375
tag
  definition, 20
TagTable function
  Word-XML conversion application, 562
target attribute
  ProcessingInstruction interface, 130
text
  definition, 24
  see also character data
  surrounded by markup, 24

Text interface, 122
  splitText method, 122
    INDEX_SIZE_ERR DOMException, 122
    NO_MODIFICATION_ALLOWED_ERR exception, 122
text nodes
  always leaf nodes, 92
  may not have child nodes, 92
TEXT_NODE
  Text, 100

Text node type
  TEXT_NODE, 100
text()
  description, 164
tidy tool for converting HTML to XML
  flaws, 554
time
  extension types, 63
time.tz
  extension types, 63
transferring information, 548
  abstract interface
    implemented by
      DummyTransfer, 548
      HTTPTransfer, 548
      MailTransfer, 548
  DummyTransfer class, 549
  HTTPTransfer class, 549
  Internet Transfer Control
    must reside on form, 549
  MailTransfer class, 550
transformation
  XSLT or the DOM
    comparison, 284
transforming to another schema
  default reorder document
    destination details
      reorder information, 545
  XSLT stylesheet
    create, 545
transforming to CSV, 546
Tree View control
  populates
    frmMain form, 150
Treeview_Expand event handler
  XML applications, 267

U

ui1
  extension types, 63
ui2
  extension types, 64
ui4
  extension types, 64
unicode
  design goals
    efficient, 28
    unambiguous, 28
    uniform, 28
    universal, 28
  UTF-8
    default encoding, 29
Uniform Resource Identifier
  see URI

UNKNOWN
  additional values, 86
UpdateProductFile method
  back-end application class, 433
  SoapWrappers class, 435
uri
  extension types, 64
URI
  definition, 32
  description, 45
URI file
  creating, 420
URL
  description, 45
url property
  parseError object, 98
URN
  description, 45
user interface
  HTML page, 484
uuid
  extension types, 64

V

valid
  definition, 30
validation
  definition, 38
  necessation of, 37
  sharing information, 38
    check if file conforms to specified format, 38
    read from a file in specified format, 38
    write to a file in specified format, 38
validation rules, specifying
  DTD, 37
  referential integrity, 37
  XML schema, 37
VerifySoapVersion function
  SoapUtils program, 320
Visual Basic
  INI files
    configuration information, 12
    use XML files instead, 12
  struct, does not have
    XML-RPC, 297
  web objects
    building, 398
  XML editor
    editing options menu, 385
    interface
      create, 371
    local menu, coding, 384
    opening a file, 385, 386, 388
Visual Basic ActiveX DLL project
  create, 493

Visual Basic application
client/server program, 305
ActiveX DLL, 305
error handling, 310
Class Initialize method, 314
ErrorUtils.ErrorInfo, 305
XMLEncode, 306
header content, retrieving, 313
HTTP headers
Entity, 307
General, 307
HttpUtils.Utils, 307
manipulating, 307
Request, 307
Response, 307
HttpUtils.Utils, 307
loading the correct object, 314
CallByName function, 314
M-POST request method, 310
POST method, 312
property accessor methods, 308
XML editor
ActiveX XML test box
building, 366
data entry fields, coding
product example, 380, 381, 382, 383
developing, 365
editing options menu, 392
frmMain
setting up, 380
menu, coding, 384
module file
create, 380
previewing a file, 391
product editor application, 375
product example, 365
product information file
can accept additional elements, 365
saving a file, 388
tab control, creating, 375
product example, 376, 377, 379, 380
tab controls
add, 375
Visual Basic COM object
methods can accept parameter of type string
String as an XML document, 12
Visual Basic EXE project
SOAP client/server application
BuildPOSTRequest function, 337
Visual Basic IDE
create new EXE project
XML object
reference, 84
IntelliSense feature
specific node interfaces
list methods and properties, 116
Visual Basic objects
XML use of
HTTP, 13
can speak to remote objects on any platform, 13
Vivid Creations ActiveDom, 34

W

W3C
create standard to define the DOM, 80
DOM level 1 recommendation, 79
DOM level 2 recommendation
not yet official, 95
DOM requirements
accessing elements of the document, 84
Core DOM for both HTML and XML, 82
CSS, work the same way, 82
extensions for HTML, 83
independent of the user interface, 83
language and platform independent, 82
promote common protocols, 10
recommendations for XML, 10
compatible with SGML, 10
design prepared quickly, 10
documents to be easy to create, 10
documents to be legible and clear, 10
formal and concise design, 10
optional features kept to a minimum, 10
processing programs easy to write, 10
support a wide variety of applications, 10
terseness, minimal importance of, 10
usability over the Internet, 10
web menu item
add to frmMain, 446
implementing, 446
Web site
designing, 513
configuring global.asa, 515
default page, 516
global.asa, 513
purchasing items, 521
resolving XLinks, 519
Search.asp, 517
SearchResults.asp, 518
web transaction utilities class, 416
data services object
declare, 417
error information object
declare, 417
object context
reference
declare, 417
SQL statements
constructing, 418
web transactions
efforts to standardize, 351
BizTalk, 352
goals, 352
WebClasses, 398
definition, 398
disadvantages, 398
introduced in Visual Basic 6, 398
not designed to be used with MTS, 398
do not provide same scalability as MTS components, 398
used to build and debug ASP code, 398

webPOST function
POST request, 336
WebTx class, 442
well formedness
definition, 30
Windows
UNIX
moving text files between, 342
WinInet library
CombineURLs method, uses, 469
Word
converting to XML, 553
principles similar for other packages, 553
creates code, 554
Word Application object
holds collection of Document objects, 554
Word-XML conversion application
ActiveDocument object
GetDocProperties, 565
AddRoot method, 560, 564
gives root element and XML declaration, 564
BookmarkTags method, 560, 564
ClearFormatting method, 558
ConvertToXml function, 556
CustomDocumentProperties collection, 565
DoAllTables method, 560, 562
DoEvents statement, 558
PrepareDoc method, 557
Selection object
Extend parameter, 559
TagLineBreaks method, 559
TagTable function, 562
World Wide web Consortium
see W3C
wrapper functiions
error handling, 79
provided by class project, 79
WRONG_DOCUMENT_ERR, 85

X

XBEL
browser neutral way to define web site
bookmarks, 14
XHTML
accessing nodes by ID
performance, maximizing, 273
W3C specified
must be valid XML document, 226
XLink
attributes for all link types
table, 259
element as link, 246
extended link
arc element, 253
diagram, 255
used for, 253, 254

definition, 251
locator element, 251
diagram, 252
resource element, 253
local resource element, 253
remote resource element, 253
external linksets
syntax, 258
implementing, 245
linking, 235
out-of-line links, 257
definition, 257
relationships between products established, 451
simple link, 247
examples, 250
xlink:actuate attribute, 249
onLoad value, 249
onRequest value, 249
Undefined value, 249
xlink:role attribute, 248
xlink:show attribute, 248
embed value, 248
new value, 248
replace value, 248
undefined value, 248
used to link to another resource, 248
xlink:title attribute, 247
xlink:type attribute, add
give value simple, 247
specification, 235
still under construction, 235
xlink:actuate attribute, 246
xlink:from attribute, 246
xlink:href attribute, 246
xlink:role attribute, 246
xlink:show attribute, 246
xlink:title attribute, 246
xlink:to attribute, 246
xlink:type attribute, 246
arc value, 246
element becomes a linking element, 246
extended value, 246
locator value, 246
resource value, 246
simple value, 246
title value, 246
XLink component, 463
handle links it finds, 463
object model overview, 463
classes required, 463
Location class, 464
XLink simple class
table of attributes, 465
XLink specification
correct order of events, 456
defines only attributes, 246
XLinkArc class
combines two location objects, 474
table of attributes, 466

XLinkedDocument class
  description, 466
  Location object
    table of action, 467
  makeLinked method, 467, 477
  table of attributes and methods, 467
XLinkExtended class
  buildLinkset method, 465
  creates collection of XlinkSimple objects, 474
  table of attributes and methods, 465
XLinks
  resolving, 519
XLinkSimple class
  combines two location objects, 474
XlinkSimple objects
  XLinkExtended class
    creates collection of, 474
XML
  ADO, will not be replaced by, 17
  benefits of using, 553
  can use HTTP and SMTP, 537
  case sensitive, 19
  Corel WordPerfect 9
    supports, 14
  CSS
    combining to produce HTML, 12
  data format, 12
  defining the elements
    gives flexibility, 13
  definition, 11
  disadvantages, 17
    *handling many large documents
      may need power of SGML, 17*
    HTML, will not be replaced by, 17
    tags and attributes add bulk to data, 17
  DTD
    also uses, 9
  easy to read, 14
  elements, 19
    must have closing tag, 11
    *invent to
      organize content, 12*
  examples of uses, 16
  exchange documents
    non-propritary format, 553
  extensibility, 7, 11
  HTML
    differences to, 7
    similar to, 18
  HTML and SGML
    comparison, 18
  introduction to, 7
  Markup, 19
  object method parameter encoding, 12
  Office 2000
    supports, 14
  open exchange
    *XSLT
      handles transformations, 13*

  platform independency, 537
  retrieving from a DOM, 99
  root element
    not required to have content, 19
  rules concerned with markup sytax, 11
    allows simple, standard data format, 11
  sample document, 17
  SGML
    similar to, 18
  styling the content, 222
  syntax, 18
  text that follows rules, 11
  text, (character data), 19
    *Markup
      distinction between, 19*
  uses, 15
  using CSS, 224
    styling, 225
  VB
    enhances features of, 15
  W3C standardized stylesheet languages
    CSS, 222
    XSLT, 222
  XSL
    combining to produce HTML, 12
XML applications
  performance, 263
    add visible nodes into tree view, 264
    AddNode method, 265
      parent node not specified, 265
      parent node specified, 265
    AddNodeList method, 267
    asynchronous loading of large documents, 268
    creating nodes in tree view for each element, 264
    load document into memory, 264
    loading into DOM, 264
    recursively cycling throughall levels of documents, 264
    Treeview_Expand event handler, 267
  performance maximizing, 263
    accessing nodes by ID, 263
    asynchronous loading of large documents, 263
    showing nodes in a treeview on demand, 263
    using SAX, 263
XML browser
  XLink, 237
    CSS styling, 237
    *transformation
      does not mix, 237*
    XSLT styling, 237
  XLink syntax, 238
XML comments
  HTML notation, uses, 29
XML data
  storing and retrieving, 397
XML documents
  creating in ASP
    using VBScript, 280
  declaring, 37
  external DTD
    using, 281

inline DTD
  using, 281
must specify validation rules, 37
parsing
  using DOM or SAX, 282
  with and without validation
    table, 281
  with validation against a DTD, 281
  without validation, 281
producing from scratch, 277
  used by Visual Basic developers
    construct a string, 277
    usually faster than using the DOM, 279
  using DOM objects, 278
    faster with very large documents, 279
removal of declaration, 39
see also payload
specify validation rules, optional, 39
  extensibility, 39
  performance, 39
validation
  disadvantages
    extending document format, 39
    performance, slows, 39
  DTD
    DOCTYPE declaration, 42
  whether or not to, 40
    good way to use, 41
    robustness or flexibility, 40
XML editor
  ActiveX XML test box
    AutoCheck property
      add, 368
    building, 366
    properties, methods and events
      table, 367
    txtXml_Change event
      add, 368
  checking for well formedness, 365
  data entry and parsing, 365
  data entry fields, coding
    product example, 380, 381, 382, 383
  developing, 365
  dynamic resource files, 370
  editing options menu, 392
  frmMain
    setting up, 380
  local menu, coding, 384
  menu, coding, 384
  module file
    create, 380
  opening a file, 385, 386, 388
  previewing a file, 391
  product example, 365
  saving a file, 365, 388
  tab control, creating, 375
    product example, 376
  user interface, 365
  using resource files, 365

Visual Basic
  resource files
    description, 370
XML file
  loading, 138
  update, 421
XML file server
  ASP application, 407
  consists of single page
    PutFile.asp, 407
  declare object variables, 408
  runs on IIS, 407
  writing files to disk, 409
  writing the XML file, 410
XML links
  visual representation, how to, 237
XML namespaces, 30
  declarations, 32
    how they work, 32
  URI
    refers to, 32
  used for, 31
    example, 31
XML parsing error
  SOAP utilities class
    uses methods from, 436
  SOAP:Fault elements, 436
XML parsing tools
  Apache Xerces, 34
  DataChannel XJ Parser, 34
  DTD, 39
  IBM xml4j, 34
  IE5, 33
  James Clark's Expat, 34
  Vivid Creations ActiveDom, 34
  XML schema, 39
XML processors
  unicode, must handle, 29
  VB, easily manipulated with, 15
XML product description file, 292
XML Query
  first stages of development, 162
  W3C initiative, 162
XML schema
  attributeType element
    default attribute, 68
    ElementType element
      attribute element, appears within, 68
  complex type declarations, 74
  content model can be open or closed, 58
  creating new datatypes, 75
  DTD
    all values are string values, 60
  ElementType
    order attribute
      one value, 66

ElementType element
order attribute, 66
many value, 66
seq value, 66
refers to W3C project's working draft, 58
validation, 58
specifying rules, 37
XML parsing tools, 39
XMLD OMXSL Processor object
param element
passing to a template, 203
XmlEncode helper method
SELECT, 406
XMLHTTPRequest object
declare, 440
XML-RPC
array type
data element as child element, 294
value elements, 294
description, 293
uses, 293
function, (example), 295
history, 293
HTTP post request, 293
methodCall element, 294
methodName element, 294
params element, 294
scalar data type
<base64>, 294
<boolean>, 294
<dataTime.iso8601>, 294
<double>, 294
<i4>, 294
<int>, 294
<string>, 294
Tag
table, 294
SOAP
more complex version of, 297
struct
description, 295
Visual Basic does not have, 297
XPath
context node
as starting point for queries, 162
description, 161
IE5 conformance, 172
axes, 172
abreviated syntax, 172
built in functions, 172
table of functions supported by, 172
used in XSLT and Xpointer, 161
W3C recommendation status, 161
XPath expressions
built in functions
boolean functions, 172
node set functions
count, 169
id, 169
last(), 169

namespace-uri, 170
position(), 169
number functions
number(), 171
round(), 171
sum(), 171
string functions, 170
starts-with, 170
string, 170
translate, 170
inner expressions
evaluated by outer results, 167
description, 167
predicates
built in functions, 169
Xpath extensions
Xpointer defines, 240
XPath queries
abbreviated notation, 165
table, 165
valid in IE5 implementation, 166
absolute or relative paths, 165
axis, 162
diagram, 163
table, 162
building a path, 165
examples, 164, 173
general and specific, 284
node test, 162
operators
table, 168
selecting subsets, 166
expression is true/false, 166
expression returns a number, 167
expression returns node set, 167
predicates, 166
XPointer
defines XPath extensions, 240
designed to link parts of documents, 238
syntax points to fragments, 238
linking, 235
shorthand notation, 238
references document element by child numbers, 239
referencing by ID, 238
specification
still under construction, 235
standard syntax, 238
appending to URL, 238
using XPath
examples, 239
XPointer expressions
character point
specified by its container and index, 240
node point
specified by its container and index, 240
points
location, 241
specified by container and index, 240
used for defining a range, 241

ranges
  example, 242
  limited to order of information in document, 241
    problems of knowing what is selected, 241
  some combinations not acceptable, 242
  syntax for defining, 242
returns a location, 240
  node, 240
  point, 240
  range, 240
XPointer extension functions
  boolean unique origin function, 244
  empty result sets
    considered an error, 245
    ways to avoid, 245
  examples, 244
  location-set end-point function, 243
  location-set here function, 244
  location-set origin function, 244
  location-set range function, 243
  location-set range-inside function, 243
  location-set start-point function, 243
  location-set string-range function, 243
XQL
  see also XPath
  syntax
    has support from IBM, 162
XSLT
  adding style, 226
  author summary
    count() function
      example, 221
    example, 220, 221
    sum() function
      example, 221
  clientside styling, 231
  converting data to HTML page, 455
    broad reach, 456
    example, 456
      XLink elements to be converted to HTML, 456
  creating links, 229
  definition, 173
  destination document, 174
  examples, 218
  generating CSV data
    example, 547
  history, 173
  IE5 implementation, 215
    MSXML 2.0, 215
  IE5 implementation, complete
    choose, when and otherwise elements, 215
    element, attribute and comment element, 215
    for-each element, 215
    if element, 215
    literal elements and attributes, 215
  IE5 implementation, partial
    apply-templates element, 215
    processing instruction element, 216

  stylesheet element, 216
  template element, 215
  value_of: disable-output-escaping not supported, 216
IE5 implementation, unsupported
  apply-imports, include, import elements, 216
  attribute-set elements, 216
  call-template elements, 216
  copy-of elements, 216
  current() function, 217
  document() function, 216
  format-number() function, 216
  generate-id() function, 216
  key elements, 216
  key() function, 216
  many top-level elements, 216
  number elements, 216
  param, with param, variable elements, 216
  sort elements, 216
  text elements, 216
  transform elements, 216
IE5 version
  strip all whitespace from stylesheet, 547
Macbeth example, 229, 230
messages
  same content but different formats, 538
    abstract interface required, 539
    Flowchart, 538
product information import
  example, 218
  transforming XML descriptions
    example, 219
start node
  as document root, 174
styling the article, 227, 228
transformation
  description, 174
  diagram, 174
transformation rules document (XSLT stylesheet), 174
W3C recommendation status, 161
XSLT stylesheet
  templates, 174
XSLT documents
  preserve space, 207
  strip-space, 207
XSLT elements
  apply-templates element, 180
    mode attribute, 180, 197
    select attribute, 180
  attribute-set element, 207
  built in functions
    complementary to those in XPath, 210
    current() function, 211
      example, 212
    document function, 213
      example, 213
    format-number function, 210
      table of symbols, 210
    generate-id() function
      example, 214

commands
  apply-imports command element, 194
  apply-template command element, 194
  call-template command element, 196
composing the XSLT stylesheet, 176
control of flow keywords
  choose element, 199
  for-each element, 200
  if element, 199
  otherwise element, 199
  sort element, 200
    case-order attribute, 201
    data-type attribute, 201
    order attribute, 201
  when element, 199
eval and script elements
  not in XSLT recommendations, 193
  only available in MSXML implementation, 193
generate output elements, 184
  attribute element, 186
    limitations, 186
  attribute value templates element, 186
  comment element, 189
  copy element, 184
  copy-of element, 185
  element element, 185
  number element, 189
    attributes, 190
    diagram, 190
    number calculation attribute, 190
  processing-instruction element, 188
  text element, 188
  value-of element, 184
import element, 178
include element, 178
key element, 208
  description, 208
  uses, 210
message element, 198
namespace-alias element, 208
number element
  format attribute
    table of common formats, 192
    table of examples, 192
  table, 191
param element, 202
  name attribute, 202
  passing to a stylesheet, 203
  passing to a template, 202
    XMLD OMXSL Processor object, 203
  select attribute, 202

pre-defined templates, 182
  xsl : apply templates element, 183
  xsl : value-of element, 183
processing-instruction element
  href attribute
    must be created as text node, 189
  type attribute
    must be created as text node, 189
simplified syntax, 214
stylesheet element, 176
  as root element, 176
template element, 178
  implementation, 178
  matching pattern, 178
  mode attribute, 197
top-level settings
  example, 205
  output element, 204
    html method attribute, 204
    text method attribute, 205
    xml method attribute, 204
transform element, 177
variable, 201
  description, 201
  syntax, 201
XSLT processors
SAXON, 175
  create output document, 182
XT, 175
XSLT specification
IE5
  assessing priority of templates
    bottom up strategy, 198
  rules for assessing priority of templates
    does not implement, 198
language extensions, 214
several matching templates
  rules to astablish most appropriate, 196
  tree diagram, 196
template element
  priority attribute, 197
    table, 197
XSLT stylesheet
create
  transforming to another schema, 545
XSLTester
define a template, 187
VBXML mailing list, 187
XSLT document, create, 187

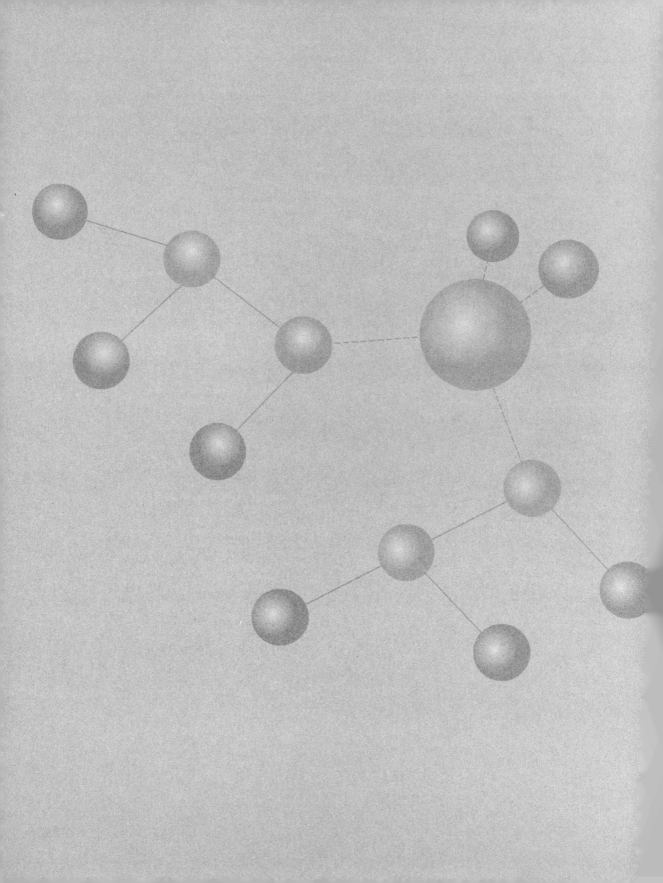

wrox
PROGRAMMER TO PROGRAMMER™

Wrox writes books for you. Any suggestions, or ideas about how you want information given in your ideal book will be studied by our team.
Your comments are always valued at Wrox.

Free phone in USA 800-USE-WROX
Fax (312) 893 8001

UK Tel. (0121) 687 4100   Fax (0121) 687 4101

Professional Visual Basic 6 XML - Registration Card

Name _____

Address _____

_____

_____

City_____ State/Region _____

Country_____ Postcode/Zip_____

E-mail _____

Occupation _____

How did you hear about this book? _____

☐ Book review (name) _____

☐ Advertisement (name) _____

☐ Recommendation _____

☐ Catalog _____

☐ Other _____

Where did you buy this book? _____

☐ Bookstore (name)_____ City _____

☐ Computer Store (name)_____

☐ Mail Order _____

☐ Other _____

What influenced you in the purchase of this book?

☐ Cover Design

☐ Contents

☐ Other (please specify) _____

How did you rate the overall contents of this book?

☐ Excellent   ☐ Good

☐ Average   ☐ Poor

What did you find most useful about this book? _____

What did you find least useful about this book? _____

Please add any additional comments. _____

What other subjects will you buy a computer book on soon? _____

What is the best computer book you have used this year? _____

Note: This information will only be used to keep you updated about new Wrox Press titles and will not be used for any other purpose or passed to any other third party.

3323   Check here if you DO NOT want to receive support for this book ☐   3323

wrox
PROGRAMMER TO PROGRAMMER™

NB. If you post the bounce back card below in the UK, please send it to:

Wrox Press Ltd., Arden House, 1102 Warwick Road,
Acocks Green, Birmingham B27 6BH. UK.

Computer Book Publishers